This book has been bound in "Malabar," a cotton fabric woven by Dan River Mills, Inc., Danville, Virginia. "Malabar," in a range of attractive patterns, is more commonly used in making sportswear, dresses, shirts, and outerwear for the entire family.

Mill on the Dan

Mill on the Dan

A History of Dan River Mills, 1882-1950

Robert Sidney Smith

Duke University Press   *Durham, N. C.*   *1960*

HD
9879
.D3
S6
1960

ⓒ 1960, Duke University Press

Library of Congress Catalogue Card number 59-7086

Cambridge University Press, London, N. W. 1, England

338.4767721

D167S

LIBRARY
FLORIDA STATE UNIVERSITY
TALLAHASSEE, FLORIDA

Printed in the United States of America
by the Seeman Printery, Durham, N. C.

Preface

Unlike an individual, a corporation reaching three score years and ten need not contemplate retirement, senility, or death. But it may share the human weakness for reminiscing. Dan River Mills in 1950 looked back on nearly seven decades of growth, which began when six Danville businessmen invested $75,000 in a new enterprise, the Riverside Cotton Mills. At mid-century the company valued its assets at $55 million; it manufactured cloth at the rate of fifteen million yards a month; and it employed 12,000 men and women—almost twice the population of Danville in 1882.

So far as I can discover, the idea that the business records of the mills on the Dan contained grist for the historian's mill was first suggested by Mrs. Kate Schoolfield Tillett. Writing to President H. R. Fitzgerald in 1926, Mrs. Tillet declared:

I think that what you and some of my kin-folks have made of these mills is one of the business wonders of the world, just like a fairy-story! A real "dream come true"! Has it ever been written up? The mills, and the men that have made them? If so, I wish you would tell me where, as I would like to read it. If not, there is a fine story yet to be written.

In 1934 President R. R. West corresponded with the secretary of the Business Historical Society at Harvard University. In response to the latter's inquiry, West wrote:

Your letter leads me to wonder if there would be anything in the records of our organization here which might be of interest to this Society. These mills, of course, represent one of the outstanding industrial developments in the South. They were organized, and have been kept supplied, by local capital and local management. I have a feeling that in competent hands the story of the development of this industrial enterprise could be made to clearly represent the change from agrarian to industrial life, which has occurred in so many southern industrial communities.

President West advised the Society's secretary, F. C. Ayres, to get in touch with the company's secretary, W. W. Ayres, who had "all of the records at his finger tips." F. C. Ayres wrote W. W. Ayres, suggesting "a loan or a contribution" of some of the oldest records for possible use in the study of textile history at the Harvard Graduate School of Business Administration. Neither the archives of the company nor the files of the Society yield any evidence that W. W. Ayres replied.

D. A. Overbey, Jr., with the collaboration of L. H. Browder, wrote a short history of the company in 1935; and in 1943, at the request of the editor of *American Wool and Cotton Reporter,* L. H. Browder composed a brief history of the New York sales office. Neither of these was intended for publication.

Although President G. S. Harris thought it was a "nuisance" to fill out questionnaires submitted by the Virginia World War II History Commission, the company's attorney, Frank Talbott, favored co-operating with the Commission. He thought the data compiled for this purpose would "contain publicity for us of a kind that we would ordinarily be glad to pay for as advertising." No Virginia corporation, he felt, with the exception of the Newport News Ship-building Corporation, had done more toward the war effort than Dan River. The company prepared the data requested, but the Commission has failed to publish a volume on industrial history.

In June 1947 L. H. Browder, the assistant treasurer, wrote President Harris of the need for a company history. "We often have need," he said, "in connection with articles for the press or for magazines, to dig back into our accumulation of historical data for some information on our Company. It would be of considerable help to us for this purpose alone, if for no other reason, to have on hand a complete written report of Dan River's history." After discussing the proposal with the president, L. H. Browder sent B. D. Browder a rough outline of desired study, which he thought could be done in four months by the firm's advertising agency.

Our idea [L. H. Browder wrote] would be to maintain the book in type-written letter-size sheets in a loose-leaf binder with, say, four or five copies. This would enable us to make additions to the history from time to time, to have it well indexed for ready reference when we are called upon for facts about Dan River's history, and to have it in shape for printing, if, at any time in the future, we decided that it was desirable to issue a printed history of the Corporation.

B. D. Browder vetoed the idea of employing the advertising agency and "for several reasons" recommended Mrs. Eunice H. Davis. Mrs. Davis had already accumulated a file of historical records; she had a "closer and more intimate knowledge" of the company than the agency; and, since she was already a full-time employee, her research and writing time would cost the company nothing "extra." Mrs. Davis continued to gather information for the proposed work but had not commenced writing when she resigned in 1949.

When I was invited to examine the records with a view to undertaking this history, it seemed to me that indifference and neglect had taken such a heavy toll of the archives that the story would have to be brief and incomplete. Much, indeed, of what might have thrown light on points that now appear obscure has disappeared; but, as more and more of the scattered and dusty papers turned up, the problem of selection became embarrassingly time-consuming. As a result, I have delayed years in doing what I expected to have done in twelve months.

The study which follows is an attempt to show how one firm got started, grew, and eventually reached a position of pre-eminence in the cotton textile industry. It is a business history, but it deals as much with men and women as with buildings, machines, dollars, and bolts of cloth. I have tried to explain the ways in which business enterprise transformed a community and contributed a significant share to the South's industrial revolution. While this is by no means a pioneer study of southern industrialization, it is, I believe, the first to rely largely on the internal records of a corporation.

Inasmuch as the data are taken from private records, I have not identified precisely the source of every statement or statistic. It seemed unnecessary, for instance, to make repeated reference to the directors' minutes, audit reports, official correspondence, and other files which are not accessible for public consultation. The result has been the suppression of several hundred footnotes; those which remain may still appear too voluminous.

Those who have co-operated in locating records and reconstructing the events of distant years are too numerous for me to make adequate acknowledgment of their contributions. Some, like C. D. Gaver, who gave me my first impressions of the men who worked under President Fitzgerald, have passed on. Others, including two of my most helpful and friendly critics, Paul P. Patteson and Waverley H. Cousins, now live in well-earned retirement. My orientation in Dan River history was enriched by conversations with Frank Talbott, chairman of the board of directors, Basil D. Browder, executive vice-president, and T. A. Bassin, the company's first controller. Raymond Hall, a former manager at Riverside Division, gave me personal glimpses of mill life at the turn of the century and loaned me useful materials from his personal files. Miss Hattie Hylton likewise made available to me personal records and scarce publications relating to welfare work in Schoolfield.

John D. MacLauchlan, Jr., formerly assistant to Vice-president Browder, first interested me in the idea of attempting this business history. Over the years he was unfailingly helpful in finding records, arranging interviews, and reading instalments of the written product. While Mr. MacLauchlan was serving as manager of Riverdan Benevolent Fund, Louis H. Fracher, now the Reverend Mr. Fracher, answered innumerable questions and walked many miles to track down records in attics, vaults, storerooms, and filing cabinets. D. A. Overbey, Jr., formerly assistant treasurer, made my work pleasant by sharing office space, lending me secretarial help, and guiding me to many landmarks in the company's history. I benefited immeasurably from the vigorous criticisms of M. A. Cross, director of public and industrial relations, who, after reviewing portions of the manuscript, undertook the tedious chore of reading all the galley proof. To these and many others at the mill, who gave cheerfully of their time and advice, I am most grateful.

My colleagues, Professors Edward C. Simmons and Frank T. de Vyver, did me the great favor of reading the entire manuscript, saving me from countless errors of fact and exposition. Two of my former graduate students, Olin S. Pugh and LeGrand Weller, assisted me in the preparation and checking of tables and footnotes. Carolyn S. Walters typed more than one of the editions through which the manuscript progressed.

The publication of this study has been made possible by a grant from the Research Council of Duke University. Dan River Mills generously financed my research in Danville. Neither Dan River nor Duke in any way shares my responsibility for faults of commission or omission, from which a book of this scope can scarcely be immune.

ROBERT SIDNEY SMITH

Durham, North Carolina
January 29, 1960

Table of Contents

Mill on the Dan

I . *Danville's Early Mills*

〜〜〜〜〜〜〜〜〜〜〜〜〜〜〜〜〜〜〜〜〜〜〜〜〜〜〜〜〜〜

Despite the handicaps imposed by the plantation—slave-labor system, southern industry developed appreciably in the ante-bellum period. While southern statesmen were warring on the protective tariff—the invention of northern industrialists designed to keep the agrarian South in vassalage—a handful of southerners saw a way out through the encouragement of industry. Men like William Gregg of South Carolina had visions of boundless cotton fields dotted at convenient intervals with whirring cotton mills; a few of them, in the quarter century following the compromise tariff of 1833, saw their dreams come true.[1] The Civil War prostrated not only the adolescent textile industry, of

[1] Broadus Mitchell, *William Gregg: Factory Master of the Old South* (Chapel Hill, N. C., 1928). United States manufactures of cotton goods for the year ending June 1, 1860, were valued at $115.7 million, of which $8.1 million was reported for the southern states. Virginia's manufactures of cotton goods (none of which were reported from Pittsylvania County) amounted to $1.5 million and were surpassed in value by the state's manufactures of flour and meal ($15.9 million), tobacco ($12.2 million), sawed lumber ($2.2 million), and sheet, bar, and railroad iron ($1.7 million) (*Manufactures of the United States in 1860 computed from the original returns of the Eighth Census* [Washington, 1865], pp. 604-639.)

which Gregg's Graniteville mill was the shining example, but virtually
every type of manufacturing. Not that the holocaust of 1861-1865
suffocated a firmly rooted industrial revolution. Too many capitalists
had too much of their wealth sunk in land and slaves not to share
Senator Willie Mangum's scorn for "those in the South that indulge in
the delusion that we are capable of becoming a manufacturing people."
Mangum believed that there were prospects of success "in the interior,
to a certain extent"; but that industry

could become the predominant interest . . . is wholly impossible. We are
destitute of all the great elements; slave labor is too careless. We are destitute of water power, on the sea-board; of navigation to water power in the
interior. We are destitute of coal, and that salubrity of climate necessary
to preserve health, in summer and autumnal months, in the fetid atmosphere of densely crowded factories. And, above all, thank God, we are
destitute of the cheap labor of a half-starved, beggared and dependent
population, fit to be packed in factories to drag out a miserable, slavish
existence for the paltry equivalent of the bread they eat, and the raiment
that they wear.[2]

Reconstruction eventually yielded the stable political and social
institutions needed for economic development and the absorption of
the surplus labor spawned by the emancipation of agricultural workers.
Manufactures of tobacco, textiles, furniture, and other industries based
upon the South's natural resources slowly opened, or reopened, employment opportunities in scattered towns and villages. No single date can
fix the rebirth of cotton manufacturing, but statistics help to establish
landmarks. In 1860 the southern states had 324,000 active spindles
and only a few thousand more in 1870, but spindleage almost doubled
in 1870-1880 and nearly tripled in 1880-1890. Neither in textiles nor
in any other industry was the process of industrialization brought to
maturity. On the contrary, at every stage of recent history students of
regional economics have picked the South as the area most urgently
in need of more, or more diversified, industries.[3]

Historians of southern industry have discovered social as well as

[2] *Speech of the Honorable Willie P. Mangum (of North Carolina) on the Tariff,
Delivered in the Senate of the United States on the 7th & 8th of Feb. 1832* (Washington,
1832). A quarter-century later a southern sociologist included cotton manufactures among
the "coarser processes of the mechanic arts and manufactures" which the South should
promote, both to give additional employment to slaves and to end dependence upon
northern manufactures (George Fitzhugh, *Sociology for the South; or the Failure of Free
Society* [Richmond, 1854], pp. 86-87).
[3] C. B. Hoover and B. U. Ratchford, *Economic Resources and Policies of the South*
(New York, 1951).

economic factors underlying the rise of cotton mills in the postwar South. Sentiment favoring manufacturing grew out of a "change in southern ideals . . . a change from a social system in which work was held to be degrading, to one in which great interest is taken in industrial enterprise" and "contempt for northern industrial methods" gave way to "an intense rivalry with those very methods."[4] The transition "from cotton field to cotton mill" got underway when "those who had saved land and capital from the wreck of the war, or had gained them since, began to tire of the never ceasing contest with the inefficiency and unreliability of the freedman. . . . Hundreds of well-to-do farmers, disgusted with the struggle, practically abandoned their farms and moved to town, there to seek profitable occupation and investments. The country merchant also began to dream of managing greater enterprises."[5] Relatively modest capital requirements and comparatively minor prerequisites of experience or technical know-how recommended cotton manufacturing above most of the alternative channels of industrial promotion and investment.

Northern textile men rose to disparage southern enterprise. In hopes of arresting the spread of competitive mills, they gravely warned prospective investors that the climate was unsuitable to spinning, that humidity would ruin the machinery, that native labor could never acquire adequate skill, that managerial ability would be unobtainable, and that, in any case, it would be uneconomical to shift labor from the the production of cotton into the manufacture of cotton goods.[6] These arguments had been refuted by Gregg and his contemporaries, who successfully demonstrated that in the South Atlantic states, especially in the Piedmont, natural and human factors favored life and work in mill villages. Now, after the war, the half-forgotten pleas for industrial expansion were rehearsed for presentation at such public gatherings as the Immigration Convention in Charleston (1870). Northern machine shops, whose profits depended more directly upon sales of textile machinery than upon the market for cloth, sent agents south with

[4] M. T. Copeland, *The Cotton Manufacturing Industry of the United States* (Cambridge, Mass., 1923), p. 33.
[5] Holland Thompson, *From the Cotton Field to the Cotton Mill* (New York, 1906), pp. 63-64. The founders of the Cone mills in North Carolina were wholesale grocers in Baltimore. "In those days the wholesale grocers were also jobbers of cotton plaids. They used to sell these goods by the bale to every crossroad store throughout the South." Impressed by the opportunities in textile manufacturing, in 1887 Moses and Caesar Cone liquidated their grocery business and established a cotton mill in Asheville (Cone Export & Commission Company, *Half Century Book, 1891-1941* [New York, 1941]).
[6] Thompson, *op. cit.*, p. 65.

specifications and price lists. At the International Cotton Exposition in Atlanta (1881) they were able to make mill owners unusually attractive offers, while the falling price of cotton gave would-be manufacturers the double inducement of cheap raw materials and, as farming became increasingly unattractive, abundant labor.[7] In 1882 the Baltimore *Journal of Commerce,* which for thirty years had specialized in commercial and shipping intelligence, met the need for a "representative industrial paper of the new South" by inaugurating the *Manufacturers' Record.* Its enthusiasm for cotton manufacturing in the southern states echoed views widely expressed long before the journal's birth. "The decree has already gone forth," said the issue of August 25, 1883, "that 'the South, that produces the cotton, must also spin it.'" That the "New South"—a term used by industrial enthusiasts as early as 1880—was "destined to be the center of the cotton manufacturing interests of this country admits of no questioning."[8]

Technological developments in 1865-1880 favored the building of new cotton mills. In 1870 American manufacturers commenced to use the English slasher, a machine "so efficient . . . in performing the function of sizing the warp yarn that in less than ten years the old-style dresser had been driven from the market."[9] Similarly, the Foss and Pevey card, patented in 1875, supplanted the carding machinery, which, basically, had not changed since the days of Samuel Slater. English roving frames began to appear in the United States before the Civil War, but the general acceptance of this machinery and of the competitive lines of intermediate and fine speeders developed by the Lowell Machine Shop was delayed until the 1870's. Most significant of the technical changes was the "spindle revolution of the 1870's." Commencing in 1866 four inventors—Atwood, Rabbeth, Pearl, and Sawyer —experimented successfully with light-weight, high-speed spindles. "Amidst the pains of recurrent and bitter law-suits over conflicting patent claims," the Sawyer spindle had by 1879 "won the market on

[7] Copeland, *op. cit.,* pp. 33-34. Recovering from a low of 299,000 bales in 1864, cotton production mounted steadily to 4,000,000 bales in 1870 and over 6,000,000 bales in 1880. Meanwhile, the price, which topped $1.00 a pound in the war years, fell to 16.5 cents in 1869 and to 11.1 cents in 1875; and for the rest of the century the annual average price seldom passed 10 cents a pound (*Historical Statistics of the United States, 1879-1945* [Washington, 1949], p. 136).

[8] M. B. Hillyard in *The New South* (Baltimore, 1887) says he used the term in a pamphlet published eight years earlier: "the name 'New South' is one as much my own as it is that of any one."

[9] G. S. Gibb, *The Saco-Lowell Shops* (Cambridge, Mass., 1950), pp. 210-214.

the basis of technical superiority."[10]   Ring spinning frames, equipped
with spindles running up to 9,200 revolutions per minute, proved "so
far superior in cost of operation and quantity of production of cotton
yarns that the mule was relegated to a very narrow field—that of spinning fine and soft yarns."[11]   New mills, equipped with improved carding, spinning, and dressing machinery, possessed an immediate advantage over the older mills, excepting those which had followed depreciation policies that made prompt modernization possible.[12]   Ring
spinning possessed another advantage over mule spinning: the new
spinning frames could be operated by women and children, usually at
lower wages than those of male operatives.[13]   And "cheaper labor" was
one reason why the South "ought almost monopolize the cotton manufacture of the world."[14]

Precisely how these and other factors influenced the founders of
Danville's postwar mills is not a matter of detailed record.   Danville's
first cotton mill, the Danville Manufacturing Company, appears to have
flourished from 1829 to the 1860's; but the census of 1880, which enumerated eight cotton mills in Virginia, located no mill in Danville.[15]
Two years later three mills were under construction on the banks of the
Dan, and in 1885 the author of the *Illustrated Sketch Book* extolled
the "merry music of their looms and spindles" which "finds harmonious
echo in the hearts of the progressive citizens, whose ambition it is to
see their beloved town some day the successful rival of the New England
cities as a cotton manufacturing center."[16]   Partly because of its proximity to the bright-leaf tobacco farms of southern Virginia and northern

[10] T. R. Navin, *The Whitin Machine Works since 1831* (Cambridge, Mass., 1950), pp.
180-203.
[11] *Five Generations of Loom Builders* (Hopedale, Mass., 1950), p. 11.
[12] S. J. Kennedy, *Profits and Losses in Textiles* (New York, 1936), p. 6.
[13] *Report on Condition of Woman and Child Wage-Earners in the United States*, vol.
I: *Cotton Textile Industry* (Senate Document 645, 61st Congress, 2nd Sess.; Washington,
1910), p. 37.
[14] Hillyard, *op. cit.*, p. 34.
[15] Two were in Chesterfield County, six in Dinwiddie (*Tenth Census of the United
States*, vol. 2: *Report on Manufactures of the United States* [Washington, 1883], p. 955).
In *The History of Pittsylvania County, Virginia* (Lynchburg, 1929, p. 240) Maud Carter Clement fancifully describes the Danville Manufacturing Company as "the fore-
runner of the great Dan River and Schoolfield mills of today."   The charter of the
Danville Manufacturing Company was granted February 10, 1829, and in 1835 the legislature approved a bill "to revive and amend an act, entitled 'an act to incorporate the
Danville Manufacturing Company'" (*Journal of the House of Delegates of the Commonwealth of Virginia* . . . [Richmond, 1835], pp. 143, 208). Although its existence in
the 1860's can be verified (see, for instance, the William T. Sutherlin papers, Duke
University Library), the Danville Manufacturing Company almost certainly was not a
going concern in 1880.
[16] Edward Pollock, *Illustrated Sketch Book of Danville, Virginia* (Danville, 1885), p. 8.

North Carolina, Danville became an important center of tobacco trade and manufacturing, with numerous warehouses, stemming plants, and factories making plug, twist, and smoking tobacco. Warehouse sales of tobacco brought in from nearby farms rose steadily from 10.6 million pounds in 1870 to 30.5 million pounds, valued at $3.3 million, in 1880. There is no uncertain connection between the prosperity of warehousemen, speculators, and tobacco manufacturers in the 1870's and the town's industrial expansion in the 1880's.[17]

Danville, known in the eighteenth century as Wynne's Falls (or Wynne's Ford), grew up on the south bank of the Dan River, sixty-two miles from the confluence of the rivers Dan and Staunton, which forms the Roanoke River. Shallow craft (batteaux) navigated the Dan, at least seasonally, and in the 1870's enthusiastic supporters of river transportation envisioned steamboats moving up from the Albemarle Sound as far inland as Danbury, North Carolina, seventy-seven miles above Danville.[18] Postwar schemes for improving navigation on the Dan ended abortively, but the resumption of railroad building gave Danville superior rail facilities in all directions. The Richmond and Danville Railroad, completed in 1856, linked Danville with the state capital, where connections were made with roads to the north and south. Crossing the state line a few miles southwest of Danville, the Richmond and Danville operated over the tracks of a subsidiary, the Piedmont Railroad, to Greensboro, North Carolina, where main routes entered from New Orleans and Atlanta. The Virginia Midland Railway provided a through route to Alexandria and met the east-west Norfolk and Western at Lynchburg and the Chesapeake and Ohio at Charlottesville. The Danville and New River Railroad, incorporated in 1873 and partially financed by the town of Danville, inaugurated service to Martinsville in 1881 and later formed a junction with north-south feeder lines of the Norfolk and Western system. Finally, the Atlantic and Danville Railroad, though not finished until 1890, opened a direct route to Virginia's ports.[19] Thus Danville acquired ample

[17] *Headlight* (Chicago, 1896); Danville *Daily Register,* Oct. 11, 1884; Duval Porter, *Men, Places and Things as Noted by Benjamin Simpson* (Danville, 1891), pp. 208-210. Simpson was disturbed by the "invasion" of Danville by "an army of pin-hookers and tobacco sharps" and the depressing effect upon culture of the "Goths and Huns of tobacco speculation."

[18] "Report of the Chief of Engineers," in *Report of the Secretary of War . . . Second Session of the 46th Congress,* vol. 2, pt. 1 (Washington, 1879), pp. 652-672; *Annual Report of the Chief of Engineers, United States Army, to the Secretary of War for the Year 1880,* pt. 1 (Washington, 1880), pp. 788-790.

[19] Details of the development of Virginia's railroads are furnished by the annual

rail facilities for bringing cotton to its mills and for shipping out finished products.

The census of 1880 reported a population of 7,526 for the town of Danville (not including 1,200 enumerated in North Danville, or Neapolis), while the population of Pittsylvania County was 52,589. Both in the town and in the county Negroes outnumbered whites; in Danville the Negroes comprised almost three-fifths of the population. While tobacco warehouses and factories furnished employment for colored workers, "there was nothing open for the white working man" and "race conflicts were constantly brewing."[20] Since white and colored laborers generally constituted non-competing groups, the promoters of cotton mills "started a development for the express purpose of affording work to the poor [white] families of the community who were having a hard time."[21] Doubtless, unemployment was a familiar problem to all those interested in the community's welfare; but mill promoters, honestly desiring to provide jobs for white workers, must also have counted the reserve "army" of labor as a favorable factor in estimating the profitableness of the proposed enterprise.

No doubt the decisive factor was power. As early as 1867 one of Danville's leading citizens urged Virginians to develop industries and "save untold strength of water power from wasting."[22] In Danville the defunct Roanoke Navigation Company,[23] having failed to create a bus-

reports of the Railroad Commissioner of the State of Virginia (Richmond, 1877–). The Virginia roads are also discussed competently in John F. Stover, *The Railroads of the South, 1865-1900* (Chapel Hill, N. C., 1955).

[20] D. A. Overbey, Jr., "History of Riverside and Dan River Cotton Mills" (MS). Actually, the only serious riot occurred in November 1883; and by this time three cotton mills were employing white laborers. In May 1882 the Coalitionists gained control of the municipal government and appointed Negroes to the police force and to other town offices. The riot broke out the following year as an outgrowth of a political rally at which the Coalition party held out to Negro voters—and "carpetbaggers"—the prospect of controlling state and national elections. An investigating committee, which included "a number of citizens of Northern birth" and two of the promoters of Riverside Cotton Mills, blamed both factions for the shooting which resulted in the death of four Negroes and the wounding of two white men (*Report of Committee of Forty, with Sworn Testimony of Thirty-seven Witnesses* . . . Richmond, 1883). See also excerpts from a pamphlet, "Coalition Rule in Danville," in Danville *Daily Register*, Oct. 16, 1888; and the *Report of the Adjutant General of the State of Virginia, November 1, 1883* (Richmond, 1884), pp. 42-44.

[21] H. R. Fitzgerald to W. D. Anderson, April 13, 1928. "Of course," Fitzgerald continued, "the mill immediately became a center to which all these unfortunate people would flock, and instead of the mill being responsible for the conditions among them, it proved to be a godsend in offering them an opportunity for employment, which was the first and most important step and what they needed more than anything else to obtain food and clothes and a reasonable measure of independence."

[22] William T. Sutherlin, *Address delivered before the Mechanics' Association of Danville, Va. March 11, 1867* (Richmond, 1867).

[23] The Roanoke Navigation Company was chartered by the state of North Carolina in

tling riverport, left behind a dilapidated log and plank dam, spanning the river above the Union Street bridge. To bypass the shoals opposite the town, the dam diverted water into a canal, running parallel to the river for a distance of 3,600 feet and emptying into a creek near the Richmond and Danville Railroad trestle. Army engineers reported in 1879 that about one-third of the dam, at the north end, had washed away and that the canal locks were out of order and no attempt had been made to keep the canal open for shipping. They also observed that "Danville's resources of water power *for manufacturing*" were very great though utilized "to but a slight extent."[24]

There seems to be no record directly linking the engineers' report with subsequent industrial developments; but in November 1881 a court order required the receivers to sell at auction the property of the Roanoke Navigation Company. Purchasers of the land and water-power rights along the canal were Danville citizens who had at least tentative plans for starting manufacturing enterprises. C. A. Ballou, later city engineer of Danville, surveyed the property and divided the canal frontage into twelve lots, each of which had the right to one-twelfth of the available water power. Subsequently, the owners of these lots organized the Danville Water Power Company for managing the power development, including the dam and the Morotock Canal. Minutes of the Water Power Company, covering a period of five years (1882-1887),[25] furnish much of the available information concerning the origins of Danville's cotton mills. While the records do not prove that the mill builders were moved to enter industry solely to mobilize their water-power investments, obviously they could not have visualized manufacturing without access to power.

In April 1882 the firm of Gerst Brothers and Company was operating a "cotton factory" on one of the water-power lots, probably at the site if not in the building formerly used by the Danville Manufacturing Company.[26] In September the five-story mill of the Morotock Manu-

---

1796, but in 1818-1826 the state of Virginia made instalment payments on a subscription of $80,000 to its capital stock (J. S. Davis, *Essays in the Earlier History of American Corporations,* vol. 2, Cambridge, 1917, p. 179; "Second Auditor's Report on Canal and Turnpike Companies," in *Journal of the House of Delegates of the Commonwealth of Virginia;* Richmond, 1824).

[24] *Annual Reports of the Army Chief of Engineers* (as in note 18, *supra*).

[25] There are two minute books in the files of Dan River Mills: one is a "Record Book of Meetings held by Owners of Water Power," April 7, 1882—May 7, 1883; the second covers the period Jan. 31, 1884 to Sept. 21, 1887.

[26] Part of the Gerst property consisted of real estate acquired by J. B. Pace from the Danville Manufacturing Company in August 1865.

facturing Company (then the largest building in the city) was almost finished, and the Riverside Cotton Mills had laid the foundations of its first building.[27]

The head start of E. L. and A. Gerst—for it seems they were the first to start producing yarn or cloth—created some friction among the owners of water-power rights along the canal. Negotiating "in a spirit of conciliation and fairness," in August 1882 the Water Power Company finally persuaded the Gersts to move their wheelhouse to make room for a road and other improvements deemed necessary for the effective use of the other power sites.[28] With this, the Gerst factory disappears from the records until the sale of its power rights to Riverside Cotton Mills in 1895.

F. X. Burton, C. G. Holland, and C. H. Conrad, identified in local annals as tobacconists, organized the Morotock Manufacturing Company on March 8, 1882, "for the purpose of manufacturing cotton cloths, cotton yarns, and other cotton fabrics."[29] Morotock's promoters had bought seven of the water power lots, but in June 1882 they sold Lot No. 1 to T. B. Fitzgerald. Practically all of the records of the Morotock Company have disappeared; its merger with Riverside Cotton Mills in 1890 will be discussed later.

While we may gather from records of the Water Power Company that mill building was inaugurated by men in search of gain from the exploitation of water-power sites, it appears equally important that they were businessmen looking for new investment outlets for earnings accumulated in the tobacco trade and other enterprises in and around Danville. In varying degrees this was true of the six organizers of Riverside Cotton Mills. Three of them were brothers: Robert A., John H., and James E. Schoolfield. They were sons of the Reverend William M. Schoolfield, a Methodist preacher of Henry County, who died in 1858, leaving eight children in the care of their mother, Sarah Harrell Schoolfield. A small ministerial income, a large family, and the early death of the father robbed the Schoolfield children of educational

---

[27] Danville *Daily Register*, Aug. 31 and Sept. 16, 1882.

[28] The Gerst firm received a guarantee of 50 H.P. continuously, additional power not exceeding 50 H.P. free of cost for five years and at the rate of $7.50 per H.P. per annum thereafter. At this time the twelve water-power lots were owned by the Gersts, the Riverside Mills, the Morotock Mills, Crews, Westbrooks & Co., J. M. Walker, and J. R. Noell.

[29] Burton, Holland, and Conrad got their start in the tobacco trade or manufacturing and, like the promoters of Riverside, financed their cotton mill with earnings from tobacco (Duval Porter, *op. cit.*, pp. 344, 353-355, 366-367). In September 1882, Conrad sold his interest to Burton and Holland for $8,556.17.

opportunities; none of the scattered references to their early life even mentions their schooling. Born in Patrick County in 1853, Robert Addison Schoolfield went to work as a clerk in a country store at the age of sixteen; later, he acquired an interest in his brother's store but left this partnership in 1881. Company records explain that R. A. Schoolfield was "out of business" when he "came to Danville to take active management" of Riverside Cotton Mills in 1882. J. H. Schoolfield was a general merchant and tobacco manufacturer. He and his brother, J. E. Schoolfield, were two of the promoters and directors of the Danville and New River Railroad. J. E. Schoolfield was also the senior partner in a Danville plumbing and hardware business. Sometime after the founding of Riverside Cotton Mills he became interested in a revival movement and was well-known throughout the state as a lay preacher. It was said of him in 1896 that "he gives but little attention to the hardware business . . . his time is almost wholly occupied in evangelical work."[30]

Carpenter by trade and a Confederate veteran, Benjamin F. Jefferson was a coal, wood, and lumber dealer in North Danville.[31] Dr. H. W. Cole came to Danville as a physician in 1858 and had "a large and lucrative practice"; but at the time the mills were started he served the town as coroner and ran a drug store. Thomas Benton Fitzgerald was recognized as the "originator and founder" of the enterprise. Born in Halifax County in 1840, after serving in the Confederate Army he settled in Danville and established the firm of T. B. Fitzgerald and Company, contractors and brickmakers. Fitzgerald was one of the most active members of the Water Power Company; both he and Cole acquired land and water-power rights from the Roanoke Navigation Company, which they later transferred to Riverside Cotton Mills. The prospect of contracts for constructing mill buildings gave Fitzgerald a further inducement to join the other five capitalists in promoting a manufacturing concern.

The exact sequence of events leading to their decision to go into the textile business cannot be reconstructed. Undoubtedly the promotors had many informal conversations, weighing the advantages and

[30] *Headlight* (Chicago, 1896), pp. 25-33. See also Duval Porter, *op. cit.*, pp. 330-332, 359-360, 391-392.
[31] A native of Fairfax County, Jefferson was a seaman in the U. S. Navy and served under Commodore Perry in his famous visit to Japan in 1853. Enlisted in the Confederate Army, he was assigned to make coffins. He made his home in Danville after having been mustered out there in 1865. (From notes kindly furnished by Norman J. Waugh, a grandson.)

disadvantages of the new enterprise, prior to their first recorded meeting.[32] As intelligent and energetic southerners, they must have been conversant with current discussions of the outlook for cotton manufacturing if not with the more abstract issue of the role of industry in the renascent South. These public discussions, as has been pointed out, emphasized the timeliness and comparative ease of establishing cotton mills in the southern states. Many of the new mills failed; for decades Riverside Cotton Mills was extraordinarily successful. It remains to explain why this mill prospered, though it commenced, as its founders confessed, with "limited means, no trade and no experience in the business by any of its promotors."[33]

The Company

On June 10, 1882, Fitzgerald, Cole, Jefferson, and the three Schoolfields met at the home of J. E. Schoolfield and instructed R. W. Peatross (the first counsel of the firm) to draw up a contract binding them to form a joint stock company "for the purpose of manufacturing cotton and woolen fabrics, rope, etc."[34] To provide the initial capital of

[32] On Nov. 6, 1905, the Richmond *Times-Dispatch* published a letter from the Reverend J. B. Buckley, D. D., under the caption "The Cotton Mill Industry in Danville." Dr. Buckley, it seems, attended the Virginia Conference of the Methodist Church in Danville in November 1880. His host at the Conference was T. B. Fitzgerald. Describing himself as a "preacher who came to Conference from a region of cotton factories," Buckley says he "expressed his surprise that such a splendid water-power should be running to waste" and asked Fitzgerald, "the man of all men capable of organizing and starting such an enterprise," why he hadn't undertaken to start a cotton mill in Danville. Fitzgerald replied that he and his friends had considered the matter but needed "a capable man to take charge." Buckley promised to secure the services of "one of the finest manufacturers of plain white goods that the South had ever produced," but eventually was not able to persuade the mill man he had in mind to come to Danville. No one, least of all Fitzgerald himself, has left a corroborative note on this incident; but there seems to be no reason to consider it apocryphal.

[33] According to R. A. Schoolfield, in the director's meeting, Jan. 9, 1893. Later, Schoolfield related that "because of a severe illness in 1881 he had been sent to the milder climate of Columbus, Georgia, to spend the winter, and there had been impressed by the cotton mills in operation with white labor. On his return he had spoken of it to his brothers. Later, when the question was to be decided as to the kind of mill to be started, he was invited to attend the meeting and give his impressions of the cotton fabric industry as he had seen it in operation in Georgia. The result was that the founders decided to engage in that type of manufacturing, feeling that it would attract a good class of white citizens to Danville" (Janie Gray Hagan to L. H. Fracher, Aug. 2, 1952). Mrs. Hagan also refers to this incident in *The Story of Danville* (New York, 1950), p. 59.

[34] The "Record Book of the Directors and Stockholders, 1882 to 1893," contains not only the preincorporation agreement but also the other documents and contracts referred to in this section. The charters and amendments have been published: *Charters and Amendments of The Riverside Cotton Mills* (1882-1909): *The Dan River Power & Manufacturing Company* (1895-1909): *The Riverside and Dan River Cotton Mills, Incorporated* (1909-1937): *Dan River Mills, Incorporated* (1946) (Danville, n.d.).

$75,000, the incorporators subscribed to 750 shares of capital stock, as follows:

	shares	par value
T. B. Fitzgerald	210	$21,000
J. H. Schoolfield	200	20,000
B. F. Jefferson	105	10,500
R. A. Schoolfield	105	10,500
J. E. Schoolfield	70	7,000
H. W. Cole	60	6,000

In October 1882, for reasons undisclosed, Cole became dissatisfied with the venture and sold his interest to Fitzgerald and J. H. Schoolfield.[35]

On July 27, 1882, the Circuit Court of Danville issued a charter authorizing a joint stock company "for the purpose of purchasing the necessary property, machinery and appliances, and constructing the necessary buildings for conducting and carrying on the business of manufacturing cotton and woolen fabrics, rope, flour &c at Danville, Virginia." A few weeks earlier the corporate name, The Riverside Cotton Mills, had been decided upon.

In part payment for their shares, Fitzgerald and Cole conveyed to the corporation, at cost to them, land and riparian and power rights on the south side of the Dan River. These two incorporators were excused from making cash payments on their stock subscriptions until the other shareholders had paid the same proportion of their subscriptions as Fitzgerald and Cole contributed in real property. Apparently, less than $16,000 was involved in these exchanges of real estate for stock.[36]

Fitzgerald was elected president. Under the terms of the preincorporation agreement he was engaged to build the mill at cost plus 10 per cent, but he accepted no salary as president. The office of vice-president, first held by Cole and then by J. E. Schoolfield, carried no remuneration; but R. A. Schoolfield, who was selected to "take charge

[35] Cole originally transferred to the company property valued at $5,774.22 and was paid $7,151.44 for his interests, in an assignment dated Oct. 6, 1882.

[36] On June 1, 1882, Fitzgerald bought Lot No. 1 of the water-power property for $3,535. This, together with three lots on Bridge Street, was conveyed to the Riverside Cotton Mills for $700 in cash and a credit of $9,340.89 on Fitzgerald's stock subscription.

The oldest document in the Dan River files is an original deed of trust executed by John F. and Elizabeth Beavers on Sept. 14, 1853, conveying "one certain lot and tenement" on Bridge Street, together with a slave, Louisa, and her child, to W. M. Tredway. This appears to be one of the parcels of land acquired by the company in 1882.

of the business . . . as its general manager and secretary and treasurer," received $1,500 a year for the first three years. Although the vagueness of the preincorporation agreement later occasioned a serious rift among the promotors, the infant business was able to start life, not with watered stock as so often happened in nineteenth-century promotions, but with organizational expenses, construction costs, and managerial salaries held to a minimum.

With 2,240 spindles and 100 looms installed, Riverside Cotton Mills began to produce yarn and cloth in April 1883. The year before R. A. Schoolfield, accompanied by C. G. Holland and C. H. Conrad of the Morotock Company, went North to purchase machinery for the diminutive mill. For technical help in the selection and installation of the machines, the two firms jointly employed Henry Rishton at a salary of $125 a month. As superintendent, the Riverside management hired S. I. Roberts, paying him $2,500 a year. Roberts, a native of Maine, came to Danville from a mill in Columbus, Georgia, bringing with him W. E. Thomas, a machinist, T. D. Wall, a carding overseer, and several skilled operatives to train the new employees of Riverside. A year later (1884) George W. Robertson, a native of Oldham, England, left a position in Columbus, Georgia, to become Riverside's overseer of weaving, and W. G. Benefield came from Alabama to take charge of dyeing. F. L. Chapman joined the company as overseer of spinning in 1889.

Bricks, Machines, and Power

Mill No. 1 was erected on the south bank of the river, taking water for its wheel near the east end of the canal. Production commenced as soon as the first looms and spindles were in place, but the building had been designed to facilitate the expansion which the directors soon found desirable. In less than three years Mill No. 1 reached its capacity of 260 looms and 6,000 spindles and employed 200 operatives. The Real Estate and Machinery account exceeded $300,000 at the end of 1886.

Meanwhile, the Water Power Company carried on the work of widening the canal and restoring the dam. On August 30, 1882, a large crowd gathered to see the "turning on of the water" as the head gates were opened to allow ten feet of water into the forty-foot canal— which was double the original width. The local press observed that the water power was sufficient to run all the factories along the canal and would "give our enterprising young city the long-desired prosperity and happiness of a first-class southern manufacturing centre."[37] The agreement to rebuild the dam was signed (July 1882) by the owners of water rights on both sides of the river; but it was not until May 1883 that the company "decided that the construction committee [of which T. B. Fitzgerald was chairman] go to work at once on dam." Apparently, the work was completed by 1884, for in September of that year the company decided "to have a McDonald Fish Ladder constructed at the Dam. . . in compliance with the laws of the state."[38]

At the same time the Water Power Company had its eye on north-shore power sites and in April 1885 offered to buy the "Water Power of G. W. Yarbrough on North side of Dan River with riparian rights at a price not to exceed Fifteen Thousand Dollars ($15,000) and the debt of said G. W. Yarbrough due Danville Water Power Company for the construction of Dam across Dan River." Yarbrough, who was liable for half of the dam construction costs, had apparently made no move to meet this obligation; nor did he accept the proposal of the Water Power Company. As a matter of fact, Riverside Mills had already displayed an interest in the north-shore power, having purchased several lots in North Danville in August 1882. The first suggestion that the mill might expand in this direction occurs in the directors' minutes for January 4, 1887, when Fitzgerald was instruced to buy Yarbrough's "upper water power." Although Mill No. 1 had increased its power 50 per cent by installing new wheels, the limited amount of power available on the Morotock Canal and the increasing demands for power in Danville must have raised the value of power sites and made it desirable for the company to acquire power rights across the river.[39]

Construction of Mill No. 2, just below the north end of the dam,

[37] Danville *Daily Register*, Aug. 31 and Nov. 2, 1882.
[38] "Record Book of the Water Power Company, 1884-87." The dam history of Danville is obscure. The *Illustrated Sketch Book of Danville*, published in 1885, refers to the dam "recently thrown across the river just above the upper bridge" (p. 8), obviously the one built by the Water Power Company. In 1884 the company named a committee of one "to see Dr. Sydnor and if in his judgment [i.e., the committeeman] the timber of the old Dam should not be removed, that he forbid him to move it." Apparently, the old dam was the "wing" dam mentioned in the Army engineers' report. Dr. Sydnor is identified as the unsuccessful promoter of steamboat service on the Dan River (*Progress,* vol. 4 [Danville], June 1 and 8, 1923).
[39] On Oct. 1, 1887, T. B. Fitzgerald conveyed to Riverside Cotton Mills the following property: the so-called Yarbrough water-power sites at the north end of the dam ($12,750); the Motley property in North Danville ($900 in cash, plus a note for $2,400); two other parcels of real estate in North Danville, for $3,500 and $2,500 respectively.

commenced in 1887; and in June 1888 Fitzgerald reported to the stock-holders that the new mill, including machinery and water power in-stallations, cost $227,260. The mortar was scarcely dry when the direc-tors began to discuss the feasibility of enlarging the building. Un-certainty over the means of financing new construction caused some hesitation, but Fitzgerald's insistence that "it is to our interest to de-velop our entire power as soon as practicable and in so doing diversify our production" encouraged the stockholders to furnish funds for Mill No. 3. A picker house and a four-story cloth hall were also added to the North Danville properties in 1888-1889. In the latter year the Real Estate and Machinery account exceeded $750,000, and there is no reason to doubt the president's claim that the plant of Riverside Cotton Mills was "one among the largest and best equipped in the South."[40]

While the young Riverside Mills flourished, the Morotock Mill under the management of Holland and Burton found it difficult to secure a profitable trade. Statistics published by the Chamber of Com-merce, while Holland was serving as its first president, reveal that in 1884 the Danville mills together produced 3,000,000 yards of brown sheeting and 2,400,000 yards of stripes and plaids. Since Riverside's production records account for all of the colored goods, the Morotock Mill must have specialized in sheeting. A stray letterhead with an 1886 date line describes the firm as a manufacturer of "standard sheetings, shirtings, drills, warps, twine, &"; and in 1888 the local paper reported that Morotock was installing new waterwheels, buying new looms, and setting up an Edison dynamo for lighting. It employed 330 "hands."[41] Nevertheless, as early as 1884 the owners offered to sell the plant to Riverside. The Riverside management found the terms unattractive and made a counterproposal, which the Morotock stockholders rejected. In August 1890 T. B. Fitzgerald, R. A. Schoolfield, and Superintendent Roberts inspected the Morotock factory and reported that it was "not in first class and satisfactory running condition." But the Morotock management declared its "wish and intention to have it so—and to ac-complish this . . . we propose to sell to you on the terms before stated." On September 15, 1890, the merger was consummated by the exchange of Morotock's assets for $190,000 in 6 per-cent bonds and 10,000 shares of Riverside common stock at $110 per share. Thus, Morotock became Riverside Mill No. 4. Included in the transaction were six of the

[40] Stockholders' Meeting, Jan. 8, 1889.
[41] Danville *Daily Register,* Oct. 17, 1884, and Dec. 7, 1888.

twelve water-power lots, a number of tenements, Pocahontas (or Sullivan's) Island, just above the dam, and other pieces of real estate.

At the end of 1891 the four mills ran 36,432 spindles and 1,246 looms.

Riverside's next expansion followed the unusually good business of 1892. At the board meeting of January 9, 1893, R. A. Schoolfield put his recommendation in the form of a question: "Your Company has been progressive in the past, why should it not continue to be so in the future, and develop the unimproved property, adding to the prosperity of the Town and bringing an increased revenue to its stockholders?" Authorized "to purchase additional Land and Water Power if in their judgment they deemed it desirable," the president and treasurer soon completed plans for new construction. Their original intention was to build along the canal, but in April Schoolfield reported to the directors: "on account of the exorbitant price asked by the Committee from the [City] Council and the illiberal spirit in which our proposals for improvements on the Danville side of the River were met by them, backed up by Public Sentiment, the additions to your Plant will all be located on the North Side of the River and the improvements on the Danville side have been abandoned." The City of Danville, which in January 1886 commenced to light the streets by electricity, operated a small generating plant on the banks of the canal with water power leased from the Gerst brothers. The "exorbitant price" refers, apparently, to the terms under which the city agreed to sell or share its water-power contract with the Riverside company. But in 1895 Riverside Mills purchased for $14,000 all the water power and land along the canal controlled by the Gersts, who, perhaps as early as 1885, had abandoned their cotton manufacturing business.[42]

Mill No. 5, a three-story building housing 10,000 spindles and 417 looms, was completed late in 1893. It represented, according to the management, a smaller investment than a similar unit in Danville would have cost; in effect, it was an enlargement of Mill No. 3 and therefore some of the installations of a detached mill were unnecessary.

In January 1894 the foundations were laid for Mill No. 6 on a north-shore site, purchased (for $5,000) from the City of Danville. This 20,000-spindle mill shared with Dan Valley Mills (a flour mill) the

[42] *Annual Reports of the Superintendent of the City Water, Gas and Electric Light Works . . . for the Year Ending December 31st. 1899* (Danville, 1900); Danville *Daily Register*, March 20 and May 25, 1889; May 30, 1895.

water impounded by a new 400-foot wing dam, spanning the river diagonally, just above the Main Street bridge.

The rapid growth of the physical plant in the early 1890's is illustrated by a memorandum prepared for a directors' meeting in October 1894. Capital outlays for the period January 1, 1893, to October 1, 1894, were listed as follows:

Real estate (Danville Mill Company and City of Danville)	$51,900
Bulkhead and lower dam	13,086
Outside bulkheads	10,037
Improvements, Morotock Canal race	1,897
Canal retaining walls	12,802
Improvements, old dam	11,750
Stone for river walls	1,550
Picker, wheel and boiler houses	88,173
Extensions, Mills No. 2 and No. 3	47,000
Improvements on wheels	940
Flour mill, outside realty, water power, etc.	12,250
	$251,385

In the same period of twenty-one months the Real Estate and Machinery account rose from $1,222,655 to $1,601,153, indicating additional permanent improvements—mainly machinery—valued at $127,-000. When Mill No. 6 commenced production (1895), Riverside was operating 15,000 more spindles than any other mill in the South.

In June 1895 Schoolfield advised the directors that all the improvements planned and authorized were virtually completed. There were then in place 65,000 spindles and 2,217 looms, of which 192 were classed as broad looms (76 to 90 inches). Less than six months later the secretary-treasurer told the board that "since the organization of your Company, we cannot recall that we have ever been in a more awkward shape as to delivery" of cloth. Estimating that additional capital expenditures of 6 per cent would increase earnings by 12½ to 15 per cent, he recommended the immediate erection of a new building to hold 336 looms. Plans were drawn for Mill No. 7 and the building constructed, adjoining Mill No. 5, in the winter of 1895-1896.

In 1897-1898 a new dye house was built on the north bank of the river. "You have today," R. A. Schoolfield told the stockholders, "one of, if not the most complete and modern dye-house to be found anywhere in the United States, the power for same being furnished by a 100 H.P. Bates-Corliss engine."

This rounded out the physical growth of Riverside in the period 1882-1901. At the turn of the century the mills operated 67,650 spindles and 2,772 looms. By way of comparison, the Pepperell Manufacturing Company then had over 200,000 spindles installed.[43]

The period in which mill buildings mushroomed on the banks of the Dan raised a number of technical and financial problems. A production difficulty arose in 1893, when the new looms in Mill No. 3 outran the supply of yarn. Since there was no space for additional carding and spinning machinery, Mill No. 1 ran day and night. The acquisition of many wide looms again created a gap between spinning and weaving capacity, and in November 1895 the directors approved Schoolfield's recommendation to scrap some Sawyer spindles and replace them with the improved Rabbeth spindles at a cost of $115,000. In the opinion of a "practical mill and machinery man" the company now possessed "colored mills . . . equal to any, North or South; and if I were to build you machinery for another mill on brown goods, it would be a duplicate of the one you have. . . . In my experience of thirty-two years . . . I have never seen any machinery that had received better care or was giving better results."[44]

Night work in spinning was again necessary after the purchase of 170 new looms in 1897, and the dyers also had to work two shifts. But it was a new procedure in dyeing that made a new dye house an absolute necessity. As Schoolfield explained to the directors in May 1897: "We have recently commenced to dye a color in cotton that we were not [dyeing] some time ago. There is perhaps a larger reduction in the cost of coloring this color in the raw state than any other, up to recently however we have been apprehensive about adopting this color, but the dyestuff has been so much improved, we think it safe and perfectly satisfactory to dye this particular shade in the raw state." He did not identify "this particular shade"— presumably it was one of the so-called "Congo" colors discovered in 1884 and perfected so as to permit the dyeing of cotton without use of mordants. Rawstock dyeing required more space than yarn dyeing, but the direct dyeing of raw cotton saved the labor of preparing hanks for dyeing and quilling the yarn after dyeing.[45] (On the other hand, much of the dyed cotton had to be re-

[43] E. H. Knowlton, *Pepperell's Progress* (Cambridge, Mass., 1948), p. 420.
[44] Directors' Meeting, Jan. 8, 1897. The decision to install Rabbeth spindles was not necessarily a belated recognition of their superiority, since as late as 1896 only 36 per cent of the spindles in the country were of this type (S. J. Kennedy, *op. cit.*, p. 6).
[45] Copeland, *op. cit.*, p. 96; C. E. Pellew, *Dyes and Dyeing* (New York, 1928), pp. 71-76.

baled.) Riverside's cost books indicate that the direct labor cost of dyeing ranged from .25 to .30 cent per pound of manufactured cloth in 1896-1897; it fell to .23 cent at the end of 1897 and stayed within the narrow range of .14 to .17 cent in 1898-1900.

A reduction in the length of the working day (1901) brought about a relatively greater decrease of output in carding than in spinning and weaving. At the same time the load of the cards was reduced in an effort to improve the quality of the yarn. The balance in production was restored by installing twenty revolving flat cards,[46] additional roving fly-frames, and new picker-room machinery. Although labor troubles and unsettled markets, which in 1901 curtailed production by 29.5 per cent, delayed the more extensive replacement of obsolete machinery, 198 broad looms were bought to replace the narrow sheeting looms in Mill No. 6.

Water power, at first the lodestar of Danville's mills, became surprisingly early the nemesis of successful operations. The river ran low in summer; and on some occasions, as in 1892, Riverside Mills operated at night when other firms were no longer drawing water for power.[47] In 1895 the company spent $6,000 to wall up the canal banks, which added "materially to the water power"; and in 1898 the spillway of the upper dam was raised eighteen inches. The undependable flow of the river and the inadequacy of the dams in Danville had two consequences: the first was the decision to supplement water power with steam power, and the second was the search for new water-power sites upstream.

By 1900 American cotton mills were using about three times as much steam as water power, and the use of electric power had passed the experimental stage.[48] In some ways the experience of Riverside

[46] "In the early 1880's a great controversy was raging in American textile circles" over the "reputed superiority of English carding methods over American" (Gibb, *The Saco-Lowell Shops*, pp. 344-346, 783). The Pettee Machine Works was the first (1885) American firm to manufacture the English-style revolving flat card, replacing the old stationary card. In 1896 Riverside was one of three large southern firms that had not adopted the Pettee card, although it may have acquired some of the competing models of Lowell or Whitin.

[47] In October 1897 there was "less water in the river than we have ever seen before," and both day and night operations had to be curtailed. In March 1893 ice and high water hampered the utilization of the power.

[48] Copeland, *op. cit.*, p. 28. Virginia's nine cotton factories, reported by the census of 1890, used 620 H.P. generated by steam and 2850 H.P. derived from the turbine water wheels (*Eleventh Census of the United States: Report on Manufacturing Industries in the United States*, pt. 1 [Washington, 1895], p. 932).

mirrored the stages through which the industry passed in its search for
more, or more economical, power.

The idea of using steam boilers matured in the plans for Mill No.
7. The estimate that one 1500 H.P. engine would furnish auxiliary
power sufficient, in case of water-power failure, to operate all the mills
on the north shore proved incorrect; and in 1898 a 100 H.P. engine was
installed to supplement the water power in Mill No. 6.

The early plans for developing the property of a new concern, the
Dan River Power & Manufacturing Company, envisaged the storage of
water at the "upper water power" for use at the Riverside Mills. If
the shortage of power could not be overcome in this way, Schoolfield
said in January 1901, "it can be done by adding an Electric Plant there
[i.e., several miles upstream] and transmitting a sufficient amount of
power to Riverside."[49] Actually, as I shall explain in the following
chapter, this solution of the mill's power problem was never tried.

The vagaries of the water supply affected communities on both sides
of the river. In 1894 North Danville needed additional water power
"for the purpose of pumping water and also perhaps for running the
Electric Light Plant." The mill company granted the town the right
to install one wheel (at an annual rental of $500) for a term of twenty
years; but a few years later, when North Danville was brought into the
corporate limits of Danville, the municipal power plant was dismantled
and Riverside Mills acquired the building and reservoir near Lovers'
Leap.

In June 1895 the company purchased the Gerst water-power lot.
As pointed out previously, the Gersts had leased this power to the city
for the use of the municipal electric plant, an arrangement which the
Riverside management regarded as a "standing menace" to its control
of the water power on the canal. In 1898 the city engineer informed
the company that Danville needed new water wheels and additional
water for the electric plant; but the mill officials replied that they could
not "furnish . . . a larger amount of power than we are now doing for
the city's use at night" and denied the city any power during the day.
The Danville Street Car Company (of which T. B. Fitzgerald was president) had, since the inauguration of trolley-car lines in 1888, generated
electricity at a thermal plant; and the "grand success" of the "electric

[49] Directors' Meeting, Jan. 25, 1901.

car people" was thought to recommend steam generation for the municipal electric service. In 1899 the city renewed its lease on the Gerst site, with an option to terminate the contract on six months' notice "should they procure power elsewhere." An opportunity to secure power elsewhere presented itself before the end of the year; and, after buying the 307-foot water-power lot of Crews and Westbrooks (founders of the elevator manufacturing firm) the city leased 45 H.P. to Riverside Mills for daytime use at $1,400 a year. The century ended with Riverside Cotton Mills in control of all the power sites on the north shore and eleven-twelfths of the south-side water power.[50]

Apparently, the charter provision of authority to carry on the business of manufacturing "flour &c." was not an idle gesture. The purchase or construction of tenement houses, stores, a grist mill, and a box factory are mentioned in early records. The box factory, originally the business of Worsham & Company, was acquired through the Morotock merger; but in 1891 the machinery was sold outright and the building leased to the firm of Noell and Woodward for $1,000 a year. In its 1890 statement Riverside placed a valuation of $3,000 on the corn mill, but the fact that James I. Pritchett was willing to rent it for $1,500 a year, commencing in April 1893, suggests gross undervaluation of this asset. One of the north-side water-power sites—capable of developing 1,000 H.P., according to a survey made by Captain Ballou in 1890— was owned by the Danville Mill Company, a flour milling concern. In 1893 Riverside Cotton Mills purchased for $38,500 the land, buildings, electric-light plant, four water-wheels, and other assets of the Danville Milling Company. Subsequently, part of this property was conveyed to a new corporation, the Dan Valley Mills, organized by J. I. Pritchett and W. H. Hill. Convinced that the mill would "fill a want much felt by Danville people as well as farming interests around the Town," Riverside subscribed to $17,500 of the stock of Dan Valley Mills.[51] The business prospered; and by 1901, when Riverside held a

[50] Stockholders' Minutes, Jan. 14, 1896; Danville *Daily Register*, Jan. 6, March 20, and May 25, 1889; May 30, 1895; *Annual Reports of the Superintendent of the City Water, Gas and Electric Light Works . . . 1900* (Danville, 1901).

In August 1899 Riverside was advised by Peatross and Harris, attorneys, that the "dam you have constructed across the tail race is a breach (if insisted on) of the provisions in said deed" (i.e., to water-power lots 5, 6, 7, 8, 9, and 10). As owner of Lot 9, the city had the right to excavate and deepen the tail race—all of which must have made it seem desirable (to the company) to acquire the city's lot.

[51] Stockholders' Meeting, Jan. 9, 1894. In 1891 the charter had been amended to permit the company to own stock in other corporations up to 10 per cent of its own capital.

two-thirds interest in Dan Valley, its $40,000 investment in flour milling
earned $8,000 a year in dividends.

In 1893 the directors approved a subscription to 100 shares of the
stock of the Citizens' Bank of Danville.   J. H. Schoolfield was president,
T. B. Fitzgerald, vice-president, and three other directors of the mill
served on the board of directors.   The bank did not prosper.   It paid
small dividends for a while (2.5 per cent in 1901), but its liquidation
in 1905 seems to have wiped out most of Riverside's investment of
$10,000.

Before the end of the period covered by this chapter Riverside Cotton Mills had invested some of its earnings in a new enterprise, the Dan
River Power & Manufacturing Company.   Although it leaves a hiatus
in the history of Riverside down to 1902, the discussion of this venture
has been postponed to the following chapter.

Financing Growth

The rapid expansion between 1882 and 1901 was financed by borrowing, by stock issues, and by plowing back earnings.   Twice the
directors authorized the mortgaging of the mills; fortunately, it never
proved necessary to go to this extreme.   An issue of $190,000 in 6 per-
cent bonds, outstanding from 1890 to 1899, and $300,000 in 5 per-cent
bonds issued in 1899, created the only fixed charges on earnings in this
period.

Appendix 1, consisting of the available balance sheet data, summarizes the financial history of Riverside.

The first stock ledger was opened on February 15, 1883, and 780
shares issued, as follows: T. B. Fitzgerald, 250; J. H. Schoolfield, 250;
B. F. Jefferson, 105; R. A. Schoolfield, 105; and J. E. Schoolfield, 70.[52]
The day before (February 14) the directors, realizing that $78,000
would not suffice to commence business, voted to increase the paid-in
capital to $100,000.   Four of the directors immediately subscribed to
220 additional shares.   At the same time President Fitzgerald was
authorized to sell 250 shares more, "in case it can be placed in the
hands of a party or parties agreeable to all the present stockholders."
The president experienced no difficulty in disposing of the stock; indeed, he had to return to the board for authority to sell a larger

[52] "Stock Ledger of the Riverside Cotton Mills, No. 1."

amount, bringing the outstanding shares to 1,504 at the end of 1883 and to 1,860 shares at the end of 1884. All but 225 shares were owned by the five promoters. In October 1883 Richard I. Anderson, a coal and lumber dealer of North Danville, purchased 100 shares; and the following year, having bought an additional 75 shares, Anderson became a director. In August 1884 John Lee acquired 50 shares, paid for in part by the transfer of land and water rights. Lee, too, was made a director.

In January 1885, having represented to the court that "the operations and business prospects of said Company have so increased as to make it desirable that they be allowed a Greater Maximum Capital," the corporation secured a charter amendment which raised its authorized capitalization to $500,000. At this time 2,031 shares were held by eleven stockholders.[53]

After the treasurer reported earnings of $20,308.77 from the commencement of operations to the end of 1884, the directors declared a stock dividend of 9 per cent, the first of a series of stock distributions designed to capitalize a portion of the earnings. Profits for the year 1885 amounted to $33,189.47, and a stock dividend of 10 per cent was voted. This was followed by the unusual distribution of a 28.9 per cent stock dividend in January 1887. Schoolfield reported that although the earnings for 1886 justified a dividend, it would be unwise to pay out cash.[54] Accordingly, he proposed—and the directors agreed—to issue 673 shares of stock pro rata to the holders of the outstanding 2,327 shares, bringing the capital account up to an even $300,000.

Applying for the second charter amendment (1888), which increased the authorized capital to $1,000,000, the company disclosed that the 5,000 shares of stock outstanding were owned by thirteen shareholders, as follows:

	shares
T. B. Fitzgerald	1115
J. H. Schoolfield	1000
J. E. Schoolfield	612
B. F. Jefferson	447

[53] As of Dec. 27, 1884, T. B. Fitzgerald held 600 shares; J. H. Schoolfield, 550; B. F. Jefferson, 188; J. E. Schoolfield, 160; and R. A. Schoolfield, 137.

At the end of 1885, there were 2,245 shares outstanding. In 1886 an additional 224 shares were issued, but 142 shares were repurchased and canceled.

[54] Earnings for 1886 and 1887 are not entered in the directors' minutes. However, the surplus stood at $83,000 at the end of 1886.

R. I. Anderson	426
J. G. Penn	375
J. N. Wyllie	375
R. A. Schoolfield	309
E. H. Schoolfield	100
Kate O. Schoolfield	100
George W. Taylor, Jr.	84
Charles Forbes	42
Jennie Fitzgerald	15

Significant is the fact that a more than sixfold increase in the paid-in capital was accompanied by a fivefold increase in the investment of five of the organizers (excluding the stock held by relatives or members of their families). "Outsiders" now included Forbes, a resident of Culpeper, and Taylor, the latter having acquired stock in part payment for building materials. In June 1887 Wyllie and Penn, Danville tobacco manufacturers, offered to buy 750 shares of stock at par, conditional upon the prior distribution of a 50 per-cent stock dividend. They pointed out that the "actual net assets as determined by the books would not represent the real value of the property, as it would not show the appreciation of the same by reason of improvements made, and the business developed, which has been built up by the united efforts of the present stockholders." Therefore, the present stockholders might object to a new subscription at par, unless the outstanding shares were diluted to a figure approximating par value. Actually, the Wyllie-Penn deal netted the corporation only $50,000 in new capital, as it was necessary to buy in and cancel 250 shares in order to avoid exceeding the charter limitation.[55]

Prior to obtaining the second charter amendment, the directors approved a mortgage loan of $250,000, but Schoolfield reported on returning from a trip to New York that he "failed to receive such encouragement as would induce him to think he could succeed" in placing mortgage bonds advantageously. Since the improvements in North Danville were practically complete and permanent funds were needed to replace short-term loans, the stockholders approved the sale of 1,500 shares of stock at not less than 125. All of this had been issued by April 1889, bringing the outstanding capital to $650,000. The president reiterated that "the policy of the Directory has been, as far as possible, to make ours a close corporation, therefore they have not gone

[55] Directors' Meeting, June 1, 1887.

outside to solicit purchases of stock, and have only sold to such parties as made application for it of their own accord."[56]   Nevertheless, the stockholders' list grew to 63 names by November 1890, when the outstanding capital reached the authorized limit of $1,000,000.

The first cash dividend was 8 per cent, declared in January 1889 and paid to the holders of 6,123 shares.   The next year, with 6,500 shares outstanding, the directors voted a cash dividend of 7.5 per cent and a stock dividend of 20 per cent.   Earnings for 1889 barely covered the cash dividend, while the stock dividend absorbed the surplus of $134,000, made up of undistributed earnings and premiums on stock sales.   The 8 per-cent dividends paid in 1891 and 1892 (both amply covered by earnings) failed to satisfy some of the stockholders, and in January 1892 the officers were authorized to buy in as many as 500 shares of the company's stock at 110 or less.   The stock became more attractive with the announcement of the expansion program a year later.   At this juncture Schoolfield came forward with a recapitalization scheme, the adoption of which saddled the company with the quasi-fixed charge of a 10 per-cent cumulative dividend on $1,000,000 of preferred stock.   The directors' minutes do not fully reveal what was on Schoolfield's mind.   He seems to have believed that future financing by common stock issues would be more attractive to stockholders who already had "salted away" a comparatively safe investment in the company's preferred shares.   No one questioned Schoolfield's judgment in the matter.   Consequently, in January 1893 the entire issue of 18,000 shares of capital stock was exchanged for an equal number of preferred shares; a 20 per-cent dividend in common stock was distributed; and 3,000 shares of common were offered for sale at par—both classes of stock having a par value of $100.

The third charter amendment (1893) increased the authorized capital to $2,000,000.   A privileged subscription to 3,000 shares of common to finance the improvements made in 1894-1895 and another privileged subscription to 2,000 common shares in 1896 brought both the common and the preferred stock accounts up to the legal maximum. Prior to the 1896 subscription the two classes of stock were divided among 130 stockholders, as follows:

[56] Stockholders' Meeting, Jan. 8, 1889.

number of shares per stockholder	number of stockholders	total number of shares owned
1-99	93	2,538
100-199	17	2,408
200-499	8	2,288
500-999	9	6,495
1,000 and over	3	4,271
	130	18,000

In 1890 there were three stockholders owning, respectively, 1,000, 1,116, and 1,418 shares; in 1896 the three largest shareholders held 1,264, 1,407, and 1,600 shares, respectively. Prominent among the additions to the stockholders' list in the 1890's were the North Carolina tobacco manufacturers, Washington Duke and his sons, James B. and Benjamin N. Duke. The Virginia statesman, Claude A. Swanson, purchased stock in this period and added substantially to his holdings over a period of thirty years. With very few exceptions, the stockholders were residents of Virginia or North Carolina. In 1889 Randolph-Macon College became the first institutional stockholder, apparently as the result of a gift of 80 shares by T. B. Fitzgerald, J. E. Schoolfield, R. A. Schoolfield, J. N. Wyllie, J. G. Penn, and R. I. Anderson.

The available sales, earnings, and dividend data are found in Appendix 2.

I estimate that sales were $130,000 in 1884, the first full year of operations, and that they rose steadily to about $1,975,000 in 1900, dropping to $1,673,169 the following year. For a period of sixteen years the company realized net earnings of approximately 15.8 cents on every dollar of sales. The lowest ratio of net earnings to sales was 8.8 per cent in 1901; the highest, 21.1 per cent in 1892. In the same period Pepperell Manufacturing Company averaged net profit of only 8.2 cents per dollar of sales. Producing a higher proportion of fine goods, Pepperell led Riverside in dollar volume of sales; but in 1897-1900 (that is, prior to Pepperell's acquisition of the Laconia mill) Riverside's production, in yards, exceeded the northern firm's output.[57]

Net earnings rose from $14,709 in 1884 to a peak of $369,341 in 1899. At the beginning of 1899, in the first published report to the stockholders, the secretary-treasurer observed that the "condition of your Mills and machinery has never been better than now, and your business, credit and property has never been in so favorable condition

[57] Knowlton, *op. cit.*, pp. 435, 468-469.

to earn dividends for the Stockholders as at present."[58] Earnings were almost as high in 1900 as in 1899; but labor trouble, poor business, and high production costs reduced earnings to $147,880 in 1901. As there had been no stock dividends since 1893, the surplus grew steadily to $442,225 at the end of 1900. Much of it came from premiums on the sale of stock, but the balance sheets make no distinction between earned and capital surplus.

As a further illustration of Riverside's financial success in these first two decades, I offer the following hypothetical case of a stockholder who acquired 100 shares upon organization of the company and terminated his investment at the end of 1901:

date		shares held		dividends (per cent)		dividend income
		preferred	common	preferred	common	(cash)
July	1882		100			
Jan.	1885		100		9*	
Jan.	1886		109		10*	
Jan.	1887		119.9		28.9*	
June	1887		154.5		50*	
Jan.	1889		231.8		8	$ 1,854
Jan.	1890		231.8		7.5	1,738
Jan.	1890		231.8		20*	
Jan.	1891		278.2		8	2,226
Jan.	1892		278.2		8	2,226
Jan.	1893		278.2		10	2,782
**Feb.	1893	278.2			20*	
July	1893	278.2	55.6	5		1,391
	1894	278.2	55.6	10	10	3,338
	1895	278.2	55.6	10	10	3,338
	1896	278.2	55.6	10	8	3,227
	1897	278.2	55.6	10		2,782
	1898	278.2	55.6	10	8	3,227
	1899	278.2	55.6	10	8	3,227
	1900	278.2	55.6	10	8	3,227
	1901	278.2	55.6	10	18	3,783
						38,366

* Stock dividends.
** Common exchanged for preferred.

Taken at par, the holdings of 278.2 shares of preferred stock and

[58] *Report of the Board of Directors of the Riverside Cotton Mills . . . January 10th, 1899* (Danville, 1899).

55.6 shares of common represented a capital gain of 233.8 per cent from 1882 to 1901.   The dividend income of $38,366 is equivalent to an annual return of 19.7 per cent; but if the stockholder had liquidated (at par) the stock held at the end of 1901, he would have earned 36.7 per cent per annum on his original investment.

Despite these generally satisfactory results, the management did not escape criticism.   In January 1898 Schoolfield reported "dissatisfaction among some of your stockholders" and called the demand for larger dividends a "suicidal policy."   He noted the inconsistency of pleas for larger disbursements of earnings and criticism of the management for excessive borrowing.   "The trouble with your Company," he said, "is not that they have been paying too little in dividends, but that they have paid too much, and that some of the stockholders have fixed their expectations too high."   President Fitzgerald supported the treasurer's view, recommending to the stockholders "the most conservative and positive policy of economy," not only for the sake of meeting the "close competition" and "small margins" in selling "but also with an eye single to the importance of building up a working capital as rapidly as possible, to relieve you of the necessity of depending so largely upon a borrowed one to run your business."[59]

Information on the relations between Riverside Mills and its creditors is scanty.   When Schoolfield went north to buy the last instalment of machinery for Mill No. 1, he had authority to arrange for credit up to a term of two years; but the record of this transaction has disappeared.   A statement of Riverside's account with the Holyoke Machine Company in 1893-1894 shows payments on a debt of $25,000 spread over more than 15 months; and in January 1897 the Crompton Loom Works accepted a promissory note for $10,220.56 payable in July 1899. Various individuals, including directors, made short-term advances to the company, while loans for $5,000-10,000 were negotiated at the Chatham (Virginia) Savings Bank, the Wachovia National Bank (North Carolina), and the Citizens' Bank of Danville.   A $10,000 loan for four months (May 1898) and a $15,000 loan for three months (June 1898) at the National Park Bank perhaps initiated the company's long history of short-term financing at New York Banks.   In 1882-1898 interest on all borrowing (less small amounts of interest received) totaled $194,516.

[59] Stockholders' Meeting, Jan. 11, 1898.

In June 1888 the president told the stockholders that "it would not be prudent to incur any greater liability for permanent improvements until the present indebtedness of the mill shall have been reduced or paid." He did not reveal the size of the debt at this time. In fact, liabilities were first reported in the statement of December 1890. Excepting 1893, when current assets ($229,000) barely equaled current liabilities, current assets remained considerably below current liabilities until 1898. New financing in 1899 provided fresh working capital, and in 1901 the current ratio rose to 6 to 1. Since net worth at the end of 1890 totaled $1,127,000, while the real estate and machinery valuation was $1,193,000, it is evident that the stockholders had not furnished all of the fixed capital. Creditors financed the entire inventory of supplies, finished goods, and goods in process, supplied the cash, and furnished credit to the company's customers. Undistributed earnings gradually put more of the stockholders' money into the business, and by 1901 net worth exceeded the property account by $345,778, or approximately the equivalent of cash and inventories at the end of the year.

A small amount of working capital was raised by the sale of bonds in 1899. In February the president and the treasurer were studying the suggestion that "it might be advantageous . . . if we could make a loan for a term of years to give us money to operate on, instead of having to borrow on short time notes"; and in April the Peoples National Bank of Lynchburg purchased an issue of $300,000 in ten-year, 5 per-cent coupon bonds. Only $110,000 was added to working capital, however, as $190,000 had been earmarked to retire the Morotock 6 per-cent bonds.[60] In view of the fact that borrowed funds cost 5 or 6 per cent per annum, while both classes of stockholders expected and usually received 10 per cent on the par value of their shares, trading on the equity was not necessarily as "suicidal" as Schoolfield supposed. On the other hand, considerably more working capital might have been raised through a wider distribution of the company's stock, without threatening the control of the business by the original management.

Cotton manufacturing, the management often reminded the stockholders, requires the producer to sell on time and to pay cash for his

[60] The original issue of 38 coupon bonds ($5,000 each) was equally divided between C. G. Holland and F. X. Burton, but in 1899 Burton held $55,000; J. W. Langhorne owned $65,000; a Mr. Winfree held $55,000; and the remaining $15,000 was held by the Lynchburg bank.

raw materials. The lag between the purchase of cotton and the sale
of cloth may extend into many months, especially when a short supply
of desirable grades of cotton forces the manufacturer to build up inventories soon after the end of the growing season. Furthermore, unless they hedge[61]—and I have not encountered a case of hedging by
Riverside Mills in this period—an aggressive management tries to accumulate stocks at cyclically low prices in order to profit when cloth
prices rise or avoid loss in case cloth prices rise less rapidly than the
advance in cotton prices.

The mills' consumption of cotton rose steadily from 538,000 pounds
in 1884 to 11,479,000 pounds in 1899. Net manufacturing cost—the
cost of raw cotton, less sales of waste—reached a peak of $934,000 in
1900. The value, but not the physical volume, of inventories is reported after 1889. Year-end inventories in 1890-1901 ranged from 7.3
per cent (1898) to 26.6 per cent (1890) of the cost of cotton entered for
manufacturing in the following year.

In October 1892 Schoolfield said that during the preceding year the
company had bought unusually large quantities of both cotton and indigo dyestuffs. Indigo prices advanced during 1892, but the cotton
market declined. No one could say for certain that the downward
trend had been halted, but the treasurer believed it prudent to contract with S. M. Inman & Company for delivery of 5,000-10,000 bales at
a fixed price, over a period of months. Since Inman shipped from
Atlanta, the freight was "against us," but the cotton would be better
and cheaper to work up than North or South Carolina staple. In
November 1898 the mills had 2,000 bales of cotton in storage and 1,850
bales under contract for delivery before the end of the year. It cost 5
to 5.25 cents a pound, and Schoolfield regretted that the lack of storage
space prevented him from buying a great deal more at the prevailing
prices. (Cotton prices did advance in 1899 and again in 1900.) From
the frequent reports the treasurer made to the directors, it appears that
Schoolfield followed the cotton market closely, read the current reports
on cotton acreage and yield, and tried to pick the best periods for buying. Generally, he regarded a large crop as favorable, though some-

----

[61] Organized trading in futures grew rapidly after the opening of the New York Cotton Exchange in 1870, but as late as 1895 many manufacturers regarded the practice of
hedging with suspicion (M. B. Hammond, *The Cotton Industry: An Essay in American
Economic History* [Ithaca, N. Y., 1897], pp. 300-315). In the 1890's Congress debated
a number of bills to restrict or impose heavy taxes on "dealing in fictitious farm products." See: 52nd Congress, 1st Session, H. R. Report 969 (1892).

times bumper crops failed to yield a proportionately large supply of the desirable grades of cotton. In 1901 an unduly optimistic forecast of cotton ginnings "had a very depressing effect on the Dry Goods market, affecting manufactured goods more adversely than it did the actual cotton." Cloth prices declined, according to Schoolfield, to a basis of 6.5 to 7 cents for cotton, although the fiber remained 2 or 3 cents higher. Conversely, a short cotton crop often caused raw material prices to advance more than prices of finished goods.

366 Million Yards of Cloth

Riverside Mills began business as a manufacturer of 27-inch plaids, woven with no. 14 yarn and averaging 4.3-4.6 yards per pound. Southern plaids, "particularly popular among the Celt descended highlanders,"[62] have been described as a "light sleazy fabric . . . composed largely of air holes and starch and selling for less than a dime a yard."[63] From an output of two million yards in 1884, the production of Riverside plaids rose to 31.6 million yards in 1899; and 250 million yards were turned out in 1884-1901. Their popularity, perhaps, rested upon a better grade of starch—or fewer air holes. An old employee recalls that the mill had no designer in the early years. "Mr. Robertson, then boss weaver, made up most of the designs himself"; or, sometimes, "different ones in the weave room would strike off a pattern or combination of patterns and take it to the office, and if 'the office' liked it, they started making it."[64]

In addition to plaids, the company made work-shirt cheviots every year and 30-inch checks in nine of the eighteen years. As compared with later periods in its history, the mill seems to have experimented little with new fabrics; and it dropped some types of goods after producing a small yardage. Thus, 30-inch drills disappear from the list after 1,522 yards were made in 1889; small quantities of cottonades (cheap trousering) were produced in 1885 but not again until 1900; chambrays were first manufactured in 1897 and again in 1901; 28-inch denims were made in 1900, and 28-inch India stripes in 1901. Brands of merchandise included the "Peconic" cheviots (1891), "Clinton"

[62] V. S. Clark, *History of Manufactures in the United States*, vol. 2 (New York, 1929 ed.), 397.
[63] "Cone Mills: Old King Denim," *Fortune*, vol. 47 (1953), 87.
[64] E. H. Davis to L. H. Browder, Dec. 19, 1956 (from an interview with Alice Thompson).

cheviots (1898), "Danbury" stripes (1898), and "Queen" cheviots (1900). In applying for registration of "Dan River" in 1909, the company stated that it had sold plaids and checks under this name since 1892.

Production of "brown" (unbleached) sheeting commenced in 1889 and rose sharply with the acquisition of the Morotock Mill in 1890. The output of sheeting ranged from 10 to almost 24 per cent of the annual output. Seven widths of sheeting, from 30 to 90 inches, were made in one year or another; but the volume of 36-inch cloth overshadows all other widths. This was a staple cloth of the dry goods trade, especially in the southern and western states, where it served not so much for bed linen as for cheap dresses, shirts, undergarments, and a variety of non-apparel uses.

Yardage statistics in Appendix 3 supplement the poundage data shown in Table 1. In reaching the peak output (for 1884-1901) of almost 10 million pounds, production doubled four and one-half times: the output in 1887 was almost twice that of 1884; production rose nearly 100 per cent from 1887 to 1889; output more than doubled between 1889 and 1891; it doubled again between 1891 and 1896; and production in 1899 was 36 per cent greater than in 1896. Modest curtailment in 1900 was followed by a severe cut-back in production the following year.

Production records reveal not only the persistent growth of the business up to 1899, but also the way in which the firm adjusted output of different types of goods to changing market conditions. The monthly data record clearly the short-run adjustments in production to take advantage of a good market for some lines while contracting output in others. Yet the treasurer's reports frequently refer to the loss of sales because weaving schedules could not be changed quickly enough to turn out goods in great demand. Thus, in 1899, when the mills had a large inventory of wide sheeting, Schoolfield wanted to "change off the weavers to the narrow looms" but could not do it "without loss of a considerable number of our best weavers, as it is not only difficult to run the narrow looms at night, on account of their higher speed, but it is hard to get a satisfactory grade of help."

The available records have comparatively little to say about Riverside's early sales organization. "At first," the secretary recalled in his 1899 report, "we of course had no trade, but as fast as the excellent

Table 1.   Cloth Production, 1884-1901
(thousands of pounds)

year	colored goods	sheeting	total
1884	461		461
1885	638		638
1886	849		849
1887	896		896
1888	1,596		1,596
1889	1,710	7	1,717
1890	1,958	576	2,535
1891	2,523	1,111	3,633
1892	3,190	905	4,095
1893	3,337	895	4,232
1894	4,235	803	5,037
1895	4,780	1,856	6,636
1896	5,561	1,826	7,387
1897	6,605	2,061	8,666
1898	7,495	2,294	9,789
1899	7,745	2,235	9,980
1900	7,519	2,186	9,705
1901	5,767	1,174	6,941

Discrepancies in totals are due to rounding.

fabric of the Riverside Cotton Mills was introduced and became known, the demand for same increased faster than the capacity of the Mills." Launching their enterprise in a period of depression in the cotton goods trade, the founders ignored the general complaint that the increase in southern mills in the early 1880's was "positively alarming."   Riverside did not send a representative to the convention of southern spinners which met in Augusta, Georgia, in April 1883, with the object of getting mills to agree on a plan for curtailing production.[65]   In these formative years, the management seldom complained of the lack of buyers.   On the contrary, looms and operatives often seemed too few to meet the demand for plaids and sheeting.   In September 1885, local gossip credited Schoolfield with the statement that "he could ship 500,000 yards of goods at once if he had the stock made."[66]

[65] *Manufacturers' Record*, Jan. 25, 1883, and Jan. 5, April 12, and Oct. 4, 1884.   The *Manufacturers' Record* conducted its own census of "every cotton mill now in the Southern States" (as of Jan. 1, 1884) and found 314 mills in 13 states operating 1,276,422 spindles and 24,873 looms.   The editor believed this was evidence of the "abiding faith" of "long-headed New England capitalists in the future of cotton manufacturing in the South."   Riverside, of course, was only indirectly dependent upon "long-headed New England capitalists."

[66] Danville *Daily Register*, Sept. 12, 1885.

Schoolfield occasionally mentioned his work in making contacts with jobbers, converters, and dry goods firms. In 1892 he spoke of "getting jobbers interested in our goods in Territory that was not very well covered and that we have been working for some years." In his report to the directors in January 1893 the secretary noted "quite a demand for all goods that we throw out as imperfect." Not only did this keep inventories free of all but first-quality cloth: "in more instances than one, we have introduced our goods into houses by selling them Seconds, which have been so satisfactory that they have been induced to buy the Firsts, and have become valuable customers." The company made foreign sales for the first time in 1891; but, prior to the crisis of August 1893, domestic sales ran so far ahead of production that the management had "not exerted itself much in foreign markets." In 1901, however, the closing of Chinese markets by the Boxer incident was given as one of the causes of the slump in sales.

In March 1891 Riverside Cotton Mills opened its New York sales office at 34 Thomas Street, with Noble A. Hamilton in charge. Less than a year later Schoolfield reported that this step had already brought about a reduction in selling costs. Shortly thereafter, N. H. Jones & Company proposed to distribute the firm's products in the Chicago area on the basis of brokerage at 2 per cent of sales, or "if large sales require a little less brokerage to help a sale, we will make it less." There is no record of the company's reply, but in January 1899 the directors approved the opening of the Chicago office and placed Orin C. Schoolfield in charge. In his annual report for 1897 the president pointed out that salaries for supervision, management, and selling amounted to slightly over $30,000, which was less than the minimum of 2 per cent charge by commission houses for selling alone.

The treasurer's reports often discuss price trends and the competitive aspects of the goods market. "Our competitors," Schoolfield remarked in the fall of 1894, "are anxious to sell goods in a number of cases seemingly regardless of prices"; but Riverside met the competition both in price and in terms of sale. There must have been exceptions. In 1894 the New York office advised Danville that the H. B. Claflin Company was interested in 40-inch sheeting containing 3.15 yards per pound. Claflin buyers, Hamilton reported, "talk on the basis of 17 cents per pound," which was considerably *below* the manufacturing cost of Riverside's 40-inch cloth (averaging 3.6 yards per pound).[67]

In 1895 the company had to contend with jobbers who anticipated an active fall demand and made "liberal contracts" during the summer; and the next year the treasurer noted the "unfortunate or one-sided method that has been existing for a number of years in the sale of cotton goods, that is, protection in prices." Presumably, the company had to fall in line with this "one-sided method." After 1900 a frequent complaint was that merchants "seem to be pursuing a 'hand-to-mouth' policy," that is, buying only for immediate needs and reordering frequently. Nevertheless, the management was convinced that "on account of the changes going on in the dry goods trade and the active competition," Riverside must "keep abreast of the times . . . maintain our reputation" and "keep before the trade goods adapted to their wants."[68] This determination was expressed early in 1901, which turned out to be the most disappointing year in the company's first two decades.

Long after the name had ceased to be appropriate, Riverside was one of a group of firms known as southern plaid mills. The mushroom growth of small mills manufacturing coarse colored goods led to numerous attempts to control production and end the "ruinous" competition. In January 1889 President Fitzgerald told the stockholders that "the year just closed has been an unfavorable one for Plaid manufacturers. The market has been greatly demoralized." The presidential campaign and the prevalence of yellow fever in the South were cited as "depressing influences." The following year the company seriously considered the proposal of the North Carolina mill owner, Moses Cone, for an agreement among leading plaid manufacturers, "looking to formulating some plan by which the evils existing in the trade might be corrected." R. A. Schoolfield attended a meeting in Columbus, Georgia, in October 1890; and in November a directors' committee reported favorably on the plan to form a sales and commission company owned jointly by Riverside and its competitors. In January 1891 Riverside's charter was amended to permit it to own stock in other corporations up to 10 per cent of its own capital.

But R. A. Schoolfield and J. E. Schoolfield returned from a meeting

[67] Only average costs of colored goods and sheeting combined are available in this period. For the four weeks ending August 25, 1894, the estimated cost of production was 21.08 cents per pound, though it dropped to 17.27 cents in October.
[68] Directors' Meeting, Jan. 25, 1901.

of plaid manufacturers in New York with the report that Cone's plan seemed impractical. In a letter to Cone they expressed the hope that "some plan not so radical in its nature might be devised that our Company could have consistently become a party to." Nevertheless, Riverside promised to "cooperate with that Company [the Cone Export & Commission Company] in maintaining prices. It is well known to the dry goods trade and mill men that our policy has never been to cut prices. Our Company has always been on the 'bull' rather than the 'bear' side of the market."

Cone attended a meeting of the Riverside board and urged acceptance of a contract under which the Cone Export & Commission Company would sell Riverside products. The Riverside management was almost persuaded; in fact, R. A. Schoolfield accepted a vice-presidency in the Export & Commission Company and prepared three promissory notes of $10,000 each for Riverside's contribution to the capital of the export firm. But in March 1891 Cone returned to Danville with the report that he had been "unable to get similar contracts to that made with Riverside with three or four of the mills making plaids"—though he claimed to have agreements by which he could "control the production" of all but two mills. Schoolfield restated the conditions under which Riverside would participate in the Cone Export & Commission Company, but before the end of the month Riverside definitively rejected the Cone offer on the grounds that too many other mills had failed to join. The matter ended with a vote to reimburse Cone for a reasonable share of his expenses in carrying on negotiations with Riverside.[69]

Although the *Manufacturers' Record* could brag of its success in "educating the Southern people to the great importance to them of a protective tariff," the campaign made little impression on the Riverside management. Schoolfield and the president of a Georgia mill were the only prominent mill executives in the South who failed to respond to Senator James Z. George's request for recommendations on the "proper duty upon cotton yarns to be levied under the new [Wilson-Gorman] tariff bill" in 1894. The bulk of American imports consisted

[69] Directors' Meeting, October 24, 1890—March 18, 1891. The establishment of the joint sales agency for marketing southern plaids is discussed briefly in the *Commercial and Financial Chronicle*, vol. 53 (New York, 1891), 351. Cone claimed that the Export & Commission Company, which opened its New York office in 1891, had contracts to market 90 per cent of southern mill production (*Half Century Book, 1891-1914*). The firm name became Cone Mills, Inc. in 1952.

of fine goods, and the duties on coarse cloth, though reduced in 1890 and again in 1894, generally satisfied the southern mills.[70]

Costs

It is quite possible that no other cotton mill has preserved as detailed a story of the cost of manufacturing cloth as that found in six "Cost of Manufacturing" books, now in the vault of Dan River Mills.[71] These volumes analyze costs of production for every four weeks' period from January 1884 to the end of 1931. The first book was opened by Lewis Garner, one of the experienced mill men whom Superintendent Roberts brought with him from Georgia.

Each cost sheet shows the four weeks' output of cloth, classified by type and width. Output is reported in both yards and pounds. Direct labor costs for carding, spinning, dressing, weaving, finishing, dyeing, and repairs are divided by the total production for the period in order to arrive at labor cost per pound for each production process. Costs of supplies are similarly allocated to the appropriate departments and unit costs calculated from the output figure. Total expenditures on (1) fuel and light, (2) "expense" and (3) cotton are divided by output to obtain costs per unit of product for these items, respectively; and the aggregate of these unit cost figures makes up the over-all cost of production per pound for the period. Finally, the over-all cost per pound is applied to the yards-per-pound data to find cost of production per yard of each class of cloth.

The cost sheets for 1884-1895 cover the entire output of the mills, i.e., colored goods in 1884-1889 and colored goods and sheeting in 1890-1895. In September 1895 separate sheets were set up for Mill No. 6. Thus, for 1896-1901 we have two sets of cost data: (1) cost for the production of sheeting in Mill No. 6 and (2) costs for colored goods and sheeting in the other mills. Yearly averages of these cost figures are presented in Table 2.

Most striking of the changes in unit costs is the downward move-

---

[70] Alfred B. Shepperson, Secretary, Subcommittee on Cotton, Committee on Agriculture and Forestry, U. S. Senate, to R. A. Schoolfield, March 7, 1894; Copeland, *op. cit.*, pp. 235-236; *Manufacturers' Record*, March 29, 1884; F. W. Taussig, *Tariff History of the United States* (New York, 1914), pp. 266-267, 296-297, 336.

[71] They are large, heavy volumes, sturdily bound in cloth and leather, meticulously compiled and written in perfectly legible handwriting. They furnish the best surviving evidence of the care with which the company managed its accounts in the manufacturing department.

ment of direct labor cost per pound of product. From 6.93 cents in 1884 labor cost dropped to a low of 4.37 cents per pound in Mill No. 6 (1896). Cost in the sheeting mill crept upward to 4.72 cents in 1900, an increase which seems to be associated with changes in the types or quality of the goods. But unit cost continued to fall in the other mills until 1901. Since the period was one of slowly rising wage rates, the higher outputs per dollar of wages must have been achieved through economies of scale, increased labor skill, and improved machinery, the separate effects of which it would be impossible to trace. In 1901 the company in effect raised wages by reducing the average working day one and one-half hours without changing daily rates of pay, thus increasing the hourly cost of labor 18 per cent. Perhaps equally important in its effect upon the year's average cost was the strike which, commencing in April, slowed production without causing the mills to stop work completely. In one period of three months unit labor cost rose to 5.50 cents, or more than a cent above the 1900 average. Unit labor cost in Mill No. 6 rose more than a cent a pound in 1901; it was also one cent higher on sheeting than on colored goods.

Except for possible economies of large-scale purchasing, supplies represented uncontrollable costs, and the fluctuations shown in the table reflect principally the movement of market prices for dyestuffs, finishing materials, lubricants, and shipping supplies. The cost of fuel and light is largely dominated by the price of coal; the unit cost rose during periods of drought, when steam was required to furnish a larger proportion of the power.

"Expense" in the 1884 cost sheets represented salaries, $4,960; interest, $4,151; freight, $697; and unspecified expenditures of $3,774. Later on, insurance, taxes, discounts, and commissions entered this category of costs. Since salaries rose less rapidly than total output, the unit cost of managerial services declined significantly as production rose. The 1884 salaries were 15.5 per cent of the amount paid out in wages, but in 1901 salaries amounted to only 7.7 per cent of total wage payments. (Salary and wage payments are entered in Table 3.)

Losses on bad debts were an insignificant element of expense, averaging less than $300 per annum in 1893-1896. Selling expenses, too, were almost unbelievably low: in 1898, for instance, the cost of sales was 1.41 per cent of sales, including the "salaries of your Secretary

Table 2. Costs of Production, 1884-1901
(cents per pound of cloth)

year	labor	supplies	fuel-light	expense	cotton	total
			All Mills, except No. 6			
1884	6.93	2.08	.40	2.94	12.16	24.51
1885	6.02	1.98	.36	1.92	12.13	22.41
1886	6.29	1.98	.29	2.54	10.40	21.50
1887	6.42	2.03	.34	2.05	10.71	21.55
1888	6.21	1.89	.25	1.29	11.50	21.14
1889	5.94	1.97	.21	1.43	11.72	21.27
1890	5.66	1.59	.21	1.16	12.03	20.65
1891	5.50	1.63	.18	1.04	9.94	18.29
1892	5.68	2.63	.19	1.50	9.14	19.14
1893	5.78	3.11	.19	1.39	11.45	21.92
1894	5.53	2.86	.16	1.16	10.59	20.30
1895	5.24	2.60	.16	1.19	8.49	17.68
1896	5.23	2.43	.15	1.05	10.19	19.05
1897	4.89	1.91	.26	1.05	9.22	17.33
1898	4.60	1.70	.20	.96	7.31	14.77
1899	4.53	1.74	.21	1.27	7.88	15.63
1900	4.46	1.70	.22	1.30	10.46	18.14
1901	4.81	2.11	.26	1.57	11.62	20.37
			No. 6 Mill			
1896	4.37	1.12	.18	1.35	10.29	17.31
1897	4.38	.63	.11	1.09	9.28	15.49
1898	4.40	.56	.09	1.07	7.32	13.44
1899	4.56	.66	.15	1.45	7.92	14.74
1900	4.72	.63	.15	1.51	10.38	17.39
1901	5.88	.82	.26	2.82	11.51	21.29

and Treasurer, Assistant, Paymaster, and office men—in fact, all of the office force, as well as our New York salesman and the expense of the office there, also our traveling salesman and his expenses."

Some of the variability in the unit "expense" cost may be attributed to expenditures not closely related to the scale of operations. For instance, the amount paid out for borrowed funds was only $900 in 1885, but it rose to $7,600 the next year. Taxes, first entered under expense in 1885, when the amount was $1,424, rose gradually to $24,242 in 1901. They represent mainly local levies on real property. The rate was generally $1.50 per $100, but valuations for tax purposes were low. Under the ordinance approved by the municipal council in

February 1885, cotton and woolen mills established in Danville between April 6, 1880, and January 1, 1885, were exempt from personal property taxes for a period of ten years. When the initial period of exemption expired, Danville prepared to assess all of the mill's property for taxes; President Fitzgerald reported in June 1892 that he and Attorney Peatross had persuaded the municipal government to extend the exemption another ten years.[72] In January 1887, while Riverside was making plans to expand across the river, the Common Council of North Danville enacted a twelve-year tax-exemption ordinance for all manufacturing concerns investing $5,000 or more.

All items of "expense' totaled $134,776 in 1901, but the great increase in overhead per pound of cloth resulted primarily from the 29.5 per cent reduction in output this year.

The cost of cotton in a pound of cloth (Table 2) represents the actual cost of cotton consumed in a given year (less sales of waste) divided by the pounds of finished cloth. I have been unable to verify the basis of inventory valuation: presumably, it was the lower of cost or market, which would have the effect of inflating the manufacturing cost of the raw material when cotton prices were falling. The trend of market prices was downward in 1884-1901, although the 1900 price equaled that of 1884. The "judgment price for the season as reported by farmers on December 1" dropped from 9.19 cents in 1884 to 4.59 cents in 1894; it rose irregularly to 9.13 cents in 1900 but fell back to 7.03 cents in 1901.[73]

The differences (on an annual basis) between reported market prices of raw cotton and the mill's cost of cotton per pound of cloth ranged from a minimum of .80 cent in 1892 and 1899 to a maximum of 6.00 cents in 1894. Little of this variability can be explained by changes in the manufacturing processes. In the cost sheets, which employ a "standard" or accounting cost of cotton, the cost of cotton per pound of cloth ranges from 101.9 to 116.7 per cent of the cost of a pound of cotton.[74]

---

[72] Directors' Minutes, April 11 and June 13, 1892; Danville *Daily Register*, Feb. 21, 1885 and Feb. 9, 1887.

[73] *Historical Statistics of the United States, 1789-1945*, pp. 90, 108.

[74] Perhaps it should be pointed out that these percentages are distorted slightly by the inconsistent treatment of waste. Sales of waste were irregular, and the cost of cotton consumed is credited with sales of waste in the month in which sales were realized, not in the months in which the waste was produced. I have only one statistic for waste: in 1901 visible waste was 8.9 per cent of the cotton consumed, and the invisible waste, 6.7 per cent.

More important explanations of the spread between the December market prices and the mill's cost of cotton per pound of cloth may be found (1) in the price differentials of various grades of cotton and (2) in the differences between December prices and prices paid by the mills in other months of the year. In 1901, for instance, the company appears to have purchased most of its cotton near the peak prices for the year. Given a fixed cost of cotton, the cost of cotton per pound of cloth (in the period under study) shows a maximum variation of only 6 per cent. In the short run, at least, fluctuations in the cost of cotton are the main determinants of changes in the cost of cloth.

Chief among the defects of the cost data presented above is the inconsistent treatment of depreciation. Although the concept of depreciation policy remained foreign to the Riverside management even after 1901, depreciation was accounted for irregularly by charging replacements and new equipment to expense, surplus, or earnings. Thus, in 1899 the cost of a "substantial four-story Brick Cloth Storage House; a large Covered Platform for Storage of Cotton at Dye-House, and a similar Cotton Storage Platform at Mill No. 6, and a Lot adjoining No. 6 Mill property . . . aggregating $11,057.80, was charged to Expense Account, besides some improvements of minor importance."[75] In 1901 the surplus absorbed the cost ($64,326.52) of new carding machinery, but at the end of the year another $84,713.54 was "charged to Loss and Gain to Reduce Real Estate and Machinery Account to $2,000,000, same am't as the capital stock." Obviously, the erratic accounting for depreciation lessens the significance of the unit cost data and makes them non-comparable with any other series in which depreciation enters *evenly* into the periodic calculations of cost of production.

Data on prices of the company's products are almost completely lacking. In 1900 the cost records indicate an average selling price for colored goods of 20.18 cents, or 2.04 cents above the net cost of 18.14 cents. Colored goods which cost 20.37 cents per pound to produce in 1901 sold for an average of 20.69 cents, a margin of only .32 cent. Similar computations are lacking for other years. Reported earnings may be used to obtain estimates of the average prices for all classes of goods, but no records have been preserved of prices of the different classes of goods.

For American manufacturers of gray goods the period 1890-1901

[75] *Statement: Riverside Cotton Mills, Danville, Va., January 1st, 1900.*

was one of slowing falling "margins" between cotton prices and cloth prices. In 1890 the spread between the average price of cotton and the average selling price of dry goods was 11.0 cents per pound; it rose to 12.7 cents in 1892 but dropped to 8.3 cents in 1898. The lowest monthly margin for the decade was 7.2 cents in August 1898.[76] Riverside's costs on gray goods for 1896-1901 stayed below the average market prices, except in 1901; but the lack of periodic sales data makes it impossible to say how well the following statistics measure the changing profitableness of the Danville mills:

	cost of production, Riverside (cents per pound)	average market price, U. S. (cents per pound)
1896	17.3	17.6
1897	15.5	15.9
1898	13.4	14.3
1899	14.7	16.9
1900	17.4	19.2
1901	21.3	17.9

Wages and Hours

Riverside Cotton Mills disbursed over $4,300,000 in wages during the first nineteen years of its history. Data on salary payments are not complete but may be estimated at $275,000. Both series are shown in Table 3.

Until 1901 questions of wages, hours of work, and working conditions are rarely mentioned in the minutes of the directors' meetings, and few other sources of information disclose the company's policy on these matters. As the business grew, men in key positions received increases in pay, commensurate with their added responsibilities. Thus, the general superintendent's salary increased from $2,500 to $5,500 in the course of 18 years. In his report for March 25, 1897, the treasurer observed that a "boss weaver" who earned $2.50 per day when the mill started with 100 looms was then earning $5.00 a day. The "boss machinist" earned $2.50 in 1884 and $4.00 a day in 1897. "We had an incompetent dyer then," he went on to say, "to whom we paid $2.00, and now we have a good man at $4.50." In 1898 the salesmen in charge of the New York and Chicago offices received $3,000 and $3,200 re-

[76] S. J. Kennedy, *Profits and Losses in Textiles* (New York, 1936), pp. 238-241.

Table 3. Wages and Salaries, 1884-1901
(thousands of dollars)

year	wages	salaries
1884	32	5
1885	38	5
1886	53	6
1887	57	7
1888	99	8
1889	102	8
1890	144	9
1891	200	15
1892	233	not available
1893	245	"
1894	279	"
1895	348	"
1896	365	"
1897	413	"
1898	446	"
1899	454	"
1900	441	"
1901	340	26

spectively. In 1900 the office force in Danville (besides the officers of the corporation) consisted of J. B. Guerrant, the chief clerk and bookkeeper, whose salary was $125 a month; G. F. Lipscomb, a clerk at $75 a month; G. H. Martin, R. A. Morris, and Raymond Hall, clerks at $50 per month; and Ormond Vass, probably a janitor or messenger, at $16.67 a month.

One of the unique pieces in the archives of Dan River Mills is the "Pay Roll Book No. 4," which contains complete data on wages for every two-week period between November 26, 1888, and November 23, 1889. Unfortunately, this is the only volume of its type which has survived the insistent pressure upon the company to get rid of the old in order to make room for new records.

In the two weeks ending December 8, 1888, the mills paid wages to 447 individuals, of whom 205 worked at day rates and 242 were paid at "job" or piece rates. Those who worked by the day averaged 88.5 cents per day, or $10.62 for twelve full days. The average earnings of 127 piece-rate workers who worked full time was $10.88.

An analysis of wage payments for November 11-23, 1889, when the payroll had grown to 554 names, is presented in Table 4.

Table 4. Daily Wage Rates, November 11-23, 1889

department	number of workers	wage rate per day		
		lowest	highest	average
Mill No. 1				
carding	44	$ .35	$2.50	$ .92
spinning	65	.25	1.50	.64
dressing	30	.40	2.25	.89
weaving	42	.40	3.25	.84
cloth	21	.65	2.50	.90
repairs	11	1.00	2.25	1.29
dyeing	20	.90	3.00	1.26
yard	4	.83⅓	.90	.85
Mill No. 2				
carding	21	.40	2.50	.92
spinning	25	.15	2.50	.81
repairs	8	1.00	3.50	1.93
All	291	.15	3.50	.88

In addition to the 291 workers on the payroll at day rates, 263 employees were hired at piece rates, of whom only 126 worked twelve full days. These 126 wage-earners averaged $10.87, as compared with the average full-time wages of $10.52 for day workers. In other words, the average pay at Riverside at the end of 1889 was 88 cents for a 12-hour day, or 7.4 cents per hour.[77] This average includes the pay of supervisory employees (overseers and second hands), which makes it noncomparable with the data presented in Table 5. A similar but not strictly comparable study of northern mills shows an average hourly wage of 9.7 cents for a 10-hour day.[78]

Statistics published by the Virginia Bureau of Labor and Industrial Statistics disclose the rates of pay at Riverside in 1897.[79] Errors in reporting, possibly with an upward bias, and imperfect processing doubtless vitiate the results; but the evidence (Table 5) indicates that River-

[77] A southern mill submitted figures to the *Manufacturers' Record* (June 14, 1884) showing the payment of $4,728.39 in wages to 488 operatives in a two weeks' period in May 1884. This averaged $.968 per day per worker, but in June a 15 per cent wage reduction was "cheerfully submitted to by every one."

[78] Robert G. Layer, *Earnings of Cotton Mill Operatives, 1825-1914* (Cambridge, Mass., 1955), pp. 34-39, 43.

[79] *First Annual Report of the Bureau of Labor and Industrial Statistics of the State of Virginia for the Years 1898 and 1899* (Richmond, 1899), pp. 205-209. Data are given for three reporting mills, one of which shows sales and capitalization figures corresponding to those of Riverside Cotton Mills, although the company is not otherwise identified.

side's average wage had increased to about 8.5 cents an hour. In northern mills workers were now earning 10 cents an hour for an average working day of 9.67 hours.

Table 5. Daily Wage Rates, 1897

department	number of workers	average daily wage
weaving		
males, over 16	415	$1.26
females, over 16	277	.98
cloth		
males, over 16	25	1.03
females, over 16	20	.65
spinning		
males, over 16	34	.84
males, under 16	221	.84
females, over 16	110	.56
females, under 16	170	.56
carding		
males, over 16	160	1.11
slasher		
males, over 16	30	.96
males, under 16	34	.96
females, over 16	130	.68
females, under 16	34	.68
dyeing		
males, over 16	64	1.41

The data disclose no difference in rates of pay for workers under 16 years of age and those over 16 years. On the other hand, women, who worked 10 hours a day, earned less than five-sixths of the wages of men working 12 hours in the same department. In 1897 about 43 per cent of the employees were female, whereas the October 1889 payroll showed 48 per cent women. Men and women were then distributed by departments, as shown in Table 6.

Twelve hours was the working day for males over 14, but by act of the Virginia legislature (1890) "no female and no child under fourteen" could work "as an operative in a factory or manufacturing establishment more than ten hours."[80] A prohibitive child labor law was yet

[80] Chap. 193, Acts of 1889-1890, in *General Laws of Virginia, 1887-94* (Richmond, 1894), p. 99.

Table 6. Distribution of Employees by Sex, October, 1889

department	male	female
carding	37	3
spinning	32	38
dressing	41	64
weaving	93	110
cloth	11	11
repairs	8	0
dyeing	21	0
	243	226

to be enacted. In 1896 President Fitzgerald said "perhaps 700" children and young persons were in the employ of the company; doubtless many were under 14 years of age. The company's retirement roll in 1950 included Alice Thompson, who began working in December 1888 at the age of eleven, and William Morgan, who entered the mill in June 1888, before his ninth birthday.

Two samples of absenteeism, though not conclusive, suggest that both in winter and in summer workers lost time for a number of reasons not associated with availability of work. Thus, from August 19 to 31, 1889, only 277 out of 494 operatives worked the full 12 days; 80 worked 11, 11.25, 11.5, or 11.75 days; but 137 worked less than 11 days. In the payroll period, November 26–December 8, 1888, 28.5 per cent worked less than 11 full days. Labor turnover tended to be high in the summer months, when farm employment lured workers away from the confining labor of the mills.[81] Although the difficulty of obtaining a "good class of help" for night work worried the management, there is no evidence that the company faced a severe labor shortage prior to 1900. In February 1897 the treasurer noticed that 25 weavers quit "because of a reduction in the price of weaving the class of goods on which they worked; but their places were soon filled by others." Excepting shutdowns to make repairs or install new machinery —running infrequently to a month or more—involuntary idleness was not a problem of the Riverside employee in the 1884-1900 period. A

[81] In 1884 a number of southern mill owners challenged the idea that southern operatives were less efficient than northern workers. On the other hand, it was admitted that the irregularity of work habits among people newly arrived from rural areas interfered with an efficient organization of the labor force. One mill kept 423 hands on the payroll, whereas 335 would have sufficed if all worked full time (*Manufacturers' Record*, June 14, 1884).

source of pride to the management was its ability to furnish continuous employment and pay wages in cash throughout the crisis of 1893 and the recession preceding the elections of 1896.

Though fragmentary, the descriptions of mill life in Danville re-mind one of New Lanark under Robert Owen. If Danville, a century later, produced no Owen, still it would be incorrect to say that mill owners were indifferent to the lot of their employees. The secretary recalled that in the beginning, "as Danville was a new place in the manufacture of cotton goods . . . we either had to import or teach the operators how to run the machinery. The imported labor was, as a rule, migratory and unsatisfactory." After commenting on the lack of help in 1891, Schoolfield reported to the directors that "we are gradually getting a better class of operatives and . . . the habits of our people are steadily improving . . . and a number of our People are buying homes." Credit for the moral improvement of the laborers was given to "our efficient Superintendent [Roberts], whose views on the liquor question has [sic] done much good."[82] As evidence of im-proved morale among the workers the management cited the fact that the mills closed on December 24, 1898, "with instructions that they be again started up on Tuesday morning, December 27th following. At that time the Mills were promptly started up, without an exception every one of the 2,771 looms . . . being put into operation without any trouble."

Whether the company had any responsibility in regard to the illit-eracy which, even more than insobriety, characterized a community of mill operatives, no one seems to have discussed until 1896. At the December board meeting President Fitzgerald asked the directors to consider the advisability of establishing a night school equipped and staffed at the expense of the company. "An interest of this character taken by the mill owners," he said, "would be of manifest advantage to the help and would result in compensating advantage to the Mills, not only in that intelligent, cultivated help can do more and better work, but at the same time [he] thought such interest would be a means of cultivating close and better relations between the two parties at a time when outside influences seemed to tend to produce different results."

[82]Directors' Minutes, Jan. 8, 1892. Danville gave birth to a temperance paper, *Anti-Liquor,* edited and published by the Reverend J. R. Moffett in 1890-1892. Moffett was killed in Nov. 1892, for motives at least partly related to his temperance crusade (*Was Rev. J. R. Moffett Murdered? Clark vs. Commonwealth. D. M. No. 432. From the Corporation Court of the City of Danville;* Richmond, n.d.).

The reference to "outside influences" was not clarified, nor were steps taken immediately to combat them in the way suggested by the President. In January 1900 a committee of directors appointed "to look into the question of bettering the condition of the operatives of the mills" recommended as a "fixed policy" of the company "that every comfort and convenience compatible with the surroundings be provided as fast as practicable, looking to the general welfare and comfort" of the laborers. A few days later H. R. Fitzgerald, T. B. Fitzgerald's son, submitted to the directors the following resolution:

Recognizing the importance of having always in the employment of this Company the most intelligent labor obtainable to secure the very best results and at the same time to show our appreciation for faithful service rendered by our employees, we desire to do what is in our power to enable each one to acquire an education that will enable them in coming time to render even more valuable service and to better qualify them to discharge their duties as Citizens and Artisans, therefore be it,

Resolved, That we as stockholders of the Riverside Mills Company recommend our Board of Directors to expend a sum not exceeding one tenth of one percent per annum of the capital stock, to be paid out of the net earnings of this Company, to build, equip, and supply competent teachers for a night school for the exclusive benefit of the employees and their families, of the Mills, free of cost to them. It is distinctly understood that this school is not to have any connection whatever with any institution of learning either private or public, no political affiliation with any party and no connection with any church or denominational work. That the sole purpose of this expenditure is to give our employees at least the advantages of securing a rudimentary education for themselves and families.

The resolution, which limns the ideas that guided the younger Fitzgerald's labor policy in later years, was adopted by the stockholders, and the night school opened in December 1900.[83] The first sessions were "slimly attended"; attendance picked up later in the winter; but in March the strike of Riverside workers overshadowed all other aspects of labor-management relations.

In January 1900 the directors listened to the "long and tedious" text of a bill, introduced in the Virginia legislature by Senator Edward Lyle of Roanoke, which proposed to regulate the employment of children in manufacturing industries. Considering it "very iniquitous and sui-

[83] The company had perhaps opened a night school earlier than this, for in October 1897 the school board of the city of Danville made arrangements to use the "Riverside Chappell" for public school purposes during the day, while the mill was "to have it at night for a Night School" (letter from the Danville School Board to T. B. Fitzgerald, Oct., 9, 1897).

cidal to the Labor Employing Interests of the State," the board appointed a committee to accompany the company's counsel to Richmond. Three months later Schoolfield reported that D. A. Overbey and H. R. Fitzgerald had rendered "valuable services" before legislative committes and that the Lyle and other proposed labor bills had been defeated.[84]

About the same time the management reported "some agitation going on among some of the Mill operatives, being incited by one of the Attorneys of the town, who, it seems, has political aspirations." In October, however, the secretary-treasurer assured the directors that the excitement has subsided. "The union has held quite a number of meetings," he said; "to some extent coercive measures [have been] adopted, in order to get the operatives into the union." Their aims are "very far reaching and their object . . . to control or dictate to the management."[85] Without recognizing the union, or admitting that public opinion had influenced the decision, on January 1, 1901, the company reduced the working day from 12 hours to 11 hours in April-September and to 10 hours in October-March. The average reduction in time of 1.5 hours per day (9 hours per week) was accomplished without reducing the daily wage rate. A preliminary report of the effect upon production indicated that output of the weave rooms increased per hour worked but carding and spinning showed a loss of production proportionate to the reduction in hours.

The union movement gained strength during the months (January-March) that the ten-hour day was in effect. On March 30, two days before the mill returned to the 11-hour schedule, Samuel Gompers, president of the American Federation of Labor, visited Danville. In recognition of its industrial coming of age, Danville had been selected as "the focal point for the entering of the wedge" in the Federation's drive "against the injustice and wrong of child labor and overlong hours in the South."[86] One morning Gompers talked with local or-

[84] *Journal of the Senate of the Commonwealth of Virginia, 1899-1900* (Richmond, 1899), pp. 174, 339, 518; *Journal of the House of Delegates of the State of Virginia for the Session of 1899-1900* (Richmond, 1899), pp. 91, 343, 366, 389, 453. The senators from Danville and Pittsylvania County were Rorer A. James and Joseph Whitehead, both of whom were financially interested in the Riverside Mills. One of the House bills on child labor was introduced by W. H. Buntin of Pittsylvania.

[85] Directors' Minutes, Oct. 9, 1900. It would be interesting to compare this statement with the views expressed in the *Labor Advocate*, a Danville paper edited by S. J. Triplett in 1901-1902; apparently, all copies of this publication have disappeared (L. J. Cappon, *Virginia Newspapers, 1921-1933* [New York, 1936], p. 77).

[86] "The Awakening of the South," *American Federationist*, vol. 8 (Washington, 1901) pp. 167-169. (Based on a story in the Danville *Labor Advocate*.)

ganizers; in the afternoon he conferred for two hours with R. A. School-field and Director D. A. Overbey; and in the evening he addressed a mass meeting of workers, at which Mayor Harry Wooding "eulogized" the labor leader in an "interesting and eloquent speech." For his part Gompers observed that "the cotton mill operatives of Danville had had a taste of freedom, and now realized that they needed time to improve themselves, to learn, to love, to breathe. . . . A citizenship based on 12 hours' work per day was a poor citizenship. They had no time to in-form themselves on issues of government and politics and become valu-able, self-thinking, reading and reasoning citizens." He frowned on strikes but "showed the value of striking power when arbitration fails." This, in effect, was an invitation to strike, since Gompers had already related the failure of his conferences with officials of Riverside Mills.[87]

At the conclusion of his discourse President Gompers read, and the assembly adopted, the following resolution:

Resolved, That in the present state of developments in the textile in-dustry, it is necessary, from the standpoints of economy, progress, civiliza-tion, or humanity, to work ten (10), certainly not more than ten (10), hours a day.

Resolved, That inasmuch as we have tasted the beneficient [*sic*] effect of the ten (10) hour work day since January 1st. 1901, we are unalterably opposed to the inauguration of the eleven (11) hours a day in the Riverside Mills of this City of Danville, Virginia.

Resolved, That we the operatives of the Riverside Cotton Mills, hereby declare that, though we deplore the necessity, we hereby pledge ourselves not to return to work for the said company unless the ten (10) hours a day is accorded us.

Resolved, That we do hereby declare that we will remain away from the Mills Monday, April 1st., 1901, and that the Chairman of this meeting shall appoint a committee of five to wait on the management of the Company on Monday, to lay before them the decision of the meeting of organized and unorganized textile workers, employes of the Riverside Cotton Mills; that the Committee shall report to a meeting to be held of all the textile

[87] A first-hand account of the earliest personal contact between a labor-union official and an officer of Riverside Mills emphasizes that Gompers "had little or no information as to textiles or the conditions existing in the south concerning the manufacture of cotton cloth." Schoolfield "constantly endeavored to get an expression from Mr. Gompers as to whether he knew we were paying higher wages in Danville than were being paid in Greensboro and other southern textile centers." As the Riverside management saw it, the carpenters—apparently the ringleaders of the union movement—"really had no grievance but . . . a few hot-heads had started something which they were not in a position to finish." For his part, Gompers seems to have been content with reiterating the "then well known quotation of William Jennings Bryan in 1896, saying that we should not press down on the brow of labor the crown of thorns." (Taken from a memorandum prepared by Raymond Hall, July 14, 1949.)

operatives inclusively, at the Odd Fellows Hall, at three o'clock Monday afternoon.

Resolved, That we pledge to each other our honor, our manhood and our womanhood, to stand by each other through sunshine or storm until the ten (10) hours a day is secured, not only in the Riverside Cotton Mills, but throughout the entire textile industry of the country. And in the righteousness, justice and humanity of our cause and our struggle, if needs be, we appeal to the conscience of our fellow men, and urge their sympathetic support and co-operation.

Bearing the signatures of Price Greene, E. T. Cole, L. S. Wilkerson, W. H. Barber, and M. S. Belk, the resolution was delivered to officials of the company on April 1.[88] Simultaneously, a strike was called.

Meeting on April 2, the directors instructed the officers to reply that, since the company faced stiff competition in the cloth market and was already paying higher wages than other mills in the South,[89] it could not afford to grant any benefits beyond the reduction of the working day already in effect. A week later the union advised the company that a committee of ten workers and eight Danville clergymen had been formed "to seek a Christian settlement of our differences." Mill officials were adamant; workers trickled back to their jobs; and by mid-summer, judging by the statistics of production, the strike and probably the union, too, had passed into limbo.[90] One of the organizers declared: "Through the efforts of President Samuel Gompers about $4,000 was contributed to the Textile Workers and had they followed the policy outlined by brothers Gompers and Price Greene, I am positive the fight would have ended differently. But they allowed outsiders to influence them to dabble in politics. After the politicians used them on election day and told them to return to work under the 11-hour system, they realized who their friends were, but too late."[91]

[88] The text given here is that of a copy inserted in the directors' minutes, April 2, 1901. It was also reproduced in the *American Federationist,* vol. 8 (1901), 168-169. Prince Greene and M. S. Belk were A. F. of L. organizers. In April Belk reported that seven new unions (street railway employees, cigarmakers, printers, garment workers, sheet metal workers, machinists, and ship carpenters) had been formed in Danville since March 5.

[89] Riverside's average daily wage of $.97 in 1901 was $.18 above the average wage of 1,276 employees, in similar occupations, of six other cotton mills in Virginia (*Fifth Annual Report of the Bureau of Labor and Industrial Statistics,* pp. 22-26).

[90] In January 1902 the state Labor Commissioner reported that he had found only one textile workers' union. It had 40 members, none of whom was employed. "We are praying," they wrote the Commissioner, "for the enactment of a law prohibiting the employment of children in our mills" (*Fourth Annual Report of the Bureau of Labor and Industrial Statistics for the State of Virginia* [Richmond, 1901], p. 205.

[91] M. S. Belk, "New Unions in Virginia," *American Federationist,* vol. 8, p. 244.

Officers and Directors

Under the by-laws approved on May 28, 1883, the stockholders of Riverside Cotton Mills at their annual meeting elected a board of directors composed of six stockholders owning at least fifty shares each. There is no record of a stockholders' meeting before June 4, 1884, when R. I. Anderson and five of the organizers of the company were formally installed as directors.   John Lee became a director in June 1885, and J. N. Wyllie and J. G. Penn were added to the board in May 1887, in consideration of their substantial purchases of the company's stock. Lee was not re-elected in 1888; thus the board had eight members until 1891, when F. X. Burton and C. G. Holland became directors, following the merger of the Riverside and Morotock Mills.   Upon the death of Holland in 1896, Daniel A. Overbey was elected to the board. Thereafter, until the board was increased to twelve members (1902), the following men served continuously as directors: T. B. Fitzgerald, R. A. Schoolfield, J. H. Schoolfield, J. E. Schoolfield, J. N. Wyllie, J. G. Penn, F. X. Burton, B. F. Jefferson, R. I. Anderson, and D. A. Overbey.

The directors appointed the officers and fixed their compensation, usually at the first board meeting following the stockholders' meeting. Few changes took place in the roll of officers during the first two decades.   The increased amount of work required of the secretary-treasurer led to the appointment of H. R. Fitzgerald as assistant secretary-treasurer in 1898.   J. E. Schoolfield withdrew as vice-president in 1887 and J. H. Schoolfield replaced him.   The most significant change was the retirement of T. B. Fitzgerald as president, under circumstances presently to be discussed.

The by-laws prescribed monthly meetings of the directorate, but the minutes reveal that formal meetings were much less frequent. After adopting the by-laws in May 1883 the directors did not meet again until June 1884, and their next meeting came in January 1885. As long as most of the stock was in the hands of board members decisions were easily reached in informal conversations, and formal meetings were infrequently necessary.   But in 1892 President Fitzgerald noted that, since the shareholders were more numerous and the business of the company more extensive, monthly meetings ought to be held "to have a record of the way in which the directors have attended to the stockholders' business." Thereafter, board meetings were more frequent but never as regular as the by-laws specified.

In default of other records, the minutes of the directors' meetings furnish the best guide to the ways in which the management planned the life and nourished the growth of the corporation. Although they fail to record in full measure the individual contributions of the directors, these prosaic manuscript pages leave no room for doubt that T. B. Fitzgerald and R. A. Schoolfield furnished all but a small part of the energy, enthusiasm, and skill which guided the company into profitable ventures. Schoolfield's reports as secretary-treasurer particularly reveal a comprehensive understanding of all phases of the business, from the purchase of machinery and the buying of cotton to the sale of cloth and borrowing of money. Among the directors who were not officers, a number served on committees to prepare recommendations for action by the directors. There were few occasions on which a commitee report was not accepted. Indeed, there were very few instances in which unanimity did not prevail, until a breach in the amicable relations between the president and the secretary-treasurer produced a serious managerial crisis.

The preincorporation agreement, as has been pointed out, put R. A. Schoolfield in "charge of the business . . . as its business manager and secretary and treasurer"; and the by-laws gave him the responsibility of keeping all the books, correspondence, accounts, and funds, and making "a full report of the condition of the affairs of the Company" at meetings of the stockholders. The founders of Riverside, as Schoolfield later confirmed, borrowed from the long-established practice of New England mills, where the treasurer was typically the chief officer and sometimes the only executive of the corporation. Schoolfield's work and responsibility grew as the company expanded, and the directors rewarded him with increases in salary: from $1,500 to $2,500 in 1886; to $3,000 in 1890; to $5,000 in 1891; finally to $7,500 in 1892.

As for the president, the by-laws specified that he should call and preside over directors' meetings and exercise "general supervision of all the affairs of the Company." At the time, no one asked for clarification of the phrase "general supervision," perhaps because it was understood that Fitzgerald would be almost wholly occupied with the construction work and problems of real estate and water power. Nor did anyone suggest that the company should pay the president a salary, since it was obvious that construction contracts with the firm would benefit him personally. Nevertheless, in January 1890 Fitzgerald resigned, alleging that he had not been adequately compensated for his services to the company.[92]

In February a committee of directors named to "settle with T. B. Fitzgerald for services rendered during the years" reported that the president had received $5,000 in connection with the building of Mill No. 2 but that it would be fitting to offer him $1,500 more for supervising the construction work in 1888-1889. The committee also recommended paying the president a salary of $1,000 a year, with the understanding that he would be required "to keep informed as to general conditions, look after real estate and water power and to assist in the placing of stock to be sold." All the recommendations were adopted by the board and Fitzgerald accepted re-election.

In March 1891 Fitzgerald declined re-election. After voting to rescind its previous vote and make the office of president nominal (i.e., without specific duties or salary), the board persuaded Fitzgerald to accept the presidency, but in April the president again resigned. Director Burton told the board that Fitzgerald "had some grievances," the nature of which he did not specify. However a committee of directors managed to mend the hard feelings and Fitzgerald resumed his office. In February 1892 a motion to make the president's salary $2,000 a year was lost; the next year the board fixed the president's compensation at $7,500 a year, including $2,500 for his work as "supervising architect" of new buildings.

After organization of the Dan River Power & Manufacturing Company in 1895, Fitzgerald occupied himself to a great extent with the affairs of the new company, surveying power sites, purchasing land, and selling stock. The finishing touches had been put on the building program of Riverside Mills, and the directors may have felt that Fitzgerald's services were less valuable than in the period when he was supervising construction. At any rate, in January 1898 the board reduced the president's salary to $2,500, while they kept Schoolfield's pay at $7,500. In February, Fitzgerald asked the directors to recon-

[92] This is based upon statements found in the directors' minutes for 1898, inasmuch as the only case in which the minutes are mutilated consists of the removal of pp. 55-62 from the "Record Book of Directors' and Stockholders' Meetings, 1882-1893," comprising the minutes for the meeting at which Fitzgerald submitted his resignation.

sider his election "or if you deem it wisest and best, to make the position entirely nominal without salary, duties or responsibility." The latter suggestion was adopted, and Fitzgerald continued this "nominal" relation with the company until November 1898, when he wrote the directors that "acting upon your suggestion in January last, that I seek other employment than the operations of your mills—for myself, my position to be with you simply a nominal one, I beg to say, now finds me with engagements outside the city and so situated that even the nominal duties as President and Director in your Company cannot be properly and conveniently filled by me longer."

A committee appointed by the board to interview Fitzgerald reported that he would not say on what conditions he would resume his position as president, but the issue was forced in December by Schoolfield's letter to the board. The secretary-treasurer said he would not remain with the company "if the Company's interest is subordinated to other interests and I am trammeled in the discharge of my duty to its stockholders collectively." The issue, he declared, was "the single question, whether the present management is to continue, or a radical change be made, by putting the President in absolute control of your business, under the Board of Directors, requiring him to take the management of the business, giving close personal attention to all of the details and holding him responsible as to results." If Fitzgerald became president, with active duties, Schoolfield said he would remain only long enough to help familiarize him with duties performed by the secretary-treasurer.

The report of a committee appointed to "harmonize all differences of opinion" and recommend a definitive settlement of the dilemma was submitted on December 30, 1898, by J. E. Schoolfield, J. G. Penn, and D. A. Overbey, chairman. The report did not come to a vote, but it is important for the light it throws on the nature of the controversy. After reviewing the disagreements between Fitzgerald and Schoolfield, the committee proposed a division of managerial responsibility so that Fitzgerald, as president, would (1) control all real estate outside of the mill yards, (2) remain in charge of the program for developing the Dan River Power Company property, and (3) look after insurance and legal matters. H. R. Fitzgerald was to succeed R. A. Schoolfield as secretary-treasurer, in which capacity he would disburse funds of the company and in general act as his father's

assistant.   R. A. Schoolfield was to become general manager of manufacturing, purchasing, and sales, having control, under the board of
directors, of machinery, supplies, water power, employment, and was
to be held responsible "for the quantity and quality of the product of
the mills."   Roberts would continue as superintendent and report to
Schoolfield.   The offices of the president and the secretary-treasurer
were to be maintained in Danville, while the general manager and the
superintendent would set up their offices in North Danville.   All
salaried officials were forbidden to engage in any business that would
take time from their duties to the company, and no officer or employee
was to be permitted to accept a commission on "any sales made to or
purchases made by, or for, any of the employees of this Company."
Finally, it was recommended that board meetings be held monthly
without fail and that each director receive $5 for attendance.

The committee report was shown to the officers of the company
prior to the directors' meeting on December 30.   Schoolfield and
Roberts accepted the recommendations unqualifiedly, but T. B. Fitzgerald replied ambiguously that he "could not accept your proposition, as one calculated to in any respect better or improve the present
existing conditions of your Company's interests."   Later, in a personal
conference with Fitzgerald, the committee found that his decision to
withdraw as an officer of the company was final.   In conclusion, the
committee expressed the conviction that "the only real difference"
separating Fitzgerald and Schoolfield was "one of business judgment."

In January 1899 the board accepted the resignation of T. B. Fitzgerald with "profound regret."   It further resolved that "we recognize
him as the originator and founder of the Riverside Cotton Mills, and
that the success and extraordinary prosperity of the Company is mainly due to him and his untiring efforts and wise and prudent administration as its president."   The directors also expressed the hope that
"his removal to country air will soon restore his health."   By this time
Fitzgerald had established his permanent residence in Byrdville,
though for the remaining thirty years of his life he came to Danville
regularly to attend meetings of the board of directors.

At the board meeting on January 16, J. H. Schoolfield was nominated for president but refused to permit consideration of his name.   Burton's name was then placed in nomination but was withdrawn when
T. B. Fitzgerald asked for information: What were to be the duties

of the president? No one knew; the committee which made the December report was instructed to restudy the question. On the basis of the new report, handed in three days later, Burton was elected president, with nominal duties such as signing the corporate name and presiding over board meetings. His salary was $1,000 a year. J. H. Schoolfield continued as vice-president, without salary. R. A. Schoolfield was re-elected secretary-treasurer, with the additional titles of general manager and executive officer. H. R. Fitzgerald was re-elected assistant secretary-treasurer at a salary of $3,000.

Thus ended an unfortunate incident in the history of the Riverside management. If, in addition to disagreement over business policies, there were elements of personal incompatibility which separated the two principal officers of the company, nothing of this sort was put into the official record of the controversy. No one ever minimized the contribution of Fitzgerald to the success of the enterprise, and Schoolfield's industry, skill, and good judgment remain unchallenged. The continued growth of the firm made it necessary for Schoolfield to divide his labor and responsibility with other officials. Of these, as later chapters will demonstrate, none shared Schoolfield's confidence to a greater degree than Harrison Robertson Fitzgerald.

At the annual meeting in 1899 Schoolfield told the stockholders:

I wish to commend to you my esteemed associate and friend, and valuable assistant, Mr. H. R. Fitzgerald, who came with your company, nearly ten years ago, as a boy, and at once studiously applied himself to the work assigned him, and has since taken up one detail after another, and has ever faithfully discharged his duties, and studied the interests of the Company that he is connected with, and today is a most valuable man to you.

Finally, I think it appropriate to notice that the management did not consider diligent officers, faithful operatives, and loyal stockholders wholly responsible for the success of the business. "We should feel thankful," Schoolfield said, "to Him who has enabled us, by His divine goodness and help, to accomplish such results, which have been so beneficial to the Stockholders of the Company, as well as furnishing honest labor for thousands of people, to earn a livelihood for the support of themselves and their families."

2. *More Mills and a Mill Village, 1902-1909*

The success and rapid growth of Riverside Cotton Mills, made possible in part by easy access to water power, stimulated landowners along the banks of the Dan to speculate on new ventures in harnessing the river. Riverside Mills frequently lacked adequate water; and it was apparent, perhaps by 1890, that manufacturing would outgrow the power supply on the river front in Danville and North Danville. The search for power sites outside the city was an obvious outgrowth of the industrial expansion of the community, to which Riverside Mills made the principal contribution in the last two decades of the nineteenth century.

The Search for Power

Much of the story of this search for power is contained in the record books of the promoters, stockholders, and directors of the Dan

River Power & Manufacturing Company.[1] Although the earliest minutes refer to a meeting on April 26, 1895, of "parties owning and interested in the Upper Danville Water Power," they reveal that the group had met in December 1894 and commissioned Robert Robertson to make surveys and maps of the river above Danville. In June 1895 the promoters examined the plans of a site several miles southwest of the city where, it was estimated, a dam could be built to develop 3,200 H.P. The surveyor's report named the owners of the land on both sides of the river and calculated their respective interests, as follows (per cent owned):

	North	South
Rorer A. James	44.9	46.9
Clement Lipscomb	23.7	24.7
Abram Wimbish	14.1	14.8
W. P. Bethell, H. W. Cole, and		
M. P. Jordan	13.0	13.6
George C. Cabell	4.3	0.

T. B. Fitzgerald, president of Riverside Cotton Mills, attended all the meetings of the promoters, exercising the power of attorney obtained from Clement Lipscomb. Fitzgerald worked out a plan for incorporating the Danville Power & Manufacturing Company, with initial capital of $90,000; and on July 8, 1895, he reported that subscriptions in hand amounted to $85,000, including $30,000 payable in land and riparian rights.

Encouraged by this response, Fitzgerald and his associates decided to increase the authorized capitalization to $750,000 and change the name of the company to the Dan River Power & Manufacturing Company. A charter giving effect to this plan was granted by the Corporation Court of Danville on July 12, 1895. The broad powers of the certificate of incorporation include building dams and developing water power, erecting and operating factories for the manufacture of cotton, woolen, iron, and other ware; the generation, transmission and sale of electricity; the laying out of town sites and the "construction, operation, or lease of other mills, factories & enterprises as may be deemed well in connection with said water power"; and the manufacture and sale of "Flour, Meal, Aluminum, &." Fitzgerald became presi-

[1] "Minutes of the Meetings of the Directors of Dan River Power & Manufacturing Company, 1895-1909."

dent of the new concern; W. P. Bethell, vice-president; and R. A. James, secretary-treasurer.   Fitzgerald, Bethell, James, Burton, and the three Schoolfields comprised the first board of directors.

In October 1895 the charter was amended to increase the capital to $1,000,000, one half in 7 per-cent cumulative preferred stock with dividends accruing from April 1, 1897.   On this basis a new stock subscription book was opened and subscriptions entered, as follows:

	preferred	*common*
R. A. James	$13,400	$ 5,000
F. X. Burton	10,000	
G. C. Cabell	6,000	4,000
T. B. Fitzgerald	7,500	
R. A. Schoolfield	7,500	
C. Lipscomb	7,100	
J. H. Schoolfield	5,000	
J. L. Pairo	2,500	2,500
J. G. Penn	5,000	
S. I. Roberts	3,500	
W. P. Bethell	1,300	1,200
H. W. Cole	1,300	1,200
M. P. Jordan	1,300	1,200
G. W. Dame	2,400	
A. Wimbish	900	900
J. E. Schoolfield	1,500	
J. T. Watson	500	400
	$76,700	$16,400

Fitzgerald had already shown the directors plans for a 40,000-spindle mill which, he estimated, would use about half of the power developed at the proposed dam.   In November the board authorized the president to "solicit and accept such subscriptions only as in his judgment will be to the best interest of the Company"; but on December 6 Fitzgerald told the directors that he had taken the subscription book to eight men, "from none of whom did I get a subscription"—in addition, that is, to the $93,100 already subscribed.   Instead of appealing to a wider circle of investors, however, Fitzgerald proposed to make Riverside Cotton Mills the dominant stockholder in the Dan River Power & Manufacturing Company.   At the December board meeting he explained his scheme: the Dan River development, connected with Riverside Mills by highway and railroad, would form a valuable addition to the plant of the older firm and would bring "incalculable benefit to our present Towns and Community. An enterprise of this magnitude must and will attract attention, and . . . give employment to a large number of People. . . . It is an enterprise that we can put into operation and carry successfully through if we will put our shoulders to the wheel and have for our motto 'Go forward.' " R. A. Schoolfield agreed. In his opinion it would be easier to increase Riverside's capital by a privileged subscription than to sell stock in the Dan River company: "Making a subscription to the Riverside Cotton Mills is investing in an established Plant and one that has a valuable trade and a most desirable reputation for its product, and is putting your money where it will at once begin to earn a Dividend, while in subscribing to a new enterprise it is more or less an experiment." Forgetting how careful they had been to keep Riverside a close corporation, Schoolfield argued that "to an enterprise of this kind we ought to be able to attract outside capital."

Dan River's stockholders accepted Riverside's subscription to $150,000 of the common stock and gave Riverside an option on the balance of the unsubscribed shares. The directorate of the Dan River Power & Manufacturing Company was increased to ten members; thereafter, the two corporations had the same officers and directors.

Early in 1896 the Dan River Company secured a charter for the Danville and Riverside Rail Road Company.[2] Surveying, constructing an iron bridge across the river near the dam site, clearing land, and cutting ties for the railroad progressed with moderate enthusiasm; and in July the president made the following financial report:

assets

real estate and water power	$ 59,068
labor on roads	2,490
bridges and surveying	6,239
wood and cross ties	693
interest paid	25
livestock	1,100

[2] The charter granted on Jan. 30, 1896, authorized the building of a railroad from Neapolis or Danville to the North Carolina, Tennessee, Kentucky, or West Virginia state line. In July the Company spent $4,000 for a right of way on the land of the Dan River Power & Manufacturing Co., and a roadbed was graded along the north shore; but the plans of the interested companies changed before the rails were laid. Only three pages of the "Journal" of the railroad company were used: these account for disbursements on account of construction totaling $13,680. In December 1899 outside interests offered to buy the charter of the railroad, and the directors voted to "encourage . . . any reasonable effort to secure an independent line of railroad westward from Danville"; but the extant minutes of the company end without revealing how the matter was settled.

cash	17	
receivables	179,652	
		249,284
liabilities and capital stock		
stock subscriptions	243,100	
payables	6,184	
		249,284

Another balance sheet, drawn up in January 1897, showed $150,327 still due on subscriptions to $78,900 in preferred stock and $166,400 in common. Depression, falling prices, and the declining earnings of Riverside Mills brought to a halt the work on the upper power site, and three years passed without a stockholders' meeting. Although in January 1897 the directors called for an assessment of 10 per cent on stock subscriptions, bringing the total assessments to 35 per cent of par value, they had little to say about resuming work. Finally, in March 1899 the Riverside management proposed to buy all the outstanding stock of Dan River "provided the directors think the property can be developed in the near future." The board approved, and soon after this President Burton reported that he had acquired all the Dan River stock except directors' qualifying shares (one for each director). In January 1900 the directors took steps to merge the two firms and surrender the Dan River charter;[3] but later in the year they decided to complete the power development as a separate corporation. The following year a charter amendment raised the capitalization to $2,000,000.

In November 1901 R. A. Schoolfield outlined plans for a dam and an 80,000-spindle mill. He also advised the board of the purchase of additional land on the south side of the river. A shorter dam, he observed, could be built farther down stream than at the site first selected, which was opposite the House Rock Wheel Club (near the present Country Club Inn). Three of the directors, R. A. Schoolfield, B. F. Jefferson, and D. A. Overbey, accompanied by W. W. White of the Holyoke Machine Company, crossed the river in a rowboat, comparing different sites, and found the best location at Lynch's Falls. Here, a dam 1,180 feet long and 25 feet high would flood 542 acres and store enough water to develop almost 4,000 H.P. Estimating that the dam and water-power equipment would cost $300,000 and require

[3] Surrender of the charter was actually effected by act of the Virginia legislature in Feb. 1900 (*Journal of the House of Delegates of the State of Virginia for the Session of 1899-1900*, pp. 281, 325, 339).

annual operating expenses of $18,000, the engineers calculated a saving of $31,500 per annum on 3,300 H.P., as compared with the prevailing cost of $15 per H.P. for steam power in the southern Piedmont.[4]

The officers decided to erect the factories on the south bank of the Dan, since surveys showed that foundations would be more costly on the marshy land along the north shore. The management's preference, according to Schoolfield's letter to the engineers, Lockwood, Greene & Company, was for "one long mill running parallel with the river, with the power distributed from the center." The most appropriate site seemed to be on land belonging to the Park Place Land Company, and this property had the added advantage of providing "a desirable location for the operatives to live." In December 1901 Dan River arranged to buy the Park Place property (165 acres) for $11,000; and if the City of Danville had not challenged the company's right to carry out its original project, new mills operated principally by water power would have lined the water front near the present George Robertson bridge.[5]

Horsepower versus Bacteria Count

Anyone who supposes that southern industrialization was achieved by "robber barons" who trampled on community rights and suborned public authorities at will would do well to study the quarrels between Danville and its leading business enterprise. The early differences between municipal and mill officials were mild in comparison with the dispute engendered by the expansion program launched in 1901. In November the directors of the Dan River Power & Manufacturing Company "anticipated trouble" with the municipal corporation on account of possible pollution of the river. A short distance below the proposed dam the city took water from the Dan and pumped it into a reservoir lying on a bluff overlooking the south bank. As news of

[4] The estimates of the cost of water power seem to have been overoptimistic. D. A. Tompkins, in *Cotton Mill, Commercial Features* ([Charlotte, N. C., 1899], pp. 122-123) put the cost of water power at a minimum of $7.50 per H.P. (or $24,750 annually for 3300 H.P.) for a "low cost development, not seriously troubled with droughts or floods." A more expensive development, with less regularity in stream flow, would cost $15 per H. P., or $2.50 more than steam power using a Corliss compound condensing engine.

[5] "Directors Record Book of the Park Place Land Company." The company was organized in 1890 by Orlando Wemple and associates. Its only asset was a tract of 165 acres purchased (but not paid for) from C. D. Noell. The company had run up liabilities in excess of $16,000, but on the advice of Wemple the stockholders accepted Dan River's offer of $11,000 and dissolved the land company.

Dan River's plans spread about town, city officials asked embarrassing questions about its effect upon the public water supply. It took three years to answer them satisfactorily.

In May 1902 the company invited Dr. E. C. Levy of the Medical College of Virginia and the University of Virginia chemistry professor, J. W. Mallet, to come to Danville and give expert testimony on stream pollution.[6] In a statement "To the Public" the mill officials cited expert opinion[7] that "the mere building of a dam and impounding the water" was not "in itself pollution of the stream"; furthermore, they quoted a "distinguished local authority" (the superintendent of the Danville City Water Works) to the effect that the company's decision not to erect mills alongside the dam "removes the fear of having the city water supply contaminated from this source." The water superintendent said he had been informed that the Dan River Company "did not intend to build mills on the site of the power" but that the mills "would be located *in Danville* and operated by electric power generated at the water power plant and transmitted to the city."[8] As late as May 1902 the company did have plans for constructing mill buildings on the banks of the river, near the dam; clearly it was the dispute with the city which evoked the alternative decision to build on high land away from the river front.[9]

[6] Requests for advice were also sent out to southern mills and to public officials in towns where mills were situated on rivers which furnished drinking water. In June, J. E. Schoolfield wrote to a personal friend, a Col. Hodges of the University of West Virginia, asking him to secure from "Professors of Chemistry or Doctors in your institution" signed answers to the question, "Will the mere fact of building a dam 25 feet high or higher, and impounding the water in Dan River, a stream flowing about 90,000 cubic feet of water per minute, at the rate of two to four miles an hour, in your opinion render the water unfit for domestic use, or be harmful to it in any way from a sanitary point of view." There is no record of the answers received.

[7] Apparently, that of Prof. Mallet. J. E. Schoolfield complained that Dr. Levy had been paid for a written statement on the Dan River but had not furnished the promised material; and on June 10 Schoolfield wrote Levy: "Your report having been delayed until now, it will hardly be worth while to send same at this time, and you need not therefore forward the report to us."

[8] *Annual Report of the Water and Light Departments* (Danville, 1901).

[9] H. R. Fitzgerald was in Boston in May 1902, conferring with Lockwood, Greene and Company on the plans for the dam and mill. Writing him on May 29 R. A. Schoolfield said: "Some of our people, we think, are very strongly inclined to transmit the power by electricity out of the reach of the interference of the City of Danville, and if the obstinate position taken by the Council, Doctors, etc. is persisted in, others of our people will probably become of the same opinion." Fitzgerald was asked to get information on electric power plants and transmission systems, in case it became necessary to give up plans for water-powered mills.

"As to the question of our rights, both moral and legal," Schoolfield said, "I am of the same opinion . . . that the position taken by the City, if sustained, practically means confiscation of property without compensation. . . . Don't understand that I mean we have a right to deliberately pollute the water in the river. . . . But we have a right in my opinion to use our property in a legitimate way, and I think those rights will be eventually established by the Courts, if the City persists in bringing it to an issue."

Under pressure from the city, the Dan River management promised to carry mill sewage away from the plant and empty it into the river below the water department's intake. But, as the city objected on other counts, Dan River officials began to talk of getting "out of reach of the jurisdiction of the city officials, who, we fear from past experience, will continue to harass us." On May 28, 1902, Schoolfield wrote Lockwood, Greene: ". . . we are still at a loss to know what to do. Some of our city friends seem to be disposed to give us all the trouble possible." A few days later the company wired the engineers: "Our Board today decided to adopt electrical transmission but desire to keep it confidential for the present." In a letter Schoolfield explained that the "unfriendly attitude" of the city had finally led the directors to put the mill "outside of the jurisdiction of the town, so as not to be interferred with by them. There is still the question of building the dam, but the sewerage from the houses, etc. being eliminated, we think this will be greatly simplified, and that there probably would not be the same delay in the litigation should it come to that, as there would be if the mill buildings and houses were on the river as at first contemplated." Reporting the decision to the stockholders, Schoolfield observed that "electrically driven mills have passed the experimental stage."[10] Freed from the natural limitations of the river-front, the company could obtain a superior layout of plant and at the same time save $60,000 or more on excavating and foundation work. An elevated location would also eliminate the difficult problem of running spur tracks from the main line of the Southern Railway down a steep embankment to the river's edge.

The Park Place land possessed some of these advantages but did not promise to keep the mills "out of reach of the interference of the City of Danville"—it would be too easy to extend the city limits. No such misfortune (for the mills) was likely to overtake "Stokesland," a 290-acre farm three miles southwest of the new dam; and in June 1902

[10] John W. Hammond, in *Men and Volts: The Story of General Electric* ([New York, 1941], pp. 210-212) describes the "first historic installation in a textile mill" of electric power. It was the Olympia Mill in Columbia, S. C., which inaugurated its 1,000-KW. water-driven generating station in April 1894. See also: H. C. Passer, *The Electrical Manufacturers, 1875-1900* (Cambridge, Mass., 1953), pp. 302-340.

By 1904 southern cotton mills derived 39,279 H.P. from electricity, or 10.1 per cent of the total H.P. used in the industry; but the Virginia mills (10) obtained only 162 H.P. out of a total of 9,502 H.P. from electricity (U. S. Bureau of the Census, *Census of Manufacturers: 1905:Textiles* [Bulletin 74; Washington, 1907], p. 62). See also T. V. Bolan, "The Electric Drive and General Driving in Cotton Mills," *Proceedings of the Seventh Annual Convention of the Southern Cotton Spinners' Association* (Charlotte, 1903), pp. 116-123.

negotiations were opened to acquire this property, which had been offered by the owner, W. C. Townes, for $4,400. Thanks to the good offices of the Business Men's Association of Danville, Dan River soon abandoned the Stokesland site. For several weeks the local press published the correspondence exchanged between the Association and the company and the Association and the city. In an open letter (July 10) the Water Committee of the City Council expressed "hearty sympathy" with the proposed expansion of the mills, which it thought would further the "general welfare of the city." Two weeks later the company relented, announcing its willingness—but not any legal responsibility—to assist the city in relocating and improving its water system. The directorate outlined a proposal for laying pipes to a new intake, above the dam, and remodeling or rebuilding the pumping station, offering a guarantee that the cost of water to the public would be 10 per cent less than during the past five or ten years. Although, in August, the Dan River management told the Business Men's Association that it could not accept the suggestion to build the new mills within the city, they agreed to leave Stokesland and "locate the plant within close proximity to the city limits, and at such a place as would contribute largely to the welfare and business growth of Danville. . . . As citizens of Danville we would deplore the necessity of locating the plant at such a distance as to have the city lose its benefits."

Though the prospect of a definitive settlement was still remote, the company lived up to its promise to build closer to the city. The site was to be known as Schoolfield. On August 21, R. A. Schoolfield wrote Lockwood, Greene: "We have at last definitely decided upon the location for the mill. . . . It is our purpose to utilize the property just beyond the City Park. . . . We will arrange so that we can throw the sewerage from the mills and dyehouse on the other side of the R.R. from the river." After voting to build a 36-foot dam, the directors reconsidered the matter and agreed upon a 25-foot dam, in view of the additional cost of $25,000 to compensate the owners of flooded land. This decision was particularly disappointing to Schoolfield, who had hoped to store enough water to generate surplus power for transmission to the Riverside plant. In September the J. W. Bishop Company of Providence, Rhode Island, signed the contract for the dam and power house at a cost of $278,465; while the Holyoke Machine Company contracted for water wheels, gates, and other machinery and equipment for the power plant. E. B. Wood, Lockwood, Greene's civil engineer, supervised the removal of the iron bridge from its original site to a point below the dam. (Wood acepted employment as Dan River's engineer in 1904 and remained with the company until his retirement in the 1940's).

Discussion of the city's water problem was resumed in 1903. Early in the year Danville sought to extend the city limits and take in much of the land owned by the Dan River Power & Manufacturing Company; but a bill to amend the city charter, introduced in the legislature by George C. Cabell, Jr., was defeated in committee with the help of "friends" of the mill corporation.[11] Again in May, after Cabell introduced a bill concerning "pollution of potable water used for the supply of cities and towns," the company wrote Representative John E. Taylor to "keep a close watch on this bill. . . . If you can avoid letting Cabell know that we want to oppose it, we hope you won't let him find it out, but of course if it comes to an open fight, we must fight it out." No further reference appears in the company's correspondence to this "iniquitous bill."

Meanwhile, Schoolfield had told the directors that "some of our friends" believed the company should build a pumping station for the city. The board agreed, and on May 14 the Dan River Power & Manufacturing Company proposed: to instal in its own power house a pump with a daily capacity of 1,500,000 gallons (50 per cent in excess of current consumption); to pump water into the city reservoir; and to sign a 25-30 year contract with the City of Danville, under which the city would obtain its water for 10 per cent below the average annual cost in the preceding five years. This proposal the city found unacceptable, but both parties continued to search for a solution.

Frank Talbott, speaking for the City Council, had already advised the company that the "purity of the water which would be supplied from the pond behind the proposed dam cannot be relied upon." Toward the end of May the city and the mills joined in employing

[11] H. R. Fitzgerald and D. A. Overbey made several trips to Richmond to lobby against the bill, and in May the directors extended a vote of thanks to Senator R. A. James "for the able manner in which you assisted our Company in defeating the iniquitous amendment" to the city charter. Another friend of the Company was Senator Joseph Whitehead. In writing Whitehead about the promissory notes he had given on his stock subscription, Schoolfield said: "We hope that you will keep an eye on the Legislature and not let any adverse legislation to our interests be enacted during the session."
Frank Talbott, J. W. Carter, and W. R. Mitchell, chairman of the Water Committee, worked on behalf of the municipal corporation.

three sanitary engineers[12] to make an impartial survey of the water system. Their report was ready on June 19. The observation that the river water was characteristically brownish-red confirmed the daily records of turbidity maintained by the water department since 1888. Besides being "far too turbid to be satisfactory for public consumption, even after improvement by sedimentation," the experts declared that the water was "not above suspicion as to its sanitary character." Danville's mortality from typhoid fever, accounting for 37 per cent of all deaths in 1890-1902, was "seldom found in a city provided with a safe water supply."[13] Sewage contamination entered the river at Leaksville and Spray, and insufficient self-purification took place between these towns and Danville. Lacking any other source of water, the city had to depend upon the river; but the engineers recommended a new system, originating in the river channel opposite the Club House, and a mechanical filtration plant to supplement the existing practice of sedimentation.

In rejecting the company's offer to instal a pump in the mill's power house, municipal officials declared emphatically: "The water supply of the City is its most important utility, and should be controlled absolutely by the City; nor do we think it wise for any private company to be even remotely connected therewith." Objection was also made to the proposed twenty-five year contract, since "conservative cities" did not enter into contracts for such a long period. Furthermore, the proposed basis for computing the cost of water ignored the fact that a new pump would be twice as efficient as the twenty-five-year-old pump then in use. In short, the city thought Dan River Mills should bear all the expense of carrying out the recommendations of the engineers, except the cost of a new pump and pumping station. Since the erection of the dam would materially lessen both the quantity and the quality of water available for public consumption, the municipality could seek an injunction and sue the company for damages. Under its charter the City of Danville had authority to "establish or enlarge water works or gas works within or *without* the City" and to "protect from injury or pollution . . . said works . . . within or without said City . . . for a distance of three miles above the limits of the city."

[12] Prof. W. P. Mason of Troy, N. Y., Nisbet Wingfield of Augusta, Ga., and George C. Whipple of Brooklyn, N. Y.
[13] In August the company sent the following telegram to the President of Cornell University and the Mayor of Ithaca, N. Y.: "Kindly wire at our expense cause of recent epidemic typhoid fever in your city." There is no record of the replies.

Denying that the building of the dam materially affected the water supply, the company nevertheless made several counterproposals for co-operating with the city in obtaining a new water system. Finally, on August 5, 1903, the company submitted the proposal which became the basis for settling the controversy. In substance, Dan River Mills promised:

(a) to exchange for the site of the old pumping station land on which the city could build a new pumping station;

(b) to pay the city a fair price for the buildings at the old pumping station;

(c) to pay the cost of piping for the difference in distance to the reservoir from the old pump house and the new one;

(d) to contribute $10,000 in cash toward the cost of the new pumping station;

(e) to arbitrate the disagreement, if these terms were unacceptable to the city.

Danville refused to arbitrate, though it found the company proposition satisfactory with the exception of the cash offer. Figures published in the newspapers on September 8 purported to prove that, since the new water system would cost $44,444, the community would in effect "give" the company $8,444 (assuming that the mills met the city's demand for $35,000 in cash), in addition to the privilege of "running its sewerage of all kinds into the Dan river at a point of safety." But the city's calculations ignored the fact that the new plant would include a filtering system, which the engineers considered indispensable in any event. Although the company was convinced that it had been "liberal and public spirited in the various propositions and that it had "no duty or obligation . . . to pay for a New Pumping Station," in September attorneys for Dan River promised the city $25,000 in cash and a quantity of rock for use in building the pumping station. This offer was accepted by Danville and approved by the Dan River stockholders. The next year land titles were exchanged by the two corporations, and in 1905 the city commenced to bring water from above the dam to its filtering plant and pumping station at the foot of Park Avenue. In his report for 1904-1905 Frank Talbott, Superintendent of the Water Department, expressed complete satisfaction with the outcome of the "Water Question"; it gave Danville "a pumping station that will be an ornament to the city and a water supply second to none in the country."[14]

Water for the mills and the mill village was drawn from the river at a point near the intake installed for the city's system. In discussing the plans with Lockwood, Greene, the company expressed a desire to have the water "as pure as possible" and had the engineers move the intake some distance above the dam in order to avoid pollution from three brooks that passed through a Negro settlement and emptied into the river near the dam. The company's first filtering plant was built to purify 500,000 gallons of water daily but a new plant to filter an additional 1,300,000 gallons was put up in 1908. Despite these precautions, Schoolfield village was visited by a typhoid epidemic in the fall of 1907.[15]

The New Mills

Work on the dam and power installations, scheduled for completion in December 1903, proceeded at a much slower pace than the management desired;[16] but on November 7, 1904, the president assured the directors that the power would be turned on "within a few days now." By this time Mill No. 1 was practically complete, and the first carding was done on Thanksgiving Day.

Advertising in the *Manufacturers' Record,* the Company received bids from fourteen contractors, scattered from Florida to Massachusetts. Excavating and grading contracts were awarded to the Virginia firm of Macgruder and Joyce. Outsiders observed that the "inequalities of the land [were] cleverly adapted to the needs of the mill, one of the ravines being utilized in forming a reservoir." The fill was ob-

[14] *Annual Report of the Water and Light Departments* (Danville, 1905). In the *Bacteriological Report of Municipal Filtration Plant at Danville, Virginia* (Pittsburgh, 1905), Dr. Ernest C. Levy reported numerous tests showing that the filtration removed 99.9 per cent of the bacteria, although the contract with the manufacturer, the Pittsburgh Filter Manufacuring Co., guaranteed the removal of 98 per cent in water containing not more than 3,000 bacteria per c.c. In 1908 Danville again petitioned the legislature for a charter amendment which would extend its jurisdiction with respect to public utilities. The Dan River Company considered the bill inimical to the interests of the mills and sent a directors' committee to Richmond to oppose it. Eventually, the matter was "amicably settled" (Directors' Minutes, Feb. 15 and 22, 1908).

[15] Local doctors and physicians from Richmond and Charlottesville were employed to inspect the village, but there is no record of their opinion as to the cause of the epidemic.

[16] There was "something radically wrong as to management and progress" on the Bishop job, Schoolfield complained. They had not kept their promise to bring fifty Italian laborers to Danville and they did not pay high enough wages to attract capable men for the hard work at the river.

tained by leveling a hill, the highest elevation in the area, which became the site of the weave shed. In February 1903 the contract for the weave shed, spinning mill, and cloth hall was awarded to George B. Hinman of Atlanta for $274,804; in July, Hinman signed contracts for the cotton houses, boiler house, dye house, transformer house, office, and stores on the basis of cost plus 10 per cent. Dan Valley Brick Company made bricks for Hinman, using firewood on the mill's land.

The designing and building of the Schoolfield mills contributed to the prestige of Lockwood, Greene & Company,[17] though the correspondence of R. A. Schoolfield and H. R. Fitzgerald with F. E. Sheed, chief engineer for the Boston firm, indicates that the mills incorporated numerous features conceived by the Dan River management. Twenty years later, however, it was easy to point out costly mistakes. The saw-tooth roof on the weave shed, for instance, furnished the maximum light without direct sunshine; but it required more than ordinary maintenance.

As the buildings neared completion, the directors determined to equip them with the "latest and most improved machinery, adapted to the manufacture of such goods as are most profitable to make, to supply the increasing demand for a diversity of product of the Riverside Cotton Mills which is being constantly called for by the customers." In March 1903 Schoolfield went to New England to buy spinning and weaving machinery. A $238,000 contract with Saco and Pettee Machine Shops covered 98 warp- and 94 filling-spinning frames (43,000 spindles), 12 slubber-, 14 intermediate-, and 28 roving frames and 16 spoolers. Saco and Pettee also furnished carding machinery; the opening and picking machinery came from the Kitson Machine Company; and Lowell Machine Shops supplied warpers, drawing-in frames, and slashers.

The company haggled over loom prices. Crompton and Knowles Loom Works first offered their best 4 x 1 drop-box looms (38 ½-inch) for $115 each; but in July, when Dan River ordered 1,266 looms, the manufacturer cut the price $15 per loom and equipped them all with

[17] *Manufacturers' Record*, Nov. 3, 1904, p. 387. A recent article refers to the competition for the Schoolfield job between Lockwood, Greene and J. E. Sirrine, a one-time Lockwood, Greene engineer, who had taken part in the preliminary survey of the mill plan. There is nothing in the Dan River files which lends any support to the statement that Lockwood, Greene lost $110,000 on the contracts for designing and supervising the construction of the first mill unit ("Men," in *American Wool & Cotton Reporter*, June 15, 1950, p. 37).

warp stop-motions for $15 extra, although this new device had been first quoted at $28. These were non-automatic looms. Two years later (1905) Crompton and Knowles marketed their first automatic looms, but Dan River deferred buying the new loom until 1909. By this time Crompton and Knowles engineers had perfected the stationary multistack magazine, with the weft detector attachment, which "has remained standard to this day for automatic fancy cotton and worsted looms."[18]

Five "latest-improved" raw-stock dyeing machines were supplied by the Delahunty Dyeing Machine Company, while drying machinery, which the company insisted should be "something better" than that in use at Riverside Mills, came from the Philadelphia Drying Machine Company. The spinning and weaving rooms were equipped with 183 humidifiers and 5,994 Grinnell automatic sprinklers. A 1,500 KW. Allis-Chalmers turbine generated power at the steam plant, and the Westinghouse Electric and Manufacturing Company installed the transmission system, including transformers and relays which "mixed" the hydro- and the thermo-electric power. Various contractors furnished the heating, cooling, and water-supply systems, pumps, tanks, elevators—and a bathtub for the office building.

Although less than half of the machinery had been set up in Mill No. 1, on April 28, 1905, President Schoolfield told the board that the demand for the company's cloth justified completing the second half of the original building program at once. The directors unanimously accepted Schoolfield's recommendation to finance the new work by selling $500,000 in preferred stock and $500,000 in debentures; but when the question came before the stockholders, the idea of issuing debentures was discarded in favor of a $1,000,000 issue of preferred stock.

N. A. and T. J. Fitzgerald started excavating and making bricks for Mill No. 2 in the summer of 1905. The contract with J. F. Gallivan Building Company of Greenville, South Carolina, called for an extension of No. 1 weave shed, a carding and spinning mill, a cotton house, and a bleachery. The original basis of the contract was cost plus 10 per cent, not to exceed $209,000; but a number of supplementary contracts brought the total outlay for the mill buildings and a second block of stores on Greensboro Road to over $270,000.

---

[18] J. F. Tinsley, *Looms for the World* (New York, 1949), pp. 16-19. By making the fancy-goods loom automatic, Crompton & Knowles "stepped into as commanding a position in the fancy-goods loom business as the Drapers occupied in the plain-goods loom field" (T. R. Navin, *The Whitin Machine Works*, p. 276).

The decision to build a bleachery is noteworthy. As Schoolfield explained it, the bleachery would enable the company to take advantage of a strong demand for wide, bleached sheeting; and the bleachery could also "be used to advantage in bleaching some of the yarn used in the colored mill, to brighten the colors. There is a large demand for this class of goods, with comparatively few mills making it." Since they regarded muddy water as a "great enemy to correct shades of color," the management had already provided filtered water for dyeing; the same supply proved to be good for bleaching. Curiously, as late as 1920, an informed writer thought there were "practically no bleaching, dyeing or printing works in the South, as the water is not suitable."[19]

For Mill No. 2 the Kitson Machine Company supplied machinery for the opening and picker rooms—"all to be of our latest construction." The labor-saving Barber warp-tying machine had been put on the market in 1904, and a number of these were purchased for the new mills.[20] Loom orders included 1,128 "Ideal" broad looms, purchased from the George W. Stafford Company for $250 each. This newly developed automatic loom, according to the manufacturer, permitted an increase in the number of looms per weaver to effect savings in labor costs up to 60 per cent.[21] From the Draper Company Dan River ordered 602 30-inch Model E looms for making chambrays. The Draper (or Northrop) automatic loom had been introduced in 1894, "a perfected machine"; but it was not in general use a decade later. Thus, the Dan River mills were able to start production with the most up-to-date weaving machinery, while many firms hesitated to adopt the new looms because of the high cost of scrapping common looms in good working condition.[22]

Before the completion of Mill No. 2 the president discussed with

[19] M. T. Copeland, *The Cotton Manufacturing Industry of the U. S.*, p. 37. Later on, Copeland notes that southern water supplies were unsuitable for bleaching without filtering. Dan River, of course, had filtered water. But the *Manufacturers' Record* (Aug. 16, 1884) had insisted that there was no lack of water in the South and no mystery in the process of bleaching: "Why should Southern manufacturers send their cloth from Georgia or South Carolina to New England to be bleached when the market for their goods lies at their own door?"

[20] *Ibid.*, p. 81. The warp-tier "ties about 250 knots per minute, and does the work of twenty girls."

[21] G. P. Erhard, in *Proceedings of the Tenth Annual Convention of the American Cotton Manufacturers' Association* (Charlotte, 1906), pp. 176-181.

[22] Copeland (*op. cit.*, pp. 84-87) describes the development of the automatic loom. The Draper Company's own story is in W. H. Chase, *Five Generations of Loom Builders* (Hopedale, 1950). Knowlton (*Pepperell's Progress*, p. 139) reveals that Pepperell first bought Draper automatic looms in 1902.

the directors "some inventions of new machinery for the Dressing Room . . . which effect a great saving of labor in drawing in the warps." Subsequently, three drawing-in machines were bought at a cost of over $15,000; but the management estimated a saving of $15 a day in direct labor costs.[23]   Other improvements made in connection with the erection of the second mill at Schoolfield included an addition to the boiler house, additional electrical equipment (Westinghouse), and a second Allis-Chalmers steam turbine.

At the end of 1907 the Dan River mills had installed 91,392 spindles and 3,018 looms, and the investment in land, buildings, machinery, housing, and utilities for the mill village had grown to $3,225,000.

Net earnings for 1908 topped half a million dollars, which encouraged Schoolfield to go before the board and speak confidently of the "opportunity to further diversify your product and make some of your lines more complete."   The proposal appealed to the stockholders, and in February 1909 they approved a stock issue to finance a new mill designed to house 43,000 spindles and 1,400 looms.   In May a $350,000 contract for Mill No. 3 and a new cloth hall (an addition to the original building) was awarded to John T. Wilson of Richmond; and in December Gallivan signed a contract for a new boiler house which would "more than double" the capacity of the steam plant.

Generally, the manufacturers who had equipped the other two mills supplied the opening, carding, and spinning machinery for Mill No. 3.   Loom contracts (March-October 1909) called for 1,549 units, as follows:

Crompton-Knowles:
     56 automatic gingham
     28 narrow (37½-inch) magazine

Draper:
     390 Model E narrow (30-inch)
     260 Model E special pillow-tubing (30-inch)
     575 Model E narrow (36-inch)
     50 single-fork (50-inch)
     12 Model D (64-inch)
     58 Model D (72-inch)
     80 Model L (100-inch)
     40 Model L (110-inch)

[23] Copeland (*op. cit.*, p. 82) states that "one man operating a drawing-in machine will draw in about six times as many warps per day as a girl can draw in by hand on the same grade of goods."

Most of the Draper looms represented improved models of the North-rop automatic loom.[24]

The Riverside Plant

At Riverside, capital improvements realized in 1902-1909 took the form of replacement and modernization. In February 1902, while plans for the Dan River Power development were still uncertain, the directors authorized a new building to house the 12,000-15,000 additional spindles needed to make yarn for 400 denim looms. Although twelve new spinning frames were acquired in 1903, the building plan was dropped. "The outlook for an investment" at Dan River, Schoolfield argued, "is much more favorable, and we think satisfactory, than it would be here."

In 1906, when both plants suffered from a shortage of labor, new carding machinery capable of turning out the same quantity of sliver with 20 per cent fewer workers was installed in three of the Riverside mills. A new engine and boilers, picking and carding machinery, and a blowing system to facilitate the cleaning of cotton preparatory to raw-stock dyeing were the major items in the $114,000 worth of improvements completed in 1906.

Power continued to be a perplexing problem. In a letter to the City Council in May 1902 the company complained that the municipal engineers were "continuing to use the water as they deemed proper, regardless of conditions, and instead of their using 75 H.P. for lights . . . they have increased it . . . for electric lights and other purposes, using double or more than double. . . ." Two years later, in the midst of an early-summer drought, Riverside reminded the city officials that the municipal light plant was entitled to less than 2,500 cubic feet per minute: "kindly instruct man in charge of your wheel not to use more than your share." The ice plant also tended to encroach upon the company's share of the water supply in the south canal.

On the north side of the river the Holyoke Machine Company installed governors on three Hercules turbines in an attempt to control the irregular speed of the 42-inch wheels at Mill No. 2. In January 1908 Lockwood, Greene submitted plans for increasing the power by constructing a breakwater, from a point opposite Mill No. 7 to the

[24] The *Manufacturers' Record* (Feb. 25, 1909) described twenty models which the Draper Company had set up in its Exhibition Weave Room at Hopedale, Massachusetts.

wheel-house of Mill No. 2, thus protecting the tail race; but the recommendation was apparently rejected.   A few additional horsepower were
secured for Mill No. 4 in 1908 by the substitution of 42-inch wheels
for the two old 39-inch ones.

Indirectly, an important contribution to the power supply at Riverside was made by the dam at the Dan River plant.   President Schoolfield frequently remarked that the storage capacity of the new dam
allowed Riverside to run during seasons of light rainfall.   As for the
Schoolfield mills, the steam plant had been expanded by 1909 "so that
we can operate all of the machinery, if necessary, independently of
the water supply."   That is, under the most unfavorable conditions
water in the upper dam could be allowed to fall below the turbine-in-
take level in order to maintain the flow at Riverside.   Under the most
favorable conditions Dan River produced almost enough hydroelectric
power to run the entire plant, and the steam generating system alone
was large enough to meet all the power and light requirements of the
mills and village.   The productive equipment of the two mills in 1909
comprised 230,000 spindles and 7,362 looms.

Financing Growth

The balance sheets (Appendix 1) summarize the financial growth of
the two companies.   The real estate, plant, and machinery account of
Riverside remained constant at $2 million from 1899 to 1907, rising
during the latter year to $2,081,956; but in December 1908 write-offs of
fixed assets reduced the property account to an even $2 million.   Mean-
while, the Dan River Power property account rose from $583,516 in
1903 to $3,224,129 in December 1908.

Having decided to go ahead with the power development, in
February 1902 the directors of Dan River Power & Manufacturing
Company solicited subscriptions to 8,500 shares of common stock.
(The 1,500 shares held by Riverside Cotton Mills would bring the
subscribed capital to $1,000,000.)   Including joint accounts, there were
89 subscribers to the new stock issue.   An innovation in financial
policy was the sale of a block of 1,750 shares to James T. Catlin & Company, a Danville brokerage and insurance firm.   The Catlin deal resulted in a wider distribution of the stock than had been customary in

Riverside financing, yet nearly all of the new capital came from Virginia and North Carolina.[25]

After Riverside's charter was amended (January 1904) to permit it to hold stock in other companies up to 30 per cent of its own capital, the older company bought 3,500 shares of a new 5,000-share issue of Dan River common stock. The rest of the issue, the president reported in November, was "selling very slowly." Acting upon his suggestion that the unsold stock could be placed in "strong hands and parties representing large means," the directors approved the sale of 1,406 shares at 104 to a "syndicate . . . gotten together through Mr. Catlin."

In view of the slow absorption of common stock, new financing in 1905 took the form of a preferred issue. A charter amendment raised the authorized capitalization to $2,500,000, and in May the stockholders voted to issue 10,000 shares of 6 per-cent cumulative preferred. The local market responded slowly to this offering, too; and in December the directors ratified the sale of 3,400 shares to the Richmond brokerage firm of Thomas Branch & Company. The terms—par less a commission of 2 per cent—were regarded by the management as "very beneficial."[26]

Sales, earnings, and dividend records of the two firms are shown in Appendix 2.

Dan River's first financial statement, covering the period from the commencement of operations to the end of 1905, showed net earnings of $128,058 (of which, however, only $55,784 was operating profit) on sales of $474,764. Only preferred dividends ($15,864) were paid. Both classes of stock sold well above par at least as early as December 1905, when the preferred brought 111 and the common, 113.

Sales rose steadily to $3,350,703 in 1909. Preferred dividends were distributed from earnings of $230,629 in 1906 and $381,392 in 1907. After increasing the capitalization to $3,000,000 in March 1908 the directors authorized an issue of 5,000 shares of common stock. Twenty-five hundred shares were distributed as a stock dividend (16⅔ per

[25] The stockholders list in 1902 included addresses in Baltimore, Knoxville, New York City, and Worcester, Mass. Significant was the purchase of 500 shares by Stephen Holman, president of the Holyoke Machine Company, contractor for the dam and power-house equipment.

[26] According to Schoolfield, the preferred issue was "dragging on the market, notwithstanding we were making an effort to dispose of it through a few parties to whom we were paying a small commission." In May 1906 the price had "materially advanced," the President said, "which would not be the case if the Company had waited to get rid of it in our local market." Schoolfield himself first subscribed to 500 shares, then took 134 more, and later subscribed to an additional 266 shares for himself and 50 for his wife.

cent), and the remainder were sold in a privileged subscription at 125. The response was "very gratifying." Upon completion of this financing, the president told the stockholders, the $3,000,000 capitalization represented "nearly but not quite the total cost of your complete Plant."

The common stockholders, who were "patiently awaiting" the time when the company could "prudently" pay dividends, were rewarded with a cash dividend of 4 per cent in October 1908. Reported earnings for the year amounted to $529,953, including the $62,500 premium on the stock sale.

Another charter amendment was obtained in March 1909 to bring the capitalization up to $3,500,000, and in April 5,000 shares of common were offered in a privileged subscription at 133⅓. Much to the president's embarrassment, stockholders asked for 10,000 shares. "Of course, it is gratifying," Schoolfield remarked, "to note the active demand for the stock, and we regret that the speculative tendency should have entered into the subscriptions." One hundred and eighty-five shares were allotted to employees who applied for stock; 3,512 shares were prorated among the stockholders who subscribed by rights; and the other 1,303 shares were doled out to a group of shareholders who owned both common and preferred stock. No consideration was given to applications from "outsiders."

Riverside Mills undertook no new financing in 1902-1908. Recovering from the nadir of 1901, earnings more than doubled the following year, while sales rose 14 per cent to $1,904,756. Payment of the regular preferred dividend and a common dividend of 8 per cent, out of earnings of $319,240, left $139,240 to carry to surplus. In March 1903 Harrison Robertson of Charlottesville, a stockholder who said he had the greater part of his estate in Riverside stock, urged the directors to increase the dividend rate, since (as he had predicted) the market price of the common had risen above the preferred. Instead of paying the 10 per cent which Robertson recommended, the board declared dividends totaling 14 per cent and in 1904-1908 maintained the rate at 10 per cent. Except in 1906, when earnings barely covered the preferred dividend, the common dividend was fully earned each year.

The few recorded transactions in Riverside stock show the common selling for 161 in September 1904 and 150 in December 1905, while the 10 per-cent preferred brought 166½ in January 1906.

Dan River Power & Manufacturing Company and Riverside Cotton Mills merged into a new company, the Riverside and Dan River Cotton Mills, in August 1909; but separate as well as consolidated earnings statements were prepared this year. It was a thirteen-months' year (December 1, 1908—December 31, 1909), inasmuch as the new federal income tax made it desirable to adopt a fiscal year ending December 31. Riverside earned $342,014 (including dividends of $65,400) and Dan River earned $616,667 (including the premium of $166,667 on the issue of 5,000 shares of common stock). The three companies distributed dividends, as follows:

	rate per cent	amount
Riverside, preferred	10	$100,000
Riverside, common	7.5	75,000
Dan River, preferred	6	60,000
Dan River, common	4	80,000
Riverside and Dan River, preferred	3	135,000
Riverside and Dan River, common	4	100,000

In the eight years 1902-1909 the Riverside common stockholder received cash dividends of 84.75 per cent on the shares held in January 1902—an average return of 10.6 per cent per annum. He earned an average of 19.6 per cent per year, if he sold (at par) the 75 per-cent stock dividend distributed upon the merger of the two companies in 1909; but at the end of 1909 he held 6 per-cent preferred stock in place of common paying 8 to 14 per cent yearly. The Dan River common stockholder fared poorly. He received cash dividends of 14 per cent, an average of 2.8 per cent per annum, if the investment is assumed to commence with the beginning of operations late in 1904; he earned 5.7 per cent a year if he sold his stock dividend. Neither corporation had matched the earnings of the most profitable firms in the industry. Pacific Mills declared a dividend of 32 per cent in 1907 and averaged 15.5 per cent for the eight years ending with 1907. The best record for eighteen cotton mills was made by Pepperell, which averaged almost 27 per cent over the eight-year period.[27]

[27] *Manufacturers' Record,* Oct. 28, 1909.

The Merger

As we have seen, at one time the directors resolved to surrender the charter of Dan River Power & Manufacturing Company and carry out the Schoolfield development under the Riverside name. The board minutes give no inkling of disadvantages experienced in operating the two plants under separate corporate names; but in July 1909 the president had ready the complete plan for merger. The directors approved it, practically without comment; and on August 12 Riverside's stockholders ratified the proposal by large majorities: 6,085 preferred shares for merger, 576 against; 7,374 common shares for merger, 1,060 against. The charter of the Riverside and Dan River Cotton Mills, Incorporated, granted by the State Corporation Commission on August 20, authorized a capitalization of $10,000,000, of which $6,000,000 was outstanding upon the exchange of stock.

Prior to the merger the two firms had the following capital structures:

	Riverside	*Dan River*
preferred stock (10%)	$1,000,000	
preferred stock (6%)		$1,000,000
common stock	1,000,000	2,500,000

To effect the merger, both classes of stockholders of Dan River Power & Manufacturing Company exchanged their holdings for the same type of stock in the Riverside and Dan River Cotton Mills, share for share. Riverside's stockholders, both common and preferred, received new 6 per-cent preferred stock in the ratio of 1.75 shares for each old share. Since the Riverside preferred carried a dividend of 10 per-cent, the extra .75 share roughly compensated the holders for the lowering of the dividend rate to 6 per-cent. The common stockholder received the "bonus" of .75 share in consideration of the difference in book value (about $50 per share) between the Riverside and the Dan River common stock.[28]

After merger the capitalization consisted of $4.5 million in 6 per-cent preferred stock and $2.5 million in common stock. Surplus accounts were adjusted in the following manner:

[28] In July 1909 Riverside common was selling for about $170 per share, while the Dan River common brought about $135.

Dan River

surplus, Dec. 1, 1908		$650,000
earnings, Dec. 1, 1908–Dec. 31, 1909		450,000
premium on common stock		166,667
		1,266,667
dividends paid		270,000
		996,667

Riverside

surplus, Dec. 1, 1908		820,436
earnings, Dec. 1, 1908–Dec. 31, 1909		276,614
dividends received		65,400
		1,162,450
dividends paid		280,000
		882,450
combined surplus		1,879,117
debit 15,000 new shares issued in merger		1,500,000
surplus (earned and capital), Riverside and Dan River Cotton Mills, Dec. 31, 1909		379,117

The following balance sheet of the consolidated firm, as of December 31, 1909, was the first financial statement certified by independent accountants (Barrow, Wade, & Guthrie):

assets

real estate and equipment			
Riverside Division			$2,000,000
Dan River Division			
machinery			1,398,664
mill construction account			984,466
electrical equipment			275,722
water power development			601,504
tenements			341,376
water supply			99,247
inventories:	*Riverside*	*Dan River*	
cotton	293,410	886,973	
finished goods	22,499	15,169	
goods in process	182,522	287,032	
supplies	29,979	35,903	
horses, mules, wagons	3,102	2,500	
	531,512	1,227,577	1,759,089
accounts receivable			925,286
bills receivable			52,446
treasury stock			510,000
investments			90,000
cash			440,373
			9,478,173

capital and liabilities

preferred stock (45,000 shares)	4,500,000
common stock (25,000 shares)	2,500,000
bills payable	2,045,000
accounts payable	6,459
dividends payable	12,597
reserve for improvements (Riverside)	35,000
surplus	379,117
	9,478,173

The treasury stock was acquired through the exchange of 5,100 shares of Dan River Power stock, owned by Riverside, for an equal number of shares in Riverside and Dan River Cotton Mills. The investments represented 500 shares of Piedmont Mills and 400 shares of Dan Valley Mills stock.

Working Capital

Both corporations, in 1902-1909, paid for fixed assets with stock issues and reinvested earnings; and they made some progress in forcing the stockholders to provide working capital.

At the end of 1902 Riverside's capital and surplus exceeded the stated value of its fixed assets and investments in other companies by $250,000, and the excess grew to $375,000 by the end of 1903. During the next three years purchases of Dan River stock exceeded undistributed earnings, and at the end of 1906 the entire surplus represented investment in Dan River Power & Manufacturing Company. Thereafter, retained earnings grew faster than new purchases of Dan River stock, although at the end of 1908 the stockholders' equity in working capital was only $230,000. That is, all receivables and cash and more than half of the inventories had been financed by creditors. The debentures issued in 1899 (and retired in 1909) accounted for $300,000; bills payable totaled $770,000.

As President Schoolfield explained, Dan River's new stock issues barely kept pace with the growing investment in plant and real estate. But the retention of earnings, as indicated by the steady rise of the surplus to $650,000 in 1908, financed inventories and provided a substantial share of the cash. As of December 31, 1909, the Riverside and Dan River Cotton Mills capital stock and surplus amounted to $7,379,117, or $1,678,138 in excess of the book value of the fixed assets; but the excess fell $80,950 short of covering inventories. The distribution of $550,000 in dividends in 1909 left current assets only 1.5 times current liabilities.

It is impossible to reconstruct completely the pattern of short-term debt in this decade. Suppliers of machinery extended credit up to three years, but the Danville mills did not adopt the practice followed by many southern firms of swapping stock for machinery. The first Dan River contract with Saco and Pettee Machine Shops required a down payment of one third, with the balance payable in six-months' notes subject to renewal up to three years. Crompton & Knowles accepted a down payment of one fourth and took one-, two-, and three-year notes for the balance. Unpaid balances carried interest at 6 per cent. Since this rate usually exceeded the rates in the money market, the company preferred to discount its promissory notes with New York bill brokers and banks in order to pay cash for machinery or retire before maturity the notes held by manufacturers. Apparently, the first account with bill brokers was established with the Boston firm of W. O. Gay & Company in October 1904. Later correspondence relating to loans shows frequent dealings (at least by 1908) with E. Naumberg, the National Bank of Commerce, and the Chase National Bank. The Merchants National Bank of Richmond furnished some short-term loans, though at one time the company protested that the Virginia bank charged 6 per cent while New York lenders took "a good deal of our Paper as low as 3⅓ and 3½%." Borrowing usually took the form of $50,000 and $100,000 notes, due in one to six months and often replaced at maturity with new notes.

While the company was borrowing large sums from the banks, the stockholders borrowed liberally from the company. Although he paid interest (at 5 or 6 per-cent) on balances due against his subscription, the Dan River stockholder had from three to twelve months to pay as much as 85 per cent of the purchase price.[29]

Riverside's investment of $40,000 in the Dan Valley Mills yielded dividends of $8,000 yearly in 1902-1904. In the latter year the flour-mill firm saw a favorable opportunity to expand and persuaded Riverside to join them in buying the flour and feed mill of S. C. Hurt and Sons in Lynchburg. Riverside and Dan Valley organized a new com-

[29] From the commencement of operations to Dec. 2, 1905, interest on stock subscriptions amounted to $61,742.

pany, the Piedmont Mills, as a result of which Riverside's investment in the milling business increased by $50,000.

Meanwhile, Dan River made large investments in housing and public utilities in connection with the building of Schoolfield village. Since this phase of the company's activities relates largely to problems of labor supply and employee welfare, it will be examined under another heading.

Production

To discuss the growth of Riverside and Dan River Cotton Mills in terms of output of goods we may refer to statistics in yards or in pounds. The yardage data (Appendix 3) for the two plants show a total product of 402 million yards of cloth in eight years, or 36 million yards more than the total for 18 years, 1884-1901. On a poundage basis the record output of almost 10 million pounds in 1899 was not equaled at the Riverside plant until 1909, but production at Dan River climbed steadily from 2.6 million pounds in 1905 to 11.5 million pounds in 1909. Thus, in five years the total output of the mills had doubled.

The distribution of output by classes of goods is shown in Table 1. Riverside's looms continued to specialize in the plaids which formed the basis of its early growth: but the chambrays and cheviots together accounted for a greater poundage of cloth in 1901, 1905, and 1909. The production of denims and coverts reached a peak of 856,000 pounds (of which 815,000 pounds were denims) in 1906, but neither class of fabric was made in 1909.[30] "Other colored" goods include India stripes, cottonades, checks, twill shirting, drills, and ginghams— all produced in relatively small quantities or for short periods. The manufacture of 27-inch drills began in 1908 and jumped to 268,000 pounds in 1909. Riverside made 359 pounds of "staple ginghams" in 1902, but the "gingham period" in the company's history did not commence until after 1909.[31]

As far as colored goods are concerned, Dan River in 1904-1909 was

[30] The *Manufacturers' Record* (Feb. 26, 1903) quoted E. S. Draper as unwilling to "take a pessimistic view of the outlook for denims," despite the fact that mills under construction would be prepared to double the production in this line. I have not seen any explanation of Dan River's withdrawal from the market.

[31] As early as 1903, southern dry goods merchants had urged that "it would pay the Southern mills to manufacture a high grade of gingham for the home trade." Some southern mills were making ginghams "but none of the best grades" (*Manufacturers' Record*, March 26, 1903).

Table 1. Cloth Production, 1902-1909
(thousands of pounds)

year	sheeting	plaids	chambray	cheviots	denims and coverts	other colored	total
			a. Riverside				
1902	1,749	3,184	1,953	1,459	187	343	8,875
1903	1,598	4,122	973	1,197	362	127	8,379
1904	1,432	3,904	1,310	1,383	111	111	8,251
1905	1,386	3,012	2,251	1,336	352	33	8,370
1906	1,300	2,328	2,028	1,074	856	62	7,648
1907	1,269	3,220	1,531	1,214	382	13	7,629
1908	1,445	4,367	805	2,032	137	22	8,808
1909	1,526	3,173	3,631	1,384	0	266	9,980
			b. Dan River				
1905	0	0	2,530	0	14	34	2,578
1906	8	0	4,565	0	235	297	5,105
1907	651	0	6,079	0	218	96	7,044
1908	2,369	0	7,191	0	42	30	9,632
1909	2,853	0	8,621	0	30	4	11,508

a chambray mill. Chambrays made up 96.7 per cent of the colored cloth manufactured at Dan River and half the total output of colored goods from the two plants. In addition to denims and covert cloth, the Schoolfield mills made relatively small amounts of cable cloth and pin checks in scattered years.

"Riverside" plaids represented approximately the same quality of coarse cloth as in the company's infancy, although the goods became somewhat lighter in weight. Thus, the 25-inch cloth, which averaged 5.5 yards to the pound in 1890-1891, ran above 6.2 yards in 1910. Production of the 27-inch plaids was nearly three times that of the 25-inch goods. "Golden Rule" chambrays, manufactured at both plants, were made of No. 15 filling yarn and No. 13 warp; and the cloth averaged 4.4 yards per pound in 28-inch widths. "Defiance," a coarser chambray, ran about 3.8 yards to the pound. "Ideal," the finest grade of chambray, came from Dan River's Mill No. 2. This cloth averaged 4.9 yards per pound and contained No. 26 yarn in the filling and No. 20 in the warp.

A batch of specification sheets, with samples attached, prepared for Oshinsky and Valentine in October 1907, show thirteen styles of "Golden Rule" chambray in blue, blue drab, tan, slate, and black. The specifications uniformly call for 1326 warp ends in cloth 31.3 inches wide (unfinished), with 42 picks per inch in the filling. This was one of the company's "confined" lines; others are identified in the cost sheets by the initials of Sweet, Orr & Company (chambrays) and Bradbury and Wilson (covert cloth).

When the Dan River mills were built, Riverside was using "about 25 different shades of colors," according to Fitzgerald. The same colors were to be used at Dan River, and the first section of the dye house was designed to raw-stock dye 14,000 pounds daily. Some dyed cotton was rebaled, but most of it was stored loose in a row of bins, one for each color. The inventory of February 1906 showed 127,000 pounds of dyed cotton in the following colors: black, indoine, sky blue, pea blue, blue drab, new blue, fawn, slate, red, brown, olive brown, and tan. The "sulphur colors," Fitzgerald noted, were "coming more and more into practical use." Actually, sulphur dyes, which had been perfected around 1900, were limited to blues, blacks, yellows, and browns; but they had the advantages of being extremely fast to washing and generally fast to light.[32]

Table 1 shows a drop in the production of sheeting at Riverside from 1902 to 1906; thereafter, some gains are recorded, but the most rapid rise in sheeting output took place at Dan River. The 17.6 million pounds of sheeting produced at both plants represented 16.9 per cent of the total output of cloth in 1902-1909. Although eighteen widths, from 36 to 108 inches, were made in at least one of the eight years, the narrow sheeting previously produced in great volume practically disappears from the schedules. Riverside made no 36-inch sheeting after 1902, and very little of its output was under 76 inches. Of all the sheeting produced at both mills, the 76-inch cloth accounted for 34.0 per cent (by weight); the 81-inch width, 23.8 per cent; the 86-inch, 15.2 per-cent; and the 90-inch, 11.7 per-cent. Riverside's 76-inch sheeting consistently averaged 2 yards to the pound, but at Dan River sheeting in the same width ranged from 1.75 to just over 2 yards per pound.

The Dan River bleachery opened in the fall of 1908, and in February 1909 Schoolfield reported a "favorable reception" for the bleached sheeting. "Some of our largest customers," he said, "are clamoring for additional widths" and also asking for pillow slips, "which very few mills make." In 1909 over 70 per cent of the sheeting

---

[32] C. E. Pellew, *Dyes and Dyeing*, pp. 104-105.

of both plants was sold bleached; and in June 1909 bleached sheets, as distinct from sheeting, were put on the market for the first time.

Costs

Dan River's "Cost of Manufacturing" book was opened in November 1904 in the form established in 1884 for Riverside's cost records; and the cost sheets for the two mills yield essentially the same statistics that were available for the earlier period. All the records are perfectly legible, practically complete in details, and almost free from mechanical error.

Average unit cost for the combined outputs (colored goods and sheeting) varied, as follows (cents per pound):

	Riverside	*Dan River*
1902	17.88	
1903	19.36	
1904	21.88	
1905	19.28	18.77
1906	22.39	20.38
1907	23.51	21.23
1908	21.93	20.66
1909	21.52	21.62

In four years out of five Dan River's total unit cost was lower than Riverside's but the period is too short for any significant comparison.

Cost sheets for colored fabrics show a lower unit cost for Dan River, excepting the first year of operations. The maximum difference appears in 1907, when Dan River's cost of 21.66 cents per pound was 1.18 cents less than Riverside's. In general, the Schoolfield mills made chambrays at a lower cost than that of producing somewhat coarser cloth at Riverside. Most of the gain derived from a lower labor cost per pound of product, reflecting the greater efficiency of the new machinery. The unit cost of supplies, which included repair parts, also remained consistently low at Dan River; and these advantages more than offset the higher cost of cotton (per pound of output) for the finer yarns used at Dan River. Because of the nature of the cost system, the unit cost figures represent the average cost for *all* colored goods manufactured in a given year. Consequently, the averages understate the true unit cost of producing relatively fine goods, which require more labor and a higher investment in machinery per pound of output than the coarser fabrics. By the same token, the unit cost of producing coarse cloth, such as Riverside's plaids, must be overstated.

For white goods we have comparable data for only three years, in two of which Dan River's unit cost ran 1.14 to 1.65 cents per pound higher than Riverside's. A relatively high overhead on a small volume raised the cost in 1907, and in 1909 a large proportion of Dan River's sheeting bore the additional expense of bleaching. Wages and bleaching supplies added .77 cent per pound to the cost of bleaching 3,400,000 pounds of sheeting in the thirteen months ending December 1909.[33]

Table 2 focuses attention on the variability of the direct labor cost and its components. The increase of .17 cent from 1902 to 1903 is easily explained by the half-hour reduction in the working day, with no corresponding decrease in daily wage rates. The "hump" in 1906-1907 resulted from high labor turnover and an upward revision of wages in the face of a scarcity of laborers. Relatively large increases occurred in the cost of cloth-room labor, repair work, and in spinning and dressing; the change in carding labor cost was small, while the variations in the cost of weaving were insignificant. Most of the component labor costs drop significantly in 1908-1909, reflecting stable wage rates, lower labor turnover, and, perhaps most important, the increased proportion of improved machinery in use.

Some of the effects of technological change may be discovered through comparison of the percentage distribution of direct labor costs

Table 2. Direct Labor Costs, Colored and White
Goods (Riverside Mills), 1902-1909
(cents per Pound)

	1902	1903	1904	1905	1906	1907	1908	1909
carding	.70	.75	.71	.68	.79	.83	.76	.65
spinning	.68	.73	.69	.66	.95	1.07	.87	.75
dressing	.43	.45	.46	.47	.55	.64	.55	.50
weaving	2.49	2.51	2.50	2.51	2.55	2.67	2.52	2.45
cloth room	.18	.19	.20	.22	.24	.25	.23	.23
repairs	.19	.22	.21	.29	.35	.41	.31	.27
dyeing	.16	.15	.15	.15	.16	.17	.16	.17
total	4.83	5.00	4.92	4.98	5.59	6.04	5.40	5.02

[33] In the four weeks ending Dec. 26, 1908, it took 4,000 pounds of bleach (costing $76), 2200 pounds of vitriol ($37.74), 5200 pounds of caustic soda ($169), and unspecified quantities of soap, corn starch, potato starch, filler, etc. to bleach 147,346 pounds of sheeting. The materials cost amounted to .4 cent per pound of cloth.

in different periods (Table 3). Relatively, weaving labor cost stays remarkably stable at 47.7-49.8 per cent of total labor cost from 1885 to 1909. But in the newest mill (Dan River Mill No. 2), after the installation of Draper and Stafford automatic looms and the increase in the number of looms per weaver, labor cost of weaving dropped to 34.2 per cent of the total labor on unbleached cloth. Carding and spinning labor was relatively more costly in 1902-1909 than in the 1880's, as the mills gradually turned to finer yarn. The relative decline in the cost of dressing reflects the use of labor-saving warp-tying and drawing-in machinery.

Table 3. Percentage Distribution of Direct Labor Costs

	Riverside: 1885, 1888-1891	Riverside: 1902-1909	Dan River, Mill No. 1; 1909
carding	9.5	14.1	11.7
spinning	11.4	15.3	13.6
dressing	16.3	9.7	8.9
weaving	47.7	48.3	49.8
cloth	4.7	4.2	5.4
repairs	4.6	5.4	4.0
dyeing	5.8	3.0	5.4
electrical			1.2
	100.0	100.0	100.0

Cost per pound of cloth for supplies, fuel, and "expense" are found on separate sheets for white goods and colored goods at both divisions. For supplies, Dan River's cost on colored fabrics was consistently below Riverside's, seemingly as a result of improved processes in the newer dye house. Dye-stuff prices affect year-to-year changes in the unit cost, which ranges from a low of 1.06 cents per pound of cloth (Dan River, 1908) to 1.92 cents (Riverside, 1902). Supplies for bleached sheeting (1909) cost 1.44 cents per pound of cloth, or about twice the average for unbleached goods. Unit fuel cost held stable at about .25 cent per pound of colored goods, but the cost sheets for white goods record a steady rise from .18 cent per pound to .45 cent (Riverside, 1908) and .59 cent (Dan River, 1907). Some of the variability stems from the growing use of steam power to replace undependable water power; it is also probable that the cost of coal for generating power and for manufacturing steam for the bleachery and dye houses was more or less arbitrarily allocated to the various classes of goods.

Costs classified as "expense" (including an undefined "expense account") rose less rapidly than output; generally, this unit cost declined in 1902-1909. Taxes at Dan River increased as the plant expanded, and in 1909 the Schoolfield mills paid slightly less taxes than Riverside on real and personal property worth one and one-half times the value of the mills in Danville.[34] But all taxes amounted to only $53,678, so that tax-wise the advantage of location in Schoolfield must be considered slight. The cost of borrowed money fluctuated widely: it was $13,660 in 1903 and $52,788 in 1908. Salary payments rose steadily at both divisions and in about the same ratio as the increase in total wages. Both series are shown in Table 4. In 1902 salaries amounted to 6.5 per cent of the total of wages and salaries; in 1909, 7.4 per cent. Salaries took 1.5 cents of each dollar of sales, both in 1902 and 1909.

Table 4. Wages and Salaries, 1902-1909
(thousands of dollars)

year	Riverside	Dan River	total
		wages	
1902	$429		$ 429
1903	419		419
1904	411		411
1905	417	$112	529
1906	400	229	629
1907	458	351	808
1908	471	446	916
1909	533	587	1,120
		salaries	
1902	29		29
1903	32		32
1904	31		31
1905	35	14	49
1906	34	23	57
1907	36	35	71
1908	36	38	74
1909	42	48	90

Discrepancies in totals are due to rounding.

[34] Assessments for county tax purposes in Schoolfield rose from $405,168 (real property) and $163,343 (tangible personal property) in 1905 to $1,505,871 and $418,270, respectively, in 1909.

Monthly averages of middling cotton on the New York Cotton Exchange ranged from a low of 7.2 cents per pound in January 1905 to 15.4 cents in March 1904. Despite frequent fluctuations in the market price of cotton, the mill's cost of raw cotton and the cost of cotton per pound of cloth stayed unusually stable. The following statistics refer to Riverside Mills, which consumed approximately 10 million pounds of cotton annually:

	actual net cost	*cost per pound of cloth*
	(cents per pound)	
1902	8.5	9.9
1903	9.4	10.8
1904	11.8	13.5
1905	9.1	10.5
1906	10.9	12.1
1907	10.7	13.0
1908	10.6	12.6
1909	11.1	13.2

The spread between the net cost of a pound of cotton and the cost of cotton per pound of cloth tends to widen, reaching 2.3 cents in 1907. Relatively, the cost of cotton per pound of cloth varied from 111 per cent to 122 per cent of the net cost of a pound of cotton. In all probability, increasing amounts of waste resulting from carding and spinning finer yarns tended to raise the ratio of the cost of cotton in cloth to the cost of raw cotton. Sales of waste—card fly, bagging, sweepings, and colored and white thread—were entered meticulously in the Petty Ledger. One of the best customers was Riverside Mill of Augusta, Georgia.

Early in 1904 speculation in cotton pushed the spot price to more than 17 cents a pound. Schoolfield noted with satisfaction the collapse of the so-called "Sully corner" in March 1904. Professing a desire to secure higher prices for growers, Daniel J. Sully and his associates commenced heavy trading in cotton futures in the winter of 1903-1904, while much of the crop still remained in the hands of planters. Sully overextended himself and was forced into bankruptcy with liabilities of over $3 million. But even the *Manufacturers' Record* considered the subsequent break in cotton prices "a serious loss to the whole South. ... A 'bull' leader as daring and as resourceful as Sully," the paper commented, "is practically a necessity to the South."[35] A movement to

[35] *Manufacturers' Record*, March 24, 1904, p. 200.

secure voluntary reduction of acreage, sponsored by the Southern Interstate Cotton Convention, soon petered out.[36]

Riverside's year-end inventory of cotton varied from 5.9 per cent (1907) to 22.6 per cent (1908) of the following year's consumption. On December 1, 1907, both plants had on hand less than $100,000 worth of cotton, as the management anticipated (correctly) the downward movement of prices in 1908. The unusually high inventories ($567,000 for both divisions) on December 1, 1908, preceded the rising cotton market of 1909. At the end of 1909 Dan River had on hand more than half the following year's consumption; and the accumulation of inventories worth $1.2 million accurately anticipated the higher cotton prices of 1910.

Dan River's "Cotton Purchase Book 1" (1904-1909) furnishes a continuous record of bales purchased, grades, prices, and suppliers. S. M. Weld & Company, members of the cotton exchanges, handled the mill's dealings in futures, which appear to have been speculative rather than hedging operations. The records describe many option contracts, which must also be regarded as generally speculative. Thus, on May 20, 1905, the Company bought 300 bales of cotton from Inman, Akers & Inman of Atlanta, "the price to be fixed any time between now and June 25 at 43 points on July." On June 13 the mill bought 500 bales, with a four months' option to fix the price at "70 points on October"— i.e., .7 cent per pound above the October quotation on the day the mill decided to establish the delivery price. President Schoolfield made all the decisions on cotton policy, but in 1905 Henry Roediger came into the company as Schoolfield's assistant and in 1912 was named cotton buyer.

As in the previous period, the erratic treatment of depreciation distorts the reported cost figures. In 1902-1905 relatively minor charges for renewals were absorbed by the "expense" account; in 1906 over $100,000 in Riverside's "Improvement" account was charged to profit and loss.[37] The Improvement account amounted to $81,956 in 1907, $109,549 in 1908, and $86,028 in 1909. Commencing with the 1908 statement the improvement charges were deducted from gross income.

[36] *Manufacturers' Record*, "Southern Cotton Prospect Supplement," Feb. 16, 1905. See also issues of Jan. 21, Jan. 28, March 3, April 7, May 5, May 12, July 21, Sept. 15, Oct. 13, 1904, and March 16, 1905.

[37] The specific items were: remodeling the old flour mill for a waste house ($1,220), remodeling No. 6 cotton house ($4,675), humidifying system, No. 6 Mill ($5,550), new equipment for carding, drawing, and picker rooms; blowing system, and new engine and boiler ($86,301), remodeling No. 3 cotton storage house and new picker room ($16,595).

At Dan Diver depreciation was accounted for by the adjustment of surplus *after* calculating earnings for the year. These charges were $60,000 in 1907, $124,168 in 1908, and $129,169 in 1909. The 1909 deduction had the effect of leaving net earnings an even $450,000!

Table 5 furnishes a comparison of mill margins—the spread between the cost of cotton and the price of cotton cloth—on gray goods and the price of goods produced at Riverside.

Table 5. Selling Prices and Mill Margins, 1902-09
(cents per pound)

| year | Riverside Mills | | U. S. mills |
	selling price	margin above cost	mill margin, gray goods*
1902	21.13	3.25	11.0
1903	23.21	3.85	10.9
1904	25.61	3.73	11.1
1905	20.73	1.45	14.6
1906	25.09	2.70	14.6
1907	27.28	3.77	17.7
1908	25.47	3.54	11.3
1909	24.42	2.90	12.2

* S. J. Kennedy, *Profits and Losses in Textiles*, pp. 241-243.

Riverside's fabrics (colored and white combined) yielded a maximum profit per pound of 3.85 cents in 1903, the year in which the mill margin in the gray goods market reached its nadir; but almost as large a profit (3.77 cents) was obtained in 1907, when the mill margin was greatest. The correlation between the company's unit profit and mill margins is not close, nor do the data at hand lend plausibility to the thesis that profits are sustained by a relatively low price of cotton. In 1902-1909 the mill margin on gray goods averaged 2.5 cents higher than in 1890-1901.[38]

Customers and Cycles

Dan River's "Sales Book No. 1" was opened on February 28, 1905, with an order placed in July 1903 by Ely & Walker Dry Goods Company. The request of the St. Louis firm for the first case of goods pro-

[38] S. J. Kennedy, *Profits and Losses in Textiles*, pp. 241-243.

duced by the new mills at Schoolfield was filled with the shipment of 2,161 yards of 28-inch "Conqueror" chambray, billed at 5.75 cents per yard. Ely & Walker also took the first bleached sheeting: nine cases of 81-inch "Foxcroft" sheeting at 16 cents per yard. Hundreds of customers—dry goods stores, wholesalers, jobbers, converters, manufacturers, and even penitentiaries—parade through the pages of these early sales books. Many of them, like Ely & Walker, began to buy at Dan River because of their satisfaction with the products they had been buying from Riverside Cotton Mills.

Very little remains of records which would explain sales policies or methods employed to gain customers and maintain sales under adverse as well as favorable business conditions. In April 1902 the management complained of lagging production, although two thirds of the spindles and half the looms ran night and day. Demand continued strong in 1903, and Riverside closed the year, as it had entered it, with no inventory of finished goods. During most of 1904 the mills fell behind on orders for wide sheeting, though Mill No. 6 worked two shifts; but in the colored-goods market buyers seemed to be holding off, waiting for lower prices. Riverside's officers were not wholly unconcerned about the general deflationary tendency that overtook trade and industry in 1904. In January 1905 Schoolfield remarked that the Sully manipulation of the cotton market and a general recession had left in their wake millions of idle spindles and numerous cotton-mill failures. "The wise policy for us to pursue," he said, "is to profit by the experience of the past, make the best that we can of the present, and persevere to the accomplishment of better things in the future." Better things were not long in coming. During 1905 the company experienced an "exceptionally large demand from the cutting trade for our heavier grades of goods." Production moved steadily upward in 1906, and in September the president told the directors: "We are shipping the goods out as fast as they are made." The upward trend was scarcely affected by the panic which paralyzed the financial centers in the fall of 1907, although in the following year the management was troubled briefly by an accumulation of finished goods at the Dan River mills.

The accelerated southward march of the cotton industry increased capacity in the South from 4,368,000 spindles in 1900 to 10,494,000 spindles—37.1 per cent of the nation's total—in 1910. "No fact relating to the industrial progress of the country is more interesting, more important, or more significant to the student of social and economic conditions . . . than the vigor, the persistency, and the success of the South in introducing this branch of manufacture," the Bureau of the Census noted.[39] But even southern mill men found the pace too rapid at times. Meeting in Charlotte in May 1903 the American Cotton Manufacturers' Association (originally the Southern Cotton Spinners' Association) recommended voluntary curtailment through abandonment of night work and the adoption of a four-day work week.[40] There is every reason to believe that Riverside and Dan River (both nonmembers of the Association) were disinterested in the proposals. The following record of year-end inventories of finished goods indicates that maintaining production was a more serious problem than curbing the accumulation of unsold cloth:

	Riverside	*Dan River*
1902	none	
1903	,,	
1904	$90,088	
1905	4,649	$ 6,297
1906	none	1,990
1907	,,	12,197
1908	,,	83,825
1909	22,499	15,169

One item concerning the sales organization appears in the directors' minutes: N. A. Hamilton died in January 1904 and was succeeded by A. T. Cockefair. In 1905 George P. Ray joined the sales staff, about the time that the New York office moved from Thomas Street to 56 Worth Street.

Management

Changes in the directorate in 1902-1909 resulted from losses by death or from changes in the size of the board. The passing of J. E. Schoolfield in August 1902 marked the first death among the promoters of Riverside Cotton Mills. J. R. Jopling, a hardware merchant, was elected a director in February 1903, and in July the board was increased to fourteen members. R. A. Schoolfield, T. B. Fitzgerald, J. H. Schoolfield, J. G. Penn, J. N. Wyllie, B. F. Jefferson, James I. Pritchett, F. X.

[39] Bureau of the Census, *Census of Manufactures: 1905: Textiles,* Bulletin 74 (Washington, 1907), p. 37.
[40] *Proceedings of the Seventh Annual Convention of the Southern Cotton Spinners Association* (Charlotte, 1903), pp. 158-159.

Burton, J. R. Jopling, and D. A. Overbey were re-elected; and H. R. Fitzgerald, John I. Pritchett, E. S. Reid, and Joseph Whitehead were newly elected directors.[41]

Because of failing health, Burton declined re-election as president in July 1903. He died the following April. One of the founders of the Morotock Mills, Burton was as much a pioneer in Danville cotton manufacturing as the Riverside promoters. R. A. Schoolfield eulogized him in the board meeting of January 1905, concluding with Scriptural advice: "Watch, for we know not what hour or day the Son of Man cometh."

R. A. Schoolfield succeeded Burton as president; but in 1904 the directors reversed the policy adopted in 1899 and made the president the active executive head of both corporations. T. B. Fitzgerald, now living in semi-retirement in Fitzgerald, North Carolina, was one of the committee of five directors who proposed the change. At the same time H. R. Fitzgerald became secretary-treasurer, with no formal change in the responsibilties he carried as Schoolfield's assistant; and J. G. Penn was elected to the vice-presidency, without salary.

Burton's death and the retirement of Whitehead left two vacancies in the board; instead of filling them, in November 1905 the directors reduced the membership to twelve. J. G. Penn died in August 1907, and he was succeeded by his son, J. Pemberton Penn. The board of directors, as constituted after the changes noted above, became the first directorate of Riverside and Dan River Cotton Mills in August 1909.

The directors fixed the compensation of all salaried employees until 1906; thereafter, the directors determined the salaries of the officers and authorized the officers to set the pay of all other employees. The board approved the following salaries at Riverside in 1905-1906;

president	$10,000	per annum	
secretary-treasurer	5,000	"	"
superintendent	6,500	"	"
salesman (New York)	3,700	"	"
salesman	3,000	"	"
clerk (bookkeeper)	125	per month	
clerk	91.66	"	"
two clerks @	75.00	"	"
one office worker	40.00	"	"
one office worker	35.00	"	"

[41] These names were reported to the Corporation Commission on July 28, 1903. On the copy of this letter someone penciled the name of R. I. Anderson, who had been a director for a number of years; but it appears from the minutes that he was not re-elected, perhaps at his own request. He died in January 1906.

As officers of the Dan River Power & Manufacturing Company, the secretary-treasurer, the assistant secretary-treasurer, and the superintendent commenced to draw pay from this corporation in January 1903. As secretary-treasurer and later president, Schoolfield received $5,000 a year for the entire period, 1903-1909. H. R. Fitzgerald's salary was raised to $5,000 in 1905 and to $10,000 in December 1906. This made Schoolfield's and Fitzgerald's total compensation the same, i.e., $15,000 a year from the two companies. Both men also received a bonus of $5,000 in 1910 for services in connection with the erection of the Schoolfield mills.

S. I. Roberts resigned in March 1905, and H. W. Kimball came from Atlanta to succeed him as superintendent of the Riverside plant. In 1904 George W. Robertson, overseer of weaving at Riverside, became superintendent of the Dan River mills at a salary of $3,000.

Stockholders found few reasons for criticizing the management. The annual meetings varied greatly with respect to the proportion of the stock represented in person or by proxy. In January 1904, 18,002 out of 20,000 shares were represented at the Riverside meeting; but a Dan River stockholders' meeting in December 1908 adjourned for lack of a quorum. At the Riverside meeting in January 1906 it was voted to mail a copy of the president's annual report to each stockholder; and Dan River's annual report for 1907 was also printed and distributed to stockholders. But it did not become an established practice in this period to inform the stockholders of the company's progress, except through verbal reporting at the annual meeting. Both companies handed out printed folders giving condensed balance sheets at the end of each year, but no income statement was distributed to stockholders.

Riverside had 305 stockholders (owning preferred stock, common stock, or both) at the time of merger. About a third of both classes of stock (6,775 shares) were in the hands of shareholders owning less than 100 shares each. Twenty-five stockholders held from 100 to 199 shares each, while almost half (9,960 shares) of the stock was held by 28 stockholders with 200 to 1,072 shares each. The twelve directors owned 2,738 shares. With 5,100 shares, Riverside was the largest stockholder in Dan River; I do not know how the other 29,900 shares were distributed.

The merger left a few disgruntled shareholders in its wake. The principal hold-outs were the estate of Harrison Robertson and certain

Winfree and Lloyd holdings. A member of the Robertson family protested: "I, and I believe all of the members of my family, have decided
not to accept the merger scheme of the two mills, and unless we can get
what we consider a fair price for our old stock, we shall be forced to
take such legal steps as we may deem best . . . let me know what your
Board will offer as a compromise." Understandably, the directors ignored this demand. W. R. Winfree, the owner of 48 shares, brought
suit against the company, and the case went on appeal to the Virginia
Supreme Court. The decision handed down in September 1912 declared the merger binding on all stockholders; soon after, the last of the
old shares were turned in for new stock, with dividends accumulated
since August 1909.[42]

The Worker

The ten-hour day (six days a week) for which the Riverside workers
had struck unsuccessfully in 1901, was put into effect by the directors—
upon R. A. Schoolfield's recommendation—in the spring of 1903. In
December the management chafed at the loss of production from the
shortened work day but thought it would be "impractical" to go back
to the old schedule of eleven hours during April-September.

In reducing the average working day by half an hour the company
in effect granted a general wage increase of 4.76 per cent. Specific information on other changes in rates of pay is lacking; in fact, the only
direct source of wage data for this period is a set of time books from
the Riverside sample room. These give daily wage rates and biweekly
earnings of a "forelady," a loom fixer, a weaver, and three or four
piece-card hands. Selected figures for 1907 (the earliest year available)
through June 1910 are shown in Table 6.

Perhaps significant are the reduction of the loom fixer's rate from
$1.85 to $1.75 per day in 1909-1910 and the drop in the second highest
wage rate from $0.95 to $0.90. After October 1908 the lowest rate paid
in this room was $0.65 per day; after October 1909 it was $0.75.

Wage data for 1901-1909 have been obtained indirectly from the

[42] Winfree v. Riverside Cotton Mills and Others, in *Cases Decided in the Supreme
Court of Virginia*, CXIII (Richmond, 1913), 717-727. Since under Virginia law a merger required only the affirmative vote of the majority of the shares in each corporation,
the Court found the appellant entitled only to "fair cash value of his stock as of the
day before the vote for consolidation."

Table 6. Daily Wage Rates: Riverside Sample Room, 1907-1910

daily wage	July 1907	August 1907	October 1908	October 1909	June 1910
		number of workers			
$1.85	1	1	1	0	0
1.75	0	0	0	1	1
.95	1	1	1	0	0
.90	0	0	0	1	1
.85	0	0	0	0	1
.80	2	2	2	1	1
.75	1	1	0	1	3
.65	0	2	2	2	0
.60	2	0	1	0	0
average	$.91	.92	.90	.92	.94

reports furnished yearly (except 1902) to the state Bureau of Labor and Industrial Statistics.[43] Although the companies are not named in the published sources, the returns furnished by Riverside and Dan River Mills may be easily identified. For Riverside, all the wage data on occupations uniformly reported for three of these years are presented in Table 7.

Apparently, the average daily wage at Riverside fluctuated around $0.97 in 1901-1905, then rose abruptly to $1.09 in 1906. (Since spinners and weavers—workers typically paid at piece rates—are included in the statistics, it would probably be more accurate to regard them as average daily earnings.) The labor shortage was acute in the summer of 1906, but the company had a "large number of families engaged to come in during fall months. Most of these families are country people and cannot move until they harvest their crops." Although, judging by obviously meager data, wages dropped noticeably the following year, it was in 1907 that unit labor costs reached their peak—perhaps because a large proportion of the help was still untrained. President School-field thought the price of labor in 1907 (prior to the panic) was "higher than has probably ever been known in this country before."[44] At Dan River the average wage of 938 employees reached a peak of $1.15 per day, but dropped to $1.10 in 1909 (1,521 employees). Dur-

[43] *Fifth* to *Twelfth Annual Report of the Bureau of Labor and Industrial Statistics for the State of Virginia* (Richmond, 1902-1910).

[44] *Report of the Board of Directors of the Dan River Power and Manufacturing Company* (Danville, 1907).

Table 7. Reported Daily Wages, Riverside, 1901, 1906, and 1909

	1901	1906	1909
carders and pickers			
male	$0.85	$1.20	$1.00
female	.85	.95	.95
cloth hands			
male	.85	1.10	1.10
female	.65	.83	.85
dressers			
male	1.00	1.00	1.00
female	.60	.83	.83
machine repairers	1.40	1.67	1.67
spinners			
male	.85	.90	.85
female	.80	1.00	.95
dyers	1.00	1.00	1.00
weavers			
male	1.15	1.20	1.10
female	1.15	1.10	1.00
average daily wage	.97	1.09	1.01
number of workers included in averages	1705	1529	1476

ing the lull in business resulting from the panic of October 1907 wages were paid in scrip furnished by local banks.[45]

A booklet prepared by the company in 1906 for the purpose of recruiting workers invited "a comparison of our scale of wages with that of ANY OTHER MILL IN THE COUNTRY." Emphasis was placed on the high level of family earnings: thus, a family of five—father, two sons, and two daughters earned $76.36 in two weeks, "probably five times as much as they ever made on the farm." Published data, which may lack considerably in accuracy, indicate that Riverside's average daily wage of $0.97 in 1901 was $0.18 above the average for 1,276 operatives in six other Virginia mills. The gap narrowed in 1903-1909; in the latter year seven Virginia cotton mills paid an average daily wage of $0.94 to 1,796 workers. Riverside's average was $1.01 or 10.1 cents an hour; Dan River's was $1.10, or 11.0 cents an hour. Layer's study of New

[45] D. A. Overbey, a director of Dan River and president of the National Bank of Danville developed a permanent pen paralysis from signing large quantities of scrip.

England mills shows the average hourly wage rising from 11.3 cents in May 1902 to 14.3 cents in November 1909.[46]

The cost of living in the United States rose approximately 17 per cent between 1889 and 1909. The Riverside worker's wage, on an hourly basis, increased about 36 per cent, indicating a rise of 17 per cent in real earnings per hour.

Data on the salaries of office workers are included in the reports of the Bureau of Labor and Industrial Statistics. The Riverside figures for 1901 and 1909 are summarized in Table 8.

Table 8. Average Monthly Salaries of Office Workers

	Riverside, 1901		Riverside, 1909	
	number	salary	number	salary
manager	4	$381.25	3	$583.33
salesman	1	266.67	3	187.50
bookkeeper	5	60.00	3	108.33
clerk			3	102.78
stenographer	1	50.00	2	76.14

The relatively high proportion of children in the southern mill, although not the only factor in the North-South wage differential, undoubtedly exerted downward pressure on the average wage in the South. The Bureau of the Census found 22.9 per cent of southern textile workers under sixteen years of age in 1904, as compared with 6.0 per cent in New England and 8.7 per cent in the Middle Atlantic states.[47] In Virginia, according to a Senate report, only 14.7 per cent of 3,292 employees were under sixteen in 1907-1908.[48] The only data available for Riverside and Dan River are found in a report of the Bureau of Labor and Industrial Statistics. In 1901, 211 boys and 100 girls under sixteen years were working at Riverside; in 1909, Riverside's 1,690 employees included 75 boys and 36 girls under sixteen, while Dan River's

[46] R. G. Layer, *Earnings of Cotton Mill Operatives, 1828-1914*, pp. 34-39 A Senate inquiry into textile wages put the average wage of male workers in Virginia mills (1907-1908) at 13 cents per hour, and of female workers, 11 cents per hour. At the same time male and female operatives in Massachusetts mills averaged 16 cents and 13 cents per hour, respectively. In both cases the averages appear to include the pay of supervisory employees (*Report on Condition of Woman and Child Wage-Earners in the United States*, vol. I: *The Cotton Textile Industry* (Senate Doc. 645, 61st. Cong., 2nd Sess.; Washington, 1910), pp. 324-325, 726-727.
[47] *Census of Manufactures: 1905: Textiles* (Bulletin 74; Washington, 1907), p. 39.
[48] *Report on Condition of Woman and Child Wage-Earners*, pp. 16, 37.

payroll of 1,593 included 64 boys and 59 girls under sixteen. A book-let published for recruiting purposes (1906) listed jobs in the spinning room for girls and boys twelve years old and work in the dressing de-partment for fifteen-year-old boys. At the other end of the scale, the company had jobs paying $5 a week for men as old as sixty.

Although the Danville *Register* fulminated against the socialistic tendency of the legislation and found "no sound reason for the regula-tion of labor by law in a free country,"[49] the Virginia legislature in 1903 forbade the employment in mines, stores, and factories of children under twelve years of age and, furthermore, restricted the employment of children under fourteen to the hours between 7:00 A.M. and 6:00 P.M. The law of March 13, 1908 raised the minimum working age to thirteen years, as of March 1909, and fourteen years beginning in March 1910; but local magistrates were authorized to issue work certificates to thirteen- and fourteen-year-old orphans, self-supporting children, or children of invalid parents.[50]

A dearth of employable labor coincided with the opening of the new mills at Dan River; and, as more and more machines were in-stalled, the management had to tap more remote sources of supply. "It is quite a job," Schoolfield said, "getting the quantity of help to-gether necessary to operate or start up the Dan River Mills, but we have men out in different places endeavoring to procure it." The opinion was widely held at this time that "cotton manufacturing in the cotton states has outgrown the supply of native labor," and mill owners frequently accused fellow-employers of raiding their labor force. One of the recruiters employed by Dan River, W. P. McCain, was canvassing in the north central counties of North Carolina in the winter of 1905-1906. From Stokes County, a poor and isolated farming area, he wrote Superintendent Robertson: "I am doing (I think) tolerably well & hoping to be in a locality where we will do better than I have

[49] As quoted in the *Manufacturers' Record*, Jan. 29, 1903.
[50] *Sixth Annual Report* (Richmond, 1903), pp. 187-196, and *Eleventh Annual Report of the Bureau of Labor and Industrial Statistics* (Richmond, 1908), pp. 225-228.
    Thomas R. Dawley, a former employee of the U. S. Bureau of Labor, contends that the Bureau's study of textile mill labor was slanted to show the evils of the prevailing conditions, without recognizing that mill people might be better off than on the farms and mountain homes from which they migrated. "Let us then give due credit," Dawley pleaded, "to the cotton mill, and if there are evils in the employment of children in our cotton mills, let us search out those evils and stop them, but not bar the progress of our mountain people through the doors of the cotton mill" ("Our Mountain Problem and Its Solution," *Proceedings of the 14th. Annual Convention, A.C.M.A.* (Charlotte, 1910), pp. 150-155, and *The Child That Toileth Not: The Story of a Government In-vestigation That Was Suppressed* (2nd ed.; New York, 1913).

been doing for several weeks past." Earlier, he had announced his intention to "canvass in Surry & Stokes [counties] as long as I can be successful. . . . I dont think I will come home for Christmas."

It is impossible to measure the results of the company's direct recruiting or the response to its advertising for help. A small sample of letters from prospective employees has been preserved. Most of the inquiries came from Virginia, North Carolina, and South Carolina, but a young fellow in Firthcliffe, New York, wrote to say that he and his father were thinking of moving South and wanted "full particluars" about wages. In 1906 the land and industrial agent of the Southern Railway, in response to Dan River's "application for hand," supplied information concerning workers seeking jobs with the railroad. The usual reply to the request for railroad fare to get to Danville was "no"; but in one case the employment office was instructed to write a North Carolina applicant a "good letter and tell him we will advance him transportation."

Keeping workers on the job was often as difficult as finding new help. "Since the open weather," Schoolfield complained in May 1906, "we have had quite a number of people leave us for outdoor work on railroads and other construction work." But in the fall labor was still so scarce that the officers fumed: "we have been at our wits end to know what was the best thing to do." A fresh explanation of the "unprecedented shortage of labor" was discovered in the "re-opening of Saloons in our City." In April 1907 the president told the directors: "The demoralization among our operatives on account of whiskey drinking and drunkenness has been wide-spread and hurtful to the operations of our machinery. . . . On account of the shortage in labor supply, we are taken advantage of by people who only seem to want work just days enough to enable them to live. In other words, if they can get by working three days in a week, they are disposed to drink, loaf or rest the balance of the time." The absence of similar complaints in 1908 and 1909 suggests that the situation had improved—or the management had ceased to fight Demon Rum.

Schoolfield

So far as I have been able to ascertain, the company made no official announcement that the community surrounding the Dan River mills would be called "Schoolfield." Perhaps R. A. Schoolfield demurred. But no other suggestion for a name seems to have been made; another name could scarcely have been as appropriate.

The rise of a village on company land and in close proximity to the mills was a corollary of the decision to locate the new manufacturing plant several miles away from existing residential areas. The immediate need of shelter for workers and their families, the uncertainty and high cost of speculative building for rental, the desire of the management to supervise every aspect of community life that related to the workers' efficiency, and the possibility that, even if Danville did not extend its corporate limits, another incorporated town might arise in the shadow of the mills—these and other considerations led the Dan River Power & Manufacturing Company to acquire large areas of land for non-manufacturing purposes and to launch into a building program that made the company the landlord, policeman, fire department, and purveyor of utilities to most of the men and women who made Dan River fabrics.

Over a period of years Dan River selected numerous parcels of land suitable for its long-run program for the mills and the adjacent village. The tax roll for 1900 showed 1184.74 acres of company land. In 1902-1909 an additional 619.76 acres were purchased, but 309.31 acres were disposed of in the same period. Purchases included the 50-acre Garvin estate, lying on both sides of the railroad south of the mills, which was acquired to give the company "better control of the situation." This land had an assessed valuation of $16 per acre; several parcels of real estate along Greensboro Road were assessed for as much as $50 an acre; and a plot on Park Avenue was listed for taxes at $370 an acre. The assessed value of 1423.50 acres held in 1906 was $20,124, perhaps one half their market value.

The housing program in 1903-1909 entailed expenditures of $292,-422 for 445 units. The first contract, awarded in February 1903, provided for ten four-room houses on Park Avenue, costing barely $600 each. Between April 1903 and October 1909 the Company erected three-, four-, five-, six-, and eight-room dwellings on Wood, Baltimore, Washington, Dallas, Richmond, and other avenues surrounding the mills. Also constructed in this period were a 13-room boarding house (rebuilt with 21 rooms, after a fire in 1904) and a $9,000 hotel on Baltimore Avenue.

W. G. B. Fitzgerald, a cousin of T. B. Fitzgerald, obtained the first contract for houses as well as a large proportion of the construction work subsequently awarded; but some of the housing and non-manufacturing building at Schoolfield was done by J. H. Fitzgerald and the firm of Burge Brothers. The Dan Valley Brick Company supplied bricks; N. A. and T. J. Fitzgerald, sand; and the Danville Lumber and Manufacturing Company and the Snow Lumber Company of High Point, North Carolina, lumber. All houses were of frame construction but well built, if the company's repeated demands for "first-class workmanship" were carried out. Each house, or cottage, occupied a plot which provided generous space for gardens. The monotony of row upon row of houses, essentially the same in design, materials, and color, was accentuated by standard outhouses, fifty paces removed from each back door. Water was supplied at hydrant taps out of doors; streets were electrically lighted, but electricity in the home was a luxury denied the Schoolfield worker until 1917.

Rentals were fixed at the following rates in March 1905 (a reduction of 20-25 per cent on the rents initially charged): 3-room houses, $2.00 for two weeks; 4-room houses, $2.50; and 6-room tenements, $3.75. Some 4-room houses, apparently built for overseers and secondhands, rented for $10 per month, while single employees in the boarding house and hotel paid $25 a month for board and room. Though incomplete, the financial records suggest that housing was not profitable —nor was it intended to be. All the rental property in Schoolfield, valued at $183,333, produced gross rentals of $16,852 in 1908; depreciation and maintenance seem to have been absorbed in various manufacturing expenses, but it is doubtful that the net income represented more than a nominal return on the investment.

There is no evidence that the company used the "rough rule that the house ought to furnish one operative for each room."[51] By 1907 company housing made available 1,150 rooms, but the payroll had not yet reached 1,000. Thompson's generalization on mill housing in North Carolina may well fit the case of Schoolfield: "So far as convenience and comfort are concerned, these houses, when new at least, are superior to those in which the operatives lived in the country."[52] Schoolfield, so far as I know, was never referred to as a model mill village; but the keen competition for desirable laborers in the period

[51] Tompkins, *op. cit.*, p. 116.
[52] H. Thompson, *From the Cotton Field to the Cotton Mill*, p. 142.

when most of the houses were built forced the corporation to adopt a tolerable standard of convenience and attractiveness. Reminiscing, H. R. Fitzgerald in later years explained that "we had about digested the supply [of labor] in our immediate community, so that it became necessary to develop the village of Schoolfield." Housing in the village had to be furnished by the company, since

experience shows that the character of houses that could be rented from outside parties or that the people would build for themselves are so much below the standard maintained by the mills that it would constitute a grave difference in the facilities for homelife. Furthermore, it would have been impossible to have made the progress along educational, moral and sanitary lines if the people had been scattered thruout the city. We find, however, as the years go on that more and more of our people are disposed to buy small farms or plots of ground and build homes for themselves, which with their improved resources and experience after having worked in the mills for some years enables them to live on a higher basis than they previously did and we think that this is healthy growth.

Housing was only the first step in implementing the Dan River policy "to provide such means as would best promote the interests of its operatives, and to uplift and make them better and more efficient people." Writing to another mill executive, Fitzgerald said: "I would not now attempt to describe the conditions that existed among virtually all of these families [from the mountain districts of Virginia and the Carolinas] in their state of run-down poverty and ignorance, and eking out a precarious existence on mountain farms. Some of the worst cases of disease and a long chain of evils and vices that had grown into their methods of living, were enough to shock the sensibilities of anyone who loves humanity."

President Schoolfield had dealt at length with health problems in the 1907 report:

Sickness among your operatives is a great drawback to the operation of the Mills, and especially when it becomes epidemic. Many of the people when they first come here seem to have acquired but little of the art of living, and several times since your Mills began operation our village has been visited with epidemics, resulting in a large amount of sickness and a number of deaths.

We endeavored first to meet this situation by the employment of District nurses, and having them visit from house to house, not only to care for the sick, but also to keep in touch with the people, and administer, as far as practicable, the "Ounce of prevention, worth more than a pound of care."

We found, however, that in addition to this it would be necessary to equip a hospital, where urgent cases could receive proper attention.

A number of ladies have interested themselves with us in this work, and have organized and associated themselves together to look after and manage this department, and to extend its influence and effectiveness among the operatives as far as possible. Good results have already been achieved, not only in the number of cases that have been treated and the number of cures that have been effected, but also by bringing these good ladies in closer touch and sympathy with our people.

The directors authorized the building of a hospital in June 1907. Medical attention and milk were furnished at the day nursery, which cared for the children of women employees during working hours. General supervision of the hospital, nursery, and home nursing service was entrusted to a Lady Board of Managers, composed of wives of officers and directors of the Company. In 1907 the Board employed Miss Hattie Hylton to open a kindergarten in Schoolfield, and the following year Miss Hylton became superintendent of welfare.

In Danville, too, the company concerned itself with the health and welfare of the mill worker. In December 1902, Danville physicians, supported by a citizens' committee, sought funds to enlarge the Home for the Sick, then the city's only hospital. Satisfied that "our own people are frequently treated there," President Schoolfield recommended a contribution of $5,000, conditional upon the raising of the goal of $25,000. Regular contributions to the Ministering Circle of the King's Daughters began in 1904 with a pledge of $100 to match the city's gift. As the Circle expanded its work, which included the employment of a trained nurse to wait on "the sick and afflicted poor," the company increased its annual contribution.

Facilities for recreation improved slightly in the period covered by this chapter. In the 1890's a group of young workers organized a cycling club, the House Rock Wheel Club, and held outings near the present site of the Inn. Use of the property was restricted by agreements with the company (1899 and 1909) which prohibited the use of "spiritous or malt liquors," card playing, and dancing. By 1906 bowling alleys, a pool room, and motion pictures, in company buildings but under outside management, were opened in Schoolfield; on the cultural side, the company sponsored an occasional band concert.

After receiving favorable comments from mill owners in North and South Carolina, Riverside commenced to support the Danville

Y.W.C.A. in 1905. Organized especially to meet the needs of the working girl, the Association enrolled 1,200 "self-supporting young women" in Danville, 900 of whom worked at Riverside. The company's initial subvention of $41.66 per month was raised to $50 in 1906; but in 1908 the directors complained that the work of the organization "had not been so helpful to our people." Continuance of the monthly grant was made "upon the condition that the organization will return to its former policy and employ a Secretary who will do practical and effective work among our people and endeavor to uplift and make them better."

News of the night school which Riverside inaugurated in the winter of 1901-1902 disappears from later records; but in December 1902 the company began to support the night school conducted by Dr. Laird and sponsored by the First Presbyterian Church. Nearly half of the students were employees of the mills, and the company's contribution, only $50 the first year, soon became a yearly grant of $250.

Schoolfield was located in the Tunstall School District of Pittsylvania County. Lacking funds to erect a school in the mill village, the trustees obtained from Dan River a gift of land and a loan for building purposes. The first Baltimore Avenue School opened in the fall of 1905, with four teachers employed by the school board; and in 1907, with another loan from the company, the school officials enlarged the building to eight classrooms.

In order to attract "a desirable class of families to become residents of our village," President Schoolfield observed, it was necessary not only to supply suitable living quarters but also to arrange for a shopping center and service establishments. In 1906-1907 the two buildings on the south side of Greensboro Road housed a motion picture theater, which paid the company a rental of $25 per month: the Dan River Lodge, I.O.O.F., using a meeting hall on Monday nights at $5 per month; the office of Dr. H. A. Wiseman; a bowling alley and pool room; a barber shop and baths; and the Park Place Mercantile Company. The latter had been organized by the mills in 1904 to operate both a general store and a coal and wood yard. Dan River owned 76 shares ($7,600) of the capital stock; five Dan River directors owned qualifying shares to serve as directors of the mercantile firm; and the remaining 69 shares were purchased by Swanson Brothers & Company. It was the "policy of the Company Store to make prices on all commodities handled by it so attractive that it will command the bulk of the trade of the operatives. Prices are not allowed to go higher than the city stores, and in most cases [were] considerably lower." Coal and wood were promised at 20 per cent less than the prevailing prices in Danville. Despite the obvious advantages to the mill worker, who at best had little free time to shop in Danville, the management soon admitted the "disadvantage to our Company to own Stock in a mercantile institution selling goods direct to the operatives, which was sometimes misconstrued and misunderstood." In 1909 Dan River's stock in the Park Place Mercantile Company was sold to the Swansons and D. A. Overbey, but the mill corporation retained the coal and wood business.

Though piety, perhaps even more than sobriety, was considered an essential characteristic of an efficient working force, the mill management could not meet all the requests for assisting the communities' churches. And it was difficult to discriminate among the calls for help without appearing to favor one faith over another. In March 1903 Riverside gave the (Methodist) Washington Street Tabernacle $500 to help pay off a debt; but a year later the company declined to contribute to the cost of repairs on this church. Though admitting that Methodism "as far as we can learn is the predominant faith" of the mill people, the management thought there were other churches that needed and deserved support—and the mills could not accommodate all of them. Dan River turned down a request from the Methodists in Schoolfield but reconsidered the case when T. B. Fitzgerald urged the directors to lend the church enough to avoid foreclosure of the mortgage. In 1909 the directors gave the Grace Methodist Church $150 "for pastoral support" and later lent the church $1,800, after hearing E. S. Reid's "appropriate remarks" concerning the good work of the church among the company's employees. At Schoolfield, the company gave each of three denominations the land on which to erect their churches and in 1909 built a parsonage for the Methodists. The Presbyterians were substantially aided by Mrs. Alice Burton, and the church built as a memorial to the former president followed the plans worked out by Mrs. Burton and the directors of Dan River.

"We have much to be thankful for," was President Schoolfield's frequent comment on life and work in the mill communities. Particularly gratifying was the responsiveness of the three thousand men and women in the mills to management's solicitude for their welfare and "improvement" after working hours. Convinced that they had found the right road to industrial peace, the officials of Riverside and Dan River Mills expanded their contributions to employee welfare in the following decade and in 1919 crowned their efforts with a noble experiment in industrial relations called "Industrial Democracy." Chapter 5 is devoted to a full account of this experience.

3. *Prosperity, War, and Depression, 1910-1921*

In the twelve years following the merger of Riverside Cotton Mills and Dan River Power & Manufacturing Company the physical plant grew steadily in size and value. Real estate and machinery, which stood at $5.7 million at the end of 1909, rose to $17.6 million in 1921. Sales jumped from $2.5 million (1909) to a peak of $30.6 million in 1920, a figure not attained again until 1941. Earnings exceeded $4 million in 1920, the highest of all years prior to 1946; and the average rate earned on the stockholders' investment (capital and surplus) was 12.3 per cent per annum.[1] Much of the expansion in dollar values reflected the inflation of the war years, but even after allowance is made

[1] Computed by dividing earnings by stated capital and surplus at the end of the *preceding* year, the yearly rates are as follows:

year	per cent	year	per cent
1910	8.4	1916	19.8
1911	7.3	1917	17.6
1912	9.1	1918	24.9
1913	7.9	1919	13.2
1914	3.4	1920	20.8
1915	14.1	1921	.7

for the higher price level the period stands out as the most flourishing
period in the company's history until it reaches another war era, the
decade of the 1940's.

Dollars, Buildings, Machines

A concise view of this expansive decade is furnished by the balance-
sheet data in Appendix 1. Total assets, which amounted to $9.5 mil-
lion at the end of 1909, rose to $26.9 million in 1921, while fixed as-
sets alone more than trebled in value. Capitalization grew from $7
million to $13.5 million and, despite the distribution of $12 million in
dividends, the surplus increased from less than half a million dollars to
a peak of almost ten million.

The depreciation accounts (Table 1) depict in summary fashion the
growth of the physical plant at both divisions. For land, buildings,
and machinery the company spent $17.9 million in this twelve-year
period. Depreciation charges absorbed $6 million; on the average,
however, two dollars of new or reinvested capital were spent on improvements for every dollar written off for depreciation.

Table 1. Summary of Depreciation Accounts, 1910-1921
(thousands of dollars)

	ledger value Jan. 1, 1910	improvements, 1910-1921	depreciation, 1910-1921	ledger value Dec. 31, 1921
Riverside division				
land, building, machinery	2,000	11,564	3,193	10,371
Dan River division				
land, water power	602	146	80	667
mill construction	984	1,064	244	1,805
machinery, electrical, water supply	1,774	4,039	2,246	3,566
tenements, Y.M.C.A., Hylton Hall	341	1,140	286	1,200
depreciation, not specified			1	
depreciation, excess over book value				—4
total	5,701	17,953	6,050	17,604

Errors in totals due to rounding.

Dan River's Mill No. 3, finished in March 1910, added about 50,000 spindles and 1,500 looms to the Schoolfield plant. Saco-Pettee built the carding machinery, drawing frames, slubbers, intermediate, roving, and spinning frames, and spoolers and warpers. Most of the looms, which were installed in the top floor of the building, were Draper models for making chambrays. As the increased consumption of colored cotton required additional dyeing facilities, in February 1910 the John T. Wilson Company of Richmond was employed to enlarge the Dan River dye house. At the same time new equipment— raw-stock dyeing machines, Butterworth indigo dyeing machinery, and automatic cotton stock dryers—was purchased for the dye houses at both divisions.

In 1911 Riverside acquired a four-story cloth hall (near the Long Mill) and a machine shop, but the major change in Danville was the remodeling of Mill No. 6. This unit—then called the "white mill"— was the "least profitable of any of the group of the Riverside Mills," the president told the stockholders;[2] and the management decided to convert it into a colored-goods mill. The factory's 422 broad looms— "of the old type [which] cannot now be operated very profitably"—were traded in as part payment for 805 high-speed automatic looms for making 30-inch chambrays. In June 1912 the production of sheeting at the Riverside plant was discontinued.

Other important changes in 1911-1912 were designed "to equalize the looms, carding, and spinning at the Riverside Plants to its proper proportions." After tearing down the corn mill and block of stores on Bridge Street, the company enlarged Mill No. 1, "practically doubling the size of this mill," and installed new carding and spinning machinery. To speed the flow of raw materials and eliminate the labor of rebaling and hauling dyed cotton, Saco-Lowell Shops (Saco-Pettee and Lowell merged in 1912) installed a conveyor system comprising units to carry colored stock from the dye house to the cotton storage house and from the cotton storage house to the spinning mills. Foundations for the cotton warehouse below Mill No. 6 were laid in the fall of 1912, and the following year Riverside's dye house was thoroughly remodeled and equipped with new dyeing machinery.[3] "While it is ex-

[2] In 1910 Mill No. 6 produced 1,569,833 pounds of sheeting at a cost of 25.84 cents per pound, including the labor cost of 5.50 cents; in 1911, the cost of making 1,428,978 pounds of cloth rose to 28.14 cents per pound, including 6.00 cents for labor. At Dan River the cost of producing sheeting rose from 25.66 cents in 1910 to 26.20 cents per pound in 1911, but the unit labor cost dropped from 5.37 to 5.09 cents per pound.

[3] In Aug. 1913 the company bought two Morton dyeing machines, with the "under-

pensive to have to throw out old machinery, and put in new," Schoolfield reminded the directors, "at the same time we believe it the wise
policy to pursue, as conditions are constantly changing and it is necessary to keep abreast with the times to hold your business and prestige
with the Trade."

In March 1912 President Schoolfield told the directors of the need
for a new mill at Dan River to operate 75,000 spindles and 2,200 looms
on finer grades of goods, "some of which we have been importuned a
number of times by our large customers to manufacture." Not only
the high level of demand for the company's products but the relatively
low price of machinery seemed to recommend immediate expansion.
The directors took a few weeks to think it over but on April 4 approved the construction of Mill No. 4. Built by T. C. Thompson of
Birmingham, the new mill was described by the president as "most
modern and substantial. . . . We doubt if it will be equalled by any
in the country."[4] Saco-Lowell equipped the new mill with carding and
spinning machinery. Crompton & Knowles 40½- and 43½-inch gingham looms and Draper Model E looms (including 300 purchased second-hand for $25,000) filled the weave shed.

Over a period of thirty years, as the president observed in 1915,
Riverside and Dan River Mills had grown at the rate of 10,000 spindles
and 300 looms a year. The three weave sheds at Dan River Division
had 1,673 Draper, 2,518 Crompton-Knowles, and 1,323 Stafford looms.
Riverside's five weaving mills housed 1,093 Draper and 1,986 Crompton-Knowles looms.

Heating and humidifying systems in Dan River's Mill No. 4 were
installed by Carrier Air Conditioning Company. The consumption of
water in the mills and village now exceeded the capacity of the filter
plant erected in 1908, and Hungerford and Terry were employed to
add four units with a filtering capacity of 5,200,000 gallons daily.

standing and agreement that you will guarantee the operation of the machines, and that
you will furnish us the stipulated number of beams (fifteen for each machine) properly
equipped to do satisfactory work, and further that you guarantee to hold us absolutely
harmless against any infringement of patents owned by anyone else, and that if at any
time notice should be served upon us to the effect that anyone else is being infringed
upon, you will at your own cost and expense defend such action and guarantee to hold
us harmless from the same, so that we are to suffer no loss or expense on this account."
[4] Within six years it was necessary to make "very extensive and expensive repairs" on
No. 4 weave shed, "due to the decaying of the timbers" in the roof. Lockwood, Greene
explained the trouble: "It sometimes happens in saw-tooth weave sheds with wooden
roofs that the temperature and humidity conditions just under the roof are extremely
favorable to the growth of fungi that cause rot."

Further improvements in the water supply system were made in 1913 by Thurban York–Continental Jewell Filtration Company.

Urgent additions and replacements during the war years included the building of Dan River's No. 4 cloth hall and an addition to one of Riverside's cloth halls; a new cotton storage house at Dan River; and about $250,000 worth of opening, carding, and spinning machinery for both divisions. Loom replacements and additions included 375 Draper looms for sheeting (1915), 274 narrow Draper looms (1916-1918), 376 Stafford wide looms (1915), 87 Crompton & Knowles gingham looms, and, curiously, one 82-inch blanket loom.

For mills manufacturing large quantities of colored goods, maintaining satisfactory dyeing equipment and obtaining good dyestuffs became increasingly serious problems after the outbreak of war in Europe. In 1914 Riverside and Dan River Mills purchased from the Elton Cop Dyeing Company of Bury, England, a shop right to "certain new, original, and useful processes and patented machinery and apparatus for dyeing and bleaching cotton and other textiles in the form of cops, cheeses, beams, etc." One of the Brandwood brothers came to Danville in 1916 to instal four vacuum warp-dyeing machines in the Riverside dye house. In August the management reported that they had been "quite successful with some of the light shades of Indigo and also with such colors as Sulphur Black . . . but for the past few weeks we have been trying out some of the darker shades of Indigo such as we use in our standard Chambrays, and we very much regret to find that although the work is nicely done and apparently shows very uniform and good results, at the same time it requires more material than the old process. . . . In spite of anything they can do to prevent it, the cost is greater than the long-chain system." The Brandwoods had guaranteed that that their beam-dyeing process would be at least as economical as the long-chain system; in fact, it cost nearly a cent a pound more to dye with the Brandwood method. In 1919, when dyes were cheaper than during the war, the dyers complained that the Brandwood process not only used too much indigo but also failed to produce the same "bloom or appearance in the goods that we got by the long-chain process." The Delahunty Dyeing Machine Company installed the Brandwood system at Dan River Division in 1919, although Fitzgerald wrote John Brandwood that the mills still needed the advice of "some one thoroughly familiar with the system as well as with practical expert knowledge of dyeing such as your brother [Thomas] has." In order to get away from the "old process of re-quilling the filling, which is slow and wasteful," Fitzgerald suggested compromising with the "fad or hobby with the buyer to demand indigo blue" by dyeing warps with indigo and the filling with a vat, or sulphur, blue.

In 1916 the company negotiated with Block Chemical Laboratories of Chicago for the installation at Riverside of "an apparatus or plant for the production of Primuline yellow dye." After the failure of the contractor to produce satisfactory dyes, Dan River's chemists managed to put the equipment in working order, and toward the end of 1918 the Primuline plant was making dyestuffs in excess of the company's needs. Although insisting that "we do not contemplate embarking in the dye-stuff manufacturing business in a general way," Fitzgerald was glad to arrange for the sale of surplus Primuline dyes through the New Jersey Newport Chemical Works, a supplier of the para toluidine dyes used at Dan River. Reported earnings of the Primuline plant amounted to $125,000 between 1919 and 1924, when the plant was dismantled.

In addition to the improvements in dyeing facilities, the war years brought about important changes in the power installations (to be discussed below). In general, however, rising prices, the scarcity of materials, and the high level of demand, which made it less urgent to maintain the quality of consumer goods, held in abeyance major changes in productive facilities.[5] At Dan River Division expenditures on new machinery dwindled to a mere $16,266 in 1917, and total capital expenditures for the year fell almost $80,000 short of the amount charged to depreciation. One of the consequences of rising prices and the low level of capital replacements was a reconsideration of depreciation policy.

Depreciation accounting, in 1910-1917, consisted of choosing a round sum to charge against each year's operating results and dividing this sum, in varying proportions, between Riverside's Land, Buildings, and Machinery account and Dan River's Machinery ledger. Depreciation allowances were: $200,000 in 1910-1911; $246,000 in 1912; $200,000 in 1913-1914; $250,000 in 1915; and $300,000 in 1916-1917. In the audit report for 1910 Barrow, Wade, Guthrie and Company suggested: "It would be better, we think, to calculate depreciation

[5] In Jan. 1921 Chairman Schoolfield told the stockholders that the quality of Dan River's products had deteriorated during the war but he thought it would "not be long before our pre-war standard will have been re-established."

more on scientific principles based upon the probable life of the Plant
than to take a round sum and arbitrarily deduct same from the assets."
The next year the auditors found that the depreciation allowance
amounted to less than three per cent of ledger values and again proposed a policy "more in accordance with recognized accounting principles."

Depreciation, a leading mill executive told the American Cotton
Manufacturers' Association, is "something we have been accustomed
in the South to charge at will—a little one year and more another year,
according to how we felt at the time and how much money we made."[6]
The federal income-tax law of 1913 and the excess-profits tax of 1917
compelled mill owners to reconsider their depreciation practices, since
the new levies had the effect of penalizing those who had taken advantage of prosperous years to write down fixed-asset values excessively.
Engineers had a field day in reappraising plants, and in the case of Saco-
Lowell Shops revaluation raised ledger values 82 per cent.[7]

Riverside and Dan River Cotton Mills employed the inspection department of the Associated Factory Mutual Insurance Companies to
appraise the two plants. Their report, submitted in September 1915,
showed the following valuations:

	Riverside	*Dan River*
buildings	$ 712,318	$1,622,773
machinery	1,429,681	4,517,064

These were insurable values, based on cost less depreciation ranging
from 5.3 per cent per annum on buildings to 33.3 per cent on such
items as belting. The appraisal shows a total valuation of $8.3 million
for buildings and equipment subject to the risk of loss by fire—excluding, however, company-owned housing. The balance sheet for December 31, 1915, valued *all* fixed assets—land, buildings (including housing), and non-insurable equipment such as dams and reservoirs—at $9.8
million. Land and other real property excluded from the insurance
appraisal easily account for the $1.5 million discrepancy between the
two statements. In other words, the lack of a "scientific" depreciation
policy had not seriously distorted net asset values. A few cases of excessive depreciation and, hence, unduly low ledger values can be veri-

[6] S. W. Cramer, in *Proceedings of the Twenty-fourth Annual Convention of the Ameri-can Cotton Manufacturers' Association* (Charlotte, 1920), pp. 146-153.
[7] G. S. Gibb, *The Saco-Lowell Shops*, pp. 506-507.

fied; but the management, apparently, saw no advantage in a general revaluation of the plants. A few completely depreciated assets were restored to the books, and the recalculation of the 1918 income led to the payment of additional federal taxes of $38,000. Further adjustment of depreciation reserves, under the prodding of the Federal Treasury, left the company with another bill for $162,000 on income and excess profits taxes for the period 1914 to 1918.

Commencing in 1918 the depreciation allowances were applied specifically to each of the major ledger accounts shown in Table 1, and in the audit report for 1920 the average rates of depreciation are shown for each account. The highest rate, 7.5 per cent of original cost, applied to Dan River's electrical equipment; the Mill Construction and Water Power Development accounts were depreciated at only 3 per cent. A rate of 3 per cent was also applied to the new Y.M.C.A. building; but this property had already been written off completely, so that the depreciation reserve at the end of 1921 amounted to $4,140 in excess of cost.

After the war, the rounding out of the physical growth of the company was accomplished through the building of Riverside's Mill No. 8 on the south side of the river. R. A. Schoolfield, now chairman of the board, explained the problem to the directors in October 1919: the Riverside plant had four picker rooms in four separate buildings, but in each instance the cards needed cotton faster than the picking machinery could prepare it. The spinning departments also tended to run ahead of the output of the carding rooms. The solution recommended by the management was a new building to house the looms in ten scattered weave sheds, thereby releasing space for additional picking, carding, and spinning machinery. At the same time at least 30,000 spindles and 1,500 looms would be added to the Riverside plant. To make the proposed changes a large amount of machinery would have to be scrapped and new machinery purchased at abnormally high prices. On the other hand, anticipating the criticism that the program was too costly, the officers insisted that the company could not afford *not* to carry out the improvements. The directors approved the plan with little discussion, and in January 1920 the stockholders were informed of the project.[8]

[8] The contract for the new mill had been awarded before the stockholders were told about it. The next year (1921) Harrison Robertson moved in the stockholders' meeting that the directors be prohibited from undertaking new construction costing more than $500,000 without prior approval of the stockholders. Robertson was the only one voting in favor of the resolution.

Lockwood, Greene & Company—the Boston firm which had planned and supervised all Riverside and Dan River construction since the turn of the century—designed Mill No. 8 and at the same time worked out extensive plans for reorganizing production at Riverside Division. The new mill, a reinforced concrete structure 144 feet by 840 feet, was built by the Aberthaw Construction Company of Boston. Aberthaw had been erecting mill buildings of this type since 1894, and they recommended concrete construction for Riverside after some years' experience with this type of building at northern mills. In the course of bargaining with Crompton & Knowles, President Fitzgerald stressed the advantages to the loom manufacturers of placing their "most modern equipment in the best and most modern mill in the United States." The new looms for Mill No. 8 were 464 Crompton & Knowles automatic gingham looms (costing $347,000) and 1,271 Model E Drapers ($440,000); the rest were looms moved from the old weave rooms of Riverside Division, all looms having been equipped for individual electric motors. An American flag was unfurled as the last of the new mill's 5,040 looms—1,741 more than previously operated at Riverside— was started on Thanksgiving Day, 1921.[9]

While Mill No. 8 was under construction, other buildings at Riverside underwent extensive modernization. A story was added to the new part of Mill No. 1, providing space for new cards and spinning frames "to counterbalance the shortage at other mills and at the same time support about 80 additional looms."[10] Orders placed with Saco-Lowell in 1919 called for over a million dollars' worth of pickers, cards, drawing frames, slubbers, intermediate and fine-fly frames, spinning frames, spoolers, slashers, and warpers. Supplementary contracts in 1920-1921 added another quarter million dollars to the Saco-Lowell bill. Much of the old machinery was sold, at half the Saco-Lowell list price, to J. Hannon Schoolfield, who had organized the Southern Cotton Yarn Company.

The Riverside "Improvement" account for 1920 listed expenditures of $5.3 million, including the following major items (in thousands of dollars):

[9] "There is so much to be thankful for, say the fellows over there, for every machine that moves furnishes employment for people who need it.
"There are 5040 looms running today at a merry clip, under the supervision of that fine young scout, Rushworth, assisted by Capt. Tom and the most efficient bunch of overseers and second hands and weavers in the South" (*Progress*, Nov. 25, 1921).
[10] In February 1918 Dan River had to buy 50,000 pounds of warp yarn from a spinner in Burlington, N. C.

No. 6 Mill, picker, etc.	$ 363
No. 8 Mill	3,370
raw stock dye house	539
boiler house, equipment	166
turbine	63
bridge (from Mill No. 8 to No. 5)	205
houses (40)	204
Lockwood, Greene & Co.	189

Aside from outlays on Mill No. 8, the largest postwar investment (over $600,000 for building and equipment) was made in the new raw-stock dye house. Fitzgerald had long felt that Riverside's dye house had an "uncouth appearance," as compared with a northern mill he and Benefield had visited in 1916.[11] H. M. Chase, the boss dyer and chemist after Benefield's death in 1918, helped plan the layout of the new dyeing plants, which now included facilities for long-chain dyeing as well as the Brandwood process and raw-stock dyeing.

From an engineering point of view, a noteworthy feature of the new layout of the Riverside plant was the 900-foot bridge connecting Mill No. 8 with Mill No. 5 on the north side of the Dan. The bridge supported an 8-inch steam line from the boiler house, a 4-inch return line for heating steam, and the electric power lines. Extensive piping, both inside the mills and crossing the river, was installed by Parks-Cramer Company, which also put sprinklers, humidifiers, and air-cleaning systems in the mills and dye house.[12]

At Dan River, the principal capital expenditures in 1919-1921 consisted of an addition to the main office building (costing $62,130), the erection of an employment building (the present telephone building), and village improvements—Hylton Hall, a fire station, a school building, and employee housing.

A shortage of labor seems to have encouraged the purchase of three warp-drawing machines in 1919;[13] and in 1918, apparently for the first

[11] Visiting the Massachusetts Mills in Lowell, Fitzgerald was "struck with the general atmosphere of your Dye House—that is to say, its cleanliness and absence of excess steam and moisture and the apparent good order of everything about it."
That the mills had not entirely avoided the problem of disposing of dye-house wastes satisfactorily is suggested by Fitzgerald's concern over a bill in the state legislature of 1918 concerning "putting dye-stuffs or coloring matter into streams." He urged the company's attorney, M. K. Harris, to "keep a watch on this bill and see that nothing comes of it."
[12] Descriptions and photographs of much of this work are found in *Parks' Piping Parables*, Dec. 1921 and Feb. 1922.
[13] In September 1918 the Company advertised in the Danville *Bee* for 12 to 15 young women to work as drawing-in hands.

time, carding was improved by the installation of vacuum card-stripping devices.

Miscellaneous improvements included the laying of sidewalks and the paving of roadways within the mill yards. With the advent of the automobile, the company accepted a share of the responsibility for making it convenient for workers to travel to and from work by car. Thus, a contribution of $5,500 to the Schoolfield-Martinsville Road Improvement Fund (1919-1921) and $20,000 to the Good Roads Fund (1920) assisted public authorities in making the highways of Pittsylvania County suitable for motor transport.[14] The corporation gave the City of Danville about $7,500 in 1920 toward the cost of paving West Main Street. Although Dan River used motor trucks in 1913, and possibly earlier, as late as 1919 it still relied upon the services of Mollie, Tom, Pet, and Lizzie, four faithful quadrupeds whose declared value was $975.

Power

New mills demanded more power to drive their speeding spindles and clacking looms. Under a full head of water the hydroelectric plant at Dan River could generate enough power to run the two mills in Schoolfield; but the construction of Mill No. 3 made additions to the steam plant indispensable. The contract for a new boiler house, with a 220-foot chimney, was given to the Gallivan Building Company in December 1909; the Edge Moor Iron Company supplied eight 542 H.P. boilers; and the Westinghouse Electric and Manufacturing Company installed a 4120 KW turbine generator, along with transformers, motors, and transmission lines. Completed in 1910, the improvement doubled the steam-power capacity of the Dan River plant.

At the same time, impressed by the relatively low cost of hydroelectric power, the management seriously considered a plan to develop more power by raising the level of the dam. In seasons of low stream flow the engineers obtained a higher head by using 30-inch flash boards, which washed away harmlessly as the crest rose. But in 1912-1913 the company had on its hands a number of suits for damages to land from "sobbing" along the shore of the pond and from flooding below the

---

[14] While contributing to the cost of the Martinsville road, Fitzgerald protested that "we have already been more than liberal and . . . our Company ought not be called upon in connection with general improvements outside of our village" (H. R. Fitzgerald to Board of Supervisors, Pittsylvania County, Aug. 29, 1919).

dam in time of freshet. In October 1913, President Schoolfield offered
R. A. James (a director of the company) $12,500 for "the right to raise
the dam three feet above our present rights, which would enable us to
use flash boards or (if we should ever desire) raise the dam itself to the
extent of five feet over its present height . . . but this price is the top
limit to which we could go." James demanded $15,000, which the di-
rectors agreed to pay him, although ultimately the plan to raise the
dam was abandoned.[15] No one seemed able to suggest a remedy for a
more serious problem—the silting of the pond. As Fitzgerald explained
it in a letter to Lockwood, Greene:

> . . . the greater part of the area has now formed into islands that are
> growing up very thickly with willows; this of course has contracted the
> space to a very large extent and there is now really nothing more than a
> narrow river channel for the water to pass through.
> During the years since the dam was built we have had many suggestions
> for removing the sylph [*sic*] and mud by various mechanical means, the
> most popular idea being that of a pipe line with power-driven fans . . . the
> idea has been apparently in every instance to sell us the equipment and
> let us take the risk of its operation. We have not had any confidence in the
> ultimate success of such a scheme, and we of course realize that if the dirt
> were removed it would come back again unless there was some arrangement
> by which to continue the dredging.
> It has been my theory that the formation of these islands would not
> materially injure the water power so long as the main channel of the river
> is kept open and that the only real injury sustained is the lessening of the
> storage capacity of the pound which . . . has already reached a very low
> point. . . .
> It may possibly be wise to try to keep open the channel on the north
> side and yet I do not see how this can be done without some sort of dredg-
> ing scheme to be operated regularly, which of course raises the question of
> whether the result to be achieved would be worth the cost.

The idea of building a new dam farther upstream was considered
briefly; it was discarded when investigations showed that land values
were prohibitive.

Some additional power was secured by improving the generating
equipment. In May 1909 the Holyoke Machine Company replaced

[15] In settling the claim of a Dr. Withers for $5,000 the company acquired the right to
raise the dam as much as it wanted. The payment of $9,127 to the heirs of Dr. John R.
Wilson also anticipated damages in case the dam were raised. In the suit of L. T. Waugh
for the flooding of his property below the dam, as a result of the freshet of March 1912,
the Circuit Court awarded the claimant $3,000, but the decision was reversed in the
Virginia Supreme Court (*Cases Decided in the Supreme Court of Appeals of Virginia,*
CXVII [Richmond, 1916], 386-395).

the 21- and 24-inch water wheels with six 27-inch Hercules turbine wheels, each guaranteed to develop not less than 775 H.P. under a full head (25 feet); and in 1917 three new 24-inch wheels were added to the Dan River waterpower. While waiting for a new generator for the lighting plant, the company issued a circular to residents of Schoolfield (November 28, 1917), urging extreme economy in the use of electricity in the homes.

Dan River's Mill No. 4 created a new power need, which was met entirely by additions to the steam plant. In 1913 Allis-Chalmers installed a new 4,400 KW steam turbine, the Edge Moor Iron Company supplied two 764 H.P. boilers, and General Electric furnished the major portion of the motors, transformers, and other electrical equipment for the new mill. In 1920 the company acquired a second-hand boiler, which the Edge Moor Iron Company moved from Nitro, West Virginia; and in 1921 General Electric sold the company a 5,000 KW turbo-generator and other electrical equipment for the Dan River steam plant. But the fear of litigation from the unpredictable behavior of the river, the rapid silting of the dam pond, and the natural limitations of the watershed in this section chastened those who at first saw an inexhaustible source of hydroelectric power in the Dan River.

Eventually, Riverside's power problem had to be met without dependence upon the dam at Schoolfield. Although the storage capacity of the upper dam made it possible to operate the machinery at Riverside "practically on full time" during the drought in the winter of 1909-1910, the next summer the Danville mills had to stop several times, "which was more or less demoralizing to the help." In order to "furnish badly needed auxiliary power" at the Long Mill, two 542 H.P. Edge Moor boilers to drive a Corliss engine were added to the boiler house at Mill No. 5. In 1912, in order to "supplement the weak points of power over the present capacity of the water wheels," an electric power station was built at the Long Mill and two new sets of wheels were installed to drive two generators. Riverside's first hydroelectric power system, furnishing 800 H.P. "under favorable river conditions," soon proved inadequate for the plants in North Danville, and in 1914 a 764 H.P. Edge Moor boiler and a 1,250 KW Curtiss steam turbine were set up to generate current for a 500 H.P. and a 400 H.P. motor.

On the South canal the company improved its position by buying (for $50,000) the power site and electric light plant owned by the city. An improvement in the tail race at Mill No. 4 yielded "much needed

additional power there"; and new wheels were placed at the site of the
old grist mill—"one of the best falls on the Canal"—to furnish power
for the addition to Mill No. 1. Still "quite short at this point," the
power was finally supplemented by electric motors.

The next major change in Riverside's power plant took place during the war. In 1917 Holyoke Machine installed seven new wheels on
the north shore, increasing the water power supplied to the Long Mill.
At the same time the steam plant was enlarged to accommodate a new
boiler and 1,500 KW turbo-generator, furnishing power for two 500
H.P. motors. New wheels were also placed at Mill No. 6; but when
Dan Valley Mills also put in a new wheel, Riverside protested that the
flour mill was drawing from the north-shore canal more than the 125
H.P. to which it was entitled. Although Holyoke Machine Company
recommended improvements in the head gates and other changes to
increase the water flow in the canal, this work was postponed until 1922-
1923.

The following data, taken from the report prepared for the U. S.
Fuel Administration, furnish a resumé of the power developments as
of July 1918:

	Riverside	*Dan River*
number of steam boilers	10	14
capacity of steam boilers, H.P.	3,180	8,000
coal consumed in 1917, tons	15,000	60,000
steam turbines	1	3
steam engines	2	0
water wheels	26	27
capacity of water wheels, H.P.	4,300	7,000
generators	3	11
electric energy output in 1917, KWH	5,411,940	28,080,000

Early in 1920 a private power company drew up plans for producing electric power outside Danville for sale to the mills and other consumers. The scheme was abandoned when Riverside and Dan River
Mills declined to subscribe to "a large amount of stock" in the enterprise. On recommendation of Lockwood, Greene, the new power needs
at Riverside were met by building a new steam plant on the site of
the old raw-stock dye house and installing four boilers (3,572 H.P.)
and two 3,000 KW steam turbines.

In 1917 W. T. Hogg, the master mechanic at Dan River division, developed and patented a "compensating damper regulator," which enabled the company to operate coal-fired boilers more economically.[16] The question of substituting fuel oil for coal was raised on several occasions, especially in periods of rising coal prices.

Although the 1919 appraisal lists 29 electric motors, capable of developing 3,100 H.P., in the various mills at Riverside division, many of the buildings had not yet been wired for motor-driven shafting. Prior to 1922 only Mill No. 8 had individual machine motors. As late as 1939 the machinery in the Long Mill was operated directly by water power, although the shafting was also belted to synchronous motors.

The balance sheets show a net increase in Real Estate and Machinery values of $7.5 million in the three years, 1919-1921. Depreciation allowances of over $3 million raised gross capital expenditures in this period to over $3.5 million annually. An even million dollars of depreciation represented an arbitrary, but not unwise, write-off to offset abnormally high construction costs in the period of postwar inflation.

The Chicago firm of Coats and Burchard, employed to appraise the company's physical plants, reported the following valuations as of November 1919:

	reproduction value	*commercial and accounting value*
Dan River division	$16,983,131	$13,003,074
Dan River power development	1,032,792	843,730
Riverside division	7,296,219	5,268,294
	25,312,142	19,115,098

Insurance records show $4.8 million of insurance in force on the Riverside plant in October 1918; and $14 million on the Dan River plant in June 1919.

Coats and Burchard's first annual upkeep report, finished in November 1920, accounted for recent additions to plant substantially at cost; but the second annual revision report (December 1921) reflected the drastic deflation of values resulting from the depression. Thus, the sound value of the Dan River property, which rose to $14.4 million in

[16] Patent no. 98,062 (Feb. 10, 1917). Dan River offered the City of Danville the right to use this device for $100.

the 1920 appraisal, shrank to $11.4 million in 1921, $3.7 million having been written off "due to price fluctuations."[17]

"The "enormity of these improvements" (1919-1921) seems to have troubled some of the directors, and in January 1922 President Fitzgerald took occasion to review the circumstances which counseled the large expenditures on plant. At the Riverside plant, the president noted, conditions

had reached a point that we could not longer hold and maintain the high character of workmanship that had won the enviable reputation of your Company. . . . It was either a question of abandoning the old buildings and developing a modern layout at some other point or else remodeling and extending the old plant so as to thoroughly modernize its conditions to provide suitable preparatory machinery as well as the absolute necessity of improving your equipment to enable you to operate at a reasonable cost, the only alternative being that you would have faced an economic situation that would have soon shown the old plant to be an elephant on your hands to be run either at a loss or shut down entirely. . . .

It is inconceivable to me that any one acquainted with the facts as to what every industry in the country has had to pass through since the war, should feel other than grateful at what your organization has accomplished during this period. When you consider that the stockholders have in no sense been neglected but that each year they have received substantial returns in dividends to say nothing of the handsome increase in the value of their holdings . . . and, that in addition to the above, after wiping your surplus clean as of March 1, 1913, you now find it at approximately $8,650,000, it does not seem to me a bad performance.

Money

The twelve-year record of earnings and dividends is shown in Table 2. For the sake of comparability the data in the audit reports, which exhibit slight year-to-year changes in form, have been partially rearranged. Thus, welfare expenses have been treated uniformly as an operating cost, although after 1919 the accountants deducted this item *after* computing net trading profit. Interest constituted a net charge against trading profit except in 1919 and 1920, when interest on government bonds exceeded the cost of borrowed funds.

"Other income" consisted primarily of tenement rents and dividends on the stock of Dan Valley and Piedmont Mills. These two in-

[17] These data are taken from the Coats and Burchard "Appraisal" (Nov. 1, 1919), the "First Annual Upkeep Report" (Nov. 1, 1920), and the "Second Annual Revision Report" (Nov. 1, 1921). The 1920 and 1921 volumes for Riverside are missing.

vestments, carried on the books at $90,000, yielded average dividends of $28,860 annually. Small amounts were received from the W. R. Moore Dry Goods Company on $7,738 worth of stock acquired (1917) in partial settlement of a mercantile debt. The Primuline dye plant earned $22,078 in 1919, $37,799 in 1920, and $23,177 in 1921. Losses on sales of government bonds—$15,795 in 1919 and $37,409 in 1920— were greater than the gain of $15,732 in 1921. Losses on the sale of machinery exceeded "other income" in 1912, and in 1918 and 1919 extraordinary expenditures for housing maintenance amounted to more than the rental income.

Net profit in this twelve-year period exceeded dividend disbursements by over $7 million. The net profit excludes $1.1 million in premiums on stock, although—much to the disgust of the auditors—the amounts were carried to surplus in the same manner as undistributed earnings. Thanks to the stock dividend declared in 1924, $1.5 million of the surplus was capitalized; but the amount thus erased as a potential source of dividends was considerably less than the surplus derived from stock premiums in previous decades.[18]

New stock issues were used for the first time to provide working capital. Some of "our leading financial friends," the president told the directors, found fault with the large floating debt shown in the 1911 statement. "This," Schoolfield said, "we have recognized as the one weak point, if any, in your statement." To reduce the indebtedness, the board approved the sale of the 5,100 shares of treasury stock derived from the merger of Riverside and Dan River. Sales of 3,300 shares in 1911 and 1,800 shares in 1912 brought an average price of $161.50.

To finance the construction of Mill No. 4, in April 1913 the company offered 5,000 shares of common stock in a privileged subscription at $166.67. Underwritten by a syndicate organized by J. T. Catlin & Company, the issue was oversubscribed and yielded a net premium of $323,333. The improvements proved to be more costly than anticipated, and in December the board voted to offer 5,000 shares of 6 percent preferred in a privileged subscription for common and preferred

[18] In the audit report for 1914 the auditors proposed "that the Premiums on the issue of common stock be taken out of the Surplus Account and put in a special Reserve Account, as we do not think it would be proper, at any time, to pay away such amounts as Dividends." At least one stockholder protested the addition of stock premiums to the Profit and Loss account, but the management asserted that the stockholders had approved his practice; furthermore, "there was no other account to which it could properly go."

Table 2.   Earnings and Dividends, 1910-1921
(thousands of dollars)

year	net trading profit	interest (net)	other income (net)	net profit	dividends in cash
1910	$ 682	$116	$ 57	$ 622	$ 429
1911	579	83	62	557	487
1912	832	112	—2	718	511
1913	718	124	52	646	545
1914	410	167	65	308	630
1915	1,471	161	70	1,380	630
1916	2,111	96	62	2,077	660
1917	845	127	65	2,783	1,830
1918	4,291	128	—3	3,559*	1,160
1919	4,643	—11	14	2,269†	1,560
1920	5,298	—92	70	4,156‡	2,250
1921	2,284	88	121	164§	1,350

* After tax reserve, $600,000.
† After taxes on 1918 income, $2,398,695.
‡ After taxes on 1918-1919 income, $1,304,308.
§ After tax on 1920 and additional taxes on 1914-1918 incomes of $2,153,368.

stockholders. This issue, too, was greatly oversubscribed; and in January 1914, in order to accommodate "some of our valuable stockholders," the company floated a second issue of 5,000 preferred shares.

Preferred dividends and a 10 per cent common dividend absorbed more than twice as much as the company earned in 1914. "We recognize that it [the common dividend rate] is subject to criticism," Schoolfield confessed in a letter to the Philadelphia National Bank; but the stockholders "have been very loyal to the Company in putting in new capital when called for, and you will note that we sold 10,000 Shares of Preferred Stock last year, so under the circumstances we thought it better not to make any changes in the rate. By paying the regular dividend we think it was appreciated by our Stockholders and that at any time we might want to place additional stock, it could be more advantageously done."[19]   Confidence that the 10 per cent dividend would be maintained kept the market price of the common around 165 throughout 1915, while the preferred sold close to par.

The sale of a third block of 5,000 shares of the preferred stock to the

[19] "The question arises," Schoolfield said in September, 1914, "whether it is better to . . . keep the Stockholders satisfied and in a good humor, or postpone the payment of this dividend for the time being, say until April 1st. and then pay 10 per cent if conditions warranted. . . ."   The following March, too, he thought the dividend should be reduced to 3 per cent semi-annually, "so as to husband our resources and put us in a better condition to meet any unfavorable contingency."

New York brokerage firm of Philip M. Shaw (May 1916) brought the total capitalization to $9,000,000, of which $6,000,000 was represented by the preferred. In recommending these preferred issues, Schoolfield described them as "practically a transfer of interest from the banks for that much borrowed money to the stockholders. . . . Stockholders will get the interest in the way of dividends on this investment, which otherwise would be paid to the banks on short time paper." But bank loans generally cost the firm less than 6 per cent and the interest had to be paid only for the period of the loan. The preferred stock carried a *cumulative* dividend of 6 per cent; and in 1914, for the first time in the company's history—but not the last—the preferred dividend was not earned.

In June 1917 the company paid a dividend of 39 per cent ($1,470,000) on its common stock. All but 5 per cent of this represented undivided profits accumulated prior to March 1, 1913, which under the federal income-tax law were non-taxable if distributed as dividends before July 1, 1917. Simultaneously with the dividend payment, the company offered 10,000 shares of common stock in a privileged subscription at 150. Since rights were issued in the ratio of one for three, the June dividend paid 78 per cent of the purchase price of the stockholder's new shares. In sum, the company capitalized the entire amount of the dividend and obtained $330,000 in additional capital.

Two stock issues financed Riverside's Mill No. 8 and the other improvements carried out in 1919-1921. Although "some of the stockholders . . . felt that a stock dividend should be declared or that an increased rate should be paid," the management thought "establishing any precedent of a higher rate of dividend than 10% on the Common Stock" would be "a menace to the interest of the Company." Managerial resistance to the importunities of stockholders was one of form rather than of substance. In January 1919 the directors declared an extra dividend of 15 per cent and then offered 20,000 shares of common stock in a privileged subscription *at par*. Since the stockholder who sold his rights realized $100 to $120 per right,[20] he may have been per-

[20] Since the stock reached a top price of 360, the theoretical value of a right touched 173.3 at one time; but T. J. Catlin purchased 31 rights at 120 in February 1919 and the company accommodated stockholders holding fractional rights by buying them at $50 per half-right.

On behalf of some disgruntled preferred shareholders, Thomas Branch & Company of Richmond brought suit against the mill on the ground that the preferred stockholders were illegally excluded from the privileged subscription. The case reached the Supreme

suaded that the company in effect paid him another extra dividend. The regular semi-annual dividends of 5 per cent were paid in March and October. After selling for 215 in April-May 1919, the common climbed to 335 in February and again in May 1920.

In January 1920 Riverside and Dan River Cotton Mills offered 15,000 shares of preferred stock, which was heavily oversubscribed. This brought the capitalization to $13.5 million: $7.5 million in preferred and $6 million in common. Earnings reached a new high in 1920, and the amount distributed in dividends was the largest in the company's history down to 1946. But declining sales and a big tax bill dragged the net earnings for 1921 down to a mere $164,000, the smallest since 1901. The common stock declined to 270 in January 1922.

A charter amendment in January 1919 allowed an increase in capitalization to $15 million, equally divided between preferred and common shares. "We do not propose to sell all of this stock at this time and probably may never wish to do so," Schoolfield wrote to the First National Bank of Richmond. A proposal to increase the capitalization to $20 million, brought before the stockholders in January 1921, did not come to a vote; and the outstanding capital did not reach the full $15 million until 1924.

Numerous stock issues and the growth of the capitalization from $7 million to $13.5 million in less than a decade spoiled the founders' dream of a corporation closed to all except those personally acceptable to the management. The preferred stock was more widely distributed than the common. Prior to the 1920 issue one stockholder held 500 shares, three had from 300 to 400 shares each, four held 200 to 299 shares, thirty-two owned 100 to 199 shares, and 686 shareholders held less than 100 shares each. The number of common stockholders reached 374 in June 1917, with individual holdings distributed as follows:

Court of Virginia, which in June 1924 exonerated Dan River's officers from the charge of fraud but found that they had violated the state corporation code in not permitting the preferred stockholders to subscribe to the 1919 issue of common stock. Damages were also awarded for the exclusion of the preferred shareholders from the stock dividend declared in 1924. Final settlement of the claims of owners of 847 preferred shares cost the company $39,786 (Branch v. Riverside Mills, 139 *Virginia* 291 (1924) ; Riverside Mills v. Branch, 147 *Virginia* 509 (1927); Branch v. Riverside Mills, 147 *Virginia* 522 (1927).

shares	stockholders
1-99	305
100-199	34
200-299	8
300-399	11
400-499	6
500-599	76
1,000 and over	3

The largest common stockholder (R. J. Reynolds) owned 3,602 shares, while 10,302 shares, or slightly more than a third of the outstanding common, were owned by ten stockholders. The twelve directors held only 5,519 shares (18.4 per cent) of the common stock; but they effectively controlled, in all probability, several thousand shares held by relatives and heirs of former directors.[21]

The directors, on January 4, 1921, approved an issue of Class A stock for sale to employees; but the number of shares represented at the stockholders meeting on January 27 was not large enough to permit a vote on the proposal. Although the president thought "permitting the operatives to participate in the profits of the Company" was "nothing but right," at the March board meeting he recommended dropping the idea of Class A stock for the time being. A few days earlier he had posted a notice to the effect that the company held a few shares of preferred stock for sale to the employees "in order to enable them to save their money."[22]

As in earlier periods, the company's stockholders furnished capital for land, power, and buildings but were slow to finance the large inventories of cotton and supplies which cotton manufacturing requires. Northern machine manufacturers frequently financed equipment purchases for periods of one to three years. Saco-Lowell Shops and the three loom manufacturers customarily accepted 5 per-cent promissory notes for three-fourths of the cost of the machinery, occasionally discounting the paper with the Textile Securities Company of Boston. When H. R. Fitzgerald went north to select new looms in 1915, Schoolfield had occasion to write him: "While under the present conditions of the money market we could easily pay for and take care of the situation, but if you can make as favorable a deal with the privilege of deferred payments, it might be the part of prudence to do so, but I think

[21] The widow of a former director owned 1,210 common shares.
[22] Circular Poster No. 87 (March 16, 1921). Fitzgerald had to reassure several influential stockholders that the Class A stock would not jeopardize their voting position. No employee, he said, would have more than $1,000 of stock.

that we could afford to take the chances to pay for them cash rather than to pay a premium of any consequence for the privilege of time." Past experiences persuaded the officers that the Draper Company would be more lenient than the Stafford Company in pressing for settlement of a "cash" transaction.[23]

In order to carry seasonally large purchases of cotton, extend credit to its customers, and build up inventories of dyestuffs and supplies when prices were favorable, the company continued to depend heavily on metropolitan banks and New York bill brokers for short-term credit. At the end of 1910 accounts and notes payable amounted to a little over $3 million, dropped to $1.8 million at the end of 1911, and rose irregularly to a record $4.7 million at the end of 1921. Because cotton purchases usually mounted in the winter months, year-end statements ordinarily reflect the peaks of borrowing: but in three cases (1911, 1915, and 1916) the average amount of notes payable during the year exceeded current liabilities on December 31. Only in the summer of 1920 did the company get out of debt completely, and for a few months the officers had the unique problem of finding a suitable short-term investment for half a million dollars.[24]

The company transacted what Schoolfield referred to as the "bulk of our business in Danville" with the First National Bank, of which Dan River's director James I. Pritchett was president. Drafts drawn by cotton shippers were presented for collection at the Danville bank; as the amounts were too large for a country bank to handle, the drafts were promptly covered by the company's notes, discounted in Richmond, New York, or Boston.[25]

[23] When the Stafford Company pressed for a partial payment on a bill, prior to completion of the shipment on an order, Fitzgerald responded with a $10,000 check and the comment that, "We are always glad to apply the principle of the Golden Rule" (Oct. 13, 1913).

[24] "Our financial condition has never been stronger than at this time," Schoolfield wrote to the president of the Hanover National Bank. "We . . . have no paper outstanding, either with our depository banks or on the open market, and . . . we are writing to know what rate of interest you would be willing to pay us on daily balances. . . ." In September, the National Shawmut Bank of Boston solicited a deposit of $250,000-$500,000, agreeing to pay 5 per cent.

[25] A letter to Philip M. Shaw & Co., Nov. 24, 1917, describes a typical transaction:
"We are giving to the First National Bank, Danville, Va., today two notes of $25,000.00 each, three of $10,000.00 each, four of $5,000.00 each and one of $3,074.06, all dated today and payable to our order at National Park Bank, New York, on May 27, 1918. These notes aggregate $103,074.06 and are given to the First National Bank in payment for cotton. When presented by them, we will thank you to pay to their order the face value of the notes and charge to our account the amount of interest and send us statement of the same. It is not necessary, nor do we wish any statement sent to the First National Bank as to interest or discount—all that it is necessary for you to do is to take the notes and give them the money for the same and charge the interest to our account. We are enclosing check on Citizens National Bank, New York, for $5,000.00 which you

In dealing with Richmond banks—the First National and the Merchants' National—Riverside and Dan River frequently complained that the discount rate "looks pretty steep." Disclaiming any desire to " 'Jew' you down in your rate," Schoolfield told officers of the First National Bank (1914) that the company would be "pleased to do what business we can with you" but not at rates out of line with the New York market. On several occasions the Richmond banks met the northern competition; and in October 1913 Schoolfield advised a New York bank that "one of our friends in a neighboring town in Virginia took $150,000.00 of our paper at 5½% a short time ago." And he added: "We are not mentioning this as naming a rate for you to take this paper at [i.e., a note for $100,000] but only as a matter of information." A small amount of discounting was handled by Thomas Branch & Company of Richmond.

For reasons best known to Schoolfield and Fitzgerald, the company stopped discounting its paper with E. Naumberg & Company. Director James I. Pritchett intervened, apparently in hopes of re-establishing relations with Naumberg in 1919. Schoolfield replied: "They are Jews, but stand well and handle the paper of a number of Southern mills. They have been pretty regularly soliciting our business. . . . Other brokerage concerns have been doing the same thing. Our connection is very satisfactory at this time and I see no reason to make a change." At that time Philip M. Shaw & Company was discounting practically all of the company's commercial paper, although prior to 1916 W. O. Gay & Company had handled most of Dan River's notes, except those discounted at the banks. Shaw took none of the company's paper in 1920-1921, but Naumberg discounted a little in 1921. The City of Danville loaned the Company $25,000 in 1913.

In at least one instance Gay sold some of the company's paper in London, with the understanding that the notes would not be rediscounted in Virginia. In an active bill market banks and brokers competed for the business. "Want one hundred thousand your paper six months at five half for special customer," Gay wired the company in November 1910. It was "important" to fill this order, Gay advised; and the company responded by sending its notes for $100,000. In

---

will please place to our credit. This will make $10,000.00 we have sent you for our credit for you to charge interest against.

"This is all the cotton we have to pay for today, but there will probably be a good deal more Monday and during the week. The paper will be sent you as the cotton drafts come in."

January 1915 the Bank of New York wrote that it would be "an accommodation to us if you can use $100,000 four to six months at 4½." "You have been so nice to us," Schoolfield replied, "we will be pleased to forward the paper." Notes for $100,000 were discounted at the Merchants National Bank, Richmond, in October 1918. "We do not need this money specially," Chairman Schoolfield explained, "but we are doing it as an accommodation to you, as we wish to cooperate with you whenever possible." In January 1920 President Leroy Springs of the Lancaster Cotton Mills offered to buy some of Dan River's notes, but the company replied that "for the time being . . . we do not wish to put out any additional paper. Our bank connections are very satisfactory and we usually can get money in New York and Boston at a lower rate than we can South."

Borrowed funds cost the company over $100,000 yearly. Variations in the amount of interest paid reflect changes in the rate of interest as well as fluctuations in the volume of borrowing. On short-term loans Dan River often borrowed at discount rates as low as 3.25 per cent and seldom had to pay as much as 6 per cent. A notable exception occurred in the fall of 1914, following the outbreak of war in Europe and the closing of the New York Stock Exchange. Schoolfield found the situation "perplexing" but had to enter the money market for funds costing 7 per cent.[26] Although I cannot reconstruct completely the twelve-year record of short-term borrowing, I believe the company consistently obtained funds at rates *below* the average discount on prime commercial paper.[27]

After the entry of the United States into World War I the company commenced purchasing Liberty bonds (partly for resale to employees),[28] and by the end of 1920 its holdings of government securities reached almost $3,000,000. Although one purchase of $1,000,000 in Treasury certificates was financed by a bank loan (at a higher rate of interest than the yield on the certificates), the transaction was not specu-

[26] "During the stringency last fall," Schoolfield wrote to the president of the Citizens Central National Bank (Jan. 29, 1915), "your bank and another that we do not keep a very active account with were the only ones that did not accord us the accommodation suggested by us. We wrote you for $100,000.00. You replied that $50,000.00 was all that you were willing to loan us at that time . . . but in both instances later on the additional $50,000.00 was loaned us by you and the other bank. The other banks that we do business with conceded all requests made upon them. . . ."
[27] *Historical Statistics of the United States*, p. 278.
[28] A poster on "The Fighting Fourth Liberty Loan" (October 1918) announced that the Company would receive subscriptions and deduct payments from wages at the rate of $1 a week for each $50 bond. "Your subscription," Fitzgerald wrote, "will be the eternal record of your patriotic service to God, your Country and Right."

lative by design. Losses on bond sales exceeded gains by $37,000. The liquidation of all holdings of Victory bonds and Treasury certificates furnished cash for the federal income tax of $2,147,251 on the 1920 earnings.

The working capital position tended to improve in 1910-1921. Capital and surplus in 1910 barely covered the fixed-capital accounts of $6.9 million, borrowed funds having been used to finance inventories, receivables, and cash. Ten years later the capital and surplus accounts ($23.4 million) exceeded the value of the fixed assets, inventories, and receivables by a margin of half a million dollars. But this trend turned downward with the slump in sales and earnings in 1921.

Of Plaids, Ginghams, Chambrays, and Sheets

Paralleling the growth of the plants, average yearly production expanded approximately 50 per cent in the twelve-year period, 1910-1921. Peaks of 54.9 million yards at Riverside and 82.1 million yards at Dan River were reached in 1916 (Appendix 3). The older division accounted for 43 per cent of the 1,332 million yards manufactured in this period, while the Schoolfield mills made 57 per cent.

On a poundage basis (Table 3), total output rose to 33.8 million pounds in 1916 but contracted thereafter, so that output in 1917-1921 averaged a little less than 150 per cent of the 21 million pounds produced in 1910. White goods (mainly sheeting) represented 77.2 million pounds of the total production of 323.9 million pounds.

Riverside continued to make large quantities of coarse plaids; but, after averaging well over two million pounds annually, the production dropped to 915,000 pounds in 1921. As early as 1912 the president reminded the stockholders: "While we are still making some of the goods that we first commenced to manufacture and on which we made money and established our reputation, the demand for these goods is very limited now. . . . We could not possibly run our Plant at this time if we were dependent upon the manufacture of these fabrics to do so." Over the years "Riverside" plaids appeared in a myriad of patterns. One of the many style books stored in the sample department shows 39 patterns of 27-inch plaids—including a solid blue and some stripes! As somewhat finer yarns were used, the 25-inch plaids that averaged 5.5 yards per pound in 1890-1891 ran up to 6.2 yards and over in 1910.

Table 3.   Output of Colored and White Goods, 1910-1921
(thousands of pounds)

| year | Riverside division | | Dan River division | | total |
	colored	white	colored	white	
1910	8,472	1,570	7,578	3,374	20,994
1911	8,655	1,429	7,857	4,085	22,026
1912	9,690	645	7,686	3,680	21,701
1913	11,451		7,181	3,977	22,608
1914	10,976		7,670	5,497	24,143
1915	12,206		10,307	7,059	29,572
1916	12,994		12,680	8,183	33,857
1917	12,538		11,077	7,689	31,304
1918	10,793		9,980	6,315	27,088
1919	11,587		10,122	6,931	28,640
1920	12,123		11,141	8,215	31,479
1921	11,357		10,621	8,516	30,494

Discrepancies in total due to rounding.

Both divisions of Riverside and Dan River Mills found growing markets for chambrays and ginghams, the two fabrics which made up over 75 per cent of all colored cloth produced in 1910-1921.[29] "Ideal," the finest chambray, running well over five yards per pound in 28-inch widths, made up 36.8 per cent of the colored goods produced in 1910. "Defiance" chambrays, made at Riverside, were comparatively coarse, running under 4 yards per pound.   Both divisions manufactured "Golden Rule" chambray, a grade of cloth in between "Defiance" and "Ideal."   "Reliance" chambray was made on special order for the Reliance Manufacturing Company.   All lines of chambray made up 70.2 per cent of all colored goods in 1910 but only 49.8 per cent in 1921.

Gingham production commenced in 1911[30] with the manufacture of 903,000 pounds of 27-inch "Quality" gingham, 783,000 pounds of 27-inch "Special" gingham, 384,000 pounds of 32-inch "Zephyr" gingham, and 382,000 pounds of 32-inch "Special" gingham—in all, 14.8 per cent of the colored goods made this year.   By 1921, when Riverside's looms turned out ginghams for the first time, ginghams amounted to nearly a third of the colored goods output.

"Quality" gingham in 27-inch widths averaged close to 6.5 yards to

[29] Goods classed as chambrays amounted to something over twice the volume of ginghams.   Since one line of goods was sometimes referred to as "gingham chambray," it is difficult to make a completely accurate classification.

[30] Actually, 405 pounds of "gingham," not otherwise described, were produced in 1910.

the pound; "Zephyr" gingham, made principally in 32-inch widths, ran as high as 6.2 yards but varied considerably, falling sometimes as low as 5.6 yards; and "Security" ginghams (or gingham chambrays), because of changes in yarn or construction, varied from 5.5 to 6.3 yards per pound. Sample books for 1912-1921 show the great variety of styles and patterns in which chambrays and ginghams were marketed. One book of Dan River dress goods, brought out in January 1912, contains 296 patterns; and 230 different patterns were available in June under 47 style numbers. One of the fall (1917) lines of "Fancies," or dress ginghams, listed Styles 768 to 794, each with four patterns in plaids and stripes; the "Fairy Zephyr" line in May 1914 contained 346 patterns; and the "Security Solids and Staples" of 1918 consisted of 66 styles, each in four patterns.

As for other colored goods: Riverside made 2.9 million pounds of cheviots in 1910—mostly 28-inch "Golden Rule" cheviots—but toward the end of the period sales of this type of cloth dropped drastically. On the other hand, the output of drills—all made at Riverside Division —after averaging half a million pounds annually in 1910-1914, rose to a peak of over three million pounds in 1917. Over 60 per cent of the drills were entered as No. 300—a 27-inch cloth measuring about 3.2 yards to the pound. "Dog's Head" drills were sold through G. A. Stafford & Company, and a similar grade of cloth was "confined" to Yglesias, Lobo & Company for export to South America. The rest of the colored goods comprised special suitings (1915-1921), mohair (1915-1917), whipcord (1915-1916), denims (1914-1915, 1919-1920), and covert cloth (1910-1911)—all fabrics produced only intermittently. In September 1915 the president reported "experimenting with some new fabrics that seem to promise a good business in the line of automobile coverings, which is a class of goods that this country has heretofore obtained largely from Europe." But in 1919 the company was "not interested" in a customer's request for whipcord: "it did not turn out to be satisfactory when we made them before."

Only a few constructions of cloth have been verified. In 1911 the "Ideal" chambray was made of no. 18 warps, with no. 30 filling yarn and a count of 66×50. "Quality" ginghams, using no. 30 yarn in both warp and filling, had a count of 64×54, while "Zephyrs" ran up to 74×64. In ordering warp drawing-in machines the company advised the manufacturer that its 28-inch cheviots contained 1,540 ends; 28-

inch plaids, 972 ends.   All these warps were no. 14 yarn, although by
1919 the mills were spinning some yarn as fine as no. 40.

Separate labor costs for designing appear in the Dan River cost
sheets after 1911, and both divisions shared the cost of materials used
in the sample room.   There is no other direct information on the development of designing and the preparation of samples in this period.
Creating hundreds, and eventually thousands, of styles and patterns
entailed the risks of consumer nonacceptance on the one hand and the
unwanted compliment of imitation on the other.   "Some of our larger
friends," the president complained, placed small orders for "Defiance"
chambrays "to get the styles and samples and then buy cheaper ones
from other parties to fill their orders with.   This makes it pretty hard
on us, having to help out the other fellow's sale of goods."

The 74 million pounds of sheeting manufactured in 1910-1921
comprised 25 different widths but almost two-thirds of all sheeting
measured over 80 inches.   Less than half of the sheeting was sold unbleached, and increasing amounts of bleached sheeting were finished
into sheets and pillow cases.   In 1919 President Fitzgerald sought the
advice of Lockwood, Greene & Company on the problem of improving
the quality of the bleached sheeting.   "We have never been able to get
our goods to feel as heavy as they really are," he said, "and they seem
to lack the necessary body to the feel which makes them appear lighter
than they really are.   In comparing them with Pepperell, Dallas, and
other goods of this class, the other people seem to be able to give their
goods a body that makes them show up heavier than ours whereas in
actual weight our goods are a few points heavier than any of the others."
Fitzgerald thought that the difficulty arose from the use of a caustic
bleach and wondered whether a lime bleach should be substituted.   I
do not know what recommendation the engineers made.

For its numerous customers Riverside and Dan River Mills offered
"Bob White," "Dan River," and "Dan Valley" sheets.   The "Foxcroft"
line was assigned to Ely & Walker in 1918; other confined lines were
"Pride of Virginia" and "Queen of the Home."   On colored goods as
well as on sheets and pillow cases "tickets" became more numerous as
new and widely scattered customers were secured.   According to company officials, the practice of product differentiation by "tickets" originated in this fashion:

. . . new lines came in direct competition with old established mills who
owned brands which had been on the market for a long term of years. . . .

To meet or overcome this situation Riverside inaugurated the plan of offering its goods under fancy non-conflicting brands as well as its own mill brand so that no one ticket was in the hands of more than one jobber in a given territory—in fact in a great many instances two and three jobbers in the same city would have the goods under different tickets and with each one striving to introduce his brand on a profitable basis. A large number of these special tickets inaugurated twenty or twenty-five years ago are popular today. . . .[31]

The principal "other white" goods were duck and bunting, made only in the war years; "DuPont" and "Special DuPont" cloth, produced in 1919-1920; and about 1.5 million pounds of burlap, manufactured in 1916-1921.

Selling Cloth

Selling a hundred million yards of cloth a year, the officers often reminded the stockholders, was a job requiring high skill and unremitting diligence. The company continued to cater to garment manufacturers, cutters, jobbers, dry goods stores, and mail-order houses, depending almost entirely on its own sales organization. Cockefair, in charge of the New York office, was assisted by D. L. Reardon, commencing in 1917, and Walter Willcox in 1919. Fitzgerald made frequent trips to New York to confer with salesmen and maintain contacts with the most important customers. As head salesman, George P. Ray, too, was frequently absent from his Danville office. The Chicago sales office served a growing business in the Midwest; but the Baltimore office, in charge of R. H. Pritchett, was closed in November 1917.

"For the benefit of those interested," Chairman Schoolfield explained the sales organization at the stockholders meeting in January 1921: "it may be in order to say that your Management not only has to act as manufacturers but merchants as well, selling your product through your own salaried organization instead of through commission houses as most manufacturers do. The commission that we would have had to pay, if in line with what other manufacturers have to pay, would have been three times as much as that paid to your entire salaried force, consisting of officers, superintendents, engineers, salesmen and office force."[32]

[31] D. A. Overbey, Jr., "History of Riverside and Dan River Mills, Danville, Va.," a typescript dated No. 27, 1936, "revised and improved by Mr. L. H. B[rowder] and Mr. Ray."

[32] In 1920 salaries totaled $408,500, or 1.3 per cent of gross sales.

Little precise information has come to light regarding marketing methods. The traditions of the trade still required personal contacts, and Dan River salesmen had to carry larger sample books to show old and prospective customers. By 1916 the company offered 37 classes of goods, in hundreds of styles, many of which were changed twice a year "to meet the requirements of the Trade." As compared with later years, advertising in 1910-1921 was infrequent and inexpensive. In connection with a feature article, "Riverside & Dan River Cotton Mills —the Model Plant of the South," the company ran a full-page advertisement in the supplement of *Mill News* (August 7, 1913). In September 1915 Dan River bought 10,000 lines of advertising in the *Daily News Record,* to be used over a period of a year.

Great reliance was placed upon repeat sales and volume business with large firms, such as Ely & Walker Dry Goods Company and the Reliance Manufacturing Company. Among the Dan River memorabilia is a picture of a train of freight cars loaded with sheeting purchased by Ely & Walker in 1914.

An analysis of the "Customers' Ledger No. 1" (1910-1911) reveals that 32.4 per cent (by value) of all sales were transacted with firms in New York. Sales in Maryland, Missouri, and Illinois accounted for 14.4 per cent, 14.1 per cent, and 11.8 per cent of total sales, respectively. Altogether, sales were made in 34 states. In the "Customers' Ledger No. 7" (1920-1921) New York sales drop to 27.9 per cent of total sales. Relatively, sales declined in Maryland and gained in Missouri and Illinois. Dan River then had customers in 40 states and the District of Columbia, but 5 states accounted for nearly 75 per cent of all sales. New York sales include Dan River's export business, which was done mainly on consignment to G. A. Stafford & Company. The Stafford orders amounted to 3.6 per cent of all sales in 1910-1911 and 3.3 per cent in 1920-1921. In the latter years three customers, Ely & Walker, Claflin's, and Sears, Roebuck, accounted for 22.8 per cent of the company's sales. Other large buyers of Dan River fabrics were the Carter Dry Goods Company (Louisville), Lamport Manufacturers' Supply Company, Montgomery, Ward, and the Missouri State Prison Board.

Gross sales[33] are shown in Table 4. After averaging $6.6 million for five years (1910-1914), sales passed $8 million in 1915 and climbed

---

[33] Commencing with the income statements for 1913, "discount" consisting of (a) discounts actually taken by customers and (b) 3 per cent of the accounts receivable at the end of the year was subtracted from gross sales. On the average, net sales are 2.3 per cent less than gross sales.

steadily to $30.6 million in 1920. The 1921 slump cut sales to $19.1 million, the same as in 1918, although the physical volume of output dropped only 3.1 per cent. But the figures tell only partially the story of the company's efforts to win customers and influence consumers.

Table 4. Gross Sales, 1910-1921
(thousands of dollars)

year	Riverside	Dan River		total
		white	colored	
1910	2,722	1,362	2,215	6,299
1911	2,781	1,458	2,688	6,927
1912	2,628	1,244	2,642	6,514
1913	2,896	1,157	2,528	6,582
1914	2,697	1,529	2,543	6,770
1915	2,997	1,874	3,368	8,240
1916	3,885	2,423	5,533	11,842
1917	5,015	3,034	6,145	14,195
1918	6,616	3,581	8,954	19,150
1919	8,505	4,818	9,711	23,034
1920	10,493	6,185	13,892	30,570
1921	6,155	4,797	8,198	19,149

Discrepancies in total due to rounding.

In March 1910 the president commented on the increasing production of finer goods, mainly ginghams, for which the demand was relatively good; but he told the directors that merchants and manufacturers generally considered the situation "a very trying one." Prices were generally firm. "Defiance" chambrays, which brought the mills 24.87 cents per pound in August 1909, sold for an average of 26.38 cents in May 1910. In the same period "Ideal" chambray advanced from 29.66 cents to 30.16 cents, brown sheeting from 27.61 cents to 30.44 cents, and bleached sheeting from 31.21 cents to 32.53 cents. In September the president still found business conditions "perplexing," in view of the high price of cotton and the tendency of jobbers and cutters to hold off buying in hopes of depressing cloth prices.[34] By December, ap-

[34] Speaking before the American Cotton Manufacturers' Association in May 1910, President Lewis W. Parker observed: "As a general proposition, it is not to be expected that the buyer shall be the one to seek the advance of that which he has to purchase"; but he felt strongly that the industry would do better to use its energy in persuading consumers to pay higher prices for cloth than to join those trying to depress the price of cotton (*Proceedings of the Fourteenth Annual Convention of the American Cotton Manufacturers' Association* [Charlotte, 1910], pp. 115-123). On a few occasions President

parently, the tide had turned. Cautioning the buyer to "treat this transaction strictly confidential," Fitzgerald accepted an order for 25 cases of "Ideal" chambrays at the price prevailing earlier in the year, although it did "not show scarcely any profit whatever to the Mills." Taking into consideration the many adverse factors, the stockholders were asked to accept the results of the year's operations as satisfactory. "Your management has endeavored to study the conditions closely and to follow the same progressive and yet conservative policy that has characterized our Company since its beginning."

During February and March 1911 all the looms were in production, but the margin of profit was "not what it should be." Writing to Fitzgerald, then in New York, Schoolfield declared he could not "understand the weakness in the situation and the demoralization in prices, except it is on account of a general demoralization all around, for conditions do not warrant it so far as I can see. The country at large is in a good condition." Quoting prices to a Texas customer in April, the company offered to shave prices on colored goods a quarter of a cent a yard "if you will send a nice order promptly." Promptness in ordering sheets was also recommended, "as our prices are liable to be advanced at any moment." But in September the sheeting market was demoralized because of "overproduction by some of the old established mills"; and, in face of "the most severe and drastic shrinkage in prices . . . in wide sheeting," Dan River's accumulated stock "had to be sold not in proportion to cost but at what the market would pay." Some of the difficulty, as Schoolfield saw it, came from abroad. As long as political unrest in Europe persisted, one could not expect "much snap to business" in America.

As far as Riverside and Dan River Mills was concerned, the "snap" did reappear in 1912. In February the mill's problem was to "furnish the Plaids and Chambrays as fast as wanted," and gingham demand was not far behind. Later in the year the president noted that the finer grades "continue to increase in favor with our customers." Prices were lower than in 1911; on the other hand, Dan River obtained large quantities of cotton at relatively low prices in the winter of 1911-1912. The favorable outlook continued into 1913, although Schoolfield warned the stockholders that a complication of the Balkan question or "some radical action on the tariff question" might cause a reversal. In

---

Schoolfield admitted that a relatively high price for cotton made for the prosperity of the South and, indirectly, benefited the makers of cotton goods.

October "Defiance" chambray brought an average price of 26.55 cents per pound and "Ideal" chambray, 31.72 cents—in both cases only a fraction of a cent more than in May 1910—while both bleached and brown sheeting averaged four cents below the May 1910 prices. Fitzgerald wrote R. A. Schoolfield that one customer "laughed" when reminded that "we wanted to get more money for our goods." But Fitzgerald and Cockefair sold him 2,250 cases of wide sheeting, making a "very wise deal," despite the buyer's warning (to the Dan River executives) that "we will have to go very slow in advancing our price, as they think we would simply force our customers to buy competing goods which are plentiful at a less price."

Actually, the Underwood tariff, which became law in October, did not constitute a radical downward revision of the rates on cotton goods;[35] and in January 1914 Schoolfield admitted that the "harmful results . . . as predicted by many have not resulted to anything like the extent that was feared, but, on the contrary, the settlement of the question removed perhaps the most disturbing factor in the business." A year later, however, he thought the effects of the tariff had been "in some respects more drastic . . . than was generally believed."

The passage of the Federal Reserve Act (1913) met with the approval of Dan River's management, since it held the promise of lower interest rates; but the Administration's "insistence upon legislation detrimental to the business and manufacturing interests of the country" was thought to be largely responsible for widespread distrust and lack of confidence on the part of merchants who bought Dan River products. The president decried the "tendency of Southern newspapers and some of the Representatives in Congress to encourage the people to look to the Government for aid beyond its power to render instead of appealing to their self-reliance."

The directors heard, in March 1914, the familiar complaint that, while demand was good, the margin of profit was unreasonable because of the high price of cotton. The outbreak of war changed all this precipitately: in one hour and fifteen minutes (July 31) the price of cotton dropped 200 points on the New York Cotton Exchange. The Exchange closed its doors and contracts for cloth, made on prewar cotton bases, were canceled. On top of this, strikes and the unemployment of western miners and railroad workers cut into Dan River's

[35] F. W. Taussig, *The Tariff History of the United States* (6th ed.; New York, 1914), pp. 432-436.

sales of chambrays for work-clothing. Demand for wide sheeting held firm; and, after "more than the usual number of adverse influences to contend with," the results for the year seemed to the president "truly remarkable."

For manufacturers of colored textiles 1914 marked the beginning of a long dearth of dyestuffs, as the western hemisphere was shut off from German suppliers. Although the management "put in a supply for several months, before the situation became generally known," Dan River lacked certain dyes for chambrays before the end of 1914, and the condition became more critical before it improved. Many colors could not be obtained at any price, and for limited quantities of Swiss dyes and of German dyes brought across the Atlantic by submarine the company paid "as much as $32 per pound."[36] Vegetable dyestuffs, especially indigo from the Far East, and American sulphur dyes tided the industry over the period of crisis, while the infant American dye industry established itself behind the protective wall of war in Europe.[37]

The "Indigo situation" in 1915 was an argument for resisting the pressure of a large customer for price concessions. In July the firm of Salant & Salant wanted 500 cases each of "Defiance" and "Golden Rule" chambrays, offering .125 to .25 cent per yard less than Dan River's best prices (6.25 cents for "Defiance" and 5.2 cents for "Golden Rule").

[36] The New York firm of A. Klipstein & Co. supplied limited quantities of Swiss-made synthetic indigo throughout the war. As for the cargo of dyes brought from Germany by submarine in the summer of 1916, distribution to manufacturers was carried out in great secrecy. Fitzgerald reminded a New York importer of the "very serious situation" at Dan River with respect to certain colors and asked for help in arranging "to pick up a few thousand pounds of them, either in a confidential manner or otherwise." Specifically, the mills needed a fast red for raw-stock dyeing, a fast Bordeaux or wine, and a fast pink. Benefield is credited with obtaining dyes, in New York or Baltimore, from German submarines.

[37] In September 1916 the company exchanged 100 "chests" of vegetable indigo for a new synthetic "indigo Zeta," manufactured by the Ernst Zobel Company. In 1917 five casks of Asiatic indigo were opened and found to contain "nothing but Chinese mud." Zeta blue and other American-made synthetics were gradually improved, and in 1921 Fitzgerald wanted to substitute a sulphur blue for both warp and filling yarns of Dan River ginghams, believing that it was only a "fad or hobby with the buyer to demand Indigo blue." The sulphur blue was more expensive, but indigo was more costly to process, since indigo was unsuitable for raw-stock dyeing.

Of the sulphur colors, Dan River had a surplus of black in the fall of 1916 and, fearing that other firms might accuse it of hoarding, arranged for the "strictly confidential" sale of 25,000-30,000 pounds. In December 1916 Fitzgerald observed that "most of the Aniline colors are being made in this country at prices ranging from five to six times normal, and it is also true that Sulphur Black is being made in this country in large quantities at prices from five to six times normal." He urged Virginia's representatives in Congress to assist dye manufacturers in getting larger quotas of electric power from Canadian power plants at Niagara Falls.

Dan River commenced to receive indigo from the DuPont Company in 1918, but DuPont had not been able to supply 25,000 pounds a month, which was "about the lowest quantity that we could pull through on" (H. R. Fitzgerald to E. I. DuPont de Nemours, Oct. 2, 1918).

Fitzgerald explained, in a letter to Schoolfield, who was vacationing in Waynesville, North Carolina: "We have a good demand for the Plain Blue, and as our production is well covered, there is no reason why we should sacrifice the price for additional business at present. . . . The situation on colored goods, generally speaking, is far from satisfactory, but most people seem to think that conditions will be better in the near future." At the end of the year a very satisfactory treasurer's report was submitted to the stockholders "with grateful acknowledgement of the kind Providence that has always guided in the management of your Company's affairs."

Early in 1916 cotton rose to "record prices," but newly built storage houses gave Dan River room for 12,000 more bales of cotton—enough fiber for all unfilled orders. Prices on colored goods advanced .25 cent per yard in September; but, in telling Cockefair of the change, Schoolfield wrote: "should you have any proposition that you might wish to put to us at less than these prices, we will take it under advisement." But on October 25 Fitzgerald instructed Cockefair to withdraw all goods from sale, except wide sheeting, because the "price of cotton has advanced so rapidly that even with the advance we made in the price of goods on yesterday our prices are entirely too low." The 1916 financial report, even more satisfactory than that of 1915, made the president feel that the "Company has much to be thankful for and every reason to trust in the kind Providence that has been with and piloted us in the past, feeling assured that if we do our part everything will come out alright [sic] in the end."

Nevertheless, the year 1917 opened, in Schoolfield's opinion, with the country in "chaotic conditions." Despite the strong demand for textiles, with orders on hand to cover production for several months, Dan River's president feared "unforeseen things of demoralizing character may occur at any time to effect business unfavorably." In March cotton seemed "to be in a very strong position and with the present unsatisfactory outlook for the coming crop, prospects for low prices are not encouraging."[38] On the other hand, Schoolfield wrote optimistically to the *Textile World Journal:* "the business of the country, as a

---

[38] This was written to President Leroy Springs of Fort Mill Manufacturing Co., Lancaster, S. C., in reply to an inquiry as to what the Dan River management thought of "cotton, cotton goods and trade in general." Schoolfield surmised that, "At the end of the war, while it will take a good deal of cotton to fill up the waste places in the central powers that have been unable to get it for sometime past, if they have the money to pay for it, it may stimulate the price of cotton for the time being, but it looks to us though it will only be a temporary matter. . . ."

whole, is in a strong position . . . the certainty of peace in Europe coming on ought not to effect business materially either way for sometime
to come. . . . We think that . . . business should continue in a healthy
condition for the near future, but later, when normal conditions in
Europe prevail, there will gradually be a readjustment of values of all
kinds." The president had won the war before the United States
entered the conflict!

Transportation became a serious problem for the Virginia mills
soon after the United States went to war. Much of the cloth sent to
northern buyers was shipped by steamer from Norfolk or West Point,
Virginia.[39] The rail-water route to New York made possible a saving
of about 50 per cent over the all-rail route, but space for coastwise
shipping became virtually unobtainable during the war. Temporary
embargoes hampered rail shipments even after the end of the emergency. It was particularly difficult for Dan River to get shipments
through New York into New England, and in May 1917 the company
solicited the help of officials of the Baltimore & Ohio Railway, with the
reminder that "We have given your line a large amount of highly
competitive southbound machinery in the past." In April 1918 an
accumulation of 30 cases of sheeting (about 15,000 pounds) for the
American Red Cross Hospital in Paris prompted Fitzgerald to complain
to the Old Dominion Steamship Company: "We have been unable to
forward these shipments due to various embargoes. We dislike to
hold them in our warehouses with the prospect of same being badly
needed by our Expeditionary Force."

The high price of coal, the Fuel Administrator's order reducing
the operations of steam plants, and ice and high water in the Dan
River plagued the production schedule in the early part of 1918. By
April the company had orders on hand, including government and
Red Cross purchases, to keep the mills busy the remainder of the year;
and for once the management admitted that cotton prices declined
without a corresponding softening in the prices of fabrics. Federal
price control of textiles, the Dan River management thought, was successful because of the "splendid spirit of cooperation on the part of
manufacturers."[40] But the aftermath of the armistice (November)

---

[39] Correspondence with insurance companies reveals that shipments valued at $1,500,000,
or about 25 per cent of sales, went by water in 1911-1912.

[40] H. R. Fitzgerald was a member of the committee of the National Council of American Cotton Manufacturers which, in the spring of 1918, promised to "cheerfully accept
control and price fixing . . . if necessary to win the war" (*Proceedings of the American
Cotton Manufacturers' Association* [Charlotte, 1918], pp. 56, 153).

was a "demoralized" dry goods market and a "critical" labor situation. In common with other suppliers, Dan River suffered from the abrupt cancellation of government contracts. The "disturbance to confidence amounted almost to panic for a few weeks," but as businessmen realized the extent to which the war had depleted stocks in trade, the market "worked back to practically the same level as before the Armistice." In January 1919 an important customer in St. Louis wired: "Cancel everything on order; cannot wait longer." By May the mills had a backlog of orders and cotton on hand to last until October. Yet, it was doubtful, Fitzgerald reasoned, "if the advances in the goods market have more than kept pace thus far with the increase in the cost of cotton." In February Dan River had initiated a price stabilization agreement among chambray manufacturers, which Fitzgerald believed would "operate to the advantage of all parties in the long run." But two prominent chambray mills declined to enter the agreement, and in January 1920 the Dan River management protested that some plaid and chambray producers "continue to lose their heads," raising prices and destroying the "opportunity for an active and prosperous business." An association of gingham manufacturers (of which, apparently, Dan River was not a member) was also found guilty of "making a very serious mistake in putting their prices so high . . . if this policy is persisted in the result will be to shorten the period of prosperous conditions and thereby pull down the situation on themselves, as they did once before."

In November 1919, when Pepperell announced increased prices on sheeting, Fitzgerald thought that if Dan River "were to offer any wide Sheeting, we would have to advance our price; but my idea is for us to stand quiet for the present and await developments for a few days." A year later, when Erwin's "White Star" sheeting was reduced, Cockefair and Ray promptly followed suit in cutting the price of "Dan River" sheeting. In October (1920) Fitzgerald wrote Ray that "no price that can be made would attract any very large business" in sheeting: "the lower the price is made, the more it will disturb confidence and check business." A freight differential, however, seemed to make it necessary "to name a price somewhat under Pepperell."

Except for the menace of organized labor—"the apparent determination of large bodies of working people to produce less and consume more"—the year 1919 was satisfactory, though not as profitable as 1918. "The year 1920," Schoolfield reported, "was a checkered one with its ups and down, largely down during the last few months. There has been no parallel to it in the dry goods business in the memory of the present generation." In March the company "really had to turn away a large amount of business," and in June the production of sheets and pillow cases was "sold ahead for several months," while "Golden Rule" and "Ideal" chambrays were "sold ahead well into the Fall." The peak was passed in early summer. In July Fitzgerald suggested shading prices on certain lines to build up foreign markets: "this is a case in which we could show some preference for the export business without any real detriment to our domestic business."[41] In August Fitzgerald and Ray agreed to wait for competitors to name their fall prices. "While I should hate to see a drastic reduction," the president said, "I am frank to say that if only a slight reduction is made, it will not meet the expectation of the trade and in all likelihood would simply cause another period of stagnation with propaganda for another mark-down later on." Deflation in the cotton goods market might end, in Fitzgerald's opinion, with a 25 per-cent reduction in prices.

On September 15 Dan River fell in line with other price-cutters, reducing its chambray lines, as follows: "Defiance," from 31 cents per yard to 21.5 cents: "Ideal," from 28.5 cents to 20 cents: and "Golden Rule," from 27.5 cents to 19 cents. Late in October Fitzgerald felt that the "hysteria through which so many of our friends have apparently been passing seems to be quieting down." Producers of cotton goods would realize that "there is little sense in giving them away at less than it costs to replace them." But deflation persisted, and in November the three lines of chambrays were cut to 17 cents, 16 cents, and 15 cents, respectively. On the average, a pound of cloth which sold for 104.7 cents in August 1920 brought in 52.9 cents in July 1921.

Wages were cut in November 1920, but the mills furnished practically full-time employment throughout the year. The inevitable consequence of continued production and declining sales was the building up of inventories to the unprecedented 4.6 million pounds of cloth, valued at $2.2 million.

Lower prices were announced in January 1921, ranging from 8 cents a yard for "Danville" 25-inch plaids to 11 cents for "Golden Rule"

[41] In a letter to G. A. Stafford (Jan. 27, 1917) Fitzgerald said that Dan River had endeavored to protect Stafford's export sales by withholding from other customers styles of cloth which they might use in competition with Stafford. Stafford claimed to have assured his customers that no one made drills equal to Dan River's. Fitzgerald hoped "that you have been consistently correct in this position . . . . we have certainly done our best to make it so."

chambrays, 12 cents for "Ideal," and 12.5 cents for "Defiance." In February Fitzgerald noticed that three firms were selling plaids and cheviots below Dan River's prices, but this was "something that no one can help." The president doubted that a "lower price would sell any more goods, but on the contrary, if we should announce a lower price, to say nothing of the fact that we cannot do so as it would simply add that much to our loss on every bale that we sold, I am afraid it would also affect the price of chambrays." Instead of lowering prices on the coarse goods, or producing for inventory, many of Riverside's plaid and cheviot looms switched to ginghams, though this necessitated a "somewhat radical change in carding and spinning" to make the finer yarns.

In the third quarter of 1921 Dan River pulled out of the doldrums and by mid-September had sheeting sold ahead for two months, coarse goods on order to keep the mills working for the rest of the year, and gingham orders to maintain production until March 1922. The extremely unsatisfactory financial results of the year's operations arose from the high rate of depreciation on additions to plant made at inflated costs, the overhead costs during the partial shut-down of the Riverside plant, and the lag in goods prices behind the rising price of cotton.

Table 5. Average Selling Prices, 1913-1921
(cents per pound)

| year | Riverside | Dan River | |
		colored	white
1913	26.34	34.95	28.59
1914	26.31	35.82	29.72
1915	23.14	32.69	28.01
1916	29.66	40.97	32.25
1917	39.97	56.61	45.21
1918	62.86	88.70	66.84
1919	73.02	95.80	74.07
1920	94.31	124.26	96.71
1921	47.82	70.60	59.09

Average selling prices (before discounts) are shown in Table 5. The data depict a more than three-fold increase in the average sales value of a pound of cloth between 1913 and 1920. This was somewhat more than the rise in the index of wholesale textile prices, which advanced from 57.3 to 164.8 (1926 = 100). The depression cut the average selling price of Riverside colored goods 49.3 per cent; Dan River colored goods, 43.2 per cent; and white goods, 38.9 per cent. But prices in 1921 averaged about twice the level of 1913.

While the United States mill margin on gray goods was rising from 10.6 cents a pound in 1910 to 52.8 cents in 1920, the spread between costs and selling prices of Riverside and Dan River products moved upward irregularly to the 1920 peaks of 23.50 cents (Riverside division), 31.18 cents (Dan River, white goods), and 38.79 cents (Dan River, colored goods). With the decline in prices these margins dropped to 14.80 cents and 13.81 cents at Dan River division, while Riverside's output sold for 2.87 cents below cost.

Costs

Soon after the merger of Riverside Cotton Mills and the Dan River Power & Manufacturing Company the New York firm of Barrow, Wade, Guthrie and Company was employed to study the mill's accounting practices. In their first report the accountants said, in part: "We wish to say frankly that in reviewing your system we did not find a great deal to criticize. Your books and accounts are remarkably well kept. . . ." Although in some instances (e.g., shipments from weave rooms to the bleachery) not enough data were recorded, many of the books of record required excessive clerical work. The cost sheets were "not as accurate and reliable as they might be made." Specific objections were the inclusion of interest on short-term loans as a manufacturing expense, the failure to separate selling costs from manufacturing expenses, and the overpricing of cotton and supplies for costing purposes.

In 1910 the company paid $3,770 for advice on the revision of its labor-cost methods; but the cost-of-manufacturing sheets for the period 1910-1931 exhibit only one significant change from the form introduced in the 1880's—depreciation is finally treated as a manufacturing cost.

Three series of average unit cost figures are shown in Table 6. It will be observed that the minimum cost for Riverside colored goods as well as the lowest unit cost for Dan River white goods was achieved in 1915, the cost per pound in each case having fallen about five cents below the 1910 average. The decreases were due almost entirely to the lower price of cotton; but the cost of making Dan River's finer colored goods did not drop below the 1910 figure. All series move upward under the impact of higher wage and materials costs during the war; they drop roughly to the same degree in 1921.

Table 6.   Unit Cost of Production, 1910-1921
(cents per pound of cloth)

year	Riverside division	Dan River division	
		white goods	colored goods
1910	24.39	25.66	26.54
1911	25.59	26.20	30.36
1912	21.06	23.81	27.86
1913	23.85	23.81	30.29
1914	24.84	26.11	33.24
1915	19.41	20.12	26.72
1916	25.64	25.09	33.50
1917	33.83	33.87	45.05
1918	55.11	51.21	62.78
1919	59.47	57.05	73.38
1920	70.81	65.53	85.47
1921	50.69	44.29	56.79

Uniformly, throughout this period of twelve years, the unit cost of the colored goods made at Dan River exceeded the cost of Riverside's colored lines; the spread widens to a maximum of 14.66 cents in 1920, while the newer division of the mills built up its lines of fine ginghams; it dropped to 6.1 cents in 1921, the year in which Riverside, too, employed many of its looms on ginghams.

With important exceptions, the components of the total unit cost of production exhibit fluctuations primarily associated with inflation in 1910-1920 and contraction in 1921. All the cost sheets for this period show cost per pound of output in terms of labor, supplies, coal, expense, cotton, and depreciation.

Supplies

The movement of the unit cost of supplies paralleled price changes for the chemicals, dyes, and other materials used in dyeing, dressing, bleaching, and finishing. Most significant was the extreme rise in dyestuff prices, which persisted long after the war. Although the company had purchased in 1914 "all the Drugs and Dye Stuffs it was possible to secure," shortages of the most desirable dyes could not be avoided for long. By December 1916 the management complained that the dye market "ranges from six to ten times normal; in fact, in a few instances small quantities have been offered at approximately twenty times normal." At Riverside dyes cost .57 cent per pound of cloth in 1910 and rose to a peak of 3.33 cents in 1921; while at Dan River the unit cost soared to a high of 4.10 cents per pound of cloth in 1919. The highest cost for all supplies was 5.89 cents per pound of colored goods (Dan River) in 1921.

While American firms, according to President Fitzgerald, "made considerable progress" in developing colors formerly imported, there was "still a long list that they have not attempted to make." Domestic costs of production were high, and the textile industry looked with favor on the resumption of competition with foreign suppliers. In March 1921 Fitzgerald reminded the Bureau of Imports that American producers charged $24 per pound for Indanthrene blue powder, which German firms were willing to supply for $10 a pound. Dan River asked for a license to import 5,000 pounds of the German-made dye on the grounds that the color was needed for goods "used largely by the working classes."[42] Yet, Fitzgerald contended, "we are in hearty sympathy with the desire to protect our domestic dye industries."

During the war the company had used waste cotton to make a substitute fabric for the burlap customarily employed in making cotton-bale covering. Under the threat of a duty on burlap, in December 1920 President Fitzgerald wrote the Tariff Commission, urging that burlap be kept on the free list.

Coal

Changes in the unit cost of coal reflect not only the rising price of fuel but also the substantial growth in the proportion of power developed by coal. It is impossible to separate the two influences accurately. Riverside's coal cost per unit of output stayed consistently below Dan River's cost, as water- and hydro-electric power furnished a larger share of the power requirements of the mills in Danville. But both divisions steadily increased their consumption of coal. Contracts for coal ran from April 1 to March 31. The highest price, $4 per ton,

---

[42] A difference of $14 per pound in the cost of blue dye would have made a difference of approximately $.07 in a pair of overalls weighing four pounds.

was reached in the contract for 1920-1921; this was four times the cost of coal in 1910-1911. The 1921-1922 contract called for 80,000 tons at $3.50 per ton.

Absolutely, the coal cost of a pound of Dan River colored goods rose from .4 cent in 1910 to 3.06 cents in 1920; at Riverside the cost moved from .24 cent per pound of cloth in 1910 to 1.55 cents in 1921.

Expense

Expense, as in the earlier records, comprises salaries, interest, insurance, taxes, and miscellaneous expenditures. These contributed in varying proportions to the four- and five-fold increase in expense cost per pound of product. In 1918, expense per pound of Dan River colored cloth was 10.04 cents but only 5.28 cents for white goods and 7.03 cents for Riverside cloth. (The comparable figures for 1910 were 2.12 cents, 2.53 cents, and 1.55 cents.) Apparently, some items of expense, particularly taxes, were allocated, more or less arbitrarily, in proportion to the profitability of the different products.

Table 7. Total Wage and Salary Payments, 1910-1921
(thousands of dollars)

year	Riverside		Dan River		salaries as a percentage of wages and salaries
	wages	salaries	wages	salaries	
1910	507	49	632	57	8.5
1911	528	51	833	77	8.6
1912	571	53	876	80	8.4
1913	632	53	906	79	7.9
1914	600	61	1,059	91	8.4
1915	640	61	1,287	91	7.3
1916	749	87	1,550	130	8.6
1917	816	86	1,643	129	8.0
1918	1,125	136	2,227	203	9.2
1919	1,590	135	3,057	202	6.8
1920	2,118	163	4,109	245	6.2
1921	1,886	163	3,127	244	7.5

Salary payments rose *pari passu* with increases in wages and, as Table 7 reveals, varied from 6.2 to 9.2 per cent of total salaries and wages. As a percentage of gross sales, salary payments ran from 1.39

per cent to 2.65 per cent. The percentage tended to fall as sales rose, but no significant downward adjustment of salaries accompanied declining sales. Although the wages bill in 1921 was 20 per cent less than in 1920, the total amount paid out in salaries declined imperceptibly.

In March 1916 the directors approved salaries in excess of $2,000 a year, as follows:

assistant secretary-treasurer and head salesman	$15,000
superintendent, Dan River division	15,000
salesman, New York office	10,000
superintendent, Riverside division	10,000
manager, cotton department	5,000
boss dyer	5,000
head designer, Dan River	4,800
salesman, Baltimore office	4,800
head, bookeeping-credit department	4,000
assistant superintendent, carding and spinning	3,600
assistant superintendent, weaving	3,600
manager, Dan River colored goods department	3,600
manager, Riverside clerical and shipping department	3,300
assistant superintendent, dressing	3,000
manager, Dan River white goods department	3,000
master electrician	2,808
chief engineer, Dan River	2,700
assistant superintendent, finishing	2,500
chief engineer, Riverside	2,500
master mechanic	2,500
manager, Dan River auditing and cost department	2,500
manager, Dan River payroll department	2,400
manager, Riverside payroll department	2,400
head designer, Riverside	2,100

Salaries for these 24 administrative officials amounted to $116,100, whereas total salary payments for 1916, including the remuneration of the president, vice-president, and secretary-treasurer, came to $216,066. In all probability, most salaries had doubled by 1920, when all salaries totaled $408,500.

After averaging about $75,000 annually in 1910-1915, state and local levies rose to $118,052 in 1916, most of the increase going to Pittsylvania County.[43] In preparation for the payment of federal in-

[43] Pittsylvania County and the City of Danville both levied a tax on corporate income.

come taxes, a tax reserve of $600,000 was set up at the end of 1917. Income and excess profits taxes took $2.4 million in 1919, $1.3 million in 1920, and $2.4 million in 1921. The tax bills for 1921 included additional taxes on income for 1914-1918 as well as the tax on 1920's record earnings; but the drop in earnings reduced the tax on 1921 earnings to $314,972. In 1925 the Bureau of Internal Revenue insisted on a re-audit of the 1918 and 1920 income-tax returns. As a result, the company had to pay an additional tax and penalty on the 1918 income; but the Bureau found an almost equal overpayment of 1919 and 1920 taxes.[44]

The cost of borrowed funds moved erratically, reaching a maximum (net) of $167,158 in 1914. In 1919 and 1920 interest earned on government securities exceeded the amount paid out for borrowed funds.

Losses on bad debts remained an inconsiderable item of expense. The usual terms of sale were 2 per cent discount within 10 days, net in 60 days; but confidential terms to selected customers provided for as much as 4 per cent discount for settlement within 10 days. Occasionally the company accepted interest-bearing notes for unpaid balances, but this was regarded as risky. "Our experience has been," Schoolfield wrote Cockefair, "that when customers were slow and did not pay their bills at maturity but let them run behind they would sooner or later come to trouble. . . . We do not think it wise to continue to do business with people who do not pay their bills promptly."[45] On the basis of salesmen's reports and his own investigations, Fitzgerald established lines of credit for each customer and wrote firm reminders to companies which ordered above their credit ceilings.

The 1916 county tax bill follows:

	rate per $1000	amount
tangible personal property	$1.50	$ 525.00
capital	.70	15,473.23
income	1.00	13,616.54
land, buildings and machinery	1.50	41,909.10
		$71,523.87

[44] The additional tax on 1918 income, plus some unspecified taxes, totaled $412,109, the exact amount of the overpayment on 1920 income, for which interest of $6,076 was refunded. Dan River tried to recover the $391,402 additional tax on 1918 income on the ground that the company had waived the statute of limitations, permitting the reaudit, under duress, inasmuch as the Bureau had threatened to proceed on the basis of a fraudulent return if the company declined to sign the waiver. After years of litigation the Court of Claims found the waiver valid, and the case was closed in 1935 (37 *Federal Reporter* 965; 11 *Federal Supplement* 134).

[45] June 14, 1912. "We do not, as a rule," Fitzgerald wrote a Tennessee dry goods firm, "accept notes in payment of bills, in fact rarely have occasion to pass upon a question of this kind"; but in consideration of "the pleasant relations that have always existed with your good firm" the company accepted the buyer's note for $1,835.

This meticulous attention to credits and collections kept losses on receivables extraordinarily low. Exceptional was the suspension of payments by the G. A. Stafford Company in 1913, but the estimated loss of $35,000 on this account was recovered in later years. The "gigantic" failure of H. B. Claflin Company in 1914 left Dan River with a claim of $7,000; this, too, was repaid by the successor firm. Indeed, in a period of eight years (down to 1920) the write-offs for "bad debts" ($62,949) were less than the amount collected from accounts previously written off as uncollectible ($76,034). The depression of 1920-1921 forced the G. A. Stafford Company and C. B. Haywood and Company into receivership, with unpaid obligations to Dan River totaling $336,000. On account of these and other overdue accounts the company wrote off $343,850 at the end of 1921.

Depreciation

Depreciation enters the cost sheets for the first time in 1910, when it amounted to .71 cent per pound of cloth at Riverside, 1.06 cents per pound of Dan River colored goods, and 1.18 cents per pound of white goods. The minimum values for unit depreciation cost were .64 cent per pound at Riverside (1917), .76 cent for Dan River colored cloth (1915), and .46 on Dan River sheeting (1916). Much higher unit costs, reaching 2.64 cents per pound of cloth at Riverside (1921), are clearly associated with the rapid write-off of fixed assets in a period of falling prices; some of the increase in depreciation cost per unit of output is related to the decline in the volume of production.

Cotton

The following selected data are representative of the variability in the cost of cotton per pound of cloth (cents per pound of cloth):

	Riverside	Dan River (colored)	Dan River (white)
1910	16.12	14.95	14.89
1915	9.52	10.48	10.41
1920	41.08	39.45	42.54
1921	17.97	17.86	18.39

While the statistics reflect primarily the wide fluctuations in the cost of raw cotton, the relationship is not measured precisely, inasmuch as the computations are based on the accountants' "standard" cost of cotton. The auditors proposed several times that cotton cost should be "based on the average cost price of all the cotton in stock"; but the management preferred to stick to "standard" cost, a round figure generally slightly above the price paid for cotton. The discrepancy, however, does not greatly impair year-to-year comparisons of cotton prices and the cost of cloth.

The lowest cost of cotton per pound of product was 9.52 cents (Riverside, 1915), or 49.0 per cent of the total unit cost. Generally, cotton advanced more rapidly than the prices of labor and supplies; and in the extreme case (Dan River's white goods, 1917) cotton constituted 68.5 per cent of the cost of the finished product.

Buying lower grades of cotton was not regarded as a practical way to save money on the cost of producing Dan River fabrics. In 1910 the company ordered "strict middling" for Riverside and "good middling" for Dan River's finer goods. It also purchased 500 bales of "light good middling tinges," with $1''$-$1\frac{1}{16}''$ staple; and when the cotton broker had "more trouble than expected getting grades," Schoolfield advised him: "You are quite right in not shipping the cotton until you get the grade we purchased. . . . We do not need the cotton and are much more interested in the grade and character of the cotton. . . ." Contracts for cotton provided for grade inspection by Henry Roediger, who became Dan River's cotton buyer in 1912, and the arbitration of differences over classification.[46]

One way to hold down the cost of cotton consists in the judicious timing of purchases, in the light of the available information on acreage under cultivation, weather during the growing season, amount of fiber brought to the gins, foreign demand, and a number of other variables— all of which makes it impossible for any individual to claim exact knowledge of the best time to buy. Schoolfield and Fitzgerald learned the art of cotton buying in the school of experience, and the frequency with which they were asked to prognosticate the "cotton situation" indicates that financiers and manufacturers respected their judgment. In 1912 (and probably earlier) the company subscribed to the confidential information service of the National Ginners' Association of Memphis; but Schoolfield doubted that the reports were worth the subscription

[46] Roediger came to Dan River in 1905. In 1914 Schoolfield referred to him as "a very clever and competent young man." At that time he was in charge of receiving and classifying but did not buy any cotton except in company with Fitzgerald or Schoolfield.

price.[47]   Private advices, especially toward the end of the growing
season, came into the Dan River offices from individuals and firms in
touch with conditions in each of the cotton-growing states.   Only a
complete record of prices and quantities purchased, month by month,
would yield an adequate picture of how wisely the management employed the information at its disposal.   No such record exists.

As the mills expanded, a month's supply of cotton required more
storage space.   But the management often deemed it advantageous to
buy cotton in excess of requirements for the orders on hand, and the
building of new cotton warehouses resulted in part from this policy.
"My opinion is," Fitzgerald wrote Schoolfield in the fall of 1912, "that
if the market should drop so that we could get another 1,000 bales of
Strict Middling at 11¢, we ought to buy along moderately, following it
down until we are completely covered, and perhaps a little margin left
over. . . .   I merely submit this as an opinion and will await a further
expression from you before doing anything else, unless there should
be a sudden drop in the market."   In July 1914 the company owned
2,000 bales "against which goods had not been sold"; and the war,
"coming like a clap of thunder in a clear sky," necessitated a drastic reduction of inventory values.   In December 1914 the company had to
explain to W. O. Gay & Company that "your opinion we never bought
cotton in excess of goods sold . . . would be in error, as there are some
seasons of the year and conditions prevailing that it is very desirable and
advantageous for us to carry a larger stock of cotton on hand than
others, but we never buy cotton on speculation to resell, but always
for consumption, but there have been times that we have resold cotton from one party back to the parties from whom we have purchased
and bought from others at the same times more advantageously."

In February 1917 cotton futures declined sharply, while the spot
market held firm.   The company might have taken advantage of the
situation, Schoolfield said, by buying futures; but "we have never
operated on the contract market in this way, finding it much more
satisfactory to buy the actual cotton."   The following year, however,
the company made a neat profit of $379,185 dealing in futures!   Al-

[47] The Association raised the subscription from $100 to $200 a year in 1912, but later
accepted Dan River's offer of $150.   In 1916 the president declared, "if we have to get
the information as to your reports from the newspapers it would seem that the $150
paid you for the same is not wisely spent, as notwithstanding the uncertain condition
on account of heavy rains and storms it seems that we are getting fewer reports from you
than ever before, and unless you give us more satisfactory information than you have
been doing for some weeks past, we most assuredly cannot afford to subscribe to your
reports."

though "not specifically purchased with speculative intent," the auditors explain, "the market was taken advantage of with the above result."[48] In May 1918 Dan River bought on margin 1,500 bales of cotton for October to December delivery. The purchase agreement, based on the October futures price of 24.75 per pound, required the buyer (Dan River) to furnish margin to the cotton merchant if the price dropped more than $10 per bale (the dealer to pay the mill, if the price rose). President Fitzgerald observed: "This is a new departure for us and one with which we have had no experience." By this time Fitzgerald and Roediger had relieved Schoolfield of much of the work of managing cotton purchases. Instead of relying on the speculative "on call" contracts, the mills now entered the futures market to hedge. True hedging requires (*a*) the purchase of futures equivalent to the cotton required for orders of cloth or (*b*) the sale of the futures protecting excess stocks of cotton on hand, as orders are received. But hedges do not furnish sure protection against adverse movements in cotton and cloth prices. A shift in the basis, or the spread between spot and future prices, may also cause losses in the covering transactions. All this the Dan River management learned in 1920, when hedges were closed out at a net loss of $564,864.[49]

Year-end inventories of cotton which had been as low as $328,000 (1914) rose to a peak of almost $4 million in 1919. Inventory values were based on the average price paid for cotton during the preceding year, which in 1919 rose to over 30 cents a pound. The auditors remonstrated: "we are not entirely in agreement with the methods," although "we understand that they conform more or less with the custom of the trade." The 1920 inventory was valued at the closing price on the New York Cotton Exchange on December 31; but the market price exceeded cost at the end of 1921, and the inventory was priced at the average of purchases during the year.

[48] In one transaction (February) the company bought 1,500 bales of July cotton at 30.0726 and sold 1,500 bales of March cotton at 30.8726, making a profit of $60,000.

[49] Experiences of this sort partly explain the unrealistic position of many manufacturers that the government should restrict the use of the cotton exchanges to growers of cotton and manufacturers of cotton goods. There was "no necessary conflict between the manufacturer and the producer" of cotton; but men who had no cotton to sell and never expected to own any manipulated prices to the disadvantage of both groups. See: "The Fight Against the Cotton Grower," *Manufacturers' Record*, March 24, 1910, and *Proceedings of the Fourteenth Annual Convention of the American Cotton Manufacturers' Association* (Charlotte, 1910), pp. 115-123.

Actually, it was hard for a manufacturer to resist "bearish" thoughts. "Won't we be glad," Schoolfield remarked in August 1918, "when this cruel war is over, and can also have a large crop of cotton again?"

Labor

Labor cost per unit of output depends upon (*a*) the price of labor per unit of time or task, (*b*) the quantity of labor employed, and (*c*) the efficiency with which labor is applied to the various processes of manufacture. Unfortunately, the data are lacking for a thorough investigation of these related factors in the wage history of Riverside and Dan River Cotton Mills. Internal records provide only one complete payroll, that for the two weeks ending April 11, 1914, when the earnings of 4,805 employees averaged 13.9 cents an hour. Broken files of time books for Riverside division show the wages of three groups of workers, as follows: in a spinning room earnings rose from 8.3 cents an hour in September 1910 to 9.0 cents in December 1913; in eight weave rooms the average wages of 75-99 workers (including loom fixers) went from 15.3 cents an hour in August 1912 to 17.1 cents in September 1917; and in a carding room earnings increased from 10.5 cents an hour in April 1914 to 12.5 cents in August 1917. Roughly indica-

Table 8. Average Hourly Wages, Sample Room, 1907-21

month and year		number of workers	average wage (cents per hour)
July	1907	7	9.2
Oct.	1908	7	9.0
Oct.	1909	6	9.3
June	1910	7	9.4
July	1911	16	13.2
March	1912	17	14.4
April	1913	14	17.8
March	1914	15	15.8
Sept.	1915	17	16.8
Sept.	1916	19	20.7
Aug.	1917	18	22.2
Feb.	1918	12	26.2
Aug.	1918	10	30.4
March	1919	10	40.5
Sept.	1919	13	41.9
Jan.	1920	13	47.6
May	1920	13	53.2
Dec.	1920	9	37.2
May	1921	12	35.8
July	1921	17	31.9
Oct.	1921	19	35.2
Aug.	1922	18	32.0

tive of the spread in wage rates in August 1918 are the sweeper's rate of 9.0 cents an hour, the filling carrier's 13.5 cents an hour, and the loom fixer's 25 cents an hour. These were base rates, excluding the bonus which was inaugurated in April 1917.

A set (1907-1922) of time books for the sample room furnished the average hourly earnings presented in Table 8. The wages include bonuses and represent the average earnings of a forewoman, a loom fixer, a drawing-in hand, and several piece-card hands. It will be observed that the average for May 1920 (53.2 cents) is more than five times the average of July 1907; a part of the gain is spurious, since the 13 workers in 1920 do not represent the same distribution by jobs as the 7 workers in 1907. The average for August 1922 (32 cents) gives effect to three wage cuts in 1920-1921, but it somewhat overstates the decline in average hourly earnings. Under a system of "Industrial Democracy" economy dividends, ranging from 5 to 10 per cent of wages earned, were distributed every month from August 1919 to the end of 1921.

Average weekly earnings for 1914, 1921, and 1922 were reported to the Federal Reserve Bank of Richmond, as follows:

	1914 (60 hours)	*1921* (55 hours)	*1922* (55 hours)
weavers	$10.60	$24.26	$24.57
spinners	9.48	20.01	20.26
common laborers	6.17	13.95	14.13

These data are obviously incomplete; but for three classes of labor they show that post-war wage reductions left full-time earnings considerably more than twice the prewar level. And the work-week had decreased five hours. One index of the cost of living in the United States registers a rise of 92 per cent between 1910 and 1921; another puts the cost of living 81 per cent higher in 1921 than in 1913.[50] On either basis the real earnings of the Dan River worker made a substantial gain.

Something may be said of the job spread in wage rates, as of October 1919. At the bottom of the ladder were scrubbers and sweepers with a base rate of 9-10 cents per hour. A few other grades of labor were rewarded at these rock-bottom rates, and even a forewoman on the spinning room blow pipes earned only 10 cents an hour. The lower end of the wage ladder was also the colored end. "As regards

[50] *Historical Statistics of the United States*, pp. 235-236.

colored people," President Fitzgerald declared, "we only employ them as sweepers, scourers, truck drivers, and in the dye-house and picker-rooms: we do not have them in the mills proper, except in the above-mentioned menial capacities." The top of the heap—so far as the 1919 data go—was occupied by a shipping-room worker, probably a foreman, at 35.5 cents per hour. Second hands were paid at seven rates between 18 and 30 cents, whereas the highest pay for a head grinder (carding) was 31.5 cents and fixers and overhaulers received up to 27.75 cents per hour. The maximum spread in base hourly rates of pay, therefore, appears to be 26.5 cents; in other words, the highest wage was 295 per cent above the lowest rate. In 1889 the lowest daily wage was 15 cents; the highest, $3.50. In the interval of thirty years some narrowing of the gap between skilled and unskilled wages appears to have taken place, partly as a result of the virtual elimination of child labor. The available data do not measure the phenomenon exactly, as there were undoubtedly some hourly-rated employees in 1919 at rates in excess of 35.5 cents.

In contrast with the paucity of data on absolute changes in wages, abundant information is available on the relative wage levels, as measured by wartime and postwar bonuses. Long before the United States entered the conflict, war in Europe induced an increased demand for American goods, caused prices to rise, and made labor scarce. In the opinion of Dan River executives, an unwise government aggravated the situation. Thus, Wilson's position on the railroad strike, President Schoolfield thought, showed that "the President was representing the labor organizations rather than the people of the United States." In 1918, after the Governor of Virginia had issued a proclamation on the critical need for industrial laborers, H. R. Fitzgerald penned a jingoistic piece entitled, "Go to Work or Go to Jail." It was printed and distributed as a handbill over the signature of the mayor and the chief of police.

The problem of the Danville mills was that of competing with industries engaged in munitions manufacture and shipping, and in an effort to hold its workers Dan River introduced a system of bonus payments. A week before Christmas, 1916, a notice "To the Operatives" announced: "In keeping with the policy of our Company to study the interest of its employees as well as its stockholders, we are glad that circumstances enable us to pay an extra bonus of 5 per cent" on total earnings for the year. The first of a series of regular bonuses was established on April 16, 1917: it was 10 per cent of the base pay of every worker who worked full time at "standard efficiency." But Fitzgerald urged the operatives not to depend on wages to beat the high cost of living—they should plant gardens, avoid extravagance, and work regularly.

A complete record of bonus rates is presented in Table 9. All these changes were "across-the-board" increases (or decreases) of wage rates. In 1916 the raising of wages gave the management an opportunity to make adjustments in different job rates "where irregularities had crept in." Again in 1917, the management told the directors that individual adjustments in rates of pay would be made "in a quiet and confidential way." Probably, the index of bonus payments understates the wartime rise in the average wage.

Table 9.   Relative Changes in Wage Rates, 1917-1921

effective date of change	increase or decrease of "flat" rate	net wage rate: per cent of rate April 1, 1917
Apr. 16, 1917	10 per cent bonus	110.0
Aug. 5, 1917	20 " " "	120.0
Oct. 29, 1917	30 " " "	130.0
Apr. 2, 1918	50 " " "	150.0
Sept. 9, 1918	100 " " "	200.0
Mar. 10, 1919	90 " " "	190.0
Apr. 7, 1919	80 " " "	180.0
May 5, 1919	70 " " "	170.0
May 19, 1919	80 " " "	180.0
July 7, 1919	100 " " "	200.0
Jan. 5, 1920	120 " " "	220.0
Apr. 26, 1920	10 " " "	242.0
Nov. 29, 1920	22.7272 per cent reduction	187.0
May 9, 1921	10 per cent reduction	168.3
Aug. 1, 1921	10 " " "	151.5

Between April and August 1917, Riverside and Dan River Mills lost 500 men to the armed forces. Women were drawn into mill employment in increasing numbers, but the shortage of help persisted.[51] In hopes of making factory work more attractive, four changes in hours and pay were introduced on August 1:

[51] In April 1917 Fitzgerald complained to the secretary of the Chamber of Commerce that labor agents in Danville "probably exceed the scope of their license in their efforts to persuade people who are already employed to leave and go elsewhere."

1. The work week was shortened from 60 to 56 hours, ending at 1:00 P.M. Saturday. For some time workers had been asking for the Saturday half-holiday, in order to shop in downtown Danville. Commenting on the change, Fitzgerald observed that "instead of working longer the other five days, as other mills do, we must overcome the difference as far as possible by keeping the machinery in operation the full actual time and do all that we can to keep up the production by increased efficiency."[52]

2. Hourly rates of pay replaced the practice of paying by the day, half-day, and quarter-day.

3. The company began to pay wages every Saturday, instead of fortnightly.

4. The bonus was increased to 20 per cent.

The net effect of these changes was an increase of 1.8 per cent in full-time weekly earnings for a week of 6.7 per cent fewer hours.

In October 1917 the bonus rose to 30 per cent (20 per cent for those who reported less than full time); and in April 1918 it jumped to 50 per cent, which, the president said, "stopped somewhat the exodus of our help." Finally, in September 1918 notice of the increase in the bonus to 100 per cent was posted, with the admonition: "Back up our Boys who have gone to the Front. Truly your friends. Riverside & Dan River Cotton Mills, Inc." But the president told the directors that the management had delayed raising wages as long as possible. With machinists earning $8-10 a day in the shipyards, it was almost impossible to keep loom fixers in the cotton mills for $3.75; and Dan

[52] But Fitzgerald wrote a fellow-manufacturer that "our action was based not upon any desire to get away from the sixty hours . . . . furthermore, it is my impression that our people would have been perfectly willing and satisfied to have worked the sixty hours on the same schedule that you are using [in North Carolina] . . . . we have very grave doubt that any of us are acting wisely to go too far toward reducing the number of working hours. . . . While under present prosperous conditions . . . the mill people can of course afford to work the shorter hours, when the inevitable time comes for adjustment . . . it will be found that our working people cannot earn a sufficient amount to supply their needs and give them prosperous conditions by working such a small part of their time. . . .

"It is all very well in theory from the politician's or the labor agitator's standpoint, to talk about eight hours per day but if our farmers and a great many of our manufacturers were only allowed to work eight hours at their trade I think you would find that it would make a vast difference in the result of their achievements, and if either you or I personally were not allowed to work longer than eight hours, we would feel the difference very quickly."

As for office workers, the management was content to let the "honor system" prevail. If the work were finished, office employees might have Saturday afternoon off; otherwise, they would "stick to their work as long as . . . necessary." Fitzgerald frowned upon the "habit of a few of our men" of unduly prolonging the dinner hour, which broke the normal 8:00 A.M. to 6:30 P.M. office day.

River had to meet the competition of "some southern mills" which had already advanced fixers and machinists to $5 a day. It would have been less expensive, Fitzgerald told the board, to adjust rates of pay job by job, according to the non-mill demand for various grades of labor; but this procedure would tend to disturb the parity of "long-established relations between certain classes of work," lead to inequalities between departments of the mill, and make it difficult to secure readjustments when conditions returned to normal.

The postwar lull in business prompted the first downward revision of wages at Dan River. Commencing in March 1919 the bonus was to drop 10 points each month until it reached 50 per cent. "We sincerely hope," the management said, "that conditions may never again make it necessary to go back to the old rates paid before the war."[53] For two weeks in May the bonus fell to 70 per cent; it was held at 80 per cent through June; but in July, "in the spirit of 'Industrial Democracy' and realizing that the cost of living is still high," the 100 per cent bonus was restored. There was another reason for increasing wages at this time. In letters to nine mill executives, requesting information on their pay scales for loom fixers, Fitzgerald announced that Dan River had just raised the fixer's pay from $25.20 to $30.80 (for 56 hours), because management "saw that something would have to be done to avoid friction." With this increase, Fitzgerald believed, the Dan River loom fixer's wage was "above what other mills in our section are paying."

Business prospects brightened, and in its New Year's greetings (1920) to employees the company announced new wage rates. Existing "flat" rates increased by 120 per cent became new "flat" rates and bonuses were dropped. In addition, the company paid for group life insurance, the amount of insurance ranging from $500 for those employed less than a year to $1,500 for workers on the payroll ten years or more.

The last of the increases in pay in this period followed recommendations of a joint payroll investigating committee of the Industrial Democracy organization. Bills passed by the Senate and the House of Representatives resolved, "That a premium offer of 10% increase in

[53] In "strict confidence" Fitzgerald sent a copy of the bonus-reduction notice to the treasurer of the Martinsville Cotton Mills (and probably to other mills). As early as December 1918 Dan River's president suggested to another mill executive that four or five mills get together for "a little confidential talk among ourselves with a view of trying to solve the question [of the wage bonus] intelligently and of course without any attempt to bind the action of any one but merely in the spirit of mutual co-operation and helpfulness." The records fail to disclose whether the proposed conference was held.

wages be made to all Operatives . . . who have in full time each week
. . . and that this premium offer is to remain in force so long as business
conditions justify, the said premium offer to begin with Monday, April
26th, 1920." The management approved, and wage rates approximately 142 per cent above the 1917 level were effective for six months.

Hard on the heels of a general business recession, the retreat of
wages commenced in November. The 10 per-cent premium was
lopped off, then the flat rate was cut 15 points, which amounted to a
reduction of 22.7272 per cent (the figure used by the paymasters). This
decrease in wages, like the raise in April, went through the "legislature." The preamble to the resolution on wage reduction reasoned
that "In the spirit of Industrial Democracy we should accept as gladly
and unselfishly the movement toward deflation as we formerly displayed
when advances were made, recognizing that as deflation progresses the
purchasing power of the dollar increases." A circular-poster (No. 80)
signed by the president expressed regret over the necessity of cutting
wages, but "to those who have Industrial Democracy in their hearts,
we are confident it is unnecessary to assure them that your Management earnestly desires to protect the interests of our people and to
keep them employed at as good wages as we possibly can . . . if there are
any that are not satisfied . . . we shall ask them to kindly notify their
Overseer promptly and receive their time." Concurring in management's view that the "continued and unprecedented drop in the market value of cotton goods" necessitated further economies, in May 1921
the "legislature" accepted a 10 per-cent wage cut; and another reduction of 10 per cent, authorized by the Senate and House, went into
effect in August. The last reduction in pay was postponed for several
weeks, on the ground that "the cost of living has not come down in our
community as fast as it has in many others."

A further consideration of the effect of wage changes is suggested by
the data on labor costs per unit of output. In Table 10 three sets of
unit labor costs have been reduced to index numbers on the same base
as the index of wage rates for 1917-1921.

Most striking is the tendency of unit labor cost on white goods to
move ahead of the increases in wage rates, creating a spread of 44.9
percentage points at the 1920 peak; and when wages drop, in 1920-1921,
unit labor cost falls less rapidly. In the latter part of 1921 the labor
cost per pound of product was 124 per cent above the cost in early
1917, although wage rates stood only 52 per cent above the 1917 level.

Table 10. Indexes of Wages and Productivity
(January-March, 1917 = 100)

period		wage rates	labor cost per unit of output		
				Dan River	
			Riverside	colored	white
Jan.-April	1917	100.0	100.0	100.0	100.0
April-Aug.	1917	110.0	109.2	108.1	113.1
Aug.-Oct.	1917	120.0	117.3	110.0	129.2
Oct.-April	1918	130.0	144.9	128.9	147.6
April-Sept.	1918	150.0	171.7	152.8	195.0
Sept.-March	1919	200.0	239.7	214.7	260.7
March-April	1919	190.0	224.8	205.6	245.6
April-May	1919	180.0	212.3	193.7	230.2
May-July	1919	180.0	215.7	204.4	237.1
July-Jan.	1920	200.0	237.6	216.2	246.0
Jan.-April	1920	220.0	257.6	225.6	257.7
April.-Nov.	1920	242.0	278.2	256.7	286.9
Nov.-May	1921	187.0	276.0	196.6	247.4
May-Aug.	1921	168.3	277.8	193.6	236.1
Aug.-Dec.	1921	151.5	231.4	174.7	224.2

As explained above, the wage index tends to understate the rate of increase in labor cost. After making a reasonable allowance for this discrepancy, it seems to me that the statistics furnish clear evidence of the relative inefficiency of labor in a period of violently fluctuating wages and prices, aggravated by scarcities of supplies and high labor turnover. In the case of Dan River white goods, no significant upgrading of the product accounts for the higher labor costs; in fact, the management admitted a deterioration of quality during the war years. On the other hand, some of the discrepancy between the relative changes in wages and unit labor costs on colored goods do represent important shifts in the proportion of fine and coarse goods: thus, more labor per unit of product was required for ginghams, manufactured at Riverside in 1921 but not in 1917.

Relatively, as Table 11 suggests, direct labor costs shifted considerably over the decade between 1910 and 1920. The data, of course, measure simultaneously the effects of technological improvement, alterations in the wage structure, and the varying efficiency of different types of labor. One cannot be sure, for instance, that the drop in the cost of dressing Dan River's white goods from 14.2 per cent to 6.0 per

Table 11. Percentage Distribution of Direct Labor Costs, 1910 and 1920

	Riverside		Dan River colored goods		white goods	
	1910	1920	1910	1920	1910	1920
carding	12.8	15.8	14.0	12.9	12.5	13.6
spinning	14.1	15.0	15.1	14.6	14.5	17.3
dressing	10.2	11.5	9.8	11.4	14.2	6.0
weaving	48.7	34.8	42.9	39.9	34.6	42.1
cloth	5.7	6.1	7.2	10.0	2.6	3.2
repairs	5.3	9.7	4.3	5.0	5.4	3.9
electricity	0	1.0	1.5	1.3	1.8	1.1
samples	0	1.0	0	0	0	0
blowing	0	.5	0	0	0	0
dyeing	3.2	4.6	5.2	3.8	0	0
bleaching	0	0	0	0	8.8	5.6
sewing	0	0	0	0	5.6	7.2
designing	0	0	0	1.1	0	0
	100.0	100.0	100.0	100.0	100.0	100.0

cent of all direct labor costs developed mainly from the substitution of drawing-in machines for hand work; but the magnitude of the change favors this presumption. It is less easy to offer an explanation of the relatively large increase in the cost of weaving labor on white goods, although references to the lowered quality of Dan River sheeting during and after the war suggest a rise in the average age of looms in these mills and a corresponding reduction in labor efficiency. The share of total labor costs borne by the four processes of carding, spinning, dressing, and weaving for white goods was 79.0 per cent in 1920, as compared with 75.8 per cent in 1910. In the colored-goods divisions, where new styles and finer fabrics made new equipment imperative, labor in carding, spinning, dressing, and weaving represented 85.8 per cent (Riverside) and 81.8 per cent (Dan River) of total labor costs in 1910 but only 77.1 per cent and 78.8 per cent, respectively, in 1920.

Child labor virtually disappeared in the period covered by this chapter, but the influence of this factor upon costs is indeterminate. Moving several years in advance of neighboring states, in 1914 Virginia prohibited the factory employment of children under fourteen and limited the work of persons under sixteen years to ten hours a day.[54]

[54] The 10-hour law applied to women, too. According to an anonymous letter to the president (1920), women and girls commonly worked 11 hours in contravention of the

In 1920 the state imposed an eight-hour day for workers under sixteen and in 1922 limited their work week to forty-four hours.[55] The federal Keating-Owen Act, which became effective September 1, 1917, banned the employment of minors under seventeen years of age but provided a system of certification for hardship cases. President Fitzgerald observed that the company employed "not a great many children between the ages of 14 and 16. . . . Frankly, we have endeavored for many years to have as few as possible of this age, but of course it is highly desirable not only on account of the practical necessity for the family for children of this age to work but also because of the training which at this age is a very important part of their education." After September 1917 Dan River employed workers under seventeen only in the spinning rooms: these were children with federal work certificates and they worked only half a day (five hours).[56]

The earnings of women, according to the management, were "practically as good as the men." There was lacking a "system of promotion for women to managerial positions," but the company was studying the problem of training women who aspired to the supervisory positions traditionally reserved for men.

Until the passage of Virginia's workmen's compensation act of 1918, injured workers received first-aid and such additional medical attention as was provided under the contract between the mill and a private insurance carrier.[57] No provision was made for the compensation of lost

---

state law. Attorney Harris gave his opinion that the company could not legally contract with women and children to work more than 10 hours, but such workers might *voluntarily* allow their machines to run through the lunch hour and so increase their earnings.
[55] E. H. Davidson, *Child Labor Legislation in the Southern Textile States* (Chapel Hill, N. C., 1939), pp. 244-246.
[56] In April 1917 Fitzgerald wrote to the Secretary of Labor, protesting the introduction of a child-labor law during the war. Though labor was exceedingly scarce, he pointed out, mills would have to do without the fourteen-sixteen year-old workers because of the practical inconvenience of operating 10 hours a day and letting the younger workers quit after 8 hours. In a letter to Senator Claude Swanson (April 14, 1917) the president said: "If the Keating-Owen child labor bill is to go into effect . . . all of the mills will practically have to discontinue employing any help between the ages of 14 and 16 years, as they will be unable to observe the eight-hour clause in employing that class of labor without introducing great lost motion"—i.e., because some of the labor force would leave at the end of 8 hours, while the mills kept running for ten.
In 1916 the company paid David Clark, secretary-treasurer of the Southern Cotton Manufacturers, $500 for lobbying against federal child-labor legislation. In 1918, after the Supreme Court found the Keating-Owen law unconstitutional, Fitzgerald complimented Clark for his "splendid fight. . . . You certainly are to be congratulated on the result of your work in having the law annulled, and I earnestly hope that you will continue the fight, as it would be extremely unfortunate to lose the ground we have gained and to have this bill come up in some other form."
[57] Writing to a private physician who presented a bill for services to an injured worker, President Fitzgerald declared (Aug. 31, 1917): "In case of accident, we are authorized by the Accident Company to obtain what is called first aid treatment . . . . for

time or disability. Prior to the act of 1918, the corporation enjoyed the common-law defenses of negligence, contributory negligence, and assumption of risk; and it was not easy for a worker to press a successful suit for compensation.[58] The 1918 law required employers to carry insurance (or to self-insure) to cover the cost of medical care, hospitalization, and scheduled benefits for dismemberment and disability.[59] In 1921 Dan River's president declared the workmen's compensation act "quite satisfactory, but it is my impression that representatives of organized labor are making an effort . . . to stretch the principle involved and to make the law more drastic."

Only the following scattered data on accidents have been uncovered (number of accidents):

	Riverside	Dan River
1914	69	213
1916	55	213
1918	69	123
1919		195

Of the 195 workers injured at Dan River in 1919, four did not return to work, 88 lost no time, and 103 lost a total of 10,060 hours of work.

Officers, Directors, and Stockholders

The officers prepared the directors' report to the stockholders, including an abbreviated financial statement, which was read at the stockholders' meeting. The annual reports, showing operating results and earnings in detail, circulated among the officers of the company;

any subsequent treatment, however, we are not authorized to furnish the service unless it is a case in which the Accident Company is liable.

"You can, of course, appreciate that in most of these minor cases the accident is due to negligence or want of reasonable care on the part of the injured party. . . . We could not undertake to be responsible for treatment rendered to such cases except upon authorization given by us."

[58] In 1912 the company chose to settle out of court (for $200 each) two suits instituted by two women injured at work. A watchman, required as a part of his duties to oil machinery, was injured in a cog wheel. Alleging negligence on the part of the employer, the watchman sued in the Corporation Court of Danville, which found in his favor; but the decision was reversed by the Supreme Court (*Cases Decided in the Supreme Court of Virginia,* vol. 113 [Richmond, 1913], pp. 346-352. On the other hand, when the chief electrician was badly injured, in 1917, the company reimbursed him for the loss of wages (about $500), while the insurance company paid his hospital and medical bills.

[59] Industrial Commission of Virginia, *The Virginia Workmen's Compensation Act* (Richmond, 1938).

but this information was not made available to stockholders. Commencing in 1910, the books were audited annually by the New York firm of Barrow, Wade, Guthrie & Company.

Condensed earnings statements were sent to the banks from which the company borrowed; and a two-page printed folder, "struck off merely as a matter of convenience for some of the Stockholders who ask for 'A financial statement of the Company,'" showed a much abbreviated balance sheet. In answer to a stockholder who thought he deserved more information, Fitzgerald replied: "We . . . beg to assure you that there is no disposition whatever on our part to withhold from the Stockholders any information pertaining to the affairs of the Company, on the contrary we endeavor to report fully all items of interest to the Stockholders at their annual meeting, and in addition to this either the President or some member of the Board of Directors frequently invites the Stockholders to ask any questions that they may desire and it gives us pleasure to acquaint them fully with the affairs of the Company. . . ."

"We do not," Fitzgerald continued, "make any statement for publication and it has never been the policy of the Company to give out to the public information pertaining to its private affairs, nor has any provision ever been made for mailing out to the Stockholders, who were absent from the annual meeting, such information, for the reason . . . that in many instances it would be giving information to competitors and to the public at large."[60] In 1912 the company did send to a Richmond stockholder a carbon copy of the directors' report to the stockholders, with the request that it be kept confidential.

Only six of the twelve directors in 1910 remained on the board at the end of 1921. E. S. Reid died in May 1910, and R. A. James, owner and editor of the Danville *Register,* was elected in his stead. In September 1910 J. N. Wyllie, though regretting "the necessity which forces this step," sold his stock in the company and resigned as director. William H. White, president of the Richmond, Fredericksburg, and Potomac Railroad, took Wyllie's place in January 1911.

In August 1913 J. R. Jopling died; and in October of the same year, B. F. Jefferson, one of the founders, passed away. John I. Pritchett

---

[60] Until 1921 *Moody's Analyses of Investments* carried nothing more than the name of the officers and directors of the company and kinds and amounts of stock outstanding. Fitzgerald objected (Feb. 2, 1918) to the proposed publication in this investment manual of "private information that the Company does not care to have published." Beginning with the 1921 issue Moody published balance sheets obtained from the company.

resigned for personal reasons. The three vacancies were filled by Edwin T. Lamb, an official of the Southern Railway Company, and Julian C. Jordan and W. B. Hill, Danville businessmen.

Lamb died in November 1919; J. H. Schoolfield, a founder and vice-president of the company, died in February 1920; and White died six months later. These vacancies were not filled; and in January 1921 the directors voted to keep the board at nine members.

James died in 1921, while serving his first term in Congress. His successor was Malcolm K. Harris, who had succeeded Peatross as attorney for the Company about 1912.

New by-laws adopted in 1910 required a meeting of the directors at least once every three months. Those who were not salaried officers received $25 for each attendance at a board meeting.[61]

The president and the secretary-treasurer received $20,000 each in 1910, but in 1911 they asked for, and received, a $5,000 raise. Schoolfield's letter to the board (pasted into the directors' minutes) furnishes a number of interesting sidelights on management in this period:

DANVILLE, VA. Jan'y 26th, 1911

To the Board of Directors:
   I dislike to mention the question of Salary, but I feel that I owe it to myself and to Mr. Fitzgerald, to state to you in a candid and businesslike way, our feelings in the matter. For many years past, both of us have given the Company about the best we had in us, and our record speaks for itself as to what has been accomplished, with your cooperation and the guidance of a kind Providence.

   Some of you are doubtless not in a position to fully appreciate the large amount of work and energy that has been expended, but if you would go over the property, and see what has been and is being done, and the amount of judgment and constant vigilance required to accomplish it I can but feel that you would see the justice of our position.

   Your business is now a very large one, and its responsibilities are heavy and exacting. The complicated market conditions through which we have passed during the last few years, have been a pretty good test of the strength of your organization, and while I am far from any spirit of boasting, I feel safe in saying that I do not believe you could have gotten, for the same amount of money, the services that we have rendered.

   During last year, I was talking with a Gentleman, who is largely interested in a number of Mills, having a total capacity about the same as yours; he told me that these Mills paid their Commission men for selling their

[61] *By-laws of the Stockholders of the Riverside & Dan River Cotton Mills Incorporated* (Danville, 1910). In 1920 the directors agreed not to accept this stipend when the purpose of the meeting was to draw up a resolution upon the death of a member of the board.

goods alone, about $300,000 per annum. These Mills were only running four days per week, and kept up the curtailment for a long period. Your Mills were run, without curtailment, and your years work was fairly profitable, whereas your total expense for Salaries of your executive Officers, Office Force, Salesmen, Superintendents and Designers was less than two percent of your sales.

It is not a small thing to develop and organize so large a business, purchase its supplies, and attend to the many details of manufacturing its goods, provide its financial needs, seek out the varied avenues of trade in which to sell its products at a profit, and carry all the while, by night as well as by day, the responsibilities incident to the well-being of your stockholders on the one hand, and your several thousand employees on the other.

Without claiming any patent upon the ingenuity or quality of judgment necessary to accomplish these things, I am certain that no one with sufficient capacity to do them, would undertake it for the amount of salary you have paid us, and I do not feel that we are asking anything unreasonable or that we are not entitled to, in requesting that you make our salaries $25,000 each.

Last year, we both felt that we are getting less salary than our efforts deserved, but recognizing the conditions and that your new Mill had not been completed, I refrained from saying anything to you about it. Another thing, I do not want the Board to feel that we expect or want an increase of salary every year, and if you prefer to fix upon it for say three or five years, it will be agreeable to me.

Your officers appreciate the cordial and harmonious support of each member of the Board, but in considering this question, I ask that you eliminate entirely any personal considerations, and act purely in accordance with your business judgment, as to the interests of the Company that you represent.

Very respectfully,
R. A. SCHOOLFIELD

I have found no evidence that other companies sought the services of either Schoolfield or Fitzgerald; but this is not the sort of thing one would expect to find in the company's files. In 1912 Schoolfield answered a proposal to erect a cotton mill in Chattanooga with the terse comment: "We are sufficiently amused with our undertaking in Danville and would have no time to devote to interests elsewhere." The following year the president informed Thomas Branch & Company that he would not be interested in "taking up properties away from home at this time . . . we think that the interests of our stockholders can be best served at this time by our undivided attention to their interests here." These relate, apparently, to suggestions for expansion outside of Danville; but they carry the implication that both officials considered themselves unexpendable and immobile.

In January 1916 the directors increased the salaries of Schoolfield and Fitzgerald to $35,000 a year, retroactive to January 1915. Both officers declined the five-per cent bonus paid to all other employees at the end of 1916, but they did accept the bonuses paid from 1917 on. Fitzgerald also received $30,000 for extra work in connection with the building of Mill No. 8. The 1921 salaries of the chairman and president were $56,218.75 each, and in 1922 Fitzgerald's (but not Schoolfield's) pay was raised to $65,000. This year Ray's salary was $40,000, Vice-president Jordan's (his was a nominal position), $3,200, and Secretary Ayres', $12,000.

Previously, in January 1918, the president had recommended changes in management "in order to provide for any contingencies." Schoolfield assumed the new position of chairman of the board of directors, retaining however general supervision of all company affairs; Fitzgerald became president, but also retained his post as treasurer; and W. W. Ayres was promoted to the office of secretary. The changes were approved by the stockholders and the by-laws amended accordingly.[62] Underneath the formal changes was the gradual shift in the relative positions of the two men who had managed the firm for two decades. During periods of Schoolfield's illness, as in the winter of 1918-1919, Fitzgerald was *de facto* chief executive of the company; and growing friction between the two men foreshadowed the waning influence of Schoolfield—the nemesis of his earlier triumph over an elder Fitzgerald.

[62] *By-laws of the Stockholders of the Riverside & Dan River Cotton Mills Incorporated* (Danville, 1918).

4. *Elusive Prosperity and a Crisis, 1922-1931*

In the ten years following the sharp postwar depression of 1920-1921—the fifth decade in the company's history—Riverside and Dan River Cotton Mills experienced reverses unequaled in the preceding forty years. Although physical output rose to a peak of almost 40 million pounds in 1927, production in 1929-1931 was less than in 1919-1921. Sales topped $24.5 million in 1923, but the average for the next eight years barely exceeded $15 million. In 1922-1923 earnings almost reached the wartime level, but in 1924 the company reported a loss—the first in its history—of over $900,000. Labor unrest, which complicated the futile efforts to reduce costs and secure markets at profitable prices, finally exploded in the strike of September 1930. The excitement of this unfortunate affair had scarcely subsided when, on February 24, 1931, President Harrison Robertson Fitzgerald died. His father, Thomas Benton Fitzgerald, had died in December 1929; and on October 25, 1931, death claimed Robert Addison Schoolfield, the last of the founders. The reorganization of management after Fitzgerald's death, the collapse of Industrial Democracy, and the passing of dividends on preferred stock (for the first time since it was issued in 1893) constitute landmarks uniquely convenient as the terminal date of the present chapter. To keep it within manageable length, however, the discussion of the program of welfare and labor relations developed under the name of Industrial Democracy has been left to the fifth chapter.

Improvements

In seven of the ten years ending with 1931 the cost of improvements fell short of the reduction in fixed-asset values arising from depreciation and retirements. In 1922 new buildings and machinery represented an outlay of $1,833,442, precisely the amount written off as depreciation. In round figures, the net increase in real estate and machinery accounts was $1,125,000 in 1923 and $225,000 in 1930; but at the end of 1931 the depreciated value of the plant ($17,972,802) was only $345,000 greater than at the end of 1921. Other asset values for the period are shown in the balance-sheet summaries (Appendix 1).

The business outlook at the beginning of 1922 encouraged the president to recommend important improvements in both spinning and weaving. At Dan River's No. 3 Mill 1,488 belt-driven looms were changed to direct drive at a cost of $125,000. Savings of $25,000 a year, it was estimated, would be achieved through a 10 per-cent increase in output, a 14 per-cent decrease in the number of weavers, and a 20 per-cent drop in unit cost of production. Similarly, the exchange of 820 belt-driven looms in No. 2 weave shed for new 90-inch sheeting looms (at a cost of $450,000) promised an annual saving of $41,500, since output would rise by a third while the number of workers dropped by a third and the unit cost fell by 40 per cent. Another $25,000 was spent to equip 1,591 Draper looms with improved warp-stop motions.

Labor troubles in New England mills created an opportunity to acquire from Saco-Lowell Shops new opening, carding, roving, and spinning machinery "at an attractive basis." A half-million dollar order, placed in August 1922, called for openers, breakers, slubbers, 7 intermediate fly frames, 33 fine fly frames, 2 jack frames, and 66 ring spindle frames. Space for this new equipment was provided by raising the roof (literally) and adding a story to Dan River's Mill No. 2. The high cost of this unusual construction job was defended on the ground that it made possible a more economical machinery lay-out. Looms purchased in 1922 "in order to better enable us to handle the gingham lines," included 581 Crompton & Knowles automatic box looms. Since old-style looms were a drug on the market, the manufacturer allowed Dan River to keep the looms traded in and store them in the basement of No. 4 weave shed. "At such time as we can run them advantageously, we can do so," Fitzgerald said. Parenthetically, this opportunity never came.

The contract for Mill No. 5 was awarded to the J. P. Pettyjohn Company of Lynchburg in June 1922. Constructed on the basis of cost plus 8 per cent, the new five-story bleachery and finishing plant, with an adjoining kier building, represented an investment of over $900,000[1] Machinery and power installations cost another $300,000, while additions to the steam plant and generating equipment required almost $200,000. The need for improved bleaching and finishing facilities was explained to the stockholders in January 1923: "From the fact that the coarse-yarn goods have continued to sell at very close prices, the policy of your Management has been to work more and more toward the finer grades and we have moved in that direction even faster than your machinery equipment justified, which has made necessary a good deal of night work." Because of the "very limited space of our Cloth Rooms and the lack of sufficient equipment for bleaching and finishing . . . it was imperative to meet this requirement by the construction of a modern bleaching and finishing plant." The new plant necessitated an increased water supply, and in 1922-1924 almost $200,000 was spent on a new pump house, improvements of the filter plant, a 300,000-gallon hemispherical storage tank, and additions to the sprinkler system. In the following seven years, 1925-1931, capital expenditures on the water supply, filter systems, and fire protection amounted to less than $25,000.

Construction carried out in 1923 included a $60,000 supplies warehouse and an addition to the No. 3 cloth hall at Dan River division. A new weave room was provided by excavating under Mill No. 4. At Riverside Division an addition to Mill No. 5 was designed to hold about $200,000 worth of new machinery. A new cotton storage house

[1] Costs ran high because of last-minute changes in the plans, including the addition of a fifth floor. In June the directors voted Pettyjohn extra compensation of $21,246, considering the fact that certain losses on the contract were beyond his control.

was erected at Mill No. 6, and Mills 1, 4, and 6 were equipped for electric power.

The decision to turn toward the manufacture of fancier, finer, and wider cloth led to large purchases of new equipment for weaving. In 1923 orders were placed with Stafford for 128 Model K-1 73-inch looms and 22 Model CA-1 32-inch looms.[2] Early in 1924, after the president had explained the necessity of replacing the Draper looms with up-to-date box looms in order to increase the proportion of fine goods manufactured at Riverside division, Crompton & Knowles accepted an order for 1,008 automatic (43.5-inch) looms at a price of $419,000 (after deducting a trade-in allowance on old Draper looms of $104,000).[3] In January 1925 the directors approved the expenditure of $300,000 for 625 Crompton & Knowles 36-inch four-box automatic looms equipped with 16-harness dobbies to replace 695 narrow looms in Dan River's No. 1 weave shed. At the same time over 1,700 dobbies (8-, 12-, and 16-harness) were acquired from Stafford and Crompton & Knowles to equip the older looms for weaving fancy patterns. On several occasions substantial sums were spent on parts to widen the older looms in order to meet the demand for dress goods and suiting in 32- and 36-inch widths.

Meanwhile, several additions and improvements had been made in the preparatory machinery. In 1923 Saco-Lowell received orders for new opening machinery, 29 cards, 72 spinning frames, and 4 beam warpers for Dan River's No. 2 Mill. The Whitin Machine Works delivered 8 long-chain quilling machines, and Brandwood supplied new continuous raw-stock dyeing machinery. Patented starching and back-filling mangles and drying cylinders were purchased from the English firm of Hampson and Kelsall.

In order to supply its customers with better finished dress goods, in 1925 Riverside division commenced to bleach some of its colored cloth. Two 8-beam bleaching plants, using the Brandwood process, were acquired from the patentee at a cost of $45,000. It was in 1925 also that Dan River began to use rayon yarns, having acquired 40 gangs of 20-spindle winding machines for quilling rayon.[4]

[2] The smaller order amounted to only $5,500, after deducting the trade-in value of $50 for each old loom. Actually, the old looms were broken up and the scrap sold for $101.50.

[3] Since the wider looms took up the space occupied by 1,170 27- and 36-inch Draper looms, only 1,008 looms were traded in. The rest were stored in Dan River's Mill No. 4.

[4] Superintendent Robertson visited a number of North Carolina mills using "artificial silk" and reported a "most profitable" trip. "If we wish to go into the silk combination,"

In January 1925 the two divisions of Riverside and Dan River Mills had installed 467,400 spindles and 13,530 looms.

Capital expenditures of only $188,565 in 1926—$350,000 less than the amount written off for depreciation—were the lowest for any year in the decade. The following year (1927) several major improvements were realized. At Riverside, 400 new looms, costing almost $100,000, were set up in Mill No. 2, and automatic spoolers were installed in Mill No. 6. Seven 120-spindle spoolers and seven high-speed warpers were put in Dan River's Mill No. 2 in order to improve the quality of the warps used in wide sheeting. The new Barber-Colman spoolers and warpers, President Fitzgerald explained, would save money as well as produce better yarn. With an investment of $100,000, he estimated, the labor cost would be cut in half at a saving of $20,000 a year. Space for some of the new machinery was provided by building a three-story structure connecting No. 4 weave shed with Dan River's Mill No. 4.

In January 1928 Fitzgerald discussed several changes at Dan River Division which seemed to him urgent. "Our policy," he reminded the directors, "has always been and we think the wisdom of it has been fully vindicated, especially during the past few years, to keep your plant in excellent physical condition and to make it as elastic as we reasonably can with a view to the maximum of manufacturing efficiency and economy." The improvement recommended, and promptly approved by the board, included excavating under No. 1 and No. 2 weave sheds to make room for 542 new looms. Another floor was added to the picker building of No. 1 Mill while the preparatory machinery was rearranged so as to leave the third floor free for new carding and roving machinery. An immediate objective was to "cultivate a somewhat higher class of goods and gradually get away from our dependence upon Ginghams to such a large extent for our box looms."

Riverside division obtained 140 new 32-inch looms in 1928 as well as additional spoolers and warpers—about $125,000 worth of new machinery in all—but when the president recommended (May 1928) the purchase of 756 second-hand looms, R. A. Schoolfield demurred and the proposal was dropped. In September, however, Fitzgerald con-

---

he said, "I have no fear but that we can master it." Ray felt that there were "too many people" making rayon goods but favored trying out one line of rayons "in a small way, so we can get our experience without going in too deep" (G. P. Ray to H. R. Fitzgerald, Sept. 12, 1925).

vinced the directors that something had to be done about the "heavy
trend toward printed goods" and the problem faced by mills like
Dan River that had a large proportion of box looms. Early in 1929
the Company ordered 604 of Draper's new high speed Model X
looms, costing $233,675.[5] The mills still had 1,257 non-automatic
box looms which could not be run economically, but within a year
or so half of these were sold and replaced by 686 new Draper looms.
No other loom orders were placed until late in 1931, although over
1,000 old looms were widened to produce 36- and 40-inch cloth.

Engineering and Research

As cotton manufacturing entered the doldrums, textile engineering approached full employment; and, judging by the dusty tomes
tossed into the attic archives, Dan River was a good customer of the
engineers. One of the most extensive studies is the "Survey Report
of the Riverside Division" made by Textile Development Company
in 1925. In general, the consultants found the mills "very efficiently
run", while the physical condition of the looms was judged "better
than in any mill previously surveyed." Proposed improvements in
the organization of spinning promised to increase yarn output 17.7
per cent (from 271,300 pounds to 319,347 pounds per 55 hours)[6] and
effect a payroll saving of $2,282 per week, despite an increase of 10
per cent in the wages of all workers whose tasks were changed or
increased.

Recommended changes in production included: running all cotton
through the bale breakers and vertical openers; making cotton mixes
from not less than ten bales; drying dyed stock thoroughly to keep
damp cotton out of the pickers; using uniform standards for machine
speeds, drafts, and twisting; and keeping records of output per spindle,
efficiency ratios in spinning and weaving, and percentages of waste.
Further improvements were to be carried out after tests of washing
and lubricating in the dye house, causes of breakage in dyeing, size
and moisture content on the slashers, causes of poor yarn in creeling,

[5] Draper's Model X line, introduced in 1929, increased loom speeds from 160 to over
200 picks per minute. Although Draper had been making automatic looms for over 30
years, as late as 1929 over one fourth of the country's 483,653 looms were non-automatic
types (S. J. Kennedy, *Profits and Losses in Textiles*, p. 165).

[6] Or 313,085 pounds of cloth per week from 154,528 spindles and 4,595 looms. Temporarily, the stepped-up production of yarn would have made it necessary to operate 500
looms on a 60-hour night shift.

spooling, and knotting. With a very small investment in new equipment but with more effective control of operations, labor could be "extended." Thus, if loom stoppage were cut in half—it averaged 1.2 stops per loom hour—the weaver could be "stretched" from 48 to 64 Draper looms. The number of spinners would be reduced by more than 50 per cent. Most of the weavers eliminated would be employed as battery hands, while spinners thrown out of this employment would be hired as machine cleaners.[7]

In the fall of 1928 Textile Development made a similar survey of Dan River's Mill No. 2. In this instance, as at Riverside, the engineers found the mill "in unusually good condition . . . exceptionally well run, and . . . well managed in every respect." One of its "greatest weaknesses" was found in the cotton mixes, which one day averaged more than the specified staple and another day, less. "The survey is not asking that *better* cotton be bought, but that the present cotton be laid down and blended so that the mixes, from day to day, will be more even." There were also comparatively minor deficiencies in machinery, which contributed to the uneven quality of the yarn and sheetings produced in this mill. Extended spinning and weaving were recommended—but only after improving the machinery lay-out and processing—in order to realize a saving in wages of $977 per week.

After several years of absence from Danville, Lockwood, Greene[8] (now styled Lockwood, Greene Engineers) returned in 1928 to study the reorganization of Riverside Division. The object of the investigation was to "suggest any changes in yarn, fabrics, machinery and other equipment, also labor, to produce more marketable merchandise at a lower cost." The engineers concluded that Mills 1 and 4, the oldest buildings in the Riverside group, should be abandoned; although their alternative suggestion was to retain Mill No. 4 as a waste mill. The latter recommendation was accepted, and in 1930-1931 new machinery was acquired to process waste for the manufacture of three-ply no. 8 yarn.[9]

[7] J. E. Sirrine & Company also made a loom reorganization study for Dan River division in 1927.
[8] Asked why he had not called on Lockwood, Greene since 1922, Fitzgerald wrote Edwin F. Greene (March 7, 1928) that he could hardly expect "our worst competitor" to be Dan River's confidential adviser and engineer. Through control of several mills, including Pacific Mills, Lockwood, Greene competed with Dan River in manufacturing; and in one instance, Fitzgerald was informed, Pacific Mills had offered Dan River's customers sheets guaranteed to be better than Dan River's at a price five per cent lower.
[9] In March 1929 Fitzgerald wrote John Brandwood in England that "for some time past George [Robertson] and I have been thinking of developing a Waste Mill." He had heard that in England and Germany there had been a "wonderful evolution in the preparatory

Lockwood, Greene's proposals for improving the other mills included the following points:

Mills 2, 3, 5, and 7 were to be organized into an economical and balanced unit by increasing capacity from 76,032 to 106,656 spindles. Floor space for the additional frames (moved in from other mills) would become available after replacing old and slow-operating machinery with one-process pickers and high-speed spoolers and warpers. Mill No. 6, after acquiring some of the machinery thrown out of Mills 1 and 4, would be used to produce only colored warp yarns. The proposed capital outlay for these improvements came to $490,000, of which $250,000 represented the cost of changing 100,000 spindles to long draft, and another $72,000 was needed for spoolers and warpers. The estimated saving in labor amounted to $60,500 annually. But the winter of 1929-1930 was hardly an opportune time to recommend spending money in order to save.

Not all the suggestions for improvement of machines, methods, and products came from "imported" specialists. George Fuller, who joined the management staff as the president's assistant in 1925, devoted much of his time to manufacturing problems, writing—in longhand—numerous careful but (from the president's viewpoint) probably too lengthy reports. In 1926 Fuller's study of sheeting called attention to the persistence of a "reedy" appearance and excessive "slugs" and bad weaves. Faults of workmanship and poor cotton were soon to be corrected; and Fitzgerald thought that "quietly" changing from no. 22 warp and no. 25 filling to no. 23-23½ yarn in both warp and filling would improve the cloth's appearance and feel and increase its tearing and tensile strength.[10] In October 1928 Fuller found that both warp and filling yarns, though somewhat more uniform than "a number of years ago," showed too frequent "bunches" and heavy places. The remedy seemed to be more careful work on the fly frames. Again in March 1929 Fuller blamed the unevenness of filling yarns for a deterioration in the quality of "Ideal" chambray, which was "not nearly as high as it was a month or more ago." At the same time he

---

machinery for handling this class of material" and asked for advice. "My own theory," Fitzgerald said, "is that a plant the size of ours ought to use up all of the waste that it produces."

[10] H. R. Fitzgerald to G. W. Robertson, June 24 and Sept. 9, 1926. In 1930 a "cooperative" inspector passed a shipment of sheets on a government contract, despite the failure of many samples to meet the minimum break for warp threads of 75 pounds. The inspector "kindly" neglected to average in the tests showing less than 75 pounds (B. D. Browder to H. R. Fitzgerald, Aug. 19, 1930).

told the president that money could be saved in No. 3 spooler and warper room, where too many workers were idling, "then making an effort to find a job just because someone is looking."

One of the major problems in production was that of holding down the proportion of seconds. "We are having entirely too many seconds from almost every department," Fitzgerald wrote Superintendent Robertson in May 1925; and this complaint was echoed and re-echoed over the years. Correspondence with another mill confirmed Fitzgerald's suspicion that Dan River's rate of 15 per cent seconds on sheeting was "unreasonable and too high" (1930), but he was offered the consolation that manufacturers had established too high a standard of inspection.

Dan River's laboratory concerned itself mainly with problems of dyeing. In 1921 Dr. H. M. Chase, superintendent of dyeing, described the laboratory as a "training field for future overseers and second hands," so that "in the future" these positions would be held by "men who have both practical and technical experience." But the training phase of the laboratory yielded a few practical by-products. Two United States patents and Canadian letters patent were granted to Dr. Chase and Superintendent Robertson for dye-house equipment perfected in 1922-1923. One invention was a device for "treatment of what are known as long chain warps up to the point of beaming, where indigo or other dyes are employed." Whereas "in all known apparatus for the treatment of long chain warps the rewinding in balls after dyeing and transportation of said balls at least once before drying is an essential though costly operation," the new technique made it possible to boil out, wash, and dry "in a continuous manner so that at the end of a single run the long chain warps may be delivered ready for beaming without re-rolling or winding." The second invention was an "apparatus for treating cotton threads in the form of long chains." It was a "machine wherein the dye is maintained in approximately full strength by the intermittent or regular addition of dye stock, as distinguished from those in which the warps gradually use up the dye in the first passage through and are reversed and passed through a second bath in order to render their color uniform."[11]

In 1927 Robertson and Chase visited a North Carolina mill to in-

[11] U. S. Patents 1,500,298 and 1,500,299, granted July 8, 1924, and Canadian Letters Patent, dated August 12, 1924.

spect a Thies dyeing machine. Dr. Chase was persuaded that this apparatus was "by far the best method of producing those colors which cannot be made on raw stock . . . . If we can dye naphtols, we can not only make some of the very fastest colors but also save money in some cases as compared with vat dyes." Within a year or two Dan River acquired at least one unit of the Thies dyeing equipment.[12] About the same time equipment was purchased for piece-dyeing, mercerizing, and pre-shrinking. Until Dan River acquired its own machinery, apparently late in 1931, the new suiting department depended upon the Lewisburg Mills in Pennsylvania for dyeing and finishing cloth in the piece.

In 1925 Textile Development Company recommended the reorganization of the laboratory. A comparatively small investment, the engineers pointed out, would equip it to make routine tests of size and moisture content of roving and yarn; to make micro-photographic tests of the evenness of cloth and yarn; and, finally, to initiate a limited amount of "academic" research, such as studies of the relative absorbencies of the different colors and other phenomena which might be "the causes of certain parts of the mill's 'going bad' from no apparent cause." In 1926 President Fitzgerald was looking for "a young man of good character and of good technical training capable of doing simple research work"; but as late as March 1930, although Dan River had made "some little progress with our own limited facilities," the company was still searching for top personnel in quality control, testing, and research.[13]

One of the purposes of a "capable research department," as envisioned by Fitzgerald in 1929, was "to keep out of the mills the almost limitless experiments and loss motions that we have experienced, especially the past year, and at the same time be able to furnish us a constant supply of ideas." The president's new assistant, Robert R. West, drew up a report on research in April 1930 and several individuals were considered to take charge of a new program of research, but the idea scarcely got beyond the planning stage prior to Fitzgerald's death in 1931.

[12] By way of contrast, other mills sent dyers to Danville to study Dan River's indigo dyeing. Amoskeag set up indigo dyeing in 1928 and, "rather than take any possible chances," sent its dyeing supervisors to observe Dan River's methods before starting up their own machinery.

[13] Dan River became a contributing member of the new U. S. Institute for Textile Research in 1930. H. R. Fitzgerald was a vice-president and director.

Power

Power problems were not insignificant in 1922-1931, although the frequent curtailment of operations made the limitations of the power plants less acute than if the mills had operated at capacity. In April 1922 Lockwood, Greene furnished a report on water power at Riverside Division. Along the south canal the engineers found excessive silting and inadequate head gates, so that under the most favorable conditions not over 1,000 H.P. could be developed. Before the end of the year Holyoke Machine Company replaced the 42-inch wheel at Mill No. 4 with two 33-inch wheels guaranteed to produce not less than 297 H.P. under a 20-foot head; generators were moved from Mill No. 6 and connected with two new units of 30-inch wheels at Mill No. 1; and a new bulkhead and head gates were installed. In 1923 Riverside acquired the one-twenty-fourth interest in the canal power owned by the Danville Ice Company. Although President Fitzgerald thought $75,000 "a very high figure for the amount of power," he recommended its purchase from the Ice Company (whose president was a Dan River director) in order "to settle the question in a mutually pleasant and satisfactory manner." The cotton mills now controlled all of the power available from the Morotock Canal.

Lockwood, Greene's "Report on Electrification of Mills Nos. 1, 4 and 6" (May 10, 1922) was "occasioned by the decision to increase the production of spinning frames by substituting four-frame motor drive for present mechanical belt drive." The report reviewed the evolution of the Riverside power system: originally, five widely separated installations of water wheels and steam engines furnished power for the mills. Beginning in 1912, these isolated power stations were "welded into one power system by installing steam turbines in the power plant and a synchronous motor connected to each water wheel shaft." Then a small hydroelectric station was added, and additional steam turbines followed the building of Mill No. 8. At this stage, picking and spinning rooms had electric power; carding, roving, and some spinning depended upon mechanical power.

The logical development, according to the engineers, would be to complete the process of electrification, using the water only to generate electric current; but the cost—$400,000-$700,000—seemed prohibitive at the current price for coal. The electrification of the spinning rooms was completed, but about 1,450 of the 9,500 H.P. available at the water wheels was delivered directly to drive shafts.

In 1928 Riverside's hydroelectric system comprised 29 wheels, with generators rated at 3,300 KW. The steam plant consisted of eight boilers and turbines developing 8,750 KW. In 1930 the General Electric Company made a "Power Plant Study," recommending an investment of $474,000 to modernize the boiler house and steam turbines; but this improvement had to wait.

Only minor improvements in power were made at Dan River Division. Lockwood, Greene made a survey of the power plant in June 1930, but the recommended improvements were postponed. In 1928 Dan River's power system consisted of 35 wheels developing 5,200 KW. and 14 boilers supplying turbines rated at 14,400 KW.

Only the partial statistics of electric consumption shown in Table 1 have been located.

Table 1. Electric Power Consumption, 1922-1931
(thousands of kilowatt hours)

year	Riverside division		Dan River division		
	steam	water	steam	water	total
1922					58,242
1923					63,259
1924					47,611
1925	13,756	3,580	30,087	7,090	54,513
1926	12,671	3,312	32,397	8,544	56,924
1927	15,170	4,177	35,025	10,667	65,039
1928					
1929	11,115	5,592			40,990
1930	9,326	3,618			35,005
1931					40,628

Land

Several parcels of land were sold in 1922-1931, but there was a net increase in real-estate holdings (exclusive of housing) of about $150,000.

Following the fire which destroyed the Main Street bridge in 1927, the city purchased a strip of land on the east side of Main Street, in order to widen the southern approaches to the bridge. This necessitated razing and rebuilding, with a 12- to 15-foot wider setback, the company's office and store building adjoining Mill No. 1. The $40,000 which the mill received from the city represented approximately the cost of replacing the structures torn down; only a nominal sum was realized from the sale of the land.

In 1925 the company sold a lot ($1,500) to Dan Valley Mills, and in 1930 the Standard Oil Company purchased (for $15,000) a filling-station site on West Main Street.

Parcels of land added to the Real Estate account included a $10,000-strip between the railroad and Greensboro Road (in Schoolfield), acquired from two of the directors in 1922, and the Dix property on Greensboro Road, purchased for $15,000 in 1923. In 1922 the company also bought the Motley property in Danville for $50,000. The so-called Motley block of stores, opposite Mill No. 1, was remodeled so as to increase the setback on this side of Main Street by four or five feet.[14]

Valuation and Depreciation

Depreciation statements for 1921 and 1931 appear in Table 2. The total capital outlays for the decade amounted to $14,414,599, of which all but $346,224 were charged to the depreciation reserve. Depreciation charges averaged $692,785 annually but fluctuated between the 1922 high of $1,883,442 and 1930's low of $155,478. The average increase in net fixed assets of only $34,622 yearly represented an insignificant rate of growth as compared with the company's early expansion.

The depreciation charge for 1922, calculated "at the rates adopted in prior years,"[15] amounted to $1,303,969; but the directors approved charging off an additional $579,473 "to apply against the estimated excess over original estimates of cost of work done, thus reducing combined net Real Estate and Machinery Accounts to the same total as at the beginning of the year." Schedule rates were used to arrive at the $1,421,965 charge against the 1923 income; but in 1924 the management cut the depreciation allowance to only $740,721 "due to the fact

[14] Under the terms of the sale, the former owners, the hardware firm of B. S. Motley & Company, obtained a lease on the store space at an annual rental of $5,000. The rental was reduced a few years later, when the hardware company vacated a part of the building. The firm, in which President Fitzgerald was personally interested, was an early casualty of the depression.
[15] Audit Report, Jan. 1923. The rates were: 6 per cent on Riverside's buildings and machinery, 3 per cent on water power equipment, 6 per cent on Dan River's machinery, 7.5 per cent on electrical equipment, 5 per cent on water supply and filter systems, 3 per cent on Hylton Hall and the Y.M.C.A., and 5 per cent on tenements.

Table 2. Comparison of Depreciation Statements, 1921 and 1931
(thousands of dollars)

	as of Dec. 31, 1921		as of Dec. 31, 1931		
	accrued depreciation	net ledger value	original cost	accrued depreciation	net ledger value
Riverside division					
real estate		1,065	1,202		1,202
buildings & machinery	3,151	9,306	13,886	7,375	6,511
Dan River division					
real estate		224	237		237
machinery	2,049	2,816	8,849	4,041	4,808
mill construction	244	1,805	3,322	761	2,561
electrical equipment	220	563	1,793	806	987
water supply, filter plants, fire protection	44	187	450	130	320
water power development	79	443	522	165	357
tenements	161	971	1,343	591	753
Y.M.C.A.	69	0	69	69	0
Hylton Hall	121	229	350	131	219
*Total**	6,136	17,608	32.023	14,068	17,954

* Errors in totals due to rounding.

that repairs to the amount of $770,604.85, which have been charged to
Operations, were considered to be more in the nature of Replacement
and, therefore, properly chargeable against Depreciation previously
provided." Exactly the same amount was written off in 1925, but the
following year the company adopted the rates prescribed by the Bureau
of Internal Revenue. This held depreciation charges below $700,000
a year in 1926-1929; but in the annual report for 1930 the company's
officers admitted that "for many years we have deducted very liberal depreciation in addition to maintaining the physical condition of your
plants, written off as Repairs and Renewals, and for the deliberate
purpose of reducing your net plant investment." Since tax officials
insisted that 43 per cent of the value of the plant had already been
written off, the depreciation allowance for 1930 was limited to $155,478.
The following year depreciation was boosted to an even $500,000, which
prompted the auditors to protest:

This amount is considered adequate by the officials who are of the opinion that the charge for renewals and replacements during the year, amounting to $204,816.22, obviates the necessity for any higher depreciation provision. . . . We are of the opinion that . . . a definite and continued policy of depreciation should be adopted . . . . We understand that officials of the Company are of the opinion that the cost of repairs and renewals should be considered in connection with the adequacy of depreciation . . . . This may be true to some extent, but nevertheless we believe that uniform practice is to be preferred from a management standpoint.[16]

A check on the adequacy of the depreciation policy is furnished by the Coats and Burchard property appraisal, completed in 1928. The reported net sound value of $28 million may be compared with the 1928 balance sheet, which carried real estate and plant at the depreciated value of $18 million. Logically, net sound values may exceed original cost less depreciation; but a difference of $10 million might be construed as evidence of unreasonably accelerated depreciation. The tendency to underestimate depreciation in years of low earnings had been more than offset by overstating depreciation (and understating earnings) in years of plenty. In 1930-1931 depreciation and maintenance dropped drastically; no thought was given to the downward adjustment of asset values in response to falling reproduction costs.

Earnings and Dividends

Net profit in 1922-1931 (Table 3) averaged less than $900,000 a year. Including the two years, 1924 and 1930, which piled up losses of $1,570,000, earnings averaged less than 6 per cent on the outstanding $15 million in preferred and common stock. Dan River's unsatisfactory earnings record paralleled the experience of the industry. Records of over 800 firms show a steady decline in the number of companies reporting profits. In 1924, for instance, Dan River was one of 634 mills which realized losses totaling $68 million, while 342 companies had earnings (after taxes) of $25 million. Again in 1930, when only 200 companies reported net earnings, Dan River was one of the 686 firms whose combined losses exceeded $100 million.[17]

In addition to net trading profit of $12 million for the ten-year

[16] Audit Report, Jan. 1932. S. J. Kennedy (*op. cit.*, pp. 130-131) discusses the Internal Revenue Bureau's investigation of depreciation practices in the cotton textile industry.
[17] Bureau of Internal Revenue, *Statistics of Income for 1930* (Washington, 1932), p. 232.

period, the company received (net) $1,242,740 from investments and non-operating assets. Of this sum, the amount realized from the rental of houses and other real property accounted for $775,000. This was considerably less than the expenditures for "welfare." Net interest and provision for income taxes reduced net profit for the decade to $8.8 million.

The Primuline dye plant contributed (net) $14,064 in 1922 and $28,584 in 1923; but in 1924 a small loss was charged to the operation of this equipment, and the following year some of the machinery was sold to the Industrial Dye Stuff Company for $3,000.

Table 3. Profit and Net Income, 1922-1931
(thousands of dollars)

year	net trading profit (after depreciation)	other income (net)	welfare expense	interest (net)	provision for income taxes	net income
1922	3,570	123	150	173	315	3,056
1923	3,525	145	129	293	496	2,751
1924	—317	123	126	173	411	—905
1925	1,498	109	114	214	0	1,279
1926	1,329	131	96	143	112	1,109
1927	2,117	130	93	122	93	1,939
1928	447	144	97	193	184	117
1929	226	152	95	250	13	20
1930	—499	96	60	203	0	—665
1931	148	90	38	105	0	94

The 500 shares of Dan Valley Mill stock, valued at $50,000, earned $20,000 in dividends in 1922 and $16,000 annually in 1923-1929. In the latter year James I. Pritchett, upon retiring as president of the milling company, asked Dan River Mills to sell him 100 shares of the Dan Valley stock. Although this deprived the company of a controlling interest in Dan Valley Mills, which shared the water supply of the lower dam with Riverside's No. 6 Mill, President Fitzgerald recommended the sale of stock to Pritchett in view of his "long, distinguished, and successful service" to Dan River. A gain of $30,000 was realized on the sale of 100 shares.[18]

Dan River's 400 shares of Piedmont Mills stock earned $12,500 in 1922 and $10,000 annually in 1923-1929. In the latter year 100 shares of Dan Valley stock were exchanged for 100 shares of Piedmont stock. Dividends on the Dan Valley stock dropped to $12,000 in 1930 and $6,000 in 1931, while the Piedmont stock paid $5,000 both years.

[18] In 1924 the management admitted that the stocks carried on the balance sheet at $97,738 "can be readily sold at any time for at least $250,000."

The stock of the W. R. Moore Dry Goods Company, carried on the books at $7,738, paid dividends of $1,548 yearly in 1922-1927. In 1928 the stock was disposed of at a gain of $12,149.

The failure of G. A. Stafford in 1927 led to the reorganization of the business as a subsidiary of Riverside and Dan River Mills. After the auditors reported that "the business offers a valuable connection and an established organization for dealing with the export trade,"[19] the Dan River management decided to retain the Stafford firm name and operate the business as a division of the New York sales office. R. A. Schoolfield, H. R. Fitzgerald, G. P. Ray, J. I. Pritchett, and M. K. Harris held 10 shares each to qualify as directors of G. A. Stafford & Company, Inc., while Dan River Mills owned the remaining 200 shares. After paying dividends of $1,000 in 1927 and $2,000 in 1928, the Stafford Company failed to make a profit; and in 1932 Dan River's investment in the Stafford stock, carried on the books at $20,000, was written off as a loss.

In July 1930 the directors authorized the management to purchase shares of the company's own stock. At the end of 1931 the treasury stock consisted of 100 shares of preferred bought for $6,055 and 360 shares of common acquired for $3,986. The market value of the two blocks was $2,500 below cost.

In sharp contrast to its previous policy of capitalizing a good share of earnings, in 1922-1931 Dan River paid out in dividends $1,400,000 in excess of net profits. The quarterly dividends of 5 per cent on the common stock continued through 1923, but at the board meeting in December President Fitzgerald suggested the payment of a stock dividend to conserve cash. There was another argument in favor of a stock dividend, since the Supreme Court had recently ruled that stock dividends were not taxable as income.[20] The directors approved two dividends, both payable January 1, 1924: (a) a 5 per cent dividend in cash and (b) a 25 per-cent stock dividend "in lieu of all other or further dividends on the Common Stock for the period prior to April 1, 1925."

Dividend policy came before the directors again in March 1925. "The question of whether or not we should pay any dividend on the Common stock," Fitzgerald announced, "has caused your Management

[19] Barrow, Wade, Guthrie & Company, "Report of a Special Investigation" (April 5, 1927).

[20] Eisner v. Macomber, 252 U.S. 189; S. J. Kennedy (*Profits and Losses in Textiles*, pp. 232-234) lists 156 textile firms which capitalized surplus through the medium of stock dividends ranging up to 900 per cent. Dan River's 25 per cent dividend absorbed less than 20 per cent of the surplus at the end of 1924.

deep concern." There were good reasons for passing the dividend. "However, when we consider that a large number of our stockholders are more or less dependent upon the returns that they receive from your Company, it becomes a question of whether it would do less harm in the long run to pay a small dividend than to pass it by." The directors accepted the president's recommendation to pay a dividend of 2.5 per cent, and this remained the quarterly rate for the next five years. In September 1925 Fitzgerald reiterated the questionable view that omitting the dividend would do more harm than paying an unearned dividend. Finally, in September 1929, he felt that the dividend should be passed; now the directors thought differently and voted to pay the 2.5 per-cent dividend on October 1 and again on January 1, 1930.

The preferred dividend was paid regularly until 1931. In December 1930 Fitzgerald straddled the issue of maintaining dividends on the preferred stock. The dividend, which had not been earned, ought not to be allowed to reduce cash on hand; but if not paid "it would be a liability just the same . . . . In addition to this our Stockholders, many of whom have been through a very hard time during this year, would feel the omission quite keenly." Director John M. Miller strongly opposed the payment of the dividend but was outvoted; and the directors declared a 3 per-cent dividend payable January 1, 1931. The dividend was passed in July and not resumed until 1934.

From limited information relating to stock transfers, it appears that investors considered the Riverside and Dan River Cotton Mills common stock a better investment immediately after the war than during the wartime boom. Shares changed hands at 330-335 in February, May, and September 1920; but in 1921 the price dropped below 300.[21] It reached 310 in December 1922 and sold for 315-317 in March and April 1923. Dilution of the stock by the payment of the stock dividend pulled the price down to 225 by April 1924. Subsequent declines to 175 in December 1926 and to 171 in April 1927 reflected mainly the poor earnings record.

Most of the time the 6 per-cent preferred stock sold at a slight premium—e.g., 105 in January 1924—but by December 1929 the price declined to 80-90. With the common bringing only a few dollars above par, the situation seemed opportune, the president told the directors, to modify the company's capital structure, which was "by no means in

[21] Data on stock prices have been furnished by James T. Catlin, Jr., who kindly took the time to go through his father's stock salesbook to tabulate prices over a period of twenty years.

keeping with modern conditions." Since the local market for the stock was "very narrow and does not really afford a fair opportunity to the stockholder either to buy or sell," Fitzgerald thought splitting the common ten for one would broaden the market, enhance its value, and "bring both the Preferred and Common Stocks into alignment with modern conditions." A directors' committee appointed to study the president's plan recommended a four-for-one split, with a change in par from $100 to $25, which the stockholders approved unanimously in January 1930. At the same time, through a charter amendment, the preferred stock—previously preferred only as to dividends—became preferred as to assets and dividends and also was made callable at 110 after January 1, 1935.

Doctoring the capital structure was, of course, no panacea for low earnings. The preferred stock dropped to about 50 toward the end of 1931, and the new common fell to 7½. Although the common stockholder had five times as many shares as in 1920, five shares in 1931 were worth only 10 per cent of the highest value of one share in 1920.

Over-the-counter quotations on the Riverside and Dan River stocks, published in textile journals on the basis of reports from brokerage firms, often seemed to the management unduly low and sometimes "harmful" to the company's interests. In March 1929 Chairman Miller concurred in Fitzgerald's view that the common stock should be listed on an exchange, preferably the Richmond Stock Exchange, since the market would be too narrow for trading in 100-share lots on the New York Stock Exchange.[22] After the common was split in 1930, the president renewed his suggestion for listing, but the board chairman had changed his mind about the advantages of listing and the matter was dropped.

Vice-president Pritchett strongly opposed Fitzgerald's proposal to organize a syndicate (February 1929) for the purpose of supporting the market for the common shares. Undoubtedly, Pritchett's guess that not enough capital could be raised to take up all the stock offered was more accurate than the president's hunch that a syndicate would return "a nice profit for those who had the nerve" to hold on.[23] For several years

[22] Although it was not listed, Miller said the Richmond Exchange regularly quoted the Dan River preferred stock.
[23] In February 1930 one of the vice-presidents proposed that the company buy all the common shares offered at 85 and "retire this stock and reduce our capital." The only thing that saved this suggestion from being completely silly was the author's misguided concern for the good citizens of Danville who had put the stock up as collateral for bank loans.

Fitzgerald participated in a pool to buy and hold common stock which came on the market at what seemed to be distress prices. His paper loss at the end of 1930 (not counting interest on money borrowed to carry the stock) amounted to over $45,000.

According to the president, it was the "very difficult and trying situation through which the textile industry has been passing" that persuaded the directors to commence (in 1924) mailing to each stockholder a copy of the annual report. The declared policy of the board "not to make public the affairs of the Company" remained in effect, but it was impossible to keep financial editors from publicizing the information sent out to stockholders.[24]

In June 1930 the preferred stockholders numbered 1,666; and there were 852 owners of the common.

Goods

Statistics of cloth production in linear yards are furnished in Appendix 3. The total output for the decade amounted to 1,291 million yards, of which all but 201 million yards consisted of colored fabrics. Dan River division, which manufactured all of the white goods, also produced 538 million yards of colored fabrics, while Riverside's share of colored goods was 552 million yards.

Average yards per pound of cloth dropped from 4.3 yards to a fraction over 3 yards; that is, the trend toward finer and lighter fabrics was more than offset (in computing yards in a pound) by the constant increase in the average width of fabrics. Thus, in 1922 three widths (27, 28, and 32 inches) made up 99.6 per cent of the entire output of colored goods. By 1930 only 42.5 per cent of the colored cloth was under 32 inches in width, 38.2 per cent measured 36 inches, and 6.9 per cent came off the loom at 37 inches.

Statistics of production in pounds are shown in Table 4. The output of all classes of goods averaged 32.4 million pounds annually, but deviations from the average are wide. After turning out 37.5 million pounds in 1923, the mills dropped back to 26.3 million pounds the following year; and, after reaching the record high of almost 40 million pounds in 1927, production slumped to 25.5 million pounds in 1930—the lowest point since 1914.

[24] Reluctantly, Fitzgerald promised to raise no objection to the publication in the *American Wool & Cotton Reporter* of the 1925 financial statement, "with such notes as you may care to make" (H. R. Fitzgerald to E. H. Bennett, Feb. 9, 1926).

Table 4. Cloth Production, 1922-1931
(thousands of pounds)

| year | colored goods | | white goods | total |
	Riverside	Dan River	Dan River	
1922	15,424	11,703	8,341	35,467
1923	16,004	12,519	8,932	37,456
1924	9,805	8,908	7,552	26,264
1925	12,466	11,711	10,280	34,457
1926	12,440	10,834	9,034	32,309
1927	14,832	13,983	10,854	39,669
1928	12,056	9,693	8,465	30,214
1929	11,267	9,963	10,606	31,836
1930	9,060	7,066	9,390	25,516
1931	11,212	5,802	14,235	31,249

Errors in totals due to rounding.

Chambrays, ginghams, and sheetings made up 86.1 per cent of the combined poundage of both divisions. In an exceptional year (1924) drills accounted for 12.1 per cent of all cloth produced but the average for the period was only 4.6 per cent. Plaids, the old stand-by of Riverside, held fairly steady at 2 to 3 per cent of production. All other classes of cloth represented less than 7 per cent of output on the average; but by 1931 these "other" classes of goods—broadcloth, suitings, flannels, seersucker, and coverts—made up nearly a fifth of the mill's output.

In view of the general decline in the demand for coarse goods, Riverside's output of the traditional plaids (mainly 27-inch cloth) held remarkably close to the ten-year average of 830,000 pounds (Table 5). Riverside drill was also a coarse cloth, running three yards to the pound in the 27-inch width. Other lines of drills were started, chiefly in response to the export demand; and in 1924, the best year for drills, the production consisted of 1,787,000 pounds of "300" drills, 518,000 pounds of a 26-inch "485" weight, 511,000 pounds of a 25-inch "600" type, and smaller quantities of seven other weights.

The virtual collapse of the gingham market brought the gingham looms almost to a standstill by 1931. In this year ginghams made up only 9.9 per cent of all colored goods, as compared with 45.7 per cent in 1922. Riverside Division continued to make the 27-inch cloth but began in 1922 to manufacture some of the 32-inch "Security" line, a 26-

Table 5. Production of Colored Goods, 1922-1931
(thousands of pounds)

year	chambrays	ginghams	drills	plaids	suitings and other cloth	total
a. *Riverside division*						
1922	8,734	4,987	950	753	0	15,424
1923	9,381	4,276	1,403	869	75	16,004
1924	3,659	1,840	3,168	836	302	9,805
1925	5,624	3,676	2,138	753	275	12,466
1926	7,971	1,921	1,320	979	249	12,440
1927	9,109	2,738	1,689	1,205	91	14,832
1928	8,252	963	1,900	854	87	12,056
1929	5,514	1,432	1,251	816	2,254	11,267
1930	5,275	1,018	689	487	1,591	9,060
1931	8,690	877	525	747	373	11,212
b. *Dan River division*						
1922	4,258	7,445			0	11,703
1923	4,138	8,381			0	12,519
1924	3,265	5,639			4	8,908
1925	4,180	7,493			38	11,711
1926	5,485	5,138			211	10,834
1927	8,898	5,068			17	13,983
1928	6,581	3,107			5	9,693
1929	6,754	3,170			39	9,963
1930	4,726	2,331			9	7,066
1931	3,513	809			1,480	5,802

inch cloth called "Navarre," and a no. 40-yarn zephyr gingham, branded "Pride of America" and offered in 203 patterns. At Dan River Division "Security" and "Dan River" dress ginghams predominated. A new "Feature" gingham was introduced in 1928, but a more promising de- velopment for the employment of gingham looms was found in colored handkerchief cloth. Thirty patterns, worked out by Designer J. A. Becher, were ready for prospective customers in the fall of 1929, and in 1931 production of handkerchief cloth reached 664,000 pounds.[25] As early as 1924 Fitzgerald thought the "strong demand" for outing flan- nels recommended using the narrow looms on this fabric, "even if it should take us into a different line of merchandise from what is com- monly called ginghams." The high cost of napping equipment delayed

[25] In 6 widths, 29 to 36 inches. In July 1929, when the mills were "up against such a serious situation on . . . box looms, "Fitzgerald urged Ray to "push forward the idea of the new handkerchief gingham."
    After the war designing was in charge of the German-trained J. A. Becher. Although he enjoyed Fitzgerald's confidence, as early as 1924 Ray reported confidentially that the superintendent and certain overseers were "down on him." The president thought Becher "could be developed into a very good style man if he traveled more" (H. R. Fitzgerald to G. P. Ray, Nov. 14, 1929). After a trip to Germany in 1930, Becher re- turned to Danville and worked in the designing department until the 1940's.

the venture into flannels but production began at Riverside Division in 1928.

As for chambrays, "Golden Rule" and "Defiance" at Riverside division and "Ideal" at Dan River were the main lines at the beginning of the period. "Golden Rule," once the most popular work-shirt chambray, steadily lost ground. Production in 1931 was only 10 per cent of the output in 1922. To an inquiring customer, the president furnished advice on "what we consider the salient talking points on our work shirt material." The excerpt which follows furnishes, I think, an interesting commentary on the management's idea of the character of Dan River products in this period:

Our three standard Chambrays (Golden Rule and Defiance coarse-yarn and Ideal fine-yarn) are made from the best staples of cotton that we can obtain. Using this class of staple and our improved spinning process we obtain yarns that are even and of superior breaking strength. This accounts for the wearing quality of the woven goods.

With the exception of the plain blue shade, which is dyed of pure indigo on the beam, our cotton is dyed in the raw-stock. In this state it has been proved by test that the fibres absorb approximately 20% more dyestuff than when dyed in the yarn or piece, and while it is an expensive process from that standpoint, we feel that we are repaid in the long run by the correspondingly increased permanency and lustre of the colors in our fabrics. Here you have one of the reasons for the staying quality of our colors; another is the fact that we use only the highest grade of colors, carefully selected for fastness and richness.

Finally, from an experience of several decades in the making of these cloths, we have gained much valuable information on every step in the production of an honest, durable work shirt material, and when you combine this with the fact that we are constantly on the lookout for ways to improve our goods, it is easy to understand why our Chambrays are regarded today— as they have been for years in the past—as the standard work shirt materials and the best values that can be obtained for the money.[26]

Riverside Division began to manufacture suitings in 1923, turning out 75,000 pounds of a 26-inch "Pocono" suiting in 1923 and over 200,000 pounds in 1924. The "Pocono" line was dropped in favor of a 28-inch suiting and 31- and 36-inch "London" twills in 1925-1929. The real drive for the suitings market began in 1930 under the direction of Thomas J. Corcoran, who had joined the executive staff to work with

[26] H. R. Fitzgerald to Van Wert Overall Manufacturing Company, Nov. 28, 1928. But in 1929 an important customer complained bitterly that the company had delivered 3-yard cloth on a million-yard order for 2.85-yard chambrays. He found the company's explanation that the goods had "dried up, or something of that sort . . . very funny!"

Robert R. West and J. A. Becher on problems of production and new fabrics. At the end of 1930 the management approved the allocation of 1,000 looms at Dan River Division for manufacturing suitings. The result was the production of over 1.5 million pounds of suitings, pantings, and trouserings in piece-dyed cottons, worsteds, and serges. It was this development, the management felt, which saved 1931 from repeating the operating loss shown in 1930.

Riverside Division made denims in 1924 but the looms were stopped after producing 86,000 pounds; production on "Oxford" crepe ended with the output of 110,000 pounds (1925); and relatively small quantities of flannels, coverts, and mattress cover were manufactured in 1928-1931. Most of the "other" Riverside goods shown in Table 5 are accounted for by "plain cloth" (1,657,000 pounds in 1929; 99,000 pounds in 1930) and broadcloth (462,000 pounds in 1929; 845,000 pounds in 1930).

The "other" colored goods manufactured at Dan River division included relatively small quantities of motor twill (1924 and 1925), about 250,000 pounds of "rayon silk" cloth (1925-1927), some seersucker (1929-1931), and moderate quantities of coverts and suitings.

Sheeting comprised 84.9 per cent of the white goods produced at Dan River division in 1922-1931. To meet the demands of customers, 28 widths of sheeting were manufactured (though not every year); but the poundage of cloth measuring 70 to 108 inches was three to nine times greater than that under 70 inches. In 1927 82 per cent of the sheeting was bleached (as compared with 59 per cent in 1919). Small quantities of colored sheets were marketed, and hemstitching was featured on some lines.[27] Introduced in 1924, "Morotock" sheets corresponded with the government Type 116 (56×60), while "Dan River" sheets met the standard for Type 128 (64×64). Type 140 (68×72), a fine muslin sheet, was introduced in 1927 under the name "Riverside." The principal confined lines were manufactured for the S. C. Lamport Manufacturing Company and John P. Maguire & Company, while numerous "ticketed," or private-brand, sheets were made for jobbers and mail-order houses.

Dan River division began to make bedspread cloth in 1924 and by 1927 built up volume on the cloth and finished spreads ("Admiration" and "Lady Jane") to almost a million pounds. Part-rayon bedspreads,

[27] Some customers complained that the hemstitching was "not as pretty in appearance as some of our competitors" (B. D. Browder to H. R. Fitzgerald, Aug. 30, 1927).

introduced in 1926,[28] represented the company's first attempt to develop a trade in a fabric containing cotton and rayon; but difficulties in manufacture, styling, and merchandising cut production to a mere 33,000 pounds in 1931.[29] No bedspreads were made after this year. In contrast, the market for birdseye (diaper) cloth held fairly steady; output in 1931 was almost as great as in 1925, when this cloth was introduced. In the meantime "Health" diapers had been marketed.

Though lacking finishing equipment, Dan River began to manufacture broadcloth in 1929 and quickly pushed production of the gray goods from 438,000 pounds to 3,473,000 pounds in 1931. Broadcloths were made in six constructions (from 90×60 to 128×68) and, after finishing, distributed under such unrevealing labels as "Yuken," "Mekong," "Yazoo," and "St. James."

President Fitzgerald's close friend, S. C. Lampert, appears to have been the first to suggest the manufacture of printed fabrics at Dan River. The idea of printing interested the management for many years but was never brought to fruition. Manufacture of 25- and 27-inch 64×60 print cloth, for sale to converters, commenced in 1929; but stocks on hand soon built up to an unwieldy volume and production was stopped.[30] A similar fate—production for a short time and dropping of the fabric for lack of markets—overtook such new lines as whipcord, auto cloth, furniture cloth, shade cloth, and toweling.

While the management searched desperately for "something that we can make a little profit on to afford us a living," its efforts were frequently inhibited by the fear of excessive diversification. "It is worse than foolish," Fitzgerald told George Ray in January 1929, "to continue the mad scramble to multiply the number of constructions of staple fabrics that are already overloaded and many or most of them sold at a loss." A month later the president was "firmly convinced that

[28] President Fitzgerald sent Governor and Mrs. Harry F. Byrd a gift of some of the first rayon bedspreads made at Dan River.

[29] In January 1926 George Fuller noticed mistakes of styling in some striped bedspreads already manufactured and predicted "some trouble" with new styles of "artificial silk spreads." He also thought the bedspread cloth sold in the gray was not up to the standard of ordinary sheetings. Fitzgerald was disturbed by Ray's suggestion that a cheaper line of spreads would make more profits. ". . . each time we have come out with a new line we have had to close out at a sacrifice whatever stock we had left from the old one, the result of which has been a step-down in values received from a basis of 82¢ per pound in 1925 to a basis of 57½¢ per pound in 1928, although the spreads sold in 1928 cost considerably more to make. . . . It is also true . . . that the first two or three years that we made the spreads there was a fairly good margin of profit in them; but for the past two . . . there was no margin worth mentioning" (H. R. Fitzgerald to G. P. Ray, Feb. 25, 1929).

[30] An inventory of 2,250,000 yards was reported in October 1929.

our best prospect for improvement is in the direction of increasing the
sales and volume of movement of our *standard lines of goods,* and, instead of keeping the mills cut up with all sorts and varieties of odds
and ends, to endeavor to standardize our work and keep our lines as
free from complications as good engineering will admit . . . we should
avoid putting into the hands of our salesmen anything that will divert
their attention from the sale of our standard lines in volume—for instance: if one of them told you that he could carry a side-line of hardware, or overalls, or something else, without really subtracting from
his effort on our lines, you would . . . probably (and reasonably) doubt
his competence . . ." Repeatedly, Fitzgerald denounced the "continuous and endless novelty business in special styles," but it proved
impossible to resist the temptation to try things that seemed to be making money for other mills. In March 1928 the management wanted "a
good posting on the automobile trade," with the idea of getting into
seat cover lines; and in 1929 the denim market looked sufficiently
promising to justify putting in new dyeing equipment for making this
fabric. By 1931 the mill was foundering between the devil of over-
diversification and the deep sea of stagnation in the markets for its
"standard" lines.[31]

Markets and Prices

Average selling prices for Riverside's colored goods and Dan River's
white and colored goods are shown in Table 6. The postwar recovery
continued to boost textile prices throughout most of 1923, but next
year's averages fell off, commencing a decline which continued almost
uninterrupted throughout the period. From 1923's high of 65.06 cents
per pound the average selling price of cloth manufactured at Riverside
Division declined 55.4 per cent to 1931's low of 29.02 cents. Colored
goods from Dan River sold for an average of 42.15 cents in 1931, 48.2
per cent below the 81.43 cents average of 1923, while the white goods'
average of 66.23 cents slumped 45.8 per cent to 35.90 cents in 1931.
These shrinking unit selling prices, combined with a reduced physical

[31] The president's remarks at the board meeting in September 1929 adumbrated the
dilemma: "While we are confident that most of our standard grades of Colored Goods will
continue to hold a valuable place in the same distributive channels as heretofore, we are
convinced that we cannot rely in the future upon so large a volume of these respective
lines . . . it will be necessary for us to diversify to a greater extent," because of the demand for finer-yarn goods and more modern finishes and styles. Fitzgerald said a start
had been made but the greatest handicap was the lack of proper finishing equipment.

Table 6. Average Selling Prices, 1922-1931
(cents per pound of cloth)

| year | colored goods | | white goods |
	Riverside	Dan River	
1922	60.94	75.61	59.74
1923	65.06	81.43	66.23
1924	58.01	69.50	62.83
1925	57.28	64.03	59.83
1926	48.40	60.48	55.05
1927	45.06	55.38	48.20
1928	46.53	54.41	50.84
1929	43.99	55.39	49.58
1930	39.50	48.56	46.25
1931	29.02	42.15	35.90

volume of sales, are reflected in the dollar sales recorded in Table 7. Only in the white goods division at Dan River did volume rise with lower unit prices, so that net sales for 1931 showed a gain over the preceding year. The over-all 55.6 per cent drop in net sales between 1923 and 1931 portrays the distress which Dan River shared with the majority of mills in a "sick" industry. The years were not equally bad; a

Table 7. Net Sales, 1922-1931
(thousands of dollars)

| year | Riverside division | Dan River division | | total |
	colored goods	colored goods	white goods	
1922	9,481	8,645	4,534	22,660
1923	9,501	10,154	4,846	24,501
1924	6,369	6,302	3,814	16,486
1925	7,188	7,377	5,789	20,354
1926	5,868	7,250	4,672	17,789
1927	6,817	7,462	4,582	18,861
1928	4,547	5,594	3,550	13,690
1929	5,439	5,120	5,606	16,166
1930	4,054	3,758	3,902	11,713
1931	3,352	2,917	4,613	10,882

Errors in totals due to rounding.

few were fairly profitable; and, characteristically, the management expected "next year" to be better.

One of the consequences of declining price levels was the recurrence of losses on inventories of finished goods. In all but two years (1926 and 1930) production exceeded sales, and in 1923 and 1928 the excess surpassed three million pounds. In value, the highest inventory was $3.5 million at the end of 1928. This worked down to a little over $1 million at the end of 1931, partly as a result of lower unit prices.

Although he was able to report, in March 1922, that production had already been sold through the fall season, Fitzgerald reminded the directors of several factors which disturbed confidence: the "menace of unsound financing" in connection with the soldiers' bonus, uncertainty over the new tariff, and the resistance of labor to wage reductions. By June the chief worry of management was the rapid advance in the price of cotton and the prospects that the crop would be a small one. In September a railroad and a coal strike were mentioned as adverse factors; but the company had an ample coal supply on hand, and its production was "comfortably sold ahead for practically the remainder of the present year." The financial results of this year's operations, the president thought, were "very gratifying," considering "the large amount of curtailment in the textile industry." Indeed, Fitzgerald told the stockholders, the long shutdown of New England mills "helped the market for some lines of goods by preventing excess production."

In June 1923 President Fitzgerald reported a quiet period in the goods market. The cotton crop was short for the third consecutive year, and by November many lines of goods were selling below the cost of production. In order to halt the piling up of inventories, Fitzgerald instructed Superintendent Robertson to stop all the Draper looms in the colored goods departments for three days a week. The shortened work week extended into 1924; and in June Fitzgerald reminded the directors that depressed conditions throughout the textile industry "had continued without abatement." Never before had the company experienced "for so long a period . . . such an unsatisfactory market." In a letter to Senator Swanson he observed that Congress had turned its back on "a splendid opportunity to do something substantial to lift the almost intolerable burden of taxes from the shoulders of legitimate industry and thereby give the honest, hardworking business man some measure of hope and encouragement."[32] The president noticed "decided improvement" following the national elections, but he found no

[32] H. R. Fitzgerald to C. A. Swanson, April 15, 1924. Senator Swanson, a prominent stockholder, frequently requested Fitzgerald's opinion on business conditions; and Fitzgerald was unusually profuse in his replies.

satisfaction in the annual report which showed a loss of $905,000. Nevertheless, stockholders expressed their "utmost confidence in the management and a desire to assure them that the Stockholders are perfectly satisfied they have conducted the affairs of the Company during the past year as well as could have been done, considering the unprecedented conditions."[33]

In March 1925 Fitzgerald reported some improvement in the demand for various lines of ginghams and sheeting "but at distressingly low prices." He also remarked at the tendency of mills, both northern and southern, "to overload the market on some lines of goods." The president's report for 1925, which showed earnings of $1,279,214 despite narrow profit margins, contains a diagnosis of the ills of the industry:

There has been a decided trend on the part of the merchant—both wholesale and retail—to buy in smaller quantities and to carry less stocks on hand, which has not only thrown an additional problem upon the manufacturer but with the bewildering array of styles and constructions and novelty effects, many of which became fads for a brief period and then with the fickleness of fashion change as suddenly as the wind, it of course adds to the expense of production both in preventing a volume output and also on account of the risk that would be involved in making up any stock of such styles ahead of actual orders. . . .

We are encouraged to believe that the markets are gradually approaching a more favorable trading basis, and that the attitude of the American people which has prevailed for the past two or three years—namely, "Millions for luxuries but very little for the wardrobe," is slowly but surely giving place to economic law, which should bring a material increase in the per capita consumption of cotton goods.

Fitzgerald scouted the notion that the "advent of Rayon will revolutionize the industry."[34]

In March 1926 Fitzgerald admitted that "Thus far the rosy prospects predicted by many of the industrial leaders of the country and the newspapers early in the year have not materialized." The difficulties arising from "heavy overproduction" and hand-to-mouth buying of finished textiles were aggravated by a record-breaking cotton crop. In Dan River's case, inventory values fell "approximately a million dollars" in response to the lower price of the fiber. As Fitzgerald saw it, the year had one "outstanding achievement," because it

[33] *Sixteenth Annual Report of the Riverside & Dan River Cotton Mills, Incorporated* (Danville, 1925).
[34] *Seventeenth Annual Report* . . . (Danville, 1926).

brought a firm conviction among textile leaders that the industry must find some means to meet the changing conditions that have developed in the distribution of its produces. A small group of manufacturers, after intensive study of the problem advanced the idea that the regulation of production to demand and the collection of statistics showing the conditions throughout the entire industry was of vital importance if indeed the industry was to ever reach a more stabilized plane. They pointed out that the textile industry, made up of widely separated units operating as individuals, could through intelligent cooperation overcome many of the most adverse conditions that were hindering the success of the Mills.[35]

The organization of the Cotton Textile Institute was "thought by many to be the most important step that has ever been taken in the true history of textile manufacturing." Stocks of cotton textiles, as reported by the Association of Cotton Textile Merchants of New York, reached the lowest point in five years on November 1; while unfilled orders of 312.4 million yards exceeded stocks by almost 100 million yards.

The first half of 1927, after adjustments had been made to the lower price of cotton, turned out to be "more satisfactory in profit margin than during any similar period for three years." But forecasts of the cotton crop were disappointing; and in September Fitzgerald complained that "the price of manufactured goods has been very much below a parity with the cost of raw materials." Nevertheless, the mills ran 90 to 100 per cent of capacity most of the year, and the net trading profit—over $2 millions before income taxes—was the highest since 1923. Furthermore, "from a manufacturing viewpoint," the president told the board of directors, "your organization has never performed better—both as to quantity, quality, and economic efficiency of output." The "educational work" of the Cotton Textile Institute furnished one of "many encouraging evidences of a broader and more intelligent cooperation throughout the industry."[36]

Although the Institute made "perhaps the greatest effort in the history of the industry to stabilize the market and overcome the evils that have grown out of overproduction," 1928 proved to be a profitless year. In September, generally "the most active season on staple goods," Sales Manager Ray encountered "more resistance to buying than I have ever seen. Practically all the buyers said they were looking for lower prices." Amoskeag knocked two cents a yard off the price of a dress

[35] *Eighteenth Annual Report* . . . (Danville, 1927).
[36] *Nineteenth Annual Report* . . . (Danville, 1928). S. C. Lamport wrote Fitzgerald that the 1927 report "created a great deal of intensely interesting talk in textile circles and bears out my abiding faith in your generalship."

goods similar to Dan River's "Security" gingham, despite the fact that cotton cost more in the fall than in the spring. "Every influence that reasonably could be brought to bear" was used by the Dan River management to avert this price cutting, but Amoskeag's President Dumaine insisted on lower prices in order to achieve a satisfactory volume of business. Understandably, Dan River retaliated.[37] The fine-goods mills in New Bedford were closed for almost six months, as a result of a strike precipitated by wage reductions, but the withdrawal of 8-10 million yards from the market failed to stiffen prices. Most important to Dan River, Fitzgerald thought, was the fact that

since the Ladies have been wearing fewer clothes, and Ginghams more or less out of vogue, those mills which were especially equipped for that class of goods have had hard sailing. It is undeniable that the advent of multi-colored prints has made serious inroads upon the woven goods for Dress purposes, but we are glad to say that the demand for our Ginghams has continued at something over fifty per cent of our former volume. The greatest disadvantage with which we have had to contend has been the cut prices made by large competitors in their desperate efforts to dislodge our lines.[38]

At the beginning of 1929 President Fitzgerald felt the most serious problem facing the company was "that of selling and of so merchandising your production that the Mills can be kept in operation without serious loss motion." As the year wore on, the continued falling off in the demand for ginghams and the "remarkably competitive conditions affecting others of your large volume lines, made it practically impossible to sell the goods at a profit." Although Fitzgerald and Ray were "confident that most of our standard grades of Colored Goods will continue to hold a valuable place in the same distributive channels as heretofore, we are convinced that we cannot rely in the future upon so large a volume of these respective lines." The management had no panacea, but it seemed clear that the company would have to diversify its production even more than in its past and offer more numerous lines of fine-yarn goods. "It is not an easy thing," Fitzgerald told the stockholders in January 1930, "to change over a considerable part of a plant equipped as yours has been, notwithstanding its flexi-

[37] Amoskeag posted a price of 12.5 cents on their competing line, despite Fitzgerald's suggestion to F. C. Dumaine that "the time has arrived that we could put them [ginghams] back to a basis that would return at least a little profit" (H. R. Fitzgerald to F. C. Dumaine, Oct. 29, 1928).

[38] *Twentieth Annual Report of the Riverside & Dan River Cotton Mills, Incorporated* (Danville, 1929).

bility, so as to be in a position immediately to compete advantageously on the finer yarn goods; but given a reasonable time, we can see no reason why it cannot be done successfully."[39]

Labor conditions overshadowed other developments in 1930. The repeated promise of a larger volume of business on the basis of lower cost, following the reduction of wages and salaries on February 1, proved elusive. Prices went down rapidly but buyers held off, expecting still lower prices. The strike (discussed in Chapter 5) which commenced in September disrupted production but at the same time prevented the piling up of inventories which could not be sold at a profit. "We consider that it was providential," the president told the stockholders, "that the disturbance should have come during 1930, if it had to come at all, for in no year of our experience has it been more necessary to get down to bedrock principles and to pursue the utmost limit of economy and efficiency in manufacturing." Nevertheless at year-end Fitzgerald spoke with confidence of the "active demand" for some of the new line of goods. "We do expect that the New Year will witness a larger distribution of cotton goods and that there will be a gradual recovery toward a more active demand and more profitable operations."[40]

After president Fitzgerald's death (February 1931) the two vice-presidents, George Ray and Robert West, reported to the directors on changes in production and sales. In April they spoke optimistically of "feeling our way quietly into the men's suiting and panting business . . . . In addition to the original line of Suiting, we are merging into other fabrics, such as cotton serges." Another new development was the marketing of "some very handsome and attractive lines" of shirtings under the "Dan River" label. Although 3,800 looms were idle in September, many of the 9,500 looms in use ran overtime on suitings and other 36-inch goods. The annual report closed with the hope "that the low price for cotton will result in a greater demand for your product during this year" (1932).[41] Measured by dollar sales, 1932 turned out to be the dullest year since 1915.

The annual report for 1928 declared that the management was "under no delusion as to the complications that modern progress has brought, and we recognize that the Textile Industry has not kept pace

[39] *Twenty-first Annual Report* . . . (Danville, 1930).
[40] *Twenty-second Annual Report* . . . (Danville, 1931).
[41] *Twenty-third Annual Report* . . . (Danville, 1932).

with the other major industries of the world, especially in its system of selling and of keeping its production schedules in proper relation to the demand as a stabilizing force . . . . More than ever before we are confronted with the necessity of scientific management in your Sales Department." Previously, in March 1928, Fitzgerald had remarked that the selling force was "inadequate for our volume needs . . . . We do not have the follow-up of the medium sized and small jobbers and cutters . . . . It is among this class that better prices are obtained than we can get from the big fellows."[42] But it seemed advisable to stick to the company's traditional merchandising policy, that is, "to sell . . . to the jobbing and manufacturing trades, together with some of the mail-order houses . . . . We believe in the jobber and that he has a necessary function to perform in the distribution of textiles, and want to give him every ounce of support we can."[43]

To carry out Fitzgerald's notion of "scientific management" in selling, Ray moved to New York in 1929. In broaching the matter to the general sales manager, the president said that "after long and careful thought" he reached the conclusion that Ray should be "in closer touch with the center of activities" and "as often as practicable . . . go over first one territory and then another . . . with your salesmen, both for the purpose of educating and broadening them and also to keep personal touch with the trade." Fitzgerald promised "to make an occasional trip" with Ray, and plans were discussed for strengthening the sales organization throughout the country.[44]

To secure more office space the sales departments moved into a building at 40 Worth Street (1928); and in response to the apparent

[42] H. R. Fitzgerald to G. P. Ray, March 15, 1928. This was not the first time that this thought had occurred to the president. In January 1924 he spoke of the need for "closer and more frequent personal touch with the trade. . . . Times have changed and with as large a business as ours it is not safe to rely on as few channels through which to operate" (H. R. Fitzgerald to G. P. Ray, Jan. 30, 1924).

[43] H. R. Fitzgerald to Wyman, Partidge & Co., May 23, 1927. In answering an inquiry, the company explained: "We only solicit the large jobbing, manufacturing and converting trade. We have repeatedly and consistently declined to sell syndicates of retailers or chain stores organizations that do only a retail business. We do sell a few of the mail order houses . . . who buy in very large volume. . . ."

[44] H. R. Fitzgerald to G. P. Ray, Jan. 1 and Feb. 25, 1929. Fitzgerald admitted that he was no longer able "to keep in touch with the actual conditions" and was often "compelled to form judgments without full and adequate facts upon which to base them. For instance: our men start out on their routes and sometimes for days and days we hear nothing at all from them, and really do not know what they are having to contend with except for the occasional small orders that are sent in. . . . It seems to me that it would be much more thorough and businesslike if when our salesman visits a market he would remain there long enough to work it very thoroughly and go into the situation very intelligently, and then write us such a report as would enable us to know something of the existing facts as they may apply to all of our various standard volume lines. . . ."

need for more frequent and intensive contacts with customers, the number of salesmen (exclusive of Ray and Cockefair) grew from 7 in 1927 to 16 in 1931.

Although the unprofitable Baltimore office had been closed, new offices were opened in Boston, Atlanta, and San Francisco. One of the consequences of the expanding sales organization was a decrease in the proportion of sales classified as direct, i.e., sales coming to the mill unsolicited. The change is shown in the following percentage distribution of billings:

	1927	1931
direct	28.67	7.97
G. P. Ray	24.86	29.16
A. T. Cockefair	14.69	18.83
other salesmen	31.78	44.04

Commission sales through H. L. McClearn & Company averaged about 1 per cent of billings.

Customers, or the number of accounts sold, totaled 801 in 1926 and rose to 1,102 in 1931. In 1926 two accounts, Ely & Walker and S. C. Lamport, made up 17 per cent of all sales. Sales to firms in New York represented about one-fourth of the business, but this figure includes export sales through G. A. Stafford & Company. A sampling of records for 1929-1930 indicates a high concentration of sales in a few states, although some progress had been made in the search for customers in new territory. In 1929-1930 there were only four states—Montana, Nevada, South Dakota, and Wyoming—in which the company made no sale.[45]

An important change in the sales organization took place in 1927, following the failure of the export firm of G. A. Stafford & Company. Stafford, who staged a successful comeback after his 1913 failure, suffered reverses in the postwar depression and at the end of 1921 owed the mills $385,000. The company voluntarily canceled $192,500 of the debt (which Stafford, nevertheless, paid off in part) and resumed busi-

[45] In 1924 Fitzgerald wrote to Ray of the large area in the Northwest "from which we have had very little regular business." He thought it would be cheaper to employ a salesman on commission than "to travel a man on salary." In January 1931 the Pacific Coast territory was divided between G. E. Polentz (Los Angeles and Utah) and W. H. Lawrence (San Francisco and other California cities, plus the states of Idaho, Oregon, and Washington.) The salesmen agreed not to sell competing lines and to make regular visits to the jobbing and cutting trade. They earned a commission of 1 per cent, not only on their own sales but also on any unsolicited orders from buyers in their territory.

ness with him on an agency basis. Stafford was the sole owner of the business. Employing salesmen in South and Central America and selling through brokers in other foreign markets, he built sales up to $1,130,000 in 1922 and kept them over a million dollars a year in 1923-1925. The decline in sales to $703,000 in 1926, Stafford asserted, was "due to the competition he has met from other concerns in the export business to which you [Dan River Mills] have sold your goods." But the auditors discovered that the insolvency which Stafford admitted early in 1927 resulted in great part from violations of the agency agreement with Dan River and from personal withdrawals of funds in excess of earnings. In partial settlement of Dan River's claims against him, Stafford deeded to the company his $100,000 home at Stafford Park, Stamford, Connecticut.

In June 1927 G. A. Stafford & Company, Inc., chartered in Virginia, became the exclusive export subsidiary of Riverside and Dan River Cotton Mills. The initial capitalization of $10,000 was increased to $25,000 in December 1927. G. P. Ray was chosen president; A. T. Cockefair, vice-president; W. W. Ayres, secretary; E. V. Strodl, treasurer; and G. A. Stafford, business manager at a salary of $1,000 a month. In 1928 the new corporation earned $15,713 (after taxes) on sales of $800,994. Sales dropped to only $255,214 in 1931, and losses for three years in succession totaled $36,792. Ray attributed the unsatisfactory results to the "great upheaval of foreign affairs," resulting in "confusion and demoralization unparalleled in the history of the present generation of exporters." Although, in January 1933, preparations were made to dissolve the subsidiary, the move was reconsidered and Stafford lasted as a separate corporation until 1950.[46]

What would advertising do for Dan River's sagging sales curve? In 1921 R. A. Schoolfield was skeptical: "I have not made up my mind that it is wise to pay the large amounts that the *Saturday Evening Post* and *Ladies' Home Journal* want for the advertisements in these papers."[47] Sales Manager Ray made a rather thorough study of adver-

[46] Fitzgerald was annoyed by Ray's suggestion that Stafford might be used to sell abroad the products of other firms. "Our sole purpose in acquiring the Stafford business," he noted, "was to save as much as we could of a heavy impending loss, and to preserve the channels of distribution for our own products" (H. R. Fitzgerald to G. P. Ray, Nov. 7, 1928). But the Stafford report for 1928 showed sales of $735,221, of which $638,764 were "our goods." The difference presumably represented non-competing lines of other manufacturers.

[47] R. A. Schoolfield to H. R. Fitzgerald, Jan. 4, 1921. The proposal, perhaps made by Fitzgerald, to spend $150,000 advertising chambrays seemed to the chairman "a very large sum" and he wanted the directors to pass on it. I find no mention of advertising in directors' minutes for this period.

tising media and came to the conclusion that a one-page advertisement
in the *Simplex Buyer's Guide* would be fruitful. Apparently, the first
advertisement in this publication featured "Health" diapers; and in
1926 reprints of this advertisement, with a covering sales letter, were
mailed to jobbers, retailers, and institutional buyers. In January 1929
Fitzgerald told the directors that "the time has come that we should do
some national advertising to popularize certain of our standard brands";
but Fitzgerald's administration ended without developing a well conceived plan for advertising.[48]

In 1931 a stockholder expressed the opinion that the sales organization "needs a sharp prod." He recommended dividing the country
into sales districts (which had already been done) and hiring energetic
salesmen to build up business in the "great markets for cotton goods"
in the Far East. Other stockholders, when dividends dried up, imagined that excessive overhead and high salaries for salesmen had swal-
lowed up the profits of the business. But Fitzgerald had gone into this
question in the annual report for 1929:

it will doubtless gratify you [he told the stockholders] to know that so far
as the cost of Management and of operating your Sales Department is concerned, your entire salaried list, including all officers, superintendents, engineers, office and clerical force, Salesmen, etc., amounted for the past year
to less than three per cent of your annual sales, which is considerably less
than is paid by most mills for selling their goods alone. You can go further
and add to the above the General Expense Account of the plant, including
selling and advertising expenses, Sample Departments, etc., and the total
will be less than five per cent of your sales.[49]

For a year or so the company sold its broadcloths through a converting house, paying a commission of 5 per cent. This arrangement,
however, "never was satisfactory"; and in February 1931 the company
opened a shirting department within its own sales organization.

---

[48] The company had plenty of free advice on the subject. One customer wrote: "Any
intelligent housewife can tell you about Pepperell Goods. . . . Why on earth don't you
all advertise at least some of your merchandise which goes to the average home? . . . If
I were an advertising man, I certainly would go down to Danville and camp on your
office steps until you said, 'Yes we will advertise'" (S. J. McCawley to H. R. Fitzgerald,
June 21, 1929). T. H. Price of *Commerce and Finance* wanted Dan River to advertise
as the "largest cotton mills in America;" and E. Howard Bennett of the *Wool and Cotton
Reporter* reported on a test among workers in his office. Forty girls were familiar with
half a dozen brands of sheets but "not one of them has ever heard of Riverside and Dan
River Sheets" (E. H. Bennett to H. R. Fitzgerald, Sept. 30, 1929).

[49] *Twenty-first Annual Report* . . . (Danville, 1930).

Industry-Wide Stabilization

In the 1920's Riverside and Dan River Mills was an active party to two major efforts to make cotton manufacturing a more profitable enterprise. The first, and probably most far-reaching, of the industry's schemes to achieve stability bore fruit in the organization of the Cotton Textile Institute in 1926. Harry Riemer, editor of the *Daily News Record,* credits Lee Rodman of Indiana Cotton Mills with the germ of an idea for an institute but considers George S. Harris, then with Exposition Cotton Mills and later president of Dan River, B. E. Geer of Judson Mills, and W. J. Vereen of the Moultrie Cotton Mills as the "fathers" of the Institute. They made the "first suggestion taken seriously by the industry" at the May 1926 meeting (in Atlanta) of the American Cotton Manufacturers' Association.[50]

Actually, Harry Fitzgerald had written and talked, since 1924, of an organization to collect data on production, prices, and sales from member firms of the A.C.M.A. Congress, he thought, might amend the Sherman Act to permit "a reasonable measure of cooperation on the part of trade associations in a legitimate way." The following year he discussed informally with members of the Association a plan for "more effective cooperation," which would embrace the northern National Association of Cotton Manufacturers as well as the southern Association.[51] In a speech before the Cotton Manufacturers' Association of Georgia (June 1926) Fitzgerald spoke vigorously of the opportunity for "men of large caliber both in the manufacturing and the selling divisions of the industry" to perfect a plan of co-operation:

The disease of the Textile industry—its one great weakness, is its lack of organization. Each unit tries to function independently and in utter disregard of its effect upon others . . . .

[50] *Daily News Record,* July 23, 1926, and Oct. 23, 1946. Perhaps W. F. Edwards' proposal for a Textile Research Institute (*Textile World,* Sept. 6, 1924) was another "germ" of the Institute.

[51] H. R. Fitzgerald to W. D. Adams, June 6, 1925. Fitzgerald thought that "if a comparatively small number of the large and leading spirits in the industry would get together with a thorough determination to consider the whole question from an unselfish viewpoint and to take some constructive action, I candidly believe that there is brains and intelligence enough in the industry to accomplish the desired result." Adams considered Fitzgerald's views "eminently sound" and offered his own plan for "inaugurating a constructive educational campaign to emphasize to our manufacturers individually, the necessity, in fact, the imperative requirements, for co-operative action, not through any centralized control, but by developing the facts as they bear upon the situation, and then leaving the individual mills to act according to their best judgment" (W. D. Adams to H. R. Fitzgerald, March 4, 1924).

There is a deep-seated impression that if the individual is keen enough he can in some way manage to outstrip his competitors and succeed even if others fail . . . .

There are two theories. One is to let things go until enough of them die out to relieve the "crowdings"; the trouble here is you cannot tell which will die, and meantime there is fearful economic loss. The other theory, which seems to me much more sensible, is that there is great scientific value in cooperation; if all would cooperate the disease would be checked and possibly the entire trouble eradicated.

Think of what a fine thing it would be for the Mills of this country to create a great Textile Institute for the purpose not only of gathering facts and statistics but of studying their problems, and to standardize their methods of distribution as well as work out better selling policies, and to discover by scientific research new fields for diversification as well as by advertising and building up new markets, etc., and seeking to popularize their products throughout the world![52]

The organization meeting of the Cotton Textile Institute was held on July 21, 1926. Fitzgerald, a member of the committee of ten to draft the Institute plan, and Harris gave liberally of their time in working for the Institute; and both Dan River's president and president-to-be became members of the first executive committee. One of their fellow organizers congratulated Fitzgerald for his "splendid work. I do not know of any one who has contributed more to the success of the movement than you have, and your splendid, clear-headed, progressive spirit has been an inspiration to all of us."[53] Another source of inspiration to the group was the report that Herbert Hoover, then Secretary of Commerce, might accept the presidency of the Institute.[54] Congress failed to amend the Sherman Act (except for the Webb-Pomerene Act of 1918), but the decisions of the Supreme Court in the Maple Flooring Association and Cement Manufacturers' Protective Association cases (1925) appeared to legalize trade associations formed to compile and distribute among members information on costs and prices.[55]

Although Fitzgerald told the directors that the "educational work done by the Cotton Textile Institute has aided to some extent in stabi-

[52] "What it Takes to Put the Plan Over," *Textile World,* vol. 69 (June 1926), p. 41.
[53] S. W. Cramer to H. R. Fitzgerald, July 6, 1926. Fitzgerald was disturbed by David Clark's running attack on the Institute in the pages of the *Textile Bulletin,* but Cramer urged him to pass it over. Clark, he said, "thrives on controversy. . . . No one takes him seriously." G. S. Harris, too, regarded Clark's anti-Institute editorials "a blow under the belt."
[54] Although given the chance to name his own salary (up to $100,000 a year), Hoover declined. Textile men guessed that he was more interested in promoting his candidacy for the Republican presidential nomination.
[55] 268 U.S. 563 and 587.

lizing the markets," the annual report for 1926 cautioned that it was "too early for anyone to attempt a definite appraisal of the movement." Dan River's president shared the view of the Association of Cotton Textile Merchants of New York that "the next five years ought to be a period characterized by a substantial upward swing in cotton manufacturing and distribution at prices which will afford reasonable profits." But "your Management," Fitzgerald told the stockholders, "does not wish to convey the impression that we can safely assume that all of our troubles will end with the functioning of the above mentioned movements. On the contrary, we believe that highly competitive conditions will continue and that the greater success will come to those plants which are handled efficiently and progressively and that, by the exercise of rigid economy and close application to the details of every department, hold themselves in line with the exacting requirements of this progressive age."

Permanently organized under the presidency of Walker D. Hines, with George A. Sloan serving as secretary, the Institute immediately plunged into an ambitious program of industry research, trade promotion, lobbying, and fact-finding. One of its earliest jobs was to set up advisory committees for various selling groups, several of which were in the formative stage when the Institute was conceived. It was Fitzgerald's constant prodding which brought the principal manufacturers of wide sheeting into an agreement to "co-operate." The "sheeting, sheet and pillow case plan," adopted in November 1926, called for a minimum price of 35.01 cents (i.e., 42 cents, less discounts of 10, 5, and 2.5 per cent) on 90-inch 64×64 bleached sheeting. Any member of the group had the privilege of trading as much as 5 per cent below this price without reporting "exceptions"; nor would it be necessary to report a price lower than 33.26 cents on sales of over 300 cases. Otherwise, members agreed to report to each other transactions at a price below 33.26 cents and to discontinue protecting their customers' stocks against downward price movements.[56]

The partially successful attempts of the wide sheeting group to hold the line on prices may be studied against the background of average prices for Type 128 bleached sheeting (Table 8). This was sheeting

[56] G. P. Ray to H. R. Fitzgerald, Nov. 20, 1926. The group had nine members at the outset. Pepperell and two smaller mills did not join, but Ray did not think this would defeat the group's objective. Joshua L. Bailey & Co., selling agents for Erwin Mills, entered the group after W. A. Erwin wrote Bailey that H. R. Fitzgerald had "thoroughly convinced me beyond any opinion that I have previously had of the benefits that should be derived from group reportings" (W. A. Erwin to H. R. Fitzgerald, Sept. 23, 1926).

of the same construction as "Dan River" brand, which was offered at
40 cents net in the July 1925 price list. The average wholesale price
dropped from 45.49 cents a yard in January 1926 to 40.80 cents in
June, when the price at Dan River was 37.5 cents net. The market
average fell to 36.86 cents in January 1927 and stayed at this level for
six months. Dan River raised the list price to 45 cents in August and
48 cents in November, and the wholesale price moved upward during
the last half of the year. How much of the higher price of cloth may be
attributed to group action, and how much to the steady advance in the
price of cotton, it would be difficult to say. In June at least one manufacturer complained to Fitzgerald, who was chairman of the group advisory committee, that the controls were ineffective.

Sheeting prices declined in the first half of 1928 but recovered and
held firm at over 42 cents from August to February 1929. In March
1928 Dan River lowered its list price to 46 cents (37.37 cents net), but
Fitzgerald was confident that the group plan was working. "From the
fact that no 'exceptions' have been reported for quite some time, the
inference is that there has not been any among the Group." But the
problem of getting sheeting prices up to a profitable level met the
opposition of producers who argued that if the goods wouldn't move at
low prices, they would certainly not sell at higher prices. "I confess,"
Fitzgerald remarked, "this is the selling agent's viewpoint, but it is by
no means conclusive." Agreement was reached in July to raise the

Table 8. Wholesale Price of 90-Inch, 64×64 Bleached Sheeting, 1926-1931
(cents per yard)

	1926	1927	1928	1929	1930	1931
Jan.	45.49	36.86	40.37	42.75	41.68	33.35
Feb.	43.88	36.86	40.37	42.75	41.68	33.35
Mar.	43.88	36.86	40.37	41.80	38.35	33.35
Apr.	43.88	36.86	40.14	41.68	35.49	33.35
May	41.66	36.86	39.36	41.68	35.60	39.90
June	40.80	36.86	39.36	41.68	36.43	28.51
July	40.80	37.14	39.83	41.68	36.43	26.88
Aug.	40.80	40.37	42.12	41.68	34.77	26.39
Sept.	40.80	40.37	42.12	41.68	33.35	24.63
Oct.	40.80	40.37	42.35	41.68	33.35	23.46
Nov.	38.59	41.84	42.75	41.68	33.35	23.02
Dec.	38.17	41.11	42.75	41.68	33.35	22.40

Source: Bureau of Labor Statistics, *Bulletin*, nos. 473, 493, 521, 543, 572.

basis from 46 to 48 cents, and in October 1928 the list price went to 50 cents.   Often, however, when the list price went up, the group approved longer discounts, especially on large orders.[57]   During the latter part of the year Dan River officials became concerned over defections from the group.   The company, Fitzgerald said, had lost some of its "largest and best customers by holding firmly to our prices while some one else has had the business at a lower basis."   In view of its large inventory, the company would like to "go in and get these customers back."   But the "demoralization that would almost immediately follow" and the fact that once price-cutting began, "there would be no bottom to the market" sounded (to Fitzgerald) "a word of warning against doing any thing to break up the present arrangement."[58]

Sheeting prices in the wholesale market dropped to a slightly lower basis in 1929, but the average stayed at 41.68 cents for nearly a year. In March 1930 the list price dropped back to 46 cents (35.5 cents net). Within a month price-cutting was renewed, despite Fitzgerald's warning of the "extreme folly" of breaking up the group.   Lack of solidarity caused the mills to be "victimized to an extent that certainly does not reflect credit upon their managements."   They "simply played into the hands of those who are shrewd enough to drive the market down mercilessly."   Sales Manager Ray wrote from the New York office that in trying "to work up volume business with Sears Roebuck . . . each time somebody has under-bid us and we have lost out."   In June the Sears buyer asked Ray for discounts up to 40 per cent on an order for 3,100 cases of sheets: "he understood there had been an armistice declared in the Wide Sheeting Group, and if we could not see our way clear to put the transaction through that we must honorably promise not to mention it to anyone."

In August Dan River's price list offered sheeting at 30.87 cents net. In February 1931 Ray made a forlorn plea against lower list prices and deplored the growing practice of selling "on memorandum," with prices to be fixed later—an obvious subterfuge for price-cutters.   The downward trend of the average, from 33.35 cents in September 1930-April

[57] On Nov. 4, 1927, Fitzgerald wired Erwin Mills that "Pepperell made price 48-cent basis early this week.   We are naming same price list. . . .   If you will take same action . . . it would greatly strengthen the situation and go a long way toward stabilization." Erwin fell in line promptly.   Discounts on the 50-cent list brought the net price down to 38.07 cents.

[58] H. R. Fitzgerald to G. P. Ray, Sept. 22, 1928.   At this time the group covered 90-95 per cent of the broad looms in the U.S.

1931 to 22.40 cents in December 1931, continued until the bottom was reached at 18.17 cents in December 1932.

The chambray and gingham market, prior to the organization of the chambray and gingham group, was just as badly demoralized as the sheeting trade. In March 1925 Amoskeag "surprised the markets" by lowering prices on its most prominent line of ginghams, which forced Dan River to reduce prices on its fall lines, as follows:

	cents per yard
"Pride of America"	16.5
"Security"	13.5
"Dan River"	11.5
"Navarre"	8.5

Even these "disappointing" prices had to be shaved to get customers, and the company's "more or less promiscuous offers during the summer of 'confidential' discounts" upset jobbers and other loyal customers. "I have become convinced," a salesman wrote to Fitzgerald,

that nothing you do for a customer confidentially is kept confidential. The trades we made last summer on Chambrays, Plaids and Sheetings were pretty well broadcast . . . . I cannot help but feel that the confidence of Riverside has been undermined . . . . Not that we have done anything un-ethical, but we enjoyed a reputation for fair dealing that has made us unique among the mills and commission houses, and many of our friends have expressed the fear that this enviable reputation is not being upheld now as it has been in former years.[59]

The manufacturers' chambray group, organized in 1926, co-operated with the chambray group of the Association of Cotton Textile Merchants of New York. It was the mercantile group which compiled statistics of sales, prices, and output; and when the proposal was made to have all members report daily sales to the secretary of the manufacturers' group, Fitzgerald protested the duplication of effort. In any event, he observed, "statistics alone cannot fully stabilize the market . . . unless we develop the spirit to cooperate, all else will fail." In August 1927 the group agreed on a .5 cent increase in the various chambray

[59] John Hughlett to H. R. Fitzgerald, Nov. 17, 1925. S. C. Lamport gave Fitzgerald a report on his trip through the Carolinas, where mills had "burdensome" stocks of ginghams and were offering the goods at "unreasonably low prices." Lamport also sent Dan River's president a copy of the March (1925) report of the Association of Cotton Colored Goods Manufacturers, which Fitzgerald had not seen (apparently because Dan River was not a member of the Association) but which Lamport said was "loaded with T.N.T." Thirty reporting mills (29,679 looms) showed sales for March of 45.6 million yards, bringing orders on hand to 70.4 million yards and stocks at 63.9 million yards. Lamport was sure this information would get into the hands of buyers with ease.

lines, but members were allowed to sell at .5 cent less without reporting exceptions.[60]

In January 1928 Ray described the chambray group as "a sick lot." One of the major members withdrew, and Dan River promptly sent its salesmen confidential instructions to stop the rival mill from "making any inroads on our chambray trade." In June Amoskeag's President Dumaine considered chambray prices "simply ridiculous . . . this unremunerative state of affairs has continued now for a number of years without the slightest change in methods."[61]   After complaining that one of the largest firms had been frequently guilty of not reporting exceptions, Ray reported a satisfactory meeting of the chambray group in December—everybody agreed to raise prices .5 cent a yard.[62]   But reports on a meeting of twenty-one members of the group showed that not over five of them "had much of an idea as to actual cost of the different fabrics and in this respect the Chambray Group was less efficient than the others."   Although President Fitzgerald had been tempted (in 1929) to "resign all groups and go out independently to sell our goods," the company stood by the chambray group until depression dispelled any hope of salvation through "co-operation."   At the end of 1930 Fitzgerald and Ray were looking for "any way in the world" to get rid of a stock of nine million pounds of ginghams and chambrays.[63]

Night Work

Another solution of the industry's ills—the elimination of night work—President Fitzgerald championed uncompromisingly.   He re-

[60] Dan River's list prices were announced, as follows: "Defiance," 12 cents a yard; "Ideal" and "Tot-Wear," 11 cents; "Golden Rule," 10.75 cents; and "Riverside" plaids, 10.25 cents.
[61] F. C. Dumaine to H. R. Fitzgerald, Nov. 1, 1928. Dumaine, who professed to share Fitzgerald's philosophy of business, regretted that the two men met so seldom. "Why," Dumaine wondered, "should our industry, speaking broadly, be the one always obliged to exact the lowest wages for the workers, the longest hours and the poorest conditions. It is ridiculous on the face of it, I am sure you will agree, when a little human effort on the part of the men charged with the responsibility of management could without hardship to anybody change a desperate situation to one of reasonable profit."
[62] According to Dan River's sales manager, Pepperell made a contract which called for a .75 cent differential on seconds and then classed 71 per cent of the goods delivered as seconds. "How is that for a modern sales organization merchandising policy? . . . . We will have to watch our Yankee friends."
[63] Judging by Ray's correspondence, the chambray group was inoperative by July 1930; but Dan River had a "gentleman's agreement" with one or two mills not to cut prices on "Golden Rule" chambray below 10.75 cents. When other mills started selling on memorandum in September 1930, Dan River followed suit (D. L. Reardon to G. P. Ray, Sept. 16, 1930).

membered that in the early history of Riverside Cotton Mills running at night was considered economical: "as help was plentiful and cheap our Management followed the custom that then prevailed . . . . I should say that the maximum number of employees at night during that period of some ten or twelve years was not over five hundred, about half each men and women, or boys and girls." But experience led him to believe that night work "not only made inroads upon the physical condition of the plant" but was "detrimental to the health of those who worked at night" and "the strain upon the morals of the operatives was greater than any wise Management could justly permit." Furthermore, "the efficiency of night work was never as good as in the day time and we found it not only more expensive but that it had a tendency to lower the grade of our workmanship and make more seconds or bad work in our production."[64] It was the dubious profitability of night work which led Fitzgerald to exclaim: "Some of the biggest fools in the world are among the textile manufacturers." As soon as a little cloth could be sold "at a little fraction above the actual cost," many mills, especially small ones, "immediately put on a night force and begin to run their mills night and day, thereby heading at once for an over production that just as surely knocks the bottom from under their market as night follows day." When Bernard Cone gave an address at the University of North Carolina, analyzing the ills of the industry, Fitzgerald complimented him for his "sound" views but protested that, contrary to Cone's notion, there was a way out: "the policy of a great many southern mills in running their plants at night is responsible for most of the trouble."[65] In 1930 a number of southern mill executives began to discuss federal legislation "to eliminate night work in cotton mills." On this count President Fitzgerald had reservations. Dan River's "Legal Department," he said, doubted that a federal law would be constitutional. Furthermore, "if such a law could be gotten through, it would open the way for the domination of organized labor to an extent that might be very dangerous."[66]

[64] H. R. Fitzgerald to H. E. Spessard, Oct. 27, 1927. Fitzgerald wrote in a similar vein to C. H. Clark, editor of the *Textile World*, in January 1926.

[65] H. R. Fitzgerald to B. M. Cone, Feb. 13, 1930. According to the *Daily News Record*, S. C. Lamport had found not more than ten men in the South responsible for the gross disregard of industry and public opinion which night work signified. "A handful of greedy men is all that is involved," Lamport said. "If it becomes necessary, I will be glad to mention names." In February 1931 the Cotton Textile Institute reported that 83 per cent of all cotton spindles were represented by subscribers to the Institute's recommendation not to run regular night shifts and not to employ women and children on night shifts (*Fifth Annual Report of the Cotton Textile Institute, Inc.*, New York, 1931).

[66] H. R. Fitzgerald to W. D. Anderson, Aug. 18, 1930. But Fitzgerald, whom Ander-

Rumors of Merger

Like a fever, interest in making Riverside & Dan River Cotton Mills a principal in the merger of textile firms rose and subsided during the decade ending in 1931. The ailing Amoskeag Manufacturing Company appears to have been the first serious candidate for union with Dan River. Although the northern firm was losing money at the rate of $2.5 million a year, Dan River's management was urged to take into consideration that "your ginghams and their [Amoskeag] ginghams and your fabrics would together make a complete line." This was in 1923. Amoskeag's reorganization gave control of the business to an energetic New England capitalist, F. C. Dumaine, who was reported to be "ambitious to make himself the Judge Gary of the American Textile Industry." In guarded correspondence with Fitzgerald, Dumaine spoke of the "mutual advantage" of a "close working connection" between the two companies, probably through a holding-company device. According to a reliable informant, bankers had ready a financial plan which would provide enough cash to buy up Dan River's common stock.[67] These trial balloons collapsed; but in 1926 an Amoskeag stockholder wrote directly to Fitzgerald, complaining of the unsatisfactory conditions at the northern mill and promising to identify "at least two prominent banking houses" willing to finance a consolidation of the two firms. Fitzgerald replied that Dumaine "understands our situation pretty well" and would, if interested, take the initiative. Word leaked out that Amoskeag and Dan River were negotiating; and in April 1927 Leroy Springs, owner of a group of mills in South Carolina, wrote to Fitzgerald: "Why not consider my mills in the same merger?" Fitzgerald replied that the northern concern had actually made no definite offer.[68]

Dan River's unprecedented loss of almost one million dollars in

son considered "so far ahead of the crowd in matters of this kind that we would naturally look to you for leadership," promised that he "would personally . . . join in such a movement as will put a stop to the evils of night running."

[67] F. C. Dumaine to H. R. Fitzgerald, Sept. 8, 1924; T. H. Price to H. R. Fitzgerald, Sept. 8, 1925. R. A. Schoolfield thought there was "sound logic" in the Price information and urged Fitzgerald to follow it up. In January 1924 Dumaine wrote Dan River's president that he had not given further thought to the merger question since his conversation with Fitzgerald "some years ago." Fitzgerald expressed surprise: "I do not recall ever having discussed the matter with you."

[68] Leroy Springs to H. R. Fitzgerald, April 11, 1927; H. R. Fitzgerald to Leroy Springs, April 15, 1927. Springs confessed that he was "getting old and would like to retire. . . . I have no one to succeed me, for my son does not take to the manufacturing business."

1924 made Fitzgerald think more seriously of merger as a way out of the troubles caused by excessive competition. He was interested in a plan advanced by T. H. Price, editor of *Commerce and Finance,* but felt that any move to buy a controlling interest in Dan River would show the common stockholders unwilling to accept the current market price of $200 to $250 a share. Price persisted. He wanted Fitzgerald to take the initiative in forming a holding company, "in which your present stockholders would, in the first instance, be the only stock-holders. This corporation would be used as a nucleus . . . in which other properties could be included . . . . From the conversations that I have had with several large Southern cotton manufacturers, I am in-clined to believe that at least five of them would soon be knocking at your door and asking for permission to come in . . . . The time is ripe to put across a big consolidation of Southern cotton mills. I want to see you at the head of it."

When Fitzgerald pressed him for the names of interested parties, Price could only cite one mill owner, who "likes the idea in principle but hesitates to surrender his independence."

It remained for President Fitzgerald to evolve, in his own way, a plan for uniting the resources of a number of rival mills so that the tendency to over-produce certain types of cotton goods might be checked. Fitzgerald's scheme was "to bring together into a unit the four large and splendid corporations [Cannon Mills, Cone Mills, Er-win Mills, and Dan River] that would of itself be a stabilizing factor around which the structure of the balance of the plan could more readily be built." The ultimate objective was control over one-fourth of the spindles in the South. The original Fitzgerald plan had to be abandoned, as the Cannon management anticipated difficulty in getting the stockholders to assent; and the Cones, too, had increasing doubts of its feasibility.[69] On the other hand, the Springs Mills liked the merger idea and the smaller Hightower group of mills in Georgia was interested. In September 1928 Erwin, Springs, and Hightower met Fitzgerald in Greensboro and agreed to have an independent appraisal made of the four groups of mills. Lockwood Greene Engineers and

[69] C. A. Cannon to H. R. Fitzgerald, April 20, 1926; H. R. Fitzgerald to J. W. Cone, June 30, 1928. Fitzgerald especially regretted that the Cones lost interest. "If it were not for the serious state of affairs confronting the industry," he wrote, "and the fact that there does not seem to be any way out unless some constructive step of this kind is taken, I would drop the matter entirely." In the meantime, S. C. Lamport, one of Fitzgerald's closest friends, had engaged an investment banker to prepare a plan for the merger of Dan River with Cannon Mills.

Charles T. Main made surveys of the plants and Haskins and Sells prepared audits. Capitalizing ten-year average earnings at 10 per cent, it was proposed to distribute the interests in a new corporation on the basis of the following values:

	millions of dollars
Riverside & Dan River Mills	31.2
Erwin Mills	23.4
Springs Mills	19.4
Hightower Mills	1.8
	75.8

The new company would have controlled 1,028,896 spindles and 27,490 looms.

At this point—early in 1929—the scheme collapsed. It is not entirely clear why the promoters disagreed. In one instance, at least, the appraisal deviated so greatly from the valuations shown on the company's own books that the owners refused to pay their share of the fees for making the appraisal. The defection of this firm caused another company to withdraw, and there was no feasible basis for further negotiations.[70]

While negotiating with Springs, Erwin, and Hightower, Fitzgerald had asked another southern mill executive to find out whether the Pepperell Manufacturing Company would put its "southern properties" into the proposed consolidation. At the same time, S. C. Lamport was sounding out the Pacific Mills, hoping to see this mill's southern plants brought into the group.[71] In an effort to use Pepperell as a wedge for bringing Pacific into the plan, Fitzgerald finally wrote directly to Pepperell's treasurer, R. H. Leonard. A merger involving Pacific, Pepperell, and Dan River would permit the "working out of a very unique and at the same time a very strong plan and in that way create

[70] H. R. Fitzgerald to W. A. Erwin, March 21, 1929. Later, Fitzgerald explained that the "intense individualism" of several important mill owners had made it "entirely impractical" to carry through any important merger during the past few years. Dan River's management felt some embarrassment at the premature publication of news of the prospective merger. Erwin and Fitzgerald flatly denied that a merger was being considered; Springs and Hightower admitted their mills might be involved in a merger (*Textile World*, vol. 74, Dec. 15, 1928, p. 38).
[71] H. R. Fitzgerald to W. J. Vereen, Nov. 8, 1929; S. C. Lamport to H. R. Fitzgerald, Jan. 20, 1929. Lamport, always eloquent in writing Fitzgerald, wanted Dan River's president to have "the opportunity for building one of the most worthwhile enterprises in American industry . . . . I do hope, Fitz, that you see the romance of this whole situation and that you will put some of that God-given energy and keen discretion that you have been so richly endowed with to the end that we may all soon enjoy the satisfaction of seeing this big job well done."

the most scientific management that we could get." Leonard replied that Pepperell had its "own plans for future development." After Fitzgerald's death, Pepperell expressed an interest in a joint marketing agreement with Dan River, with the possibility of "physical merger" if the sales venture succeeded. President Pritchett was interested, but the worsening state of the textile market undoubtedly dispelled any hopes of a successful promotion.[72]

There was no single factor which defeated the merger schemes sponsored by or on behalf of the Dan River management, but Fitzgerald believed that the preferred stock was a major stumbling block. The decisions in the Branch case, he maintained, "virtually acts as a cloud upon the title of the common stock." The "cloud" was the opinion of the court that the Dan River stock, preferred only as to dividends, was entitled to share pro rata with the common if the common holders were offered more than par in case of merger or dissolution. "On two occasions . . . there might have materialized a very attractive situation for the holder of our Common stock if it had not been for the obstruction caused by the Preferred."[73]

Costs

The cost-of-manufacturing books were kept up, substantially in the form in which they were started, until the end of 1931. As in the preceding period, cost per pound of cloth, in terms of labor, supplies, coal, expense, cotton, and depreciation, was computed separately for (a) all goods manufactured at Riverside division, (b) colored goods made at Dan River division, and (c) Dan River white goods.

Employed in 1927 to study the mill's cost accounting, Ralph E. Loper & Company observed that the cost sheets, "while affording nothing in the shape of individual fabric costs," were nevertheless helpful in identifying departmental labor and supply costs and useful for showing fluctuations in composite costs. Loper prepared fabric cost sheets "for a wide range of styles" and set up skeleton records for costing new styles. Significant modifications of the company's costing pro-

[72] J. M. Cecil to J. I. Pritchett, July 6, 1931. In June Pritchett reviewed the question of a merger of Springs, Erwin, and Dan River mills but got very little encouragement from the bankers.
[73] H. R. Fitzgerald to R. R. King, Jan. 15, 1930. In Oct. 1929, E. Naumberg had proposed to organize a new Virginia corporation, to get around the anomalous privilege of Dan River's preferred stock, but Fitzgerald considered the time unpropitious (E. Naumberg & Company to H. R. Fitzgerald, Oct. 25, 1929).

cedures had already been accomplished under the direction of Waverley H. Cousins, and Dan River was better prepared to estimate the cost of producing cloth than many other cotton mills. As late as 1929, a Cotton Textile Institute survey of 110 cotton mills disclosed that 70 per cent of the mills had no cost systems.[74]

In 1922 it cost 51.04 cents a pound to manufacture cloth at Riverside division, 59.76 cents for Dan River's colored goods, and 49.99 cents for white fabrics. These costs increased to 66.01 cents, 76.76 cents, and 62.41 cents, respectively, in 1924, the highest values for the decade. Thereafter, a fairly steady decline, reflecting mainly lower labor and cotton costs, brought costs per pound down to 29.58 cents, 43.90 cents, and 33.76 cents, respectively, in 1931.

Depreciation

Depreciation for costing purposes was a round sum: $1 million in 1922, $1.5 million in 1923-1924, and $1.3 annually in 1925-1931. In 1922 the Riverside cost sheets absorbed 40 per cent of the depreciation allowance, while 36 per cent was allocated to Dan River colored goods and 24 per cent to white goods. But these percentages shifted: in 1925-1926 Riverside division bore 50 per cent of the load, and in 1927-1931, only 35 per cent. The amount set aside for Dan River division was also divided in varying proportions between white and colored fabrics. Consequently, the fluctuations in the cost of depreciation per pound of cloth stem from the arbitrary distribution of the total charges as well as from changes in the volume of output.[75] Furthermore, over the ten-year period depreciation allowances for costing purposes exceeded the amounts actually charged against income by $5.2 million; thus, while the 1925 cost sheets assume depreciation of $1.3 million, the depreciation charges for the year were only $931,848, including $191,126 for repairs and renewals, charged to depreciation "this year for the first time." On the average unit depreciation cost has been

[74] *Third Annual Report of the President of the Cotton Textile Institute* (New York, 1929).

[75] Loper recommended an annual allowance for depreciation of $925,000, equally divided between the two divisions.

As early as 1923 Cousins had pointed out to the management that Riverside's share of the depreciation ought to be allocated in approximately equal shares to the coarse-yarn goods and the fine-yarn goods, although the latter constituted only 30 per cent by weight of the total cloth produced. This made depreciation per pound of fine goods 2.29 times the unit depreciation cost on coarse goods, or about the same ratio as the additional machine hours required to produce fine-yarn fabrics (W. H. Cousins to H. R. Fitzgerald, Sept. 24, 1923).

overstated by 65 per cent, but I have not attempted to measure the extent to which cost for a particular period, or of a given class of goods, has been inflated. On an annual basis depreciation per pound of cloth at Riverside Division rose from 2.59 cents in 1922 to a maximum of 6.12 cents in 1924. The 1924 figure exceeded Dan River's costs of 6.06 cents (colored) and 4.76 cents (white); but in 1931 Riverside's cost of 4.06 cents per pound was below Dan River's 4.48 cents per pound on colored goods and 4.11 cents on white goods.

Supplies, coal, expense

Generally, the unit cost of supplies fluctuated with changes in the market price of these commodities. The somewhat finer and better finished colored goods of Dan River division required supplies costing from 1.25 to 2.51 cents per pound of cloth more than Riverside's goods. The cost of supplies for white goods (bleaching and sewing-room materials) reached a peak of 2.34 cents per pound of cloth in 1929, as compared with only 1.21 cents in 1923. Some of the increase, however, was only nominal. Increasing percentages of the white goods were sent to the bleachery and sewing room, but the cost sheets uniformly figure unit cost of all supplies on the basis of total production in the white goods departments.

The total cost of coal and expense was distributed among the three producing units in the same ratio as depreciation. The cost of coal per pound of cloth (.91 to 1.26 cents) stayed consistently lower at Riverside Division, which used proportionately more water power than Dan River Division. Operation of the bleachery also tended to keep Dan River's unit cost relatively high: the highest values were 1.78 cents (colored goods) and 1.66 cents (white goods) in 1923.

Items of expense—salaries, taxes, insurance, interest, welfare, and miscellaneous expenditures—remain fairly constant, averaging a little over $1.4 million until 1930. Expense per pound of Dan River colored cloth (generally the highest of the three series) rose from 8.14 cents in 1922 to 10.78 cents in 1924, fell to a low of 5.55 cents in 1927, and climbed to 7.73 in 1930; but salary cuts and a somewhat greater output reduced it to 5.66 cents in 1931.

Salaries, as Table 9 indicates, rose gradually to $476,775 in 1927. By 1931 the total had been reduced by $100,000. In 1922-1923 salaries averaged only 7.5 per cent of the total amount disbursed in wages and salaries, but in 1930—one of the two least profitable years in the period —this ratio rose to a high of 13.1 per cent. At the same time the ratio of salaries to sales mounted to 3.59 per cent. "Huge salaries," together with high wages, accounted for the company's inability to earn dividends, according to some stockholders. But the president reiterated his stand that the management was comparatively underpaid, since many firms paid as much for selling alone as Dan River spent on salaries for all its officers, salesmen, superintendents, overseers, and clerical help.[76]

Table 9. Wages and Salaries, 1922-1931

	wages	salaries	salaries: per cent
	(thousands of dollars)		of net sales
1922	5,225	434	1.91
1923	5,793	458	1.87
1924	3,934	452	2.74
1925	4,848	457	2.25
1926	4,443	472	2.65
1927	5,164	477	2.53
1928	3,582	463	3.38
1929	3,791	474	2.93
1930	2,737	421	3.59
1931	3,267	375	3.45

State and local taxes, excluding income taxes (Table 10), reached a high of $387,663 in 1924 and dropped steadily thereafter (except in 1928) to a low of $207,981 in 1931. A revision of the company's city and county tax list brought about a reduction of nearly $300,000 in taxable property in 1925; and in 1926 the state of Virginia lowered the capital stock tax, replacing some of the lost revenue with an increased income tax.[77]

In 1927 Fitzgerald began making comparisons of Danville's tax rates and the taxes paid by textile firms in other areas. F. W. Reynolds ad-

[76] As early as 1921 Vice-President Pritchett felt that, in accepting a salary, he was "getting something for nothing!" but the president insisted that his advice was valuable. Again in 1924 Pritchett thought it "wrong for me to allow you to pay me a salary as vice-president any longer, in the face of existing conditions" (J. I. Pritchett to H. R. Fitzgerald, Aug. 13, 1924.

[77] Governor Byrd consulted President Fitzgerald on proposed changes in the tax laws. Fitzgerald thought he would prefer the capital tax at the old rate to an increase in income taxes but recognized that "if high taxes must be paid, it is better to pay them on income than on capital, for at least then the tax payer is supposed to have the income out of which they can be paid" (H. R. Fitzgerald to H. F. Byrd, Jan. 29, 1926).

vised him that Pepperell's New England mills had valuations as low as
$13.10 per spindle, or not much more than a third of the Danville as-
sessment of $35 per spindle. The "death grip" was relaxed by the
reassessment of the Riverside plant in 1930, and over $20,000 was pared
from the 1931 tax bill. Similar savings were achieved by revaluation
for insurance purposes: premiums dropped from $125,672 in 1929 to
$56,669 in 1931.

Table 10. State and Local Property Taxes, 1922-1931
(thousands of dollars)

year	Riverside division	Dan River division	total
1922	138	182	320
1923	135	208	343
1924	155	233	388
1925	151	155	306
1926	117	158	275
1927	93	134	228
1928	127	159	286
1929	114	136	249
1930	112	125	238
1931	92	116	208

Interest, after deducting the amount earned on bank balances,
reached its highest point ($293,196) in 1923. Over a period of nine
years (1923-1931) bills payable averaged a little less than $5 million,
dropping to lows of $3.2 million in 1927 and $3.4 million in 1931.
Borrowing to meet cotton drafts and maintain a comfortable cash position[78] presented no problem: the banks were eager to buy Riverside
and Dan River paper and the rates were usually the lowest available
in the commercial paper market. But the management became increasingly concerned over the company's dependence upon bank credit for
working capital. The ease of raising equity capital in the summer of
1929 prompted Fitzgerald to inquire about a public offering of Dan
River common stock, but before a decision could be reached the opportunity to float industrial stocks had been lost in the whirlpool of the
Wall Street crash.[79] The passing of dividends and the shrinkage of in-

[78] Average balances (as of the fifteenth of each month) were $1.31 million in 1925;
$1.25 mlilion in 1926; $1.20 million in 1927; $1.32 million in 1928; and $1.53 million in
1929.
[79] Fitzgerald wrote to at least two banking groups in New York, asking for advice
on an issue of $2.5 million in common stock. "Under ordinary circumstances," he ob-

ventories put the stockholders in a relatively more favorable position: in 1931 they furnished 60 per cent of the $4.8 millions in working capital.

Other items of "expense" had comparatively little influence upon changes in the unit cost of production. Losses on uncollectible accounts continued low. Although the amount written off for bad debts exceeded $50,000 in 1927—the year of the Stafford failure—the sums recovered on accounts written off in prior years reduced the average loss to about $2,500 a year. Advertising cost over $15,000 in 1926 and 1927, but the average annual expenditure was barely $5,000.

In 1930-1931 sharp cuts were made in welfare expenditures. Employees' group life insurance was dropped, while the company pruned its list of contributions to various religious, charitable, and social activities. Discussion of these phases of the business in 1922-1931 appears in the following chapter.

Cotton

American cotton production rose steadily from 7.9 million bales in 1921 to 18.0 million bales in 1926, dropped sharply to 13.0 million bales in 1927, and averaged 14.5 million bales in the following three years. Production rose to 17.1 million bales in 1931, declining in 1932 to 13.0 million bales. Meanwhile, the annual average price rose from 17.00 cents per pound in 1921 to 28.69 cents in 1923. After declining to 12.47 cents in 1926, the average climbed to 20.19 cents the following year; but in 1928 a decline set in which carried the season's average price to 5.66 cents per pound in 1931, the lowest figure since annual average prices were first reported in 1908. Although the annual averages for the ten-year period exhibit a range of 23.03 cents, ever greater variability shows up in the intraseasonal movements.[80]

The annual average cost of cotton opened for manufacturing at Riverside Division ranged from a low of 8.11 cents per pound in 1931 to 27.42 cents in 1924. Monthly values show a wider range: the cotton used in September 1923 was priced at 32.39 cents a pound, while the fiber consumed in September 1931 (after credits for waste sales) cost

---

served, "we would not want to issue any additional stock"—probably because of the risk of a shift in control. Fitzgerald was particularly bitter because R. A. Schoolfield was openly critical of the precarious working capital position. The "wise head that now seems to bemoan this weakness" was the one who in years gone by thought it perfectly proper to borrow working capital (H. R. Fitzgerald to J. I. Pritchett, Oct. 14, 1929).

[80] *Historical Statistics of the United States, 1789-1945*, p. 108.

only 1.89 cents! Loper had recommended using a constant multiplier of 1.129 to convert cotton cost in the bale to cotton cost per pound of cloth; but the cost sheets preserve the established practice of deducting irregular sales of waste from the cost of cotton consumed in the period in which waste was sold.   After allowance for waste sales, the cost of cotton per pound of cloth fluctuates within a range of 1.36 cents to 4.57 cents above the cost of a pound of cotton.   The highest cost of cotton per pound of cloth was 31.99 cents in 1924; the lowest, 9.47 cents in 1931.

Cotton inventories varied from one million pounds, priced at $78,000, at the end of 1930 to 14.7 million pounds, worth $3.1 million, at the end of 1922.   Cotton on hand at the end of 1922 represented more than a third of the following year's consumption, and the 10 million pounds in inventory at the end of 1926 amounted to about one quarter of the next year's requirements.   In both cases the high inventories anticipated rising prices.   After 1926 year-end cotton inventories decline; but steadily falling prices caused losses on inventory revaluation.   At the end of 1931, however, the cost of cotton on hand was less than its market value.

Cotton policy in 1922-1931 combined hedging with speculation. In September 1921 R. A. Schoolfield reported that the mill had 20,000 bales of cotton "provided against an equal quantity of goods sold." It was a "serious proposition" to decide whether to go long 800 bales, then offered at 24 cents a pound.   I do not know whether the chairman bought the 800 bales; but the cotton market was strong in 1922, with an average price fully six cents above 1921.

In June 1923 President Fitzgerald thought the company was fortunate to have on hand a four months' supply, "not only because of the high price now prevailing for the old-crop cotton, but it is doubtful if you could obtain the same grade at this time at any price."   In September, returning from a trip to Texas, Henry Roediger advised Fitzgerald to "start buying on any breaks, as we certainly cannot hit the bottom, but had rather buy on a scale down than on a scale up."   By November the company owned 22,680 bales of cotton in excess of goods sold (including 2,500 bales of July futures).   It also had 13,000 bales of May cotton on option, but Fitzgerald wrote Ray that there was "nothing to worry about."   The continued rise in the price of cotton persuaded the president to stop selling cloth "for the time being . . . as it seems impossible to get prices for goods in keeping with the cost of making them."

Early in 1924 Fitzgerald observed that "if conditions were normal and fluctuations within narrow limits," there would be no justification for dealing in futures, except to hedge. But, with cotton at 32 cents and "the further incentive that goods cannot be sold on that basis," he saw "no harm in selling a reasonable amount when I thought it was too high and buying a reasonable amount if or when I thought it low enough to be attractive." This sort of speculation seemed to be no more risky than going long 45,000 bales at 32 cents.[81] At the same time Schoolfield and Roediger berated speculators for the excessive fluctuations in price and suggested that the government change the limit on the daily price variation on the New York Cotton Exchange from 200 points to 25 points (i.e., .25 cent a pound).

In March 1925 Fitzgerald found the cotton situation "quite a conundrum . . . . Notwithstanding the apparently large crop there is an undoubted shortage of the better grades and staples which has kept them at a high premium." Undoubtedly, the relatively high price for select grades of cotton accounts for this year's reported loss of $15,000 on "unclosed hedges."

Early in 1926 the cotton market became bullish, but both Fitzgerald and Roediger expected a break. On February 10 the company had options on 36,000 bales of May cotton. May contracts were then at a premium of 60 points over July and 150 points over October, spreads which Fitzgerald considered "entirely illogical . . . brought about by the manipulation of certain cotton firms who apparently find it profitable to create this situation." Yet the president proposed to "take my chances" on 12,000 bales, fixing the price "on the downward trend if it occurs." The other 24,000 bales he proposed to cover by sales of July and October contracts. This plan "would come about as near equalizing your risk as could very well be done."[82] Fitzgerald proved correct in predicting a bearish market, but the change did not occur as soon as he expected. It was the government crop report late in September, adding 600,000 bales to previous estimates, which "like

---

[81] H. R. Fitzgerald to R. A. Schoolfield, Feb. 2, 1924. In April Schoolfield wondered whether production would use up all the cotton on hand and contracted for before the new crop came in. If not, he thought the inventory should be protected by a sale of futures.

[82] H. R. Fitzgerald to R. A. Schoolfield, Feb. 10, 1926. Fitzgerald had already written to C. A. Cannon, Julius Cone, and others, asking them to confirm his impression that the outlook for a favorable crop made current cotton prices too high.

a slap in the face to the goods market . . . immediately put a stop to the active demand for goods." It seemed strange, Fitzgerald wrote Senator Swanson, "that an intelligent Congress should insist upon inflicting these reports upon the public with the direful consequences both to the farmer and the manufacturer."[83]   President Coolidge named a special committee to assist in the orderly marketing of the 1926 crop, but putting the brakes on the downward spiral of cotton prices came too late to wipe out Dan River's loss of almost a million dollars on inventories of cotton and goods.

In May 1927 Fitzgerald told Ray that he was "frankly worried about the cotton situation" but intended to persevere in "our plan of buying each week about the amount consumed."[84]   In October the company had enough cotton on hand to last until May 1928, and Roediger wanted to buy 12,600 bales more. The following month, although he could not understand why the market broke, Roediger resumed the familiar device of buying 1,000 bales or so with each decline of a fraction of a cent.

Once again, in September 1928, a "flurry" swept through the cotton exchanges with the publication of the government crop report, and Dan River had "a pretty tough time of it to stem the tide of bearish sentiment." President Fitzgerald polled the sentiment of fellow manufacturers and also studied a scheme called "protective hedging" advanced by George S. Harris. Dan River's president-to-be had denounced "blind hedging," i.e., the purchase of futures to balance sales of cloth, or short sales against unsold goods. Instead, he proposed a plan based upon an estimate of the range of cotton prices for a given crop year. As the price rose toward the predicted upper limit, the manufacture would hedge an increasing percentage of his unsold stock of finished goods. Whenever cotton dropped to the lower limit of the assumed scale of prices, hedges (i.e., sales of cotton) would be removed on finished goods but sales of cloth would be hedged 100 per cent.[85]

[83] H. R. Fitzgerald to C. A. Swanson. Fitzgerald had much more to say about the erratic performance of the Crop Reporting Board, no suggestion for improving the service.

[84] In September 1926 Fitzgerald thought the "safest plan is to cover your sales with actual cotton at the time you sell your goods and never speculate." Roediger was skeptical. He quoted a "successful manufacturer" to the effect that a mill executive "had to be a good manufacturer, an organizer of labor . . . as well as a successful merchant and gambler, all combined." It was Roediger who proposed the plan of buying only as much cotton each week as was consumed during the preceding week.

[85] G. S. Harris, "A Cotton Hedging Plan that Avoids Speculative Extremes of 'Blind Hedging' and an In-and-Out Policy," *The Textile World,* Vol. 74, Oct. 6, 1928, pp. 47, 103, 105. An academic study of hedging arrived at the conclusion, quite in keeping with Harris' views, that "A single mill cannot assure itself of adequate protection by hedging

Another bumper crop in 1929 kept prices on the weak side. Instead of waiting for the market to reach bottom, Roediger proposed (September) to buy cotton "when the movement is heaviest, so you can select your grades and staples." A year later (September 1930) Roediger was buying liberally on the downward trend, confident that the price would not go as low as 10 cents a pound. Fortunately, he resisted the president's suggestion to buy substantial amounts of May (1931) futures.

The new management in 1931 inaugurated the practice of making a detailed cotton report at each board meeting. The April 1 report showed 22,000 bales of cotton on hand, of which 16,000 bales were needed for goods on order. In addition to this long position of 6,000 bales, the mill had contracts for 17,500 bales, "the pricing of which is subject to our call." By October the long position had dropped to 4,166 bales, and West announced that "in the event cotton prices remain at their present level of work lower, it is our intention to buy in our sold futures, which will lengthen our position by 14,600 bales." The year-end inventory comprised about 7,000 bales.

Labor

Unit labor costs correlate partially with wage rates. The wage increase granted early in 1923 made this year's unit labor cost .11 to 1.39 cents higher than in 1922. Lower labor costs in 1925 resulted from the wage cut put into effect during the latter half of 1924, while 1930's unit labor costs declined 1.07 to 1.24 cents per pound of cloth following the reduction of wages on February 1. The details of wage changes are considered in Chapter 5.

At Riverside division a dollar in wages yielded a minimum of 6.92 pounds of goods (1924) and a maximum of 11.70 pounds (1931). A dollar of wages spent on Dan River's colored goods yielded 5.15 pounds in 1923 and 7.83 pounds in 1930. On white goods, a dollar in wages turned out 7.38 pounds in 1926 and a maximum of 9.34 pounds in 1931.

These calculations provide a very imperfect measure of labor productivity, since they combine the separate effects of technological

---

so long as most of its competitors speculate in their purchases of raw cotton." Mill managements, it was found, generally had "too great confidence" in their ability to "beat the market." (M. T. Copeland, "Professor Copeland on Hedging Theory," *The Textile World,* vol. 74, Nov. 3, 1928, pp. 100-101).

change, varying efficiency of the worker, and changing proportions of different types of goods. Somewhat better evidence is furnished by data for the principal manufacturing processes. In carding, for instance, Riverside's 1931 cost of 1.75 cents per pound was 29.5 per cent below the highest cost of 2.48 cents (1924). The gains at Dan River division fall somewhat short of this figure, but these mills were carding for the production of increasing amounts of fine yarn. In spinning, too, significant reductions in the labor cost per pound of finished cloth were achieved, despite the requirement of increasing amounts of high-count yarns. The data on dressing are erratic. Minima occur in 1928, 1930, and 1931, while the corresponding maxima are found in 1926, 1929, and 1931. Undisclosed changes in the allocation of process labor costs may have affected these series, but relatively high costs in dressing would appear if a large number of different warps had to be drawn in, each for a comparatively small output.[86]

Table 11. Direct Labor Costs in Weaving, 1922-1931
(cents per pound of cloth)

		Dan River	
year	Riverside	colored goods	white goods
1922	3.93	6.35	3.77
1923	3.96	6.54	3.84
1924	4.14	6.30	3.99
1925	4.52	6.39	3.79
1926	3.92	6.32	4.13
1927	3.90	5.48	3.94
1928	3.32	5.15	3.79
1929	3.44	4.92	3.63
1930	2.89	4.14	3.27
1931	2.26	4.90	3.25

Labor costs for weaving are shown in Table 11. Between 1922 and 1931 the unit labor cost of weaving dropped 43 per cent at Riverside division, 23 per cent in the manufacture of Dan River colored goods, and 14 per cent on white goods. These gains reflect the lower wage rates of 1931, but they also measure the increased productivity achieved by using better looms and increasing workloads. Generally, average hourly earnings at the end of 1931 were 12 per cent lower than in 1922.

---

[86] Thus, the high unit cost on Dan River's colored goods in 1931 appears to be directly related to the unusually large number of styles of suitings manufactured this year.

Other things equal, a dollar spent for weaving labor would have turned out 13 per cent more cloth in 1931 than in 1922. Actually, the 1931 "weaving" dollar bought from 16 to 75 per cent more woven cloth than in 1922.

In 1927 President Fitzgerald wanted to know why labor costs in the manufacture of white goods had not declined as much as in making colored fabrics. Cousins pointed out that the apparent decreases of 21.13 per cent in the labor cost of brown sheeting and 31.14 per cent in the cost of colored goods was misleading. If the mills had been making, in 1927, the same fabrics as in 1919, and in the same proportions, the labor cost of brown sheeting would have been 18.55 per cent lower and the cost of colored goods, 15.06 per cent lower. In other words, some of the increase in labor productivity had taken the form of better cloth.[87]

Loper's cost study was based upon the current (May 1927) loom occupation of 82.7 per cent at Riverside division and 89 per cent at Dan River. The experts estimated that if all of Riverside's 8,562 looms were operated, costs would decline $.80 per loom week; at 50 per cent of capacity, cost would rise $3.63 per loom week.

Management

Until 1930 R. A. Schoolfield continued to serve as chairman of the board, but failing health forced him into a position of decreasing responsibility. As Schoolfield's duties diminished, Fitzgerald's increased, at first with the approval and gratitude of the chairman. At the di-

[87] Splicing Riverside's cost sheets for 1895-1912 and Dan River's cost sheets for 1907-1911, it is possible to present an estimate of variations in labor productivity over a period of 37 years. It is assumed that output per man-hour may be estimated by dividing average hourly earnings by the direct labor cost per pound of gray goods, as shown in the cost sheets. Apparently, at Riverside output fluctuated narrowly between 1.6 and 1.9 pounds of cloth per man-hour. At Dan River production rose from 1.6 pounds per man-hour in 1907 to a high of 4.4 pounds in 1917. Thereafter, product per man-hour averaged considerably under 4.0 pounds, dropping to a low of 3.0 pounds per man-hour in 1926.

The results are vitiated by the lack of homogeneity of product. Until the 1920's gray goods were predominantly sheeting; after 1920 the cost figures cover varied lines of white goods, including sheeting. Thus, there is no way of following precisely the output of sheeting per man-hour separately. In general the data for 1922-1931 indicate stabilization of output per man-hour at 3.0-3.5 pounds, despite rising wages (until 1930) and upgrading of the product.

An engineering study of textile labor costs places the gain in man-hour output in an ideal sheeting mill at 55 per cent between 1910 and 1936 (Boris Stein, "Mechanical Changes in the Cotton-Textile Industry, 1910 to 1936, *Monthly Labor Review*, vol. 45 [Washington, 1937], pp. 316-341).

rector's meeting in January 1922, Schoolfield commended "the excellent service rendered by the president and treasurer." A department head, he said, told him "on one or more occasions" that Fitzgerald was doing the work of four men. Indeed, Schoolfield's praise of Fitzgerald seemed even more generous than was necessary to persuade the board to vote the president additional compensation of $30,000 for his services in 1921.

There is no clear-cut explanation of the deterioration in the relations between the chairman and the president during the following five years. Schoolfield, perhaps, persuaded himself that the business would have been more profitable if, as in years gone by, he had been the chief architect of policy. In December 1926 Fitzgerald reminded the directors that "our esteemed chairman has had to contend for some months with impaired health," a circumstance which made it "unwise" to annoy him any longer with "active details of the business." Changes in the by-laws were approved to strip the chairman of all responsibility beyond calling and presiding over directors' meetings and serving "in an advisory capacity to the officers of the company." The president became the "executive head of the company" with "general supervision and control over all its affairs."[88] Chairman Schoolfield outwardly accepted the situation: "It is a relief," he said, "to be relieved of responsibility." He was chagrined that the changes in the by-laws were worked out by the president and Attorney Harris and approved at a board meeting from which the chairman was absent. Nevertheless, he offered the following resolution: "That we try to forget past controversies . . . that we be faithful to the trust committed to us, and pledge our attention and close cooperation to the direct affairs to the Mill." In January 1928 the chairman's salary was reduced to $25,000 a year, "on account of his being freed from the worry of active management."

In May 1928 President Fitzgerald outlined a proposal to acquire a number of second-hand but practically new Draper looms at a price which represented only a third of their cost. Chairman Schoolfield was silent while the directors discussed and approved the purchase, but later he protested vehemently. "While I get but little information from you direct," he wrote President Fitzgerald, "I am not unmindful of what is going on in a general way from outside information and some of your competitors with whom I have come in touch . . . and from commercial

[88] *By-Laws of the Stockholders of the Riverside and Dan River Cotton Mills, Incorporated* (Danville, 1927).

reports . . . I have felt for some time that we should go slow in additional expenditures in the way of enlargement under present conditions." Then he apologized for "an unsolicited opinion," observing that having "practically all of my accumulations of nearly fifty years" invested in the company's stock, he was anxious to see the investment safeguarded. On June 1 President Fitzgerald broke off negotiations for the purchase of the looms.[89] The next year (January 1929) President Fitzgerald submitted to the board a long statement on the problems of management and supported his written comments by a personal appeal to the directors to eliminate the office of chairman of the board. Speaking "as kindly and as candidly as possible," Fitzgerald remarked that he had been the butt of "unwarranted criticism and derogatory remarks" which had not only hindered him in developing a "harmonious atmosphere" among the executives but reflected upon the reputation of the company on the outside. Chairman Schoolfield replied, expressing his disappointment "at the turn taken relative to the office he was holding." At first he offered to sever his connections with the company completely, providing the directors would pay him "the intrinsic value of his stock"; but on second thought he requested his reelection as chairman of the board, "assuring all present of his sincere wish and desire and intention in the future to avoid criticism and to work in harmony with the Management of the Company." A majority of the directors voted to keep the chairman in office.

The showdown came in January 1930 when Fitzgerald offered his resignation. "The Board of Directors has stood by me," he said, "but the Chairman of the Board has shown no such attitude and notwithstanding the assurances made at the beginning of the past year, I am convinced that there can be no cheerful cooperation between us and that we can no longer work together." The resignation was not accepted. Instead, on motion of M. K. Harris, the board retired Schoolfield on a pension of $12,000 a year and left the office of the chairman of the board vacant. Disappointed, Schoolfield defended his stand: "For some years I have felt that the organization has not been a protective one . . . . I feel as a Stockholder and a Director . . . that major changes should be made in the methods of doing business and the handling of the employees . . . to the end that the investment of the Stockholders

---

[89] But, as he reported to the directors later, Fitzgerald found it difficult to close the deal. The original price on 756 looms was boosted from $200 to $300 per loom on the excuse that the New England mills were mustering forces to prevent the looms from going South.

may be made more secure and remunerative." As for Fitzgerald, "I tried to cooperate with him as far as possible, and at the same time be consistent with my best judgment."

Scarcely free of what he considered the harassments of R. A. Schoolfield, Fitzgerald was thrown into the maelstrom of a labor disturbance of unprecedented proportions for Danville and the village of Schoolfield. Although he was able to report to the stockholders in January 1931 that the strike cost the company "but little inconvenience" since "old and loyal employees" reported for work as promptly as the company had need for their services, the strain of managing mills surrounded by militia, like an armed encampment, the bitter abuse of those who held him personally responsible for the misery among strikers' families, and the ingratitude of those whom he regarded as the beneficiaries of his enlightened industrial leadership—these and other tensions growing out of the futile attempts to keep peace among laborers and make dividends for stockholders exhausted him. He died suddenly, after suffering two heart attacks, on February 24, 1931. Harrison Robertson Fitzgerald, the directors memorialized, "so expended his time, energy, and strength that it may be fairly said that he in truth gave his life for this Company's interests."

Nine months later, as he entered his fiftieth year of service to the firm, death ended the career of R. A. Schoolfield. The passing of Schoolfield removed from Danville the last of the founders of Riverside Mills, and for the first time in half a century neither a Schoolfield nor a Fitzgerald occupied an important executive position in the company.

The irony of fate which permitted R. A. Schoolfield to outlive H. R. Fitzgerald also granted to the older man the privilege of nominating Fitzgerald's successor. On February 27, 1931, James I. Pritchett was unanimously elected president and treasurer and Malcolm K. Harris, the company's attorney, was chosen to serve as assistant to Pritchett. Both appointments were regarded as temporary; upon election Pritchett and Harris filed their resignations "for acceptance at the pleasure of the Board." Both officers were re-elected in January 1932, but another crisis in top management arose in September, following the death of Pritchett.

In January 1929 President Fitzgerald advised the directors that "it would be a great relief to me and would strengthen your organization to have a suitable man who could relieve me of some of the details of active management." George Fuller, who had been employed in 1925 as the president's assistant, left in April 1929; and it was not until the following March that Fitzgerald brought into the organization Robert Rout West, formerly treasurer of the Lancaster Mills in Massachusetts. During Pritchett's brief presidency, West, as vice-president in charge of production, and Ray, vice-president and sales manager, shared the main responsibilities of management. West's administration as president (1932-1940) is the subject of Chapter 6.

The directorate of nine members was increased by the election in January 1922 of the following directors: G. P. Ray, the sales manager, E. S. Reid, a Chatham banker, and E. S. Carlton of Richmond. Carlton died before attending a board meeting, and the vacancy was not filled. There was no election to fill the place of W. B. Hill, who resigned in 1924, but after the death of T. B. Fitzgerald the stockholders elected two new directors: J. B. Kirby and J. M. Miller, bankers from Baltimore and Richmond, respectively. R. R. West became a director in January 1931; but financial reverses growing out of the failure of his bank forced Reid to retire, while Kirby refused to stand for re-election because of his objection to the payment of the preferred dividend in January 1931. Three directors, H. R. Fitzgerald, R. A. Schoolfield, and D. A. Overbey, died in 1931; only two new members were added to the board in January 1932: W. D. Overbey, a son of D. A. Overbey, and Duryea Van Wagenen of Richmond.

At Fitzgerald's request, in January 1931 the board designated an executive committee of three—Pritchett, Harris, and Jordan. To many of his associates it may have seemed an act of premonition.

In January 1922 the directors approved the following salaries for the chief officers of the company: chairman of the board, $56,218.75; president and treasurer, $65,000; vice president (a nominal position), $3,200; sales manager, $40,000; secretary, $12,000. On motion of R. A. Schoolfield the directors voted President Fitzgerald extra compensation of $10,000 for 1922; in 1923 the president's salary was increased to $75,000, and the salary of the sales manager was raised to $50,000. These salaries were retained until 1930, except that, as previously noted, the salary of the chairman of the board was reduced to $25,000 in 1928.

In January 1928 Fitzgerald suggested a bonus plan for officers, superintendents, and salesmen, but the board failed to act on the question. In February 1930 all salaries were cut ten per cent, and an addi-

tional 16.7 per cent decrease was put into effect in September. The
following salaries were fixed by the executive committee of the board in
January 1931: chairman of the board (emeritus), $12,000; president
and treasurer, $50,000; vice president, $2,400; sales manager, $37,500;
vice-president in charge of production, $20,000; and secretary, $9,000.

In October 1931 a disgruntled stockholder, the owner of 3,404 shares
of common and preferred stock, bombarded the directorate with letters
criticizing the management's inability to earn dividends. He was sure
that "our officials are being paid excessive salaries . . . . Our officials
decline to allow a stockholder to examine our salary lists, but it is believed many of them are huge and excessive, and wholly unwarranted
by results being obtained. To allow office holders to draw huge salaries
and be enriched at the expense of stockholders, while many of the
latter are in dire need of the bare necessities of life, is an economic
paradox which stockholders are unable to understand." In upholding
the officers in their refusal to open the books to the complaining stockholder, the directors resolved, "That it has been the policy of this
Company, in effect for nearly fifty years, that such information be held
confidential." One director suggested writing to the complaining
stockholder that "it is dangerous to rock the boat during a storm."
The storm, as the sixth chapter reveals, was of long duration.

5 · *Welfare, Industrial Democracy, and a Strike*

The decision, reached in 1919, to bring labor and welfare problems into a system of self-government called Industrial Democracy climaxed a consistent record of corporate investment in the moral and physical well-being of the workers and their families. The beginnings, during the period in which Schoolfield village came into existence, were sketched in Chapter 2. After the merger of Riverside Cotton Mills and Dan River Power & Manufacturing Company in 1909, the pace of welfare and community activity quickened, and for the two decades determined efforts were made to cement the foundations of harmony and mutual understanding between the company and its employees. That these measures failed to withstand the shock of depression does not rob them of significance for the history of Danville, its major enterprise, and southern industry in general.

Paternalism, as the management saw it, was born of necessity. It would be hard to find a more revealing commentary on this point than the letter President H. R. Fitzgerald wrote in 1928 to W. D. Anderson of the Bibb Manufacturing Company, in response to Anderson's request for help in combating the propaganda of the Southern Industrial Conference.[1] It seems worth quoting *in extenso:*

Our first mill . . . was built in 1882, at which time my father and the three Schoolfield brothers, together with two or three other friends, started a development for the express purpose of affording work to the poor families of the community, who were having a hard time. . . .

Of course the mill immediately became a center to which all these unfortunate people would flock, and instead of the mill being responsible for the conditions among them, it proved to be a godsend in offering them an opportunity for employment, which was the first and most important step and what they needed more than anything else to obtain food and clothes and a reasonable measure of independence.

We built additional mills at intervals of a few years apart until the Riverside group of seven mills was completed. . . . We then conceived the idea of developing a water power higher up the river and of starting the Dan River plant, of which the first mill was erected about 1902. It so happened that at that time other developments were going forward thruout the South very rapidly and instead of a large surplus of help we had about digested the supply in our immediate community, so that it became necessary to develop the village of Schoolfield. We had to draw upon the mountain districts of the Piedmont section. I would not now attempt to describe the conditions that existed among virtually all of these families in their state of run-down poverty and ignorance, and eking out a precarious existence on mountain farms. Some of the worst cases of disease and a long chain of evils and vices that had grown into their methods of living, were enough to shock the sensibilities of anyone who loves humanity.

While it had been our custom to promote educational work among our operatives in the city and to assist in their churches and social affiliations, we soon recognized that it was a question of business necessity to begin at the very bottom with day nurseries, kindergardens, primary departments, as well as district nursing and medical department, if we were ever to develop a nucleus of capable and efficient workers. For anyone to have seen their methods of living, cooking and sanitary surroundings they would have wondered how anyone could live under those circumstances, and it is true that the death rate was high and the health rate extremely low.

[1] The Southern Industrial Conference was organized in December 1927 for the purpose of mobilizing public opinion against the long hours and low pay prevailing in southern industries. Chairman of the executive committee was Bishop James A. Cannon. Although President Fitzgerald thought there were "a good many mills that place themselves in a vulnerable position which is very hard to defend"—in contrast with the majority of southern manufacturers, who "have the right spirit and are doing the best they can to improve conditions"—he denounced Bishop Cannon and his "Committee of radicals . . . . I consider them a positive hindrance inasmuch as they have no practical experience and their views are in many respects illogical and unwise . . . . if they really wanted to serve the present generation to the best of their ability they should stick to their respective callings of preaching a sound gospel . . . ." In a symposium on "The Paymasters on the Preachers' Wages," Fitzgerald went on record in favor of good salaries for clergymen (*The Literary Digest,* vol. 79, Dec. 29, 1923).

Furthermore, they were proud as well as ignorant, and any attempt to get at them in other than a very practical way would have been an utter failure. It required several years in which to make any real progress in this direction, but having laid the foundation we kept persistently at it and did not hesitate to gradually broaden and enlarge the scope of our work as fast as circumstances justified. . . .

After a few years we could begin to see some of the results of this work, and I may say that after ten or fifteen years we had virtually succeeded in transforming the entire community and, incidentally, in developing a corps of operatives of intelligence and efficiency which, in our opinion, has more than repaid all that it cost, to say nothing of the infinite satisfaction of having had some small share in the transformation of so many lives and in bringing happiness and reasonable prosperity to thousands of people who otherwise would never have had it.

Now, I have mentioned the above experience in order to substantiate from actual observation the basis upon which my own reasoning is constructed, namely, that what these people needed most was an opportunity to work and to make for themselves a decent living, and, along with it, the contacts that would develop individual initiative and push them to a higher plane of thought and life. This is something that apparently our critics know very little about, nor could they make intelligent allowance without the practical experience; and I am also convinced that if they had the experience and would go to work and try to accomplish something along the same line, they would have a fuller sympathy for the difficulties involved and the patience required. One of the finest things in the rapid industrial development of the South has been the educational work that has been accomplished in almost every community by the splendid men who have developed these plants and many of whom have made it a prominent feature of their life-work to uplift and benefit their people. I do not suppose that history records in any nation that has inhabited the earth a period of more rapid and substantial development than has taken place in this regard throughout the South.

As to the criticism of the mill village and the suggestion that it represents a system of serfdom, etc., the idea is so ridiculous as to show on its face that the author of the suggestion knows nothing about it. I do not suppose there is a more independent or self-asserting class of people anywhere, who know better what they want or who represent a more genuine type of Democracy than will be found among the mill villages of the South.

In the first place it would not be possible to meet the housing situation in any other way, but even if this could be done experience shows that the character of houses that could be rented from outside parties or that the people would build for themselves are so much below the standard maintained by the mills that it would constitute a grave difference in the facilities for homelife. Furthermore, it would have been impossible to have made the progress along educational, moral and sanitary lines if the people had been scattered thruout the city. We find, however, as the years go on that more and more of our people are disposed to buy small farms or plots of ground and build homes for themselves, which with their improved resources and experience after having worked in the mills for some years enables them to live on a higher basis than they previously did and we think that this is healthy growth. . . .

Many will be disposed to quarrel with Fitzgerald's interpretation of the chain of circumstances which, in Danville as elsewhere, fastened responsibility for family and community development on a profit-seeking enterprise. It may be argued, for instance, that different objectives would have hastened the process of development, or that the same objectives might have been reached in better ways. To speculate on what could have happened is not a very fruitful exercise for the historian. The guiding principles of social betterment in Schoolfield and Danville were doubtless narrow but not necessarily less enlightened than in industrial communities in no way beholden to a large corporation.

In general, the welfare program had the stockholders' endorsement. Meeting in January 1911, they approved a resolution introduced by J. T. Catlin commending the directors and officers for their "valuable assistance to various charitable organizations in the City that are striving to uplift and help humanity in general, and the employees of the mills in particular." It was only a secondary consideration, the resolution implied, that welfare work made for "increased efficiency of their employees." In January 1916 the stockholders agreed with President Schoolfield that the "untiring zeal with which the various branches of welfare work have been conducted has not only borne fruit in the contentment and happiness of the people but it has lowered the death rate, increased the standards of health and enabled you [the stockholders] to attain a far more efficient organization of help than could otherwise have been had."

As earnings dwindled in the 1920's, a minority of stockholders became more critical than in the days of lush dividends. Fitzgerald saw no reason for changing his opinions: "Contrary to the impression of many," he said "your so-called welfare departments are not, and never have been, run by your company for sentimental reasons." Recalling the desperate struggles of the company to find suitable operatives, to teach them elementary rules of healthful living, and to discipline them in the monotonous tasks of the factory, the president believed the benefits of the welfare program were worth three times what it cost.

Abstinence, Benevolence, and Worship

"Our New-Year Policy," a leaflet distributed to supervisory employees at the end of 1914, emphasized the Company's determination to minister to the "moral and spiritual welfare of the operatives." High on the list of objectives was sobriety.

When the Company started its first mill [the officers reminisced], the strong position taken by the Superintendent [Roberts] and his faithful Overseers and the vigilance that they exercised to employ only sober men achieved wonderful results not only among the help but throughout the community. One of the first questions asked of an applicant for a position was, whether or not he drank whiskey; if he did, or if it was afterwards discovered that he did, he was refused employment. Intelligent men have long since recognized that a whiskey drinker cannot be relied upon for constant and efficient service, and it is now a uniform policy of railroad and practically all progressive enterprise to require total abstinence of all whom they employ.

Few references to the liquor question are found in later records, but there is scarcely room for doubt that Dan River's officers continued to battle intemperance wherever they found it. The fight against the lesser vice of smoking waned. In 1924 the secretary of the boys' work department of the Schoolfield Y.M.C.A. considered smoking "the most perplexing problem we have to contend with . . . . I should say that nearly fifty per cent of the boys in Schoolfield use tobacco in some form or another."[2]

In supporting religious groups the corporation preferred to help congregations that included mill workers. Thus, the company gave the Third Avenue Christian Church $250 in 1918 and $500 in 1920, in view of the fact that three fourths of the membership were employees. In 1911 a building on Jefferson Avenue, formerly used by the Presbyterians, was made available to workers in Schoolfield who were organizing a Christian Church; and in 1917 the company built a church on Pelham Avenue for a congregation of Dunkards, since a number of these "quietly disposed and very desirable people" were operatives.[3] The Grace Methodist Church received an annual contribution of $150 and an extraordinary gift of $500 in 1919 to help pay for the enlarged Sunday School room. In 1911 the mill gave the Second Baptist Church

[2] *Progress*, vol. 5, no. 13 (March 28, 1924).
[3] The company also bought the pulpit, chairs, and other furnishings for the Dunkard Church, with the understanding that the church would have the use of and the company retain title to the equipment.

$500 to apply on a church debt, and similar gifts were made to the Moffett Memorial Baptist Church ($200 in 1914), the Cabell Street Methodist Church ($250 in 1917), the Keen Street Baptist Church ($500 in 1918), and the Northside Christian Church ($250 in 1918).

At the board meeting of January 1917, Fitzgerald discussed "some contemplated and necessary improvements as to the three churches located in the village, stating that while the policy of the management was to encourage this work as far as practicable, they felt it to the best interest of the churches themselves as well as the Company for the Company not to go too far in offering financial assistance but rather to insist that the churches do a reasonable part . . . ." The Presbyterians, Methodists, and Baptists presented proposals for improving their church buildings, estimating that their respective congregations could raise only $5,350 of the $36,000 budget. Dan River's directors voted to contribute not over $32,000, and in 1917-1918 the improvements were carried out by contractors employed by the mill. All the parsonages were owned and maintained by the company but furnished rent-free to the pastors.[4]

Closely related to the religious life of the mill communities was the charity work conducted by the Wesley House of the Main Street Methodist Church, to which the mills contributed regularly: $250 in 1914 and 1915; $500 in 1916, 1917, and 1918; $1,000 in 1919; and $7,500 to an improvement fund in 1922. Schoolfield commended "the excellent work that you good ladies are doing . . . we are pleased to cooperate with you and we pray that you may do even greater work in the future . . . and that His Blessings may continue to rest upon you." In March 1910 the president reported favorably on the work of the Home Mission Society among Riverside operatives, particularly in the district known as Mechanicsville. To house this organization the company repaired the old Morotock boarding house, and for a number of years the mill paid the society an annual subvention of $250. The Ministering Circle of King's Daughters continued to receive a yearly contribution of $150, and in 1919 the company contributed $5,000 to the Salvation Army. Revivalists and itinerant preachers were encouraged to

[4] In 1928 the company declined to help the Schoolfield Methodist Church in its building program, in view of the fact that not even interest had been paid on a ten-year loan from the company, negotiated in 1907. But debt to the mill was not a "big stick" to keep the preachers and the congregations in line. Fitzgerald frequently urged the church leaders to get out of debt and become self-supporting (H. R. Fitzgerald to the Reverend W. H. Hautzman, Sept. 16, 1921).

appear before groups of workers;[5] but the management protested to the Southern Railway that circuses and carnivals which made their headquarters on railroad sidings near Schoolfield engendered a "great deal of demoralization."

Contributions to Danville's medical services included a gift of $1,000 to the Hospital Improvement Fund in 1912, subscriptions of $500 in 1915 and 1917 (and probably other years) to maintain beds for charity patients in the Anti-Tuberculosis League's camp, and a donation of $5,000 in the $50,000 drive to relocate the Hill Top Sanitarium for tuberculars (1921).[6] Financial aid was also extended the Providence Hospital for Danville's Negro citizens.[7]

Red Cross contributions amounted to $5,000 in 1917 and $7,000 in 1918. In the latter year the company gave $25,000 to the United War Work campaign, and in 1920 contributed $1,500 to the *Literary Digest* Child Feeding Fund. The Travelers' Protective Aid Society received several donations, including $1,000 in 1919, "it being understood that the Management desired to secure the co-operation of this Society in looking after our mill people at the railway station."

Education

In addition to his night school, Dr. W. R. Laird conducted a mission school; and in 1916 the company lent the First Presbyterian Church $2,400 to provide suitable housing for the mission. The night school, which became the Laird Memorial City Night School after Laird's death, received annual subventions of $250 to $600. Dr. T. L. Sydnor succeeded Dr. Laird as principal; a Dan River director, D. A. Overbey, served as dean. Grants, which reached $1,500 annually in 1924-1929, were continued for the support of the North Danville Night School, of which the Reverend O. A. Guinn (a mill operative) was founder and president. In 1917 parents of some seventy-five children attending a county school just beyond North Danville asked Dan River for funds to keep the school in session two months beyond the six months pro-

[5] See, for instance, the poster prepared at the mills announcing "Gypsy Smith Coming" (November 1918) and the notice signed by Superintendent Robertson on the "Ham-Ramsey Meetings for Mill Employees" (March 1926).

[6] As a director and ex-president of the Anti-Tuberculosis League of Danville, President Fitzgerald strongly supported state aid for local sanatoriums in 1930. In 1919 he had recommended that residents of Schoolfield be admitted to Hill Top on the same basis as residents of Danville (H. R. Fitzgerald to Helen Koss, July 25, 1919).

[7] In making a personal contribution of $50 to Providence Hospital, Fitzgerald observed that it was "doing an excellent work among the colored people of our city."

vided by the county. The company responded with a contribution
of $147—60 per cent of the amount needed, since mill children made up
60 per cent of the enrollment.

Schoolfield's school population quickly outgrew the eight-room
frame building erected in 1905-1907, and in October 1912 the company
agreed to help the trustees of Tunstall School District build a twenty-
room brick schoolhouse. After buying the old school for $2,000, the
corporation lent the trustees $18,000 (at 6 per cent) to apply toward
the cost of the $33,000 structure. Enrollment rose to about 750 in the
war years, and in planning a new building the convenience of families
living on the western edge of the village was taken into consideration.
For the West End School the company donated the land and $17,000
in cash and lent the school trustees a large share of the $63,417 outlay.
At the opening of the school in February 1923 President Fitzgerald
delivered an address on "The Importance of Education as a Character
Building Process."

In the school year 1918-1919 Pittsylvania County paid the twenty-
three Schoolfield teachers $50-64 per month for six months, while Dan
River paid salaries for the other four months at a cost of $11,740.
Commencing in 1919-1920, the county paid the teachers for seven
months, the company for three. Domestic science teachers (sewing
and cooking) were added to the faculty entirely at company expense.
In 1924-1925, when the company supplemented the county salary of
$87.50 per month and paid the entire salary of $100 per month for
three months of the year, teachers' salaries cost the company $26,589.
This covered only the pay of public school teachers. Several kindergartens were operated entirely at company expense.[8]

School enrollment grew, as follows:

1920-1921	976
1921-1922	1,106
1922-1923	1,242
1923-1924	1,294
1924-1925	1,282
1925-1926	1,227

The eighth grade was added in 1922-1923; the ninth, the following
year; and in May 1924 the first junior-high school class was graduated.

[8] Payroll records for 1919 list three kindergartens, staffed by eight teachers and assistants earning $444 per month. The company also gave some support (e.g., $1900 for
improvements in 1922) to the Jackson Avenue kindergarten, which was sponsored by the
Burton Memorial Presbyterian Church.

It seemed to Principal Rose Brimmer that plans should be made for a new school building, but in the late 1920's both the mill and county school officials were bent on economy. In 1928, over the protests of Dan River officials, the county schools, lacking funds, closed almost a month short of the promised nine-months' term.[9]

Founded in 1913, the Schoolfield Educational League had a brief career as a cultural center. As a part of its program to spread knowledge of communicable diseases, the League brought to Danville (February 1916) Dr. Harvey Wiley, a noted authority on pure foods and drugs. During the war the League awarded prizes for the best gardens, yards, and homes in the village.

Overseers and second hands organized the Textile Progressive Club, and in 1919 the members were publicly debating the merits of a co-operative store. For a number of years the company paid for correspondence courses on "Modern Production Methods," offered to supervisory personnel by the Business Training Corporation. As many as 150 were enrolled at one time, and President Fitzgerald thought the studies were "very helpful."

To encourage thrift, the Schoolfield Savings Fund, with a convenient teller's desk in the Welfare building, was inaugurated in 1913.

Welfare and Recreation

A modest amount of educational activity (e.g., classes for illiterates) was carried on under auspices of the Y.M.C.A., but the primary objective of this institution was the promotion of community welfare through programs of fellowship, recreation, and physical training. In January 1914 the directors authorized the Schoolfield Y.M.C.A. building, and in February 1916 the Roman Eagle Lodge of Masons officiated at the laying of the corner stone. Rising prices doubled the original estimates of cost, but the $71,275 charged to "Y.M.C.A." in the Welfare accounts for 1917 appears to represent the major portion of the capital outlay.

In July 1919 the president told the directors of a "very pressing need" for a Y.M.C.A., with dormitory space, for workers at Riverside Division; and the following January the stockholders were advised that the company planned an "industrial" Y.M.C.A. in Danville. Within

[9] In 1925-1926 the mill's subsidy amounted to one third of the Schoolfield school budget of $47,785.

a year the plan was discarded with the explanation that it was impossible to get the work done "on anything like a reasonable basis." In 1925 the Danville Y.M.C.A. successfully completed a $75,000 drive to enlarge its building on Main Street. Company officials participated in the campaign, which provided an adequate substitute for the proposed industrial "Y" for Riverside employees.

H. E. Spessard, who became general secretary of the Schoolfield Y.M.C.A. in 1916, directed its numerous activities with the advice and approval of a board of directors selected by the mill management. The Association had 500 members when it occupied the new building in January 1917, and membership grew to a peak of 1,750 or more in 1922-1923. Complete membership rolls are not available, but the dues collected ($3 per year for men, $1 for boys) may reflect the ebb and flow of interest in the institution. The amount passed $3,000 in 1923 but fell to only $203 in 1928.

A number of "Y" activities were at least partially self-supporting (e.g., bathing privileges and motion pictures), but the company's subsidy averaged close to $25,000 annually in 1917-1929 (Table 1). Equipment for "talking pictures" was installed in 1929. After operating at a loss for two years, the directors voted to lease the theater to an outside firm for $150 per month.

Company officials viewed the "Y" program as "one of fellowship and character building." Through "evening schools, lectures and propaganda of an education[al] and constructive nature peculiar to the immediate needs of our citizenry," the "Y" conducted a "liberal line of Christian activity designed to build the fourfold life of our people." Furthermore, it "afforded opportunities for the management to mingle with operatives under a more happy and normal condition and in this way . . . helped to create an atmosphere for the successful operation of our present [1922] system of Industrial Democracy."

Besides sponsoring the traditional round of clubs, societies, and social gatherings, the Schoolfield "Y" trained athletic teams whose prowess is attested by a collection of medals and trophies displayed in the recreation building. Both men's and women's teams represented the company at the Textile Basketball Tournament in Greenville, South Carolina, in February 1922. The athletes brought back two silver cups, but President Fitzgerald found greater satisfaction in a letter from the physical education director of the University of South Carolina, a tournament official. "Never in all my experience with young people," he wrote, "had I seen a mill group like the Schoolfield delegation . . . . There was no loud talking, no boisterous conduct, no ungentlemanly actions at any time . . . . they were at all times ladies and gentlemen in looks, words, and deeds . . . . I do not know much about corporations or finance, but there must be some dividends other than dollars and cents which come to the man who heads up a corporation like yours."[10] After World War I the baseball commission of the Y.M.C.A. sponsored the Schoolfield team of the semi-professional Bi-State League, which finished in first place in the 1921 season. The Danville club of the professional Piedmont League began to use the Schoolfield ball park in 1920.

Concern for the health of the operative and his family began in the day nursery, where working women left their infants and children in charge of a matron and her staff from 6:30 A.M. to 5:30 P.M. There were forty-eight of these nursery children in 1922; for their care parents paid a nominal fee of ten cents a day.[11] Management considered the nursery "well worth the effort and expense—not only from the standpoint of providing an additional source for desirable operatives, but it contributes materially to the betterment of the babies and children thus cared for, as we have always aimed to give them better care and attention than they receive at home, which is of itself a valuable object lesson to the parents."

Medical and dental clinics attended outpatients of all ages and conducted routine examinations of the school children, while the district nursing service provided home visitations. In 1918 the clinic opened a milk station, supplied by the company's own contented cows, for the sake of supplying "every bottle-fed baby in the village with Pasteurized milk."[12] As head of the company's medical department, from 1918 on, Dr. L. O. Crumpler was in effect superintendent of

[10] J. C. Van Meter to H. R. Fitzgerald, Feb. 25, 1922. See also: *Progress*, vol. 3, Feb. 17 and 24, March 3, 1922. Dan River teams also participated in the 1923 and 1924 tournaments.

[11] In the fall of 1930, when the mill was struck, the nursery enrolled 53 children. Their parents were identified as 28 mothers earning $12.60 to $26.25 per week and 22 fathers earning $12.00 to $33.50 per week.

[12] The Riverside and Dan River Cotton Mills dairy flourished for about seven years. In the spring of 1925 H. E. Spessard reported that although "several cows are due to come fresh during the next two months . . . we can not break quite even on our cows." His recommendation to close the dairy and sell the cows to a private firm coming into Schoolfield was doubtless accepted. It was, however, a matter of satisfaction that the mill's dairy had "accomplished the purposes for which we originally started it"—i.e., to provide pure milk at a reasonable price and a better grade of milk (from Guernsey cows) than the community had previously been able to obtain.

health for the village of Schoolfield.[13] During the influenza epidemic
in the fall of 1918 the Welfare building served as an emergency hospital. Medical and nursing services were taxed to the utmost, and in
recognition of their contribution the staff received the president's
thanks and a 100 per-cent bonus on salaries for the month of October.
Shortly after the war the state Health Commissioner questioned the
purity of Schoolfield's water supply. Fitzgerald consulted Hungerford
and Terry, the builders of the filtration plant, and authorized improvements to "overcome to the fullest extent . . . the difficulties complained
of by the Department of Health." In 1920 the U.S. Public Health
Service visited Schoolfield and recommended measures to combat ma-
laria, which was traced to mosquitos breeding on the mill pond.

On the lighter side, residents of Schoolfield enjoyed community
Christmas parties and the play festival in the spring of the year. A
printed program for the 1918 "Schoolfield Patriotic Pageant" described
the line of march for the Red Cross, Garden Boys, Junior Army,
Mothers' Club, Odd Fellows, Red Men, the mill departments, and
"loyal citizens." Probably the most outstanding event in the postwar
years was the pageant of 1923, entitled "The Story of Cotton," presented in Ballou Park under the direction of Miss Brimmer. Music for
the occasion was furnished by the Dan River Concert Band, directed
by "Professor" Joseph Vezzetti. A former Italian bandmaster, Vezzetti
came to Schoolfield as director of music in 1922. The company paid
H. A. Osborne $6,320 to build the bandstand in the wooded area be-
tween the Y.M.C.A. and the Welfare building. Over a period of six
or seven years Vezzetti and his Riverside and Dan River Coast Artillery
Band appeared in numerous concerts, including a concert at the Acad-
emy of Music in Richmond (August 1925). A leading textile journal
declared: "It is freely stated in Danville that the musical department
of the mills has been productive of a greater return on the investment
than any other activity."[14]

---

[13] Dr. Crumpler also had his private practice, but in 1922 it became necessary to give
notice that he could not make house calls.

[14] *Textile World*, vol. 63 (June 2, 1923), p. 77. Expenditures on the band ran as
follows:

1921	$6,415	1926	$3,140
1922	3,680	1927	3,215
1923	7,228	1928	3,112
1924	6,248	1929	3,854
1925	3,684		

Music was an early casualty of the depression. Leaving Danville to return to Italy in
August 1930, Vezzetti wrote Fitzgerald that he was "proud to have been associated with
such a Prince of a man."

The annual pageant, too, was regarded as a builder of morale. It not only provided entertainment but helped to dispel "the lack of dignity popularly attached to the work of an operative in a cotton mill . . . . Visualizing the function of such a worker as one of the cleanest and most useful occupations in the industrial world, the company has conscientiously set itself the task of helping the worker to see his job in this light, to acquire self-respect and consequently to engender respect in others."[15] Portions of the May festival and views of men and women at work in the mills made material for a five-reel motion picture, "The Story of Cotton," which was filmed in Schoolfield by the Rothacker Film Manufacturing Company in 1923. In the belief that "most of the women who now buy the products of the mills do not know the conditions under which the products are manufactured," the producers promised to publicize the fact that "these products are *not* made by cheap labor under sweat shop conditions."[16]

The expansion of the welfare work encroached on space in the store buildings along Greensboro Road which otherwise would have produced revenue. Accepting President Schoolfield's proposal to house these activities in an "inexpensive building," the directors approved the construction of a welfare building (the present personnel and public relations building), which was built in 1916-1917 at a cost of $17,405.

Although Hylton Hall, the woman's dormitory of the Riverside and Dan River Cotton Mills, furnished space for social and recreational programs, it was primarily the acute shortage of labor in 1917 which led the company to erect this "home away from home" for young women workers. Occupied in October 1919, the building cost $387,437, of which $254,305 was capitalized in the Tenements account and $133,-132 written off as a Welfare expenditure. Accommodations were provided for 225 women and girls in 116 steam-heated rooms. Named after Miss Hattie Hylton, Dan River's first superintendent of welfare, the Hall had not only "every convenience afforded in the modern hotel" but also the "protecting and refining influence of charming women of high Christian ideals and character." A booklet circulated among prospective female operatives set the price of room, board, and laundry at $7.50 per week; but the employee-guest had free use of a

[15] *Textile World*, June 2, 1923, p. 77; *Progress*, vol. 4, June 15, 1923.
[16] "We're in the Movies Now," *Progress*, vol. 4, Feb. 16, 1923. Later, the film was revised. At least as late as 1930 the Rothacker Company, the Y.M.C.A. Motion Picture Bureau, and Dan River Mills had the film in circulation. Payments to Rothacker totaled $13,422 in 1923-1924.

gymnasium, swimming pool, infirmary, and parlors for entertaining callers. "Six lovely guest chambers" had "latchstrings on the outside to greet the fathers and mothers who may wish to visit their daughters . . . . They may stay one week at no expense to them if arrangement is made in advance."[17]   The staff of Hylton Hall included a house mother, two assistants, a physical director, a dietitian, and cooks, waitresses, laundresses, and charwomen.   Seventy-five years earlier the cotton mills of Lowell, Massachusetts, had adopted a similar plan for caring for unmarried women brought into factory life for the first time; and the New England scheme flourished until a new source of "cheap" labor made mill work unattractive to native farm girls.[18]   At Dan River employment opportunities for single women declined sharply in the 1920's, and Hylton's "home away from home" began to look like a white elephant.[19]   Including school teachers, the house roll dropped to 138 in 1928; and some of these had been unemployed for embarrassingly long periods.   Opening the Hall to single men and finally, in 1925, to married couples without children failed to close the gap between revenue and operating expenses; and in the 1940's the building was converted piece-meal into mill offices.

Table 1 exhibits a breakdown of the net charges to the Welfare accounts in 1913-1932.   Excluded (because they were treated as charges to Expense rather than Welfare) are the company's donations to churches, night schools, the Community Chest, and sundry benevolences, which reached a maximum of $17,250 in 1924 and dropped to a mere $3,000 in 1931.   Welfare expenditures reached high points in 1919 and 1922; the average stayed close to $100,000 until the economies induced by the depression cut the figure to less than $24,000 in 1932.

As has been noted, substantial portions of the capital outlays for the Y.M.C.A. building and Hylton Hall were written off as Welfare expenses.   For a year or so Hylton Hall's operating income came close to covering expenses, but as the occupancy rate slumped the revenue

[17] *A Pleasing Story of an Unusual Enterprise: Hylton Hall, a Commodious and Attractive Home for Young Women* (Danville, n.d.).   Printing an unspecified number of these booklets in 1922 cost $1,155.   Probably this was a second printing.

[18] Hannah Josephson, *The Golden Threads* (New York, 1949).   An article entitled "Sympathy" by Ella Carmichael, a clothroom worker (*Progress*, vol. 4, Jan. 23, 1923) is reminiscent of the Lowell Offering, but it is unlikely that the girls of Hylton Hall had the education or the incentive to develop literary flairs comparable to the writings of the Lowell operatives in the 1840's.

[19] In April 1920 Fitzgerald wrote Miss Hylton that the "weak point in your present system is that you have entirely too large an overhead expense for the comparatively small number of boarders . . . .   While I am not impatient . . . your present arrangement is extravagant . . . .   You will not be able to show business-like results from it."

from room rents and meals fell off more rapidly than costs declined. Hylton Hall's laundry, however, consistently showed a profit on its business among the villagers; and it was the gain from this source that kept the deficit within reasonable bounds.[20]

Table 1. Welfare Expenditures: Dan River Division, 1913-1932
(thousands of dollars)

year	Y.M.C.A.	public schools	medical director and clinics	Hylton Hall	other	total
1913						9
1914						9
1915						12
1916	71					88
1917	17					60
1918	9					75
1919	17					164
1920	23					120
1921	26	18	6	17	39	107
1922	32	57	7	14	45	155
1923	29	22	5	22	50	129
1924	27	32	7	25	37	128
1925	22	30	9	24	29	114
1926	28	21	9	9	29	96
1927	22	20	11	10	30	93
1928	28	22	9	9	29	97
1929	26	18	10	9	32	95
1930						60
1931	6	13	12	2	6	38
1932						24

Housing

New houses for Schoolfield followed necessarily in the wake of new factory buildings. In May 1912 W. G. B. Fitzgerald contracted to build 25 two-room cottages (at $600 each), and in September Fitzgerald

[20] Gross receipts of $20,500 in 1931 may be compared with receipts of $50,900 in 1927. Operating statements for all years have not been found, but the audit report for 1927 shows Hylton Hall "in debt" to the company in the amount of $158,187.
   The laundry's profit was $1,684 in its fiscal year 1921-1922; $3,476 in 1922-1923; and $3,997 in 1923-1924. One of the commercial laundries in Danville accused the Hylton laundry of price-cutting to build up business outside Schoolfield. Superintendent Spessard denied any intention of competing unfairly, but President Fitzgerald thought the two parties should make an agreement to share the market (i.e., the city laundry to stay out of Schoolfield and Hylton laundry to stay out of Danville).

started another group of 50 dwellings. A contract for 50 houses was awarded to the Hayes Improvement Company in 1912, and in June 1913 Fitzgerald started work on 100 two-, three-, and four-room cottages. A brick residence for the Y.M.C.A. secretary was built in 1916, and in 1919-1920 J. A. Jones Construction Company erected seven overseers' homes on Park Avenue extension (at $9,300 each). The latter project, recommended to the directors in 1916, was designed to enable the overseers "to live in closer proximity to their work, as well as to be identified with the village life."

Postwar housing included a group of 50 dwellings on Bishop Avenue, designed by E. R. James and built by the J. P. Pettyjohn Company at a cost of $378,864. In 1925 Dan River's engineer, E. B. Wood, supervised the building of 25 four-room cottages on Harrison Avenue, Schoolfield; and in 1927 H. A. Osborne built 50 four- and six-room houses in Schoolfield.

In 1918 E. S. Draper, a landscape architect, was employed to make a survey of Schoolfield village and to recommend the improvements which, in view of the difficulty of getting desirable employees, would make the mill village more attractive. Steps had already been taken to give the houses modern conveniences: commencing in 1911 sanitary toilets (or "closets") were installed in all the houses, and in 1917 the dwellings were wired for electricity. Recognizing that it was "very trying to the help traveling over muddy streets to get to work," in 1917 the management announced plans for grading streets and laying sidewalks. In 1923 Draper made a topographical survey and furnished blueprints for further improvements, including the opening of new streets and the location of new residential areas.[21] Serious consideration was given to the proposal to instal a sanitary sewerage system, but when it was pointed out that rents would have to be increased about 25 per cent to amortize the estimated cost of $300,000, the majority of the villagers decided to get along without sewers.[22] A visitor to Schoolfield in 1918 observed that most of the villagers used the garden space and

[21] E. S. Draper, "General Report on Improvement of Schoolfield Village" (August 1918).
[22] The proposal first came before Industrial Democracy's "legislature" (House of Representatives, Bill no. 1, 1923) but was reported unfavorably after the committee consulted with the president. Fitzgerald thought that a modern sewerage system would "undoubtedly . . . have some advantages as compared with the present method." On the other hand, the existing method of sewerage disposal was "one of the best and least expensive." Furthermore, he believed that "if all of the houses were screened, it would be a more effective improvement than sewers"; but when the company offered to instal screen for a small charge, most of the tenants declined to have them.

many kept chickens and cows;[23] and these bucolic aspects were slow to disappear. It hardly needs to be mentioned that this was an all-white settlement. When (as in 1914) the company acquired land and cabins occupied by Negroes, the tenants were required to vacate.

Annual housing and rental reports prepared by W. H. Dodson, the village superintendent, furnish information on the financial aspects of village maintenance and improvement. As of January 1, 1929, the following scale of rents was in effect:

type of house	number	weekly rental
two-room	70	$ .75-1.00
three-room	321	1.00-1.25
four-room	287	1.25-3.00
five-room	15	1.75-3.60
six-room	90	1.50-8.075
seven-room	30	4.20-8.655
eight-room	14	2.00-9.23
nine-room	6	4.80
	833	

Non-rental property included four church buildings, together with the Presbyterian manse and the Methodist and Baptist parsonages. A company-owned hotel rented for $15 a week, while a boarding house yielded $4.61½ weekly. Two barns rented for $5.76¾ per week, while the various stores along Greensboro Road paid total monthly rentals of $200. Some of the store space was unoccupied, and some of the newest houses (paying the highest rents) were also vacant at this time. I do not know what use was made of the "nannie's house," built in 1923 at a cost of $5,760.

After the war the company razed over thirty "old shacks" near the mills at Riverside Division and awarded a $334,000 contract to J. A. Jones to build 41 houses with modern conveniences. In January 1928 mill housing in Danville comprised 113 dwellings of two to twelve rooms each, yielding gross rentals of $395 weekly.

In October 1928 the company had insured 832 houses in Schoolfield for $1,625,300, but the ledger value of this property stood at only $1,068,148 at the end of 1929. Deducting "depreciation and other credits" of $395,466 from the original cost of $1,592,323, the Tenements account at Dan River Division, which included the store build-

[23] *Southern Textile Bulletin,* Dec. 19, 1918, pp. 8-12.

ings, amounted to $1,196,857. Similar data for Riverside Division
have not been found.

Was village housing a good investment? Unfortunately the available data do not answer this question satisfactorily. In 1918-1919 Dan
River division showed net losses of $126,000 on rentals as a result of
extraordinary maintenance expenditures and improvements which
might have been capitalized more liberally. Unusual economies in
maintenance pushed net income to over $66,000 in 1924 and to $68,000
in 1929; but in the latter year there were 75 more houses in the village
than in 1924.[24] The $55,025 realized from Schoolfield rents in 1930
represented a return of 4.6 per cent on the ledger values of December
31, 1929; but the Tenements ledger carried, unsegregated, various
properties not expected to produce revenue. On the other hand, current expenses of the police and fire departments were charged to the
mill's Expense account.[25]

The only complete analysis of the company's housing investment in
Schoolfield was drawn up in June 1932. It placed a value of $1,450,000
on 834 homes, one hotel, and fourteen stores. The houses and hotel
accommodated 3,250 employees, equivalent to 1.02 room per employee.
Annual costs, including interest at 5 per cent and depreciation at 3.5
per cent, totaled $165,740, while the rental income amounted to $94,-
716, leaving a net loss on the investment of $71,023. Neglecting interest and depreciation, the net income represented 3.6 per cent of the
invested capital.

A more careful scrutiny of the records may suggest expenses, such
as managerial salaries, which in part might have been properly allocated to housing costs. Certainly, it would be easier to prove that mill
housing was a poor financial venture than to show that it was the source
of gain.[26] The hopelessness of the search for a precise measure of the

[24] Village Superintendent Dodson wrote discouragingly of his efforts to keep expenses
down in 1924. He employed two carpenters regularly to replace broken windows and
repair locks and doors. Two other workmen were required to make other repairs, such
as replacing sills and floors in houses built so low to the ground that the wood rotted
rapidly. Two men kept brickwork in repair, and two more were employed to plaster
and calcimine. Dodson had seven painters on his force, yet all the houses were "suffering
for paint now." The sanitation staff kept "always busy," cleaning toilets and carrying off
garbage. It required three full-time employees to keep water in the toilets and replenish
the toilet paper: "if we do not use toilet paper, newspapers, rags, sticks, etc. are all used
and the closets fail to work. As it is, it is hard to keep buckets, old clothes and dead hens
etc. from being put through the seats . . . ."
[25] These departments cost $16,383 in 1921, reached a high of $17,465 in 1923, and
dropped to $12,129 in 1931. The costs were principally salaries.
[26] In 1924, while the mill was running only three days a week, Dodson was besieged
with requests for company houses by "people who are living in houses adjoining our

extent to which housing was subsidized helps to explain one aspect of the interminable argument over the North-South wage differential.

Schoolfield's shopping center consisted of two blocks of stores on Greensboro Road. In 1918 the Park Place Mercantile Company was leasing space for a dry goods store, meat market, restaurant, furniture store, and drug store. This firm also operated the coal and wood yards. Although Dan River had no financial interest in the Park Place business, charge accounts were settled by payroll deductions at the mill.

In 1918-1919, when coal was scarce and high-priced, the mill took over the coal and wood yards and organized the Schoolfield Coal and Wood Company, with W. H. Dodson as manager. The new company lost money in 1919, 1920, and again in 1922; but from 1923 on it never failed to turn in a tidy profit (e.g., $17,100 in 1925, the best year prior to 1933). In August 1919 the company acquired the coal yard operated in Danville by G. T. Davis. Riverside Coal Company reported losses of $8,953 in 1920 and $441 in 1921. Subsequently, this organization disappears from the records.

The annexation of Schoolfield remained the ultimate goal of civic leaders bent on creating a "greater Danville." In connection with municipal elections in June 1924 H. C. Ficklen published "Facts for Annexationists," which held President Fitzgerald responsible for blocking the annexation of Schoolfield when the city limits were extended in 1907. Four years later (1928) Ficklen brought five municipal bills before the state legislature, including one providing for the annexation of Schoolfield; but the mill's arguments for keeping Schoolfield outside the city limits prevailed.[27] An alleged misrepresentation of Dan River's position on annexation was the occasion for another of the frequent jousts between the company and the local press.[28] On another municipal issue Dan River's executives took a stand which the majority of the

property, also Danville . . . not able to pay the high rent . . . . There is more dissatisfaction on account of not being able to supply houses than I have ever known." Of course, in the emergency people in non-mill housing may have been pushed to lower their standard of housing.

[27] J. T. Catlin to H. R. Fitzgerald, Jan. 26, 1928. According to Catlin, one of Ficklen's arguments hinged on the fact that residents of Schoolfield could not become home owners. In December 1928 Fitzgerald wrote a three-page letter to Mary Cassidy, a student at George Washington High School, giving her his arguments against annexation. The student was authorized to use the material in a debate, but without quoting the author.

[28] H. R. Fitzgerald to M. K. Harris, Aug. 30, 1929. Fitzgerald and Harris talked of suing the *Bee*, but finally let the matter pass with the expression of "deep and sincere regret . . . that our local papers . . . have had an unfriendly attitude" toward the mill.

voters approved. When the city government drew up plans for the sale of the municipal gas and electric plants to a private utility, President Fitzgerald worked for the continuance of municipal ownership. The issue was decided by referendum in December 1926.[29]

If Danville had escaped the disruptions of American society brought on by a world war, clinics, nurseries, playgrounds, ball clubs, and pageants might have been enough to keep five thousand workers contented. One of the consequences of the war was to give the city and its suburbs a large "floating" population. As the more aggressive workers abandoned textile mills for lucrative employments in shipyards and munitions their places were filled by less tractable operatives than those who came to people Schoolfield and Danville in the early days of the mills. Although the management responded to this war-born unrest by increasing wages and by renewed efforts to strengthen morale through improved living conditions, restiveness, high labor turnover, and low efficiency persisted. A searching appraisal of the situation prevailing in the summer of 1917 may be found in the letter which the superintendent of the welfare department addressed to President Fitzgerald.[30] After noting that "the unrest . . . manifested here is more or less common to all our Southern industries at this time," Miss Hylton referred in detail to some outstanding causes of dissatisfaction among Dan River employees. They commonly felt, she said:

That they were not fairly treated by their "boss." That the bosses try to drive and they say *they can be led a long way, but will not be driven*. . . . They also say that this driving method is not true of any other mill. Many say that they are sorry to leave and do so on that account alone, as they cannot stand it . . . .

Another reason, often given, is that they can make so much more elsewhere, particularly at Spray, Leaksville, and Draper, and that they can live much cheaper at either of these places . . . .

There has been a growing dissatisfaction, very freely expressed, that there is no chance for a man "to get anywhere" in the mill. That there is no system of promotion. That when a man is wanted to take any position of trust that he is always brought in from some other mill . . . . Knowing your ideas along this line, I have always tried to convince them that the

[29] Although the president, in October 1926, was not sure that a vote for municipal ownership would "safeguard the future growth of the city, both as to rates and quality of service," in December he commended the participation of mill employees (at Riverside Division) in an "organized effort against the sale of the light and gas plants" (H. R. Fitzgerald to L. B. Conway, Oct. 18, 1926; and C. J. Parrott to H. R. Fitzgerald, Nov. 29 and Dec. 4, 1926).

[30] Hattie Hylton to H. R. Fitzgerald, Aug. 22, 1917. (Miss Hylton kindly permitted me to use this letter.)

real policy of the mill is the opposite of their belief, but I know of no other subject upon which I can make so little headway . . . . It makes no difference how much we stress, in the school, Night school, and clubs, the opportunity the mill affords the wide-awake, efficient boy or girl, that is lost on them because of this very pronounced feeling they are taught at home . . . .

Your Second Hands are variously charged with impurity and profanity, with driving, over-bearing, and unsympathetic administration of their powers, with discriminating unfairly against their best help because of jealousy . . . . The Superintendents and Overseers are censured for backing up the Second Hands, without due investigation of the merits of every case, so that often gross acts of injustice are committed and allowed to pass . . . .

While your own, and Mr. Schoolfield's attitude toward the Welfare Work for your employees is understood by the people to be a lofty and noble one . . . the indifference of the Superintendents and Overseers of every degree is not understood . . . .

I would suggest that there now be arranged a definite course of lectures specially designed for the overseers and second hands, to be given at the Y.M.C.A. . . . The course could take as its structural idea the beauty and joy of service, and show how the handling of men with this thought dominant, would breed more contented, more loyal, more faithful and efficient "hands" . . . .

There is real and very justifiable complaint about the condition of the interior of the houses. This complaint is general and wide-spread, and this dissatisfaction on the part of their wives plays a large part in the contentment of the men. The system of improvement is very ineffectual, and requests by the people to have their walls fixed, are in many, many cases apparently unnoticed for months and even years . . . .

Now I admit, that at first the abuse of the houses was something terrific, but it is enough to delight anybody to see the great improvement in this particular. This being true, it seems to me that everything reasonable should be done to encourage the women in their efforts to make sweet attractive homes . . . .

I do not pretend to know why, but I do know that [the handling of garbage and trash] is not done promptly or systematically, but spasmodically, and that the accumulation of trash, cans, garbage, etc., is an actual menace to the community health . . . .

The execution of your plan to lay sidewalks on the streets as rapidly as you can will certainly be an important factor in the comfort and satisfaction of the people . . . .

In this connection it is probably superfluous for me to suggest that a Landscape Architect be first secured to design our whole scheme of village improvement, as you have in all probability had such a course planned for years . . . . I am very enthusiastic over the possibilities before us for making our village the most beautiful place imaginable . . . .

I know that [the police department] does not have the support and confidence of the people as it should have, because I have heard the subject often discussed by various groups of our most loyal men and women . . . . They charged the officers with being recreant to duty . . . and generally expressed great contempt for what they call a "rotten System." . . . There has been too much bickering and strife among the men themselves . . . .

Throughout my experience in Schoolfield, I have been impressed with the frequency of the expressed wish that the mill would assess the people to secure a company physician . . . . Until now, there has been at no time, a medical man on the field suitable for such an important position. This is not the case now, however . . . .

Because of a lack of mutual understanding of the problem of each department, and a proper appreciation of the spirit and ideals governing each, and because of the consequent lack of co-ordinated effort, there is unnecessary friction and loss of conservation of all forces for community betterment . . . .

I have not found Fitzgerald's reply to this letter. It was, however, management's concern over the conditions described by Miss Hylton which inspired the move toward Industrial Democracy.

Industrial Democracy

Community and welfare programs of the type employed by Riverside and Dan River Cotton Mills were not uncommon in the southern cotton textile industry.[31] The improvement of mill villages, which all mill owners found imperative when labor was scarce, may have proceeded more rapidly at some places than in Schoolfield. Among southern textile firms, however, Dan River pioneered in introducing a plan of employee representation under which wage earners were encouraged to make their demands for improved working conditions the subject of "legislation."

So far as I have been able to ascertain from the surviving records and from conversation with his associates, Harry Fitzgerald put Industrial Democracy into Riverside and Dan River Mills single-handed. His youthful enthusiasm for schemes to harmonize the relations between labor and management bore fruit in the various welfare ventures already discussed; and in 1919 his vision was broadened by the appearance of a book, *Man to Man,* which showed how to apply the Golden

---

[31] A. Berglund, G. T. Starnes, and F. T. deVyver, *Labor in the Industrial South* (Charlottesville, 1930), pp. 105-124.

Rule to industrial relations. The author, John Leitch, began working at a tender age in Chicago's stockyards but in later life attained some prominence as the originator and promoter of a plan for improving labor relations. In the period of unrest following the war a number of firms tried his panacea for bringing labor and management together through the organization of executive and legislative bodies modeled on the federal government. This was Industrial Democracy.[32]

It requires no great imagination to suppose that Fitzgerald, after reading *Man to Man*, exclaimed: "That's just what I've always believed." What made the book so timely, from Fitzgerald's point of view, was the return of labor organizers to Danville and the founding of Local No. 1 of the Loom Fixers' Southern Association of America on February 26, 1919.[33] Industrial Democracy promised to stop the unionization movement; more than that, it offered the hope that workers would learn to appreciate how much better off they were without unions.

Fitzgerald rejected a common view of American manufacturers that labor's gains during the war were undeserved. In an address at the Blue Ridge Industrial Conference in 1920 he declared that business should recognize that:

What was perhaps right and best policy for the nineteenth century won't answer for us to go all the way through the twentieth century . . . . One of the great evils that grew out of [the prewar] system, was the tendency of those who employed labor to buy it just exactly as they would the machinery and materials required; to obtain it at the lowest possible price and get just as much out of it as they could . . . .

[32] John Leitch, *Man to Man: The Story of Industrial Democracy* (New York, 1919). Fitzgerald bought 100 copies of *Man to Man* to distribute to employees and friends. In December 1919 Leitch wrote Fitzgerald to tell him "how much happier my Christmas will be because you have added another unit to those who are helping to bring peace on earth in Industry . . . . Will you please assure your people of my warm regard and of my pride in them as members of my 'family.' " Leitch's stationery was embossed with a triangle enclosing his initials and a swastika. *Progress* (vol. 2, Nov. 25, 1921) contains "A Sketch of the Life of John Leitch."

[33] Fitzgerald wrote R. A. Schoolfield "confidentially" (March 1, 1919) that two or three attempts had been made by "outside parties" to organize the mills. "I am glad to say," he reported, "that we have apparently frustrated each such attempt."
Although there is no mention of the Loom Fixers' Southern Association in A.F. of L. publications for 1919, an A.F. of L. affiliate was apparently working in Danville. I found in Dan River files a carbon copy of a letter from L. R. Fair to W. W. Mobley, dated February 20, 1919. Fair, apparently a union official, told Mobley he had heard rumors that the Dan River management "has requested that all machinists in their employment affiliated with the International Association of machinists must either resign or withdraw from the Association . . . . Let me say however I hope I am erroneously informed as I am personally acquainted with the officials of your Mills and know they possess too high a standard of citizenship to attempt the [sic] enslave their employees . . . . I feel you can amicably adjust your troubles satisfactory to both sides and without additional complications, and last but not least *remember you are not to agitate any* of the operatives."

Then came the labor unions; you may like it or not, but they have certainly brought a great many blessings that labor would not otherwise have gotten. Shorter hours, more pay, and better working conditions are the undoubted products of militant unionism, and it not only had the approval of fairminded men and women everywhere, but for a long time the battles that they waged almost invariably commanded the sympathy and applause of the disinterested public . . . .

But unions were "simply carrying out the same principle, in virtually the same way, . . . that the employer did when he tried to get out of labor all that he could and give us little in return." It was easy to reach the conclusion that, since two wrongs don't make a right, unions did not satisfy the worker's quest for justice.[34]

In an earlier speech Fitzgerald had observed:

. . . the one outstanding fact, which to me is more alarming than any other, is that so many of our people . . . seem to have utterly disregarded the fundamental principles of our democracy. Indeed it is evident that we have already gone too far in the direction of treating this question [the labor conflict] as if it were a matter of compromise between two selfish and competing forces.

We have already discovered that advances in wages and shorter hours, which for so long have been the goal of Labor Unions, do not of themselves bring satisfaction. However desirable they may be, both have been attended with a multiplicity of evils, not the least of which is a serious decrease in the productive output and the fact that labor is less contented than before. Neither have profit-sharing schemes nor stock ownership, sick and death benefits, accident insurance, or the like, been found to any considerable extent efficacious. They accomplish a slight ripple of approval on the part of a few, and are soon forgotten or regarded as a sort of bonus which might just as well have been added to their wages.

What was labor's real grievance?

I'll tell you what we have found. The real American workingman, especially that splendid specimen which we all know in the South, is not only loyal to his government and the vital interests of his homeland, but he is far more sensible and reasonable than some would have us believe. True, he has problems which are just as real to him as ours are to us. He also has a very deep-rooted impression that he has been dealt with unjustly, and it is sadly true that in many instances the nefarious influence of the professional agitator has found fertile soil in the American workman's brain, due to the petty frictions and arbitrary methods under which he has worked.

[34] *Address of H. R. Fitzgerald, President, Riverside & Dan River Cotton Mills, Danville, Va., At the Blue Ridge Industrial Conference, Blue Ridge, N. C., July 2-4, 1920* (n.p., n.d.).

It is my belief that a vast majority of employers not only desire to accord justice to their employees, but instances are common in which large amounts are being expended in educational and welfare work and everything being done that the said employer knows how to do to bring about cordial and friendly relations among his people. Notwithstanding this fact, the old system is lacking in many respects: the overseers, the sub-bosses—and some times the superintendent himself, are autocratic and overbearing; there has been no adequate method of recognizing or rewarding individual merit; no system of promotion; the operative has had no opportunity to express himself in matters pertaining to his own well-being or that of the industry, and while we have been trying to persuade him the interests of capital and labor are identical, etc., he has been forced to regard this as more poetic than real.

How did Industrial Democracy propose to improve the situation?

Industrial Democracy is not, as some have supposed, a paternalistic or socialistic theory; it does not mean democratization in the sense of government ownership of railroads, etc. It is merely the application of true democratic principles to industry. Ethically it means a square deal in wages and working conditions; in reality it is a system of selfgovernment in which the operatives have a voice in all matters pertaining to their welfare.[35]

Although offered "any reasonable price" to help with the inauguration of Industrial Democracy at Riverside and Dan River Mills, Leitch had too many prior commitments to come to Danville in 1919.[36] Thus, it was left to President Fitzgerald to work out the details of organization, modifying the Leitch principles to suit local conditions. There is no mention of Industrial Democracy in the directors' minutes until after the plan had been adopted. On July 30, 1919, Fitzgerald explained to the board that Industrial Democracy "is a system of self government fashioned on the order of our Federal Constitution and National Government . . . . It does not contain any profit-sharing scheme nor is there anything included that encroaches in any sense upon the interests of the Stockholder." By way of explaining the timing of this innovation, the president spoke of "the whole atmosphere, especially for the past few months . . . surcharged with labor troubles. Unions

---

[35] Address of H. R. Fitzgerald at Southern Textile Association, printed in the *Southern Textile Bulletin*, vol. 18 (Oct. 30, 1919).

[36] Leitch organized the John Leitch Company, with offices on Fifth Avenue, New York. In the depression of 1920-1921 the author of *Man to Man* was less successful in selling his plan; and in order to protect Industrial Democracy "from the odium consequent upon legal procedure," a committee of his creditors appealed to a number of firms to help bail him out. Dan River put up $500, which Leitch repaid a few years later.

have been organized all over the South, and with the backing of the Government Labor Departments, all of whom seem to champion any demands that the Unions make, it has been extremely difficult to keep our situation here free from complications." Director Lamb moved that the board "heartily approve" the action taken by the management; and at the annual meeting in 1920 the president's explanation that "we have worked along this line for many years" seemed to satisfy the stock-holders.[37]

Preparations for introducing Industrial Democracy began with con-ferences among the supervisory personnel. A constitution was drafted, probably by Fitzgerald; and, after the election of a House of Repre-sentatives, all members of the Cabinet, Senate, and House signed the constitution at a ceremony held in the Y.M.C.A. building on August 12, 1919. After indoctrination, employees were invited to sign a pledge card, as follows:

I hereby subscribe to and heartily endorse the Policy of our Company as printed on the back of this card. I pledge myself to observe and be governed by its principles of Justice, Co-operation, Economy, Energy, and Service. I also agree with my fellow-associates of the Riverside & Dan River Cotton Mills, that by the help of God, I will do all in my power to aid in carrying out this Policy and to achieve the distinguished success which I believe is within the reach of our great organization.

The "Policy of our Company" embraced the principles set forth in the constitution.[38] According to the preamble, "the members of the Industrial Organization known as *The Riverside & Dan River Cotton Mills, Inc.,* earnestly desiring to improve and better the Industrial, Economic and Spiritual condition of all concerned, and believing that the Principles hereinafter set out are fundamental in our efforts to that end, do hereby solemnly announce and establish this *Constitution* . . . . We endorse and declare the following Principles to be fundamental": (1) *Justice* was "the first Corner Stone"; (2) *Co-operation* meant "to pull together, and to freely offer, and work with the spirit of that prin-ciple" in order to "develop individual and commercial supremacy";

---

[37] In February 1920 Fitzgerald wrote a director, Capt. W. H. White, that he appreciated White's "apprehension . . . in regard to the distorted views taken by radical labor agi-tators, etc., and we of course fully recognize that there is no guarantee against having a thing of this kind occur at any time . . . We did not expect Industrial Democracy of itself would prove a panacea. . . ."

[38] *Constitution and By-laws for the House of Representatives, the Senate and the Cabinet: Employee Representative Plan of The Riverside & Dan River Cotton Mills, Incorporated* (Danville, 1919).

(3) *Economy* was defined as "time, material and energy well spent";
(4) *Energy* was "the power back of action"; and (5) *Service* was the
"Cap Stone of the superstructure" since "fortune favors the performer
of worthy deeds and of unusual Service . . . . Quality shall always be
the first element of our Service and quantity shall ever be the second
consideration."

Following this lofty declaration of principles, the constitution describes the machinery of the organization:

The Cabinet, "not an elective body," comprised all the executive
officers of the company.

The Senate, "likewise not an elective body," was made up of overseers, foremen, and heads of departments.

The House of Representatives was elected by the workers, on the
basis of one representative for each forty employees. Workers in each
room or department nominated "double the number of Representatives to which said department . . . is entitled," and the names of the
nominees were posted in their respective departments for two weeks
prior to the election. Eligible for nomination was "any white person,
male or female, who is forty-one years of age, who has been continually
in the employ of the company for twelve months and who has subscribed to the five Principles of Our Business Policy."

By-laws provided for the organization of the House of Representatives, headed by a speaker, and the Senate, presided over by a president.
A majority of either house could recall any of its officers. Other articles
explained rules of order, committee duties, and arrangements for compensating representatives for legislative and committee work.

President Fitzgerald, Secretary W. W. Ayres, G. P. Ray, sales manager, W. W. Moore, superintendent of Riverside Division, G. W. Robertson, superintendent of Dan River Division, Raymond Hall, manager
of Riverside Division, H. M. Martin, manager of colored goods production at Dan River, and J. H. Schoolfield, Jr., manager of white goods at
Dan River Division made up the first Cabinet. Clayton D. Gaver,
President Fitzgerald's personal secretary, was secretary of the Cabinet.

The Senate comprised 61 overseers and department heads, 34 from
Dan River Division, 17 from Riverside, and 10 from the offices. L. J.
Rushworth, superintendent of dressing, served as the first president of
the Senate and Gaver was its secretary.

One hundred and seventeen workers—76 from Dan River Division and 41 from Riverside—constituted the House of Representatives in the First Congress. Judging by given names of the representatives, only nine were women. Speaker of the House was C. J. Parrott, a representative from No. 5 weave room at Riverside. Gaver also served as secretary of this body.

Eleven other Congresses were similarly formed in the summer of each year, the Twelfth Congress having been installed in July 1930. Following organizational meetings, the members of the Cabinet, Senate, and House dined at the Country Club as guests of President Fitzgerald. Here the president read his annual "state of the union" address.[39]

When Riverside and Dan River Mills inaugurated Industrial Democracy the New York *World* heralded the event with a banner headline: "Employees Take Charge of Great Cotton Factory and Run It Just as United States Is Governed by President and Congress." To see whether or not the workers did "take charge" of the mills one may turn to the legislative history of Industrial Democracy, preserved in a bound notebook labeled "Record of Bills."

Let us begin with the bill introduced in the House of Representatives on July 17, 1919. H. R. 1 was a bill which recommended building a Y.M.C.A. and a Community House for Ladies in North Danville. Its "patrons" were Clark and Wheatley, weavers at Dan River and Riverside, respectively. Referred to the Recreation and Amusements committee, the bill was reported favorably and passed by the House on August 14. The Senate concurred (September 26) and the Cabinet approved the measure (October 3), whereupon it became "effective" and was published in Bulletin No. 15 (January 12, 1920). Here the legislative record ends. As already explained, a company-owned "Y" and community center proved to be too costly, and H. R. 1 never bore fruit.

Between July 17, 1919, and August 13, 1925, the House received 484 bills: 304 of them were presented during the first year and only 15 came up between November 13, 1924 and August 13, 1925, the last date entered in the "Record of Bills." The same record describes only 17 Senate bills, all of them introduced between August 29, 1919, and April 30, 1920; possibly this record is not complete.

Aside from bills dealing with questions of hours and wages, the legislation brought before the House of Representatives concerned

[39] Several of these addresses (e.g., 1922, 1923) were printed as leaflets and widely distributed.

principally two problems: the health and convenience of workers in and out of the mill and technical matters relating to machinery and equipment.

The first of the latter class of bills was H. R. 6 (1919), which dealt with the speed of looms in two of the weave rooms. The "Record of Bills" indicates that this was adjusted by management in consultation with a House committee. H. R. 61 (1919), asking for replacement parts on some old Crompton looms, was tabled; but H. R. 146, "That 20-inch heads be used on all Crompton beams as far as practicable," was enacted into "law" on January 19, 1920. H. R. 91, directing management to "purchase pick ball, pick levers, box plates, pick points and filling fork slides direct from loom companies," and H. R. 131, calling for steel skeleton harnesses for Riverside's Long Mill, were enacted in October and November 1919. House Bulletin No. 6 refers to a resolution of August 7, 1919, asking for improvement in the quality of warps, "especial reference being made to gouts, knots, loose ends, missing ends, stuck ends and other poor work back of the Weave Room." The resolution enjoined every department to CO-OPERATE. H. R. 41, introduced by nine Riverside weavers and passed on January 19, 1920, repeated the demand for improvements in carding, spinning, and dressing, "so as to increase the supply of warps and filling and to prevent loss to the weavers by stopping of looms." The bill furthermore required that "any weaver who loses as much as one hour on one or more looms in any one day by reason of the stopping of his loom, waiting for warps or filling without fault on his part, be allowed pay for the lost production."

H. R. 151 (1920) directed that "an emery wheel be placed in every department . . . where necessary or needed"; and H. R. 185 (1920) called upon the company to purchase whisk brooms and require the use of brooms instead of scrap cloth in cleaning ring rails. H. R. 241, introduced in January 1920, was not brought to a vote. This bill provided for a new blacksmith shop at Dan River, "as the building we are now occupying is in a very bad condition and about to rot down." H. R. 287 (1920) requested the management to "keep on hand an adequate supply of oxygen, used in electric welding. This is a matter of economy in that castings and supplies can be welded at once and machinery kept going that now has to wait for this work."

H. R. 139, demanding better lighting in the designing department, was enacted in November 1919; and at least three bills sought improvements in the humidifying systems. The first of these (H. R. 30) was "handled with management by committee"; no action was taken on the second (H. R. 114); and the third (H. R. 238) was passed and approved in January 1920.

A bill asking that a successor to W. G. Benefield, the chief dyer, be chosen by promotion within the department, was disposed of by consultation between the management and a House committee; but a Senate bill requesting the hiring of an understudy for each overseer was tabled. In November 1919 Henry Roediger, head of the cotton department, proposed: "That the Senate . . . investigate and report on the feasibility of erecting a building where our boys can learn the art of Manufacturing cloth in all of its branches, from dyeing to finishing." The measure was passed by the Senate but subsequent action on the proposal has not been recorded.

Welfare legislation ranged from such petty questions as the demand that the "Greeks" be forced to vacate their lease of the restaurant to proposals which, if adopted, would have necessitated inordinate outlays by the company or forced it to engage in activities unreasonably remote from its principal business. Certainly futile was the House resolution (November 14, 1929) to request the corporation to provide employees with food, clothing, fuel, medicine, and hospitalization at cost. More reasonable were the bills calling for better toilet and dressing-room facilities, e.g., H. R. 12, proposing a dressing room for girls in No. 3 cloth room, "as when they work in the dress they wear up here they are not decent to go home on the cars"; and H. R. 212, providing for a dressing room and shower bath in the boiler house, "owing to the excessive grimy character of the work." H. R. 258, petitioning for a gymnasium and shower baths "for ladies" at Dan River Division, was tabled. In 1916 the mills in Schoolfield had installed six drinking-water systems manufactured by the Audiffren Refrigerating Machine Company. President Schoolfield found them so satisfactory that he wrote Lockwood, Greene, recommending their use in other mills; but Riverside Division had to wait four years for similar equipment. The passage of H. R. 130 led to the installation of 32 Audiffren drinking fountains in the older mills at a cost of $13,680.

Senate Bill No. 15 (1920) provided for a medicine cabinet in each department; but H. R. 145 (1919) to establish a company-owned hospital for employees was defeated. The high cost of medical care was the subject of a House resolution (1919), protesting that "physicians in this city, since their recent advance in the price and charges for services rendered, are charging exorbitant prices, unwarranted and unjustified." In 1926-1929 committees appointed by the House discussed with the management and the company's medical director medical and hospitalization prepayment plans. Dr. Crumpler favored a program which he estimated would require contributions of twenty-five cents per week per employee; but the management was unconvinced that any group plan would work without a heavy subsidy from the company.[40]

More successful than the movement to obtain a medical-care plan was the proposal, originating in the House of Representatives, to separate Schoolfield from the annual Community Chest drive in Danville. House and Senate conferences in December 1926 led to the organization of the Schoolfield Community Chest; in February 1928 this body was formally established with its own constitution and by-laws. One of its principal objectives was to assure adequate support to Hill Top Sanatorium; but the Chest also furnished food and medicine to numerous families not reached by the company's own welfare work.[41] Pledges in the 1927-1928 campaign totaled $9,105.

Group life insurance with premiums paid by the company was adopted under one of the earliest bills passed by the House (H. R. 10). Benefits totaling $35,000 were paid in 1921, but there appears to be no complete record of the families helped by the payment of $500 to $1,500 upon the death of the breadwinner. In the economy drive of 1930 this plan was unceremoniously discontinued.

In his message to the 1922 legislature, President Fitzgerald revealed that it had been "in my mind for some time past to suggest some practicable plan by which to recognize and reward those who, after rendering long years of faithful service, become incapacitated by age . . . . a small reserve fund could be set aside on the books of the Company out of the earnings and before the Economy Dividend is calculated." A

[40] *Progress*, vol. 1, no. 1 (1919); Dr. L. O. Crumpler to H. R. Fitzgerald, Nov. 8, 1927 and Feb. 23, 1929; H. R. No. 1 (1929)

[41] A member of a House committee wanted to introduce a bill which would make it compulsory for every tubercular patient to enter Hill Top Sanitarium, but President Fitzgerald warned him that it was "not within the province of your constitution to pass legislation of this character." It would represent an "invasion of individual liberty." (A. C. Splawn to H. R. Fitzgerald, Jan. 22, 1926; H. R. Fitzgerald to A. C. Splawn, Jan. 28, 1926).

joint committee of the House and Senate made a study of retirement programs, but all the plans submitted proved prohibitive in cost.[42]

H. R. 3, asking the company to furnish employees coal at cost, was "handled with Management by Committee." H. R. 65 (1921), requesting a 50 per cent reduction in the price of wood, was not brought to a vote, but in May the price of wood was reduced to $2.75 and in June to $2.50 per one-horse load. A bill to set up an employees' cafeteria passed both houses, but there is no record of any action on the matter. In January 1920 a bill to increase the lunch "hour" to 45 minutes was defeated; and H. R. 286, proposing to limit overseers' lunch "hour" to 90 minutes, died in committee. H. R. 106 (1919) provided sheds at all the gates to protect dinner carriers in bad weather; but no solution was offered to the frequent request for a service that would permit workers to eat without leaving the job.[43]

In November 1919 the House enacted a segregation "law," as follows:

That no colored persons of either sex or any age be employed by our Company inside of Mills in any department or capacity other than sweepers or scourers, or floor cleaners, or janitors except the picker rooms, dyeing and bleachery departments, waste houses, yard force, drivers, tuckers, and boiler house.

That no colored people can use same room for dressing or toilet that is used by white people.

In 1920 the rule was modified (H. R. 160) to permit Negroes to work at quill cleaning and waste baling.

H. R. 177, requesting an investigation of the firing of six young girls in the finishing department was tabled, and no action was taken on H. R. 37 (1920), asking for an explanation of the laying off of older employees. These, it appears, were the only measures concerning hiring and firing policy.

[42] One proposal called for an annual subsidy of $25,000 from the company and contributions of over $150,000 from employees. A stumbling block was the high cost of providing for those close to retirement, since in 1922 there were 84 workers over sixty-five and 190 over sixty years of age. Informally, the company looked after certain employees too old to work. Fitzgerald wrote F. E. Murrie (Dec. 4, 1920) that it was "nothing but fair and right" to pay $6 a week to Fannie Chapman, who had worked for the company thirty-five years.

[43] In 1930 or 1931 Superintendent Robertson protested to the president that the "custom of having refreshment places at different gates, ever since they have been allowed, has been a nuisance, the help leaving their work continuously without permission." He proposed giving the Y.M.C.A. the concession for operating a food cart, making regular rounds under regulations that would not interfere with the mill work.

A curious proposal, tabled in the House, was the demand contained in H. R. 240 (1920) that wages be paid in gold coin!

To popularize and create enthusiasm for Industrial Democracy, the magazine *Schoolfield Progress,* first published in 1914, was revamped and re-christened *Progress.*[44] With Hattie E. Hylton as editor-in-chief and A. Bledsoe Clement as managing editor, the paper made its initial bow on December 12, 1919. The first number was in newspaper format, and its ten pages included 900 column-inches of advertising. The managing editor had the lead editorial, exclaiming: "Howdy! Well, here's a little surprise for you, another result of Industrial Democracy —your own paper . . . . Things will be written so you can understand them . . . Let's proceed to issue the livest, most interesting paper in the country." An anonymous rhymester contributed this gem (to be sung to the tune of "Maryland"):

> No more we'll toil by rule of might
>   At Schoolfield and Riverside
> We each shall live the rule of right
>   At Schoolfield and Riverside
> True glory lies in noble life.
> Not sullen scorn nor envious strife.
> Nor where oppression's law is rife
>   At Schoolfield and Riverside.
>
> Justice shall always lead the way
>   At Schoolfield and Riverside
> Democracy shall have the sway
>   At Schoolfield and Riverside
> No man shall claim another's toil,
> Nor wrong his brother on thy soil.
> Each man shall haughty spirits foil
>   At Schoolfield and Riverside
>
> Thy sheets and ginghams lead the world,
>   At Schoolfield and Riverside
> Nor shall our banners e'er be furled
>   At Schoolfield and Riverside
> Some day each brother's toil shall cease,
> From work in rest shall find release,
> Till then we'll have Industrial Peace
>   At Schoolfield and Riverside.

[44] *Schoolfield Progress* (vol. 1, no. 1, Jan. 25, 1914) was an organ of the Welfare Department, furnishing news of schools, clubs, churches, and recreation. It ran irregularly through vol. 2, no. 13 (June 1919). The only issues of *Schoolfield Progress* I have seen are personal copies of Miss Hylton, who also owns early issues of *Progress.* Dan River vaults have bound copies of an incomplete file of *Progress.*

In the first flush of Industrial Democracy this "Weekly Digest of Progress, Human Interest, Social and Industrial Welfare" reiterated the editors' confidence in the triumph of Justice, Co-operation, Economy, Energy, and Service. One of the magazine's jobs was to keep alive the friendly rivalry among workers trying to raise output and increase the Economy Dividend rate. "Riverside Weavers are after Dan River's Scalp" ran the captions on letters (January 1922) describing a production marathon in No. 3 weave room. In one week, operating 540 looms over 30 years old, this group turned out 2,696 cuts of ginghams, with only 9 cuts of seconds. Individuals, too, were singled out for honors: "Here's How Davis Does It" reported that in five weeks (1921) Davis took 455 cuts off 17 Crompton looms, 85 cuts in excess of "required production." At Riverside's Mill No. 8, which one writer referred to as the "parlor mill," co-operation reached its highest level: loom fixers helped weavers when they got behind, and fixers volunteered to run "their lady weaver's looms during the lunch hour."[45] Not much space was given over to presenting the case for the opposition; although, surprisingly, *Progress* did print an article, "Why I Am a Member of the I.W.W. (by One of Them)," opposite a piece by an Industrial Democrat, "Why I Am Not an I.W.W." But "Cunneff's Column" clinched the argument: six thousand workers belonged to the "finest labor union in the world" without paying a cent in dues.

Progress was sold on a subscription basis for $1.50 per year. After the novelty wore off, subscriptions dwindled, yielding only $1,225 in 1922; but job printing done on the *Progress* presses absorbed a large share of the deficit. As a matter of fact, when the management decided to suspend publication in September 1924, Managing Editor W. M. Hundley complained to the president that "the mills, through the various department heads, have failed dismally to support the printing department by not giving it the job work required by the Company." Friendship, and probably inertia, routed most of the printing work to private shops in Danville.[46] Although *Progress* was discontinued, as Fitzgerald explained, "because in our candid judgment it is no longer necessary as an educational medium among the operatives," from the

[45] *Progress*, vol. 2, Dec. 9, 1921; vol. 3, Jan. 27, 1922; vol. 4, Feb. 16, Apr. 20, 1923. Although the writer of the first of these articles urged overseers to "cut out all unnecessary help, and give every efficient man a man-size job," he advised weavers: "If you have more looms than you can keep going, ask your overseer to cut them down."

[46] W. M. Hundley to H. R. Fitzgerald, Sept. 6, 1924. A professional journalist, Hundley came to Schoolfield to take charge of *Progress* in 1923.

outset the publication had furnished fuel for a skirmish with the news-papers in town. In 1921 R. A. James, a Dan River director, complained that *Progress* competed with his papers for both news and advertising. He thought the mill's magazine should be used only as "an organ for preaching the advantages of Industrial Democracy and Mill News." President Fitzgerald feigned surprise but did nothing about it.[47]

At one time the management considered a plan for linking stock ownership with Industrial Democracy's cooperation. In January 1921 the chairman of the board outlined a proposal for selling Class A stock to employees. Although many corporations were doing this, Dan River's plan was "different from any that we know of." No officer, superintendent, foreman, or any employee earning more than $10,000 a year would be permitted to own the stock; on leaving employment with the company the Class A stockholder would have to redeem his stock or exchange it for preferred shares. "In permitting the operatives to participate in the profits of the Company," Schoolfield said, "we feel that it is nothing but right that they should." Since a quorum for voting a new stock issue was not present at the 1921 stockholders' meeting, the matter was tabled; and at a board meeting in March Fitzgerald announced that the management had decided to postpone the question indefinitely. A week before this, however, a Circular Poster notified the employees that the company had acquired a small amount of preferred stock "solely for the purpose of letting our people have it . . . in order to enable them to save their money." The following June the president castigated the anonymous authors of a letter "addressed to the voters of our Industrial Democracy suggesting that Representatives be selected who would favor a bill to issue Stock of the Company to Operatives." This, Fitzgerald said, was

not only a breach of etiquette and a direct violation of the rules of Industrial Democracy for such a letter to have been issued without the sanction of the Legislative Bodies, but the suggestion that it contains is misleading and absurd and does not accord in any sense with the principles of In-

[47] After the death of James in 1921, Fitzgerald and some of his associates sounded out the prospects of gaining control of the morning *Register* and the afternoon *Bee*. When this proved impractical, they invested in a competing afternoon paper, the Danville *News*. Although Fitzgerald declined to become a director of the new company, the *News* agreed to abide by the policy of not printing anything "reflecting the policy or inner workings of the mill without approval of management." But it was not long before the James papers announced that Danville had room for only one afternoon paper and that "everything owned by the James family will be sacrificed before the *Bee* is allowed to go under." In due course the *News*, not the *Bee*, went under (R. A. James, Jr., to H. R. Fitzgerald, Oct. 30, 1923; H. R. Fitzgerald to R. A. James, Jr., Sept. 9, 1924).

dustrial Democracy. Such a bill, if offered would be unconstitutional . . . .
No one has any right to deal with a question of issuing Stock except the
Stockholders and the Company's Directors . . . . It is needless to say that
the only way in which anyone can acquire Stock in the Company is to buy
it at its market value.

Another channel of cooperation which Industrial Democracy sought
to develop was the encouragement of inventiveness on the part of the
workers. Fitzgerald wrote Leitch in November 1920 that the Dan River
employees had already turned in "many valuable suggestions . . . . We
have discovered a great deal of talent and some genius that was not
previously recognized at all." In his address to the Third Congress the
president reiterated the need for "promoting valuable suggestions for
improvement of the service and of encouraging the study of technical
problems as well as the invention of methods for greater efficiency." No
great flood of mechanical improvements arose from these suggestions
for stimulating the worker's ingenuity, but at least two devices were
noteworthy. One of these Fitzgerald described as follows:

> An old fellow who for many years has been second hand in one of our
> cloth rooms, having charge of certain finishing machines, had been working
> a long time to devise some scheme to prevent cloth from being wrinkled
> and cut while passing through steel calendar rolls. He finally succeeded in
> bringing out one of the most ingenious devices to overcome this trouble
> that I have ever seen. It is very simple, comparatively inexpensive, and will
> prove a serviceable thing to industry. One wonders why it was never dis-
> covered before. We had the pleasure of patenting it for him without any
> cost, as well as having all of the work done in the mill shop and of hand-
> ing him a check for one thousand dollars in recognition of his contribution
> to the progress of his department.[48]

A worker by the name of Lyles developed an improved bunch builder,
the effect of which was to increase bobbin capacity up to 20 per cent.[49]

Wages and Hours

Legislation dealing with welfare and working conditions cannot be
dismissed as mere window-dressing; much of it doubtless led to the removal of petty grievances and sources of friction that might have mush-

[48] *Address of H. R. Fitzgerald . . . At the Blue Ridge Industrial Conference* (1920).
[49] G. W. Robertson to H. R. Fitzgerald, Aug. 1, 1928. Robertson suggested that "we
allow Peg [Lyles] some consideration for his faithful efforts," but I do not know how he
was rewarded.

roomed into serious problems.   On the other hand, no system of employee representation could be viewed as a success unless it coped satisfactorily with the major questions of hours of work and wages.   The
records dealing with these phases of Industrial Democracy at Dan River
are abundant.

A number of House bills deal with vacations, although none went
so far as to recommend vacations with pay.   In 1919 a bill calling for a
ten-day vacation in August was defeated, while the proposal to make
Labor Day a holiday was tabled.   Though promising to abide by the
will of the majority, the management gave several reasons for running
on Labor Day: (a) there had been a holiday in June to welcome the
returning soldiers, (b) the mill closed for two days in July, (c) two
thirds of the employees averaged more than two weeks' absence during
the first seven months of the year, and (d) closing one day would cost
about 100,000 pounds in production and 2 per cent in the Economy
Dividend.   In 1925 (and probably other years, too) Labor Day was a
holiday; and Easter Monday was ordinarily a day of rest.   In 1922,
despite the disapproval of management, the House and Senate voted to
close the mills for two weeks at Christmas time.[50]   The following year,
however, the House voted 64 to 24 to substitute one week's vacation in
July for the long Christmas holiday.   After 1923 the problem of holidays faded into insignificance: for reasons beyond the control of Industrial Democracy the work week was frequently cut to four or four
and one-half days.

The decision reached in the fall of 1919 to cut the normal working
week from 56 to 55 hours (stopping at noon instead of 1:00 P.M. Saturday) originated in a proposal put before the House of Representatives
and enacted as H. R. 8.   In reporting the bill favorably, the committee
urged that "to save this time and lose nothing in production . . . all
operatives be requested to cut out every moment of loss motion, keeping all machines in operation full up to schedule time, and not more
than a few minutes be consumed in washing up."   Although the 1920
Congress had considered a bill to reduce the working day to nine hours,

[50] This was the occasion for the following note of feigned incredulity: "Here are two
unique facts.   One is the delegation to the employees of the decision as to the length
of time the mills should shut down—a startling change from the old method of posting
an arbitrary notice about 24 hours previous to the time the closing was to go into effect.
The other fact is even more interesting . . . .   When [the author] read the notice in the
mill, he was confident that the legislative bodies would take their cue from the implied
wish of the management and vote for the shorter shut-down.   But democracy is no mere
form at Danville; it is not a game of 'follow the leader' but a business of building up
independent thought and action" (*Textile World*, Jan. 13, 1923).

in 1922 the House of Representatives joined the management in opposing state legislation to limit the work of women to nine hours a day. It was a "strange and unwise move." Working ten hours, the Dan River "legislature" averred, could not be considered detrimental to the health of the 2,500 women employees. Furthermore, the workers would not "welcome any move that would render our industry less prosperous or reduce the income of our people."[51] Thanks to the lobbying of Virginia manufacturers, the state enacted no important labor law in this period, although somewhat stricter enforcement of the child-labor act and the ten-hour law for women was secured.[52] On the question of child labor Industrial Democracy had nothing to say, probably because the company virtually ceased to employ persons under sixteen years of age.[53] The management, however, kept up a running debate with the proponents of federal child-labor legislation.[54]

[51] *Progress*, vol. 3, Feb. 17 and March 3, 1922. Fitzgerald said that he was glad that the work week had been gradually reduced to 55 hours, but he saw no reason or opportunity for making a further reduction. He did not consider 55 hours "in any sense irksome"; nor did he see how the "vast majority of these people could earn a sufficient amount in a shorter number of hours to afford them the standards of living from which to derive the most happiness and satisfaction. We may quarrel with Providence . . . but my own philosophy is that the kind Father knew better than we do how important it is in the development of manhood and womanhood to do a good hard honest work for our living; nor do I believe that any people could be happy and prosperous without it" (H. R. Fitzgerald to W. D. Anderson, Apr. 13, 1928).
In addition to sending Attorney Harris and others to Richmond, Fitzgerald reported putting out "some strong propaganda among the various industries of the State" to defeat the nine-hour bill introduced in 1922 (H. R. Fitzgerald to R. A. Schoolfield, Feb. 25, 1922). The company's opposition to labor bills brought up in the 1924 legislature was equally "satisfactory" (H. R. Fitzgerald to R. A. Schoolfield, Feb. 8, 1924; M. K. Harris to H. R. Fitzgerald, Mar. 10, 1924).
[52] The Division of Women and Children in the Bureau of Labor and Industrial Statistics was created in 1922. When state inspectors complained that women were working during the lunch period, Superintendent Robertson posted a notice, calling attention to this infraction of the law, but added: "Those who run automatic machinery may leave the machines running, provided they do not require any work or attention" (June 20, 1922).
[53] Reports of the Bureau of Labor and Industrial Statistics show a steady decline in the number of work certificates issued to fourteen- and fifteen-year-old laborers. In 1929-1930 only six were issued in Schoolfield and 55 in Danville; not all of these, of course, were for mill employment.
In 1925 Riverside Division employed no one under 16; at Dan River "between 25 and 50" boys and girls worked five hours a day and went to school for five hours. They were all children of "worthy families . . . absolutely dependent upon their own effort for support and without which they would be objects of charity" (H. R. Fitzgerald to Dr. J. E. Hicks, Jan. 15, 1925).
[54] Fitzgerald objected to the support of federal legislation by the Federal Council of Churches of Christ in America. The Council, he thought, did not realize that a constitutional amendment would lead to "abuses much greater than the evil itself." The proposed eighteen-year age limit would "deprive a very large number of our young people of the opportunity of becoming adept in almost any industrial line. If you compel a boy or girl to wait until after they are eighteen years of age to learn a trade . . . the chances are very much against their ever learning it at all" (H. R. Fitzgerald to Dr. Worth M. Tippy, April 22, 1924). In writing to the secretary of the American Cotton Manufacturers' Association Fitzgerald proposed "to arouse every agency that we can to

With the inauguration of Industrial Democracy questions concerning wages and bonuses were referred to a joint payroll investigating committee. Apparently, the first of the committee's recommendations touching wages was embodied in the two bills (H. R. 285 and S. 16) which resulted in raising the bonus 10 per cent in April 1920. As has been pointed out, this brought the general level of earnings to 242 per cent of the 1917 level. Seven months later the proposal to cut wages evoked a lively discussion. When H. R. 40, recommending a 25 per cent reduction in wages was introduced, one representative, "after making a number of scriptural quotations," compared wage rates with the price of ginghams: in 1914, he said, a week's wages would buy 171 yards and in 1920 (until the price cut late in the year), only 130 yards. Therefore, he considered the proposed wage cut too severe. Another representative "took a rather drastic view of the Company's management," asserting that the enormous sums spent on Riverside's new mill and the high dividends paid during the "fat years" seemed to belie the necessity of cutting wages. He also volunteered a naïve view of the balance sheet: "the surplus rightfully, but not legally, belongs to the operatives who have earned it . . . . the Company should authorize an additional issuance of common stock and hold a sufficient amount of it in the Treasury to be used to pay the operatives as a part offset to the wage reduction." A third speaker urged a four-day week, with wage rates unchanged; but another representative, who had "studied the situation and thought over the situation and prayed over it," believed the legislature should leave the matter of wages to the president and "thank him for the privilege of working." He foresaw "a very, very critical situation ahead . . . . it was largely the selfish laboring man's fault." The debate ended with the report that the management had shown the "full facts and figures" to the joint committee and convinced them that the only alternative to lower wages was closing the mills indefinitely.[55] The upshot of the matter was the enactment by both houses (November 27) of bills approving a 22.72 per cent reduction in wages.

House and Senate bills passed in May 1921 prepared the way for a second cut in wages. Half of the recommended reduction of 20 per cent went into effect in May, but the Cabinet postponed the other half

---

co-operate in bringing the facts to light in opposing such an iniquitous measure" (H. R. Fitzgerald to W. D. Adams, April 24, 1924).

[55] Based upon notes written up by the secretary of the House, C. D. Gaver.

of the scheduled wage cut until August, since "the cost of living has
not come down in our community as fast as it has in many others."
Nevertheless, four employees appealed to the House to prevent the
application of the second instalment of the cut, as the "reduction of
wages at this time would mean a hardship." The House did nothing
until September, when a bill calling for a 10 per-cent raise in wages
was referred to the joint payroll committee. The committee called
on the president and listened sympathetically to his explanation of why
wages could not be increased: the company's wage level, Fitzgerald
said, was 80 per cent above prewar rates, whereas most cotton mills had
cut back to 40 per cent above their 1914 rates. The "drastic reduction
in prices of cotton goods" and widespread unemployment made wage
increases unthinkable at this time. "Instead of complaining as if we
had experienced a hardship, when in fact we have had steady employment and have received more money for the same period than any
other similar industry in the United States, we should thank God for
the blessings we have." A bill to pay a Christmas bonus of 4 per cent
on 1921 earnings was defeated.

No measure relating to general wage rates came before the House in
1922, but in March 1923 the representatives approved a resolution
calling upon the management to raise wages 10 per cent. The increase
was granted with the understanding that for six months "no further
adjustments are to be asked for." Actually, the new wage scale remained in effect for over a year; but in August 1924 the company put
up Notice-Poster No. 140, announcing: "It is imperative that this 10%
be removed without further delay."[56] This brought the general level
of wages back to the 1922 scale, where it remained until January 1930.[57]

Industrial Democracy had something to do with the structure of

---

[56] There are no House or Senate minutes on this wage cut, but President Fitzgerald
wrote an article on the subject. In view of "very trying business conditions," he related,
in the summer of 1924 the president "appeared before a joint committee of the House
and Senate and explained the existing situation . . . . They were told that we enter-
tained the hope that the new crop of cotton would bring about more normal market
conditions . . . . We felt it wise to remove the 10% wage increase in order to place the
mill in a position to secure as much of the current business as possible . . . . As far as
we could observe, there was not a single discordant note" ("Co-operation Needed in Industrial Leadership," *Textile World*, vol. 67 [Feb. 7, 1925], pp. 158 ff.).

[57] On Nov. 14, 1924 President Fitzgerald wrote Herman Cone that Dan River's average
earnings "last week" were $18.08 (before the Economy Dividend). He wanted to know
whether Cone thought a further reduction of wages would be necessary. (The Cone
Mills had cut wages about 12.5 per cent in August.) Fitzgerald hoped not. It seemed to
him that "with railroad labor and the various building trades, as well as the automobile
and steel industries, paying all the way from 65 cents to $1.25 per hour for labor, the
world ought not to begrudge a faithful and efficient textile operative making from 37.5
cents to 40 cents per hour. . . ."

wage rates as well as across-the-board changes. In September 1919 the joint payroll committee asked all overseers to furnish "absolutely accurate" data on the number of machines tended by different workers, "the actual work done, the energy and ingenuity required, etc." The committee promised to make recommendations to the legislature which would "straighten out any inequalities" in job-to-job rates of pay. Apparently, the only results of this investigation were two bills enacted in March 1920, which authorized an increase of 1 cent per cut in weaving "Ideal" chambrays and an increase of five cents an hour for pipe-fitters. A house resolution in March 1923 recommended "reasonable" changes in a number of job rates of pay in order "to more nearly equalize any places now out of parity," but the records do not show what became of this measure.

In July 1920 the Senate vetoed a House bill for increasing the pay of loom fixers. According to the senators, "the evidence submitted proves our loom fixers' pay, if the Economy Dividend be considered, as much as and in most cases more than anywhere else . . . . to grant the increase asked for would throw our whole wage scale out of balance. While it is true that some operatives are making more than the fixers, it is also true that practically all such operatives are working more than ten hours per day." They admitted, however, that it was "very discouraging to the fixers to see others able to take on a little more work or work a little extra time and thus make extra money, whereas they are unable to do so despite the fact that they have to buy all their tools and overalls." As a compromise, the Senate proposed to maintain the basic rates for fixers but grant them an efficiency bonus, based upon a "standard" output as determined by a committee of four in each weave room. I have found no record of how this arrangement worked, but the following year one of two factions within the Loom Fixers' Southern Association took its case directly to President Fitzgerald. The "loyal" fixers apologized for the hasty action of their colleagues; and the matter ended with a friendly reminder from the president that complaints had to pass through proper legislative channels. Again, in 1925 the fixers let it be known that "we feel like we ought to get more money"; and in 1927 the Loom Fixers' Association presented to the management a set of "trade rules for your approval." They demanded time and one-half for overtime, the maintenance of the fixer's pay scale when temporarily assigned to a "cheaper" job, and extra help for fixers in such tasks as changing warps for rush orders. Fitzgerald found this communication a "very unwelcome surprise." In a three-page letter he extolled the advantages of Industrial Democracy, urging the workers to recognize that it would be inconsistent with the principles of this organization for the company to operate "according to rules made somewhere else." For their part, the union officials not only withdrew the proposed trade rules but thanked the president for "the light you so kindly gave us on the question."[58]

There were other complaints of inequities in job rates of pay. In 1925 the slasher tenders regarded themselves as "treated very badly." They had been "neglected as a class for the last seven years . . . . Most any body in the mill is making more than the slasher tenders." Weavers at Riverside asked for a conference with the president to straighten out a "lot of dissatisfaction," while a group of weavers on dobby looms requested an adjustment of rates to permit them to earn $25 a week. "Winter is approaching," they pointed out, "and at the present wages [averaging $15 a week] some of the weavers with families will be unable to buy coal or winter clothing."

Bills dealing with overtime came before the House in 1924, apparently as the result of the discontinuance of the practice of paying extra for overtime. A committee called on Fitzgerald with the request that overtime pay be restored to the former basis, i.e., time and one-half for work on Sundays and legal holidays and two hours extra for each eight hours of overtime on other days. The president thought there "ought to be some way in which to solve the question"; but I have found no record of its solution.

The worker's earnings under Industrial Democracy comprised three elements: (a) wages at contractual rates, by the hour or piece, (b) a fluctuating bonus, and (c) an Economy Dividend, paid monthly at rates which varied with the average laborer's efficiency. Let us look first at the wage chronology, exclusive of the Economy Dividend. Complete payroll records for 1922-1931 are missing, but the data presented in Table 2 indicate the principal turning points in average hourly earnings. In the absence of figures for 1920, when the bonus reached its peak, we may estimate earnings from the bonus rates. Since increases in the bonus raised wages 142 per cent above the January-

[58] J. C. Blackwell to H. R. Fitzgerald, Jan. 7, Jan. 24, and April 25, 1927; H. R. Fitzgerald to J. C. Blackwell, Jan. 17, Jan. 25, 1927. Blackwell was secretary of Local No. 1.

March 1917 level, average hourly earnings apparently reached a maximum of about 52 cents.

Table 2. Employees and Earnings, 1922-1931

	division	number of workers	average earnings (cents per hour)
1914 (April)	Riverside	1,918	14.0
	Dan River	2,887	13.8
1922 (November)	Riverside	1,958	32.5
	Dan River	3,036	33.2
1923 (November)	Riverside	1,956	36.5
	Dan River	3,318	36.2
1924 (September)	Riverside	1,331	32.8
	Dan River	2,311	32.4
1925 (January)	Riverside	1,801	32.6
	Dan River	3,207	32.4
1926 (January)	Riverside	1,748	32.4
	Dan River	3,571	34.4
1927 (January)	Riverside	1,680	33.2
1928 (January)	Riverside	2,152	33.0
1929 (January)	Riverside	1,410	33.5
1930 (February)	Riverside	1,612	29.1
1931 (December)	Riverside	1,294	29.3
	Dan River	3,206	28.7

After three wage reductions in 1920 and 1921, hourly earnings in March 1922 were 145.5 per cent higher than in March 1914.[59]   A wage increase brought average earnings up from 32.9 cents an hour in November 1922 to 36.3 cents in November 1923.   The following year wages were reduced, and for five years average hourly earnings stayed within the range of 32.4 to 34.4 cents.   The pay cut in February 1930 pulled the average down about 10 per cent, and at the end of 1931 hourly earnings were slightly more than double the 1914 level.   For the entire cotton textile industry the 1931 average hourly wage of 28.6 cents was 87 per cent above the 1914 wage.   Measured by hourly earnings, the Dan River worker still held his gain in real wages.   The

[59] From a wage study made by Waverley Cousins. Average weekly earnings in March 1914 were $8.23 (56 hours), or 13.7 cents an hour; for the four weeks ending March 4, 1922, average earnings were $18.51 (not including the Economy Dividend).

Bureau of Labor Statistics consumers' price index for Norfolk, Virginia (none is available for Danville) shows for December 1931 an advance of only 46 per cent over December 1914.

Despite the fact that bonuses were applied at uniform percentages to the base rates of pay, job and piece-rate adjustments outside of the bonus system led to considerable disparity in the rates of increase in earnings for different classes of workers. Thus, full-time weekly earnings (adjusted to a 55-hour basis) in the spinning rooms at Dan River Division rose from $5.70 in 1914 to $17.31 in 1922, an increase of 203.7 per cent. Spinners at Riverside earned 187.3 per cent more in 1922 than in 1914, but shop and electrical department employees advanced only 112.6 per cent. Generally, the largest rates of increase are associated with the lowest earnings in 1914. Wage and employment policy (i.e., the elimination of the labor of boys for doffing) tended to narrow the departmental differences in full-time earnings.

Full-time earnings for those working at hourly rates rose in proportion to changes in rates of pay; but piece-rate workers gained both through increases in the piece rate and by increasing their output per unit of time. In 1929 the payroll showed 2,307 piece-rate workers and 2,571 hourly-rated employees. At Dan River division the hourly-rated employees (50.85 per cent) earned 46.96 per cent of the payroll; at Riverside workers paid by the hour (56.37 per cent) received 53.70 per cent of the wages.[60]

Economy Dividends

Although the Constitution provided for a committee on bonuses and dividends, with authority to "inquire into and report on all matters concerning bonus and dividends that may be referred to them by

[60] Hourly-rated workers made up the following percentages of the departmental employees in January 1929:

	Dan River	Riverside
opening, through carding	56.82	69.66
spinning	30.21	37.91
dressing	60.73	44.32
weaving	35.89	38.42
finishing and shipping:		
colored goods	79.35	71.88
white goods	93.43	
sewing room	40.09	
sample room		36.36
all other departments	100.00	100.00

the respective bodies," I have found no evidence that this committee or any other representative body had anything to do with deciding the rate of the Economy Dividend. The dividend was announced every four weeks in a Cabinet bulletin, and the rate was undoubtedly fixed by management in consultation with the cost accountants.

President Fitzgerald always insisted that the Economy Dividend was not a form of profit sharing. "This is how it works," he said.

Suppose I were the employer and you the employee. We get together in a friendly way and agree to act on the square with each other. I am to pay you the market wage—which is easy to determine—and I am also to give you the opportunity to increase that by individual effort. At the same time I am to share 50-50 in the results of that improved production. This plan is just a mutual interchange of good . . . . The Economy Dividend bears no relation to the profits of the company or to market conditions. It is possible that the company could be losing money and the operatives earning an Economy Dividend at the same time—although such an anomaly has not existed at our plant.[61]

In response to numerous requests for information on the Economy Dividend, Fitzgerald composed a form letter which furnished the following explanation:

For instance, our standard month for comparison is the period of four weeks immediately previous to the introduction of our system, which was June, 1919. Our cost sheet for that period shows the number of pounds produced and the actual labor cost from which we derive the cost per pound. The first and most substantial gain comes of course from an increase in production or a decrease in the labor cost, which shows a saving in the cost per pound by comparison. Then we also keep a record of the percentage of seconds, and, while this can only be approximated in value, we allow a certain amount for each per cent or fraction thereof saved in seconds. Also, we keep record of the absenteeism and labor turnover, both of which items practically express themselves in the gain of production. Upon putting together the savings thus derived we reach the approximate amount, and this is split 50-50 between the employees and the company at the end of every four weekly period, and out of the sum set aside for the employees we declare an Economy Dividend, which distributes their share.

It is difficult to escape the conclusion that the computation of the savings upon which the Economy Dividend was based lacked something in precision. In 1924, as a result of "improved methods and machinery additions," the 1919 base for determining labor saving yielded too high

[61] "Sees Principle of Democracy Gaining Ground," in *Textile World,* Jan. 13, 1923.

a dividend rate; and the legislature was persuaded to accept a higher base output for dividend purposes. It was estimated that this would decrease the dividend rate about 5.25 per cent. The House approved the change, however, not as a technical adjustment but as a device to cut costs, "recognizing that the Textile Industry is passing through a very serious depression."

Economy Dividends were held down by "those who allow bad work to get by uncorrected, those who are unwilling to 'stretch' where necessary to make their work more effective, or who fail to use their brain in an honest and earnest effort to help reduce the cost or improve the quality and enhance the quantity of production." The dividend rate usually dropped in months which included holidays, especially in December, when the employees insisted on stretching the Christmas vacation into a week's shutdown.[62] Absenteeism and abnormal labor turnover also kept the dividend rate down.[63]

Idle looms also adversely affected the dividend rate. In June 1925 Fitzgerald advised Superintendent Robertson:

While it is true that having some looms stopped for reasons beyond our control affects the dividend proportionately to the loss of production, the real factor that has operated against your results has been the low efficiency of the various looms on the Fancy Styles as well as Wide Sheetings and Bed spreads. We of course recognize that some of this work is new to many of the weavers . . . [but] with the splendid equipment that we have, it seems to me a direct challenge . . . . If other people can do this (our competitors are doing it right along) I see no reason why we cannot.

But in 1926 the president admitted that "at the present rate of curtailment it would be almost impossible to earn a normal average, but a study of the payrolls indicates that there has been some loss motion in the production in various departments." Economy dividends were promised if "we can gradually overcome and systematize this loss motion." In January 1927 Fitzgerald was "very glad" to answer the question raised in the House of Representatives: What has become of the Economy Dividend? "Under adverse conditions, when 1500 or more of your looms are standing idle and when a good proportion of your machinery can be run only at 70% or 75% efficiency, it is not possible

[62] See in this connection "Cunneff's Column" (*Progress*, vol. 4, Jan. 12, 1923) on the "follies of some of our people in indulging in the pleasures of anticipation and neglecting to work the limit of time they should before the Christmas holidays."
[63] In 1919 President Fitzgerald regarded labor turnover, which then ran 10 per cent *per month* at Dan River Division, as "the most difficult problem that confronts the mill operative today" (New York *World*, July 27, 1919).

to earn an Economy Dividend." In other words, if the management could find no profitable employment for some parts of the mill, wage earners could not possibly work hard enough to earn a reward, which was based upon productivity at substantially full capacity. Efficiency, through no fault of the worker, was indivisible.

Economy Dividends were distributed every four weeks from August 1919 to May 1928, excepting one month in 1925 and eight four-week periods in 1926. Cabinet Bulletin no. 1 (August 8, 1919) announced a dividend of 5 per cent "as a result of your first four weeks of Industrial Democracy." This was "truly a remarkable showing," the president declared. "When you consider that many of the improvements in various departments have hardly yet gotten fully under way and that there still remains some machinery idle, which if started up so that everything can run to its full capacity will aid very materially in getting a better production and consequently add to the Economy Dividend Account, you can readily see that the prospect is bright for larger returns." The second dividend, covering the four weeks ending August 30, 1919, was also 5 per cent. Anticipating grumbling because the rate had not increased, the Cabinet pointed out that absenteeism had curtailed output, the percentage of seconds had risen, and the unit cost of production had moved upward. Actually, output and costs showed slight changes in the two periods under comparison: production at Riverside dropped 11,000 pounds and the cost went from 14.56 to 14.66 cents per pound; the output of colored goods at Dan River fell 31,000 pounds and the cost rose from 21.24 to 21.51 cents per pound; but Dan River's white-goods production increased 4,000 pounds while unit cost fell from 12.60 to 12.32 cents. What obviously irritated the management was the decision of the legislative bodies, in August, to pay the 100 per cent bonus (instead of 80 per cent) to workers who put in less than full time.

Table 3 presents Economy Dividend rates for selected periods and indexes of rates of pay and unit labor costs for Dan River's white-goods mill. For the four weeks ending May 15, 1920, wage, bonus, and dividend payments combined rose to a peak of 263.8 per cent of the average wage in the first quarter of 1917. At the same time the direct labor cost of producing a pound of white cloth rose to a maximum of 291.9 per cent of the base period. In the early years high Economy Dividend rates are associated with low indexes of labor cost; the Econ-

Table 3. Economy Dividends, Wages, and Labor Costs, 1919-1928

four weeks ending	Economy Dividend (per cent)	wages, including bonus and dividend	unit labor cost, Dan River division white goods
			(January-April 1917 = 100)
1919			
Aug. 2	5	210.0	249.0
Dec. 24	8	216.0	250.2
1920			
Jan. 24	10	242.0*	252.8
April 17	9	239.8	260.9
May 15	9	263.8*	291.9
Nov. 27	8	261.4	275.9
Dec. 25	6	198.2†	224.5
1921			
April 16	7	200.1	255.3
May 14	7	180.1†	247.8
July 9	5	176.7	236.2
Aug. 6	5	159.1†	238.5
1922			
May 13	11	168.2	212.5
June 10	12	169.7	206.9
1923			
March 17	16⅔	176.8	209.1
April 14	14	190.0*	225.7
1924			
Aug. 30	4	173.3	248.8
Sept. 27	4	157.6†	228.7
1925			
May 16	3	156.0	251.4
June 13	0	151.5	243.5
1926			
Aug. 7	0	151.5	271.1
Sept. 4	0	151.5	281.2
1927			
Jan. 22	3	156.0	255.9
Feb. 19	4	157.6	249.6
1928			
April 14	3	156.0	230.4
May 12	2	154.5	224.1

* Wage increase effective this period.
† Wage decrease effective this period.

omy Dividend of 16.67 per cent maintained for 12 weeks in 1923 partially offset three successive reductions in the wage bonus. But after the wage reduction of 1924 and the drying up of Economy Dividends, the index of labor cost creeps upward. In August and September, 1926, when the average wage was only 51.5 per cent above the 1917 level, the unit labor cost was 176 per cent greater than in the base period. These figures relate to the white-goods divisions, which were no longer producing a homogeneous product (sheeting); but, after allowance for some upgrading of the goods, the gap between wage rates and labor cost seems significant. An Economy Dividend predicated on the worker's efficiency failed to materialize when the company, plagued by rapidly changing market conditions, failed to maintain the volume of output necessary to minimize costs.

Table 4 is a complete record of the amounts disbursed as Economy Dividends. In the banner year of 1923 dividend payments averaged 13.89 per cent of wage and bonus earnings; in 1922 the dividend was slightly lower. Both years were comparatively prosperous for the corporation. After the company's million-dollar loss in 1924, Economy Dividends dropped to 3.12 per cent and 1.38 per cent in 1925-1926. Dividends averaging 5 per cent were paid in 1927, when corporate earnings recovered to the highest point since 1923; but the following year earnings fell to less than half a million dollars, and the stream of Economy Dividends dried up.

Table 4. Economy Dividends and Earnings, 1919-1928

year	Economy Dividends		corporate net earnings (thousands of dollars)
	amount	per cent of wages and bonus	
1919	$146,729	3.26	2,285
1920	490,120	8.63	4,156
1921	322,626	6.86	164
1922	594,235	12.68	3,022
1923	712,609	13.89	2,724
1924	220,553	5.89	—905
1925	148,140	3.12	1,279
1926	61,231	1.38	1,109
1927	248,997	5.00	1,911
1928	47,186	1.30	434

The Decline

In 1923 President Fitzgerald confessed: "I am frank to say that in the absence of this practical feature [the Economy Dividend] and with human nature in its present stage of development, the system would not get very far."[64] It was not only the omission of dividends—for one four weeks' period in 1925, for seven months in 1926, and definitively after May 1928—that killed Industrial Democracy, but also the wearing off of the early fervor and determination to make the system work. The demise of the institution took place in 1930, but it had so long lived in a comatose state that its passing was unannounced. No one sang its requiem; its grave was trampled on by strikers. Yet, its declining years were marked by faint hopes of its resuscitation.

As early as 1923 Fitzgerald complained to the chairman of the Senate educational committee of the "more or less aimless drifting, so far as actual results go, of our Senate meetings for some time past." The remedy proposed was the planning of a definite program for each meeting. Interest in the House meetings was a little more lasting, but in 1926 Secretary Gaver observed that "for some months past . . . the attitude of the House has been running more and more towards indifference." Attendance had dropped as low as 67, out of a membership of well over 100. Two years earlier Gaver had compiled a small handbook of the "Object and Purposes" of Industrial Democracy, intended to keep alive enthusiasm for the system; but no action was taken on the proposal to publish the booklet.[65]

When it became impossible to show the progress of Industrial Democracy in terms of Economy Dividends, the president found it less convenient to attend meetings of the legislature. Gaver urged Fitzgerald to give the workers the bad news as well as the good: "take them into your confidence and tell them whatever you think it is wise to say . . . our people have withstood the reduction in their earnings wonderfully well." Reluctantly, and perhaps too late, the president went be-

[64] "The True Ethical Standard for Employers and Employees," in *Progress*, vol. 4, May 4, 1923; also printed separately, *Address of H. R. Fitzgerald, President, Riverside & Dan River Cotton Mills, Danville, Virginia, before Rotary Club of Danville, Virginia, March 27, 1923* (Danville, 1923).

[65] Besides general information about the principles and procedures of Industrial Democracy, the handbook contained a number of letters from a number of workers who wrote sincerely, if not spontaneously, of the benefits they had received from the system. For obvious reasons, many letters stressed the Economy Dividend, which by this time was on its way out.

fore the House in December 1929 and again in January 1930 to talk about the necessity of reducing wages.

In March 1927 the House and Senate passed a joint resolution reaffirming the members' "sincere faith in the scientific value of co-operation." Although they doubted that there were "any in our organization who do not value and appreciate the co-operative plan," the time seemed ripe to conduct a campaign for new pledges. No action was taken on the proposal to exclude non-signers from participation in the Economy Dividend, but in September the employment office began to require new employees to sign the pledge.[66]

Perhaps to convince some of his northern friends that Dan River's Industrial Democracy was not dead, in October 1929 President Fitzgerald sent C. J. Parrott, the enthusiastic and articulate speaker of the House of Representatives, to the annual meeting of the National Association of Cotton Manufacturers. Parrott made a speech, written in part by Fitzgerald, which would lead the unwary to suppose that nothing had happened to the system since it was introduced ten years earlier. Trade papers friendly to the Dan River management believed that, contrary to current rumors, Industrial Democracy was "as vital a factor in the employer-employee relations at Danville today as it has ever been."[67] But not all the doubts about the workability of the system were malicious. John Leitch found employers increasingly skeptical of his program; and in 1928 the original Industrial Democracy became "The Leitch Plan" in order to avoid confusion with the newly formed, and "Bolshevic" League for Industrial Democracy.[68]

Two things sealed the fate of Industrial Democracy: (*a*) increased workloads, introduced gradually over a period of years but employed more consistently in 1928-1929; and (*b*) the wage reduction put into effect in February 1930.

The stretch-out was grist for the union mill. Just before Christmas 1925 Local No. 1 of the Loom Fixers' Association extended the season's

[66] In canvassing for new signers, Superintendent Robertson urged supervisors to use the "proper spirit and tact." He also asked for a list of those declining to sign (G. W. Robertson to H. R. Fitzgerald, Sept. 14, 1927).

[67] "Industrial Democracy at Danville," *Textile World*, vol. 76, Aug. 24, 1929, p. 34. See also D. G. Woolf to H. R. Fitzgerald, Aug. 15, 1929.

[68] Although he claimed to have his program working in 900 industrial plants, Leitch decided to leave the East and look for greener fields in California. From Los Angeles he wrote Fitzgerald (June 1928) an urgent appeal for a loan of $1,500, but Dan River's president found it impossible to help him (John Leitch to H. R. Fitzgerald, Nov. 23, 1927, and May 10, May 22, and June 23, 1928; H. R. Fitzgerald to John Leitch, June 30, 1928).

greetings to President Fitzgerald and thanked him for the "kindly consideration given our claims during the past year, and the numerous
courtesies shown our representatives." Union officials hoped to remain
"ever . . . in a position to cooperate with you to the end that Justice
shall prevail between man and man."[69] I have not found the president's reply. Any reply, of course, might be construed as evidence of
his acceptance of collective bargaining with the loom fixers. What
went on in union councils during the following months, I do not
know; but in October 1928 the union's secretary took the unusual step
of sending the newspapers a copy of a letter to President Fitzgerald,
protesting working conditions. Specifically, the fixers complained that
their load had been extended unreasonably at Riverside Division and
that the savings resulting from the "stretch-out" had been unfairly divided between the Company and the fixers. The "bigger jobs" threatened to "sap the strength of our men to such an extent that they will
be made an easy prey to such diseases as Pneumonia, Influenza and
Tuberculosis." The loom fixers "were not organized to make trouble
but to co-operate with all to the end that the Scales of Justice might be
kept on an equal balance." They recalled that in the past union committees had "always met with a kind reception from you, though some
have lost their jobs soon after the interview for obscure reasons."[70]
There were hurried consultations among management over the union's
letter, but to the best of my knowledge it went unanswered.[71]

President Fitzgerald came before the House on January 9, 1930, to
discuss wages. The company, he said, faced an emergency, created by
the "unsound wage basis on which we are now operating, due to the
long-continued and unsatisfactory market conditions and the fact that
our present wage basis is approximately 20% higher than our immediate competitors." He asked the House to approve a measure re-

[69] J. C. Blackwell to H. R. Fitzgerald, Dec. 21, 1925. On the letterhead of the School-
field-Danville Loom Fixers' Local 199, Blackwell had written Fitzgerald (July 6, 1925) to
"accept your Piece Plan as you laid it out before the committee at the last conference."
The fixers had first asked for 60 cents an hour but accepted a compromise which promised them about $28 per week.
[70] J. C. Blackwell to H. R. Fitzgerald, October 13, 1928. The letter was published in
the Danville *Bee* the same day.
[71] Riverside's superintendent, L. J. Rushworth, reported to Superintendent Robertson
that Buford Nash, a loom fixer and Speaker of the House of Representatives, had protested over the loom fixer's load a few days earlier. Nash, it seems, had argued that increasing the section from 64 to 96 looms yielded a saving of $8.36, of which half should
have been added to the fixer's pay, bringing the base rate to $29.26 per week. Rates
applied by the company held the fixer's pay to $25.08 a week. From Fitzgerald's cor-
respondence with neighboring mills, it seems that the pay for fixers in Danville was about
as high as elsewhere—but not higher.

ducing wages 10 per cent. After some discussion, the House appointed a committee of five to meet with the president. The outcome of this conference was not reported in the House until February 13, or nearly a month after the president issued Circular Poster No. 192, addressed "To All of Our People":

The time has come when it is necessary for us to announce a vertical reduction of Ten Percent in all wages and salary rates, beginning with the President and including all officers, clerical force, superintendents, engineers, overseers, welfare workers, and all operatives of the Company, the new wage rates to become effective as of February 1st, or with the Pay Roll that begins Monday morning, February 3, 1930.

We have fought hard to stave it off as long as possible, with the hope that conditions would improve, but with the fierce competition we are having to meet and with our present wage rates approximately Four Dollars per week above the entire South, the differential against us of Twenty Percent is greater than we can hold. It would not only mean a continuation of operating without profit, but a positive loss, and in addition to this it would mean heavy curtailment which is really harder on the operatives than a wage reduction.

For instance, for the past year, if our rates had been anywhere near a fair competitive basis—or, in other words, if the rates had been reduced Ten Percent, we could have run much nearer full time, and our people would have received at least Five Hundred Thousand Dollars more for the year's work than they did; and, in addition to this, they would have earned an Economy Dividend.

We hope that this improvement in our economic position will enable us to run nearer a full time basis, which in the long run will mean that our people will receive more instead of less in their pay envelopes than when curtailment is necessary.

It will continue to be our policy, after the basic rates are adjusted, to permit efficient operatives to run more machines when practical and thereby to improve their earnings.

It is also our hope and sincere belief that each member of the organization will cheerfully accept the small sacrifice involved, and be glad to cooperate in carrying out a policy that is so manifestly to the interest of all.

With every good wish,

Yours very truly,
RIVERSIDE & DAN RIVER COTTON MILLS, INC.,

Over one hundred representatives assembled on February 13 to hear the report of the committee sent to confer with the president. The discussion, if there was any, must have seemed pointless. Surprisingly, there were four other meetings of the House, all well attended, and at one of them a bill (H. R. 1) was introduced to adjust rates of pay for drawing-in, as it appeared that the scale had been cut more than 10 per cent. Ninety-one members met on June 12, 1930, to hold the final meeting of Industrial Democracy's House of Representatives. Outside of the halls of the legislature other workers were meeting to lay plans for an entirely different approach to their problems of work and wages.

The Strike

Although its inception and progress differed little from other unsuccessful walkouts in the early days of the Great Depression, the "spectacular strike in the mills at Riverside and Dan River Cotton Mills" provided voluminous copy for newspapers from the Carolinas to New York and Boston. Several factors account for this nation-wide interest in Danville's troubles. In the first place, the strike grew out of a determined drive by the American Federation of Labor to organize industrial labor in the South. The groundwork was laid at the Toronto convention in October 1929. The report of the Federation's committee on organization pointed out that the United Textile Workers of America had been trying to organize in southern mills "for the past thirty years," but the response of textile workers was insignificant "until the stretch-out system lashed their sense of justice into action." A "spontaneous revolt" followed the outbreak of violence in Elizabethtown, Tennessee, and Marion, North Carolina; so the time seemed ripe for "all organizations to include in their organizing plans for the coming year definite provision for work in the South."[72] Egged on by an editorial in the Scripps-Howard newspapers, which called the failure of the A.F. of L to organize southern textile laborers an example of its inability to provide leadership for a national labor movement,[73] the Convention adopted unanimously a resolution introduced by President T. F. McMahon and other officers of the U.T.W.A. Observing that the "unionizing of these Southern workers means a vast outlay of

[72] *Report of Proceedings of the Forty-ninth Annual Convention of the American Federation of Labor* (Washington, 1929), p. 199.

[73] Denying that the Federation had been indifferent to the cause of southern textile workers, President William Green declared: "During the past twenty-five years the United Textile Workers' organization . . . sent to the South for organizing purposes more than $1,080,000. Is that staying out of the South? Where did the money come from? From the organized labor movement" (*Report of Proceedings*, pp. 237-240).

money," the McMahon resolution instructed A.F. of L. officials to con-
sult with officers of all the affiliated unions "for the purpose of devis-
ing a policy that will be acceptable to all interested parties in the proposed campaign of organization among all Southern workers regardless
of craft or calling."[74]

For more than a year the Danville mills bore the brunt of
U.T.W.A.'s organizing drive. Instead of launching its campaign where
labor conditions were notoriously bad, the union chose to challenge a
mill whose workers were relatively well off. If wages were not higher
at Dan River than at other southern mills, at least they were not lower;
and, with minor exceptions, labor relations had been conspicuously
good for nearly thirty years. A victory in Danville would constitute a
rich prize indeed: if an enlightened management were to accept organized labor, it would be easier to break down the barriers where workers
had even greater grievances. Other reasons for the union's choice of
Danville were advanced by a trade paper, as follows:

Danville was the most likely place for the United Textile Workers to
make their demonstration. It is the biggest mill in the South. It is very
largely on colored goods, the most difficult fabric to sell at the present time
and through the last year or two. The whole trend of purchasing has been
away from ginghams and similar cloths—they are practically unmerchantable. And because these ginghams have been nearly unsalable the great
Riverside and Dan River Cotton Mills have found it impossible to keep
their operatives steadily employed and impossible to maintain a net income
that would justify the maintenance of common stock dividends. Hence,
here was the easiest place in the South to find a large number of operatives
unemployed or only partially employed and most amenable to the orations
and expositions of the labor union organizers. And stockholders without
dividends are more apt to be critical of a mill management. Hence at
Danville there was an opportunity perhaps to disturb the equanimity of
the Riverside stockholders. And with a great number of operatives unemployed, or only partially employed, the local merchants would feel a slack-
ening in their own business and hence it would be easier to enlist the sym-
pathies of these small merchants with stories inimical to the management
of the corporation. So Danville was chosen by the United Textile Workers'
officials as the ripe spot for fomenting trouble.[75]

The use of the injunction, the calling out of the militia, and sporadic acts of violence, as well as the failure of persistent efforts to
mediate the dispute, kept the Danville strike newsworthy from the end

[74] *Report of Proceedings*, pp. 265-285.
[75] *American Wool and Cotton Reporter*, Oct. 9, 1930.

of September 1930 until early in 1931. In the account which follows I have attempted to draw out of the millions of words spawned by the strike the essential facts of the controversy, supporting the narrative wherever possible by direct use of records left by the two parties in conflict.[76]

While the U.T.W.A. was perfecting its plan to "invade" the South, the left-wing National Textile Workers Union began to raise strike funds for southern workers. N.T.W.U. literature circulated in Danville during the summer of 1929, and the State Investigation Agency (private detectives) warned the Dan River management that a number of "Communist" employees had attended N.T.W.U. meetings in Gastonia, North Carolina.[77] Boasting of the "splendid work we are doing to combat all sources of organized labor," the Agency predicted that the A.F. of L. would soon arrive in Danville "strong enough to sweep us [the Dan River management] off our feet." These representations sufficed to persuade the company that it needed the services of the State Investigation Agency.[78] During the strike agents of the Railway Audit and Inspection Company and of the Pinkerton National Detective Agency were also added to Dan River's payroll.

President Fitzgerald's "hope and sincere belief" that the wage cut would be accepted uncomplainingly was a delusion. A member of the House committee which discussed the problem with him denied the president's claim that the workers had "understood and appreciated the wisdom in making the move." The representatives were called together, he asserted, and "told the cut would be put on and those who did not like it could get out of the organization . . . ." The workers' spokesman was told by the president he had too much to say and would "look better going than coming."[79] Fitzgerald himself confounded his

[76] In addition to contemporaneous newspaper material, important data on the strike are found in the following books: Tom Tippett, *When Southern Labor Stirs* (New York, 1931), pp. 210-269; Julian R. Meade, *I Live in Virginia* (New York, 1935), pp. 3-99; Duane McCracken, *Strike Injunctions in the New South* (Chapel Hill, N. C., 1931), pp. 114-126, 257-268.

[77] In November a Danville minister reported the arrival of some Gastonia Communists but said the "labor people" (presumably U.T.W.A. officials) would have nothing to do with them. Told of the incident, Superintendent Robertson commented: "I would rather see these people [the Communists] try to get a foothold than the other people."

[78] The Agency began to work at least as early as Feb. 25. Besides professional operatives, the Agency used selected workers on the job to report on union talk within the plant.

[79] L. G. Nunn in a letter to the Greensboro (N.C.) *Daily News* (from an undated clipping). Nunn was one of the committee of five appointed by the House, and may have been talking about himself. At any rate, his employment terminated soon after the conference.

friends and gave comfort to his foes by declaring in an interview with a local newspaper that "Industrial Democracy, neither here nor in any other industry, controls wages."

Labor leaders and—for different reasons—mill officials challenged the explanation that Dan River's wages had to be reduced in order to bring them in line with rates of pay in competing mills. Near-by North Carolina mills especially insisted that their wage scales were "fully as high" as Dan River's.[80] But it was not Dan River's fault that the facts about southern wages were hard to obtain. The industry-controlled National Industrial Conference Board admitted failure in "urging that many more Southern mills give us payroll data each month." The Conference Board received figures (1929) from six southern firms employing 7,700 wage earners, but these data seemed inadequate to refute the widespread allegations of starvation wage-scales throughout the industry.[81] Early in March, after a union official castigated the company for paying as little as $6.00 for 55 hours of work, Dan River offered to show its payroll to "any responsible persons or committees that desired information." A reporter for the Greensboro (N. C.) *Daily News*[82] took advantage of the offer and published the following statistics of full-time earnings for the week ending February 6 (i.e., after the wage cut):

department	employees	average earnings
carding	499	$16.29
spinning	454	15.64
dressing	318	16.95
weaving	926	18.68
all other	976	15.74
	3,173	$16.79

[80] According to the *Daily News Record* (Jan. 29, 1930), Erwin Mills thought it was an "injustice" for Dan River to make such a claim. In Schoolfield the welfare superintendent was alarmed at the consequences of reducing the pay of the Hylton Hall staff. After a walk-out of dining-room employees, new help had been secured at rates one to two dollars less per week than the former scale of $8.00-$10.00 per week. Drivers for the laundry were already earning $5.00 a week less than employees of a private laundry, and other rates were similarly out of line *before* the cut. Four machinists at Riverside Division wrote President Fitzgerald on January 14 (the day before the pay cut was announced) that, contrary to a promise he made them "just a few years ago," they were not earning "just as high wages as any other shop in town."

[81] In February 1930 Waverley Cousins wrote Fitzgerald that the N.I.C.B. wage averages for the South (which then included ten mills, counting Riverside and Dan River as two mills) were doubtless too high, since no data came from North Carolina, Alabama, or Mississippi.

[82] Dan Meeker, in the *Daily News*, March 4, 1930.

Comparable averages for four states were: North Carolina, $16.23; Georgia and South Carolina, $14.30; and Alabama, $13.42. But there was one group of mills in North Carolina which paid an average of $19.26 a week (55 hours) as late as August 1930.[83]

For the directors President Fitzgerald had a different explanation:

We did not say that we were paying 20% above 'any other' or 'every other' southern mill; we said the 'average southern rate.' The fact is that most of the sheeting and print cloth mills in the South . . . are located in sections that have very low rates both of wages and taxes. It is also true that your mills are of an entirely different type and require a much larger percentage of skilled workers. Therefore, while the statement as made was literally and absolutely true, it is not one you would wish to talk too much about or use on an entirely different battlefront from that for which it was made.

Fitzgerald told a friend that "Only the Kind Father knows how hard it was for me to face this decision"; and there were many who, recognizing him as "one of the greatest idealists in our industry," knew he was telling the truth. "Far from wanting to cut wages, he would do everything in his power to place wage levels on a higher scale."[84] Nevertheless, the *News Bureau,* a Boston business magazine, thought the wage cut would "be deplored, both inside and outside the textile industry. The penalty of inability to regulate cotton manufacture properly is made to fall upon the operatives, the class least able to bear it, and in reality the least responsible . . . . Wage cutting . . . is a pusillanimous method of attempting to correct an unhealthy situation [and] may well do more toward organizing labor than all the previous arguments of walking delegates."[85] The day the wage reduction was announced a member of President Hoover's advisory committee on industry strongly urged Dan River's president to reconsider, "because it is generally construed as a straight wage reduction, and it is feared that it will cause a general avalanche of that sort of thing in the South." Fitzgerald answered that neither the company nor the textile industry had given Hoover any pledge to maintain wages.

[83] *Daily News Record,* Jan. 28, 1930.
[84] In his presidential address at the May 1929 convention of the A.C.M.A. Fitzgerald declared: ". . . there is nothing smart or commendable in any management that seeks to drive its costs down by lowering the standard of living of the operatives . . . . Those who are paying wage rates below a fair Southern average are jeopardizing their own interests as well as that of the whole Industry, and it is indeed a false security for them to assume that low costs derived from such a source is either tenable or justifiable . . . the result of this philosophy is a vicious system which embodies the germ of the disease from which all have to suffer" (*Proceedings of the 33rd Annual Convention* (Charlotte, 1929), pp. 19-27.
[85] Quoted in the Chattanooga *News,* date unverified.

Fitzgerald was sure that the wage reduction would have led to no trouble or discontent except for the presence of agitators. The specific object of his wrath was the eleven-year old Loom Fixers' Southern Association. Back in 1918, the fixers recalled, "we . . . saw . . . that we needed an organization for the protection of ourselves and families from the greedy, money-loving, slave-driving cotton mill kings." After perfecting their union, however, they "let the management trick us into leaving it and joining a company union, the great fake called 'Industrial Democracy.' "[86] Actually, as I have pointed out, the fixers' union managed to survive throughout the 1920's; and its leaders spearheaded the movement to unionize all the company's employees. In January 1930 a "large number of the workers journeyed to Richmond and requested President Green, of the American Federation of Labor, to send them an experienced organizer, purely for the purpose of superintending the mechanics of organization." In response to this appeal, Green chose a United Textile Workers of America vice-president, Francis J. Gorman, to undertake the organizing drive in Danville. At the first rally, held in the Majestic Theater on February 9, 1930, about 1,000 workers heard Gorman, O. E. Woodberry, publicity representative of the A.F. of L., and Mathilda Lindsay, southern representative of the National Women's Trade Union League, assert that they were "here to stay." At the conclusion of the meeting union membership cards (requiring initial dues of $1.00) were signed by some 750 workers.[87] Thus was born Local 1685 of the United Textile Workers of America, dedicated as Gorman said "to bury this system of so-called industrial democracy." B. F. Nash was elected president; J. C. Blackwell, secretary. Both were loom fixers and members of the old Loom Fixers' Southern Association.

Fitzgerald took cognizance of Gorman's arrival in the following Letter Poster No. 192 (February 12, 1930):

To all of our People

We are informed that paid organizers have appeared in our midst and that as usual they are appealing to such prejudices as they can arouse and do not hesitate to distort existing facts to carry their point.

We think that we can confidently claim to be the friends of our people

---

[86] W. I. Frye, in a letter to the *Chronicle* (Cincinnati, Dec. 27, 1930), previously printed in the *American Labor Banner* (Washington, D. C., Dec. 20, 1930).

[87] Early in May an informer for the company ascertained from the Union's executive council that the Union had 800 paying members, plus 103 who had joined but not paid dues.

and that the many years of pleasant relationships that have existed in the organization will speak for themselves as to the truth of this statement.

Our system of Employe Representation contains every element of collective bargaining that has any real merit. It is true that it does not give either employer or employee a club with which to intimidate or threaten anybody, but is based upon the principles of Justice, Cooperation, Economy, Energy and Service. It has never failed to obtain for the employees the best possible rates of pay and the best working conditions. If anyone entertains any doubt as to the correctness of this statement, it can easily be verified with actual facts and authentic figures.

We do not desire the employees of the Company to be misled by these outsiders for the simple reason that they cause discord and their whole method of operation depends upon agitation and strife. This has been so obvious and so unsatisfactory to those who have tried it that their membership among Textile workers has dwindled to almost the vanishing point. You have only to examine the history of the Textile Industry in the New England States and to observe its present condition, to see how tragic has been the result; the bitterness engendered; the severe financial losses incurred; and the rapid decline in the number of people employed, being now only a fraction of what it was before prosperity was driven away from them.

What can such a movement do for you that you do not already have (except to take your money in dues to pay a lot of foreign agitators and some few disgruntled, unappreciative persons who are continually sowing seed of discord and unhappiness)?

If there were any merit in their claims it seems to us that they would go into those sections where labor is being exploited at low wage rates, with night running, etc., and demonstrate to the world whether they can improve those conditions. They will tell you that they "are going to do this," but that they want to get started here first; which means of course that they want your money to do it with and, incidentally, to fill their own depleted coffers.

We have confidence in the good sense of most of our people and we believe that they sufficiently recognize the principle of Justice to let the facts speak for themselves.

For eleven years we have fought hard against the downward trend of post-war deflation, refusing to reduce wages when others were doing it and persistently holding the living standards of our people as high as we could. We carried this burden without one whimper of complaint, trying to gradually increase the efficiency of the organization to meet the many changes in distributive demands and to put out fabrics of superior merit that would win success both for the operatives and the Company.

The past two years have been extremely difficult, as evidenced by the fact that your Company was compelled to curtail an average of more than 25% of its normal capacity. Furthermore, with a wage differential of more than 20% above the average of the entire South it created an unsound economic condition which neither the Company nor its operatives could afford. Not until we became firmly convinced that the situation was serious in that respect and that it would mean more money in your envelopes, instead of less, did we consent to the adjustment of wage and salary rates.

Now that this has been done, we feel that your prospects have been decidedly improved, and while the goods markets are still very weak, with no real margin of profit for anyone, we are doing our level best to run the Mills as near full capacity as we can. We cannot see very far ahead and can make no promises as to what the future may bring forth, but we confidently hope that you can soon be earning an Economy Dividend; more important, however, is the fact that with your economic condition improved there will be less curtailment, and in the long run more money in your envelopes than for the past two years.

We have tried to encourage our people to think for themselves; not to be unduly influenced by superficial impressions either inside the organization or *outside of it,* but to base their judgments upon what is right and fair.

We regret the insidious temptation that is placed before you by these agitators, who appeal to your credulity with promises that neither they nor anyone else can make good. But we confidently expect that the vast majority of the members of our organization will continue to appreciate what they have accomplished by cooperation, and that they will refuse in no uncertain terms to be deluded by these false promises.

It is our purpose and desire to continue to work for the happiness and prosperity of all our people. We realize that the eyes of the world are upon the organization to see whether it is indeed possible for friendly relationships to be maintained in adversity as well as in prosperity. We believe that it is, and that this will be fully demonstrated.

However, if or when we become convinced that a majority do not care for or appreciate these principles, and that they cannot be trusted to adhere to them, of course the system will be withdrawn.

We are, therefore, putting before you this friendly message, and in the kindest spirit, with the hope that you will have nothing to do with these trouble makers. They can do you no good but they can cause you much harm.

With every good wish and kindest personal regards,

Yours very truly,

H. R. FITZGERALD

President and Treasurer[88]

A few days later, Secretary Blackwell replied, on behalf of the union, in a personal letter to H. R. Fitzgerald:

The employes of the Riverside and Danville [sic] Cotton Mills after

[88] Fitzgerald's letter was published in the *Journal of Commerce,* Oct. 24, 1930.

reading your poster No. 192 have decided to reply to the same by order of the meeting held Sunday, February 23.

First of all we want you to know that the American Federation of Labor and the officials of that organization came to Danville at our request for a union. The representatives who came here are not foreign agitators but American citizens delegated by President Green of the American Federation of Labor to assist us. When you say their whole method of operation depends upon agitation and strife we would call to your attention that the officials of the Labor movement have advised the workers in your mills to keep calm, that the American Federation of Labor is not here for strife or strike but to organize the workers and do business in an orderly manner with justice to employer and employee.

When you say that these men and women take our dues, we desire to inform you that our money is handled by local officials who are bonded and we resent the inference of thievery made in your statement. It would appear to us that as a Christian gentleman you would hesitate to charge someone you do not know with dishonesty and is entirely in opposition to the announced "Golden Rule" and justice so often set forth by your company.

You ask us to have confidence, and we ask in reply how can we have confidence when our conditions are getting worse from day to day? Our wages taken away from us, our work increased beyond reason by the stretch-out system. We would ask you again if the workers have not cooperated with the company to the breaking point. If you desire to restore our wages, meet us on a common ground and let us work out together a plan to reduce costs with fairness to the workers and to the company . . . .

Industrial Democracy is a misleading term as used here. No benefits have resulted from it to the workers. First it took away the paying of time and a half for overtime. This was done to increase the economy dividend. The payment for stoppage for lack of material has been discontinued, presumably for the same reason. Many believed stretching the people out would make the dividend grow and that the workers would share with the company on a fifty-fifty basis, as so often and persistently claimed, but on the contrary no economy dividend has been paid for the past two years, and on top of all this you reduce our wages 10 per cent without the workers having anything to say about it.

The workers in the mills want their own union and we ask you why they should not have it. They also want an opportunity to demonstrate to the company that this union will be helpful and not harmful. We believe in collective bargaining and will continue along these lines, but we cannot subscribe to a policy of so-called Industrial Democracy which forces the workers downward.

On the question of wages and the point you make about paying 20 per cent higher than the southern average. We would call to your attention that this point has been disputed not by us but by the employers in the

South, and if there should be any need for further discussion we are prepared with wage envelopes and a list of wages which is certainly no credit, but a reflection on the reputation of the Riverside and Dan River Cotton Mills.

On your point of the textile industry in New England, you very well know that for a good many years the unions there have kept the wages of the textile workers much higher than ours. In some departments of the mills doing the same work that we do a difference of $10.00 a week and more can be found.

We are sending this letter to you in good faith and ask you to accept our offer of friendship in all sincerity.

EMPLOYES OF THE RIVERSIDE AND DAN RIVER COTTON MILLS
By J. C. Blackwell

On the eve of the strike the union appealed for public support in a handbill, making the following statements which "local newspapers refused to publish":

To residents of Danville and Vicinity:

Knowing that the people of Danville are very much interested in the mill situation, we desire to place the workers' position before you in order that there shall be no misunderstanding of the issues. We have tried to bring out before the public all of the facts in the controversy, but this has covered a period of time, and we have decided to submit a résumé of the whole question to date.

In January of this year the workers of Danville sent a committee to William Green, President of the American Federation of Labor, asking him to assist us in the formation of a union. Mr. Green gave us this assistance, and since then we have formed an organization affiliated with the American Federation of Labor. With very few exceptions all of the employees of the Riverside and Dan River Cotton Mills are members of the union.

Before we became members of the American Federation of Labor we had a grievance against the company when our wages were reduced ten per cent, the officials of the company endeavored by several methods to compel the workers to vote in favor of this cut, and failing in this it was announced that the cut would go into effect anyway. The argument advanced by the company officials for the wage reduction took the form of an inducement if we would accept the cut we would get steadier work, and there would be no difference in the total amount of our wages.

We have worked under the cut for six months and our conditions have been worse than at any time in the history of the company, even though it was publicly admitted recently that the production for the first half of 1930 was better than the two previous years.

Since forming our union the company has used treachery and persecution against our people in an effort to stop them from exercising their rights as free men and women to join a union. Hundreds of workers have been laid off and discharged, and people brought here to take our places from other states. These men and women who were discharged have given years of faithful service to the company and are known as capable workers, respected in the community.

The workers in the mill have been insulted, threatened and told they would be starved into submission. Women have been bullied and their work increased until they have become physically and mentally exhausted under the strain. The workers have been fined heavily at the will of the overseer. The stretch-out system has been applied more cruelly than ever, and wages reduced to a point which has caused destitution in many homes. Children are made innocent victims of oppression.

All the while our organization has advised the workers to be patient and not permit the company to drive us into a strike which would cover up the mismanagement and waste throughout the mills. We feel confident that if the stockholders, outside of those who control the policy of the company, knew the exact conditions a change would be demanded at once. We have repeatedly tried to convince these officials that the organization could help in a substantial way, that we had a plan of cooperation which had proved successful in other mills and would bring about harmony in the industry.

To all of this the company has turned a deaf ear, and continued to punish, discharge, and browbeat the workers, and we are now informed that workers from other states will be brought in here to take the places of hundreds of workers let out recently when some of the mills closed. At our meetings we have expressed the hope that the company will consider seriously before bringing any more people here and we want the general public to know who is to blame for the present conditions, and who will be responsible when we are forced to defend ourselves and families against those who are permitting hate and passion to replace justice and decency.

Our organization is now providing for those in need, our plans for the future are laid out, we are prepared to carry through to the finish, and propose to expose a condition in these mills which is a disgrace to the community. We would ask the people of Danville to investigate these charges for themselves, and if you find merit in our cause, we expect to count you as our friends who will help us in our struggle for human rights in order that we may be treated like men and women and not dirt for those higher up to wipe their feet on.

We have made no demands on the company, all we are asking is the right to have our union and take up our grievances in an orderly manner with the employer.

This is our side of the question, if you care to discuss the situation or secure further information our officers are ready and willing to meet you.

Sincerely yours,
B. F. NASH, *President*
JAMES C. BLACKWELL, *Secretary*[89]

[89] Reproduced in T. Tippett, *When Southern Labor Stirs*, pp. 218-221.

The union's indictment contains a number of half-truths. It is certain that dismissal of workers for union activities commenced soon after the organization of Local 1685. Secretary Blackwell was fired (if he did not quit before being discharged), and the president instructed the employment manager to "write him a nice courteous note," requesting him to vacate his house. "He is not now in the employ of the Company, and, I hope, never will be again." By mid-March not less than fifty-five employees had been dismissed, "quietly" and with "no other cause or reason" than "unsatisfactory work." No one was fired "merely for joining the Union"; but there were, according to President Fitzgerald, "probably three or four dozen all told who were acting as snakes in the grass and going out of their way to induce others to join the movement; in other words, they were carrying on their activities in a stealthy way on the inside of the plant." In addition, according to one of the superintendents, the union had inspired "an organized effort on the part of the help to slow up production in any way they could .... In fighting this we found that in each room there had been a committee appointed ... operating along the lines of doing and saying everything possible to hold back production." The trouble cleared up with the discharge of a "few of the rotten ones."[90] The allegation that the company had hired Communists for the sake of discrediting and intimidating union workers, a charge which an A.F. of L. official repeated before a Congressional committee, seemed not even worthy of a denial.[91]

In the absence of complete employment records, production statistics may be relied upon to measure the extent of curtailment in 1930. Total production for the twenty-eight weeks ending July 12 ran two million pounds ahead of output in the same period of 1929. If this gain in production fell short of providing additional employment to compensate for the 10 per-cent wage cut, the increase is great enough to impugn the assertion that the average worker was worse off in early 1930

[90] C. C. Bolen to H. R. Fitzgerald, March 18, 1930. Volunteer informants kept the company advised of union activities inside and outside of the mills. In May two men and their wives were identified as "the biggest spies that ever worked in Riverside mill." They talked of the union when the overseer was absent; and when he approached, they muttered, "there comes the red headed Devel." Union workers retaliated. One supervisor was warned anonymously to "lay off the union members ... for i will find a way to make you lay off ... for i am getting old now and i will go throw hell for my chirldren. Show this too old Rosworth [Rushworth] he will be looked after too."

[91] On May 3 the company hired a frame hand who "worked very well while on the job and there was no hint of his being a Communist." A month later a detective agency produced some records of his unsavory past, but by this time the man had quit.

than the year before. But in July and August 1930, when ginghams were "practically unmerchantable," drastic cut-backs went into effect in Dan River's colored-goods department and the production of white goods slumped considerably. Total output for the four weeks ending September 6 was 1.7 million pounds, as compared with 2.3 million pounds in the preceding four weeks. From the viewpoint of the union, however, reduced production represented not a necessary economic adjustment but an attempt to "break our spirit." In closing the plant on July 29, the company "tried what they thought to be a master stroke . . . throwing out of employment over two thousand of our people, leaving them to live as best they could."[92] Inventory statistics suggest that more employment had been furnished than was economically justifiable: the nine million pounds of cloth on hand in October was equivalent to more than a third of the year's production.

As the day for the election of a new House of Representatives approached, the management seriously considered the advisability of scrapping Industrial Democracy forthwith. Only a "very small percentage of our people," it was argued, "actually put forth any real spirit of cooperation. . . . a very large majority of them regarded it only as a means of getting out of it all they can for themselves . . . . Our House meetings have for a long time been going stale in that they are almost entirely perfunctory." But for the management to kill Industrial Democracy would be a victory for "Gorman and his crowd." Subsequently, nominations were posted, and on July 3 the Representatives to the Twelfth Congress were elected.[93]

The 1930 election enabled the company to insist, throughout the period of the strike, that a plan of workers' representation remained in effect; but it also tended to buttress the union's argument that the system was unrepresentative and coercive, since Fitzgerald had broken his word to withdraw Industrial Democracy when it was no longer wanted. Instead,

when the management found that the entire working force did not care for or appreciate such a system, they refused to withdraw it . . . . the management insisted upon forcing them to continue the system of so-called Industrial Democracy by calling a certain election, strapping the ballot boxes around the necks of the overseers, who, flanked by two second-hands, carried the ballots and the ballot boxes to the workers, together with checkers, who

[92] W. I. Frye (see note 86).
[93] House Bulletin No. 89-B, July 10, 1930.

checked the ballots as they were voted by the workers, and those who did not vote were discharged from the employ of the said mills and many of those, who were coerced into voting, scratched all of the names on the ballots, only to be told that their services were no longer needed by the mills . . . .[94]

Outsiders who visited Danville in 1930 generally agreed that the last election was a vain effort to revive a corpse. A Baltimore newspaperman interviewed members of the House of Representatives, who asserted that nothing important had been done by the legislature for more than a year. "The typical meeting . . . consisted of calling the roll, reading the minutes of the last meeting, and adjourning to view a movie at the Company's expense."[95] A writer for a Knoxville paper found "a deep resentment against the paternalistic system which has made these mills famous for their elaborate welfare work." Speaking of Fitzgerald, he said: "I am convinced that he honestly believes that he has given true representation to his men. But I am just as convinced that he has failed to give them such representation . . . . They have had 'sham' industrial democracy for years; what more natural than that they should now want the real thing?"[96] The New York *Times* correspondent, Anne O'Hare McCormick, wrote that "the issue is joined between the old system at its best and the workers trained under that system groping toward a new system." Working conditions in Schoolfield were above average. "The girls I saw gathering for a union meeting . . . were as good looking and well turned out as any group of office workers on Fifth Avenue." But the defection of employees trained in Industrial Democracy was a personal tragedy for President Fitzgerald; he was "drinking the hemlock," he told Mrs. McCormick.[97] The president's "answer to the cry of paternalism that comes from the radical group" was the somewhat enigmatic declaration that "The people who work for the Riverside and Dan River Mills are going to be happy if it lies within the power of the company to make them so."

It was not until March 21 that Fitzgerald discussed with the directors the progress of the unionization drive. "Labor organizers and agitators," he said,

[94] "Answer" of Local Union No. 1685 to the injunction issued by the Circuit Court (in D. McCracken, *Strike Injunctions in the New South*, pp. 257-264).
[95] Baltimore *Evening Sun*, Oct. 29, 1930.
[96] E. J. Meeman in the Knoxville *News-Sentinel*, Nov. 15, 1930.
[97] New York *Times Magazine*, June 15, 1930.

are at work in our midst, having chosen Danville as the point of beginning
for their campaign to organize Southern Textile Workers. We have known
for some time that it was their purpose to come here, as they have kept in
touch with an old Loom Fixer Association that has existed here for many
years, and some of the more radical of these Fixers invited them to come
just at the psychologic moment to use our wage reduction as an excuse for
organizing a Union . . . . We do not conceive that the Stockholders of our
Company would ever be willing to subject it to the domination of Labor
Unions, and, as our system of Employee Representation contains all that is
worth while in collective bargaining and affords our people an opportunity
to express themselves in an orderly way . . . we have no intention of having
any conference or anything whatever to do with these organizers.

During the remainder of the year Fitzgerald made no further comment
on the labor situation at board meetings, but in his annual report to
stockholders (January, 1931) the president again exorcised the "agitators and professional propagandists" who had descended upon Danville a year earlier. "With shrewd and experienced cleverness they had
made their plans to force themselves upon us and obtain control of the
labor policies of our Company at any cost . . . . We determined from
the start not to have anything to do with them, nor to be drawn into
any controversy, nor to make replies to the many false statements and
propaganda that they immediately began to circulate." What Fitzgerald could not comprehend was that "the many years of happy and
prosperous conditions which have distinguished the relations of your
Company with its employees, instead of rendering them immune to
such an outside attack, had created in many of them a frame of mind
that failed utterly to appreciate the seriousness of the economic conditions or to realize how much better off they were than thousands of
other workers."[98]

The union's membership drive was fruitful, and by the end of
March the organizers claimed that 92 per cent of the company's employees had joined. Apparently, their biggest talking point was the
promise to restore the February wage cut. Speaking in Durham, North
Carolina, President Green assured the Danville workers that, with the
help of the A.F. of L., they would "compel the company to pay back
the reduction taken from the men."[99] Thus encouraged, the union's

[98] *Twenty-second Annual Report of the Riverside and Dan River Cotton Mills, Inc.*
(Danville, 1931).
[99] Greensboro (N. C.) *Daily News*, Feb. 27, 1930. At a union meeting on March 9
Gorman promised that the wage cut would be restored, and he claimed that three overseers or high-salaried men in the corporation were working with him.

executive council prepared to make its demands upon the company: reinstatement of those discharged for union activity, restoration of the pay cut, and a five-day (50-hour) week. It is not clear whether they planned to ask for the same pay for 50 hours as they had received for 55 hours, but the leaders talked of a 40-hour week, with the same pay as for 50 hours, as an ultimate objective.[100]

No one knew how to get these or any other demands before the Dan River management. On March 26 Geoffrey C. Brown, a "personal representative of Mr. Green," called on President Fitzgerald. Stenographic notes of the interview show that the president received him courteously. When Brown explained that his mission was to arrange a conference to discuss "alleged discrimination against your employees because they are members of the Union," Fitzgerald called him "brother" but declared firmly: "if you come here to discuss matters pertaining to the running of our business, you will have to excuse me. You are neither an employee nor a stockholder of the Company and we have nothing whatever to discuss with you." Less than a month later Brown wrote to Vice-president Ray, sending copies of the letter to each of the company's directors, and requested an opportunity to submit to the company a "union-management co-operative plan" similar to a plan in effect at the Naumkeag Mills in Massachusetts. So far as I know, none of the directors showed any interest in the proposal. Months later, a committee of union workers called on Fitzgerald in hopes of arranging a conference between the president and union officials. When Fitzgerald exclaimed: "I will have absolutely nothing to do with them," the workers' spokesman asked, "Is that final?" The president replied: "Yes, sir, as final as I can make it." He never deviated from this position.

A week before the strike two Department of Labor Conciliators came to Danville in hopes of averting the walkout. After conferring separately with union officials and President Fitzgerald, they made the following announcement:

> Having obtained the mills' side and the union's side of the controversy, we suggested to Mr. Fitzgerald that we would like to arrange a joint conference between representatives of both sides, at which the questions in dispute could be taken up and discussed. That if a plan of this kind was

---

[100] All this information was duly relayed to the management by someone present at an executive council meeting. At a "closed" meeting on March 23 Gorman said he knew there was a "spy" present, but no one seemed reluctant to pledge himself to secrecy.

adopted, we felt confident that we would be in a position to suggest a plan for adjusting the controversy, which would be fair to both sides.

Mr. Fitzgerald declines to agree to our suggestion, with the explanation that in 1919 the Riverside and Dan River Cotton Mills and its employees established an Industrial Democracy, under which the mills and its employees had worked in harmony for the last eleven years, that if the employees had any grievances which they desired to have adjusted, they could bring up their grievances and adjust them through machinery now in operation under the Industrial Democracy Plan.[101]

In March Gorman declared that the Danville local was "facing its first real test as a 'no-strike union.' " Despite the restlessness of many of the members, union leaders maintained this policy throughout the summer; but on September 9 the T.W.U.A. vice-president announced the end of the no-strike pledge. Speaking in New York, Gorman said: "the time has come for us to move against the enemy . . . . It is quite certain that our members who have been fired because they joined the union are not going to stand idly by and permit workers brought in from other places to take their jobs."[102] A few days later, one of the workers recalled,

we saw that we were going to have to call a strike for our own protection . . . . Over 95 per cent of our people voted for a strike and the International Union and the American Federation of Labor sanctioned our act, so on the 29th. day of September our strike was called. When we went to the mills . . . we found the gates locked. We were locked out but the Company made an effort to start the mills and we successfully kept the scabs out by peaceful means until the infamous injunction which was granted . . . by a judge who was indirectly connected with the company.[103]

Fitzgerald was in Charlottesville when the strike commenced. In response to a telegram from the Danville *Bee,* the mill executive sent the following message:

If strike has been called the mills will not open for the time being until we can ascertain what proportion of the employees are loyal to the company and desire to continue their work.

For forty-seven years our company has operated continuously with mutual trust and confidence between the management and employee. There

[101] Danville *Bee,* Sept. 29, 1930.
[102] Danville *Register,* Sept. 10, 1930. On Sept. 11 "Operator 99" reported that the workers had been "eager" for a strike for several months. The organizers were cautious, because an unsuccessful strike would mean that they could not win anywhere in the South. The strike became an urgent matter in September, when it became known that the mills might shut down completely.
[103] W. I. Frye (see note 86).

does not exist any real grievance or any fundamental difference between the management and the operatives.   An adequate system has for many years been in existence for the discussion and adjustment of matters pertaining to relations between the employees and the company and there has never been any trouble in handling any questions that have arisen in a thoroughly friendly and mutually satisfactory manner.

The responsibility for this strike and all that it involves upon the employees as well as the community rests upon these who have called it.[104]

On the second day of the strike the Circuit Court of Pittsylvania County issued a restraining order.   The company's bill for injunction cited two specific acts of violence: (1) on September 29 pickets forcibly prevented the paymaster from entering his office at Riverside Division and (2) on September 30 pickets forcibly restrained workers from going into the mill "to finish the process of work on certain goods which were in the slasher, which would be injured and destroyed if the process were not completed."[105]   Judge J. T. Clement upheld the right of workers to "desist from work" and to use "peaceful persuasion" to cause others to quit their jobs; but he issued the injunction because it was:

. . . unlawful to use force or violence, or to terrorize or intimidate new employees . . . congregate in large numbers . . . trespass upon, or enter without permission the private property, streets and ways which are the private property of the Riverside and Dan River Cotton Mills . . . . interfere with the business of the plaintiff . . . by patrolling the sidewalk or street in front of same or in the vicinity of the premises occupied by them, for the purpose of preventing persons from entering same by force . . . .[106]

The union's "Answer" to the injunction dealt at length with the development of the controversy and described the strike as a "protest against the inhuman, unjust and unfair treatment that they had been receiving at the hands of the management of the said mills."   Admitting that as many members of the union had not been informed of the situation before they came to work on September 29, "among some of the members there was some confusion," the labor leaders denied,

that they . . . are undertaking to direct or control the movements and actions of the complainant's foremen and employees who are not members of said Union . . . that they have called a strike against complainant but allege that the workers . . . voted, by an overwhelming majority, not to

[104] Danville *Bee,* Sept. 29, 1930.
[105] Text in D. McCracken, *op. cit.,* pp. 248-253.
[106] D. McCracken, *op. cit.,* pp. 254-256.   A similar injunction was granted by Judge H. C. Leigh in the Corporation Court of the City of Danville.

return to the mill under the inhuman, unfair, unjust and oppressive conditions existing . . . that they have placed large numbers of men at each
of the gates of the complainants' plant who, by force and intimidation,
prevent persons from passing in and out of said gates . . . that on the
29th day of September, 1930 . . . they, or any of them, or any
members of said Union, prevented fifteen (15) or twenty (20) workmen
to enter a certain gate of the complainants' plants . . . that any members of
said Union, inspired and directed by other members of said Union and
Francis J. Gorman, J. C. Blackwell and B. F. Nash, forcibly prevented the
entrance of said employees into said mill for the purpose of saving certain
goods then in process in said mills . . . that they or any members of said
Union . . . defied officers of the law . . . continued to unlawfully congregate
on the mill's property and . . . attempted by force to prevent complainant
from using and enjoying its property . . . that the acts of them or the acts
of the members of said union in picketing peaceably are illegal, unlawful
and constitute an unlawful conspiracy to do an unlawful act . . . .

Your respondents point with pride to the statement of Honorable Posie
J. Hundley, Attorney for the Commonwealth for the County of Pittsylvania,
Virginia, that there have been no law violations in the entire county of
Pittsylvania since the lock-out by the mills was put into effect, with the
exception of one lone drunk, an old man, not in any way connected with
said Union, who staggered up to an automobile driven by officers and asked
for a ride, which was given him, and he was arrested and brought to the
jail . . . .

Your respondents deny that there is any disposition on the part of its
officers or members to cause any injury either reparable or irreparable, to
the property of the River Side and Dan River Cotton Mills, Incorporated . . . .[107]

After granting the injunction, Judge Clement had to answer the
union's contention that ownership of Riverside and Dan River stock
disqualified him to sit on the case. The judge admitted owning twenty
shares—which he considered "as worth nothing"—and asked Governor
Pollard to replace him at the hearing of the union's motion to dissolve
the injunction. Judge J. L. McLemore took Judge Clement's place but
refused to dismiss the temporary restraining order.[108]

On October 2, "on account of important public interests involved,"
Governor John G. Pollard appealed to the company and the union to
consent to his appointment of "a committee of mediation for the purpose of seeking to bring about an amicable settlement of the pending
[sic] controversy." Union officials promptly replied: "we appreciate

[107] D. McCracken, *op. cit.,* pp. 257-264.
[108] Danville *Register,* Oct. 4, 1930.

and welcome this offer of the governor." Thanking the governor for his "fine telegram," President Fitzgerald wrote: "We believe that if you knew the mill situation and the history of our company that you would realize that so far as our company and its employees are concerned there is absolutely nothing to mediate." Labor organizers were dismissed as "outside professional trouble makers," bent on besmirching the company's "enviable record of having dealt liberally with its employees."[109]

"Nothing to mediate" remained Fitzgerald's watchword to the bitter end. "Nothing to Mediate," editorialized the Raleigh *News and Observer*, recalling the bloodshed at Marion and Gastonia, North Carolina. "Nothing to mediate, when the differences are so acute that 4,000 workers have quit work . . . . In such industrial situations, the side which says 'nothing to mediate' assumes responsibility for all the ills that follow industrial disturbances . . . . The saddest thing about the Danville trouble is that President Fitzgerald has in his control of the mills been far in advance of most other manufacturers."[110] Although the Virginia Manufacturers' Association passed a resolution commending the company for refusing to "consent to any negotiations in the future, as in the past, with any outside organizers and trouble makers," Roger Babson spoke up to condemn as "shortsighted" a management policy which declined to confer with representatives of the peace-loving A.F. of L.[111]

In November Secretary of Labor Davis invited the Dan River management to come to Washington and attend church with him Sunday morning, "then meet in Christian fellowship around the conference table in the afternoon." The invitation was declined.[112] A few weeks later Secretary Doak, who succeeded Davis (now a Senator) in the Labor Department, persuaded the general counsel of the National Association of Manufacturers to use his good offices in an attempt to bring Fitzgerald to Washington for a conference. Again the reply was in the negative: "There was not, or has there ever been, at any time any question of grievance between our Company and its employees." From Boston the Dan River management was offered the services of a con-

---

[109] Danville *Register*, Oct. 3, 1930.
[110] Raleigh *News and Observer*, Oct. 4, 1930.
[111] Correspondence with C. E. Michael, president of the Virginia Bridge & Iron Co.
[112] From the reports of "Operator 299" Fitzgerald knew that a strikers' committee had gone to Washington to ask Davis to intervene. Of course, it is unlikely that he would have accepted the invitation in any event.

sulting engineer, who promised to use his influence with A.F. of L.'s President Green. The scheme was to put an unnamed individual "in charge temporarily of the Union activities in Danville," whereupon "the whole thing will be settled satisfactorily to both sides without your [Fitzgerald] entering into any direct negotiations with the Union or holding any conference with them, and at no time will you be asked to recognize the Union." Fitzgerald was adamant. "I presume you understand," he wrote his would-be counselor, "that we are running practically all of the machinery that we care to run under such unfavorable economic conditions."

President Green came to Danville in December with a peace plan. He proposed that the workers return to their jobs, with the assurance that there would be no discrimination in rehiring them. Future disputes would be referred to an arbitration board consisting of two employees, two representatives of the Dan River management, and either Admiral Byrd or ex-Governor Harry Byrd. Informed of this proposal, Fitzgerald had "nothing whatever to say." In January 1931 the executive council of the A.F. of L. fruitlessly renewed the overture.

Following a visit to the president's home in Danville, early in January 1931, Governor Pollard appealed to Fitzgerald to accept mediation "in the public interest." By waiving his legal rights and "entering into some such agreement as I outlined to you in my personal interview," Fitzgerald, the governor said, could make a substantial contribution to domestic tranquility and the relief of unemployment. The governor's proposal, which Fitzgerald rebuffed, involved the reemployment of strikers without discrimination and the election of a workers' representative for a panel of arbitrators.[113]

Equally unavailing were efforts of the Federal Council of Churches to prepare the way for intervention by local church leaders. At a meeting of the Danville Ministerial Union, the Council's representative, the Reverend W. M. Tippy, proposed the selection of a committee of clergymen to study Danville's labor problem. According to the Reverend J. B. Winn, who reported the session in a penciled note to Fitzgerald, Tippy was "quite plausible and made it plain that he did not desire the [Ministerial] Union to take sides or to express itself on the merits of the present situation, but to put itself in a position to

[113] Gov. J. G. Pollard to H. R. Fitzgerald, Jan. 12, 1931. Sidelights on this incident are given by T. Tippett, *When Southern Labor Stirs*, pp. 243-244, and J. E. Meade, *I Live in Virginia*, pp. 62-67. See also: New York *Times*, Dec. 22, 1930, and Jan. 21, 1931.

tender the best service to all parties and to the community as a whole."
The ministers were divided, and at subsequent meetings a resolution
to go on record in favor of collective bargaining as well as an innocuous
motion to offer the good offices of the clergy were killed.[114] In view
of the "numerous instances of depraved conduct" associated with the
strike, Fitzgerald was "at a loss to understand how the Federal Council
of Churches, or any other respected organization, can lend their aid or
endorse such performances under the guise of humanitarian rights."[115]

Support for Fitzgerald's determination to have nothing to do with
the union came from various sources. Commenting on the president's
reply to Governor Pollard, the sanctimonious *Southern Textile Bulletin* observed, "There was, of course, nothing to arbitrate." A North
Carolina textile executive wrote Fitzgerald: "We are all your debtors
for the courageous fight which you have put up." The *Daily News
Record* declared: "Every mill executive in the South has recognized
that H. R. Fitzgerald . . . has fought the battle of each individual."
On the other hand, this well-informed textile publication deplored the
"sorry spectacle" of "mill executives who gave their personal assurances
to the president of the Riverside and Dan River Mills that they would
do everything they could to assist and support him," then "behind his
back, tried to take away his business by methods which could not
exactly be called fair." Rival firms, it was charged, had taken customers
away from Dan River by representing that labor troubles would prevent the mills from making deliveries; and Dan River styles were
pirated, "even to the point of using the same numbers."[116]

Stockholders paid for advertisements in Danville newspapers, mani-
festing their complete support of management's policy; and at the annual meeting in January 1931 the stockholders commended the conduct

[114] An Episcopal clergyman, the Reverend W. B. Spofford, representing the Church
League for Industrial Democracy, brought money and encouragement to the strikers in
January 1931. The Associated Press quoted him, as follows: "I say with shame that the
churches have not supported you as they should, but I suppose the preachers are mill-
owned."

[115] *Twenty-Second Annual Report of the Riverside & Dan River Cotton Mills, Incorporated* (Danville, 1931); W. M. Tippy to H. R. Fitzgerald, Oct. 4, 1930. The rebuff to
the Federal Council of Churches did not go unchallenged. A Methodist minister in
Norristown, Pa., told Fitzgerald he was "unworthy to enjoy the blessings of free government. For the representatives of organized capital—deriving its rights and privileges of
incorporation from organized society to 'flatly refuse,' under the circumstances stated,
to deal with the representatives of organized labor is so utterly repugnant to equitable
business ethics that it is doomed." And the industrial secretary of the Federal Council
asked: "Is Mr. Fitzgerald a big enough man to lay aside the only weapon by which he
can crush this strike—the increased privations, hunger and sickness of women and children
on short rations?"

[116] *Daily News Record* (New York), Feb. 3, 1931.

of their officers during the strike. The local newspapers adopted a neutral policy, as a result of which the union branded the press "our worst enemy" and the company, discovering eighteen cases of libel in the *Bee* and the *Register*, threatened suit if the papers published "just one more." Attorney Harris had a "plain talk" with the editors, which he thought would prevent the publication of "anything very detrimental," but he doubted that they could be persuaded to render "active help."[117] At least one of the preachers in Schoolfield "took a definite stand against the strike . . . and preached several sermons that did not at all suit the strikers"; it cost him virtually all of his income, except the subsidy furnished by the mill. Among the workers, a die-hard defender of Industrial Democracy wrote the president: "I think it is just awful that our people whom we have loved so dearly should be misled as they have, but they would not listen to a friend, but I pray that they will soon see the error of their way, and I find myself saying forgive them for they know not what they do." Finally, Fitzgerald had occasion to praise the loyalty of Negro employees, who were ineligible for membership in Local 1685.[118]

Production was resumed in some departments before the end of the first week of the strike. One of Dan River's cloth rooms commenced work with five out of a normal force of fifty employees, and in the second week twenty-eight reported for work. But overseers complained of the poor work of "green" help, as workers were temporarily transferred from closed-down departments to sections already reopened; and cutsomers got "very nervous" about scheduled shipments. Some orders were filled on time with the help of other firms manufacturing the same classes of goods, but as late as November 1 the president admitted that any estimate of the shipping date on certain goods would be "more or less of a guess," in view of lack of help in the weave rooms. Was the pressure to make prompt delivery on the limited amount of business available great enough to induce the company to employ strikebreakers? The union said "yes," and Fitzgerald repeatedly denied it.

[117] Girard Tetley, editor of the *Bee*, wrote Fitzgerald on Jan. 24, 1931, that he had "tried to be fair to both sides and to be intimidated by neither." The "policy of fairness" had been adopted by the publisher at the start of the strike. Further comments on the press during the strike will be found in J. R. Meade, *I Live in Virginia*. The author was correspondent for the United Press.

[118] A group of colored workers wrote the president (Feb. 26, 1930) that they had "confidence in you and the boss men you have placed over us . . . . We have not worked here for ten or more years and not learned who is our friend . . . . So when you hear of people joining the Union, remember, it is not us, for we know better than to bite the hand that is feeding us."

The available evidence, though inconclusive, suggests that most of the needs for labor were met by persuading old workers to return to their jobs. In mid-November the president wrote to Ray: "We do not desire any premature break in the strikers ranks, but prefer to go along quietly and pick our operatives out of the large number who are loyal at heart." By December the problem was that of finding work for as many old and loyal employees as possible, "in order to keep them from suffering."

Although the union alleged that the company's attorney, M. K. Harris, "repeatedly, both publicly and privately, expressed the wish that the workers would strike," it seems fruitless to try to find evidence that the management deliberately abetted the strike movement. On the other hand, the walkout was not entirely unwelcome. "When at the end of September," the president told the stockholders,

the situation had gotten beyond their control and even against the wishes and plans of their organizers, a strike was called, we made no attempt to check it or to offer any interference whatever . . . . They had . . . created such an atmosphere of discontent and insubordination that we did not wish to continue to operate your mills under such circumstances. We, therefore, closed the gates and shut the mills down completely (except the shipping departments) for several days until we could properly distinguish between those who were loyal and willing to conform themselves to an honest effort necessary to success and those who were not.

On September 1 Fitzgerald had written another mill president "in strict confidence" that the company would soon "make a complete shutdown which will last at least a few weeks." The growing probability that the workers would walk out held in abeyance the management's plan for closing.

The day-to-day effect of the strike upon production cannot be measured, as production records have been preserved only for four-weeks' periods. Furthermore, considering the great amount of voluntary curtailment throughout the period of the strike, the following statistics fail to isolate the losses in production attributable solely to the lack of operatives.

Convinced that no grounds existed for an injunction, the executive board of Local 1685 nevertheless "anticipated in the methods of organization practiced in Danville and elsewhere by the United Textile Workers" all the requirements and prohibitions of the restraining order. Picketing was established on four-hour shifts, and pickets were

Production
(thousands of pounds)

four weeks ending	Riverside	Dan River		total	sales
		colored	white		
Aug. 9, 1930	930	459	925	2314	1930
Sept. 6	919	60	726	1705	1873
Oct. 4	538	67	523	1128	2018
Nov. 1	121	66	0	187	1913
Nov. 29	263	123	93	479	1435
Dec. 24	338	148	230	716	3067
Jan. 24, 1931	592	283	686	1561	
Feb. 21	767	507	956	2230	

instructed on tactics to be avoided. Policing the picket lines remained
entirely in the hands of Danville's city police and the sheriff of Pittsylvania County, inasmuch as Judge Clement had denied the company's
request for permission to deputize a number of employees. After the
fracas which called forth the injunction, the strike scene became comparatively calm. Fresh excitement was furnished by the arrival of W.
T. Murdoch, the general secretary of the N.T.W.U., who had journeyed all the way from Massachusetts to fish in troubled waters. Since
he was jailed for what the court considered libelous attacks on Gorman
and the U.T.W.A., his stay in Danville was prolonged four months; he
had the company of two fellow travelers sentenced on charges preferred
by U.T.W.A. pickets.

As the number of workers crossing picket lines increased, a rash of
violence, principally in the form of reprisals against non-striking employees, increased the problem of public order. On October 14 the
Bee reported that the tires on a non-strikers's car had been slashed; the
next day a worker's house was stoned; and on October 16 (at 2:00
A.M.) the "strike situation reached the pineapply stage . . . when dyna-
mite or a bomb was thrown into the yard of J. E. Wentz" (an overseer). All this the union publicly deplored; but on October 17-18,
after a Negro worker had been badly beaten up, the city hired fifteen
additional police officers and Governor Pollard sent ten highway patrol-
men to Schoolfield.

During the rest of the month the picket lines were comparatively
tranquil, leading the Baltimore *Evening Sun* to observe that "the Danville strike, considering its importance, is probably the most gentleman-

ly and good-natured strike that was ever called." This proved to be a lull before the storm. On the morning of November 26 an estimated 600 strikers formed a human barricade on the main road leading into Schoolfield and effectively blocked the passage of street cars, automobiles, and pedestrians coming from Danville. Neither operatives, office boys, nor vice-presidents reached their places of work. Governor Pollard, who had previously turned down hysterical demands for the use of troops, reconsidered; and on the evening of November 26 nearly 900 officers and men of the state militia took up quarters in Schoolfield. "With the arrival of these troops," Meade observed, "most of Danville's citizens and all her capitalists breathed sighs of relief and began to talk of victory."[119]

For a time the presence of troops seemed to encourage the strikers to take a bolder stand. Mass picketing was resumed, in contravention of a military ruling fixing a limit of eighty on the number of men in the picket lines. After forty-five strikers had been arrested for unlawful assembly, the strikers organized a parade with the purpose of marching *en masse* from Schoolfield to Danville. Tear gas was used to disperse them, but what the *Bee* called the "worst disturbance since the race riots of 1883" resulted in the hospitalization of only one person. A few days earlier Governor Pollard had acceded to requests to reduce the militia force to half its original strength, but the fresh disturbances kept the remainder of the troops in Schoolfield (quartered in Hylton Hall) until the waning days of the strike.

Relative abundance of provisions and relief funds contributed to the holiday-like atmosphere of the strike in its early stages. In October Miss Matilda Lindsay, the Virginia-born vice-president of the National Women's Trade Union League, related that "Club and church women bring sandwiches and coffee for the pickets. The business men, who depend for existence on the mill workers, are sympathetic. It is all more like a picnic than a labor war." But on October 12 the union stopped soliciting aid among business firms, saying "Everybody is like we are—broke." It took about $1,000 a day to provide for strikers' families. On October 22 the *Bee* called "Old Man Hoar Frost" an accomplice in company ranks: with the temperature at 28° "it was a ruthless attack with little comfort in it for those men loyal to union principles and doing post duty." Now coal was added to the relief

[119] *I Live in Virginia,* p. 42.

needs, and the response of organized labor was slow and inadequate.[120] Two women strikers went to Boston to attend the A.F. of L. convention and, by their moving pleas, garnered "many a case of beans";[121] but the resolution introduced by McMahon and Gorman, calling for a special per capita tax to provide a textile strike fund, was voted down. President Green promised to send out the "strongest appeal that my mind can conceive or that my vocabulary will permit, appealing to the hardened conscience of men and women of labor to give to these men and women all the help possible in their fight"; but the response to his request for donations, issued in November, was paltry.[122] Moved by the thought of the bleak Christmas facing striking families, the Church Emergency Committee of New York solicited funds and clothing; and the Church League for Industrial Democracy sent contributions in cash amounting to at least $3,500. The outlook for better rations of milk (or beef) brightened somewhat with the "unionization" of 125 cows belonging to strikers. As the union's treasury dried up, strike leaders looked to the Red Cross for aid and accused that organization of trying to starve them out when only limited help (reportedly, a bottle of milk and a can of tomatoes) was extended. After some delay, national representatives of the American Red Cross verified sixty-odd cases of destitution among striking families and finally took over the burden of the union commissary, which closed on February 13.[123]

I cannot find a complete record of evictions of strikers from company houses. On December 5 notices, requiring removal within fifteen days, were served on 47 families. The notice reminded the tenant that "as you are not now an employee of this company and will not in the future occupy such a position with us, we desire that you should

---

[120] From doubtless incomplete accounts of relief funds, I find that Federal Local 17,649 (Danville) gave $30 monthly and unions of Danville paperhangers and carpenters voted $10 weekly, while the Central Trades and Labor Council of Richmond contributed $20 a month.

[121] J. R. Meade, *op. cit.*, p. 60. The speeches of Mrs. Lucille Humble and Mrs. Della Gilreath are found in the *Report of Proceedings of the Fiftieth Annual Convention of the American Federation of Labor* (Washington, 1930), pp. 334-335.

[122] The Baltimore Federation of Labor voted the Danville strikers $25 a week for the duration, and a like amount was subscribed by the Central Labor Council of Cincinnati. A year earlier the executive council of the A.F. of L. called for contributions to the Textile Workers' Fund and collected $41,521 between May 1929 and August 1930.

[123] As reported in the New York *Times*, the "difficulties in the path of the American Red Cross were removed today [Feb. 13], when the U.T.W.A. asked the organization to step in." A few days earlier the state commissioner of labor found the distress in Schoolfield acute, as the union commissary ran dry, and drug bills—there was an influenza epidemic—accumulated at the rate of $40 a day.

vacate." Subsequently, the management relented, and the involuntary moving day was postponed until after Christmas. "Yesterday was Eviction Day," the *Danville Strike Bulletin* (December 30, 1930) declared. "The company took back 14 of its miserable shacks, with the help of the law." Other families had their occupancy extended to January 9.[124]

None of the charges and countercharges which agitated the Danville air were more preposterous than the cry of "Communist." Among the workers there could hardly have been a corporal's guard who knew the meaning of the word. What did distinguish the strike employees of Dan River was a religious zeal. "Danville," one commentator wrote, "awaits the outcome of this unusual strike of church folks, the finest type of industrial workers against this well meaning employer, himself a prominent churchman."[125] Unfortunately, faith divided labor's ranks, and one sect which regarded union membership as inconsistent with salvation had its church building dynamited. In a lighter vein, singing and guitar-playing to while away the time yielded by-products in the form of "strike" ballads of the following stamp:

> They cut down our wages,
>   They took our freedom, too;
> The stretch-out system gave us
>   More work than we could do.
>
> They discharged our daddies,
>   Brothers, sisters, all.
> Because we joined the union,
>   When we heard freedom's call.

Other literary by-products of the strike made the company's president the butt of their jibes. "One of the many that have been here all their life" (one of numerous anonymous letter writers), wrote: "I used to think you was one of the best men in the world, when I heard you make speeches at school, but since you have refused to even talk to the people that have worked and slaved for you and the company the best part of their lives, my opinion of you has changed. . . . You dont seem to think about what we poor people have to put up with because you are rich and have every thing you want, but if you dont

[124] The obituary of the noted Socialist, Elisabeth Gilman, recites that she "worked successfully to prevent the eviction for nonpayment of rent of textile strikers at Danville . . ." (New York *Times*, Dec. 15, 1950.)

[125] The Reverend James Meyers, industrial secretary, Federal Council of Churches (from unidentified clipping).

do better you wont have every thing your way in the next world."
S.L.A. thought it was "a sin for such a thing as you to live. There you
sit in your office with plenty of money an no family to take care of an
you taking the bread out of little childrens mouths an clothes of there
backs." The author of a "Notice to Mr. H. R. Fitzgerald" recalled
that he had heard him "in the lodge rooms many times say, Trust in
GOD," and concluded some verse for the president with the couplet,

> Just as sure as there's a GOD up in heaven, which we always taught
> to believe,
> Will he look down and smile upon his children and give us the
> courage we so need.

In a song, written to be sung to the tune of "Don't Let Your Deal Go
Down,"

> Harry Fitzgerald ate the turkey
> Also the pumpkin pie.

Curiously, perhaps, most writers hoped the president would have a
change of heart and "recognize the people and let them go back to
work under a union."

Union officials declared the strike ended on January 29, 1931. Gorman left town after handing the press the following "Statement":

On September 29, 1930, Local Union No. 1685, United Textile Workers
of America, called a strike in the Riverside and Dan River Cotton Mills in
Danville, Va. In taking this action it was fully realized at the time that
economic conditions existing throughout the country, particularly the unemployment situation, made a protest of this kind on the part of organized
labor inexpedient and untimely.

The decision to strike was arrived at with great reluctance and only
after long and patient efforts on the part of operatives to find other solutions to the problem. Various questions at issue were temporarily laid aside
for future adjustment, and the decision to call the strike was made at this
time because a vital principle of labor was challenged. It was the
opinion of members of the local union that the mill management was discriminating against them because of union membership. Organized labor
would not permit without protest an infringement of this inherent right of
the American workingman to go unchallenged.

During the long weeks which have elapsed repeated attempts have been
made by labor leaders to convince themselves of the attitude of the mill
management on this point, but without success. However, during the past
weeks it has been increasingly plain, both from press statements from Mr.
Fitzgerald and by the action of the company, in taking old employees back

into the mills in considerable numbers without raising the question of union membership, that this principle of labor is being respected. We are further convinced that the justice of this principle will, in the future, be recognized by the company's representatives and will determine their policies.

With this fundamental principle no longer questioned, those especially charged with the interests of organized labor feel that the necessity for this strike no longer exists, and members of the Union are called upon to return to their work as promptly as places may be found for them. This action is taken voluntarily by the union, with the hope on their part, that the mill management will accept it as a measure of confidence and trust, which in time may become mutual and enable employer and employe to view their problems eye to eye.

"No defeat was admitted: nothing was said concerning lack of food at the commissary, the futility of struggling against the militia, the state, the public-at-large."[126]   Allegedly, a mining company executive and Fitzgerald's brother-in-law had persuaded the company's president to let them explain to Gorman the management's policy in hiring workers, so that Gorman could make a pacifying statement to the union.   This allegation Fitzgerald quickly scotched:

I, of course, know nothing of what representations have been made to some of our former employees by their so-called leaders. Neither myself nor anyone else representing the Riverside and Dan River Cotton Mills has entered into any agreement of any nature . . . . We have made no agreement, nor are we under any obligations expressed or implied to employ any individual or groups of individuals. Our company has consistently refused to negotiate or discuss such a matter with any organization, or representatives of such an organization. There has been absolutely no departure from such policy.

It has always been our policy to give preference to such of our old loyal employees whose record entitles them to be considered employees of our company.[127]

The Communists made a futile effort to capitalize on the retreat of U.T.W.A. The first issue of the *Textile Workers Guide*, published in Danville without a date-line, promised to "expose the sell-out . . . by the A.F. of L. Gorman outfit" and to collect information on "everything these fakers did in selling us workers out." According to the National Textile Workers Union, the Dan River employees needed "the Red Union to fight and win better conditions." For some months

[126] J. R. Meade, *op. cit.*, pp. 71-72.
[127] Danville *Bee*, Jan. 29, Feb. 1, and May 19, 1931.

the N.T.W.U. mill committee issued a sheet called *Riverside Worker,* and handbills of the Communist party and of the Young Communist League were distributed in Danville.

On August 10, 1931, the Danville *Bee* attempted to estimate the cost of the strike. It was probably a pointless undertaking, since the largest items were the "imputed" cost of lost wages ($416,000) and mercantile losses ($500,000); but the grand total of $1,756,423 in public and private costs may have impressed the community. The uncounted costs of labor's battle with capital included lasting resentments, enmities, and ill-will, much of which was earmarked for President Fitzgerald.

Harry Fitzgerald

Since to an extraordinary degree the outcome of Dan River's epochal labor dispute hinged on decisions made by the president, it will not be out of place to examine briefly those personal traits and abilities which contributed to his conduct of the fight against organized labor. Born in 1873, Harrison Robertson Fitzgerald ended his formal education with three years spent at Mt. Welcome High School in Culpeper County. At seventeen he went to work as office boy in Riverside Cotton Mills. Later in life, he explained that the poor health of his father persuaded him to leave school. Honors to compensate for his limited education came to him from three schools which elected him a trustee: the Ferrum School (Virginia), Randolph-Macon College, and Emory University.

Invited to write something for the students of George Washington High School (Danville) on the occasion of National Book Week (1930), Fitzgerald reminisced:

Alas! In the days of my boyhood I did not appreciate as I have since learned to do the value and importance of good reading . . . .

I have always regarded Bunyan's "Pilgrim's Progress" as one of the finest books ever written, except the Bible. Thackeray's "Henry Esmond" and Dickens' "David Copperfield" perhaps impressed me more than any of the ancient classics . . . .

However, in my younger days Mark Twain's works—especially "Tom Sawyer" and "Huckleberry Finn," the works of John Esten Cook— especially "Mohun," and of James Fenimore Cooper—especially "The Last of the Mohicans," were among the best; the works of Augusta Evans (Wilson), of George Elliot, and even the fiction of E. P. Rowe, were all enjoyable and helpful; also, I greatly enjoyed the works of Marie Corelli and of Myrtle Reed.

A self-educated man, Fitzgerald earned the highest honors attainable by an executive in the textile industry. After serving two years as a vice-president of the American Cotton Manufacturers' Association, he became its president in 1928. When Fitzgerald was elected, the outgoing president, George S. Harris (Dan River's president in 1940-1949) declared that the Association had "picked the cream of the industry to succeed me." Fitzgerald was a charter member of the directorate of the Cotton Textile Institute and was joint-president of the National Council of American Cotton Manufacturers. His leadership and pre-eminence among southern mill executives is securely established.

Fitzgerald's services to the state included membership, from 1926 until his death, on the Virginia Commission for the Blind. For a number of years he sought to get an appropriation from the legislature to build a new school for the blind, but an economy-minded administration considered the state's School for the Deaf and Blind at Staunton adequate for both groups of afflicted children. In 1926 Fitzgerald used his influence to support the request of the University of Virginia's Medical School for an extraordinary appropriation. His brother-in-law, Dr. J. C. Flippin, was for many years a member of the faculty.

A Democrat by grace of geography, Fitzgerald's political regularity was put to a test in the elections of 1928. Governor Byrd begged him to take over the leadership of the pro-Smith forces in Danville and Pittsylvania County, but Fitzgerald insisted on working in his own quiet way. He surprised many of his fellow-workers by refusing to fear the Pope. "I do not believe," he wrote for publication, "that our people realize that in the religious intolerance so commonly and insidiously employed against Governor Smith there lies a subtle poison to democracy."[128]

The whole record of his benevolences would fill many pages; indeed, in religious, educational, and charitable giving he appears to have adopted the practice of tithing. It was not perfunctory giving. He noticed a girl in church who needed medical attention, or asked for a list of boys who would benefit from Y.M.C.A. memberships, or called a youngster into his office to assure him that Santa Claus would visit

[128] The Danville *Bee*, Sept. 5, 1928.

his house. He was president of the board of directors of the Danville Orphanage and took an active part in improving its facilities, originally donated by his father, for the care of orphan and destitute children. Often he had to say "no" to the growing list of requests for gifts and loans, but no one called him stingy.

Away from the mill, Fitzgerald shared his time with his family, his church, and the golf course. He organized and for many years taught "Class 20" at Mt. Vernon Methodist Church. He wrote personal messages to members of the class, announcing the topics for forthcoming meetings and urging their attendance.

A physical handicap played an important part in his life and work, for, after experiencing deafness as a young man, he lost his hearing completely before middle age. When hearing-aids no longer served him, he was forced to carry on conversations entirely by lip-reading. Telephone conversations had to be relayed through his secretary, Clayton D. Gaver. Upon taking up his duties as president of the American Cotton Manufacturers' Association, he told his fellow executives that he was

under no delusion as to the limitations that my natural affliction places upon me . . . . While I have never suffered the supersensitiveness that so often accompanies this trouble, I long ago ceased to shed tears and regret that I no longer could hear the birds sing or enjoy the exquisite harmonies of music (I can and do hear those in my soul), there is the compensation that I am relieved from having to hear many things that are undesirable or irrelevant, whereas, the world, which is very considerate of deaf people, usually manages to make them understand what is important for them to know.[129]

Even those who held him in esteem thought that Fitzgerald had the fault, common among the deaf, of pretending to hear what he did not hear. He likewise had difficulty in making himself understood. It may be idle to speculate whether the absence of this infirmity would have changed the course of the last year of his life; it does seem possible that without it he might have gained a deeper insight into the motives of workers, labor leaders, government officials, and churchmen who urged him to sit down at the conference table. There is some evidence that Fitzgerald was not absolutely convinced of the soundness of his course of action. In 1928 he made an appointment with a New York

[129] *Proceedings of the Thirty-second Annual Convention: American Cotton Manufacturers' Association* (Charlotte, 1928), p. 145.

astrologer, telling her that "all my life . . . I have wanted to know something about astronomy." He was, he said, "daily conscious of the utter inadequacy of my own poor judgment to meet and cope successfully with the many complicated problems of life." If he could have the "guidance of the stars," he would "work with—rather than against them." In May 1930 he assured the same astrologer of his "great faith in your science." In the midst of labor troubles and poor business he wished to know "as accurately as possible the indications as they may apply to me personally for the remainder of this year—also the Industry in which my life work, thus far, has been done . . . . I sometimes wonder whether it would be best for my Company if I should get out and turn over its management to some one else."[130] Death answered all his questions on February 24, 1931.

[130] The fullest factual biography of Fitzgerald is found in the *National Cyclopaedia of American Biography*, vol. 35 (New York, 1949), pp. 320-321. A full-page portrait accompanies the text. The *Caduceus of Kappa Sigma* (March, 1912) carried an unsigned biographical article: it is effusive rather than informative. (Fitzgerald had been elected to membership in the Washington and Lee chapter of Kappa Sigma.) Notes on Fitzgerald's career were published by Laura A. Davies in the *Volta Review* (Jan. 1924). A tribute to C. D. Gaver was published in *Progress* (April 18, 1924) under the title "The Sphinx of the Cotton Mills."

6. *Nine Lean Years, 1932-1940*

Reviewing a nine-year period, the present chapter deals mainly with the administration of Robert Rout West. West was elected president and treasurer in October, 1932, succeeding James I. Pritchett, who became president after the death of H. R. Fitzgerald. This was not a prosperous era. The company lost over a million dollars in 1938, and net earnings in the other eight years averaged less than half a million dollars. Preferred stockholders received dividends (not always on time), but common stockholders waited in vain. Sales of only $9.8 million in 1932 were the lowest since 1915; the subsequent recovery, though short-lived, brought sales for 1936 close to the previous high of $24.5 million (1923) and the physical volume of output to a new peak of 57.8 million pounds (1936). The stimulus of war in Europe and defense in the United States had spread as far as Danville's mills when George Simmons Harris became the seventh president in May 1940.

The Plant

The balance-sheet data (Appendix 1) reveal a contraction in the value of fixed assets at the rate of over $350,000 a year. Except in 1937, when additions and betterments represented a net increase of $319,000, improvements ran consistently below the amounts set aside for depreciation—despite the fact that the period was generally one of rising prices.

This shrinkage of fixed-asset values as Table 1 indicates, arose in large measure from the writing down of plant and machinery accounts at Riverside Division. Mill No. 4 was demolished in 1937, and in other mills machinery was scrapped because of the falling demand for the coarse goods which it was designed to produce. At Dan River Division the mill construction account declined about $500,000, while the machinery ledgers showed a net increase of only $258,000.

I dare say that never in the company's history was so much spent for advice on improvements and so little, relatively, expended in acquiring the tools with which to carry out this advice. In addition to Lockwood, Greene Engineers, Riverside and Dan River Cotton Mills contracted for the services of the Textile Development Company, J. E. Sirrine & Company, Ralph E. Loper Company, Barnes Textile Associates, Charles M. Mumford, and Eric R. Voss. In one instance a consultant was employed to report on the report of another expert. It is hard to escape the impression that the common sense of the management, aided by technicians on the permanent staff of the company, in many instances would have yielded less costly and more realistic advice.

Power and water

Serious shortages of electric power faced both the City of Danville and its largest industry in the early thirties. President West explained the mill's dilemma to City Engineer Scott: ". . . our own generating plants have become increasingly uncertain as reliable sources of power," but the company "did not deem it advisable" to make a large investment in a new steam plant. The municipal steam-generating station also failed to meet the needs of a growing population, and city officials thought Dan River should co-operate in developing new

Table 1. Summary of Depreciation Statements, 1932-1940
(thousands of dollars)

	book value, Jan. 1, 1932	improve-ments-additions, 1932-1940	deprecia-tion, 1932-1940	book value, Jan. 4, 1941
Riverside Division				
land	1,202	0	17*	1,185
buildings-machinery	6,511	1,734	4,340	3,905
Dan River Division				
mill construction	2,561	242	727	2,076
water power: construction	357	0	93	264
water power: land	237	0	44	193
machinery	4,808	3,191	2,932	5,066
electrical equipment	987	546	683	850
water supply-filter system	320	31	110	241
Hylton Hall, Y.M.C.A., tenements	971	123	569	526
coal and wood company	†	65	11	55
Stamford real estate		49	0	49
debit depreciation reserve (1934) ‡			—282	282
	17,954	5,981	9,244	14,691

* Land sold.
† Included in tenements account.
‡ Major repairs and replacements charged to depreciation reserve.
Error in totals due to rounding.

hydroelectric facilities. In March 1933 Danville offered the company a contract for sharing power from the proposed hydroelectric plant at the Pinnacles of the Dan (Patrick County), but the proposal was rejected on the ground that within five or ten years the mills would need much more primary power than the municipal plant could supply. Eventually, Dan River would have to improve its own generating facilities; then the mills would require only secondary power, which the city might not be able to furnish on satisfactory terms. Supported by a bond election and a federal subsidy, Danville went ahead with the Pinnacles project and commenced to use power from this source in 1938.[1]

[1] In the emergency, the city had to enlarge its steam plant at the river front, the company having agreed to furnish condensing water from the south canal. The city paid $1.50 per million gallons at first (1934), but in 1937 bought 131 million gallons at $1.75 per million gallons.

Two engineering reports submitted in 1932 dwelt on the inadequacies of the steam and hydroelectric plants at Dan River Division. According to J. E. Sirrine & Company, at least three boilers, which had a maximum pressure of 175 pounds, needed to be replaced with 450-pound boilers. The 23-year-old Allis-Chalmers turbogenerator was so inefficient that it could be used only in emergencies. Sirrine's recommendations called for an expenditure of $1,250,000 on new generating equipment with a capacity of 14,000 K.W. As for the hydroelectric plant, it no longer seemed worthwhile to remove the silt which had greatly reduced the storage capacity of the pond.

Lockwood, Greene's report recognized the low efficiency of Dan River's boilers and turbines but pointed out that, since the plant had been built economically and was "pretty well written off," it would pay to "run this plant out." What the engineers regarded as the "stumbling block" in the whole power set-up was the large investment in equipment designed for 25-cycle current, whereas "by a process of evolution and the survival of the fittest" 60-cycle power had become standard for manufacturing and lighting in A.C. installations.[2] The estimated cost of complete conversion to 60-cycle power was $1,823,000, but Lockwood, Greene recommended spreading this over a ten-year period. An immediate investment of about $100,000 was required to use 60-cycle purchased power.

Negotiations with the Appalachian Electric Company led to the signing of a five-year contract for secondary power in July 1933. Under this agreement double circuits, running into substations at each division, delivered Appalachian power to the mills and returned to the Appalachian system "dump" power generated at the dams when the mills were not operating. The value of this "dump" power (at .2 cent per K.W.H.) was applied to the promissory note for $49,627 which Dan River Mills gave Appalachian Power to cover the cost of transmission lines.[3] For electricity obtained from Appalachian the company paid .8 cent per K.W.H.[4] Expenditures for purchased power rose steadily from $57,844 in 1934 to $296,846 in 1940.

[2] An opportunity to change to 60-cycle current had been "lost" in 1914, Lockwood, Greene said, when the management decided that the necessary capital expenditure could not be justified.

[3] The debt was fully retired in 1939.

[4] Lockwood, Greene made the following estimates of power costs at the mills (based on 1931 prices and output):

	cents per kilowatt hour	
	Riverside	Dan River
steam	1.23	.85
hydroelectric	1.40	.97

Table 2 presents the available data on power consumption in 1933-1939. Particularly striking is the result of closing down the steam plant at Riverside Division in 1935. As early as 1932 G. N. Miller, Riverside's engineer, pointed out that the plant produced constantly decreasing amounts of electricity per ton of coal; but it was necessary to keep this obsolete equipment in operation until the tie-in with the Appalachian lines had been completed.[5] Thereafter, Riverside's boilers were used only for heating and process steam.

Table 2. Electric Power Consumption, 1933-1939
(thousands of kilowatt hours)

	1933	1935	1936	1937	1938	1939
Riverside						
steam	17,383	8,299	0	27	59	7
hydro	5,987	9,299	8,934	11,756	10,392	9,136
bought		10,286	22,770	19,312	12,691	14,404
sold		2,299	1,862	2,590	3,973	2,445
Dan River						
steam			44,719	39,454	29,776	36,198
hydro			15,176	20,393	16,193	15,254
bought			11,034	13,520	14,869	18,875
sold			937	1,264	1,391	905
net consumption						
Riverside			29,842	28,505	19,170	21,102
Dan River			69,992	72,103	59,447	69,422
total			99,834	100,608	78,617	90,524

Lockwood, Greene re-examined the power problem prior to the expiration of the contract with Appalachian Power. The engineers' proposals were the same as those made five years earlier, but now they were more costly. Thus, an investment of $2,000,000 in new steam-generating equipment would have assured both divisions of ample power for another decade or so. Such a program the engineers judged "not sufficiently profitable to justify the entire investment. As a matter of fact, the complete generating plant at Dan River would show a substantial loss as compared to purchased power on the basis of a 40-hour week, and even at maximum production, the net saving is too

[5] In 1933 Riverside generated 17.4 million K.W.H. of current with 40,360 tons of coal, while Dan River's steam plant—not an efficient one at that—produced 44.7 million K.W.H. (1936) with 84,655 tons of coal.

small to justify the generation of power." Appalachian's price for primary power made it "extremely difficult to figure out a generating plant to compete with it on a very attractive financial basis." The upshot of the matter was the renewal of the Appalachian contract for five years, providing for the mill's sales of dump power at .18 cent per K.W.H. Including the $188,000 invested in electrical equipment in 1938, improvements in the power system averaged nearly $70,000 annually for six years (1932-1938); and in 1937 Dan River's hydro-electric station generated over five million K.W.H. of 60-cycle current.

The Lockwood, Greene recommendation for purchasing power, while improving gradually the company's own generating facilities, ran counter to the advice of G. N. Miller. Now superintendent of power, maintenance, and construction, Miller insisted that the company should either produce all its power or tie in with the city's system, purchasing surplus power from the Pinnacles plant and sending dump power to the municipal lines. He calculated that this would save the mills $40,000 annually and reduce the city's costs by $50,000 a year.[6]

Tests of the boilers at Dan River Division (1935) revealed an inexcusable waste of coal through lack of regulatory devices for adjusting the stokers to varying requirements of steam. An estimated $37,000 a year was saved by the installation of automatic combustion controls, supplied by the Bailey Meter Company, on seven of the fourteen boilers.[7]

Lockwood, Greene considered Dan River's facilities for filtering and storing water inadequate, especially after the bleachery and finishing plant took on increased loads. It was not advisable, the engineers thought, "to use pond water any more in the bleachery if an alternative at reasonable expense can be devised." The manager of the finishing plant scouted the fear of "any bad results from pond water if used in the early washes," but in 1937 Hungerford and Terry installed new filter beds and made minor improvements at the filter plant at a cost of $15,780. This was half of the entire sum spent on improvements for the filtering and water-supply system over a period of nine years.

By 1932 the Dan River bleachery required two million gallons of water daily, or about 40 per cent of the filtering capacity of 3,500

[6] In emergencies, the Riverside plant had furnished small quantities of power to the city (1936, 1937, and 1938); and small quantities of current were likewise made available to Dan Valley Mills.

[7] "Pays for Itself in Three Months," an article in the *Textile World* (vol. 89, Nov. 1939, pp. 94-95) featured this improvement at Dan River.

gallons per minute. The filter plant at Riverside Division had a rated capacity of 1,500 gallons per minute.

Machinery and processes

Several engineering reports during West's presidency dealt with efficient organization of production and plans for machinery replacements. In May 1934 Charles M. Mumford submitted an elaborate plan for the reorganization of Riverside Division. One of his two major proposals involved the demolition of three buildings (Mills 1, 4, and 6); but West presented to the directors the second and less drastic program, which called for the dismantling of Mills 1 and 4 and the conversion of Mill No. 6 into a "complete balanced unit on warp yarns." The razing of Mill No. 4—the old Morotock Mill—was commenced in 1937; Mill No. 1, after a period of idleness, was re-equipped for spinning.

Meanwhile, about $70,000 was expended (against estimated annual savings of $35,000) to convert the top floor of Mill No. 8 to spinning, replacing 1,620 looms with 107,000 spindles. The Long Mill was re-arranged so as to concentrate all of the yarn preparatory processes, through fine roving, in these three buildings. This left Riverside with only 3,244 looms in operation, all of them restricted to the manufacture of plaids, chambrays, drills, and coverts. At the same time, some of the machinery used to make sales yarn at Dan River Division was moved to Riverside's Mill No. 6. After 1933 sales yarns included carpet yarn as well as the older lines of hosiery yarn.

By all odds the most significant improvement in 1932-1940 was the introduction of long-draft spinning and roving. This technological change which has been ranked with the development of the high-speed spindle and the automatic loom, accounts for a major portion of all the labor-saving improvements in spinning mills since the 1920's. Long drafting in spinning made it possible to spin from coarser rovings, while the development of long-draft roving frames reduced the number of drawings required for a given count of yarn. One of the machinery manufacturers stressed the idea that longer drafting was better drafting, since the fine-count yarns formerly made only on mules were easily made on long-draft ring frames.[8]

[8] T. R. Navin, *The Whitin Machine Works since 1831* (Cambridge, 1950), pp. 513-527, provides an excellent summary of the invention (in Spain) and spread of long drafting. Other aspects of the development of long drafting in the United States are related in G. S. Gibb, *The Saco-Lowell Shops* (Cambridge, 1950), pp. 557-566. On labor saving from long drafting and other improvements, see: "Report on Survey of Technological Im-

In September 1932 the directors approved the expenditure of $127,000 on Saco-Lowell long-draft attachments for 77,000 spindles in Dan River's Mill No. 4. The first order for parts to change two fly frames to the "Roth" type of long drafting had been placed a year earlier; thereafter, the introduction of long-draft equipment proceeded in piece-meal fashion over a period of years.[9] In addition to long-draft changeovers for 252 spinning frames, ordered in November 1932, Saco-Lowell furnished (1932-1934) 42 "Hi-draft" drawing frames. Employed to make a "thorough study" of mill reorganization, in May 1934 Mumford recommended an outlay of $2,100,000 to convert all spinning at Dan River Division to long draft, but this phase of the engineer's report was accepted only as a long-run objective.

One reason for not going into long drafting as rapidly as Mumford advised was the uncertain performance of some of the Saco-Lowell machinery. In May 1934 one intermediate frame and eight spinning frames were equipped with Whitin (i.e., "Casablancas") long-draft attachments "to test out this method." The results were satisfactory, and even Saco-Lowell officials conceded that "we have never been able to equal the break on your regular work or that obtained on the other make [Whitin] of long-draft roving frame." But Lowell soon perfected its roving frame. With authority from the directors to make "further substitution of long-draft roving for old-style roving," in September 1936 West ordered Saco-Lowell changeovers for four roving frames in Mill No. 1; and four more frames were changed to long draft the following May. C. E. Clark, then superintendent of carding and spinning, reported an increase in output per roving spindle of 12 per cent, while "the spinner attends the same number of spindles as she did for the same amount of pay."[10]

In the development of long-draft roving, Riverside and Dan River Mills was an interested spectator in the lawsuits over conflicting pat-

---

provements in Cotton Textile Machinery during the 25-year Period, 1910-1935" (mimeographed; Barnes Textile Associates, Inc., Boston, 1935). The data compiled by Barnes was incorporated in the article, "Mechanical Changes in the Cotton-Textile Industry, 1910-1936," *Monthly Labor Review*, vol. 45 (1937), pp. 316-341.

[9] Saco-Lowell announced in March 1928 that they were ready to make change-overs of the LeBlan-Roth system, a rival of the original Casablancas method. The latter had been adopted in Whitin Machine Works.

[10] Perhaps a discriminatory price policy, as well as long-standing relations with Saco-Lowell, enabled the latter firm to obtain most of the orders for new spinning and roving machinery. In May 1936 Saco-Lowell confirmed a schedule of discounts ranging from 7.5 per cent on controlled-draft roving to 12.5 per cent on spinning machinery. Dan River had no obligation to buy Saco-Lowell machines exclusively; but, "inasmuch as you are the largest user of our equipment, we feel that special consideration is in order."

ents. Dismayed by unsatisfactory efforts to develop a worthy competitor to Whitin's "Casablancas" roving frame, in 1933 Saco-Lowell hired William G. Reynolds, an overseer and mill superintendent who had designed and built an experimental roving frame at Dan River. Reynolds was employed at the Biddeford plant of Saco-Lowell for about a year. Charging that the roving frame which Saco-Lowell finally marketed (April 1937) infringed his patents, Reynolds brought suit and in June 1943 won an award of $210,265 in back royalties.[11]

Between March 1935 and October 1938 Saco-Lowell furnished long-draft changeovers for about 125,000 spinning spindles at Dan River Division. Barnes Textile Associates, which carried out most of the tests of long drafting, recommended (September 1937) an investment of $315,000 in Saco-Lowell super-draft roving frames soon after the new machine came on the market. The estimated saving in labor was $59,000 annually, but the management tabled the proposal and spent only $4,000 (1938) on long-draft changeovers. About this time the company found it necessary to curtail its outlay for the Barnes service; but one of their engineers, D. K. Woodard, joined the Dan River organization as President West's assistant. In March 1939 Woodard reported on a test of filling yarn made on long draft from single roving, showing it to be "equal in quality from every standpoint" to yarn made on regular draft from double roving. He concluded that a return of 73 per cent could be obtained from a changeover of 50,000 spindles to long-draft roving. Notwithstanding these tempting calculations, the management was constrained to defer the complete conversion of the mills to long drafting. Because these improvements seemed more urgent, comparatively large sums were appropriated for new twister frames for the rayon and suiting yarns, for converting spinning frames to twisters, for changing spindles to tape drive and for equipping drawing and spinning frames with Veeder-Root hank clocks.[12]

In cotton manufacturing, as in other affairs of man, one thing leads to another. With long drafting firmly established, the need for a better

[11] G. S. Gibbs, *op. cit.*, pp. 562-565. Reynolds also won a case against Whitin Machine Works.

[12] According to R. W. Cutler, who was soliciting new orders in Oct. 1939, Dan River Mills had used 216,500 yards of Cutler tape, enough to equip 270,000 spindles.

Some of Riverside's spinning frames but none of the drawing frames had hank clocks in 1932; two years later only 384 of Dan River's 1,316 spinning frames had hank clocks. Both the Barnes Textile Service and the Textile Development Company recommended complete installations. According to Textile Development, operatives paid "standard" wages on drawing and spinning frames "do not have the same interest in keeping the machines running" as when paid by the hank.

sliver at the roving frame hastened the improvement of the preparatory processes. Single-process picking, first developed in England, was brought to America by Saco-Lowell shops; and, announced to the trade in 1928, the Saco-Lowell picking system "swept the industry."[13] Dan River bought ten new (1929 model) pickers and one-process changeovers for ten of the 1903 model Kitson pickers. In the carding rooms Saco-Lowell installed 445 new continuous strippers at a cost of $165 per card; while the Carrier Corporation, Parks-Cramer, and American Moistening Company made several installations of air-changing and humidifying equipment. These improvements economized in the workers' health as well as labor and, in the opinion of President West, represented a "very profitable investment."[14]

In the development of combing machinery Whitin "had stolen a march on Saco-Lowell," but after a lapse of thirty years Saco-Lowell commenced to manufacture a competitor to the Whitin comber. Dan River began to acquire Saco-Lowell combers in 1935 and had fourteen installed by 1939. Combing, as Lockwood, Greene pointed out in 1931, was one example of the "gradual transition to finer goods" which would put Dan River in competition with "higher cost mills of the North, particularly New Bedford." Combed broadcloths and handkerchief cloth were added to Dan River's lines in 1935.

Late in 1934 representatives of the T. C. Entwistle Company arrived in Danville to conduct a survey of warping. I find no reference to Entwistle equipment in use until late in 1937, when tests of the labor-saving features of an Entwistle warper, combined with either Universal or Abbott winding, compared unfavorably with Barber-Colman automatic spooling and warping. In March 1936 Superintendent Robertson found "quite an improvement in the running of yarn on slasher" from the Barber-Colman "Super-speed" warper and automatic spooler; within a few months the two dress rooms at Dan River Division had 17 automatic spoolers and 14 high-speed warpers. It was esti-

[13] G. S. Gibb, *op. cit.*, p. 566.
[14] R. R. West to J. A. Cairns, Sept. 18, 1936. A survey conducted by the State Health Commission in 1936 revealed "considerable" dirt, dust, and lint in the opening, cleaning, and picking rooms at Dan River Division. Although not regarded as a "very serious health hazard," the health officials believed it contributed to absenteeism due to colds and other respiratory diseases. The installation of a dust collecting system at Riverside Division made the opening and picking rooms "much less dusty." Since air-changing had been added to some of the weave rooms, the suggestion was made that the company keep comparative records of sickness in air-conditioned and non-air-conditioned weave rooms.

Claims for compensation for "strippers' asthma" were frequently brought before industrial commissions ("Card-room Fever," *Textile World*, vol. 90, March 1940, p. 68).

mated that the investment of $180,000 in new spooling and warping machinery would produce an annual saving in labor of $52,500.[15]

In the summer of 1931 Lockwood, Greene proposed a long-range weave-room reorganization which called for the following distribution of looms:

Riverside Division:
   3,240 looms for chambrays, ginghams, plaids and coverts

Dan River Division:
   2,539 looms for sheeting
   2,000 looms for carded and combed broadcloths
   1,000 looms for colored suitings
   1,000 looms for shirtings and diaper and handkerchief cloth
   1,000 looms for fine print goods

The program required the purchase of 1,000 new Draper looms; for, although the company had 13,060 looms, 2,900 were narrow, plain-box or non-automatic models unsuitable for weaving any goods the market would take. A "natural development" for Dan River, the engineers reasoned, would be a gradual transition to the manufacture of finer goods, in order to shift the brunt of competition from the low-cost mills farther South to the higher-cost mills in the North—"particularly New Bedford." As often happened, the advice of experts was accepted partially and eventually.

Installations of the new Draper Model X looms began with the purchase of 54 40-inch looms in 1932, at a cost of over $18,000; this was much less than the expenditure on parts to widen looms and on selvage motions for 1,825 looms weaving "Riverside" sheets. Loom widening, as an alternative to investment in new looms, appealed to many manufacturers, who felt that the competition of the two makers of automatic looms had not sufficed to keep loom prices in line with prices in the goods market.[16]

No loom orders were placed in 1933, but it cost the company nearly $100,000 to equip looms with pick counters. Pick counters made a more accurate record of loom output than measuring by the cut; it

---

[15] The great advantage of the new spooler was the automatic knotting of yarn ends moving off the bobbins. High-speed cone or tube winders required hand-knotting machines. An additional, though indirect, gain from improved spooling was a reduction in the number of bad knots, kinks, and gouts, resulting in less frequent stoppage of looms from defects in the warp. This permitted "stretching" weaving labor as much as 30 per cent ("Warping at 900 Yards," *Textile World*, vol. 81 [1932], pp. 1994-1995).

[16] Barnes Textile Service called Dan River's attention to this and reported that several mills were rebuilding their own looms "with considerable success and saving."

became imperative to use this device with the introduction of the second shift in order to record the production of different weavers on the same cut.

In January 1934 Waverley Cousins' "preliminary report" on savings from the installation of 390 Draper looms indicated an increase in loom output of 21.28 per cent and a reduction in weaving cost of 24 per cent. The proposed improvement required capital expenditures of $225,357. Actually, in less than two years (February 1934-November 1935) a much larger sum was expended on Draper's Models X, L, and XL looms, viz., 358 48-inch looms, 140 72-inch looms, and 607 90-inch looms. Prices in this period ranged from $388 to $666 per loom.

West talked of buying some Jacquard looms in 1935; none was ordered, so far as I know. Crompton & Knowles sold Dan River 59 16-harness looms, and in 1937 156 second-hand Crompton & Knowles looms were acquired from the receivers of the Amoskeag Manufacturing Company. "Satisfactory" experiments with the Crompton & Knowles "Cotton King" loom, first ordered in 1932, led to the investment of about $300,000 in 312 looms of this model in 1939-1940.[17] And, in response to the demand from cutters for wider dress goods and suiting fabrics, Dan River spent (1939-1940) over $50,000 to widen almost 600 looms from 36 to 40 inches.[18]

An issue of *Parks' Parables* (April 1936) is devoted to an improvement in Dan River's weave rooms—the installation of Parks patented air changer. According to the equipment maker, the system was designed to maintain relative humidity of 85 per cent, with a temperature of not over 84°. Previously, in the basement weave room work had to be carried on "with a dry bulb temperature oftentimes reaching 92°."

A bright spot on the dreary map of idle machinery was found in Dan River's finishing department. Thayer P. Gates, who came to Dan River from the Sayles Bleacheries, wrote a "Survey of Finishing Departments" in April 1931 and helped to reorganize the department of which he was appointed manager.[19] In July 1931 Lockwood, Greene,

[17] The "Cotton King" must have been one of the two new looms which the Barnes Textile Service said "certainly do delight the eye and must make the loom builder proud of his art."

[18] Parts supplied by Crompton & Knowles to widen a 36-inch loom to 40 inches cost $202.55, but Dan River's machinists soon discovered that many of the parts could be made in Danville foundries. The saving was close to $50 per loom (J. A. Becher to R. B. Newton, May 6, 1941).

[19] "The reorganization of the finishing plant at Riverside," Gates wrote, "has taught me something new in the speed of such a development" (T. P. Gates to D. McArthur,

noting the low demand for ginghams and chambrays, advised the management that there was "no profit in the colored lines and in general none in whites unless a mill does its own finishing." This provided a cue for informing the directors (March 1932): "As to weaving and spinning, it is too much to hope that we can manufacture more cheaply than our Southern competitors, but in our finishing and selling we are in a more favorable position." President West described the Dan River finishing plant as one "originally intended solely for the purpose of bleaching, finishing and making up our Sheets and Pillow Cases. For years it has been run more or less as a side issue . . . today this finishing plant is becoming more and more important; as a matter of fact, a great part of our business is developing along these lines." In addition to sheetings, "quite a volume" of white and colored broadcloths and some fancy shirtings went through the bleachery. "My plan," West said, "is to put the Bleachery on its own feet with its own cost system which will indicate the result of operations." As a matter of fact, the accounting department had data to show that unbleached broadcloth purchased from another mill at 5.545 cents a yard could have been sold when finished for 6.6 net, leaving a margin of .375 cent per yard over the cost of bleaching and finishing.

On the basis of West's recommendation the board appropriated $150,000 for new bleaching and dyeing machinery. In addition to purchases of up-to-date but more or less standard equipment for the bleachery and dye house, the new program provided facilities for preshrinking goods. The Morrison Machine Company, one of three companies licensed to make "Sanforizing" machinery, furnished four of the preshrinking machines which finished cloth with a residual shrinkage of not over 1 per cent. Another manufacturer, H. B. Butterworth & Company, furnished two preshrinking machines—referred to at the mill as "Rivershrinkers"—designed to reduce residual shrinkage to not over 3 per cent in warps and not over 2 per cent on average. "To meet competition of the so-called pre-shrunk fabrics," Dan River's salesmen were told in 1932, "we have added this process to our equipment and same will be known as Rivershrunk." Until the Federal Trade Commission promulgated trade practices on shrinkage (1938), some Dan River cloth carried the "Rivershrunk" tag; other goods bore the "Sanforized" label. Confusion over the difference between the two proc-

Dec. 22, 1931). Gates died in January 1934 and was succeeded by R. T. Read. Basil D. Browder became manager of the finishing department in March 1938.

esses, together with the possibility of a conflict with the "Sanforizing" patents, led to the abandonment of "Rivershrinking."[20] The Butterworth machinery was converted to Sanforizing and, since the preshrinking equipment had long been used to capacity (24 hours a day), in 1939 a $100,000-addition to Mill No. 5 was begun. An index of the importance of Sanforizing may be derived from the following data on royalties paid to the patentee, Cluett, Peabody & Company, at the rate of .25 cent per yard:

1931	$ 10,647	1936	40,126
1932	29,435	1937	46,127
1933	21,195	1938	65,510
1934	23,728	1939	115,095
1935	21,056	1940	95,814

Dan River's 1938 price lists offered Sanforized cloth at 2.5 to 2.75 cents per yard more than non-Sanforized cloth.

In 1939 Dan River adopted the "Tebilized" crease-resisting finish for some rayon fabrics. Royalties paid to the English patentee, Tootal Broadhurst Lee Company, amounted to $32,209 in 1939 and $33,750 in 1940. The fee ran as high as one cent per yard for "Tebilized" cloth containing over 49 per cent rayon.[21]

In January 1939 Chairman Miller sent President West a clipping dealing with the development by General Electric Company of an "eagle eye" for detecting skewness in filling threads. West was able to inform Miller that the company already had the device on two finishing ranges and had ordered equipment for a third.[22]

[20] Tests in 1938 showed that some of Dan River's "Sanforized" fabrics had a residual shrinkage of up to 3 per cent. When the patentee, Cluett, Peabody & Company, succeeded in finishing the same cloth with a shrinkage of only .87 per cent, Dan River sent some of its finishing men to the Cluett Peabody plants in Troy, New York, to improve their skill in the process.

[21] Dr. Chase had some doubts about the usefulness of the process. In a research report (April 3, 1939) he pointed out that Dan River rayon goods had "crease resisting tendency to some extent, after resin treatment." He also wondered whether the "Tebilized" process had not been anticipated by different resin treatments which produced crease resistance "without its being noticed." West complained that payment of the royalty (one and one quarter cents per yard initially) had forced the company to withdraw two lines of rayon plaids and two shirting lines (R. R. West to T. B. Lee Co., Sept. 9, 1939).

[22] "Automatic Weft Straighteners," an article in *Textile World* (vol. 90, Nov. 1940, p. 58), described the operation of this device at Riverside & Dan River Cotton Mills: "One of these tenters [equipped with weft straighteners] is used for wide sheetings, one for narrow sheetings, and one for handkerchief fabrics and bird's-eye cloth. The superintendent cites . . . several advantages resulting from the installation. Chief among these are the vastly improved quality of the goods and a considerable saving in material, the latter due to the fact that since the filling yarn in the finished piece is at right angles to the warp, the cloth tears true and waste is thereby reduced. Another advantage is elimination of eye fatigue."

Lockwood, Greene's 1931 report, emphasizing that the "popularity of prints seems to be well maintained," recommended the installation of four printing machines. Several buyers of print goods, the engineers said, were already Dan River customers, and the bulk of the competition was northern instead of low-cost southern. In May Thayer Gates made an estimate of the cost of setting up a printing department. A plant capable of printing 240,000 yards per week required a capital outlay of $254,706 and would add $912 per week to the payroll. No recommendation was brought before the board of directors, but the idea of going into printing interested the management for several years. In 1933 West and Ray had the prospect of engaging an outside printing plant to do contract work, which promised to "turn out very nicely for us and at no outlay of capital on our part"; but in 1935 the president, though convinced that it was "desirable and necessary for us to firmly establish ourselves in the printed goods field," turned down an opportunity to buy (and bring to Danville) the printing plant of a liquidated Massachusetts firm. "We have," West said, "approximately 8,000 people employed, and I am of the opinion that it is too highly concentrated already without adding more to it. Possibly it [the printing plant] could be put in some nearby location which would be readily accessible and capable of being handled by us."[23] A year later the directors deferred action on West's proposal to buy six used printing machines; and in 1937 the president confessed that the chances of going into printing were "remote," though this was a "logical development." The only outcome of the discussions of printing was the purchase of two single-color warp-yarn printers for the piece-dyeing plant.

Although unrelated to print cloth, it deserves mention that the company's printing shop, set up in 1932, was a source of saving. For the month of May 1933, for instance, multigraphing and the printing of tags, tickets, and labels cost $286 less than it would have cost in an outside shop.

Research and Development

The foundations of Dan River's rise in later years to a foremost position in research were laid toward the close of Fitzgerald's presidency.

[23] R. R. West to H. M. McCord, Sept. 12, 1935. In writing to the U. S. Finishing Company in May 1934 West lamented the "lack of progress . . . on this printed goods development."

In May 1930, Robert R. West, then the president's assistant, outlined the requirements for a "research, experimental and development department." The objectives of West's plan included the development of improved manufacturing methods, the maintenance of standards of quality, and experiments with new fabrics "in line with market trends." The proposed organization involved three units: (1) a designing, styling, and fabric development unit, (2) a laboratory unit, and (3) an experimental manufacturing unit. It was recognized that a great deal of the work of the proposed department—testing chemicals, dyes, and fabrics, control of manufacturing processes, and experimenting with new fabrics—was already being done in various divisions of the mills; but West considered it "advantageous to consolidate all of this work under one head, physically separated from our main production units." A pilot plant, for instance, consisting of 100 looms and 5,000 spindles, would avoid interference of experimental work with the regular manufacturing operations. It is fairly clear that President Fitzgerald's preoccupation with more urgent matters, in the year before his death, prevented any thorough consideration of these recommendations.

Two years later Dr. H. M. Chase submitted a proposal for reorganizing the Chemical and Dyeing Department, which in 1932 embraced the dyestuffs laboratory, chemical laboratory, cotton research laboratory, and chemical manufacturing plant. Another "Plan of Reorganization: Research, Chemical and Dyeing Department," submitted by Dr. Chase in June 1934, shows some progress in carrying out the recommendations made in 1930 and 1932. In 1934 the department comprised an analytical laboratory in charge of a chemist, a cotton research laboratory, a chemical manufacturing plant headed by a chemist, and piece, beam, indigo, and raw-stock dyeing plants. A dyehouse control laboratory was urgently needed, Dr. Chase thought, to train overseers and foreman; and a rayon and celanese dyeing plant would be a profitable investment, in view of the increasing use of these yarns. A dye-testing and color-matching laboratory existed on paper; no personnel had been hired for this type of work. As a matter of fact, the whole research department suffered from a lack of skilled personnel.

Weekly reports of the chemical manufacturing plant, prepared by W. E. J. McMann, showed a consistently satisfactory performance in this phase of the research program. In the week ending December 17, 1932, the cost of manufacturing relatively small quantities of gum, softeners, and oils was $684 less than the market prices of these supplies; in the period January 1—March 10, 1934, the estimated saving was $14,295. In January 1934 M. E. Bebeau reported to H. M. Chase on "oil V" for use on suitings. Igepon, the chemical formerly used, tended to "blend the carbon colors, bringing down the shade and darkening the white. Oil V overcomes this and gives a superior Scouring." Some ventures proved much less rewarding. In the hope of improving dyeing processes, in 1934 the company invited Dr. Vincent Chmielnitski to work with Dr. Chase. Chmielnitski claimed to be familiar with superior methods of vat dyeing; but, after inspecting samples of his work, the company concluded that he had not demonstrated a knowledge of any "revolutionary processes." In 1937 the Aldox Laboratory Corporation announced a continuous bleaching process which promised a great reduction in costs. Dan River sent 1,200 yards of cloth to Boston for a test run; but the results, in Dr. Chase's opinion, fell woefully short of the Aldox claim.

The idea that flax could be spun successfully with cotton had a hard time dying. Experiments conducted by Theodore P. Haughey, with the financial help of Dan River, were unsatisfactory; but on various occasions the company was asked to revive the experimental work.[24] In 1935 the firm of Jonas and River felt sure that Dan River would want to get in on the ground floor in the development of cotton goods containing an admixture of rabbit fur. No evidence has been found that President West took to heart the promise that "those houses originating fabrics with rabbit in them will be the ones who will be able to capitalize on its advantages."

At several points I have called attention to the fact that the board of directors approved specific appropriations for capital improvements. President West outlined the needs, as seen by the management, and estimated the amount of money required. Ordinarily the directors supported the management; but in December 1937, when West asked for $900,000 to carry out his 1938 "Schedule for Plant Improvements," the board demurred. In view of poor business conditions, the directors requested the president to revise his estimates and return with a streamlined budget. The following January West proposed spending $531,000

---

[24] R. R. West to Canadian Cottons, Ltd., Jan. 2, 1936; C. T. Revere to R. R. West, Dec. 7, and R. R. West to C. T. Revere, Dec. 23, 1936. Dan River files contain some samples of the cotton-flax cloth produced by Haughey in 1930 or 1931. According to West, "we were never able to get the flax fibre sufficiently clean so that we could spin it in a commercially satisfactory way."

for improvements, but the board decided to allocate only $250,000 for "items deemed most urgent." Writing to Chairman Miller, the president confessed his disappointment and regret. "I sincerely hope," he said, "that we may find our way clear to proceed with putting into effect our policy of consistent plant improvement."[25]

The board moved cautiously in granting requests for capital expenditures in 1939. In January it appropriated $100,000, added $210,000 in March, and in May approved West's request for $175,000 for new suiting looms. When the executive committee learned that heavier looms were advisable, the directors increased the appropriation by $30,000. Before the end of the year, encouraged by the sales of suitings, the directors raised the total budget for new equipment to $700,000.

The need for heavier looms for making suitings was one of the subjects discussed by the management and staff in December 1939. Suitings were being woven on converted gingham looms, which were too light and too narrow for the best results; but the expenditure of nearly $2 million to replace the 2,049 looms manufacturing suitings would scarcely win the directors' approval. Another problem, particularly perplexing in the case of suitings, was the duplication of effort in cross-hauling and handling goods in process. Yarn production, weaving, and finishing were carried out in widely dispersed operations; dyeing requirements exceeded the capacity of two shifts, and a third shift was not considered economical. One of the many plans of reorganization proposed by Lockwood, Greene envisaged the concentration of the weaving of suitings in Riverside's Mill No. 8, making a complete suitings department at the plants in Danville. These changes awaited a new administration.

Dan River's problems in Danville were sufficiently acute to keep it disinterested in merger schemes, which textile financiers continued to offer as panaceas for the industry's ills. In co-operation with the Kendall Company and two machinery manufacturers, Draper and Whitin, the Dan River management worked out plans for a subsidiary to acquire the assets of the bankrupt Pelzer Manufacturing Company (South Carolina). The success of the scheme hinged on a loan from the Reconstruction Finance Corporation; but Dan River withdrew (August

---

[25] A few years earlier the *Daily News Record* quoted West as believing that, "A mill is no stronger than its physical equipment." Referring to obsolete machines at Dan River, he said, "All these machines must go. They are in good repair, in perfect working condition . . . . But they are out-dated by new machines."

1936) when it looked as though the project might result in "buying into a lawsuit."[26] In 1935 a group of Richmond bankers urged Dan River to buy the preferred stock of the Industrial Cotton Mills of Rock Hill, South Carolina. After careful consideration, this proposal, too, was rejected. Although the mills were using increasing quantities of worsted yarns in the manufacture of suitings, no serious attention was paid to the recommendation (submitted by Duryea Van Wagenen, a Dan River director and president of the Charlottesville Woolen Mills) that the company purchase a "three- or five-set woolen mill."

In 1936, after President West had accepted the chairmanship of an American Cotton Manufacturers' Association committee to work on some scheme for the "early and orderly retirement of the Industry's less efficient machinery," Dan River invested $10,000 in the Textile Machinery & Supply Company. Organized by R. E. Loper, this company made plans for "financing the orderly liquidation of textile plants which are finding liquidation desirable or necessary." Machinery acquired by the Textile Machinery Company was offered for sale to the mills owning stock. Not enough mills, however, were interested in the plan to make it work; and Dan River withdrew without loss.

Finance

Financial developments in this nine-year period reflect closely the low level of business in the Great Depression; the expansion of trade induced by the New Deal; the sharp recession in textiles in 1937-1938; and the halting return to prosperity with the onset of war in Europe and rearmament in the United States.

Net sales (Table 3) made sharp gains in 1933. The dollar volume of sales rose relatively more than output, as the Agricultural Adjustment Act and the Cotton Textile Code combined to raise costs and unit selling prices. The gains in both net sales and the physical volume of production moved upward consistently, and both series reached their peaks in 1936-1937. The impact of the recession shows up in the statistics for 1938, but neither output nor sales dropped back to the 1932-1933 levels. Sales in 1939-1940 picked up about 25 per cent over 1938; output advanced somewhat more. Sales of yarn increased in

[26] Pelzer, a subsidiary of the New England Southern Corporation, had been a football in the consolidation movement since 1923. Ultimately, it was reorganized by a group of southern mill men. See S. J. Kennedy, *Profits and Losses in Textiles,* pp. 29-43.

importance in this period; in 1940 sales of carpet and hosiery yarn made up 3.2 per cent of total net sales.

Table 3. Net Sales, 1932-1940
(thousands of dollars)

	cloth		yarn		
year	Riverside division	Dan River division	hosiery	carpet	total
1932	3.466	6,232	120	–	9,818
1933	4,646	9,821	88	–	14,554
1934	6,230	12,528	37	238	19,032
1935	6,040	14,906	123	296	21,364
1936	5,734	17,365	298	348	23,745
1937	5,390	17,486	192	278	23,346
1938	4,195	11,962	117	117	16,390
1939		22,256*	287	219	22,762
1940		21,111*	395	309	21,815

* Both divisions.
Error in totals due to rounding.

Income and earnings data are presented in Table 4. There is not a close correlation, it will be observed, between net sales and gross profit; in one case (1934-1935) sales increased by $2.3 million and gross profit fell $.7 million. Net profit is more closely related to gross profit; on the average, about $1.2 million in gross profit was required to keep the net earnings out of the red. This fairly substantiates the management's position that unused capacity and a low volume of sales were more important than price levels in determining profitable results.

Except in 1940, "other charges" exceeded "other income," making earnings before taxes less than net profit from sales.

Other income consisted of discounts on purchases of supplies, dividends, rent, and earnings from the coal yard, cloth store, and canteen. (The items associated with welfare and housing will be discussed later in the chapter.)

The company's principal investments were stocks of Dan Valley and Piedmont Mills, from which Dan River Mills received dividends of $11,000 annually in 1932-1936, $16,000 in 1937, $11,000 in 1938-1939, and $3,750 in 1940.[27] One hundred odd shares of Regal Manufacturing Company stock were acquired in 1933 in partial settlement of a

[27] From Dan Valley Mills only in 1940.

Table 4. Summary of Income Statements, 1932-1940
(thousands of dollars)

| year | profit from sales | | other income | other charges | earnings before income taxes | income tax reserve | net earnings |
	gross	net					
1932	896	62	111	144	29		29
1933	2,029	1,047	160	245	962	225	737
1934	2,164	1,110	169	350	930	150	780
1935	1,432	278	178	222	234	45	189
1936	2,908	1,584	211	243	1,552	273	1,279
1937	3,125	1,578	183	240	1,520	250	1,270
1938	401	−949	199	267	−1,017		−1,017
1939	2,049	561	239	245	555	109	447
1940	1,775	523	188	181	530	139	391

Error in totals due to rounding.

mercantile debt. After charging off $19,110 to bad debts, the stock had a book value of $1, but it drew dividends of $79 in 1933 and $475 yearly in 1934-1937. Ten shares of Park National Bank stock were valued at $150. In order to accommodate David Clark, editor of the *Southern Textile Bulletin* and vociferous champion of laissez faire, in 1937 Dan River invested $600 in the debentures of Tompkins Realty Company, a Charlotte enterprise organized by Clark to house his publishing company. Part of the debt was repaid in the form of advertising in the *Bulletin*.

The 200 shares of G. A. Stafford stock, with a par value of $20,000, were carried on the balance sheet without value. As of December 31, 1932, G. A. Stafford's personal debt amounted to $43,406, secured by a mortgage on his Connecticut home. Stafford's business improved, and the export firm was able to pay dividends of $10,000 in 1936, $12,500 in 1937, and $6,250 in 1938 and in 1939. Meanwhile, Dan River had acquired the 50 shares of Stafford stock owned by individuals; and the cost of these shares ($7,518) became the ledger value of Dan River's investment in the wholly owned subsidiary.[28]

A non-recurrent item of income was the $135,587 (less a tax reserve of $35,635) received in 1940 as the result of an award by the Interstate Commerce Commission, directing the Southern Railway Company to refund to the corporation and to the city of Danville excessive freight charges on coal shipments in 1931-1933.

Deductions from net profit on sales (excepting village and welfare

[28] The price for the 50 shares represented par, with interest at 6 per cent since the passing of the dividend in 1928.

expenses) consisted largely of interest on borrowed funds. The average amount of outstanding notes payable ranged from $1.8 million in 1932 to a high of $5.7 million in 1939. Payables at the year-end were generally lower than the average, as the company took pains to deplete cash balances before the last day of the year to minimize the state tax (.75 per cent) on demand deposits. In 1936 the company had accounts in eleven banks. Board Chairman Miller, a banker, had the main responsibility for arranging loans, and his only consolation for what seemed to him excessive borrowing was the prevailing low interest rate. Interest absorbed upward of $100,000 a year toward the end of the period, and the management chafed at the obstacles to raising working capital from stock issues.[29] Year-end statements for 1937 and 1938 show current assets slightly less than twice current liabilities, but current ratios of about three to one were maintained in 1932-1935. In a "Memorandum to the board of Directors" (March 1937) President West projected working-capital requirements for a period of rising prices (which he supposed might increase as much as 40 per cent over 1936). He reached the conclusion that if no new working capital were made available by the stockholders, the company could avoid an "uncomfortably low" current ratio only by producing below capacity. Prices, of course, sagged significantly in 1937-1938, and production was curtailed involuntarily. Modest earnings in 1939 and 1940 brought current assets up to over twice current liabilities.

The "punitive" tax on undistributed earnings, West thought, closed the door to financing through retention of earnings. The earnings record of the 1930's gave faint hopes of augmenting the earned surplus in any case. Net earnings for a nine-year period averaged a little more than $450,000 a year (approximately the preferred-dividend requirement), or 2.1 per cent on average net worth. The rate climbed from .1 per cent in 1932 to 5.7 per cent in 1936 and 1937; and, after the stag-

[29] In November 1932 Miller reported on a visit to New York banks. "I stated to the banks," he related, "that we had no intention of borrowing through paper brokers, feeling that we were not in a sufficiently independent position to do so at this time, although the brokers' rates are from one to one and a half per cent below the rates we are paying to our banks."

Within a few years the chairman felt secure enough to shop around. He wrote the First National Bank of Chicago (August 1934) that brokers were offering lower rates than "our regular bankers" and wondered whether the Chicago bank would take "some choisest [sic] paper at less than 1½%."

Danville banks were invited to discount relatively small amounts of the company's paper. In one instance (1934) Miller supposed a rate 1 per cent above the New York market would seem "pretty low" to a local banker; "on the other hand it is about the best he can do with his money."

gering loss of $1,017,000 in 1938, the ratio of earnings to net worth eased upward to 2.1 per cent in 1939 and 1.8 per cent in 1940.

A study of cotton mill earnings in 1932-1939 shows net losses exceeding net profit in three years out of eight. In 1932 only 187 of 815 companies realized a profit; and in 1934, 1935, and 1938 more than half of the reporting firms had net losses. Dan River was one of 582 companies showing net losses totaling $27.2 million in 1938. The 271 companies reporting net profit after taxes earned only $19.2 million.

Dividends

Dan River's common stockholder received no dividends in 1932-1940. In February 1934 the president told the owners of common stock that "the resumption of dividends . . . will of necessity depend on future earnings, for it is unthinkable to reduce the present cash resources for this purpose, and as the Surplus Account is made up of bricks, mortar and machinery, it is not available for disbursement as cash." His estimate that dividends might be resumed in five years was wrong by five years. Holders of the common shares saw the market price plunge to a low of 4 in 1932, equivalent to 16 for a share that once brought over 350. Hope of a dividend raised the quotation to 29¼ in 1937, but the common was back in the bargain basement at 6½ in 1940.

As for dividends on the cumulative preferred stock, by the end of 1933 the directors were searching for "some satisfactory plan . . . for handling this growing liability." A committee of three studied the problem, but a proposal to liquidate the arrearages with a stock issue was shelved because of a "certain antagonistic spirit among some stockholders." Despite the feeling of several directors that the modest earnings of 1934 should be reserved for working capital, in November a dividend of 3 per cent was distributed; and another 3 per cent was paid in December. Regular dividends were also paid in July 1935 and January 1936. Earnings for 1936 seemed to justify cleaning up the dividends in arrears, which with interest at 6 per cent amounted to $1,313,-820 in 1936 and $1,049,349 in 1937. The sharp reversal of business after the summer of 1937 recommended the conservation of cash, and the dividend due in January 1938 was passed. Stockholders received 3 per cent in January 1940, but at the end of the year dividends in arrears again reached $18 per share. In the market the preferred touched a low of 40 in 1932, recovered to a high of 116½ in 1936, but fell back to 65 in 1939.

Earlier, in February 1937, the stockholders had ratified the management's proposal to issue 300,000 shares of common stock for the purpose of retiring the preferred shares by exchanging four common shares for one preferred.[30] In May, when arrearages of dividends had been paid in full, market conditions made the common stock unattractive to holders of cumulative preferred shares, and the possibility of conversion evaporated.

For an inquisitive stockholder, the management tallied the stock transfers for a three-year period, showing a turnover of 11,538 shares, 5,992 shares, and 5,408 shares of preferred in 1936, 1937, and 1938, respectively. Transactions in the common amounted to 60,467 shares, 64,472 shares, and 24,667 shares in the same period.

Frequently, the management was invited to list the stocks on either one of the New York stock exchanges. Chairman Miller, though "open to conviction," felt that the disadvantages of listing—listing fees, the fees of registrar and transfer agents in New York, and compliance with the requirements of the Securities and Exchange Commission—outweighed the gains from a better market and wider distribution of the stock.[31]

[30] This, apparently, was West's idea. In June 1936 Chairman Miller spoke strongly in favor of a scheme to refund dividend arrearages into second preferred stock, a plan he thought "practicable, fair, equitable and just to all concerned"; but he withdrew the suggestion when several directors objected. In his opinion, Miller told a New York banker, "we must fund these dividends or else the stockholders might become dissatisfied with the present Board and elect a less conservative one."

West's proposal, first mentioned at a board meeting in December 1936, would have attacked the problem at the root by eliminating the preferred issue. In February 1937 the president told the chairman: "There seems to be a good deal of sentiment to exchange on the part of the Preferred stockholders, and a good deal of desire on the part of some of the Common stockholders to purchase the stock on the basis offered, and it might be advisable to put this plan in operation before this sentiment cools off. As you know, I am not given to taking undue chances, but with the situation as it prevails it may be that the opportunity is right before us and we should seize it."

The proposal, which gave common stockholders the right to take up at $27.50 per share any shares not issued in exchange for preferred stock, was ratified by large majorities of both classes of stock.

[31] In response to Miller's request for advice, the vice-president of a Philadelphia bank counseled against listing: "It would appear that the stocks of your company now command an unlisted market in your own neighborhood market and that this market has been adequate heretofore to handle the small volume of transactions in the stock. If this is a fact, I should be inclined to 'let sleeping dogs lie' and not to make any change" (C. P. Blinn to J. M. Miller, July 31, 1936). In May 1937 representatives of a New York brokerage firm attended a board meeting to answer questions about listing, but the directors took no action.

Production

Table 5 presents the poundage statistics of cloth and sales yarn production in 1932-1940. From 1932's low of 34.6 million pounds output rose to a maximum of 55.9 million pounds in 1937. The peak production of 3.4 million pounds of sales yarn was reached in 1940.

Measured in linear yards, output rose steadily to 167 million yards in 1937, but the next year's production was only slightly higher than in 1932. On a yardage basis 1939-1940 averaged little better than 1932-1933; the increase in the average width of fabrics accounts for the higher rate of increase in output measured in pounds.

Table 5. Output of Cloth and Yarn, 1932-1940
(thousands of pounds)

	cloth	sales yarns
1932	34,632	2,017
1933	41,353	1,700
1934	44,665	1,159
1935	46,701	1,652
1936	54,784	2,796
1937	55,914	1,838
1938	42,371	1,181
1939	45,330	2,916
1940	50,284	3,424

Production in linear yards is reported in Appendix 3. Until 1938 the output of chambrays, ginghams, coverts, plaids, and drills made up close to half of the entire production of cloth; but in 1939-1940 these goods became absolutely and relatively less important. The shift in the relative importance of other types of fabrics, especially suitings, is shown by the following percentages (per cent of total production on linear yardage basis):

	1932	*1940*
chambrays	50.6	27.7
domestics	19.6	25.4
shirtings, sportswear	17.3	19.0
suitings	2.5	16.3
dress goods	7.8	6.6
handkerchief cloth	2.2	5.0
	100.0	100.0

Chambrays and coverts

Included in "chambrays and coverts" are the traditional "Riverside" plaids, still woven with No. 14 warp and filling yarns. Made only in 27-inch styles—there were 83 patterns in 1936 and 52 in 1937—plaids still had customers for an annual output exceeding three million yards. Coarse 27-inch drills—mostly two or three yards per pound—and coverts furnished occupation for four or five times as many of Riverside's looms as the plaids. Divided into fine-yarn and coarse-yarn fabrics, coverts ranged from 4.85 to 1.75 yards per pound (36-inches wide). In contrast with "Rapidan" and "Riverdan" and the relatively fine covert for Girl Scout uniforms, the coarse coverts went to market under a warlike array of tickets: "Armor," "Armada," "Cruiser," "Dreadnaught," "Gridiron," "Gunboat," "Invader," and "Ironclad." Among the chambrays, "Ideal" continued to hold a commanding lead. The "Quaker" and "Defiance" lines accounted for several million yards each year, but the old 28-inch "Golden Rule" became—certainly no later than 1936—a distinctly unimportant chambray line. Chambrays, including "Totwear" playcloth, were offered (1936) in over 200 styles. By 1936 many of the chambray lines were available in three finishes—regular, "Rivershrunk," and "Sanforized."

Domestics

Production of sheeting, sheets, and pillow cases—the main component of "domestics"—averaged 14.9 million gray yards in 1923-1932. For the period 1932-1940, output in linear yard fluctuated, as follows:

	thousands of linear yards
1932	17,128*
1933	20,944
1934	23,096
1935	21,495
1936	22,795
1937	20,021
1938	21,210
1939	21,217
1940	27,029

* Estimated from square yards.

The three grades of sheeting differed in construction, as follows (1932):

| | yarn count | | cloth count |
	warp	filling	(finished)
"Morotock"	24	24	61×56
"Dan River "	24	24	76×60
"Riverside"	19	24	75×69

"Sovereign" sheeting was a "low-count percale" (80×84) confined to Lamport Manufacturing Supply Company. About the time that Dan River commenced to make this type of sheeting, the Association of Cotton Textile Merchants was trying to work out an agreement on the use of the term percale, setting the minimum count at 180 threads per square inch. Dan River's first vote on the proposal was in the negative, as it seemed impractical to drop the "Sovereign" line or order the customer not to sell the sheeting as percale. Reconsideration of the question eventually brought President West to support the move, which led in 1939 to the industry-wide adoption of minimum standards for four types of muslin and percale sheeting.[32] Production of all combed-yarn sheeting commenced in 1940.[33]

From time to time tests were made of competing sheets. A test in December 1933, just after the adoption of a slightly different construction for "Riverside" and "Dan River" sheeting, gave the following comparisons:

[32] Types 112, 128, and 140 muslin; Types 180 and 200 for percale.
[33] R. R. West to G. W. Robertson, Aug. 24, 1939; D. L. Reardon to R. R. West, Nov. 17, 1939; R. R. West to D. L. Reardon, Nov. 23, 1939. At this time Dan River was looking forward to making Type 180 sheeting, both carded and combed. Though the "Sovereign" business "gave us some experience," in West's judgment it was not a satisfactory development "because being a sub-count Lamport will naturally want to always be in a position to undersell the whole market, and there is not sufficient profit in this sub-count for us to be interested in putting him in a position to do it."

	cloth count		breaking strength (pounds per sq. in.)	
	warp	filling	warp	filling
"Riverside" old	74.65	67.47	62.0	59.8
new	75.40	69.65	62.8	57.8
"Dan River" old	71.90	58.86	57.6	48.2
new	70.55	60.01	54.4	46.8
"Lady Pepperell"	75.50	70.80	53.8	61.4
"Pequot"	76.10	69.80	58.2	53.4
"Erwin"	80.00	66.80	54.3	51.8
"Cannon"	70.60	61.80	56.8	52.6

The count of the new "Riverside" sheet (145.05 threads per square inch) brought it closer to the competing lines of Pepperell, Pequot, and Erwin; but the new "Dan River" grade remained slightly below the Cannon sheet in cloth count. The new "Dan River" sheet also showed a slight reduction in breaking strength. Tests of Cannon sheets in 1936 showed a non-cotton content of 4 per cent, which seemed to belie the claim that the fabric had "no loading or artificial weighting"; but the competing "Dan River" sheet had a 10 per-cent non-cotton content.[34] The high percentages of mill seconds was a constant problem. Reports from the inspection room in 1937-1938 showed seconds of "Morotock" running as high as 43 per cent, while in one period of four weeks seconds of "Dan River" sheeting ran up to 41 per cent and of "Riverside," as high as 61 per cent.

Dan River commenced to market cellephane-wrapped sheets and pillow cases in the summer of 1936.

Production of birdseye cloth, a large part of which left Danville cut in twelve ready-to-wear sizes, amounted to several million yards yearly. In response to "numerous calls for a lower price Birdseye Cloth and Diaper," in 1936 "Charmspun" was added to the original "Health" line of cloth and diapers. The mill also had non-conflicting tickets, such as "Childhood," for its diaper lines.

Small quantities of barber cloth and drapery cloth were manufactured from 1934 on, but these did not develop into important lines. Production of toweling and burlap ended in 1934-1935.

[34] R. T. Read to G. W. Robertson, Sept. 12, 1936. In September 1935 Dan River's bleached sheets had non-cotton content of 3 per cent. Tests of 13 Type 128 sheets, made by Dan River's cotton research laboratory in Sept. 1939, showed the "Dan River" sheet ahead of its 12 competitors in breaking strength (69.6 pounds in warp, 65.5 pounds in filling) but just about average (i.e., 130.8 threads per square inch) in finished cloth count.

Production of napped outing flannels was resumed in 1936 and
built up quickly to over four million yards in 1939. "Riverside" flannels were offered for the fall of 1938 in six new constructions and in
seven colors.[35] The fancy "Dansport" flannel was introduced in 1940.

Suitings

Production of suitings, which included fabrics designed mainly for
men's pants, rose steadily from 2.8 million yards in 1932 to 21 million
yards in 1940. Fifty-seven styles were offered in 1936, each in various
color patterns of blue, black, and brown. Sales of Style No. 2500
reached 1.9 million yards in 1938, while the 2200 line accounted for 1.2
million yards. On the other hand, several styles yielded sales of less
than 1,000 yards.

The company's first suiting lines were cotton, cotton flannel, and
cotton-worsted goods. Some of the lines described in the fall 1936 price
list were: all-cotton and worsted-content pencil stripe, all-cotton and
worsted-content fancy frenchback, all-cotton and worsted-content serge,
worsted-content frenchback herringbone, all-cotton chalkline stripes,
and worsted-content sharkskins.

Manufacture of "Rivercool," a part-viscose, part-acetate rayon fabric
for summer suits and slacks commenced in 1937. To compete with
"Palm Beach" suits, which in the mid-thirties had almost half of the
summer-suit business, Dan River inaugurated extensive trade and consumer advertising of "Rivercool" and pushed sales to 2.3 million yards
in 1939. Thomas J. Corcoran, according to President West, was "Daddy
to this development."[36]

Dress Goods

Among the dress goods the familiar "Security" gingham held its own
throughout the period; in May 1937 the company offered "Security"
staple checks in 52 patterns. But the old "Dan River" and "Pride of

[35] In a circular to salesmen, G. P. Ray wrote: "We may be mistaken, but we do not
know of any other mill at the present time offering vat colors in the pastel shades."
[36] "Spun-Rayon suitings for men's wear," according to *Textile World* (vol. 89, Aug.
1939, pp. 48-49) "have been in the incubator stage for several years. The season now current, trade factors are beginning to believe, will witness the hatching and growth."
Dan River claimed the honor of bringing out "the first practical spun-rayon fabric for
men's pants, slacks, and suits" in 1937. In August five patterns had been decided upon,
and Corcoran predicted that "we will obtain for our season our full estimated production
of 60,000 pieces—forty of which will be on our books at the end of six weeks time" (T. J.
Corcoran to R. R. West, Aug. 30, 1937).

America" gingham lines were closed out by 1936. According to a prominent trade publications editor, Dan River faced the "necessity of going after the style volume market in cotton goods." He predicted that the company would "duplicate the success you have had in the men's wear and in the women's wear field, but it will be much more profitable and a much larger business."[37] Supplementing its all-cotton dress goods, the company offered a growing list of part-rayon fabrics. "Scotspun," a fancy dress goods offered in 1936 in 25 patterns, was one of a number of trade names built on the suffix "spun," although not all "spun" goods were part-rayon. "Scotspun" was woven with cotton warps and rayon filling; but the white and solid-color "Sheetingspun" ("for the low end of the dress and sportswear trade") was nothing more than "Riverside" sheeting—which salesmen were instructed not to sell as sheeting. The dress goods lines numbered 30 in 1938. A small quantity of green "Novelspun" produced on a government contract in 1938 was rejected because of the "fugitive" color: it stained "everything it comes in contact with after being wet." Sales Manager Ray thought he would have to wait for St. Patrick's Day to dispose of the cloth.[38]

Shirtings and sportswear

Shirtings and sportswear comprised a number of fine-yarn chambrays, notably the "Grande" line, as well as a wide variety of broadcloths in white, solid colors, stripes, checks, and plaids. Manufacturing schedules called for 76 styles (205 patterns) in 1936; 85 styles in 1937; and 97 styles in 1938. Seven lines sold over a million yards each in 1938: "Cresmoor," "Broadwear," "Grande," "Bonnie," "Brytysh," "Juneau," and "Swanee." "Bonnie" was an 80×60 cloth, but the carded-yarn "Juneau" and the combed-yarn "Swanee" both had counts of 136 ×60. The finest cloths were the combed-yarn "Fairmond" (152×60) and "Seine" (144×76). By 1932 some of the broadcloths used no. 40 filling yarn; finer yarns were spun later on. As the mills had limited facilities for combing, the sales emphasis was put on fast vat-dyed broadcloths made with carded yarns; and the sales manager believed that the

[37] M. D. C. Crawford to R. R. West, Feb. 19, 1936; R. R. West to M. D. C. Crawford, Feb. 22 and May 23, 1936. West informed Crawford that Dan River was approaching the problem "in a scientific manner—that is to say, we are endeavoring to obtain the best technical advice to enable us to produce satisfactory fabrics." But he was "impressed by the rather slow growth on the available spun rayon fabrics . . . we shall make haste slowly in this development."

[38] G. P. Ray to J. A. Becher, June 7, 1938. More serious was the probability that "if the green can go sour in the Novelspun, it can go sour in all the other dress goods."

company was the first to offer Sanforized carded-yarn shirtings.   One
of the biggest customers was the New Process Company, a mail-order
men's shirt distributor.[39]

Handkerchief cloth

Dan River made handkerchief cloth only for cutters and manufacturers, rejecting the recommendation of one of its salesmen that the
mill produce finished handkerchiefs.   The main lines were carded-yarn
fabrics, although by 1939 the total sales of $602,000 included $269,000
worth of combed cloth.   In 1936 the eight styles of handkerchief
cloth comprised 134 patterns in white, colors, and colored borders.
As late as 1940 the Company was one of two major producers of the
colored-border handkerchief cloth used in the five-cent handkerchief.
This was made of nos. 35 and 40 carded yarns, with a cloth count of
64×56, finished 34 inches wide with a one-inch colored or satin border.
Other types of handkerchief cloth, according to a report on the "handkerchief situation" by W. J. Fullerton (August 1940), comprised 36-
inch cloth for the ten-cent handkerchief, made of nos. 50 and 60
combed yarns; and 37-inch cloth for twenty-five cent handkerchiefs,
requiring no. 60 yarn, combed and mercerized, with a count of 80×80
or 92×92.

Sales yarns

Mills No. 1 and No. 6 at Riverside Division made a variety of
single- and multiple-ply yarns for sale to hosiery and carpet manufacturers.   The business grew, and in May 1939 the president spoke
of plans for "an additional line of blended yarns."   In October, after
a small sum had been spent for new machinery, the directors were advised that the new lines yielded "a much better return than the lines
formerly produced."   Until January 1935 sales yarns were marketed,
on the basis of a 5 per-cent commission, through the Boston firm of
Waterman-Currier.   A new exclusive agreement with Schoolfield-Sauer
& Company (with which J. H. Schoolfield, Jr., was associated) provided for the distribution of Dan River's yarns at a commission of only

[39] New Process bought over 1.5 million yards in 1936.   Although Salesman L. R. Walls
showed the firm sample of 29 styles in the "Brytysh" stripes line, New Process asked to
have its own styles copied.   Dan River hesitated, but New Process assured the company
that they were patterns which another manufacturer had discontinued (J. L. Blair to
R. R. West, June 19, 1936).

3 per cent. But in November 1939 President West thought the volume of sales had reached the point at which a separate Sales Yarn department in the New York sales office would be profitable.

Table 7, showing the value of cotton, worsted, and synthetic fibers consumed in manufacturing, reflects fairly accurately the growing importance of other materials than cotton in the making of Dan River fabrics.

Table 7. Consumption of Cotton and Other Fibers, 1932-1940
(thousands of dollars)

year	cotton	cotton yarn	wool and worsted yarn	synthetic fibers*
1932	3,202	5	118	41
1933	3,999	70	318	54
1934	6,773	144	330	64
1935	6,867	500	374	108
1936	8,944	210	437	94
1937	8,487	219	503	137
1938	4,453	158	438	368
1939	5,173	365	585	892
1940	6,160	118	762	1,202

* Artificial silk in 1932-1936; artificial silk and cut staple rayon in 1937-1948; staple acetate, staple viscose, filament rayon, and filament celanese in 1939-1940.

The lack of sufficient equipment for manufacturing certain types of cotton yarn in Danville necessitated regular purchases of yarn from other firms. Thus, in September 1939 the company accepted an order for 360,000 yards of combed handkerchief cloth, relying on a North Carolina mill to supply 50,000 pounds of 60/1 combed yarn. Similarly, woven goods were supplied by other manufacturers, either to fill out an urgent contract or to finish for marketing under a Dan River ticket. Purchases of cloth (in thousands of dollars) varied, as follows:

1932	$ 715	1937	$1,269
1933	1060	1938	675
1934	841	1939	836
1935	587	1940	799
1936	1093		

Purchases of gray broadcloth averaged 8.5 million yards in 1936-1940.[40]

[40] Sheeting was purchased from Fort Mill in August 1935, and in June 1932 Pepperell supplied over a million yards of 90-inch sheeting.

Codes and Controls

This hectic decade saw the rise of virtually new devices to cope with the old problems of overproduction and excessive competition. Under the leadership of the Cotton Textile Institute most cotton manufacturers had come to accept the philosophy of regulated competition long before the National Industrial Recovery Act made codes of fair competition a national policy. While Congress debated the Act, committees of the Institute worked rapidly on the proposed code for the cotton textile industry. The biggest stumbling block was the North-South wage differential, which was finally settled by agreement on a southern minimum of $12 a week and a northern minimum of $13.[41] The Code was submitted to President Roosevelt soon after he signed the Act on June 16, 1933. Public hearings were held on June 30; the Code was approved by the President on July 16; and it became effective, as Code No. 1, on July 17.[42]

Robert West was a prominent member of the industry committee which helped to draft the Code. He became a member of the Code Authority, which aided the National Recovery Administration in policing the Code, and was a member of the important subcommittee on code interpretations. With reservations, West viewed the Code as the answer to long-standing problems of the cotton textile industry. In July 1933 a northern mill executive, F. C. Dumaine, wondered whether the Code would "make our business a better one in which to be." West was sure it offered opportunities for "much more satisfactory business" and that it would "eliminate certain outrageous handicaps." He criticized the "Platform for Recovery" of the National Association of Manufacturers, which went "rather far afield" in recommending the abolition of controls on production. "The great weight of opinion" in the textile industry, West said, "supports the necessity of Production Control." In December 1934 West proposed a merger

[41] According to an official of the ACMA, the southern section of the industry was "caught in a vise" and had to agree to a differential which gave "a distinct advantage to Northern mills." Efforts were made to demonstrate that subsidized housing, utilities, and medical care in the southern mill village justified a wage spread of $2.16 per week (W. D. Anderson to Scott Roberts, Jan. 24, 1934).

[42] Commenting on the harmonious relations of industry, government, and labor representatives in drafting the Cotton Textile Code, Roosevelt declared: "It would be unfair to omit a word of commendation of this great industry. It has proved itself the leader of a new thing in economics and government. That took faith and courage and patriotism of the highest order. They have their reward in the results they have achieved and the example they have given."

of the Cotton Textile Institute with the wool, rayon, thread, and silk associations in order to obviate some of the conflicts arising from the application of two or more codes to a single firm.[43]

President West had vigorous objections to what he considered abuses of the Code. In December 1933 he advised the N.R.A. that proposed amendments prohibiting advertising allowances, options, and certain other sales practices "put a wholly unnecessary limitation on the means of selling merchandise; limitations which . . . will neither provide additional employment nor increase purchasing power."[44] The amendments were nevertheless written into a supplementary code approved in January 1934. As a member of the Code Authority, West took a firm stand against the petition of the Chicopee Manufacturing Company for permission to operate four six-hour shifts daily, or 144 machine-hours per week. This, he said, would be "tantamount to unleashing a gigantic over-production." The textile industry had had enough experience with the "theory of run and ruin . . . . In view of this experience, you will pardon the scepticism with which the Code Authority and the Industry generally view the claim to economic liberalism which has been embodied in this application."[45] In March 1935 West found it "irritating" that N.R.A. officials failed to see that "the details of running the business of this country simply cannot be handled by a bureau in Washington." He was opposed to "any and all price-fixing provisions in all Codes," because they seemed to him "a futile substitute for intelligent merchandising." When the Textile Fabrics Association reached an agreement to suspend trading on Saturdays, West exclaimed: "May the good Lord forgive us of the crimes

[43] R. R. West to W. D. Anderson, Dec. 11, 1934. West thought Arthur Besse, president of the Silk Institute, would be the ideal president for a consolidated textile institute.

The Wool Textile Code applied to companies making fabrics with more than 25 per cent wool content. Dan River lines in 1934 included at least two fabrics containing 25-30 per cent wool, but the company was not pressed to come under the jurisdiction of the Wool Code Authority (F. K. Nixon to R. R. West, May 29, 1934, and June 29, 1934; F. K. Nixon to P. B. Halstead, July 5, 1934.

[44] West also complained to C. A. Cannon (Dec. 7, 1933) of the "desire on the part of a good many people to get a lot of rigid specifications written into the Code . . . . I am very much afraid that if we start getting too specific and too dogmatic in our interpretations of the Code, we are going to find that it just won't work with the Industry . . . . I view with considerable alarm the tendency that is developing to issue definitive and restrictive rulings without any leeway."

[45] N. R. A., "Hearings on the Cotton Textile Industry: Modification Proposal" (April 2, 1934), vol. 1, pp. 37-48. West wrote many personal letters to mill executives urging them to oppose the Chicopee (Johnson & Johnson) application; e.g., R. R. West to Donald Tansill, March 22, 1934.

against good sense which are being committed under the name of Code conformity."

When the Supreme Court declared the National Industrial Recovery Act unconstitutional (May 27, 1935), leading cotton manufacturers wanted to go on as though the Code were still effective. West wrote President Dorr of the Cotton Textile Institute that "texile manufacturers in this section are prepared to continue operation under the conditions outlined by the Code, at least for the time being . . . . In spite of the many sources of complaint against any regulating measures . . . I believe we are going to find a way of practical industrial self-government. I wish to heaven I knew the precise way just at the moment."[46] The executive committee of the Institute adopted unanimously a resolution recommending "that the Cotton Textile Industry make no changes in the conduct of its business during the interim caused by the Supreme Court decision" and called up President Roosevelt to "exercise the prestige of his great office in a direct appeal to all industry to pursue a like policy." Subsequently, the Institute drew up a "Cotton Textile Industry Pledge," embodying the Code limitations on maximum hours of work, minimum age of employment, and minimum wages. The pledge was to become effective as soon as 90 per cent of the spindleage in each of twelve divisions of the industry had signed; but evidence submitted before a Congressional hearing in January 1936 indicated that there was no prospect of reaching this goal.[47]

President West continued to believe that some sort of substitute for the Cotton Textile Code was needed. In 1938 he characterized as "very unrealistic" a resolution of the United States Chamber of Commerce calling for the abolition of all controls on hours, wages, prices, and production; and he condemned the Chamber's opposition to federal regulation of hours and wages. These matters, he thought, should not be left to "the vagaries of the State governments." Enthusiasm for

[46] R. R. West to G. H. Dorr, June 1, 1935. In April 1935 President Roosevelt appointed a Cabinet Committee to study the problems of the textile industry. West was one of the seven men appointed by the Cotton Textile Institute to confer wih the Secretaries of State, Commerce, Agriculture, and Labor. Making its report in August, the Committee reviewed what by this time had been publicized ad nauseam: that the industry suffered from excess capacity and chronic overproduction. The remedies, too, were commonplace: limitation of machine hours, retirement of obsolete machinery, curtailment of Japanese imports, and a subsidy on exports of cotton goods (*Cotton Textile Industry: Report of Cabinet Committee:* Senate Document no. 126, 74th Congress, 1st Session [Washington, 1936]).

[47] *Hearings before a Subcommittee of the Committee on Labor, House of Representatives, Seventy-fourth Congress, Second Session, on H. R. 9072* (Washington, 1936), pp. 424-426.

new measures of self-government in the textile industry was dampened when the Justice Department brought suit against a group of print-cloth manufacturers, charging that an agreement to curtail production by 25 per cent during July, August, and September 1939 violated the Sherman Act.[48]

The Cotton Textile Institute continued its labors to promote and defend the industry. Riverside and Dan River Cotton Mills was a most "loyal" member. Besides paying annual dues of .625 cents per spindle (the 1936 rate), the company contributed to the work of the New Uses section ($1,500 in 1936) and the "Cent-a-Bale Fund," which financed publicity to increase the consumption of cotton goods. Vigorous efforts to combat the menace of foreign competition, particularly Japanese, were partly rewarded in 1936. According to Institute figures, imports of Japanese cloth rose from 1.7 million square yards in 1928 to 7.3 million square yards in 1934 and reached 5.7 million square yards in the one month of February 1935. Dan River's president thought the situation was "dangerous" but feared that "the desire of the Administration is to abandon the Cotton Textile Manufacturing Industry to the sacrifice to promote the State Department's international gestures." A complaint to the State Department pointed out that the Japanese were copying Dan River patterns, making higher-count cloth, and underselling the company by two cents a yard.[49] In April 1935 the Tariff Commission began a study of duties on cotton goods; and in May 1936 President Roosevelt, accepting the advice of the Commission that higher rates were necessary to equalize costs of production, proclaimed increases in duties of more than 40 per cent.[50]

Dan River maintained its membership in the several trade associations which endeavored, with questionable success, to stabilize market conditions. In 1932 the management thought that joining the Colored Yarn Group "would serve no useful purpose"; in 1933 President West brought Dan River into the Group, though he had some doubt of its "sincerity of purpose." Since Dan River had not been able to sell colored yarns for three months, "because we have been unwilling to accept the price offered," it seemed to West that "somebody in the Group is selling at low prices." In August 1934 the Group comprised

[48] *Textile World*, vol. 90 (Jan. 1940), p. 57.
[49] This is what C. G. Holland, on behalf of the Danville Chamber of Commerce, wrote Secretary Cordell Hull, April 13, 1935.
[50] Tariff Commission, *Report to the President: Cotton Cloth* (Report no. 112, second series; Washington, 1936).

26 firms, but one large manufacturer had just announced his withdrawal because "he was fundamentally opposed to any price-fixing arrangements." West took the same stand on price-fixing but advised the group that Dan River would not withdraw "immediately." Group leaders, knowing that Dan River's withdrawal would break up the organization, made a strong case for the "excellent job" they had done "in keeping the prices on colored yarns up to the cost of production, whereas practically everything else has been selling below cost."

As a member of the Carded Yarn Group, Dan River paid an assessment of .125 cent per spindle on 20,773 spindles in 1937. In 1935 President West opposed a mandatory curtailment of 25 per cent for a period of eleven weeks, as recommended by the Group; and, apparently, the Group failed in this effort to control production. The Group was still operating in 1940, when dues increased to .5 cent per spindle.

George P. Ray was chairman of both the Handkerchief Group and the Chambray and Shirting Covert Group, but I have found no records of the work of these Groups. Wide sheeting manufacturers continued to report to the Cotton Textile Institute on looms operating, production, shipments, stocks, and orders. The 20,170 looms of the Group members, as of March 29, 1935, represented about 58 per cent of capacity in this division of the industry. Dan River was one of 23 reporting firms.[51]

Robert R. West, intrigued by the power of statistics, often urged a more comprehensive program of gathering data for the industry's use. The Cotton Textile Institute, he believed, should be the "authoritative repository" of all relevant statistics available from manufacturers, and these figures should be supplemented by equally authoritative data from the distributive branch of the industry. "Cotton mill policies," West declared at the 1936 meeting of the Institute,

all too frequently are, of necessity, determined upon and executed on the basis of information which is wholly inadequate. Statistics having to do with our raw material supplies, and with the production and unfilled orders on the part of primary producers, mark the limits of our knowledge in that respect. Manufactured goods, once out of the hands of producers, disappear into distributing channels as into an obscure mist of vague estimates . . . the stocks in hands of converters, wholesalers, cutters-up and retailers, and the rate of movement of such stocks into consuming channels is of an importance equalling the consumption of raw cotton or the rate

[51] See, for instance, "Consolidated Report, Wide Cotton Fabrics, Bed Sheet and Pillow Case Division," Sept. 14, 1935.

of production of cloth . . . . Of necessity, undue emphasis is placed on mill stocks because of lack of knowledge as to the remaining stocks; and, sales and production policies are swayed by that emphasis. It is something like attempting to write with only half the alphabet at one's command.[52]

At the 1939 convention of the American Cotton Manufacturers' Association West argued that "periodic lapses into industrial anarchy might be circumvented" by complete and reliable statistics of production, sales, prices, and stocks on hand.[53]

Sales and Markets

Market conditions and changes in the demand for the company's products were regular topics for discussion at the board meetings. In March 1932 the management spoke of the "almost total lack of demand for gingham products. One of the results of the strike was to weaken our position . . . . To improve this position we set out to meet prevailing prices, and during the course of the year we recaptured sufficient business to operate approximately 75 per cent of our machinery and to liquidate a large part of the slow-moving merchandise which had been on hand." In July, business was "extremely dull" and prices "distressingly low." When cotton, after touching five cents, rose to nearly ten cents a pound, "a spirited demand for goods" prevailed for about a month; but the aftermath was "a very indifferent demand."[54]

The year 1933 brought about a "sequence of events . . . so amazing that one has had to give up the attempt to grasp its significance or appraise its ultimate value." But the president prophesied that the "flush of speculative excitement" (before the Code went into effect), during which the industry "outdid itself in demonstrating its productive capacity," would end with a "resumption of competition similar to

[52] "Textile Cycles and Cotton Mill Policies," *Current Information from the Cotton-Textile Institute, Inc.*, vol. 2, no. 13 (1936), pp. 19-21. West went on to argue that the problem of excess capacity or overproduction was a matter of uncontrolled output in relation to the movement of goods into consumers' hands. "Excess capacity cannot be defined in the absence of full knowledge of such movement of goods, and any capacity is excess capacity when not controlled by that knowledge." If complete information were available to producers, distributors, and consumers alike, he thought the textile industry would be a "safer field for investment, a more stable provider of employment, and a less hazardous venture for management than it has been for the last ten years."

[53] *Textile World*, vol. 89 (May, 1939), pp. 52-53. At the same meeting, B. B. Gossett, later a Dan River director, lashed out against the third shift, which many mills had introduced during the depression of 1937-1938.

[54] *Twenty-fourth Annual Report of the Riverside & Dan River Cotton Mills, Incorporated* (Danville, 1933).

that which we experienced during 1931 and 1932."[55] In fact, the next
year (1934) witnessed "a slight revival of the demand for Ginghams,"
and new lines of Dan River fabrics were "well accepted by the trade";
but "high manufacturing costs necessitated by the various Recovery
measures not only denies to us the export markets but also opens the
gates to importations which threaten our domestic markets."[56]

In May 1935 Sales Manager Ray thought the "Japanese menace"
was greater than ever, while the processing tax and government cotton
policy kept the goods market unsettled. Reviewing the year's developments, President West spoke of "a series of harassing events due to
changes in governmental participation in business affairs." The invalidation of the National Industrial Recovery Act "put in jeopardy" the
"partial stability in the industry which had been achieved by operations
under the Cotton Textile Code." In July federal courts ruled that the
processing tax imposed under the Agricultural Adjustment Act was unconstitutional; but the cloth markets remained in a "state of paralysis"
and "extreme speculation," awaiting the decision of the Supreme Court
(January 6, 1936) which upheld the lower courts. Furthermore, West
feared that an excise on cotton manufactures would be introduced to
replace the processing tax: "owing to the threats of reprisal against
processors, coming from high official sources, there hangs over textile
markets an apprehension which all but destroys that confidence in
values which is necessary to the conduct of a business such as ours."[57]

In April 1936 Ray found the trade "hesitating in placing their
orders for fall and winter, not knowing what to expect of the government"; he anticipated "very good business" as soon as Congress "adopts
a reasonable business program." Later in the year the president considered business conditions satisfactory. Unfilled orders amounting to
22,000,000 pounds were the largest in the company's history. At the
end of the year, however, the management was "not unmindful of
the possibilities of severe reactions" and promised to "continue the
direction of the business with that conservatism which has characterized
its management to date."[58]

[55] *Twenty-fifth Annual Report* (Danville, 1934). In a letter to Nixon, President West
related (what a friend had told him) that yarn manufacturers had kept their prices so
high that Dan River got "all of the suiting business . . . . I have every reason to
believe that we have obtained our share of this business," West observed, "but I hate
to think that what we have received is all of it" (R. R. West to F. K. Nixon, Dec. 7,
1933).
[56] *Twenty-sixth Annual Report* (Danville, 1935).
[57] *Twenty-seventh Annual Report* (Danville, 1936).
[58] *Twenty-eighth Annual Report* (Danville, 1937).

Record-breaking sales were reported in the first months of 1937, but by August the market came to a standstill. A "business recession of major proportions" continued into 1938. A turning point was reached in the last quarter of the year, and at the end of the third quarter of 1939 unfilled orders exceeded inventory for the first time in over two years. The first half of 1940 was a depressed period, but the end of the year found orders on hand exceeding inventories "by a very comfortable margin." The president discerned "a confidence in values that has not been evident since 1937 . . . . This we think indicates a sound market, giving us an optimistic view of the first half of 1941 and probably the entire year."[59]

Sales organization

A new departure in the sales organization took place in February 1931 with the setting up of a Shirting Department in the New York office. The new department resulted from "taking over intact an independent organization that had specialized in fine combed fancy shirting"; but for a number of years Dan River continued to merchandise fine carded shirtings in competition with combed-yarn goods.

In September 1932 the company established its Suiting Department, which T. J. Corcoran regarded as "following through a development on which we have been working for two years." Corcoran's objective was "to make cheap trouserings . . . to replace the overall that has been used by working men generally." Government statistics showed a decline in the overall industry, as workers turned to cheap trousers. There was, Corcoran believed, an "immense future" both in trouserings and cheap suitings. The first lines of Dan River suiting fabrics had been sold to two jobbers, but the new sales department, under the direction of F. K. Nixon and E. A. Dafter, brought in new customers and pushed sales directly to garment manufacturers.

In retrospect, it seemed that more departmentalization should have been attempted earlier. In 1938

the product of over two-thirds of the mill was yet being merchandised by the General Sales Manager, and without application of the specialized styling and merchandising necessary to operate successfully under highly competitive conditions. This situation drew justifiable criticism. Much of this large part of our production was distributed by underselling the market. While the selling staff had been gradually enlarged, mostly with

[59] *Thirty-second Annual Report* (Danville, 1941).

good salesmen, there existed in the sales department a fundamental administrative weakness resulting in lack of full specialization and in close
direction of the sales force.[60]

The slump in 1938 inspired further specialization in the sales organization, and in 1939 the management set up two new sales departments,
Domestics and Staple Colored Goods. One purpose of the Domestics
Department, headed by D. L. Reardon, was to broaden the market for
sheets and pillow cases carrying the company's three brand names. In
the belief that policy up to this time had resulted in "too much of our
merchandise" going to "too few of our customers, usually with a discount which seemed necessary to sell those large firms," the Domestics
Department now made plans to "confine our sales to shorter periods,
keeping us closer to the market—to sell less of our production to numerous smaller accounts—to build up nationally the mill's brand through
trade and consumer advertising and to gradually enter the retail field
broadly without disturbing our present jobbers' outlets."[61] As late as
1939 only 2 per cent of the mill's output was marketed under the
company's brand names.

The first job tackled by the new Staple Colored Goods Department,
under the guidance of John M. Hughlett, was to dispose of an inventory, "consisting largely of obsolete styles and fabrics," equivalent to
almost a year's production. New fabrics were needed to take the place
of the work-clothing lines, which had been comparatively unprofitable.
Automobile seat cover materials and fabrics for boy's wear looked like
promising ventures until the flood of war orders diverted this division
into the manufacture of uniform cloth.[62]

In 1933 the directors considered a proposal to distribute certain
Dan River fabrics through Southeastern Cottons, Inc. A committee
was appointed to work out the details, but on Ray's recommendation
the idea was soon dropped in favor of an expansion of the New York
sales force. Four years later W. J. Fullerton submitted a proposal for

[60] "The Sales Department," a mimeographed report dated January 1943.
[61] In March 1939 Ray told the directors that it was increasingly difficult to do business
with jobbers: they bought in reasonably large quantities but required the mill to ship
small quantities to many customers for their account.
[62] According to a memorandum prepared by Hughlett, Dan River sold 1,125,000 yards
of its "regular coverts" to manufacturers of automobile seat covers in 1939-1940. But
Hughlett considered it a "highly specialized business in which the best results could be
obtained only by having some one style and sell the fabrics who is thoroughly familiar"
with the trade. On his recommendation Dan River entered into an agreement with
W. H. Duncan Co. for the exclusive distribution of seat cover materials on the basis of
a 1-per-cent commission (Aug. 12, 1940). Dan River agreed to furnish samples and
pay one-half of the traveling expenses of Duncan's salesmen.

a Dress Goods Department, "laid out and operated in a similar manner to that in which Mr. Corcoran handles his department" (i.e., suitings). Fullerton wanted a separate division at the mills as well as a new department in the New York office. All of the construction and designing of fabrics would be done in the Designing Department under Fullerton's supervision, but "keeping in close contact with fabric and style trends would necessitate more time in New York than in the past. I feel that the quality of the finished goods and the efficient and prompt deliveries of orders is as essential as a well-styled line of fabrics to the success of such a department, and to avoid our unfortunate experience of the past season, I would plan to spend no small part of my time in the mill and finishing plant in an endeavor to see that quantities and deliveries were rigidly maintained." Fullerton's program was to build up sales to cutters of cotton dresses retailing for $1.00 to $2.95, since "in these price ranges . . . the greatest volume of business in cottons is done."

Furthermore, "with Spun Rayon almost within our reach," Fullerton believed a Dress Goods Department would be "a profitable and valuable asset to our organization." A few months of poor business dampened enthusiasm for the proposed expansion, and in September 1938 W. E. Willcox wrote that both he and Fullerton had "come to the conclusion" that it would be "practically impossible" for Dan River to enter the rayon dress goods business on a large scale. The company had three strikes against it: the "overwhelming demand" was for printed designs; stocks had to be carried to New York and deliveries made "as fast as possible after being ordered"; and credits were handled "more on the basis of direct knowledge of the customer . . . than on financial statements." These considerations persuaded the management to enter into an agreement with National Fabrics Corporation under which National Fabrics undertook to "act as your agent to style, convert and sell such fabrics manufactured by your company as we may from time to time mutually agree upon." The contract, which assisted Dan River in introducing some of its new rayon dress goods, was terminated in July 1939. By this time a revival of trade gave the Dan River sales organization more confidence in its ability to merchandise the dress goods lines, leading to the formation of the Dress Goods Department.

Prior to 1940 Dan River sold handkerchief cloth, through a broker, to five or six jobbers. "Under that method the prices obtained were not profitable, although colored handkerchief cloth was known to have good profit possibilities."[63] A Handkerchief Department, in charge of A. A. Buff, was established in 1940 and the list of customers enlarged by direct selling to handkerchief manufacturers.

Advertising

Advertising until the mid-thirties meant buying a half-page or more in *Cotton* or *American Wool and Cotton Reporter* to announce that Riverside and Dan River Cotton Mills were "manufacturers of cotton fabrics for the jobbing and cutting trade." At the most, such advertisements would list the classes of fabrics in which the mills specialized. In 1933 the company had the help of an advertising agency, Winternitz & Cairns; but advertising expenditures this year amounted to only $11,541, including the agency fee of $553. What West described as "our first faltering steps in this advertising business" began with specific fabric advertising in the *Daily News Record* in January 1935. It promised to "lead us to something constructive and helpful." Ray brought before the directors the question of a "greater amount of advertising" in order to match the efforts of competitors and make Dan River fabrics better known to jobbers, cutters, and garment manufacturers; and the board appropriated $25,000 for advertising in 1936. Toward the end of the year the sales manager reported that Dan River advertising had been "well received by the trade"; it was "so much liked by some that there was imitation . . . in some quarters." It was time, he thought, to use advertising that would reach the retail trade; and for this purpose the directors appropriated $15,000.

Winternitz & Cairns prepared the company's advertising budgets for 1937 and 1938, both calling for expenditures of $40,000. An additional $30,000 was earmarked for the promotion of "Rivercool" suiting fabric;[64] and in July 1939 the directors fixed the advertising budget

[63] But in June 1940 other firms had the impression that Dan River took "very large orders" for handkerchief cloth, "at times at very low prices, and by so doing set the market." On the other hand, anything that increased costs of the handkerchief manufacturer, who had to produce a finished commodity to retail at (say) five cents, put pressure on the cloth manufacture to lower his prices. Retailers gave "no encouragement" to the suggestion for marking up the five-cent handkerchief to three for twenty or twenty-five cents (M. R. Porter to J. W. Cox, June 21, 1940, on letterhead of Iselin-Jefferson Co.). It appears that after the demise of Amoskeag, the New Braunfels Textile Mills were Dan River's chief competitor in handkerchief cloth.

[64] The first advertising of "Rivercool" consisted of trade ads in the *Daily News Record*, *Men's Wear*, *Apparel Arts*, and *Men's Apparel Reporter*, together with display materials

for 1939-1940 at $75,000. The firm of John A. Cairns & Company be-
came Dan River's advertising agency in October 1939 at a fee of $1,000
per month. Another $1,000 per month was paid to the American In-
stitute of Laundering for fabric tests used by the Company's salesmen.[65]

Statistics

Statistics of net billings (Table 8) show increases in all the major
classes of goods from the deep depression to the comparatively prosperous levels of 1936-1937. Some of the advance in terms of dollars is
associated with the general inflation of values in the early years of the
New Deal. While Dan River's sales rose 142 per cent (1932-1936), the
index of wholesale commodity prices increased 30 per cent. In the best
years in this period Dan River's sales represented just under 2 per cent
of sales in the cotton textile industry, comprising 1,116 firms in 1937.

Sales of sheeting, sheets, and pillow cases averaged close to 25 per
cent of all sales, with the "Dan River" grade (Type 128) accounting
for twice as much as the other grades combined. The chambray business (including plaids, drills, and other coarse goods) reached a sales
peak of $8.2 million in 1936, but the subsequent decline reduced this
division's sales from one third to one sixth of the total. Suitings sales
increased tenfold from 1932 to 1940. In the later year sales of $5.8
million represented nearly 30 per cent of the year's business. Gains
in the shirtings and sportswear departments brought these lines up to
one fifth of all sales, while sales of dress goods and handkerchief cloth
also increased more rapidly than total sales.

The composition of sales did not become stabilized in 1939-1940,

---

for retailers and manufacturers and a mat service. Full-color ads in *Esquire* in the spring
of 1939 initiated advertising at the retail level. As "Rivercool" contained 70-75 per cent
viscose rayon, the manufacturer of the fiber, the American Viscose Corporation, was
interested in sharing the cost of advertising which identified the fiber and used the
corporation's "Crown seal of approval." One proposal called for a contribution of $7,500
from American Viscose to a display devoted to "Man—His Clothes—His Sports" at the
New York World's Fair (1939); but when the two companies failed to come to terms, the
sales office observed that "Rivercool" was doing very well without any identification of
the raw material (F. K. Nixon to R. R. West, Oct. 24, 1938; Winternitz & Cairns to
American Viscose Corporation, Oct. 17, 1938).

In March 1939 Winternitz & Cairns were preparing a "giant 15-color display to be
used as the main panel in dressing a window of RIVERCOOL garments." It was planned
to be used by a select group of customers, who would pay about half of the cost of the
display materials.

[65] The agreement covered fabrics other than shirtings, but since Dan River had submitted only shirtings in the contract year ending May 31, 1939, the Institute reduced
the fee to $720 a year. At this time the Institute was making tests of various collar
cloths.

but it may be useful to summarize: Domestics, including handkerchief cloth and flannels made up one fourth of the sales; suiting furnished another fourth; chambrays and related lines accounted for about one fifth of total sales, while shirtings and sportswear made up another fifth. The remaining 10 per cent of sales derived from dress goods and sales yarns.

Table 8. Net Billings by Classes of Goods, 1932-1940
(thousands of dollars)

	1932	1933	1934	1935	1936	1937	1938	1939	1940
sheetings, sheets pillow cases:									
"Morotock"	756	833	1225	1188	753	885	535	609	772
"Dan River"	1341	2489	2572	3836	3526	3307	2942	3036	3449
"Riverside"	479	671	234	710	960	834	731	759	841
other								75	73
chambrays, plaids coverts, drills	3879	5835	7414	6964	8152	7410	4276	4607	3615
shirtings and sportswear	1752	2106	3040	3253	4378	4669	3051	4620	3863
dress goods	215	299	1107	708	467	692	677	1756	1274
suitings	584	1652	2290	3061	3729	3699	3167	5541	5817
diapers and diaper cloth	289	233	300	427	324	414	181	246	143
handkerchief cloth	281	243	540	320	647	505	160	602	757
flannels	26					276	329	351	279
drapery and other cloth	−9		60	258	10	9	9	23	30
rags and pound goods	103	108	162	241	191	204	100	92	100
sales yarns	122	184	281	430	655	477	238	518	720
waste			188	172	234	239	156	163	200
total	9,818	14,653	19,413	21,568	24,026	23,620	16,552	22,998	21,933

On a poundage basis sales exceeded output in 1932, 1933, and 1935; and in 1934 production topped sales by only a small margin. But sales for 1936 and 1937 fell far below output, and the inventory of finished cloth and goods in process piled up to a record-breaking 26.6 million pounds, worth $8 million, at the end of 1937. Production in 1938 surpassed sales by a million pounds, but the spurt in sales in 1939 cut the inventory of finished goods in half. Although cloth inventories in 1939-1940 were almost twice as large as in 1932-1933, by the end of the period the minimum, or "normal," inventory position had risen significantly by virtue of the wider range of fabrics and styles in the company's merchandise.

Inventory control was a problem which few firms in the textile industry learned to master. Research on the subject led to the conclusion
that "the accumulation of inventories has not been the major cause of
the decline in manufacturing margins," but "in practically every case
where a substantial accumulation of inventory in relation to current
shipments did occur, manufacturing margins decline."[66]

Year-end inventories of goods in process and finished goods built up
to staggering totals of 26.6 million pounds in 1937 and 25.0 million
pounds in 1938. They were reduced to an average of just under 10
million pounds in 1939-1940. In value, the maximum inventories
(1937-1938) were $7.3-7.9 million. Statistics for the industry show for
January 1937 stocks of cotton goods equivalent to production in 2.8
weeks, while orders on hand required 18.7 weeks' output. But this
position steadily deteriorated, as stocks in March 1938 rose to 11.7
weeks' output and orders amounted to 9.3 weeks' production. For the
first time since 1936 orders (14.2 weeks' output) exceeded stocks (6.4
weeks' output) in September 1939.[67]

Operating reports furnish a comparison of quarterly movements of
unfilled orders and finished goods on hand for Dan River Mills. While
the rate of production was relatively stable, abrupt changes in the end-
of-quarter unfilled orders reflect seasonal and erratic movements in
sales. But the seasonal pattern is not pronounced: maximum unfilled
orders (for the year) occur at the end of the first quarter (1939), at the
end of the second quarter (1933), at the end of the third quarter (1932,
1935), and at the end of the fourth quarter (1935, 1936, 1940). Unfilled orders exceeded cloth inventories at the end of 14 quarters, while
inventories were greater than unfilled orders in 16 cases. At the end of
1936 unfilled orders amounted to 1,097,000 pieces of cloth, but the inventory was only 726,000 pieces: on June 30, 1938, the mills had an inventory of 1,248,000 pieces and orders for 727,000 pieces; but at the
end of the first quarter of 1939 orders requiring 1,050,000 pieces were
twice the inventory of 521,000 pieces.

The margin between unfilled orders and goods on hand is not a
completely reliable index of the effectiveness of inventory policy. At
the end of March 1939, for instance, the cloth inventory included large

[66] J. J. Madigan, "Managing Cloth Inventories in the Cotton Textile Industry," Business Research Studies No. 6, Harvard Graduate School of Business Administration (Boston,
1934).
[67] American Cotton Manufacturers' Institute, *Cotton Textile Hi-Lights: Mid-Century
Number, 1900-1950* (Charlotte, n.d.).

amounts of old styles and second-quality merchandise, which could not have been delivered against orders on hand.

Sales in 1932-1940 were classified as direct (or "house"), commission, and salesmen's accounts. The direct accounts declined to only $181,000 in 1938 but rose to nearly one third of all sales in 1940, when a number of large accounts, formerly credited to the sales manager, were treated as "house" accounts. Commission accounts, which exceeded $1.1 million in 1939, comprised yarn sales, handkerchief cloth sold through H. L. McClearn & Company, and comparatively small quantities of dress goods distributed by National Fabrics Corporation in 1938-1939.

Salesmen, including the general sales manager, numbered 18 in 1932, 20 in 1936, 25 in 1939, 27 in 1940.

Accounts (customers) dropped from 1,103 in 1931 to 934 in 1932, but rose to 1,238 in 1933.

The pattern of domestic sales showed some shifting as a result of the opening of regional sales offices in Boston and Atlanta. Sales of G. A. Stafford & Company, comprising virtually all of Dan River's export business, attained a maximum value of $700,000 in 1939, dropping to $674,000 in 1940.

Prices

Table 9 depicts the movement of selling prices for five classes of fabrics and two grades of sales yarns. A general upward trend after 1932 practically doubled prices by 1937, when the prewar peak was reached. Group averages conceal the changes arising from differences in the composition of the classes, which were pronounced in the cases of suitings, shirtings, and dress goods. Thus, the highest average price received for dress goods was 66.73 cents in 1940, reflecting principally the higher cost of a larger proportion of rayon fabrics in the dress goods lines.

The price history of "Dan River" sheeting, which the available records cover with considerable detail, probably portrays the general pattern of price movements for most of the company's fabrics. Price List 75, issued August 22, 1930, remained effective for seven years; but numerous price changes, which took the form of varying discounts on the list prices, were announced in bulletins and letters distributed by

Table 9.   Selling Prices, Costs and Profit Margins
(cents per pound)

	1932	1933	1934	1935	1936	1937	1938	1939	1940
average selling price									
suitings					62.48	68.17	57.78	61.15	61.72
chambrays coverts					36.11	40.43	30.63	30.48	33.23
shirtings, sportswear					64.20	70.27	54.27	56.65	56.46
domestics					44.08	48.22	33.49	35.95	38.20
dress goods					49.71	60.15	48.75	51.67	66.73
all cloth					44.62	50.21	30.09	43.07	45.65
hosiery yarn					28.81	32.89	26.68	21.36	26.32
carpet yarn					20.26	22.68	15.71	13.90	18.07
all goods	25.90	31.16	42.58	41.40	44.11	49.33	38.54	41.69	44.10
cost of sales	23.54	26.81	37.74	38.63	38.78	42.74	37.60	38.34	40.52
gross profit on sales	2.36	4.35	4.84	2.77	5.33	6.59	.94	3.35	3.58
selling, general administrative expense	2.20	2.11	2.36	2.23	2.43	3.26	3.17	2.26	2.53
net profit on sales	.16	2.24	2.48	.54	2.90	3.33	−2.23	1.09	1.05
pounds sold (millions)	37.9	46.7	44.7	51.6	54.6	47.4	42.5	54.6	49.5

the New York office.   The list price of 90-inch bleached sheeting was 40 cents; but in May 1931 the discount advanced to 37.5 per cent, making a net price of 25 cents a yard.[68]   In June 1932 the discount jumped to 55 per cent, and salesmen were instructed to offer an additional 5 per cent for large orders.   This lowered net prices to 16-18 cents a yard. The net price in April 1933 was 18 cents, but after the Code went into effect the price advanced over twelve cents a yard.   For almost four years the net price for "Dan River" sheeting fluctuated around 30 cents a yard, dropping to 26 cents in May 1936, and rising to 33 cents in May 1937.   The August 1937 price list retained the 40-cent basic price, but discounts tended to widen, bringing the net price down to 21 cents in June 1938.   In May 1939 a "trading" discount of 50 per cent was announced, making the net price 20 cents a yard, the same as in September 1932.   As late as April 1941 sheeting was cheaper than in 1936.

Table 10, showing the average net selling price per pound of "Dan River" sheets and pillow cases, presents another view of price movements in 1931-1940.   The monthly figures serve to emphasize the continued weakness in textile prices throughout the first half of 1933, whereas other industries experienced some improvement in prices and volume of trade before the end of 1932.   The lowest point was reached in March and April 1933 when bleached sheets and pillow cases brought

[68] "Morotock" 90-inch sheeting was listed at 35 cents (List 76), but discounts made the net 21.875 cents a yard in May 1931.   The "Riverside" list (List 203) on 90-inch sheeting was 50 cents; the net in May 1931 was 31.25 cents.

only 24 cents per pound. Prices climbed in response to the changes introduced by the Code and to the higher price of cotton induced by New Deal farm legislation. After the abrupt jump from 30.7 cents in July to 41.7 cents in August 1933 sheet prices gained steadily; and by April 1934, this product sold for just about twice its depression low. Prices softened with declines in the cost of cotton and the removal of processing taxes in 1935. Fairly stable averages in 1935-1936 were followed by a sharp rise to the decade's highest price level in mid-1937. A recession pulled prices back to lower values than in the early months of the Code, and only part of the loss was recovered before 1941.

Table 10. Prices and Sales of "Dan River"
Bleached Sheets and Pillow Cases, 1931-1940*

month	thousands of pounds	cents per pound	thousands of pounds	cents per pound
	1931		1932	
Jan.			241	33.9
Feb.			142	32.6
March			205	31.2
April			189	32.5
May	243	39.9	180	30.2
June	331	38.4	226	28.6
July	180	40.9	141	28.1
Aug.	389	32.4	372	28.5
Sept.	360	35.3	327	25.4
Oct.	402	35.5	340	27.9
Nov.	256	33.5	291	26.5
Dec.	670	26.8	599	26.2
	1933		1934	
Jan.	343	27.5	291	45.5
Feb.	158	24.9	341	46.7
March	331	24.6	230	45.4
April	307	24.6	175	48.9
May	433	26.5	184	47.5
June	506	27.3	198	45.2
July	432	30.7	197	45.6
Aug.	320	41.7	196	44.3
Sept.	457	41.7	296	43.1
Oct.	667	44.5	844	43.8
Nov.	435	46.1	379	44.9
Dec.	761	44.8	404	41.2

	1935			1936	
Jan.	481	40.7		425	38.6
Feb.	484	41.3		582	40.2
March	579	41.6		523	41.0
April	622	41.8		615	42.2
May	455	40.9		390	41.0
June	587	41.0		752	40.5
July	590	41.8		628	40.1
Aug.	613	42.3		579	40.2
Sept.	530	42.1		591	40.7
Oct.	613	43.5		812	41.4
Nov.	497	42.8		562	44.4
Dec.	716	44.5		531	47.1

	1937			1938	
Jan.	595	47.6		217	40.6
Feb.	408	49.7		233	38.0
March	465	49.7		584	36.5
April	615	50.3		526	35.5
May	326	50.7		487	35.7
June	471	50.6		733	34.3
July	568	50.8		843	34.2
Aug.	383	50.6		570	34.4
Sept.	459	50.6		587	34.2
Oct.	475	50.2		842	34.9
Nov.	297	50.5		667	36.2
Dec.	408	48.2		583	36.9

	1939			1940	
Jan.	421	38.3		285	40.0
Feb.	169	39.2		317	41.5
March	263	37.4		365	41.3
April	397	36.4		396	40.4
May	288	35.9		406	39.0
June	555	35.2		626	35.7
July	817	34.9		632	35.7
Aug.	547	34.8		784	35.8
Sept.	791	35.1		610	36.3
Oct.	939	35.5		828	37.7
Nov.	626	38.3		783	39.4
Dec.	652	39.0		893	40.5

* Type 128 (64 × 64). First and seconds, 1931-1938; first quality only, 1939-1940. Source: New York Sales Office.

The practice in pricing birdseye cloth and diapers was similar to that of the sheeting trade. Thus, the "Health" price-list of August 2, 1933, offered garments 27-inches square at $1.85 per dozen, subject to discounts of 45 per cent and five per cent ($.97 net). The discount was

lowered (and the price raised) on August 5, but prices generally worked
lower in 1934 and 1935. The net price reached $1.0175 per dozen in
March 1937, but by February 1938 the price had dropped to $.79.
("Charmspun" diapers in the same size sold for $.7125 net). Price List
119 (December 19, 1940) kept the same list prices; net prices were
list "less 45 & 5%, with privilege of submitting contracts at 50% off."

Price lists for other classes of goods usually stated the net prices,
subject only to such "trading" concessions—usually .25 or .5 cent per
yard—as might be necessary to make a sale. In the recession of 1937-
1938 the price of "Defiance" chambray dropped from 13.25 cents
(March 1937) to 9.5 cents (October 1938). On September 5, 1939, it
was priced at 9.75 cents a yard; on September 8 the price advanced to
10 cents; on September 14, to 10.25 cents; and on September 20, to 11
cents. Other chambrays and coverts rose correspondingly.

Costs

Table 9, though incomplete, shows some of the interrelations of
costs, prices and profits. Gross profit on sales rose to a maximum of
6.59 cents per pound in 1937, or seven times the minimum of .94 cent
obtained the following year. Net profit per unit showed practically
the same variability, the net loss of 2.23 cents per pound falling in the
year of lowest gross profit. Selling, general, and administrative expenses stayed within the narrow range of 2.11 cents to 3.26 cents per
pound of goods sold; as a percentage of average selling prices these expenses varied from 5.4 per cent in 1935 to 8.5 per cent in 1932. The
ratio was highest when selling price and volume of sales were lowest
(1932), and a low ratio—5.5 per cent in 1937—is associated with the
highest average price and the maximum sales volume for the period.
For other years, however, the correlation is not pronounced. When
gross profit reached 3.5 cents per pound (as in 1939 and 1940), about
one cent per pound remained as net profit. With sales of about 50
million pounds, this level of net profit yielded earnings of 2.25 cents per
dollar of capital and surplus.

The economists' concept of a system in which prices bear a precise
relation to costs of production finds poor support in the history of
textile pricing. Within the industry, everyone professed an unwilling-
ness to sell goods below the cost of production; but the varieties of

textile cost accounting in use left many managements in doubt about their costs. President West wrote a Finnish manufacturer that it was "absolutely hopeless to attempt to install an adequate cost control system directly from the use of textbooks dealing with the subject." Even empirically developed systems often failed to satisfy the needs of managerial policy.

Dan River's early cost records, as has been explained, furnished a tolerably accurate record of unit costs over periods of four weeks at a time. Thus, management was fairly well informed of costs for the period just ended; it had a less satisfactory basis for estimating current costs or for projecting them into the future. Furthermore, the "Cost of Manufacturing" sheets (discarded after 1931) failed to show any difference in the cost per yard of different fabrics, except as they differed in weight. Any two types of cloth had the same cost per yard if they measured the same number of yards to the pound. The discrepancies were, perhaps, not too unrealistic as long as the fabrics were roughly similar; but the increasing diversification of product and the use of other fibers than cotton necessitated more accurate accounting for the separate costs of each fabric and style.

The Loper cost system, installed in 1927, contributed certain refinements of the traditional cost-finding methods, making it possible to improve the estimates of individual fabric costs. Partly for reasons of economy, the Loper costing methods were dropped in 1931; but the same year Lockwood, Greene Engineers were employed to restudy the work of the cost department. Lockwood, Greene's recommendations led to the adoption of better methods for ascertaining departmental and process costs and an improved practice for allocating overhead and general expenses to different fabrics. "One-hundred-per-cent costs" for each type of cloth provided a check on historical costs. Thus, a review of actual costs for eight weeks ending in April 1932 showed the costs of 27 fabrics running from a fraction of a cent to a little more than one cent per yard above the 100 per-cent costs.

New cost problems arose with the introduction of two-shift operations in 1933. In March a Loper cost study stressed Dan River's competitive disadvantage in operating only 55 hours a week. A "typical" mill running 110 hours per week, Loper reported, could manufacture 100×60 gray broadcloth for 4.402 cents per yard, as compared with Dan River's cost of 6.633 cents. The differential was slightly more than one

cent a yard on three types of chambray, but the typical mill produced
90-inch sheeting for three cents less than Dan River's cost.

In 1934 the Barnes Textile Associates offered to instal a "modern
up-to-date cost system which . . . will be of vital assistance . . . for sales
guidance." President West seems to have doubted that the company
needed a brand-new system and he cautioned the cost department not
to "forget . . . that emphasis in this study should be placed on determining where our costs are high, and why, rather than setting up a different
kind of cost system."

The fruit of the Barnes survey, conducted with the collaboration
of Waverley H. Cousins and his associates in the cost department, was
the construction of "standard costs" for each fabric, style, and pattern
of cloth. Cost-estimate sheets were submitted to the management in
January 1936 with the admonition that the new standard costs, though
"lower than our present attainment," were about the level "we expect
to reach if we operate in 1936 at the same rate of operations as in 1935.
In other words, these costs are what we expect to make the various
fabrics for in 1936, but are lower than our actual Costs for 1935."
There were, therefore, "no 'Cushions' in these Costs." Each fabric
cost sheet showed the cost of cloth per yard, with cotton at 10 cents a
pound, and indicated the difference in cost per yard for a change in
the price of cotton of one cent a pound. A standard cost sheet for
napped flannel (May 1937) showed a cost of 6.678 cents per yard, with
cotton at 12.23 cents per pound. The cost included an allowance of 1
per cent for defective cloth and 1.1 per cent for selling expenses.

Pricing had to compromise the manufacturer's objective of selling
at a "reasonable" markup above the cost of production and the effects
of frequent shifts in demand for various styles of goods, each of which
was more or less competitive with other producers' fabrics. It was the
job of the sales organization to ascertain, under constantly changing
market conditions, how far above costs the prices of each fabric, style,
and pattern might be set without pricing the goods off the market or
reducing the volume of output predicated in the cost estimates.

We may compare some pricing experiences with the cost data. In
the 1936 fall price list for clothing fabrics, issued in March, prices
ranged from 27 cents to 49 cents per yard for thirty-odd "ranges" of
cotton and part-wool fabrics. On a range selling for 22 cents a yard
the cost varied from 17.751 cents to 18.552 cents per yard, depending

upon pattern and color. Another style, selling for 28 cents, cost from 21.691 cents to 22.763 cents a yard to produce. The selling price of eight patterns ranged from 3.448 cents to 6.309 cents a yard above cost. Commenting on the list, the director of the clothing fabrics division saw an advantage in having all patterns of a particular style priced at 48 cents, instead of offering the lowest-cost patterns at 47 cents. It was also desirable to have the prices "run even money—no fractions"; that is, all list prices were full cents per yard. Although the processing tax on cotton had been removed, there was "nothing to be gained" from a corresponding reduction in prices. Furthermore, the sales organization took the position that it would be "wise to advance prices" as soon as the volume of sales assured a season's run at the mills, "because of the strategic position it gives for the establishment of prices for the ensuing season."

The September 1940 price list for fancy shirtings offered three styles at a reduction of ½ cent a yard from the previous list, "as a result of our increasing volume of business on these numbers." In October 1940 the cost department reported that manufacturing operations averaged 65.98 hours per week (for 50 weeks) in 1936-1939, which was close to the "standard" week of 66.56 hours.[69] Two full shifts of 80 hours, it was estimated, would raise output by 30 million yards a year and yield a saving of .25 cent per yard on depreciation. No estimate was made of other savings from full-time operations; they may not have been enough to offset the additional sales expense of marketing a larger volume of goods.

Price concessions on large orders were common until the Robinson-Patman Act (1936) outlawed many forms of price discrimination and "necessitated our going on a one-price basis." At one time the company put itself in the embarrassing position of cutting prices for one customer to such an extent that the jobber was able to sell at the same prices Dan River charged its other customers.[70]

In pricing sheets and sheeting the percentage markup tended to increase as the quality (and cost) of the product increased. Thus, in April 1937 the standard cost of "Morotock" sheeting was only 27.5 per

[69] The yearly averages were 74.32 hours in 1936; 73.67 hours in 1937; 54.10 hours in 1938; and 61.85 hours in 1939.

[70] F. K. Nixon to I. Rittenberg, Sept. 25, 1939. Nixon had "been asked by some of our very big accounts some very embarrassing questions as to why your firm can sell our goods at the same price as we do .... The situation has become so complicated that I took the matter up with Mr. West ... and in the interest of the Company it seems best to say to you that we do not wish to continue our present method of operation."

cent below list; the medium-grade "Dan River" sheeting had a cost 31.4 per cent below list; and the cost of "Riverside" sheeting was 36.1 per cent under list. Similarly, "Health" diapers showed a standard cost 60.4 per cent below list (September 1939), but the cost of the lower-priced "Charmspun" was only 17.8 per cent under list. "Charmspun" was the garment introduced to meet the demand for a lower-grade product. The two brands of diapers were really different, but the price differential reflected inaccurately the difference in quality as measured by cost of production.

Early in 1940 the executive committee of the board of directors asked the cost department to prepare quarterly statements of costs and selling prices in order to demonstrate which types of goods were most profitable to manufacture. The first of these reports, covering the first quarter of 1940, estimated a loss of 37.27 per cent on small quantities of "Sovereign" sheeting; at the other extreme, the return on gray dress goods was equivalent to 22.83 per cent of the net sales. The report for the year 1940 (Table 11) revealed losses on sales of "Morotock" sheeting, plain broadcloth, and one of the lines of cotton suitings. The highest rate of return on sales (15.31 per cent) was realized on gray dress goods, but four of the suitings lines returned over 10 per cent. Relatively high rates of profit were shown on 2.3 million yards of combed handkerchief cloth as well as on small quantities of barber cloth and combed sheeting. Cloth and sales yarn manufactured at Riverside Division produced only 4.79 per cent of the total profit.

The total return of $1,013,377 was $344,652 in excess of the estimated profit shown in the monthly operating reports and almost twice the net profit from sales ($523,102) reported in the year's audit.

Although the sales executives in New York thought there was "no report coming to this office that is more constructive and of more value" than the quarterly analysis of billings, the cost department considered the work "still in the experimental stage." The report for the third quarter had been "way off, due to price used for cotton and cost at standard whereas we operated far below standard." Cousins proposed to improve the reports by figuring yardage "at standard cost on cotton as near market price as could be estimated, and then charge each department with idle looms or credit with looms running above standard hours." For this purpose the management approved an "allocation of looms to departments." Depreciation was "spread on looms only, on the assumption that if looms are idle, other machinery back of looms, as well as finishing equipment, will likewise be idle." All this improved the processes of cost finding, although losses and gains from dealings in cotton futures vitiated the estimates of the actual cost of cotton used in manufacture.

Table 11. Sales and Profit, 1940

	billings		profit	
	thousand yards	thousand dollars	dollars	per cent of sales
sheeting, sheets,				
pillow cases				
"Dan River"	16,989	3,347	29,485	.88
"Morotock"	4,537	749	−36,909	−4.93
"Riverside"	3,673	816	16,166	1.98
other	349	71	2,128	3.00
barber cloth; flannel	3,822	294	5,568	1.89
birdseye cloth	1,845	138	8,360	6.04
handkerchief cloth				
combed	2,347	315	39,413	12.50
carded	4,829	441	2,189	.50
fancy shirtings	18,139	2,692	181,529	6.74
plain broadcloth	10,665	1,114	−10,091	−.91
dress goods	8,399	1,189	90,564	7.62
suitings	18,939	5,758	541,571	9.40
pound goods	585*	95	94,898†	−
sales yarn	3,217*	704	38,481	5.47
Riverside cloth	38,940	3,628	10,035	.28
total	133,473	21,357	1,013,377	4.75

* Thousands of pounds
† Cost absorbed by allowances for defectives on other goods

Cotton

No element of cost was more important or more subject to influences beyond the control of the manufacturer than the price of cotton. Year-end inventories and the inventory value of cotton (the lower of cost or market) are shown in Table 12. One of the inventory values (1939) falls below the December quotation for middling, indicating that a substantial part of the 11.6 million pounds of cotton on hand had been acquired at less than the December prices. Inventory values in

Table 12. Cotton Inventories, 1932-1940

year	millions of pounds	value: cents per pound
1932	8.3	6.93
1933	7.1	10.77
1934	4.6	14.12
1935	5.4	12.87
1936	9.1	13.93
1937	12.2	10.07
1938	5.3	9.56
1939	11.6	10.39
1940	10.0	11.00

excess of the market price for middling cotton arise from premiums on grades better than middling.

Attracted by the weakness of the cotton markets in 1931 and 1932, the management built up inventory with each fresh decline in the price. In October 1931 the president reported a long position of 4,166 bales, bought at an average of 5.66 cents a pound, and announced that he would buy in futures contracts, if prices worked lower, in order to increase the long position to 14,600 bales. The net long position was only 6,850 bales in March 1932, but Vice-president Ray explained that the "swift fall in values of raw materials and goods manufactured" made it necessary to sell futures heavily in order to hedge unsold goods, cotton in process, and cotton on hand. Prices on option contracts were fixed on June 25 at 5.15 cents a pound, apparently the cheapest cotton ever bought. The cotton statement presented to the directors in September 1932 showed the following position:

	bales
bought, in transit, and on hand	16,092
cotton in process	10,796
cotton in finished goods	13,795
	40,683
goods sold	32,512
futures sold	2,000
cotton unpriced	25
	34,537
net long position	6,146

Chairman Miller told the directors in November that he had found it necessary to assure the banks that the company's policy was against speculation in cotton; that the current long position of 20,000 bales was "due to what we believed necessary in order to obtain proper grades, colors, and staples."[71] He would have been a prophet of the first order if he had assured them that the price of cotton would double within a year.

In February 1933 President West advised the directors that the domestic allotment plan, if passed by Congress, would "seriously handicap the successful operation of this business." With the approval of the board, he sent a telegram to President-elect Roosevelt, asserting that "while this company is in full accord with any plan to improve present conditions, we feel very strongly that the proposed Farm Relief Bill will accomplish no good but bring about great harm .... It will mean disaster to many textile institutions."[72] New Deal farm policy took shape in the Agricultural Adjustment Act of May 12, 1933. Cotton mills had to pay a processing tax of 4.2 cents a pound on cotton entered for manufacture, and market prices rose as part of the growing crop was plowed under. The Cotton Textile Institute spearheaded a drive to get the processing tax removed, and in July 1935 the industry's opposition bore fruit in a decision of the Circuit Court of Appeals, holding the tax unconstitutional.[73] Dan River promptly obtained an injunction against the Collector of Internal Revenue, which allowed the firm to pay the processing taxes in escrow. After July 25 the company promised its customers a refund of the processing taxes included in selling prices if the Supreme Court upheld the lower court. On January 6, 1936, the Court invalidated the Agricultural Adjustment Act.[74]

[71] Because the basis—the spread between spot and future prices—behaved erratically with respect to premium grades and staples, it was impractical to attempt to hedge purchases of superior quality cotton in the standard middling contracts (see W. H. S. Stevens, "The Relation of Cash-future Spread to Hedging Transactions," *Journal of Business of the University of Chicago*, vol. 2 [1929], p. 28).

[72] The company's attorney conferred with Virginia's Senator Claude A. Swanson in January 1933 but found him "somewhat favorable to the bill, provided it included tobacco." Senator Swanson owned 4,000 shares of Dan River common stock, and Harris thought he "would feel very much embarrassed to openly fight the bill with cotton included" (M. K. Harris to J. M. Miller, Jan. 25, 1933). Swanson, of course, became Secretary of the Navy on March 4 and did not participate in Congressional debates on New Deal legislation.

[73] Franklin Process Co. v. Hoosac Mills Corp., 8 F. Supp. 552; Butler v. United States, 78 F. (2d) 1. In April 1935 President West lectured a fellow manufacturer who had suggested that mills refuse to pay the tax: "How would such a refusal differ from the refusal to obey any law? In regard to closing the mills, another proposed form of protest, I cannot follow you at all .... We may be forced to close our mills down for lack of business, or because some of us insist on selling goods at ruinous prices, but for us to visit upon our people the affliction of loss of employment, purely out of spite toward an inept Government, is entirely out of reason" (R. R. West to T. M. Marchant, April 12, 1935).

[74] United States v. Butler *et al.*, receivers of Hoosac Mills, 297 U.S. 1.

Dan River refunded $825,578 to its customers and received $55,793 in refunds from its suppliers. Funds in escrow provided $743,892.[75]

Drought in 1934, combined with acreage reduction, brought the output down to 9.6 million bales, the smallest crop since 1921. The price was supported at 12 cents a pound and brought an average of 12.3 cents in the market. Next year's crop—only a million bales larger—sold for an average of 11.9 cents. In October 1935 Dan River's cotton buyer, Henry Roediger, wrote from Memphis that he had bought some "attractive lots of cotton," but he was "not so rampant bullish on the basis" and expected the market to work down to ten cents. Actually, the lowest monthly average price was 10.8 cents in September.

New proposals for the control of production, following the invalidation of the A.A.A., created uncertainty in the cotton markets. In March 1936 President West saw "so many capricious influences at work" that he was "singularly lacking in any opinion as to the cotton market." Output for the year rose to 12.4 million bales, and the price averaged 12.1 cents. As orders for cloth accumulated, the volume of hedges declined; the management, apparently, became confident of its ability to cover cotton requirements at lower prices after the new crop came to market. In closing out its hedges, however, the company lost $300,464.

In 1937 acreage restrictions were removed; the crop of 18.9 million bales was a record output; and before the end of the year the price sagged to 8.8 cents a pound. Lack of storage space prevented the company from investing more heavily in good grades of "bargain" cotton; and receipts of cotton had to be curtailed in proportion to the curtailment of manufacturing operations.

Crop control and price supports returned with the 1938 planting, but the low level of business activity kept the price of a greatly reduced crop—12 million bales—close to nine cents a pound. In April the company had on hand 83,500 bales, including cotton in process and in finished goods. Unfilled orders represented 16,800 bales. The remainder (except for 2,500 bales) was hedged, as follows: 19,500 bales in July futures (at 8.61 cents), 11,700 bales in October futures (at 8.34 cents), and 33,000 bales in December futures (at 8.65 cents). In November Chairman Miller thought the 44,629 bales of cotton on hand was excessive. "We are committed, as you know, not to speculate in

---

[75] A lengthy dispute with the Bureau of Internal Revenue over "unjust enrichment" from processing taxes collected (in effect, if not in name) but not returned to the government ended in November 1941 with the payment by the company of $50,623, plus interest.

cotton," he wrote West; but the chairman confessed that he would "never understand thoroughly the cotton business . . . . Please clear my brain on this subject." The president, I suppose, explained that much of the 44,629 bales was protected by hedges.

The relatively small crops of 1939 and 1940 (11.8 million and 12.6 million bales, respectively) brought average prices of 9.3 cents and 10.2 cents. Early in 1939 West noted a "widespread conviction that the price of cotton is artificially high. . . . if the government were to remove its loan support in any way, the price would fall substantially." From a net long position of 2,024 bales on January 7, the company sold goods ahead of cotton purchases and was short 3,698 bales on June 3. But the market remained strong, anticipating the commencement in July of federal subsidies on cotton exports; and President West had to report that fixing prices on call contracts and closing out hedges wiped out the operating profit for the first half of the year. The short position was covered in September, and on October 28 the net long position amounted to 51,421 bales. The president invited "expressions from the Board as to whether or not any part of the long position should be hedged." No answer was given to this question, but the directors did instruct the management to hold the net long position to a maximum of 30,000 bales. In December West asked for a "free hand in the market, to take advantage of the breaks"; and the directors authorized an increase in the maximum long position to 40,000 bales. They vetoed the president's proposal to liquidate the hedges on 39,000 bales as soon as he could bring the average cost of 69,000 bales (including 30,000 bales unhedged) down to 9.5 cents a pound.

Previously, West had explained to the company's auditors that "our dealings in cotton futures are purely hedging operations. They are always sales of futures to hedge cotton purchased at a fixed price . . . . Our only purchases in the future market has been the purchase to take up futures which had previously been sold. On many occasions our open short futures do not equal the excess of cotton on hand over orders accepted, owing to the fact that very frequently we have cotton on hand purchased on buyer's call." It was also true that the net long position frequently included unhedged cotton on which the price had been fixed. And this was just as speculative as a net short position. President West seems to have been influenced by George S. Harris, who had written convincingly on the alternatives to a policy of 100 per-cent hedging.[76] Harris argued that a skilful cotton policy should take into account the cyclical movements in cotton prices. Instead of hedging under all circumstances, which involved the risk of loss from a change in the basis, the mill should maintain a long position whenever the price seemed unduly low and go short of cotton at abnormally high prices. Harris did not pretend to know the exact levels at which prices should be regarded as "too high" or "too low" but thought the minor losses from mistakes at one phase of the cycle would be offset by gains at another phase.

As president of Dan River, Harris took a bearish position on the cotton market in mid-1940 and allowed the net short position to rise to 8,483 bales on November 2. By the end of the year, however, the net long interest amounted to 2,209 bales. In the meantime, as Harris admitted to Miller, "our bearish ideas have led us into a very poor job of getting out of the cotton contracts originally placed in the market March of this year." Hedges of 21,000 bales of December cotton were replaced with May (1941) futures at a loss of $51,000. "It may develop," the president observed, "that we would have improved our position if we had bought in these contracts, increasing our long position by that amount, but it seemed wise to us to re-sell in a distant month in the expectation that sometime before May we will get some decline which will enable us to recover a part of the losses we have taken in this hedging transaction."

Depreciation

No calculation of costs of production can be better than the accountant's estimate of the value of buildings and machinery used up in the process of manufacturing goods. Annual depreciation charges, including the amounts allocated to tenements and welfare property, varied as follows:

1932	$ 500,000	1937	$ 948,287
1933	1,191,238	1938	985,589
1934	1,530,620	1939	1,013,129
1935	1,155,899	1940	1,040,373
1936	1,122,307		

In general, depreciation charges seem to have been too high; the reported costs of production, therefore, tended to be overstated. In re-

[76] *Textile World*, vol. 74 (Oct. 6, 1928), pp. 47, 103, 105.

viewing the operations for 1933 the auditors deplored the fact that "the Company is taking depreciation on assets that have already been fully depreciated" and predicted accurately that tax officials would object. The management took the position that "considering the conditions under which it operates . . . the depreciation rates . . . are warrantable and fair";[77] but the Bureau of Internal Revenue restored $495,663 (including $368,878 in depreciation charges) to the 1933 income and disallowed $404,938 of depreciation in 1934, $281,871 in 1935, and $214,846 in 1936. Additional federal income taxes for the four years amounted to $359,249, and payments on account of state taxes increased by $35,420.

Treasury officials made a detailed examination of the company's records in 1939 and approved rates of depreciation, based on "estimated useful life," which should be applied to the recoverable cost of fixed assets as of December 31, 1932. In the course of the investigation new errors were found in the statements of 1935-1937. According to government accountants, the 1935 tax had been overpaid by $113,232 but additional taxes of $137,323 and $66,728 were levied on income for 1936 and 1937, respectively. President West was "outraged" by this reversal of the Bureau's previous settlement, particularly because the tax officials disallowed an inventory write-down at the end of 1937. This was not the end of the matter. In 1940 the company paid an additional assessment of $19,521 (including interest) on income for 1935-1938; and disallowance of certain items of depreciation in the 1939-1940 statements required the payment of an additional tax of $40,000.

Bad debts

The cost of bad debts is noteworthy because it remained so low. Write-offs of uncollectible accounts totaled $140,490 in the nine-year period; $8,782 in debts previously written off was recovered. A single customer accounted for $23,271 of the $32,917 written off in 1932; and one account was responsible for $19,109 of the $23,604 lost the following year. A suit for $284,900 against the Reliance Manufacturing Company, taken on appeal to the Supreme Court of New York in 1938,

[77] In December West wrote Miller that his "confidence in our schedule has been shaken somewhat recently by the appearance of certain cotton mill statements which indicate that some of the important cotton mills have accepted the schedules of the Bureau, allowing a much lower deduction for depreciation than was formerly used"; but in June 1937 the president advised state tax officials that he thought the federal government had made a "very technical, unfair and unjust disallowance."

was settled two years later by the payment of $52,000 and the return of goods valued at $184,000. The established loss was $48,900.

The question of the cost of labor leads to an examination of wages and labor relations under the Code, the Wagner Act, and federal wage and hour legislation.

Labor

In June 1931, five months after the end of a memorable strike, the management found "things . . . very quiet on the Dan, so far as the labor situation is concerned." Some of the workers held an occasional meeting "to listen to the best orators which their organizers have given them," but the union offered no panacea for the short time and falling wages which afflicted all sectors of the American economy.

New hope for a successful labor movement in the textile industry arose with the adoption of the Cotton Textile Code, which outlawed "yellow-dog" contracts and guaranteed workers "the right to organize and bargain collectively through representatives of their own choosing." Toward the end of May 1934 United Textile Workers of America, claiming a membership of 300,000 in the cotton textile industry, prepared for a general strike, protesting specifically the 25 per-cent industry-wide curtailment order of the Code Authority. An apparent victory was won, without a strike, when the N.R.A. intervened and created a place for a textile workers' representative on its Labor Advisory Board, put a union leader on the Cotton Textile National Industrial Relations Board, and selected an employee representative as adviser to the government delegate on the Cotton Textile Code Authority.

This flare-up was scarcely noticed in Danville where, according to the management, "very little organization" had been achieved. More serious was the general strike called by U.T.W.A. in September 1934. Although President West observed "no disposition on the part of our people to join in the strike," he wired the governor that "lawless elements from other states" had arrived for the "avowed purpose of shutting down by force the cotton mills in Danville." To "forestall the possibility of a calamity," the company asked for the protection of state troops. Management's fears were unjustified. Practically everyone came to work the day the strike was called; U.T.W.A.'s Vice-president

Gorman, "hurling challenges right and left," found the majority of workers apathetic;[78] and the Dan River directors applauded them for staying on the job:

The Board of Directors . . . hereby expresses its thanks and appreciation to the loyal employees of this Company, who so calmly and steadfastly continued their work without interruption during the recent General Textile Strike.

In spite of all agitations, rumors and threats, the employees of this Company have been practically 100% loyal to this, their organization.

The Board deems it just and fitting that these facts should be formally acknowledged and that it be allowed here to repeat its determination to use every effort to promote the welfare of every member of this organization.[79]

The September strike, while it brought no substantial gains to U.T.W.A. led President Roosevelt to set up a Board of Inquiry for the Cotton Textile Industry under the chairmanship of John G. Winant. The Board's report reviewed briefly the rise of conflicts over collective bargaining and workloads and recommended permanent executive agencies to cope with these problems.[80] Accepting the recommendations of the Winant Board, the President created a Textile Labor Relations Board (September 1934) and a Cotton Textile Work Assignment Board (October). In May 1935 the Work Assignment Board reported that "the great majority of employers in the cotton textile industry have not set up machine assignments that create excessive work loads"; in order to deal with the minority, the Board asked for a permanent body with power to enforce the reduction of work "in the event it is found that the machine assignment complained of creates an excessive work load." Dan River's president denounced the recommendation as unworkable, since repeated investigations had demonstrated the impossibility of reaching agreement on standards. Workers at Dan River had already carried to the Work Assignment Board a complaint against "stretching" (from eight sides to twelve) in spinning, but I am practically certain that the Board never took any action on the complaint.

West was deeply interested in the problems arising from the

[78] Sarcastically, the Danville *Bee* (Sept. 5, 1934) supposed the "active leader of the textile strike . . . has good reason to feel irritated over the attitude of textile workers in Danville, especially after his personal efforts a few years ago to lead them along the paths of economic progress by contributing to their starvation . . . ."

[79] *Twenty-sixth Annual Report of the Riverside & Dan River Cotton Mills, Incorporated* (Danville, 1935).

[80] "Report of the Board of Inquiry for the Cotton Textile Industry to the President," in *Hearings . . . on H. R. 9072,* pp. 65-76.

"stretching" of labor and personally endorsed a thorough investigation of the question undertaken by Yale University's Institute of Human Relations. In a study covering eleven northern and southern mills, including Riverside and Dan River Cotton Mills, the investigators pointed out that in four cases (Dan River was one) the stretch-out provoked strikes, necessitated demotions and discharges, and generally produced bad operating results. The other mills (with one exception) had accomplished the transition from the old to the new methods without disturbing good labor relations or resorting to the dismissal of workers. Success depended upon careful preparations for the change, such as training supervisory employees and improving "communications" between management and workers. West was impressed with these findings.[81] In a symposium on technological change in industry, he stated publicly that "industrial management is responsible for seeing that the tempo of technological change is sufficiently governed so that there occurs little or no displacement of labor. And it can be done!"[82] As well as I can determine, during West's presidency the stretch-out was allowed to displace workers only to the extent of normal withdrawals and dismissals; and the earnings of "stretched" workers generally increased.[83]

While testifying before a House of Representatives committee (January 1936), President West hedged his answers to questions about collective bargaining at Dan River. The National Labor Relations Act was clearly the "law of the land," but West did not "believe in having collective bargaining the only means of group expression or dealings between employer and employee." There were "thousands of communities in this country where harmony prevails between employer and employee, where there is collective bargaining." There were also thousands of communities "where the same harmony prevails where there is collective bargaining in the form of shop committees, or various other forms of employees' representation. Furthermore, there

[81] Elliott D. Smith, "Lessons of the Stretchout," in *Mechanical Engineering*, vol. 56 (1934), pp. 73-80. Dan River is identified as "Confederate" mill in this article. Smith later published a book on human relations in industry: *Technology and Labor: A Study of the Human Problems of Labor Saving* (New Haven, 1939). R. C. Nyman, who collaborated with Smith, was the author of another study, *Union-Management Cooperation in the 'Stretch-Out'* (New Haven, 1934).

[82] R. R. West, "Government Regulation and Technological Change," in *Personnel Administration and Technological Change: A Symposium* (American Management Association Personnel Series 17; New York, 1935).

[83] For instance, in the proposed reorganization of Mill No. 6 at Riverside (1938) weavers were stretched from 18-22 looms per weaver to 42 looms; but weekly earnings rose from $17-$18.40 to an average of $21.

are thousands of communities where harmony prevails where there is individual bargaining." Pressed to justify the feasibility of individual bargaining, West admitted that it would not afford a satisfactory solution to the problem of labor-management relations for Dan River's 8,500 employees.[84]

Officers of the U.T.W.A. were among those union leaders who bolted the A.F. of L. convention in 1935 to form the Committee for Industrial Organization. This was the group which sponsored the Textile Workers' Organizing Committee in the hope of carrying out a more effective drive for union members than U.T.W.A. had realized. In 1938 the Committee became the Congress for Industrial Organization and T.W.O.C. became the Textile Workers Union of America. In April 1937 President West told the Dan River directors that C.I.O. organizers were in Danville, distributing membership cards and organizing a local union. It was his intention, West said, to deal with organized labor "precisely as contemplated by the National Labor Relations Act, recently upheld by the Supreme Court." But the union made insignificant gains prior to the war, and it was not until 1942 that the Dan River management had to face union officials at the collective bargaining table.[85]

Wages and Employment

The wage chronology shown in Table 13 marks the turning points in average earnings over the nine-year period. The nadir reached in the first half of 1933 brought average hourly earnings down to 22.5 cents an hour, the lowest point since 1917, although this seems to have been fully one cent above the average of northern and southern mills combined.[86] The company struggled through 1931 without reducing wages, but in January 1932 the president found the pay scale "as much

[84] *Hearings . . . on H. R. 9072*, pp. 442-445.

[85] In December 1937 Lucy Randolph Mason, a public relations representative of the C.I.O., wrote West that the union organizer had found Danville a "free" town, " in contrast to many other textile centers of the South." In June 1938 Miss Mason found West the only southern cotton manufacturer in whom she could confide: "The suffering among textile workers . . . is incredible . . . . The crumbling of wage standards goes on with increasing speed . . . . The influence of T.W.O.C. is sane, constructive, temperate . . . ." West replied that he was using "all the power at my command" to get an industry agreement on a minimum wage under the proposed wage and hours legislation.

[86] A study based on a sample of 88,852 workers in 251 northern and southern mills put the March-April (1933) average at 21.4 cents an hour (*Monthly Labor Review*, vol. 53, no. 6 [1941], p. 1495). The average wage in the South, just before the code went into effect, was 20.5 cents an hour (*Monthly Labor Review*, vol. 46 [1938], pp. 36-47).

above our competitors as our rates were two years ago" and asked the
directors to approve a 10 per-cent cut.[87]   Deflation persisted; and in
February 1933 wage rates were reduced 11.3 per cent, bringing the
average hourly pay to about 65 per cent of the rates prevailing in
January 1930.[88]

The management hoped that the wage reduction in January 1932
would "provide steadier employment than has been possible in the
last two years."   Apparently, several hundred names were added to the
payroll during the year.   To spread the work, a four-day week was
adopted during the summer; but operations for the year averaged 80
per cent of capacity.   The depth of depression brought unemployment and distress to Danville, but such evidence as the company's
records yield suggests that the employable textile worker was relatively better off than many other groups.[89]   For the relief of the unemployed the directors appropriated $1,000 in December 1932, and for
the month of April 1933 tenants of company houses paid no rent.

Table 14 presents some of the wage data for three groups of workers
at Riverside Division.   The average for women workers, it will be observed, kept close to the average wage of unskilled males.   Both groups
must have had average hourly earnings of less than 20 cents after the
wage cut of February 1933.

The Code, effective in July 1933, raised Dan River's average hourly
wage approximately 53 per cent; but full-time weekly earnings ad-

[87] Circular Poster No. 210 (Jan. 13, 1932).   In November 1932 West complained that
"some of our competitors farther South have done scandalous things to their wages.   I
know a broadcloth Mill in South Carolina that has an average wage of $9.56.   Ours is
$14.50.   There is a chambray mill in Georgia that has an average of $10.25 and ours at
Riverside is about $14.00."

[88] This cut put Dan River's rates "probably 10 to 15 per cent" below the scale at the
Cone Mills, but in March the Cone management decided not to fall in line with the
Dan River rates.   Two months before the Code went into effect Herman Cone proposed
an agreement by Erwin, Marshall Field, Dan River, and the Cone Mills on increases in
hourly rates to accompany the change to the 40-hour week.

[89] In April 1932 F. E. Murrie, the employment officer, wrote President Pritchett that
he had consistently followed the policy of giving preference to local applicants for jobs.
Murrie said he interviewed hundreds of unemployed weekly, but a "large majority of
them are unskilled in our line, and many of the skilled and semi-skilled have passed
their peak of usefulness."   During the first three months of the year 269 of the 387
people hired were former employees; of the remainder, 15 were local residents and 67 came
from out of town.

Early in 1933 local relief and employment agencies complained that some workers,
including those considered desirable by overseers, couldn't "get by" the company's employment office; and Murrie admitted that the decision to become a self-insurer under
the Workmen's Compensation law had, "no doubt, made us more careful than we were
some years ago."   On the other hand, a public official in Danville said that giving a work
card to the wife of one of the strike leaders "created a very fine impression and will go
far toward allaying the idea of discrimination in the minds of those old employees who
have not been able to get on" (H. T. Williams to R. R. West, April 11, 1933).

week ending	division	employees	average hours	average earnings (cents per hour)

Table 13. Wages and Employment, 1932-1940

week ending	division	employees	average hours	average earnings (cents per hour)
1931: Dec. 26	DR	3,206	*	28.7
	R	1,294	35.86	29.3
1932: Jan. 20	DR	3,167	*	25.9
	R	1,412	51.73	26.0
1933: Feb. 18	DR	3,185	*	22.7
	R	1,801	49.37	22.6
1933: June 17	DR	3,263	*	22.5
	R	1,860	54.71	22.6
1933: July 22	R	2,407	35.84	33.7
1934: Jan. 6	R	2,219	37.25	35.4
1935: Sept. 7	DR	6,048	*	35.8
	R	2,521	35.61	35.6
1936: Nov. 28	R	2,746	29.93	38.9
1937: Sept. 18	DR	7,225	*	43.9
	R	2,870	*	43.1
1938: Nov. 5	DR	7,167	*	38.6
	R	2,144	*	38.5
1939: Dec. 16	DR	7,415	*	41.2
	R	2,398	*	39.2

* Not available.

Table 14. Average Earnings of Male and Female Employees
(cents per hour)

week ending	male, unskilled		male, semi-skilled and skilled		all female	
	number	earnings	number	earnings	number	earnings
Feb. 28, 1931	160	23.9	667	33.5	439	24.1
May 30, 1931	176	24.3	744	34.2	459	24.6
Jan. 30, 1932	196	21.9	749	29.5	467	21.9
Dec. 10, 1932	278	21.9	1097	28.5	672	21.4

vanced only 11 per cent, since the maximum work week dropped from 55 hours to 40 hours. The 27.3 per cent reduction in hours required an increase of 37.5 per cent in hourly rates to yield the same full-time earnings. Apparently, some hourly rates were adjusted to achieve just this result. On the other hand, many rates, particularly those at the lower end of the wage scale, were increased more than 37.5 per cent.

The following changes in the pay of selected employees in the sewing room suggests that generally the rates of increase in both hourly and weekly earnings were greater for those below the Code minimum than for those above it:

hourly rates (cents per hour)		full-time earnings:		percentage increase:	
pre-Code	under Code	55 hours (dollars)	40 hours (dollars)	hourly rate	weekly earnings
17.00	32.50	9.35	13.00	91.2	39.0
18.50	32.50	10.18	13.00	75.7	27.8
18.50	34.00	10.18	13.60	83.8	33.7
19.50	32.50	10.73	13.00	66.7	21.2
20.00	32.50	11.00	13.00	62.5	18.2
20.50	32.50	11.28	13.00	58.5	15.3
21.75	34.00	11.96	13.60	56.3	13.7
23.00	32.50	12.65	13.00	41.3	2.8
24.25	37.50	13.38	15.00	51.5	12.1
29.75	45.00	16.36	16.40	51.3	.2
37.00	51.00	20.35	20.40	37.8	.2

In determining new piece rates (under the Code) the management assumed that production in 8 hours would be 80 per cent of the normal 10-hour output. But the new schedules of piece rates revised, obviously by design, the job-to-job differences in piece rates. For example: one job (in the sheet put-up room) had a standard of 400 units per day, rated at .52 cent per unit, equivalent to weekly earnings of $11.44. Under the Code, 320 units were priced at .84 cent, or $13.44 for a 40-hour week. Another job, with a normal daily load of 200 units at .85 cent, or $9.35 for 55 hours, was revised to 160 units at 1.7 cents, representing $13.60 for a full week.

The adoption of two-shift operations[90] increased the number of employees from slightly over 5,000 in June 1933 to 6,700 at the end of the year. As business improved, additional workers were hired: in September 1935 the payroll had 8,500 names, and in September 1937, the number passed 10,000. Expansion of employment required a considerable amount of recruiting and training. "Some trained textile workers were available," West reported, "but a large portion of the

[90] The first shift, commencing in July 1933, was 6:30-11:30 A.M. and 12:00 M. to 3:00 P.M.; the second shift, 3:00-6:00 P.M. and 6:30-11:30 P.M.

second shift had to be trained for their work . . . this problem has been met in quite a satisfactory way, and we are certain that our second shift will be operated economically."[91] Furthermore, the president believed that the eight-hour shifts furnished "a wonderful opportunity for those living in the outlying district to obtain employment in the mills; thus adding to the family income, the other part of which is derived from the farms."

In March 1934, the Cotton Textile Institute compiled wage data from a number of northern and southern mills, which showed Dan River's full-time (40 hours) weekly earnings $0.81 below the southern average. But the unweighted average of earnings by jobs was pulled down by Dan River's extremely low rates for apprentices ($7.56) and cleaners ($9.00); Dan River also paid much less ($16.16) than the southern average ($22.01) for office employees. On the other hand, average earnings for loom fixers ($22.08) were slightly above the southern average and for "outside help" and the repair shop crew, considerably above the average for all southern mills.[92]

Rates below the southern minimum of 30 cents an hour were permissible in the cases of outside laborers, cleaners, substandard workers, and learners. If an apprentice were retained, he had to be advanced to the Code minimum after six weeks.

Although in September 1934, the directors authorized the president to make an upward adjustment in "some brackets of wages in the Mill," the average seems to have held close to 36 cents an hour until 1936. Weekly earnings, however, were adversely affected by curtailment, since the company generally "spread the work" instead of closing selected units completely. Thus, when machine hours were reduced 25 per cent under a directive of the Code Authority (June, July, and August, 1934), Dan River operated two six-hour shifts, five days a week.

[91] *Twenty-fifth Annual Report of the Riverside & Dan River Cotton Mills, Incorporated* (Danville, 1934).

[92] In August 1933 the southern average was 33.7 cents an hour, or $13.48 for a 40-hour week (*Monthly Labor Review*, vol. 46, pp. 36-47). For several job classifications, as the following data show, Dan River's averages fell below the southern average (average earnings, cents per hour):

	North	Dan River	South
learners	22.1	21.5	21.1
spinners	37.6	33.9	31.8
weavers	43.2	34.0	38.7
shipping room	44.4	33.4	35.2
card grinders	48.2	42.6	42.3
loom fixers	61.0	53.3	48.2

In the wake of the Supreme Court's annulment of the National Industrial Recovery Act (May 27, 1935) leaders of the textile industry professed a willingness to go on as though the Code were still effective. West proposed an unofficial code with a 30-cent minimum wage, a minimum employing age of sixteen years, and operations limited to two 40-hour shifts.[93] But in May 1936, Dan River's president complained to Donald Comer of the "continued breaking down" of wage and hour standards. "I, for one," he said, "cannot stand by and see conditions revert to the dog fight which existed in '31 and '32 . . . . In the absence of the ability of the Industry to persuade its members to stand by those standards, I can see no other alternative than to request Congress to devise some means of setting up legal standards and enforcing them."

In West's opinion, however, three attempts to apply federal legislation to the problem were ill-advised. In February 1935 he opposed the Black thirty-hour bill, which would have limited the work-week in most industries to 30 hours, with the same pay as for 40 hours. Testifying before a Senate committee, West said it "would be fantastic to attempt to cram into this [the textile] industry additional employees." He estimated that average hourly earnings had risen 78 per cent above March 1933.[94]

Now, a further increase of 33⅓ per cent in hourly rates, pyramided as it would bound to be, as a practical matter, in the wholesale and retail markets, would increase consumer resistance and would in all probability be the finishing touch to our export trade and to our efforts to regain that trade . . . . A candid consideration of the provisions of this bill and their probable effect on employment and unemployment therefore leads on to the conclusion that after all, this is not a bill to relieve unemployment to any great extent, but rather a bill which will result in decreasing production and limiting the individual workman's capacity to earn.[95]

[93] This was the basis of the "pledge" which the Cotton Textile Institute endeavored to persuade its members to accept, except that northern firms were to maintain a minimum wage of 32.5 cents an hour. It proved impossible to get 90 per cent of the spindles in any one of the twelve groups in the industry to ratify the pledge (*Hearings before a Subcommittee of the Committee on Labor, House of Representatives, 74th Congress, 2nd Session, on H. R. 9072* [Washington, 1936], pp. 424-426).

[94] In March-April 1933 the average hourly wage in the cotton textile industry was 21.4 cents an hour; in March 1935 it was 38.1 cents, an increase of 78 per cent. In the same period average weekly earnings rose from $9.54 to $13.52. (*In the Matter of Survey of Cotton Textile Industry Problems . . . Statement submitted in behalf of the Cotton Textile Industry Committee and the Cotton Textile Institute, Inc.*, mimeographed, 1935).

[95] *Hearings before a Subcommittee of the Committee on the Judiciary, United States Senate, 74th Congress, 1st Session, on S. 87* (Washington, 1935) , pp. 421-422. The bill was passed in the Senate but defeated (as the Black-Connery Bill) in the House of Representatives. Curiously, West had stated privately that the first of the year (1935) might be "an

While the Senate debated the Black bill, the House of Representatives began hearings on the Ellenbogen bill, described as a measure "to rehabilitate and stabilize labor conditions in the textile industry." Under unregulated conditions, proponents of the bill argued, "wages below a decent standard of health and comfort, excessive hours, child labor, overburdensome work assignments, other unhealthy and demoralizing conditions of work, the denial of the right of self-organization and collective bargaining, and excess production prevail in the textile industry, cause wide-spread unemployment and heavy financial expense to the Government of the United States, and constitute a menace to the health, safety, morals, welfare, and comfort of the citizens of the United States."

Testifying against the Ellenbogen bill, President West entered a vigorous protest over the aspersive language of the measure, "because an industry that employs some million of people, which provides the livelihood of this million people and their dependents, and which supports by its taxes whole townships, counties, and in some cases States, can hardly be looked upon as menace to American life." He was equally positive that the proposed minimum wage of $15 for a maximum work-week of 35 hours was uneconomic. "The question," he said, "of what a minimum basic wage should be is not for me to determine, whether it should be $15 a week or $10 or $12 a week. That in the long run will be determined by what the goods can be obtained for and wages that can be afforded to be paid."[96]

Conditions improved, and wage increases were general before the end of 1936.[97] Dan River's scale went up 10 per cent in November; and in March 1937, because of a "considerable shortage of skilled labor" and in view of the success labor organizers were having in Dan-

opportune time for the Industry to recommend a basic 35-hour week with the same weekly pay as now being paid for 40 hours" (R. R. West to W. D. Anderson, Dec. 11, 1934).

[96] *Hearings . . . on H. R. 9072*, pp. 432-453. A revision of the Ellenbogen Bill, which would have established a National Textile Commission to regulate the industry, was introduced in the 75th Congress. Dan River's president did not testify in opposition to the measure, as did the executives of Erwin, the Cone mills, and many other textile leaders; but West wrote Congressman Kent E. Keller, chairman of the subcommittee, that he questioned "very much the wisdom of legislation such as this having to do with a particular industry. I am in favor of Federal legislation which will make it possible to set maximum hours of work and minimum rates of wages, but I believe the best interest of all concerned would be better served by having such legislation made applicable to all industries" (R. R. West to K. E. Keller, April 27, 1937). See also *Hearings before the Subcommittee of the Committee on Labor, House of Representatives, 75th Congress, 1st Session, on H. R. 238* (Washington, 1937).

[97] On Nov. 14 Herman Cone wrote R. R. West that, because of impending increases in wages in South Carolina and New England, "it looks like we are going to have to go ahead a little faster than we had anticipated the other night."

ville, numerous changes in job and piece rates were announced.[98] This
gave a substantial lift to average earnings. For the week ending May
15, 1937, the company paid 9,800 employees an average of 43.40 cents
an hour; and for the week ending December 18 the average pay of
9,923 employees reached 43.95 cents an hour. The industry average
(North and South) was 42.0 cents in May; 42.3 cents an hour in December.[99]

As Table 16 reveals, Dan River's scales for skilled, semi-skilled, and
unskilled wage earners were appreciably above the southern average,
though the margin was slight in the case of the unskilled. The male-
female differential is pronounced in two cases, but for some reason the
semi-skilled female at Dan River earned more than the semi-skilled
male.[100]

Table 16. Average Hourly Earnings: September 1937
(cents per hour)

	Dan River	southern mills
men		
skilled	53.20	49.26
semi-skilled	41.58	38.08
unskilled	32.86	31.83
women		
skilled	46.13	42.49
semi-skilled	42.74	35.36
unskilled	31.55	31.30

Despite persistently adverse business conditions, the wage gains of
1936-1937 were maintained until mid-1938. In July hourly and piece-
rates were reduced 12.5 per cent[101]—the fourth and final pay cut in the
decade 1930-1940. This left the "cream" of Dan River's wage earners—
electricians, machinists, and welders—with a base rate of 70 cents an

[98] For the week ending Dec. 12, 1936 the average hourly wage was 39.2 cents, .9 cent
above the average for a group of northern and southern print-cloth mills, as reported by
the Cotton Textile Institute. In April and May the president received several letters,
with long lists of signatures, expressing the workers' appreciation of the increases in pay.
[99] *Monthly Labor Review*, vol. 53 (1941), p. 1495. An April (1937) study placed the
northern average at 48.9 cents an hour; the southern at 38.1 cents (*Labor Information
Bulletin*, vol. 5, no. 5 (May 1938), pp. 8-10).
[100] The data are taken from President West's files, and I have not been able to verify
the source of the average for Southern mills.
[101] It amounted to more than 12.5 per cent for 177 employees.

hour; but the modal rate for hourly workers dropped from 36 cents to 31.5 cents an hour. A tally of the payroll for the week ending July 9 showed 423 employees (390 Negro and 33 white) earning less than 30 cents an hour. The lowest rate (three laborers) was 15.5 cents, while 345 sweepers and scrubbers received 23 cents an hour.

Averages conceal the full significance of the loss of earning power from reduced wages and shortened hours during the 1937-1938 depression. By September 1937 inventories were accumulating alarmingly, but the directors, "recognizing the demoralizing effect and great expense of curtailment by closing down in the Mill for even a short period of time," decided to continue operating "as usual." In October the board still found itself "reluctant" to put workers on short time; but in December, confronted with the "virtual stoppage of orders," the directors instructed the management to go on a three-day week. The following year business failed to improve, and the mill worked 13 weeks of 16 hours, 14 weeks of 24 hours, 24 weeks of 32 hours, and closed one full week. In response to queries about workers' morale, Attorney Harris testified that there was "no open dissatisfaction" and President West thought the "people as a whole appreciated the situation and were as patient and uncomplaining as could be expected." In February and again in March the company waived one week's rent. The management brought to the directors' attention "some very serious cases of distress among our people" and the board appropriated $6,000 for the president's use in relieving hardship cases.[102]

Efforts to put floors under wages were renewed in Congress, and in October 1938 the Fair Labor Standards Act imposed a minimum industrial wage of 25 cents an hour. President West became a member of the textile industry committee—the first such committee constituted under the Act—to work out permanent wage standards on an industry-wide basis. After months of wrangling over the North-South wage differential, the committee finally agreed to a uniform minimum of 32.5 cents an hour, effective in October 1939. Dan River raised all rates already at or above 32.5 cents, adding 3.1 cents an hour to average earnings. For the week ending October 23, 1939, average earnings per hour were 41.2 cents.

A study of some 50 occupational wage-rates, following the increase of October 1939, reveals a narrowing of the spread between the lowest

---

[102] Apparently, only the yarders and folders in the piecegoods department were hardy enough to complain that the 1937 pay cut was "not justified."

and the highest rates of pay. In July 1933 (under the Code) the loom fixer earned almost three times as much as sweepers and scrubbers. In October 1939 the loom fixer's pay was less than twice that of the lowest-paid employee. The average loom fixer earned more than the lowest-paid second hand, but the range of second-hand's pay (1940) was from 55 cents to 81.5 cents an hour. Furthermore, the highest-paid second hand earned slightly more for a full week than the lowest-paid overseer. Overseer scales in March 1940 ran from a low of $32 per week in carding and spinning rooms to a high of $63 a week in weaving. Master mechanics earned from $50 to $72 per week.

The minimum wage in the cotton textile industry advanced to 37.5 cents an hour in May 1941. The average wage (North and South), which was 41.0 cents in November 1939, edged up to 41.5 cents during 1940. Dan River's average hourly earnings of 41.0 cents stayed slightly above the southern average of 39.9 cents but appreciably below the northern average of 47.4 cents (December 1940).[103]

Average weekly earnings improved after 1938, with generally higher rates of operations. In 1939 Dan River operated 15 weeks full time, 29 weeks of 24 hours, and seven weeks of 32 hours. The mills closed completely for ten days in June 1940, but employment rose during the last half of the year and the average work week occasionally exceeded forty hours. A third shift, introduced in one or two departments in 1939, was expanded in 1940 to employ a maximum of 995 employees. The distribution of workers by shift (December 1940) was as follows:

shift	Riverside	Dan River
1	1,350	3,634
2	1,033	2,225
3	357	626

On December 30 idle looms on the first shift numbered 1,411 at both divisions, or 13.5 per cent of the looms in place. Assuming other idle machinery in the same proportion as looms, operating at 86.5 per cent of capacity required 4,948 employees; and operations at capacity would have employed 5,760 workers. Mathematically, three full shifts would have furnished employment for 17,280 operatives.

A "Schedule of Information by Employers" filed with a Senate sub-

[103] *Monthly Labor Review*, vol. 53 (Dec. 1941), pp. 1495, 1501 and vol. 59 (Oct. 1944) p. 826.

committee in the fall of 1938 showed the age distribution of 9,893 employees (5,617 males and 4,276 females), as follows:

over 60 years	197	30 – 40	2,861
50 – 60	536	20 – 30	4,267
40 – 50	1,346	under 20	686

The average age (excluding minors) was thirty-four years, and the average period of employment at Dan River was 13.5 years. Thirteen hundred and eighteen employees had worked for the company over ten years; 856 had been employed less than a year. Negro workers numbered 926 in 1939 but only 750 in 1940. There were no women workers under eighteen years of age or male employees under sixteen.

Efforts to regulate working conditions by state law were consistently opposed by the Dan River management. A bill calling for an eight-hour day for women, together with proposals to tighten the controls on stream pollution and to tax industrial raw materials, were the main measures "detrimental to your company's interest" which the 1932 legislature debated. "We were successful," the management told the directors, "in defeating all three of these measures."[104] The eight-hour-day bill was reintroduced in 1936. Harris spent fifteen days in Richmond and reported his success in working against this and two other measures inimical to the company's business.[105]

Strangely, when the proposal reappeared in the 1938 legislature, Harris thought it would be futile to oppose it. The law finally enacted was a compromise: amending the statute of 1890, which had set the maximum working day for women at ten hours, the legislature prohibited factory work in excess of forty-eight hours a week or more than nine hours a day.[106]

Welfare in the City and Village

In recognition of its social responsibilities to the community, the mill continued its traditional policy of supporting selected religious

[104] In February Attorney Harris asked the president to instruct superintendents to go through the mill and get a batch of letters from women workers to send to the Senate. Harris proposed that the letters, though not stereotyped, should say in effect: "I understand somebody has brought up a bill to keep us from working more than eight hours. We do not want any such bill passed."

[105] M. K. Harris to R. R. West, March 10, 1936. The Richmond *Times-Dispatch* called the 1936 General Assembly "one of the most reactionary legislatures . . . . The magnitude and potency of the lobbies which descended upon the Capitol is one explanation . . . ."

[106] *Acts of Assembly, Virginia, 1938* (Richmond, 1938), pp. 770-771.

and charitable organizations. Annual appropriations of $2,500 to Hill
Top Sanitarium, $500 to Wesley House, and $150 to Grace Methodist
Church were approved by the directors as a matter of course. These
outlays, the executive committee observed, were "not contributions in
the ordinary sense but legitimate expenditures for the advancement of
your company's interest." Wesley House received additional donations
of $100 in 1935 and $250 in 1938. Irregular contributions to other
religious bodies are doubtless not all included in the following: $200
to Calvary Baptist Church (1935), $125 to Schoolfield Methodist
Church (1935), $250 to Southall Baptist Church (1940). In 1937 the
president was authorized to make a donation to the North Danville
Baptist Tabernacle; and regular contributions were made to the Riverside Mission, conducted by the Reverend O. A. Guinn.[107] Many requests for help were denied, especially in the depression years when
need was most acute. In hopes of getting out from under an $1,800
debt to Dan River and a $400 bank debt in 1932, Burton Memorial
Church offered to sell the manse to the company. The offer was rejected. Early in 1940 the Burton Church was destroyed by fire and
rebuilt at its present location, on a site donated by the corporation.

Riverside and Dan River Mills was part of another community, the
city of New York, which had welfare problems. In 1938 the company's
contribution to the Greater New York Fund was $2,000, and the same
amount was subscribed in 1939.

Welfare programs

The amounts devoted to the religious and charitable objectives just
discussed were separate from the company's budget for its own welfare
programs. A summary of welfare expenditures, together with data on
the village and housing accounts, is presented in Table 17.

Direct outlays for the welfare work rose from the depression low of
$23,899 (1932) to over $60,000 in 1940, suffering only one sharp reduction (1936). These are net amounts; many of the activities were
partially self-supporting. Thus, in 1932 the Y.M.C.A. realized $7,639
from memberships, room rents, lockers, baths, bowling, billiards, and
the rental of the motion-picture theater. The mill's contribution to

[107] Upon receiving a $250 donation in 1938, Guinn reported that he was aiding 72
needy families. On one occasion the president's secretary sent the Mission an unspecified amount of "conscious" (i.e., "conscience") money. This was a fund made up of
voluntary remittances by former employees who admitted to petty thefts of cloth or
padded payrolls.

Table 17. Village and Welfare Accounts, 1932-1940
(thousands of dollars)

year	welfare division expense	depreciation	village expense	rental income, net Riverside	Dan River	net cost, village and welfare
1932	24	30	27	15	68	3*
1933	26	80	27	14	67	51
1934	47	80	32	17	64	78
1935	57	72	43	17	49	107
1936	54	79	43	17	60	99
1937	36	57	50	11	35	96
1938	51	57	48	10	63	83
1939	53	57	44	11	73	70
1940	61	72	†	7‡	26‡	165

Error in totals due to rounding.
* Gain
† Charged to Rental Income
‡ Loss

the "Y" was $5,358 in 1932 and $6,216 in 1933. In 1937, which Secretary Spessard called "one of our best years," the "Y" took in $20,475 and required a subvention of $7,800, approximately the equivalent of the salaries of the general secretary, program secretary, assistant program secretaries, and a bookkeeper-stenographer. Membership stood at 1,248 in 1937.

In 1932 Hylton Hall required a subsidy of $4,845, the amount by which revenues of $35,613 fell short of operating costs. The next year receipts increased to $49,833 and the company's contribution dropped to a mere $715. The budget for 1939 anticipated income of $51,400, sufficient to cover all but $600 of the running expenses. Hylton Hall was expected to have 175 paying "guests," but in September 1940 the Hall housed only 127 men and women, of whom 14 had been unemployed for the past two months.

Support of the public schools in Schoolfield absorbed close to a third of all appropriations for welfare. School population rose sharply with the commencement of a second shift in the mills, and in 1933 the company gave the Pittsylvania County School Board land on which to build an annex to the Baltimore Avenue School.[108] Additional land

[108] West wrote to the superintendent of schools that "the step which the School Board took last year in enlarging the Baltimore Avenue School has proved to be a great blessing to this community" (R. R. West to F. B. Watson, May 2, 1934).

was made available for a vocational education building (1936), and in 1939 the company donated the site of the Wynn Hotel, which had burned the summer before, for the Schoolfield High School.

The mill-supported kindergarten, a casualty of the depression, was reopened in the fall of 1937. The budget for the first year called for expenditure of $1,250 for a 32-week term, but $448 would be paid by parents at the rate of 25 cents per week. The kindergarten report for 1938-1939 showed a cost of $1,203, of which $311 was paid by patrons. Average enrollment was 51.

The idea of a textile school probably originated with President West, who was concerned over the shortage of qualified workers after the second shift was introduced. The Danville Textile School opened late in 1935, using a room on the fourth floor of Mill No. 1 at Dan River Division. W. D. Vincent was the first principal. Forty-one male students, all workers on the second shift, were enrolled in the two-year course in March 1936. Partly state-supported, the school was under the jurisdiction of the state supervisor of trade and industrial education.[109]

The company's loan of four old looms to the Hughes Memorial School, a school and home for orphans, contributed modestly to the training of future textile workers.

Fifty-four Dan River employees enrolled with the International Correspondence Schools completed "two or more units" in 1939.

In 1931 Virginia's industrial compensation and liability agency completed a survey of Dan River's safety organization. At this time the mills had a general safety committee of five, which met monthly to review accident experience and make recommendations for accident prevention. There were also five subcommittees charged with the weekly inspection of designated departments. The state officials found the organization inadequate: it did not "meet with standard requirements as outlined by the Rating Bureau." Measures were taken to comply with the recommendations of the experts, and in 1934 a representative of the Industrial Commission complimented the management for the "efforts you are putting forth to prevent industrial accidents." In contrast with early experience under the Workmen's Compensation Act, when the Commission held as many as ten hearings in Danville, the "record made in the last few years is really phenomenal and . . .

[109] A course for girls was introduced in the fall of 1936. The school did not escape criticism. Someone in Danville wrote Mrs. Roosevelt that the company was using the school to get goods manufactured with cheap labor.

reflects great credit upon Mr. F. Ernest Murrie . . . , who seems to have the happy faculty of enforcing rules and regulations without the usual amount of friction." The Commission was also "impressed with the cleanliness and ventilation of your mills."

A feature of the safety organization, which by 1939 included the Ladies' Safety Committee and the Junior General Safety Committee, was the annual safety banquet. F. E. Murrie was secretary of most, if not all, of the numerous safety committees.

A large part of the company's outlay for medical services and the operation of clinics was transferred from "welfare" to the workmen's compensation account. After a year's experience as a self-insurer, in October 1932 the company elected to purchase workmen's compensation insurance. In President Pritchett's opinion, the risk of an exceptional loss was not worth the apparent savings in premiums. President West took the opposite position, and in 1933 the company returned to self-insurance, using reinsurance to cover the risk of extraordinary claims.

The workmen's compensation insurance account for 1939 shows the following distribution of expenditures:

medical			
	Dr. Crumpler; clinic nurses	$4,537	
	premium credit for clinics	4,647	
	outside doctors and nurses	1,352	
	hospitals	2,407	
	X-ray, drugs, braces, etc.	1,282	
	travel expenses (Richmond)	147	
	reserves	652	15,024
compensation			10,467
safety promotion			2,787
fixed costs			
	bond	250	
	taxes (Industrial Commission)	1,384	
	reinsurance	1,311	
			2,945
total			31,223

Total costs represented 67.1 per cent of the gross premium that would have been charged by a private carrier; the actual saving was $10,600 out of the net premium of $41,823. Over a period of seven years as a self-insurer the company saved $186,362, including credits of $34,593 allowed by the Commission in consideration of the maintenance of clinics. The average saving was about 50 per cent of the commercial premiums.

Monthly accident reports are extant for a short period. There were no lost-time accidents at either Dan River or Riverside Division in January 1939; in February the rate was 3.2 accidents per million hours at Dan River and 4.9 accidents per million hours at Riverside. Dan River's accident rate jumped to 7.9 in July 1939 and was 7.8 in July 1940; at Riverside Division the rates for the same two months were 3.9 and 3.5 per million hours. The data are too scattered, however, to conclude that Riverside Division was really a safer place to work. Accidents for the year 1939 totaled 861, of which two were fatal and 61 caused loss of time.[110]

Secretary Spessard of the Schoolfield Y.M.CA. seems to have taken the initiative in exploring the possibilities of providing workers with insurance for medical service and hospital care. In April 1936 Spessard reported that an employees' committee had voted to recommend a group policy offered by the Protective Life Insurance Company that would pay benefits for non-accidental disability and death. No action was taken by the management, but in December 1937 the Employees' Benefit Association of the Riverside and Dan River Cotton Mills was set up as a "non-profit coperative organization." The company made payroll deductions of the dues of $.25 per week per member; otherwise the organization was self-supporting. About 30 per cent of the employees joined the Association at the beginning. Benefits included payments on account of hospital care, surgery, maternity care, laboratory fees and X-rays.

At the same time the company gave some thought to the problem of providing systematically for "sick and physically impaired employees." The pension list as of December 1938 comprised two former overseers over 65 and a former superintendent and an office worker, both retired by illness before reaching 65. Payments at the rate of $11,000 annually were being made to six retired workers in May 1939;

[110] The case of Riverside and Dan River Cotton Mills v. Thaxton was settled in the Virginia Supreme Court, Jan. 11, 1934. Charles M. Thaxton, an electrician, was electrocuted while working for the company in May 1932. The claim of his survivors for compensation was upheld by the Industrial Commission but denied on appeal to the Supreme Court on the ground that Thaxton had been guilty of "wilful misconduct" in working near high-tension wires without pulling the switch (172 S.E. 261).

later in the year one of these was dropped from the roll and another's pension was cut from $100 to $50 a month.

Housing

Net income from the rental of company houses fell from $83,382 in 1932 to $46,386 in 1937 but recovered to $83,740 in 1939. In 1933, 1938, and 1940 tenants were excused from paying rent for several weeks, in view of the low level of employment; but the principal fluctuations in net rental income responded to the uneven rate of expenditure on maintenance and improvements charged to income. Sanitary sewer lines were provided for a number of residences, including 33 houses on Park Avenue; but the major project of furnishing the entire village with sewer system and inside plumbing, for which Lockwood, Greene drew up plans in 1938, was held in abeyance.[111]

In 1940 village expense—the cost of police and fire protection and other public services—was charged to income from rents, creating a loss on the combined accounts of $32,718. In 1937 also the village expense exceeded net rental income, but it is not clear that the entire amount of these community services was properly charged against housing income. The confusion of the accounts makes it difficult to estimate the rate of return on the company's investment in housing. At Dan River Division net rental income averaged $50,375 in 1932–1940, or about 3.2 per cent of the estimated replacement value, as of November 1933, of houses, sidewalks, streets, lighting, and water and sewer systems. This calculation undoubtedly overstates the profitability of the investment, inasmuch as new facilities were added before the end of the period and some part of village expense should rightfully be charged against rental income.[112]   Net rental income at Riverside

[111] "Budget for Construction of Sanitary Sewer System, including sewer, house plumbing, bathrooms, and pumping station in Schoolfield Village" (Feb. 18, 1938). The estimated cost of furnishing these facilities to 566 houses was $250,662.

[112] The replacement value of tenements and welfare property in Schoolfield was broken down into the following accounts (Nov. 27, 1933):

houses	$1,159,200
sidewalks	56,290
streets	218,067
lighting	40,407
water system	51,945
sewer system	25,067
Y.M.C.A. building	40,000
welfare building	20,000
Hylton Hall	250,000
fire station	15,000
total	1,875,976

Division averaged 3.7 per cent on an estimated investment of $300,000.

Some statistics of company housing are presented in Table 18. At this time (November 1933), the total population of Schoolfield Village was 4,854.

Table 18. Company Housing, 1933

	Riverside division	Dan River division
	per cent	
employees housed	15	43
employees owning homes	40	10
employees renting non-company houses	45	47
company houses with		
electric lights	95	100
running water	100	100*
sanitary toilets, inside	45	11
sanitary toilets, outside	27	89
surface toilets	28	0
bath rooms	45	11
	number	
dwellings	110	840
employees housed	330	2,182†
rooms	588	3,488
rent per room per week	$.56‡	$.33⅓ to 1.32§

* 89 per cent in yard taps
† Including 202 in Hylton Hall
‡ Not including water and lights
§ Including water and lights

There were two major additions to Schoolfield housing in this period. In the fall of 1935 the president proposed to build a steam-heated apartment house to provide accommodations for "selected families." The directors "seemed to think it would be worth while to try out this plan," and in the fall of 1936 the H. R. Fitzgerald Apartments on Greensboro Road were ready for occupancy. During the same year the directors appropriated $50,000 for a number of cottages for skilled workers, but President West had asked for about twice this amount in order to build fifty new homes.

On several occasions during West's administration the management considered proposals to sell the houses in Schoolfield; but the president was never "able to convince myself that it would be at all wise." Under the Code the industry was required "to consider the question

of plans for eventual employee ownership of homes in mill villages"
and make a report to the N.R.A. before January 1, 1934. West was a
member of a subcommittee of the Industry Committee which made the
report. On the basis of replies received from an elaborate question-
naire sent to mills owning villages, the committee concluded that it
was "impracticable at this time to offer any plan looking to home
ownership." The objections were threefold: (*a*) previous attempts of
mills to sell their houses had failed. "The employees, with few exceptions, have shown no interest in purchasing . . . . Ownership of a home
in a rural mill village . . . limits occupational opportunity." (*b*) With
few exceptions, employees preferred to live in mill-owned houses.
(*c*) The mills were generally unwilling to sell, since an employee-owner
could allow the property to pass into the hands of "those who may not
be interested in the operation of the mill and indeed into the hands of
interests that may be subversive of those things that are best for the
morals of the community and the peace and welfare of the town."[113]

Coal and wood

The Schoolfield coal and wood yard, the cloth store, and the canteen service, though operated mainly for the workers' convenience,
consistently showed profitable operations. The cloth store made only
$4,593 in 1932, but earnings rose steadily to a peak of $26,844 in 1937.
The canteen, which was taken over by the company in 1938, netted
$11,346 in 1938, $17,000 in 1939, and $18,515 in 1940. The coal and
wood yard, under the management of W. H. Dodson, greatly expanded
its operations, selling gas, oil, tires, and automotive supplies to the increasing number of car-owning employees. For the sake of "giving our
people a decided advantage over the outside market," Dodson also
stocked washing machines, radios, fertilizer, stoves, and (in the Christmas season) toys. Gross sales for three years (1934-1936) totaled $595,-
000, and profits ran as high as $37,000 a year. This was "big business"
as compared with the neighborhood store, and in October 1936 the
management gave in to the pressure of local merchants and restricted
the coal and wood yard to the sale of fuel.[114]

[113] Discussing the report, the magazine *Cotton* (Dec. 1933) pointed to a Bureau of
Labor Statistics study, which failed to show any significant difference in labor turnover
between mills with villages and those without company-owned housing. The growing
use of the automobile and shorter hours of work made a small farm or a rural home
much more attractive than a house in the shadow of the mill.
[114] The decision "took me completely by surprise," Dodson protested (W. H. Dodson
to R. R. West, Oct. 31, 1936).

Management

In accepting the presidency, following the death of H. R. Fitzgerald, J. I. Pritchett agreed to serve only until a trained textile executive could be secured for the position. No progress was made in the search for a candidate in 1931. In February, Director J. M. Miller expressed the opinion that it would be a mistake to select a Northerner—"they do not know how to handle Southern people." If any Northerner was being considered at this time, I do not know who it was; but President Pritchett's continued interest in a merger created the possibility of a transfusion of northern blood into the Dan River management. Miller thought George S. Harris would be a "good man" and argued that the relatively small size of the Exposition Cotton Mill, which Harris had managed during the 1920's, was "not altogether an index of his ability to handle a larger one."[115] Curiously, H. R. Fitzgerald had discussed with Harris a place in the Dan River organization but feared it would not work out, since he "would only be second in command." In February 1932 Allan McNab, president of New England Southern Corporation, declined the offer of the presidency for personal reasons.

President Pritchett died on September 25, 1932, from injuries received in an automobile accident. The choice of his successor was delayed scarcely a week. At the board meeting of October 5 J. M. Miller offered the motion to elect Robert R. West president and treasurer. West, in turn, nominated the general sales manager, George P. Ray; but Ray declined and seconded the nomination of West.[116] George W. Robertson was elected vice-president, retaining his position as general superintendent. At the same time Miller was chosen chairman of the board of directors. To make it clear that Miller's duties were not merely nominal, as had been those of the late Chairman Schoolfield, the directors granted him "all of the authority now specified by the by-laws and, in addition thereto . . . general charge, authority and control of the financial affairs and policies of the company, subject to the Board of Directors." Specifically, the board required that all notes and other obligations for borrowed money should be countersigned by the chairman.

[115] At this time Harris was connected with the Hunter Manufacturing and Commission Co.

[116] Born in the District of Columbia and educated at Harvard, West had been treasurer of the Lancaster Mills in Clinton, Massachusetts. Apparently, he met the test of knowing how to "handle Southern people" by reason of his three years' experience at Dan River.

The board meeting ended with the adoption of the following resolution:

> *Resolved,* That this Board expresses the utmost confidence in Mr. Robert R. West, as President and Treasurer of this Company, and in Mr. George P. Ray, as Vice President in charge of sales, and that they desire to record on the Minutes of this meeting, the intention of this Board to continue the present management of this organization in so far as its authority, conditions, and results will warrant.
>
> The Board looks upon the present organization and management as a permanent[117] one, and it believes that with the harmonious cooperation of all the members of this organization such as has existed in the past few years that the developments of the future will fully warrant the views herein expressed.

After amending the by-laws, permitting the election of a vice-president who was not a director, in 1935 the board named Henry Roediger vice-president and cotton buyer. At the same time D. A. Overbey, Jr., formerly a salesman in the Atlanta Office, became assistant treasurer. Leslie H. Browder, credit manager in the New York office, became an assistant treasurer in 1939. In November 1938, M. K. Harris, who had been responsible for most of the company's legal work since 1910, resigned. He was succeeded as counsel by Frank Talbott, Jr.

Relations between the board of directors and the management remained cordial throughout the trying years of operations under the Code as well as during the two years (1936-1937) of comparative prosperity. To a hypercritical stockholder, Chairman Miller wrote in February 1936: "Mr. West is an exceptionally good President and Manager and Mr. Ray an exceptionally good salesman." The severe recession in 1938, combined with difficult personnel problems, undermined the board's confidence in the management and culminated in the resignation of President West in 1940.

In November 1938 Chairman Miller called the directors' attention to defects in the sales organization which had come to light during a prolonged illness of Vice-president Ray. L. H. Browder was advanced to the position of credit manager in the New York office, and John M. Hughlett moved from the Atlanta office to New York to take over some of Ray's work. But the whole question of managerial organization, in Danville as well as in New York, seemed to require an impartial study by someone not connected with the company. Probably because

---

[117] In the directors' minutes "permanent" has been scratched and "ideal" written above it.

he was a banker, Miller's choice of an expert was F. W. Shibley, vice-president of the Bankers Trust Company. Shibley came to Danville, visited the mills, and discussed with the directors "some of the things important to successful operation of a manufacturing plant." Without mentioning any personal shortcomings in the officers or staff, he called attention to the "imperative necessity" of keeping inventories down, the advantages of careful controls over costs, and the desirability of using up-to-date machinery. Shibley also recommended closer contacts between management on the one hand and overseers and operatives on the other. The company ought to cultivate some "humanizing" forces in dealing with the workers and not cut wages every time sales slumped.

With the Shibley report in hand, the executive committee of the board of directors bestirred itself. In March 1939 the committee reported on two conferences with the president, in the course of which they told him their "aims and objects were to cooperate with him in every possible way to improve conditions and to assume, so far as we were able to do, a part of the responsibilities for the conduct and success of the business." Although admitting that they "should thoroughly familiarize themselves with the various departments . . . before making any recommendations," the committee had the feeling that the company "should give careful consideration to a change of sales policy and to the development of our own brands of merchandise." Vice-president Ray took up the challenge. Reviewing the development of Dan River's sales policies, he argued that "the difficulties experienced with jobbers and many other classes of the trade when trying to sell exclusively under Mill Brands" made it unwise to move farther in this direction.

In May Shibley returned to Danville and sat in on a board meeting. He said he was encouraged by the improvements that had been made, especially in the suitings and finishing departments, since his previous visit. Shibley suggested hiring one or two "executives of competitive mills" to assist in the reorganization of Dan River; but on May 27 the board's executive committee concluded that it was "impractical" to raid other firms for managerial talent. More could be accomplished by weeding out "non-productive employees" now on the payroll. No names were mentioned.

At the meeting of the board (June 24, 1939) the executive committee asked for the resignation of Ray as general sales manager. They recommended Frederick K. Nixon, a salesman, as Ray's successor and requested the board to grant Nixon "full authority to surround himself with a competent sales force" in order to "inaugurate, after consultation with the President, such policies as may be deemed wise for the best interests of the Company." Ray protested, asserting that the existing arrangements in the sales organization were "good and very satisfactory." After Ray withdrew from the meeting, President West spoke in favor of the committee report; and the directors voted to retire Ray, "owing to ill health," but to continue his salary in view of his thirty-five years of service to the company.[118] Nixon succeeded Ray as vice-president as well as general sales manager. Ray remained a director until his death in May 1941.

President West's nemesis was excessive "extra-curricular" activity. The demands upon his time from business, governmental, and civic organizations increased each year; and, like H. R. Fitzgerald before him, he found it difficult to refuse engagements which appeared to promote good-will for the company or to maintain its prestige in the industry. Frequent references have been made to his work in connection with the Code and other federal legislation. Perhaps not so clearly in the line of duty were his gracious responses to invitations to speak before educational and civic groups, to participate in community projects, and to write for trade and professional publications.[119]

The idea that West spent too much of his time on "outside matters" seems to have been aired for the first time in the board meeting of November 1938. The president observed that all of his committee work had, in his opinion, been in the interests of the Dan River: on "certain important committees the Company should certainly have some representative to take care of its interests." Nevertheless, the directors urged him to "divest himself, as far as possible, of outside demands upon his time"; and a few weeks later the president was re-

[118] In 1940 the directors reduced Ray's salary to $8,000.
[119] In addition to various committee assignments for the Cotton Textile Institute and the Code Authority, West was a member of the executive committee of the National Association of Finishers of Textile Fabrics, a director of the Virginia State Chamber of Commerce, a member of the American committee of the International Chamber of Commerce, and a member of the Virginia Labor Relations Commission. He was adviser to the U. S. employers' delegates to the Technical Tripartite Conference on the Textile Industry in 1937, and was granted a leave of absence to attend the International Labor Conference in Geneva as an employer representative in the U. S. delegation.

quested to give up all outside engagements he could get out of "grace-fully."[120]

In June 1939, after Shibley had made two trips to Danville, Chairman Miller told the directors that he wanted the New York banker "to spend a month or two with Mr. West and try to work out a plan or method to promote greater efficiency and economy." The president demurred but promised to think it over. The suggestion was not brought up again, but in August Miller asked West if anything had been done about getting an "understudy for the President." West was not prepared to make a recommendation, although he had in mind "several promising young men" already in the employ of the company.[121]

In 1938 West was elected second vice-president of the American Cotton Manufacturers' Association and the following year advanced to the position of first vice-president. In the tradition of the Association this meant that West would be elected president at the 1940 convention.

On March 2, 1940, Chairman Miller informed the board that he had advised President West not to accept the presidency of the A.C.M.A. on the ground that the "seriousness of the times and conditions in the Textile Business called for Mr. West's undivided attention and time to Riverside business." The directors supported the chairman; West resigned as vice-president of the Association; and on March 4, "with utmost regret," he tendered his resignation as president of Riverside and Dan River Cotton Mills. The board accepted the resignation on March 9. West spoke briefly of the "irreconcilable differences between the Board and the President as to policies."[122] He said he had never been more confident of the success of the business but urged the directors to "stand up for" the man chosen to take his place and to "temper pressure with judgment" in dealing with the "fine folk" working in the mill. For his part, Miller assured West that "personalities" had not entered into the board's action; on the contrary,

[120] Early in 1938 West accepted appointment as a member of the National Association of Manufacturers' Committee on the Study of Depressions but declined nomination for membership on the NAM board of directors.

[121] D. K. Woodard had been appointed assistant to the president in October 1938; apparently, he did not fit the role of "understudy for the President."

[122] The *American Wool and Cotton Reporter,* not always an informed critic of what went on in the Dan River management, concluded that "inside politics" drove West out (vol. 55, June 19, 1941, pp. 9-10, 30-33). The editor took credit for recommending West to President Fitzgerald.

West enjoyed the affection, respect, and best wishes of the directors.[123]

The search for a new president began immediately. Several candidates were considered, but it took less than a month to narrow the list to one name: George S. Harris, then executive vice-president of the Springs Mills. Meeting in Lynchburg on April 9, six members of the board of directors voted unanimously to offer Harris the presidency. He accepted and took up his duties in Danville in May.

For about two months, following West's resignation, George W. Robertson served as executive vice-president. Robertson had been with the company fifty-six years, and President West, some of the directors felt, had been less than firm in trying to persuade him to retire.[124] It was left for Harris to accomplish this bit of managerial rejuvenation. Robertson retired in February 1941 and died in April 1944. It was also Harris' chore to get A. T. Cockefair to accept "gracefully . . . the Mill's last proposition for his retirement" (June 1940).

Changes in the directorate were infrequent. Following the death of President Pritchett, his son, James I. Pritchett, Jr., became a Dan River director. After the resignation of M. K. Harris, the stockholders elected two new directors: Albert F. Patton, a Danville realtor, and A. B. Carrington, a tobacco merchant whose experience in foreign business proved useful to G. A. Stafford & Company. The membership of the board increased to eleven when G. S. Harris and F. K. Nixon became directors in 1940.

Stockholders' meetings in 1932-1940 were generally unexciting affairs. While an occasional skeptic dared to assert openly that dividends had been too long withheld, the management never lacked for staunch defenders. In February 1933 J. Hannon Schoolfield congratulated the officers and employees "for having worked together to such an extent that your Company came through the most trying year in its history without a serious loss, while competitors' losses are run-

[123] Probably of minor significance was the tiff between the president and the board chairman over coal shipments. West thought the service provided by the Virginian Railroad was entirely satisfactory, but Miller, a director of the Chesapeake & Ohio Railroad, wanted his company to have a share of the business. West hated to be "stubborn" but found "no advantage at all to splitting up this coal business between two railroads." Later on, West relented, and the coal companies were instructed to route one half of Dan River's coal over the C. & O.

[124] As vice-president and general superintendent emeritus, Robertson received $4,000 a year "subject to discontinuance at the discretion of the Board." The directors expressed their "real regret" on his retirement. ""Fifty-seven years of hard and continuous work," they believed, were "unequalled in our industry." Previously, in 1934, Robertson had been honored with a banquet, attended by 192 employees who had worked for the mill thirty years or more.

ning into millions." Riverside and Dan River Mills, he said, "stand
out as one of the most progressive organizations in the textile business."

From time to time stockholders became inquisitive about the
salaries paid to executives, but the directors took the position that the
interests of the company were best served by withholding detailed information. At the 1936 stockholders' meeting Chairman Miller announced that the compensation of the chairman, the president, and the
vice-presidents totaled $70,000, "against a figure a few years back of
$200,000." In March 1936 the directors required approval by the
board of any salary in excess of $5,000 a year. At this time the com-
pany was paying 31 salaries over $5,000, the total amounting to $318,-
442 a year. In December 1938 salaried officers, department heads, and
salesmen numbered 41, while there were 115 clerks, secretaries and
overseers on salary.

Table 19. Wage and Salary Payments, 1932-1940

year	wages	salaries
1932	$3,002,872	$330,186
1933	3,572,318	343,282
1934	4,923,045	392,238
1935	5,793,302	449,715
1936	6,487,502	481,989
1937	7,634,647	587,483
1938	5,614,159	517,441
1939	6,076,783	521,210
1940	7,031,622	534,378

Table 19 compares the total wage bill with the amount paid out in
salaries. Salaries were reduced in January 1932 and again in February
1933, but increases in salaries paralleled the rise in wage rates, and
salary disbursements reached a high of $587,000 in 1937. A graduated
cut in salaries, amounting to 20 per cent on salaries in excess of $12,000
a year, took effect in April 1938; but the total amount paid out in
salaries dropped only moderately, as new names were added to the list
of salaried employees.

The directors approved the following salaries for the principal
officers in February 1940:

chairman of the board	$4,335
president	32,000
vice-president (sales)	18,000
vice-president (production)	16,000
vice-president (cotton)	12,000
secretary	8,500
assistant treasurer (credit)	6,000
assistant treasurer	4,590

The demand of stockholders and brokers for more information about the business bore fruit in somewhat fuller statements than in the years prior to 1932. The first interim report of the president was distributed in July 1932. Thereafter, mid-year reports were irregular; but the annual report was issued in two parts: (1) a four-page leaflet containing the messages of the chairman and the president, and (2) a four-page digest of the financial statements, including the auditor's certificate. The balance sheet gave only the totals of the principal accounts, while the income statement disclosed net income, cost of manufacturing, profit from goods sold, other income, net profit, and changes in the surplus. No attempt was made to analyze sales and earnings or to compare the results of one year with previous years. Needless to say, the information furnished to stockholders did not include any of the detailed statistics of goods produced, costs, wages, and selling prices that have been presented in the preceding pages. In the Twenty-fifth Annual Report (1933), the directors are identified by name, occupation, and residence; and the following year's report listed the principal officers. In general, the information supplied stockholders was considerably less than that required of a corporation listing its stock on the New York Stock Exchange.

7. *Textiles in War and Peace, 1941-1949*

Problems of national defense, war, and postwar adjustment dominated the nine-year administration of President George S. Harris. The
war years were prosperous only by comparison with the lean 1930's, but
the end of World War II touched off an expansion of business that
pushed the company's sales and earnings to new highs. Net sales passed
$100 million for the first time in 1948, as earnings after taxes estab-
lished a record of $15 million. Preferred dividends in arrears were
paid off; the 6 per-cent preferred stock was replaced by 4½ per-cent
preferred; dividends on the common stock were resumed; and the surplus grew to an impressive $37 million. All this was accomplished be-
fore illness forced President Harris to accept the less arduous duties of
chairman of the board in the fall of 1949. He died in Danville on
February 16, 1950.

The steady growth in balance-sheet values (Appendix 1) in part
reflects the upward movement of prices which, though moderate during
the war, raised the wholesale index almost 100 per cent between 1940

and 1950. The magnitude of the company's physical growth in this period will be made clear in the discussion of plant improvement, production, and employment.

Improvements

Table 1 shows compactly the changes in fixed-asset values over the nine-year period. The net increase in ledger values was nearly 50 per cent, but the gains were unevenly distributed. For four years (1941-1944) capital expenditures totaled $1.4 million less than charges to the depreciation reserve. In the following five years outlays on improve-

Table 1. Comparison of Plant Accounts, 1941 and 1949
(thousands of dollars)

	Jan. 4, 1941	Dec. 31, 1949
Riverside division		
buildings-machinery	3,905	4,674
land	1,185	1,177
Schoolfield division		
mill construction	2,076	2,833
water power and development	264	
land	193	346*
machinery	5,066	
electrical equipment	850	
water supply-filter system	241	10,463†
coal and wood company	55	
welfare and village	526	387
general		549‡
Stamford real estate	49	
Ringgold real estate		4
construction in progress		568
credit depreciation reserve	282	
total	14,691	21,000

Errors in totals due to rounding.
* Water power development and land
† Machinery, electrical equipment, and water systems
‡ A new ledger account, comprising autos, furniture, fixtures and miscellaneous properties

ments exceeded depreciation allowances by $6.6 million, all of which was provided by earnings. The sources of each year's expenditures on capital account are disclosed in Table 2.

In March 1940, following West's resignation, the directors set aside
$437,000 for "urgently needed plant improvements." In July Presi-
dent Harris came before the board with a request, which was granted,
for $35,000 to buy three machines needed at Riverside division for
shrinking cloth. For a while requirements of new equipment were
taken care of in a piece-meal fashion, but in February 1941 the direc-

Table 2. Expenditures on Improvements, 1941-1949
(thousands of dollars)

year	offset by depreciation	provided by earnings	total
1941	1,040	*—26*	1,014
1942	973	*—181*	791
1943	1,229	*—581*	648
1944	1,265	*—568*	697
1945	1,295	111	1,406
1946	1,063	2,109	3,172
1947	894	1,722	2,616
1948	1,152	2,548	3,701
1949	1,416	1,175	2,591

Errors in totals due to rounding.

tors made a blanket authorization of $500,000 to cover such improve-
ments as the president deemed essential. As the president impressed
upon the directors the urgency of having the mills "more modernly
equipped" to meet the competition of other manufacturers, the board
made additional appropriations, bringing total capital expenditures
for the year to $1 million.

During the war obtaining priorities for new machinery and replacement parts was a more difficult job than persuading the directors to
appropriate funds. The board authorized the management to spend
not over $1 million in 1942, but the actual outlays on improvements
came to less than $800,000. By the time machinery and materials be-
came available, earnings had risen substantially and the directors did
not hesitate to appropriate the money.[1]

Although the new management did not use ex-President West as a
scapegoat for all its troubles, it complained frequently that the previous
administration had "no systematic program of maintaining machinery,

[1] "The Board is disposed to approve rather blindly all improvements that we propose" (G. S. Harris to H. L. Bailey, June 28, 1947).

part of which is explained by the pressure to economize in every possible way and in so doing proper evaluation was not put on precision maintenance, which is so necessary for sustaining quality of work and earnings of operatives where they are paid on a piece-rate basis." President Harris explained to a New York banker that he encountered "seriously deferred maintenance, which we have been working on diligently for the past two years and have made important progress." Riverside and Dan River Cotton Mills, the southern agent of Saco-Lowell Shops recalled, "had one-process, two-process and three processes of Roving, spinning frames of various gauges and ring diameters, none matching with the order allocated to them."[2]

Estimates prepared by the management in May 1941 indicated possible savings of $291,491 annually from capital expenditures of $666,796. A month later a "large-scale program for the improvement of our machinery" was underway. The project was "being conducted by our own organization without the employment of outside engineers; and we believe," the officers declared, "a better job is being done and at a much lower cost." In less than six months, of course, much of the long-range planning had to be abandoned, in deference to the urgent need for increasing product with a minimum of attention to improvements in equipment.

Modernization of roving and spinning ranked high on the list of imperative improvements. In October 1941 the management advised the directors that "our long-draft spinning change-overs are now practically completed." At Riverside's Mill No. 6, Whitin change-overs were adopted for 17,500 spindles producing carpet yarns. The rest of the long-draft equipment, including Model J-3 roving frames, came from the Saco-Lowell Shops.[3] But a tabulation prepared in November 1941 showed 113,472 spindles (plus an unstated number of spindles in Mill No. 6) not yet changed to long draft. In the sheeting division,

[2] W. W. Gayle to G. S. Harris, April 30, 1945. Speaking before the Rotary Club of Danville, Harris recounted that when he heard of West's resignation, he told Mrs. Harris: "There's one situation I don't want. God help the man who takes it."

[3] Harris had some doubt of the superiority of Saco-Lowell roving frames, since Springs Mills had reported that there was no significant difference, except ease of cleaning, between this frame and those based on the Reynolds patents. In December 1940 Harris chided Saco-Lowell for boosting Dan River's competitors in its advertising. "We may not have as much long-draft roving and 'what have you,' but with a little time and your cooperation, we might be just as good as some of your friends which you have singled out in this advertisement." (G. S. Harris to W. W. Gayle, Dec. 30, 1940.) *Saco-Lowell Bulletin* (vol. 13, April 1941) featured Saco-Lowell equipment at Dan River and paid a tribute to Harris, "whose aggressive yet canny managerial abilities will unquestionably carry the Dan River and Riverside Mills' record to new heights of accomplishment."

General Superintendent Russell B. Newton reported in 1942, there were "more spindles obsolete than in any part of the corporation." Undecided, as yet, was the question of planning an "ideal setup" for sheeting and acquisition of spindles to manufacture 60s and 70s yarns. Even after the war Harris wanted to go slow in modernizing the spinning rooms, believing that "within the next five years we are going to see radical developments in the process of spinning";[4] but over $500,-000 was appropriated in 1946 to purchase Saco-Lowell long-draft change-overs.

In March 1945 the company asked the War Production Board for priorities on the following equipment: Parks-Cramer traveling cleaner attachments for 100 spinning frames,[5] three Abbott winders, two Abbot quillers, and four 20-spindle piece-outs. The request was supported by estimates of manpower saving and increased production of tent twill for the armed forces, but no action appears to have been taken by the W.P.B. Ninety-two Atwood twisters for rayon yarn were on order in December 1947, and in May the company bought two 16-harness drawing-in machines.

After investing in 156 Lyle patented bobbin formers and finding it "almost impossible to keep them regulated," Dan River encouraged A. C. Drake, one of its machinists, to devise a bobbin former described as "nothing like the Lyle former." Apparently, J. T. Lyle accepted the company's claim that "the formers which we are now using in no way infringe on your patent."

In October 1940 the president cautioned Salesman L. R. Walls that contracts for combed goods threatened to outstrip the mills' combing capacity and suggested that he "get out of this hole" by urging customers to accept carded yarns. Saco-Lowell furnished quotations on new combers—"like the 14 you now have"—but Harris had "not brought myself to this investment at this time." Further study of the combed-goods market persuaded the president to reverse his position, and six new combers were added before Pearl Harbor. The 20 Saco-

---

[4] G. S. Harris to R. E. Barnwell, Sept. 3, 1947. The textile industry, Gibb points out, "had shown an understandable disposition to purchase 'change-overs' (the drafting element alone) rather than entire new frames." Two major improvements, long-drafting equipment for synthetic yarns and ball-bearing spindles, had been perfected before the war, and continued research by machinery manufacturers held the threat of rapid obsolescence of prewar spinning-room machinery (G. S. Gibb, *The Saco-Lowell Shops*, pp. 594-595).

[5] *Parks' Parables* (Book 46, Spasm 3, March 1949), a house organ of Parks-Cramer Company, contains excellent photographs of Dan River spinning rooms equipped with traveling cleaners as well as Parks automatic airchanger and turbomatic humidifiers.

Lowell combers ordered early in 1946 and the 32 Naismith combers purchased in 1948 increased the company's investment in combing equipment by $250,000.[6]

In May 1941 the president was "worrying" about the 1,500 36-inch looms in the shirting and dress-goods department. These were wide enough before the days of fully-shrunk cloth, but 40-inch looms were needed to manufacture goods 36 inches wide after shrinking. To widen these looms would cost $175 per loom; to replace them about three times as much. Not much had been done with this problem before Harris found a more serious dilemma in the "heavy expenditures . . . as we slip rapidly into war economy . . . to equip our looms to meet government specifications."

Let the president's own words explain this problem and how it was solved:

. . . the outbreak of the war . . . caught us with plenty of fancy looms and plenty of fancy production to meet a wartime demand that was essentially staple in character. We knew we had a job on our hands as soon as we saw what the score was in regard to the types of military fabrics that were required most urgently . . . .

The first thing we did was to appoint a mill-trained expert to study all fabrics that would be needed in large quantities by the armed forces. Because we are a big mill, set up to produce goods by the mile, there seemed to be no sense in looking over the numerous specialty fabrics that would be needed only in limited quantities and that were much better adapted to the particular manufacturing schedules of smaller, well equipped organizations. Having picked out the fabrics that would be needed in large amounts, we then gave particular attention to those goods that had not been overbid to date, and that the government seemed to be having some difficulty in securing. Again our idea was to render a service where it was most needed, rather than to duplicate jobs that were already being ably taken care of by other mills. As a result of this study, we finally settled on perhaps a half dozen cloths that the government needed "yesterday" in big volume. Unfortunately, we had never made any of these cloths before, and they were all considered too heavy for our equipment. On top of this, we were loaded up with a lot of box looms for checks and plaids and yarn dyeing equipment and these new government requirements were all staple fabrics for plain dyeing. We bought 700 new 40" Draper looms especially for these cloths and junked a corresponding number of box looms. These have been running constantly since. We also converted a lot of looms from our sheeting, shirting and trousering divisions, rolled up our sleeves and went to work.

[6] In April 1949 Saco-Lowell shipped to Dan River the first comber made in its southern machine shop in Sanford, North Carolina.

Hardly a loom in the plant was set up to do the job it was now called upon to do for this new government program. We needed new parts, and plenty of them. We needed engineering. We needed a lot of mechanical work done, even when the new parts were available. We also needed many types of brand new equipment, particularly preparatory and finishing types. Many of these things just weren't to be had for love nor money, regardless of priorities. So we set up a Machinery Maintenance Department whose job it was to make all necessary conversions in equipment and to maintain that equipment at a peak level of efficiency. Then we called in technical experts on the staffs of various manufacturers of textile machinery to help our own people in expediting the work. Their assistance proved invaluable in this emergency. When new parts were not available, we made them in our own machine shops. On many occasions entire machines were constructed from start to finish in Dan River Shops. We then set up a schedule of maintenance that provided for intensive preventive care for each machine in each mill, with most of the work done on Sundays or holidays when repair work would be least likely to interfere with normal production. We even went to the extent of hiring an outstanding expert in machine lubrication and established a special lubricating department that had no other function than to keep the machinery properly oiled. All this paid dividends, and in the space of a very few weeks we had high quality grey goods for military use come off equipment that had formerly produced lightweight fancy dress materials and similar constructions.

Anticipating postwar problems of production, in November 1944 the New York executive committee met for its "loom discussion no. 1." W. J. Fullerton reported on visits to loom factories and predicted that no manufacturer would make quantity shipments in less than two years. Tentative plans were made for replacing box looms with newer models. In July 1946 the directors appropriated $1,250,000 for 624 Crompton & Knowles 54-inch looms for Riverside Division, and in September 1948 another $700,000 was set aside for 298 C-5 looms for Schoolfield Division and 96 for Riverside. In September 1944 Draper promised Dan River one of its improved XD looms, and 10 of this model were installed late in 1946. The costing department recommended an investment of $1.6 million to replace 880 Stafford looms with Draper's XL model, estimating a saving of $321,107 annually.

Two patented processes developed by Dan River machinists were introduced in the weave rooms. Glenn F. Womble was awarded a patent for a method of making selvage on rayon fabrics, and Robert A. Littlejohn patented a pivot mounting for looms.

By June 1941 a reorganization to concentrate suitings production at Riverside Division was completed, except for moving 150 looms. "All dyeing and finishing," T. J. Corcoran, manager of the clothing fabrics division, reported, "is more successfully carried on there, in the best equipped plant of its kind in this country." Except for a few pieces of equipment obtained under priorities for war production,[7] the company had scant opportunity to re-equip its dyeing and finishing departments. A modern piece-goods dyehouse was built, "in spite of extremely difficult construction conditions," over a two-year period (1944-1945). By June 1947 plans had been perfected for installing new dyeing and finishing machinery. "We are in the midst of completely revamping our bleachery and finishing," President Harris told Elliott Springs in February 1948. In order to employ continuous bleaching processes, the bleachery was moved to the first floor of Schoolfield's Mill No. 5. The expense of relocating the bleaching and finishing plant and the cost of new wide and narrow finishing ranges, mercerizing machinery, and a 110-inch tentering unit were covered by appropriations (1945-1947) totaling almost $3 million. Early in 1948 the finishing plant handled nearly four million yards of cloth weekly, but another quarter million yards had to be shipped out for finishing at the Sayles Bleachery in Asheville, North Carolina. In 1949 the company rented a hearse to carry a scale model of the new finishing plant to the Smithsonian Institution in Washington.

In response to an inquiry from an Alabama mill, the president confirmed that "our men" had made an improved desizing machine. "Usually," Harris said, "I am pleased to show a friendly competitor anything we may have"; but in this case he firmly declined to permit its inspection. An important but inexpensive improvement at Riverside Division was a storage "Lixator" designed by the International Salt Company. Instead of hauling bags of salt to the raw-stock and suitings dye houses, up to 18 carloads of rock salt were dumped into the saturated brine "Lixator," from which the brine was pumped through 3,700 feet of pipe to the dye houses.[8]

In January 1941 President Harris wrote to Abington Textile Machinery Works that "our stripping equipment is badly antiquated, but

[7] In April 1942 the Company had an A-1-C preference rating for equipment to dye herringbone twills by the Aridye process (B. D. Browder to L. R. Walls, April 27, 1942). In March the management expected to instal, within a few months, new machinery, "the last word in piece-dyeing equipment," which would add 800,000 yards weekly to the existing 1,400,000 yards piece-dyeing capacity.

[8] *Textile World*, vol. 97 (Aug. 1947), p. 135. According to this account, the company saved more than the cost of installation in one year.

I cannot get to this in the immediate future." Later in the year Saco-Lowell promised to inspect 72 cards in Riverside's No. 6 Mill which were equipped with continuous strippers so poorly installed that the cards had to be stripped by hand. Improvements in the cloth rooms included a number of Sjostrom automatic pillow-case doffers. One person operating the new doffer displaced four persons required to doff pillow-cases from the mangle. Savings in wages paid for this $2,300 machine in less than a year. Similar savings were realized from the substitution of power tables for hand-pull tables in the inspection room. An improved cloth inspection and handling system, perfected by Oscar J. Norton in 1945, was awarded a patent in 1949. Fluorescent lighting was gradually extended to all manufacturing departments; in 1941-1947 expenditures on lighting at Schoolfield Division amounted to $193,538 and at Riverside Division, $91,625.

New construction in 1941-1949 included an $800,000 cotton warehouse at Schoolfield Division. Authorized in October 1945, the eight-story structure was built by C. M. Guest and Sons. In 1943-1945 Dan River had to depend upon the Danville city reservoir for a part of its needs.[9] After the war the company spent $250,000 for new filters and mixing basins at the Schoolfield plant, increasing the water-supply capacity from 5.5 million to 11.5 million gallons daily. In 1948 an electric sign to advertise the "Home of Dan River Fabrics" was erected on the roof of Riverside Mill No. 8 at a cost of $22,602, and $40,000 was appropriated to build a grandstand at the baseball field in Schoolfield. On a small tract of land in Ringgold, a few miles northeast of Danville, the company built a lodge for the accommodation of members of the New York sales organization, customers, and guests.

Real estate transactions included the sale at auction of the Stamford (Connecticut) property acquired from G. A. Stafford. The final accounting for this asset showed a loss to Dan River of $34,451. Property transfers in Virginia included the sale of about 185 acres on Hughes Hill (1941), the sale of 40 acres to the state (1941) and a smaller tract to the city (1948) for highway use. In 1946-1947 the company sold timber rights for $50,379.

The purpose of Table 3 is to reveal the types of "other assets" entered in the balance sheets.

Investments at the end of 1941 consisted of stock in Dan Valley

[9] G. N. Miller to E. C. Brantley, May 29, 1943. The company requested 1,000-1,500 gallons per minute for 16 hours daily.

Table 3. Description of "Other Assets"
(thousands of dollars)

year	investments	U.S. Government securities	prepaid charges	sinking fund	receivables from sale of houses
1941	98		62		
1942	98	298*	123		
1943	98	3,247*	103		
1944	94	6,346*	107		
1945	94	7,151*	159		
1946	88	5,000	247		
1947	88	2,800	353		
1948	88	2,500†	1,296‡	1,000	
1949	108	2,500†	1,226‡	150	263

* Includes excess profits tax-refunds or tax-refund bonds.
† pledged to retirement plan past service cost.
‡ Includes contributions to retirement plans, $891,146 in 1948 and $560,569 in 1949.

Mills ($30,000), Piedmont Mills ($50,000), G. A. Stafford & Company ($7,518), Park National Bank of Knoxville ($150), treasury stock ($10,041), and debentures of the Tompkins Realty Company ($82). Although the debt had been written off, Tompkins Realty redeemed one $100 debenture in 1944 and another $100 in 1946 in the form of advertising in the *Southern Textile Bulletin*. The 360 shares of treasury common stock were sold for 21½ in 1944; the Park National stock was disposed of in 1945; and the 100 shares of treasury preferred stock were sold in 1946. The "reserve" against the G. A. Stafford stock was wiped out in 1949 and the ledger value raised to $27,518.

Table 4 summarizes the available data on electric power in 1941-1949. Noteworthy is the fact that Riverside's obsolete steam plant, which produced virtually no electricity in 1940, was called upon to carry a substantial power load during the wartime emergency.[10] Purchases of power from the Appalachian Electric Power Company increased steadily during and after the war. The net cost of purchased power, after allowances for small amounts of power returned, rose

[10] In the interests of national defense, Dan River entered into an agreement with Appalachian Electric Power Company to restore the Riverside steam plant to power production. Appalachian agreed to buy all the current produced at 8.5 mills per K.W.H. Such power could be consumed at the Riverside plants only in case Appalachian was unable to meet the demand at this division. (G. S. Harris to Federal Power Commission, Oct. 6, 1941.) The company's engineer has estimated that 8 mills per K.W.H. would be a fair rate for power purchased by Appalachian (G. N. Miller to G. S. Harris, Oct. 23, 1941).

from $427,000 in 1941 to $927,000 in 1948, dropping to $791,000 in 1949.

Table 4. Power Statistics, 1941-1949*
(thousands of kilowatt hours)

	1941	1942	1943	1944*	1945*	1947	1948	1949
Riverside division								
generated								
steam	6,468	6,328	4,257			0	84	0
water	7,604	10,124	9,470			7,451	7,907	7,454
purchased	28,639	32,286	33,215				37,495	28,715
returned	1,665	933	1,420				0	0
total net consumption	41,046	47,805	45,522				45,486	36,169
Schoolfield division								
generated								
steam	45,873	49,493	41,761	39,617	34,939	40,838	32,625	19,665
water	12,897	16,224	18,612	26,261	27,093	14,903	17,751	20,821
purchased	32,675	40,491	37,231	73,568	73,250	108,634*	78,489	63,136
returned	416	176	119	0	0	0	0	0
total net consumption	91,029	106,032	97,485				128,865	103,622
consumption— both divisions	132,075	153,837	143,007	139,446	135,282	171,826	174,351	139,791

* Data for both Divisions combined. The 1946 statistics have not been located.

According to a report of R. H. Spessard,[11] in 1946 purchased power represented 56 per cent of the normal load of 25,000 kilowatts hourly on the first shift. Installed capacity and average loads are detailed in Table 5.

Schoolfield's eleven boilers, rated at 6,861 H.P., produced 140,000 pounds per hour of power steam and 160,000 pounds per hour of heat and process steam. Reviewing the history of the power installations, Spessard pointed out that because of the silting of the dam at Schoolfield, the "run of the river is all that is available." An average load of 2,000 K.W. was maintained over a 12-hour period, covering high and low flows of the river. Although in 1945 it cost only 1.09 mills per K.W.H. to produce 14,272,730 K.W.H., improvements to increase the output of power were deemed uneconomical. In the steam plant the newest boiler dated from 1921, but in 1945 seven boilers were equipped with spreader stokers costing $50,000. Savings in labor and mainte-

[11] Superintendent of power, maintenance, and construction, succeeding G. N. Miller, who resigned in 1944.

Table 5.   Power Capacity and Load, 1946
(kilowatts)

	Schoolfield division	Riverside division	both divisions
hydroelectric:			
25-cycle, installed	4,300	0	4,300
25-cycle, average load	2,000	0	2,000
60-cycle, installed	950	3,170	4,120
60-cycle, average load	0	1,000	1,000
steam:			
25-cycle, installed	12,900	0	12,900
25-cycle, average load	8,000	0	8,000
60-cycle, installed	0	8,750	8,750
60-cycle, average load	0	0	0
purchased power:			
60-cycle	8,500	5,500	14,000

nance were expected to return the cost of the investment in one year. It cost 7.93 mills per K.W.H. to generate 34,939,300 K.W.H. of electricity (1945).

The water wheels at Riverside Division operated at an average load of 1,000 K.W. on the "run of the river." The cost of the 12,820,540 K.W.H. generated in 1945 was 1.95 mills per K.W.H. The steam generating plant had been retired once more to a stand-by basis, but some of the boilers were equipped with spreader stokers and mechanical coal- and ash-hauling systems. The capital expenditure of $60,000, it was estimated, would be returned within a year from the reduced cost of manufacturing heat and process steam.

In 1944 the firm of Charles T. Main, Inc., which had been studying Dan River's power problem since 1941, made a lengthy report on "the probable results of supplying steam and power . . . with new low pressure boilers and *all power purchased* and with new high pressure boilers and *no power purchased,* so as to develop the limits between which purchased power would probably be used."[12]   Much, of course, hinged on the cost of purchased power. Appalachian's rate advanced from 7.15 mills per K.W.H. in 1943 to 7.24 mills in 1944, and 7.25 mills in 1945. According to Main's engineers, Dan River would have

[12] Charles T. Main, Inc., to G. S. Harris, Jan. 10, 1944. In January 1943 Harris observed that a complete new power plant at Schoolfield Division would show a return of 40 per cent on the investment.

saved $48,404 in 1943 (on bills totaling over $500,000) if Appalachian's rates had been the same as those of the Duke Power Company.

As long as war shortages lasted, the management could make only the most urgent replacements—and sometimes not even these. Boiler inspections at Schoolfield Division in 1943 disclosed excessive corrosion and cracked headers, but the War Production Board denied priorities on replacement parts and new equipment. Finally, in October 1945, the company signed contracts amounting to $1.3 million for new generating equipment. By the end of the year, the Schoolfield mills had installed a new high-pressure boiler, feeding steam to a new back-pressure turbine connected with a rebuilt 3,000-K.W. generator.[13]

The power report for 1947 shows total expenditures of $2,188,369 for process steam and electricity including 108.6 million K.W.H. purchased from Appalachian at 7.29 mills per K.W.H. Schoolfield Division produced 40.8 million K.W.H. of steam-generated power at a cost of 9.61 mills. In November 1947, President Harris felt that the new equipment had resulted in "a considerable reduction in the cost of the power we produce" and had in mind "reconditioning some of our older equipment, the result of which will further reduce this cost." Yet he thought that "some alterations" in the "current tariff" of Appalachian Power Company might induce the mills to increase their dependence on purchased power, advancing the peak load from 23,000 K.W. to "something in excess of 31,000 K.W. by January 1952."[14]

Appalachian may have known that Dan River engineers were dismayed by the repeated breakdown of the high-pressure boiler installed in 1946. Within six months after installation the tubes became clogged, and tests of water and chemical feed lines yielded unsatisfactory explanations of the difficulty. In July 1948 Charles T. Main's engineers outlined five "schemes" for meeting the power problem;[15] but no action was taken on the proposals. A new survey, conducted by United Engineers & Constructors, Inc., recommended one more low-pressure boiler, together with auxiliary piping and electrical apparatus, at a cost of $800,000. In May 1949 the directors approved the United

[13] In July 1946 Spessard and three other Dan River engineers visited Springs Mills to observe the operation of power-plant equipment similar to that being installed at Schoolfield (R. H. Spessard to G. S. Harris, July 29, 1946).

[14] G. S. Harris to Philip Sporn, president, American Gas and Electric Service Corporation, Nov. 17, 1947.

[15] The schemes differed with respect to the size of investment in new equipment and, correspondingly, the projected increased, or decreased, purchases of power.

Engineers' project, which had been presented with the assurance that the company would save $129,000 annually.

Production

Statistics of production show a peak of 199 million yards of cloth in 1942. The declining yardages after this reflect the wartime labor shortages and the "loss" of output (in yards, at least) occasioned by conversion to fabrics required by government orders. Output climbed steadily after 1945, and the postwar peak of 189 million yards of cloth, together with an all-time high of 11.9 million pounds of sales yarns and 857,000 pounds of "pound goods," contributed to the company's record sales and earnings. Unfavorable market conditions in 1949 necessitated retrenchment, and the production of cloth dropped to the lowest level since 1939.

Table 6 reveals the major changes in the classes of goods manufactured. So-called "government fabrics" amounted to 20 per cent of total yardage in 1942, 28 per cent in 1943, 25 per cent in 1944, and 19 per cent in 1945. The relative position of the domestics, including sheeting produced for the armed forces, fluctuated widely: the proportion of total yardage was 28 per cent in 1941 and 24 per cent in 1942; it dropped to about 12 per cent in 1944 but reached 24 per cent in 1947. Staple colored goods, the most important classification in 1941, lost rank during the war and remained in 1946-1949 the company's fourth most important class of goods. In contrast, the dress goods, which were in fifth place in 1941, gained first position in yardage in 1949. Similarly, shirtings, sportswear, and stormwear, the third ranking classification in 1941, held first place in 1948 and second place in 1949. Suitings made up something less than 10 per cent of the yardage in five years, a little more in the other four years.

The war effort

As early as September 1941 defense orders occupied about one tenth of the spinning capacity of Riverside's Mill No. 6. In January 1942 contracts for 842,000 pounds of yarn used in machine-gun cartridge belts not only proved profitable but afforded the company priorities on the purchase of supplies and machinery. The Dan River laboratories developed high-strength raw-stock dyed yarns for airplane safety

Mill on the Dan

Table 6. Production of Cloth, 1941-1949
(millions of linear yards)

	1941	1942	1943	1944	1945	1946	1947	1948	1949
domestics	51.2	47.7	30.0	20.1	19.6	27.2	42.8	41.7	29.1
staple colored	53.0	41.1	32.8	29.0	25.5	19.6	22.9	17.3	15.7
suitings	17.7	19.1	16.3	17.0	14.9	20.6	19.3	17.4	10.6
dress goods shirtings,	13.9	12.7	16.0	20.4	17.9	28.2	31.0	48.3	36.3
sportswear-stormwear	37.8	29.6	24.3	32.8	33.2	55.5	55.6	56.7	26.2
handkerchief cloth	8.0	8.3	7.4	3.1					
government fabrics	2.5	40.6	48.1	40.0	25.1				
contract gray goods							4.8	7.5	7.5
total	184.2	199.2	174.9	162.4	136.2	151.1	176.4	188.9	125.4

Errors in totals due to rounding.

belts and parachute harnesses, and several hundred thousand pounds were produced on government orders in 1943.

"The Plan for Progress, prepared by and for the Supervisor" (August 1943) describes the organization of the mills for war-related activities. An executive committee, with Walter D. Vincent as chairman, coordinated the work of thirty plant committees, whose projects ranged from beautification to ways and means of preventing seconds in yarn manufacture.

The heaviest share of the war effort fell on the thousands of looms making sheets, chambrays, and government fabrics. The so-called government fabrics produced in 1941-1945 consisted primarily of drills and twills for uniforms. Oxford cloth, raincoat cloth, and tent twill were also included under this phase of the company's contribution to the war on the textile front.

In September 1941 the government was "badly in need of unbleached Sanforized dril [*sic*]" and requested Dan River to re-equip as many looms as possible to make this fabric to government specifications. Although many loom parts had to be obtained from the manufacturers, production commenced before the end of the year and built up to 13.8 million yards in 1942. At the peak 744 looms were occupied on this fabric. "This was done at considerable expense, with the assurance that this fabric would continually be in demand throughout the emergency and that our contracts would be renewed."[16] But in November 1942 the government "placed new contracts to the extent of eighty million yards without placing one yard with us." Much to the

[16] G. S. Harris to J. M. Miller, Nov. 9, 1942.

"amazement" of the management, Army procurement offices stepped up the company's share of contracts for herringbone twill and combed shirtings. Over 56 million yards of the herringbone twill alone were manufactured in 1943-1944. After the first quarter of 1944 Dan River was bound by a W.P.B. order which forbade the use of any looms unless the number of looms on herringbone twill was equal to the greatest number of looms producing this fabric at any time since March 6, 1943.

As early as September 1942 government orders required over 90 per cent of Dan River's combed yarn, and the company told the W.P.B. that it was "suffering very much by reason of the fact that our competitors are able to supply our civilian customers." Relief was granted in 1943, when production of combed uniform twill surpassed 10 million yards; but in the first quarter of 1944 slightly over 75 per cent of the combed yarn was earmarked for two government fabrics, wind-resistant Oxford cloth and wind-resistant sateen. In March 1945 the W.P.B. announced that military needs for combed goods had almost doubled, as combed goods were "found by actual usage under grueling battle and weather conditions to be the most satisfactory fabrics for a number of highly essential uses." In a "direction" to all combed-goods mills, W.P.B. ordered increases in the output of combed goods, which in the case of Dan River necessitated the employment of all combers for government fabrics. The company appealed the order, on the grounds that it was "participating in such procurements to a greater percentage than many firms throughout the industry." Apparently, the order was not rescinded; but in June Dan River obtained priority certificates for the purchase of limited quantities of combed yarn from other mills.[17]

The first contracts for tent twill were accepted in 1944. Although nearly a million yards were produced before the end of the year, the management found it impossible to man three shifts on the fabric, and the office of Quartermaster-General assigned Captain W. R. Capers to supervise a number of textile workers released from the Army to run the third shift on tent twill. Captain Capers' influence reduced absenteeism to the vanishing point on all three shifts, and in January 1945 the management strongly protested his reassignment to other duties.[18]

[17] W. P. B. to Combed Goods Mills, March 19, 1945; W. J. Fullerton to Superior Yarn Mills, June 15, 1945.

[18] G. S. Harris to Col. R. T. Stevens, Jan. 11, 1945; G. S. Harris to Maj. J. P. Walsh, Jan. 9, 1945. "We find in Captain Capers," Harris said, "a personality peculiarly fitted to assist us greatly not only in the production of Tent Twills but in all other Army fabrics."

Chambrays

In October 1941 Dan River showed Army procurement officers "experimental samples" of raw-stock and piece-dyed chambrays for work shirts. One of the officers "seemed very much impressed with this development work and expressed his appreciation" for the mill's efforts. But it was the Navy that, by adopting blue ship and shore work uniforms for enlisted men, put pressure on the country's chambray looms. Contracts signed in 1942 required the company to sell its entire output of "Ideal" chambray to manufacturers of Navy shirts. In January 1943 the four producers of 3.90 chambray formed a pool and agreed to apportion Navy orders on the basis of capacity, as follows:

Dan River	39.338 per cent
Pepperell	39.338 per cent
Arista Mills	16.407 per cent
Avondale Mills	4.917 per cent

In June the W.P.B. issued a "freeze" order on chambray looms, directing 90 per cent of production to be delivered to work-shirt manufacturers. According to J. M. Hughlett, this was "the first effective measure taken by W.P.B. to increase the quantity of work shirtings available for work shirts. While Riverside & Dan River have adhered strictly to the letter and intent of M-207, we know there have been many leaks from other sources into such channels as children's and women's clothing."[19]

Although at the beginning of 1944 the situation had eased, so that the chambray division was able to release 190 looms to work on suitings, in February a W.P.B. directive required Dan River to deliver on Navy contracts 8.5 million yards of chambray and coverts each quarter, beginning April 1. An appeal from this order,[20] based upon the shortage of help, was sustained by the Textile, Clothing, and Leather Bureau of W.P.B. "You have represented," the Bureau observed,

[19] A disadvantage of the order, Hughlett said, was that "it disarms us to a large degree in bringing pressure on the O.P.A. for higher ceiling prices. We could also mention our objection to regimentation and Government control but that's just wasting breath" (J. M. Hughlett to G. S. Harris, June 9, 1943). Later in the year O.P.A. "practically guaranteed" an increase of 2 cents a yard in chambray prices.

[20] L. J. Ewing to Riverside & Dan River Cotton Mills, March 23, 1944; W. J. Fullerton to G. S. Harris, March 31, 1944. While the appeal was under consideration, the manpower problem at Danville became more acute and the company had "no reason to hope that these conditions will not become worse." The mill had to stop 344 looms on the second shift and another 150 looms were about to be stopped.

that because of the manpower problem . . . it will be impossible for you to comply fully with the direction involved. You state that there has been a constant drain on your manpower . . . that the third shift has been eliminated; that because of the fact that your plants are located in a predominantly agricultural area, a considerable number of employees are always lost every spring to the farming occupation; and that in order to meet the terms of the direction, it will be necessary to hire 400 new employees, 300 of which should be skilled operators, an action which is next to impossible at present. Consequently, in the face of these conditions you further state that you are able to produce only an approximate yardage of 500,000 weekly as compared to the 654,000 weekly yardage required by the direction.

In May it was the Navy's turn to issue a directive, calling upon the industry to turn out not less than 39 million yards of chambray in the last seven months of 1944. In order to turn out its share—500,000 yards a week under the revised W.P.B. directive—Dan River shifted weavers from 400 non-chambray looms to chambrays, transferred 112 looms from suitings to chambrays, and closed down the handkerchief-cloth division, freeing 372 more looms for chambrays. The loom schedules of September 21, 1944, showed 1,676 looms on 36-inch chambrays.

With 1,373 looms still frozen on 3.90 chambray, in October 1945 Dan River asked the W.P.B. to approve the transfer of 668 looms to other fabrics "essential and in short supply," such as work shirtings and trouserings. The mill believed that this was "in conformity with the policy of W.P.B. in that it will aid the reconversion of our plant, increase over-all production, and utilize finishing capacity installed in recent years at heavy cost." Permission to make the change was granted by the Civilian Production Administration in November.

Sheeting

In December 1940 the sales department reported an "absolute scarcity" of 63- and 72-inch sheets because of the "tremendous demand" for these goods by federal, state, and local government agencies. By the following May the company had to decline all civilian orders for these two widths. The needs of the armed forces rose sharply after Pearl Harbor, and late in 1942 the government requisitioned "the entire industry's production [of sheets] on practically all sizes for some months to come."[21] In an "all-out effort to supply such an important

[21] "It is military secret," D. L. Reardon wrote, "as to where these goods are to go, but we do know that they are for the Medical Department, following the United States Army in the field."

need," Dan River promised to furnish promptly over a million sheets and half a million pillow cases.

In July 1942 sheeting manufacturers were called on to make a high-count (84 × 96) cloth, dyed, mildew-proofed, and waterproofed, for use in hammocks. Dan River exercised its privilege of declining orders for this cloth, which the company had not manufactured for some time; but no such exception was granted to the W.P.B. order (May 1943) requiring manufacturers to shift all 42- to 50-inch looms to sheeting for converting into raincoat cloth. Much to the dismay of the sales department, the order had the effect of suspending the production of pillow cases; it was "not a desirable operation from the mill's standpoint" to tear wide sheeting in order to make cases. In June the entire line of sheeting, sheets, and pillow cases was withdrawn from non-government sale. In what was perhaps the most heroic effort to step up the production of sheeting, W.P.B. ordered Dan River (and other mills) to suspend production of all cotton textiles after April 1, 1944, unless its output of sheeting equaled the yardage manufactured in the first quarter of 1942. Since this meant the diversion of about 1.3 million yards monthly from "profitable dress goods and shirtings to sheetings, showing at best a very nominal profit," the company proposed to join the industry's "stiff fight" against the directive. Estimated production in the first quarter of 1944 was 6.8 million yards, as compared with 10.5 million yards in January–March 1942. It was, as a matter of fact, practically an unenforceable order from the standpoint of labor supply. In March 344 wide-sheeting looms had to be stopped for want of workers, and there was little prospect of finding enough help to man the 2,400 looms, running three shifts, which had turned out the base-period output.[22] On appeal, the order was revised downward: the company was ordered to produce 520,000 yards weekly; 2,400 wide-sheeting looms were scheduled, as of July 22, 1944; but the year's output of 18.9 million yards of gray sheeting was the lowest in over a decade. The sheeting looms were also used to produce comparatively small quantities of Navy mattress covers in 1944-1945.

In December 1944 civilian customers were offered a "share of our January, February, March production of sheets and pillow cases,"

---

[22] Furthermore, in the base period looms ran at 88 per cent efficiency, as compared with 80 per cent in 1944. Despite the usual "aversion of weavers to shifting to different types of looms and fabrics, not to mention going on the night shift," the management did plan to make up a third shift on sheeting looms by taking workers off 1,678 fancy looms.

though cautioned that if the government should take "some of the goods . . . projected ahead for civilian distribution . . . we cannot help it and, of course, it will be taken for the worthiest of causes." Output rose slightly to 20.6 million yards in 1945, while the needs of the armed services tended to rise with the increased tempo of the war in the Pacific. After doing what it could to help the government over the sheeting "hump"—the third quarter of 1945—Dan River accepted relatively small Army contracts.

In February 1945 the W.P.B. introduced the "set-aside" device for textile exports: each producer was required to allocate specified quantities and types of goods to foreign buyers.[23] In the *Dan River News Letter* of November 12, 1945, the sales department attempted to explain this feature of American policy:

We understand that the reasons largely stem from international politics, and that these export set-asides are made at the insistence of the State Department. We are told that, with world-wide textile production drastically reduced, it is essential that our country supply many of the world markets to keep down native unrest, and also to aid us in obtaining native raw materials which are badly needed. Some people in the Government think these set-asides will continue as long as there is a world shortage of textiles.

Set-asides were abolished at the end of 1946. In the meantime, Dan River had succeeded in obtaining "export rated order relief"—the language of W.P.B.—which permitted the company to sell against export orders 462,000 yards of ginghams instead of an equal yardage of seersucker, "Cord-spun," and "Cross-cord" cloth.[24]

As of August 17, 1945, all but one of the government contracts were canceled. Although the "quick change-over of a large part of our capacity was a major operation," the mills "were able to take the termination date in our stride without shutting down our machinery and without the layoff of a single employee."[25]

Reconversion was facilitated by pretermination agreements, under which the company agreed to retain "all raw cotton and all work in process up to and including cloth prepared for dyeing," while goods in the dyeing stage had to be held for government account.[26] In March 1946 the company appealed an order of the Civilian Production Ad-

[23] War Production Board, *Wartime Production Achievements and the Reconversion Outlook* (Washington, 1945), p. 77-82.
[24] W.P.B. to Riverside and Dan River Cotton Mlils, Jan. 5, 1945.
[25] *Annual Report and Financial Statements* (Danville, 1946).
[26] W. J. Fullerton to Philadelphia Quartermaster Depot, July 30, 1945.

ministration "to apply 971 looms to production of work shirt coverts or work shirt chambrays in addition to 705 looms now on that production."[27]

To the chagrin of the Dan River management, a local newspaper erroneously reported that the mills had earned the Army-Navy "E". The rumor originated in the War Department's request for data on the proportion of plant capacity devoted to war work in February 1944. At that time war contracts occupied 31.25 per cent of the company's looms and 62.5 per cent of the carding capacity, ratios which were not deemed high enough to justify the award.[28] It may not have been a matter of record in Washington that in addition to producing cloth for the armed forces Dan River "also turned over our designing and fabricating departments to government procurement agencies for the development of important new fabrics which we were unable to produce on our own equipment."[29] Again, in May 1945, the Philadelphia Quartermaster Depot was "interested in considering your two mills" for the "E"; but no award was made. In December, however, the Army Services Forces commended the company for its co-operation with the Quartermaster Corps, praising in particular the work of W. J. Fullerton, Dan River's manager of the Government Department in the New York sales offices. President Harris was satisfied "that our productive capacity was devoted to the war needs of our government without stint and that our contribution to the war effort was substantial and highly valued by the procurement offices." In a public ceremony on Sunday, January 27, 1946, General Louis B. Hershey awarded the mills the World War II Employment Flag.

At one time President Harris spoke approvingly of war orders which showed "a profit well in line with what these looms could show in civilian production." Profit could not, of course, be the sole basis for the decision to accept government contracts. Nevertheless, the management tended to regard the non-civilian part of its work as an unwelcome diversion from what the mills were best prepared to do: produce cloth to clothe the civilian population. In a letter "to our more than 13,000 employees," dated January 24, 1942, the president declared:

[27] G. S. Harris to Civilian Production Administration, March 18, 1946 (telegram).
[28] For the third quarter of 1944 orders rated AA2x or better constituted 45.75 of billings, and the total "rated" business was 58.25 per cent.
[29] G. S. Harris, "Conversion of World's Largest Cotton Mill to War Production a Man-sized Job" (typescript, Jan. 4, 1943).

Our war activities are not confined to our looms producing Army cloth, because people working in factories making war munitions, ships, etc., must have clothes and you are producing these clothes in addition to millions of yards of cloth that will be worn by our fighting forces . . . .

Every week we are working with the Army and Navy on additional yardage and our looms on these fabrics will steadily increase. At the same time, I want us to keep in mind that a man cannot build a ship until he has a pair of pants to wear and we are shipping millions of yards for that purpose. Likewise, all people in all walks of life will need clothes if we are to win this war.

Balanced production

One of the adverse effects of converting the mills to war production was the increase in the variety of goods manufactured, aggravating what Harris considered a major obstacle to profitable operations. "We are not on a very sound foundation," he wrote in December 1940. "We are confronted with the absolute necessity of reducing the number of yarn and color conditions . . . which now have us bogged down." Two reports on the problem painted a discouraging picture of the uncontrolled proliferation of "conditions."[30] In his first month in office the president urged department heads to reduce the number of yarns and colors, but between May and December 1940, the conditions increased from 1,519 to 1,583. In the departmental breakdown of conditions and yardage sold (January–June 1940) the sheeting department had "the best record by far": only 23 conditions were needed for sales of 10.2 million yards. The dress goods department was "extremely out of proportion, having many more conditions and the smallest volume of all the fancy departments"; but the clothing department, "which is in every sense a fancy department, has the largest dollar and cents volume with the lowest number of conditions."

Although, in a "fancy goods mill it is always necessary to change from one fabric construction to another, and this is generally a costly proposition," W. J. Fullerton thought department heads could be held responsible for more careful appraisal of market conditions in order to avoid producing patterns and styles that did not sell well. Concretely, any color or pattern of cloth which would not require a minimum 10,000-yard warp should be dropped.[31] The company's chemist,

[30] A condition is a combination of grade and staple length in the "mix" put into the openers, yarn size, and color.

[31] W. J. Fullerton to G. S. Harris, Dec. 13, 1940. Fullerton referred to instances in which styles had been abandoned too soon. "During 1939 we checked the market on All

Dr. H. M. Chase, confirmed Fullerton's criticisms of the unwieldly and uneconomical practice of making up an excessive number of yarn and color conditions. "During the year [1940] nineteen different mixes of cotton, strips and comber noils, rayon, have been dyed. Some colors occur on three or four different mixes, which is equivalent to three or four separate colors. These mixes not only have to be carefully kept separate in the dye house, but all through the mill. Since [July 1] one hundred and sixty-eight new conditions (new colors or old colors on new mixes) have been added." Chase, too, thought that "we should select our fabrics strictly on the basis of suitable equipment, familiarity with the same or similar lines, and the probability of volume production."

In January 1941 President Harris confessed that the great size of the mills made it difficult for him to discover why Dan River had been a "marginal earner for eight or more years . . . .

Had our producing units been smaller, I could have seen the picture more clearly months ago. Due again to the size of our producing units and the complicated operating conditions, I failed to see that we are badly out of balance . . . . Unquestionably, our size as compared with our competitors is our greatest difficulty. Theoretically, this should be solely a matter of strong men in key positions with an alert chief executive to coordinate these forces. Practically, this has its difficulties but I am convinced that in time the necessary organization can be perfected.

Many hopes for improvement were snuffed out by the fever of war production, but Harris lived to see the mills come closer to his scheme of "balanced" production.

One of the earliest steps taken to correct the excessive diversification of the company's products was the decision to stop manufacturing cotton flannels. In December 1942 D. L. Reardon was convinced that these goods could not become a profitable line and recommended the sale of the napping machines. He was overruled by the sales department's executive committee, which guessed that the machinery

---

Spun Rayon Plaids and found a definite demand . . . so we decided to go into production. During this season we made approximately 1,000,000 yards and we had a great deal of trouble, such as streaky dyeing, trouble in spinning, in warping, slashing and weaving; but our people in the mill worked terrifically hard all through the season ironing out the kinks here and there . . . and finally accomplished what at first seemed like the impossible. Toward the end of the season they had overcome all of the difficulties and could really make that type of cloth to perfection. Then the next season for this type of cloth came around. We didn't follow up our advantage. . . . during 1940 we made approximately 500,000 yards and we should have at least doubled our 1939 production because the business was there to be had.
"We had practically the same experiences on Dotted Swisses."

might be needed again; but no flannels were produced after 1943.[32] Looms weaving "Riverside" barber cloth were reassigned during the war. Until 1947 the demand for sheets was so great that few looms could be spared for barber cloth. Volume production was resumed at the instance of the sales department, which pointed out that Cannon Mills was the only firm making this fabric. But in 1948 "the goods were not moving as quickly as anticipated" and it seemed pointless to continue the line.

From 1943 on Dan River had 50 looms "frozen" on birdseye cloth, i.e., the mill could not employ more or less looms on this fabric. Market conditions in 1946 appeared to favor an increase in output, but the management felt "licked before we start" because of O.P.A. price ceilings. Production was "somewhat increased" in 1947; the trademark "Health Diapers" was renewed and a new box designed for packaging the garments; but indifferent results in the market led to the dropping of this product after the first quarter of 1948.

Another casualty of the war period was the line of automobile seat-cover cloth. In February 1941 "Dantex" fabrics were offered in 32 styles. The contract with W. H. Duncan Company for the distribution of this product was terminated in June 1943 and the looms reassigned to chambray production.[33]

While the domestics department was losing its diapers and flannels, the sheeting lines expanded to include percales. In July 1940, after the major textile merchants agreed on 180 threads as the minimum count for goods labeled percale, Dan River disposed of its stock (200 cases) of "Candlelight' percale, a combed sheeting with a thread count of only 164. Over 200,000 yards of "Dancraft" combed percales (88× 96) were turned out in 1940-1941, but the urgent need of combers for other goods halted this development. "Dancale," a carded-yarn percale (88×96) was introduced and nearly one million yards manufactured in 1941-1942. Repeated recommendation of the sales department finally led to the reintroduction of combed-yarn sheets in 1949.[34] To-

[32] The output this year was 1,578,300 yards, compared with 1941 production of 10,446,925 yards.

[33] G. S. Harris to B. Cone, Nov. 22, 1943. But Harris explained that the seat-cover trade "left us suddenly at the beginning of the war." In 1946 a proposal to produce automobile headlinings received some attention (B. B. Howard to J. F. McCarthy, July 16, 1946).

[34] D. L. Reardon to J. J. Duffy, Dec. 21, 1945; J. M. Hughlett to D. L. Reardon, Jan. 22, 1946. At the end of 1945 comber production was 105,000 pounds of yarn per week, of which 74,000 pounds were allotted to shirtings and 31,000 pounds to dress goods. New combers were ordered in February 1946.

ward the end of 1947 the sales force reported an increased demand for scalloped pillowcases and recommended making "Dan River" scalloped cases similar to those of Cannon Mills. At the same time the sales division urged "experimental work" to improve the hemstitching on the new "Dancale" line.

"Dan River" sheeting and sheets (Type 128) continued to dominate the muslin lines. Production in 1942 amounted to 23.5 million gray yards, in 15 different widths, as compared with an output of 8.4 million yards of "Riverside" (Type 140) and 8.2 million yards of "Morotock" (Type 116). In 1943 the three lines were rechristened "Old Dominion" ("Morotock"), "Shenandoah" ("Dan River"), and "Virginia Manor" ("Riverside"). Production of 6.1 million yards of "Virginia Manor" in 1943 as compared with 8.4 million yards of "Old Dominion" forecast the persistent upward shift in the demand for finer muslin bedlinen.[35] The "Old Dominion" (Type 116) line was discontinued after the war.

The war also put an end to Dan River's career as a producer of part-wool suitings. Early in 1942 President Harris surmised that, with woolen mills cut back to 20 per cent of normal wool consumption, cotton manufacturers would have to find substitutes for the wool used in blended yarns. "Our years of experience in blending synthetic staples," he thought, would give the company an advantage over woolen and worsted manufacturers who might try to adapt their equipment to the man-made fibers. There were those who were fooled, or pretended to be, by the prewar look of suits made of Dan River cotton and rayon goods. "For your information," Harris replied to one critic, "there is not a pound of precious wool in this cloth." The cloth in question was "Rivercool," the all spun-rayon "tropical" suiting, "the aristocrat of all spun-rayon fabrics for men's summer suits or for top-quality slacks." "Riverbreeze" was another all spun-rayon fabric for summer suits and slacks, "more popular in price than Rivercool." "Rivercrest" was a half-cotton, half-rayon fabric, "designed for strength . . . and the admitted leader in its price field." "Imperial" plaids, a cloth "made to resemble a very fine wool flannel," was introduced in May 1941; and toward the end of the war "Rayokool," a spun-rayon, piece-dyed cloth was added to the lines of suiting fabrics. After the war Dan River

[35] In 1949 the mill adopted a new finish on its Type 128 sheeting, inasmuch as the old "weighty feel" of this durable type of sheet seemed no longer to be important to the buyer. (D. L. Reardon to B. D. Browder, Feb. 14, 1949).

developed an even greater variety of spun and filament rayon suitings for both summer and winter clothing.

On the basis of its experience in making water-repellent goods for the armed forces, in 1945 the company set up a stormwear division in the shirting and sportswear department. The first fabric offered for sale was the combed-yarn, vat-dyed, Zelan-treated "Aquadan," promoted as a cloth "most desirable for the raincoat trade." "Stormwear" was the trade name of another water-repellent cloth "popularly used for raincoats, skisuits, golf jackets, etc." "Tattersal," a two-ply cotton fabric in checks, was designed for women's rainwear.

The numerous lines of shirting fabrics included plain and fancy Oxford cloth and white and colored broadcloths for dress shirts and sportswear. "Prince Oxford" was a yarn-dyed, mercerized cotton for shirts, shorts, and pajamas. "Spunray" was a two-ply rayon and cotton fabric for "leisure shirts, dress shirts and ensembles," while "Skytop" was a cotton mesh "comfort shirting, porous and cool, with the sheen of rayon." It was also promoted for pajamas and dress shirts. "Danscot," another cotton and rayon blend, was offered to manufacturers of boys' wear, slacks, skirts, and sport shirts.

In the dress goods department "Scotspun" was the largest selling item in 1941, but it gave way to an endless variety of styles, patterns, and colors of cotton and rayon goods. Besides the staple "Dan River," new "Starspun" in checks and plaids helped to preserve the company's traditional position in the gingham market. "Crosscord" similarly supplemented the older lines of chambrays.

Riverside's yarn mill (No. 6) continued to justify the expectations of the West management that a market could be found for yarns too coarse for the fabrics in which Dan River found it most profitable to specialize. Number 14, and even coarser yarns, were produced in single and multi-plies (up to six) for weavers of carpets, tapestries, and webbing and for knitting mills making hosiery, sweat shirts, and sweaters. The yarns were "not suitable for underwear manufacture or in any product where the presence of a little colored fly would be objectionable or cause seconds." In 1948 J. O. Petty advised an exporter that Dan River could supply spun rayon yarns, preferably "on the coarser side," since twisting capacity for sales yarns was limited.

Purchase of 32,000 pounds of nylon staple in January 1946 was, apparently, the beginning of the company's experimentation with this fiber. In July 1949 samples of four fabrics containing 40 per-cent spun nylon and 60 per-cent spun rayon were entered for production, but no nylon goods were offered for sale until the 1950's.

The shift to the production of finer fabrics and new finishes created new, or virtually new, problems of quality control. Whereas in the 1930's it sufficed to conduct routine laboratory tests and search for the causes of any unusual ratio of seconds or defective cloth, quality control in the 1940's had to be organized on a continuous basis. As long as the company worked on war orders quality control was essential to the maintenance of standards set by government specifications. After the war, quality control helped to maintain the quality of the rapidly changing array of new constructions, new colors, and new finishes, many of them marketed under the company's own label for the first time.

"The selection of a man to organize and head up a quality control function . . . from manufacturing through finishing" was one of the topics on the agenda for discussions by the New York executive committee in December 1942. Organization of the Quality Control Department under the direction of W. L. Clement took place the following year. The first job of the department concerned suiting production, and in July 1944 Superintendent Newton reported that seconds had been reduced to 2 per cent, "the lowest percentage of seconds we have ever had." In January 1945 the quality control installation was "about 60 per cent complete" and the "factual records in the hands of the operating staff" were found "increasingly effective in reducing off quality goods or seconds." But quality was ever an elusive component of textiles. In 1947 it was the "unanimous opinion of the salesmen . . . that there has been a letdown in the quality and grading of such a large proportion of our lines that the fine Dan River reputation is seriously threatened."[36] Many solutions were offered to make quality control more effective, but the "deluge of complaints on quality" scarcely receded until the company entered the astonishing "sellers' market" of 1948.[37]

[36] "I am sorry indeed," J. M. Miller wrote President Harris, "that our goods have not been holding up to our quality standard. I have been bragging about our quality for sometime past." He recalled an instance in the 1930's when "bed sheets were sent out with holes in them big enough to put your head through."

[37] In a memorandum to the president (June 13, 1947) M. Franco stressed the importance of inspection in the weave rooms at Schoolfield Division. "A great deal of valuable information is sent from Quality to the various departments," but "the sending of this information could be reduced" if mistakes were corrected before the goods reached the Greige inspection rooms. In 1948 the sales office said that it did not get prompt answers

Excessive shrinkage was one of several recurrent sources of complaint. Thus, in 1947 a "very puzzling situation" developed in connection with Sanforized broadcloth. The customer, a leading shirt manufacturer, inspected the plant without finding a significant fault; Cluett, Peabody found nothing wrong with the operation of the Sanforizers; and Dan River's experts approved of the customer's testing method. Yet samples tested in the customer's laboratory showed greater shrinkage than that of samples from the same piece of cloth tested at Dan River. A new finish on "Spunray," perfected in 1948, was found to be "out of Sanforized tolerance."[38] Even with the "tebilized" finish, goods shrank 3.5-4 per cent after ten washings. An "extensive experiment" in the Research Department finally brought the shrinkage of "Spunray" under control—i.e., not over 1 per cent in nine launderings. It was decided, however, to continue Sanforizing this fabric. On other rayon goods the new resin finishes kept residual shrinkage within 1 per cent without Sanforizing.[39]

Sheet shrinkage was a less difficult problem. In one of several tests of competitive sheets Dan River's Type 128 came out third best on the basis of the combined shrinkage of width and length after one wash at the Danville Laundry (1949). But, "for practical purposes, shrinkage in sheets is not of vital importance, as sheets are customarily bought with allowance for shrinkage. . . . the loss in length by shrinkage does not materially affect their adequacy in use."[40]

The odor of cloth, or of garments made of Dan River fabrics, gave rise to some of the most delicate letters of complaint. In October 1940 it was admitted that, with the existing equipment, the urea-formaldehyde odor could not be completely eliminated from the "Spun-

to complaints addressed to Quality Control (J. M. Hughlett, "Meeting of Department Managers," Feb. 4, 1948). A year later the complaint of delays was repeated, and it was added that some of the replies from Quality Control were "so ridiculous that we cannot possibly pass it on to the customers." For instance, it was suggested that Dan River tell its customers that if some of their workers were allergic to the resin finish on "Skytop" the workers "should be shifted from working with these goods" (W. J. Fullerton to B. D. Browder, March 21, 1949).

[38] H. M. Chase to B. B. Howard, July 15, 1948. Tests in Danville indicated that home-laundered shirts did not shrink, "but there has been trouble every time these shirts have been laundered by a commercial laundry." From the sales viewpoint it seemed impractical to caution against commercial laundering of "Spunray" garments (B. D. Browder to J. F. Grimes, July 27, 1948).

[39] W. J. Adams to W. J. Fullerton, Jan. 7, 1949. Another case of excessive shrinking (10.56 per cent in the warp) was reported for some "Rivercool" suiting which had been dyed by United Piece Dye Works (B. D. Browder to T. J. Corcoran, June 17, 1948).

[40] Association of Cotton Textile Merchants, "Considerations involved in tentative specifications for cotton bed sheets and pillow cases" (1947). Of course, this was not true of fitted sheets, which came into use after 1949.

ray" fabrics. Although new equipment promised to solve this problem, complaints persisted. At least two shipments of "Dantwill" were
returned to the mill for rehandling because of an "objectionable odor"
in the cloth.

A spray-rating test at intervals of 5,000 yards was used to control
the quality of water-repellent goods, but the Quality Control Department collected a sheaf of complaints of fabrics such as the raincoat
"Dantwill" which lacked sufficient water repellency. In 1947 the Textile Fabrics Association met to discuss possible standards for "storm
resistant" and "rain resistant" cloth, and the following year the Federal
Trade Commission called a trade-practice conference on the problem.
Dan River's director of research, H. M. Chase, was "strongly opposed
to too much Federal regulation on the subject of labeling . . . .

In the case of water-repellent goods I do not see how anything but confusion can result. There have been many tentative proposals to use such
words as 'water-repellent', 'shower-proof', 'storm-proof', 'rain-proof', etc. . . .
Of course, penalties would have to be devised for improper use of these
terms and inasmuch as what some people call a shower other people call a
rain, I do not think the public would be any better served that it is at
present, although undoubtedly some manufacturers are turning out products which are inferior to those of others.

Similarly, Chase thought a proposed commercial standard on the
flammability of textiles was "absurd"; he granted that it would be
appropriate to require labeling of "those fabrics which are hazardous."[41]

The number of customer complaints relating to unsatisfactory
colors was large but probably not excessive for a firm making such a
variety of dyed fabrics. "Shading," or the slight variations in color of
different batches of the same style of cloth, caused the return of thousands of yards of goods. In answering one complaint, the manager of
the finishing plant said: "We continue to work on the matter of shading here, and while we have not made any miraculous improvements,
there has been a steady improvement in the handling of goods, and
recent changes, both in the physical layout of the Shading Room and
in personnel, we believe, have put our shading in a much stronger and
more efficient basis than it has ever been." In February 1948 changes
in a gray dye formula were expected "to put a stop to the high per-

[41] H. M. Chase to B. D. Browder, Nov. 29, 1946. The sales department also thought
that only "dangerously flammable fabrics" should be labeled (J. M. Hughlett to Association of Cotton Textile Merchants, Jan. 30, 1947).

centage of throw-outs we have had because of too many assorted shade cases." In discussing a complaint about the "disappearance of shade" in garments made of Dan River poplin, W. L. Clement diagnosed the trouble as "abrasion"—i.e., the customer had practically worn out his pants. This was no snap judgment: "Every dye lot on goods shipped this customer were tested for fastness to washing, wet and dry cleaning, and light fastness." Although all the tests were satisfactory, Clement was hopeful that further improvement in dyeing processes would yield a cloth which would "stand more and more wear without the color going out." Complaints about the crocking of flame-color "Dantwill" prompted B. D. Browder to remind the salesmen that goods in this color had to be sold without a guarantee, since no way had been found to prevent frequent crocking.[42]

Research

In July 1940 President Harris told one of his former associates at Springs Mills that he was "developing a Research department, similar to yours, and having an interesting time of it." The Research and Development Committee, established in 1942, brought together sales executives, designers, production specialists, and chemists. "With our fully equipped Designing Department, plus a very complete laboratory in chemistry and dyeing," Harris observed in 1943, "this Committee has done . . . some excellent work. Experiments in fabric construction, especially with synthetic fiber blends, have already produced most interesting results. We hope to be ready when the war ends to 'follow the cat whichever way he jumps.' " By the end of 1945 the research department, now styled Research Engineering Division, had a staff of 13 chemists, 4 engineers, 2 physicists, 13 technicians, and 16 administrative and clerical workers. Its director, Dr. H. M. Chase, was assisted by Dr. H. Y. Jennings, who joined the Dan River research staff as a chemist in 1943. Work was conducted along two main lines: (1) operational research, furnishing "continuous and direct service to the operating divisions" and (2) developmental research, concerned with the "creation and development of new processes and products."[43]

[42] B. D. Browder to J. Daniels, May 21, 1947. In 1946 the mill advised the sales office that it preferred not to make "Dantwill Flame": "the mill will experience trouble each time this shade is dyed and . . . the percentage of seconds will run very high" (J. Daniels to L. K. Fitzgerald, Sept. 19, 1946).
[43] H. M. Chase, "Report on Dan River Research Work during 1945."

As of January 1946 projects in the field of pure research included work

on new types of synthetic resins and on the cotton fiber itself, with especial reference to the chemical transformation of the fiber . . . . No particular end is sought and all projects are contained strictly within the realm of pure research. Upon the appearance of any development which promises commercial possibilities, that phase of the pure research project is transferred to chemists and physicists working specifically in applied research.

In applied research, activity centered on "the treatment of synthetic resins and other bonding agents of textile fibers, rovings, yarn and fabrics."[44] The division (in 1945) comprised seven sections, "each . . . a separate and distinct entity, but . . . at the same time completely integrated with all the other research and development agencies of the Company."[45] The sections included a laboratory for fundamental chemical research, a practical working laboratory, a physical laboratory, a control laboratory, a pilot mill, a design department, and "a department permanently staffed, and segregated from all routine mill operations, and devoted to the development and exploration of mechanical methods and improvements." Twelve chemical and physical laboratories, spread over 23,500 square feet of floor space, were housed in the new part of Riverside's Mill No. 1.

Research in dyeing led to the perfection of two patented processes: (*a*) continuous pigment vat dyeing, and (*b*) oil-in-water pigment dyeing. As early as 1940 the sales department found Pepperell's vat stock-dyed herringbone selling at a price equal to Dan River's cost on similar fabrics dyed with less acceptable sulphur colors. The war hastened research on methods of dyeing rapidly the deep shades required on government goods; and in 1943 Dan River's chemist, Glen F. Womble, perfected a "speedy and economical" process which "yielded, in long and varied commercial operation, colors of maximum fastness and evenness in shading, from light pastels to deep solid tones, the full range of color possibilities from vat dyestuffs." The new method supplanted the straight-jig, pigment-pad jig, and reduced-pad, continuous vat dyeing methods—all "considered inefficient in that they were either slow, complex and expensive, or that coloration at high speed has been

---

[44] "A Report on Current Research conducted by the Research Engineering Division of Riverside & Dan River Cotton Mills, Inc. . . . prepared at the request of U. S. Department of Agriculture," Jan. 15, 1946.
[45] Riverside & Dan River Cotton Mills, *Review of Dan River Research and Patent Digest* (Danville, 1945), pp. 1-2. See also: W. J. Ritz, "Textile Research by the River Dan," *The Commonwealth*, vol. 13 (Richmond: July, 1946), pp. 7-10, 32.

limited to light shades."[46] During the war Dan River shared the new process with other manufacturers working on government orders, so that "hundreds of millions of yards of cloth were delivered to the Army in the correct shades and at speeds that eclipsed all the old methods." The continuous vat dyeing process was patented on March 19, 1946.

The basic patent for oil-in-water pigment dyeing was issued to Dr. Harley Y. Jennings (November 16, 1943). Dr. Jennings came to Danville to carry on in the Dan River laboratories research initiated under the auspices of Copeman Laboratories of Flint, Michigan. After he joined the Dan River staff, the company acquired several patents originally issued (1937-1942) to F. E. Bartell, L. G. Copeman, and Dr. Jennings. Four of these covered the treatment of fibers and fabrics with resins, a process commercially introduced by Dan River under the trade mark "Fiber-bonded."

The research department claimed the following advantages for the new fiber-bonding and dyeing processes:

The coloring matter bound to the material by the dry film of resinous substances is fast and permanent;

The textile materials are of a uniform color and appearance;

The resinous substances not only bind the coloring matter to the fibers in a smooth and continuous film but also serve as a finish for the treated material, so that the usual dyeing and finishing steps are accomplished in a single operation;

The finish may be made permanent as regards washing and dry-cleaning;

The resinous substance imparts added wear to the fabric by offering an additional surface against abrasion, and the tensile strength is increased;

The treated material may be subjected to repeated washings without affecting the "hand" or appearance;

Since the emulsion carrying the pigment is relatively thin, it penetrates the fibrous structure of the fabric without affecting the porosity of the fabric;

The amount of organic solvent required by the dyeing process is so small as to make it unnecessary to use any recovery apparatus;

No subsequent reaction is necessary as in other dyeing methods, because the dye pigments are already developed and in water-insoluble form.[47]

[46] *Review of Dan River Research*, pp. 20-22.
[47] *Review of Dan River Research*, pp. 5-16. The oil-in-water method also "greatly simplifies the application of pigment dyes by eliminating all explosion and fire hazards. The equipment is easily cleaned by flushing with water . . . . The outstanding characteristic of uniformity of shade is easily obtained. Phenomenal results are achieved in the surface appearance of yarns and fabrics dyed by this method which permits the use of lower grade cotton than is possible with any other dyes" (*Report on Progress Made during 1945 in Development of New Textile Products by Fiber Bonded Processes of Dan River Mills* [n.p., 1946], p. 3).

Fiber bonding developed out of research on methods of stretching cotton fibers to increase tensile strength. One of the early patents (1937) was granted to Russell B. Newton, Dan River's president in 1949-1952, for a process of stretching tire cord after saturation with water. A patent granted to Dr. Jennings (1940) covered a process employing chemicals.

His procedure consisted in applying the bonding materials in a solution or emulsion form to the yarn or cord, stretching the yarn to as near the breaking point as practical, while the resins were in the plastic stage, and then setting the bonding material on the fibers. His first work was done for the shoe thread field and shoe threads were said to have been produced in which tensile strength was increased 70% or 80%. The stretch was taken out of the cotton yarn and at the same time the strength increased so that it compared favorably in properties with linen thread.[48]

What Dr. Chase considered "an entirely new and revolutionary idea" was the application of stretching and bonding to rovings, increasing tensile strength by 75 to 100 per cent.[49]

Dan River engineers, assisted by the Walter Kidde Company of New Jersey, perfected fiber-bonding machinery. Two experimental machines, together with specimens of fiber-bonded yarns and fabrics, were exhibited by Dan River at the 1946 Convention of the American Association of Textile Chemists and Colorists. The twenty-six exhibits included samples of fiber-bonded rovings with a tensile strength of 16 pounds (as compared with 9.5 pounds untreated), belt ducking and webbing made from fiber-bonded roving, fiber-bonded pigment-dyed warps for awning fabrics, "slip-proofed" marquisette, shoe-lining fabric, florist twine, spinning tape, and conveyor-belt fabric with a tensile strength of 1,000 pounds per inch, or about twice that of the standard fabric.[50] A similar exhibit was prepared for the First National Plastics Exposition in New York, April 22-27, 1946[51]; and in May the exhibit

[48] H. M. Chase, "The Treatment of Cotton Roving and Yarns with Bonding Agents," *American Dyestuff Reporter*, vol. 33, Nov. 6, 1944, pp. 474-478 (a paper presented at the Annual Meeting of American Association of Textile Chemists and Colorists, Oct. 14, 1944). Dr. Jennings gave an "Explanation of Fiber Bonding" at a meeting of the Southern Textile Association (*Textile Colorist and Converter*, vol. 68, July 1946, p. 31).

[49] Earlier patents (1,959,723 and 2,215,633) had been granted for direct treatment of rovings but had not been utilized commercially. According to the *Rayon Textile Monthly* (vol. 26, Oct. 1945, p. 85), the "great interest shown by the world textile industry in these developments has been evidenced by the large number of mill executives and technologists who have visited Danville in the past year."

[50] *Report on Progress* (1946), pp. 6-14. The 50-end fiber-bonded machine for yarns and rovings is pictured and described in the booklet, *A Development of Dan River Research: Fiber Bonded Processes* (Danville, 1946).

[51] *Plastics Work Miracles with Textiles* (n.p., 1946); *Daily News Record*, April 22, 1946.

was moved to the Philadelphia store of Gimbel Brothers. The premier showing of "Color Bond" fabrics—resin-pigment dyed and bonded cloth —also took place at Gimbels, May 10-25, 1946.

"Florabond," a florist twine made of plied yarns, dyed and fiber-bonded, was put on the market in 1945 under the Dan River trademark. The following year Cutler Textiles marketed a fiber-bonded tape under a Dan River license. Licensees paid royalties of 2 to 3 per cent of sales.[52] Some Dan River officials seemed proud of "our willingness to share our findings on a licensing basis, as contrasted with others who would try to monopolize the results of their laboratories," but the company's advertising agency recommended a more practical view: "bear in mind that it does not become profitable for you to license a patent until the potential royalties from other firms exceed the potential amount you can save in your own operation by not paying any royalties yourself."[53] A confidential "Research Abstract" for the information of licensees was started in December 1945 but was not, apparently, continued.

Before the war the progress of American research in the application of resin finishes was promising enough to weaken the monopolistic position of the English firm, Tootal Broadhurst Lee Company, with respect to a crease-resisting finishing process. Dan River's contract for use of "Tebilized" finishes expired in October 1946. Terms for a new agreement were under discussion for several months, but in July 1947, Tootal Broadhurst Lee withdrew its "last" offer and terminated Dan River's license to use the "Tebilized" trade mark. Meanwhile, the Research Division carried on experiments with resin-finishing processes which would not infringe the "Tebilized" patents. For about two years the Monsanto Chemical Company collaborated with Dan River, furnishing a synthetic resin called "Resloom C"; and in

[52] *Rayon Textile Monthly*, vol. 27, July 1946, p. 11. In October 1945 President Harris said that the company had been licensing mills "rather extensively for the past several months." Fiber-bonded yarns produced from rovings had been practical "only in the coarser numbers" and there seemed to be "little possibility of it ever developing into the fine yarn field." (G. S. Harris to M. Beattie, Oct. 10, 1945). Tires made of fiber-bonded yarns were being road tested in November 1944, but I have found no record of the results (G. S. Harris to E. H. Lee, Nov. 27, 1944).

Rayon Textile Monthly (vol. 27, Dec. 1946, p. 80) declared: "The resin treatment process developed by Dan River Mills has become of international significance in textile manufacturing, and is now being adopted by licensees in a number of other mills in the United States and in more than a dozen foreign countries."

[53] J. A. Cairns to G. S. Harris, Nov. 22, 1943. As early as November 1944 Harris declared: "So far as the yarn development is concerned, we expect to earn considerably more through the operations of licensees than in our own production" (G. S. Harris to L. D. Brace, Nov. 7, 1944).

August 1947 "Wrinkl-Shed" fabrics were introduced.[54] First applied to
the coarser cottons,[55] "Wrinkl-Shed" had "eight amazing new features,"
including wrinkle-resistance comparable to that of fine worsteds, permanent shrinkage control, soil-resistance, mildew-resistance, faster drying and easier ironing. Continued research improved the process, making it possible to offer the "Wrinkl-Shed" finish on all Dan River
fabrics for which these qualities had some consumer appeal.[56]

In 1947-1949 the following patents awarded to Dan River scientists
were assigned to the corporation:

Glenn F. Womble and Paul Feldman: Dyeing fabrics containing cellu-
losic material treated with quaternary nitrogen compounds.

William B. Carroll, Jr.: Dyed cellulose ethers and dyeing of fabrics
therewith.

Dmitry M. Gagarine: Polymeric polyhydric alcohol condensation products and treatment of cellulose textiles therewith.

In 1948 Dr. Chase was honored by the award of the Olney Medal
for outstanding achievement in textile chemistry.

Sales

Organization

As of December 1940 the sales organization, headed by General
Sales Manager F. K. Nixon, comprised five divisions in charge of divisional managers and a number of departments and offices assigned
to specialists in designing, production, or sales. Five regional sales
offices in St. Louis, Chicago, Atlanta, Boston, and Los Angeles were
managed by general salesmen. In addition, three general salesmen
responsible to the New York office covered territory not assigned to
regional offices.

The death of Nixon in April 1941 left a gap in the sales organiza-

[54] "Rinkl-Rid" seems to have been the first suggestion for a trade name (L. H. Browder
to B. D. Browder, Oct. 31, 1945).

[55] In 1948 salesmen complained that some customers preferred to buy greige goods,
because Dan River couldn't finish the finer fabrics as well as some finishing plants.
Referring to the "Everglaze" resin process of one of these rival firms, J. Udis declared:
"I think they have it" (J. Udis to W. J. Fullerton, Apr. 28, 1948).

[56] The "amazing features" of "Wrinkl-Shed" were not immediately convincing to the
consumer. In December 1949 company officials "road tested" pajamas made of "Wrinkl-
Shed Dantone." President Newton considered the cloth unsatisfactory for pajamas—it
did not have a "smooth, silky hand." Vice-president Browder reported no improvement
as far as wrinkling was concerned over untreated cloth; while John Cairns of the advertising agency thought the fabric was "entirely too rough and sandpapery."

tion which was not formally closed for four years. There was either no candidate, or too many candidates, for the position to pick Nixon's successor as general sales manager. A compromise was found in the creation of an executive committee, consisting of the five divisional heads.[57] The executive committee held its first meeting on April 16, 1941. Because of "a certain amount of jealousy," the committee had no chairman; but President Harris felt the company had "a set-up on which we can depend . . . . In some ways we have a strength that was not present with Nixon as Sales Manager." He had, perhaps, not anticipated that the arrangement would require him to spend half his time in New York; and in July the president confessed that the sales office was "a difficult problem."

Sometimes I think we are making progress . . . and again I run into things that are quite discouraging. I still think that if it is at all possible, we should select one of our own men but, frankly, the best man we have still lacks sufficient training and would have to overcome considerable jealousy . . . . It will require some courage to make an appointment and then force that appointment through against some odds. On the other hand, it would probably require more courage to admit that our men are not equal to the task and risk the selection of a stranger, attempting to support him through a period of training.

In July 1941 the company advised its yarn customers that the Dan River sales organization would take over all sales of yarn. "This change," the announcement said, "is no reflection on Schoolfield & Company, who have so well represented us in the past, but it is effort to better service our customers through a closer contact with our mills." Kyle T. Alfriend became manager of the yarn sales division but maintained his office in Danville. The following year, in order to provide personal contacts with its principal yarn customers, Dan River opened an office in Philadelphia, placing J. W. Sauer in charge. It was closed in 1945.

The war necessitated numerous changes in the sales organization. W. J. Fullerton was appointed manager of the new government division to handle sales to the armed services. A contract dress goods division was set up with J. Udis as manager and A. Poremba as designer; while T. E. Morgan had charge of a pajama and shorts department and H. S. Van Ingen managed the new merchandising research

[57] L. H. Browder, secretary, L. R. Walls, D. L. Reardon, J. M. Hughlett, and B. P. Anderson. Anderson, who succeeded Nixon as manager of the clothing fabrics division, was inducted in the armed forces. His place was taken by E. A. Dafter.

department. In 1943 Walter Willcox was assigned to the full-time job
of preparing charts and other statistical materials for both the New
York and Danville offices.

A war casualty was the handkerchief fabrics division. The creation
of this division under A. A. Buff came about as a result of President
Harris' opposition to treating these fabrics as "loom fillers" and confining sales to one broker.[58] During the first nine months under Buff's
direction the division sold six million yards of cloth for $750,000, with
a net profit averaging 9.5 per cent of sales. In December 1943 Buff
recommended the purchase of a small plant in Passaic, New Jersey,
which was suitable for the manufacture of handkerchiefs. The executive committee agreed that Dan River was "not ready as yet to recommend to our administration that we go into any operations outside of
Danville," nor did the committee think it "advisable to buy the machinery alone for transfer to Danville at present in view of the requirements of skilled labor and the differential in the wage schedule in the
manufacture of handkerchiefs." A more important consideration behind the decision to stop making handkerchief cloth (June 1944) was
the growing shortage of combed yarns for government requirements.
Buff, who shortly thereafter resigned, told the president that Dan
River's withdrawal from this market was a "great shock" to all its
customers, "inasmuch as we were their only source of supply . . . for
the past two years."

The substitution of an executive committee for a general sales manager, which worked not too badly as long as the salesmen had little to
do, threatened to become an awkward arrangement when postwar
markets demanded aggressive selling. In May 1945 President Harris advised the directors that he proposed to appoint J. M. Hughlett general
sales manager. The board approved the appointment, and later in the
year Hughlett was made a vice-president and director.

An organization chart prepared in May 1947 showed the following
personnel:

J. M. Hughlett, general sales manager.
L. H. Browder, assistant treasurer in charge of advertising, credit, and
    New York office finance
W. J. Fullerton, director of merchandising, dress and gray goods depart-
    ments, and director of fabric development (except clothing fabrics)

[58] G. S. Harris to F. K. Nixon, June 6, 1940. "We are, in my opinion," Harris said,
"producing quality merchandise which should in some way afford us a better profit."

W. W. Lufkin, Jr., administrative assistant
E. T. Pugh, in charge of production control
J. F. Grimes, manager, shirting and sportswear department
D. L. Reardon, manager, domestics department
J. F. McCarthy, manager, staple colored goods department
J. Daniels, manager, stormwear department
T. J. Corcoran, manager, clothing fabrics department
R. H. Lennox, manager, dress goods department
J. Udis, manager, gray goods department

General Line Salesmen:

Atlanta:	G. C. Robey and E. D. Cogburn
Boston:	F. E. D. Talbot
Chicago:	D. F. Reynolds and J. D. Moir
St. Louis:	F. J. Hahn and J. S. Hammes
Los Angeles:	C. O. Vigeland and H. Houston
New York:	E. A. Anderson, S. Gibson, K. E. Pinnell, and A. J. Rowlenson

D. F. Reynolds took over the Chicago office on the death of J. C. Long in 1943. In 1949 F. J. Hahn left the St. Louis office for reasons of health, and illness forced T. J. Corcoran to resign as manager of the clothing fabrics department. In 1949 Frank L. Cassady became head of the new over-the-counter piece-goods department. Stanley Talbot succeeded his father in the Boston office (1949),[59] while new sales offices were opened in Philadelphia and Dallas.

The illness of President Harris shifted to Vice-president Newton a large share of managerial responsibility, including supervision of the sales organization. In September 1949 Newton discussed with the directors "numerous problems in the Merchandising Divisions"—the minutes are not specific—and recommended that Hughlett be requested to resign. The board thought Harris should be consulted, as he doubtless was; but on September 23 Hughlett resigned. W. W. Lufkin succeeded him as general sales manager and vice-president.

In 1940 Dan River occupied Rooms 700-712 at 40 Worth Street. Four additional rooms were rented in 1941, increasing the rent bill from $14,500 to $18,500 annually; but this included the rental of two rooms used by G. A. Stafford & Co. The need for more space grew during and after the war, and in 1947 the "deplorably crowded condi-

---

[59] F. E. D. Talbot retired at the age of seventy-three. For fourteen years he had sold Dan River fabrics in the New England area for a commission of 1¼ per cent, plus an allowance of $75 monthly for his Boston office. S. Talbot took over as a full-time salaried salesman.

tion" at 40 Worth Street compelled the company to lease additional office space on Broadway. As a result, the advertising department was separated from the rest of the sales department until 1950.

Table 7 depicts the nine-year sales record. Rising prices and the back-log of demand added steadily to the dollar volume of sales in 1945-1948, and the all-time high of $103.6 million in 1948 was almost double the sales for 1945. The general softening of textile markets in 1949 subtracted more than a third from the preceding year's record.

Table 7. Billings and Net Sales, 1941-1949
(thousands of dollars)

year	billings			net sales
	cloth	yarn	waste	
1941	35,619	2,025	684	37,747
1942	53,906	4,127	866	58,170
1943	52,331	5,069	696	57,445
1944	56,349	5,546	475	61,284
1945	49,700	4,454	457	53,628
1946	72,308	6,393	492	77,346
1947	87,861	5,640	895	92,270
1948	98,946	6,272	726	103,604
1949	61,236	4,380	748	64,998

War orders

Government contracts amounting to $65 million represented a little more than 25 per cent of total sales in 1940-1945. The bulk of defense and war orders came from the Army. The goods supplied consisted of about $6 million worth of sheets and pillow cases, over $50 million in so-called government fabrics, and relatively small amounts of miscellaneous fabrics and yarns. Navy orders amounted to slightly over $1 million.[60]

Exports

After slumping to $1.3 million in 1943, sales of G. A. Stafford & Company rose to a high of $7.3 million in 1947. The postwar boom faded in the face of high tariff walls and the recovery of the textile in-

[60] Civilian Production Administration, *Alphabetical Listing of Major War Supply Contracts,* vol. 4 (Washington, 1945) cols. 2661-2662. The list includes only contracts amounting to $50,000 or more, and some contracts for the third quarter of 1945 may have been omitted.

dustry in war-torn countries; and in 1949 Stafford suffered a net loss of $29,987.[61] The removal of the federal subsidy on cotton exports, which had amounted to as much as three cents a pound on cotton cloth, contributed to a general decline in textile exports after 1947.[62] Canada usually stood at the top of the countries in which Stafford sold Dan River goods.[63] Before the end of the war the company's products began to enter South African markets, and sales in the Union surpassed $500,000 in 1947. This was less impressive than the recovery of Far Eastern markets, where sales reached $1.5 million in 1947.

Early in 1947 Stafford had 58 agents handling Dan River cloth and yarn throughout the world. G. S. Harris succeeded G. P. Ray as president of G. A. Stafford & Company (May 1940).[64] J. M. Hughlett became Stafford's president after his appointment as Dan River's general sales manager, and W. W. Lufkin, Jr., succeeded Hughlett in these two posts in December 1949. Immediate supervision of the export business rested with J. H. Judge, Stafford's vice-president, and E. V. Strodl, treasurer. Strodl retired in June 1949 and was succeeded by M. J. Moore.

Customers

By 1949 half of all the cloth manufactured in Danville reached the final consumer—the purchaser of sheets, shirts, suits, slacks, dresses, or piece goods—identified by label, tag, or wrapper as a product of Dan River Mills. "It's a Dan River Fabric" was not just another slogan but one of the most prominent landmarks in the evolution of the company's sales policy.

"Prior to a year ago," the president told the directors in 1943, "Dan River was known to consumers principally as the producer of Rivercool Spun Rayon Suiting. Today we are preparing a broader acceptance of our products after the war by presenting Dan River's sheets and pillow cases, dress goods, shirtings, sportswear fabrics and work cloth-

[61] When Cuba increased her duties on textile imports, President Harris wired Virginia's Senators (July 21, 1948) suggesting retaliation in the form of restrictions of U.S. imports of sugar.

[62] From a record high of 1,479 million square yards in 1947, U.S. exports of cotton cloth dropped to 940 million yards in 1948 and 880 million yards in 1949 (*Cotton Textile Hi-Lights: Mid-Century* [Charlotte, n.d.] p. 26).

[63] In September 1944 Stafford signed an agreement with Canadian Cottons, Ltd., for the marketing of the Canadian company's product in other countries.

[64] In 1943 Miss Elizabeth Coates, President Harris' secretary, was elected assistant secretary of G. A. Stafford & Company, the only time to my knowledge that anyone on the distaff side of the Dan River family became an officer.

ing fabrics by name to consumers through selected periodicals having national circulation." A year later he reported "substantial headway in the field of consumer relations. Dan River fabrics have been and will continue to be widely and consistently advertised in national maga- zines, as well as in trade papers. Many of our customers are now ad- vertising our brands in newspapers from coast to coast at no expense to us. As a result, our fabrics are more broadly accepted and in more gen- eral demand than ever before in our history."

The tangible evidence of the new policy may be found in the steady increase in advertising expenditures from $120,774 in 1942 to $1,274,- 986 in 1949. Sales declined about 30 per cent in 1949, while advertis- ing cost $325,000 more than in 1948. No one, of course, was prepared to say how much more sales might have dropped without increased ad- vertising.

The company's experience with "Rivercool" was not a good omen for the new policy of aggressive advertising to secure consumer accept- ance of the Dan River label. To an enthusiastic garment maker Nixon related the development of this fabric by T. J. Corcoran, whose previous experience led him to the belief "that the ultimate summer fabric must duplicate as far as possible the similarity in appearance and pattern to fine worsteds." Dozens of Dan River employees, who had "road-tested" garments of "Rivercool" reported "coolness not possible in fabrics that contain wool," but the salesmen cautioned that businessmen would not "sacrifice too much appearance for comfort." How to merchandise such a product was "a considerable problem," Nixon said. "If we limited the sale to only the better manufacturers, the total yardage sales might be so restricted that it would not be profitable from a mill standpoint"; while "government restrictions" made mills "very timid about attempting to dictate the retail selling price." All that seemed feasible, granted that Dan River could not manufacture garments, was "to demand from our customers a cut, make and trim in keeping with the fabric"; but Nixon did not speculate on how this policy could be enforced.[65]

In 1941, after numerous conferences with manufacturers of men's suits and with the advertising agency John A. Cairns & Company, the management came to the conclusion that the best way to promote

[65] F. K. Nixon to J. Bothe, July 17, 1940. In 1941 it was discovered that one Dan River customer resold cloth to a suit maker who sold "Rivercool" suits door-to-door. It turned out that the fabric was made for pantings, three years previously, and was not designed for suits.

"Rivercool" would be to "confine" the fabric to a few firms.[66] Three suit makers agreed informally to fix the wholesale price of "Rivercool" suits at $13, which had the effect of establishing a minimum retail price of $21.50. Dan River's attorney advised the sales department that it was "on safe ground in refusing to sell to one customer with whom you have formerly done business." But it was "important not to say to this customer that our action is based on his cutting of prices or on unsatisfactory workmanship in the finished product." Nothing should be done that could be construed as "discrimination between dealers as to price because of price cutting or poor workmanship on their part." This legal strait-jacket served its purpose. In 1943 a suiting manufacturer, who claimed to have been "the first to discover and develop possibilities of this particular fabric," sued the corporation for $300,000, alleging a violation of federal anti-trust laws in Dan River's refusal to accept his orders for "Rivercool." A U.S. District Court found that the company had done no wrong. There was no evidence, the court said, that "Rivercool" was a "material of so exclusive or peculiar a nature that it cannot be imitated." Under the circumstances a manufacturer had the right to "pick his customers and refuse to sell to those who for any particular reason he does not care to do business with." The allegation of monopoly was disproved by the fact that the three suit makers named in the indictment took only 27 per cent of "Rivercool" production; the other 73 per cent went to a suit manufacturer who was not a party to the price-fixing agreement.[67]

Sagging sales suggested that something more than a favorable judicial decision was needed to keep "Rivercool" at a par with rival fabrics in the "tropical" suiting field. One suggestion was to obtain control of "Palm Beach" fabrics, but Harris almost certainly never proposed to do what Burlington Mills succeeded in doing ten years later. By 1948 the sales manager had "increasing evidence that our Suiting operation is in a dangerous spot . . . . While it is true that the new line shows a broader range of colors and includes a good many new and popular styles, there is widespread criticism from the trade that the greater part of our line is outmoded . . . . Our showing of a tremendously large number of styles of similar character . . . has missed its objective and has resulted in unfavorable comment to the point of ridicule." Particular-

[66] J. M. Hughlett to H. W. Church, Nov. 5, 1941. The year before Dan River granted A. Schreter & Sons exclusive use of "Rivercool" in the manufacture of ties (E. A. Dafter to W. J. Adams, Nov. 13, 1940).

[67] 55 *Federal Supplement* (1944), 13-16. The case was decided Feb. 16, 1944.

ly serious was Burlington's competition, but Hughlett saw no reason why Dan River could not regain its leadership. "Regardless of all the talk about Burlington, I question whether the answer lies in copying their lines or in going overboard for the men's suit trade." The pants trade, he said, was the backbone of Dan River's volume in the past.

The fight against consumer depreciation of Dan River fabrics by their use in inferior or low-priced garments was waged on many fronts. A bulletin of the dress goods department (1946) warned salesmen that "some cutters in the lower price ranges cannot possibly use our goods at present prices and make a good garment." After studying the department's accounts, the management stopped sales to some customers and reduced the quantity of cloth made available to others. Some special dress fabrics were confined to "such fashion leaders as William Bass, Josette Walker," in the hope that "these houses will successfully promote the use of cottons in the fall and winter in addition to the spring and summer seasons."[68] Did this policy boomerang? "Looking backward," Harris observed, "we can now see that we might have prepared ourselves on dress goods distribution through other than dress manufacturers. Our fabrics have been in such demand among those manufacturers, we must have thought we could depend on them through all markets. Now that they have so drastically curtailed their operations in fabrics in our category, we are finding it difficult to reduce our volume sufficiently to avoid excessive inventories." A ray of hope was offered by a new departure in merchandising—the cutting and packaging at the mill of piece-goods in dress lengths, ready for self-service sale in retail stores.[69]

In 1947 Cairns prepared "Recommendations for a Dan River Shirting Department Identification Program." It involved, as the company's attorney pointed out, dividing Dan River customers into "sheep" and "goats." The former, a small group of shirt manufacturers, would get confined fabrics or patterns for use in price-fixed garments carrying a fabric-identification label or tag. The "goat" manufacturers would comprise a selected list of about 50 concerns "whose standards of manu-

---

[68] W. J. Fullerton, as quoted in the *Journal of Commerce*, Sept. 24, 1946. Famous-Barr Co., St. Louis, featured Dan River cottons in dresses from eight manufacturers in "the largest back-to-school cotton dresses promotion of the season" (*Women's Wear*, Sept. 11, 1946).

[69] Dan River "Handi-cuts" of chambrays, ginghams, and other dress goods were first offered in the "Dan River Fabrics Shop" of Rich's in Atlanta, April 1946. Trade papers reported that the store was "swamped" with customers (*Daily News Record*, April 2, 1946).

facturing and price lines are as uniform as possible"; but these would be prevented from using the Dan River name. All this sounded illegal to Attorney Talbott. Many states had price-maintenance legislation (so-called fair-trade laws), but it was doubtful that a manufacturer could legally control the retail price of a garment made by another manufacturer.[70]

Table 8 shows the distribution of sales of sheeting, sheets, and pillow cases by customer classes in 1940-1942. Jobbers bought 41 per cent of the cases sold, and mail order houses and chain stores took 43 per cent. Comparable data for later years have not been found, but the major change in the distribution pattern was the relatively larger sales through channels which brought to the consumer branded products. No inflexible policy developed, but, as the domestics department advised its salesmen in May 1947, "the decision as to whom we shall sell must largely rest on the judgment and good common sense of our representatives in the field who will know what is good for Dan River and what type of business will not be harmful to our merchandising." On the principle of not selling to customers' customers, *small* retail stores (who normally bought from jobbers) were excluded. So, too, were "price-cutting concerns"; but exceptions were made for mail-order houses, "whose business to a certain extent we desire to keep as a back log." Hotels and institutions were to be left to jobbers, but instalment houses and firms selling door-to-door were offered goods under non-conflicting tickets. An attractive prospect was that of increasing sales to companies using sheets and pillow cases as premiums, especially if they used a Dan River brand.[71] In general, the salesmen were told, "our aim is to distribute our goods with the least conflict amongst our various types of distribution. No one has been able to avoid conflict entirely, but we plan to hold it down to a minimum. We are going to have a large production to sell and the more we can place in the hands of concerns doing a real distributive function without price cutting, the less we will have to cater to the big chains and mail order houses."

[70] F. Talbott to L. H. Browder, March 6, 1947. J. M. Hughlett stated the company's policy (1945) on selling yardage to chain stores for the manufacture of garments: "Realizing that any expansion of this type of business would tend to hamper distribution, preclude identification of our fabrics in the garments, and lose the good will of many garment manufacturers, we all agree that it is best not to encourage this type of operation. At the same time it is understood that we shall not withdraw our lines from those operators in cases where we are already serving them in a limited way."

[71] In 1947 Procter and Gamble ran a contest in which the merchandise prizes consisted of Dan River sheets. The soap company "made considerable research and cross-checking with housewives" before adopting Dan River brands, "which naturally has pleased us" (Domestics Department Bulletin No. 238).

Table 8.   Classes of Customers: Sheeting, Sheets, and
Pillow Cases, 1940-1942*

customer	number of customers	number of cases bought
mail order	5	27,381
jobbers:		
over 1,000 cases per year	2	23,726
500-1,000 cases per year	3	4,424
less than 500 cases per year	224	19,497
chain stores	9	22,657
armed services	3	6,950
manufacturers	45	5,098
retailers	14	2,757
exporter	1	1,072
rental firms	3	1,046
instalment houses	8	616
syndicate buyer	1	430
unclassified	16	956
total		116,610

* July 1, 1940—June 30, 1942.

How much "catering" to chain stores and mail order houses had to
be accepted depended upon the fabric and market conditions.   While
one firm contracted for "very large quantities" of shirting fabrics for
shipment to the manufacturers of the shirts sold in the company's retail stores, another concern was advised that the distribution of shirtings was "built around the garment manufacturer" and urged to buy
"direct from that branch of the trade."   The sales office showed a lukewarm interest in the proposal of a large department store to work out
"through its own laboratories" specifications for fabrics which Dan
River would manufacture and confine to this firm.   Although the New
York committee wished to reach "some mutual understanding" in this
case, it hesitated to see a private brand developed at the expense of the
Dan River label.[72]

In line with the decision to make Dan River brands more familiar
to the consumer, new names were selected for the three grades of
muslin sheets.   In announcing a "Sheeting Name Contest" (1942)

[72] L. H. Browder to New York Committee, Aug. 11, 1944.   In 1945 salesmen complained
that combed-yarn ginghams sold by the American Bleached Goods Company under Dan
River labels, competed with goods offered by the company's own Dress Goods Department.   The value of this "very important account" seemed to preclude cutting off sales
to American Bleached Goods, but steps were taken to persuade them to give up the Dan
River "tickets" (W. J. Fullerton to F. J. Hahn, May 29, 1945).

President Harris observed that as one of the largest producers of sheets and pillowcases,[73] "with a quality of the very best on our market," the company needed "a new brand name . . . a Virginia name that will be instantly recognized by the purchaser as being identified with the historical background of colonial Virginia." Prizes of $50 and $25 in savings bonds were awarded for the four entries which the advertising agency considered best. At the end of 1942 the old "Morotock," "Dan River," and "Riverside" labels were replaced by "Old Dominion," "Shenandoah," and "Virginia Manor." Other trade marks were registered, and in 1947 the company adopted the following assortment of "tickets" for its wholesale and retail customers:

sheets	wholesaler	retailer
Type 128	"Shenandoah" and "Dancraft"	"Bob White" and "Integrity"
Type 140	"Navarre" and "Majestic"	"Sapphire" and "Debutante"
Type 180	"Dream House"	"Dancale"

"Shenandoah" was confined to wholesalers, "because we believe by assigning our new attractive tickets to department stores they will have no price conflict with small retail stores carrying 'Shenandoah' purchased from the wholesalers."[74] It was the salesmen's duty to keep both classes of customers from dropping the Dan River brand in favor of their own labels.

"Unquestionably," Harris wrote the company's advertising agency in 1943, "we are doing a good job of advertising, but I sometimes wonder whether we are not getting too far ahead of the availability of our merchandise in the retail stores." It was hard to say how much wartime advertising contributed to the tremendous surge of sales in 1946-1948. The increase in expenditures for 1949 was justified on the grounds that Dan River's competitors would increase their advertising (probably because they supposed that their competitors, including Dan River, were going to spend more). The amount spent in 1949 was a trifle under 2 per cent of sales, which in the past had been considered a generous allowance for *all* selling expenses.[75]

[73] In May 1941 the Domestics Department stated that Dan River's current production of sheeting, sheets, and pillow cases "so far as we can learn exceeds that of any mill in the country by a considerable margin" (D. L. Reardon, May 5, 1941).

[74] In 1944 a campaign to distribute sheets directly to "prime retail stores throughout the country" brought in 109 customers in 34 states and the District of Columbia (C. J. Dore to G. S. Harris, Oct. 24, 1944).

[75] Hughlett had recommended increasing advertising expenses to 1.92 per cent of sales, raising all selling expenses to 3.70 per cent of sales (J. M. Hughett to G. S. Harris, Nov. 5, 1948). For the first 11 months of 1947 the total cost of merchandising, including advertising, was only 1.77 per cent of billings.

The "overall aim" of advertising, L. H. Browder said, was "to get people throughout the country to believe that Dan River fabrics are the best in the country." Apparently, John A. Cairns & Company first pointed out the advantage of shortening the firm name, at least as it was used in fabric identification, to "Dan River." Who dreamed up "It's a Dan River Fabric," I do not know. In registering a trade mark consisting of DR enclosed in a wreath Dan River conflicted with the prior registration of a DR monogram by a cosmetic manufacturer, Daggett & Ramsdell. An amicable arrangement was reached: Dan River agreed not to use the monogram on powder puffs and the other firm promised not to use it on textiles "outside of the cosmetics field."

The advertising budget for 1946 distributed expenditures, as follows:

	Consumer advertising	Trade advertising
institutional	$ 30,500	$ 24,465
clothing fabrics	25,823	35,071
dress goods	73,744	18,541
domestics	57,452	30,483
shirtings-sportswear	59,706	21,533
yarns		816
agency fee		12,000
special		1,591
research		1,591
	$247,225	$146,092

Error in total due to rounding.

Institutional advertising included frequent page or half-page ads in the *Daily News Record, Women's Wear Daily,* and *Apparel Manufacturer.* Clothing fabrics were advertised in trade publications, such as *Men's Wear,* but shirtings and sportswear had space in general magazines (*Esquire, Collier's*) as well as the trade papers. Dress goods were advertised in *Parents Magazine, Glamour, Vogue,* and *Good Housekeeping,* while *American Home* and *Good Housekeeping* as well as the *Dry Goods Journal* advertised the domestics.

All copy-writing was done by the agency, in co-operation with L. H. Browder, the company's advertising manager. An occasional assist came from outsiders. A girl in Elmwood, Nebraska, won $5 and a shirt for an unsolicited poem extolling "Spunray"; but she was urged not to encourage her friends to follow her example. A Danville girl, dubbed "Miss Staway Halitosis," insisted on writing jingles, which the New

York office found too "corny" for use.[76] Inevitably, a certain amount of "cheesecake" crept into the photographic side of the advertising. "It is amazing," L. H. Browder declared, "how many requests we are receiving from the boys in the service" for a pin-up picture of "Spunray Girl." It was also encouraging, since the company was "directly beaming" its "message" on "Spunray" shirts to servicemen.[77] In 1946 the agency gave birth to "Buttons." In the "flesh" "Buttons" was a rag doll, dressed in Dan River fabrics by Inez Holland House and priced at $3.00. In the ads she was a rakish waif cajoling people to get a good night's sleep on Dan River bed linen. "Buttons" shared the spotlight with Margaret O'Brien, who helped promote children's dresses, and Gail Russell, who featured "Beau Catcher" playsuits of Dan River fabrics in 1947. Queen Shenandoah XX of the Shenandoah Apple Blossom Festival (1947) wore a Tina Leser gown of Dan River cotton, while a Dan River employee, Paulyne Scott, went to Memphis as one of twenty-two finalists in the Maid of Cotton contest.

An occasional sour note sounded in the advertiser's paradise. In 1946 the president had to protest that the advertising of "Fiber bonding" was extravagant and should be revised to avoid unfavorable publicity. While many manufacturers and dealers obligingly accepted Dan River hang tags and woven labels to use on their finished products, others declined to give fabric identification "in spite of all the quality we have built into them, and the advertising we have put behind them."[78] Nevertheless, a survey conducted by Fact Finders Associates in 1949 showed that 60.7 per cent of the women interviewed in eleven cities had heard of Dan River Mills; in 1947 only 31.8 per cent were familiar with the name.

To make stockholders more familiar with the company's products, twenty minutes of the 1946 annual meeting were devoted to a style show in which employees modeled clothes made of Dan River fabrics.[79] A few days later the annual fashion show was inaugurated. About a

[76] But B. D. Browder imagined there was "more corn in New York City than in provincial communities."

[77] The president answered one request for a color print of "Spunray Girl" with the hope that "she reaches you in good form," but he declined to reveal a "military secret" —the identity of the model.

[78] L. H. Browder to M. Allen Cohen, April 7, 1949. "Some manufacturers take the position that they do not wish to be confined to any one fabric . . . . others say that they run the chance of garments similar to theirs and made of our fabrics, being sold at lower figures than theirs and still others say that they do not wish to have anyone's name but their own known in connection with their garments."

[79] "I doubt that you ever saw a stockholders meeting in that 'shape,'" President Harris commented.

hundred guests, representing trade papers and selected customers, witnessed the exercises in the City Auditorium, where Glorious Chilton, a laboratory technician, was elected "Miss Dan River of 1946."[80] The following year a payroll employee, Harriet Crute, became "Miss Dan River," as the fashion show was staged in connection with the celebration of the company's sixty-fifth year. Although the president felt that the cost of the 1947 show ($12,818) had been somewhat extravagant, the fashion show was repeated in 1948 and 1949.[81] "Miss Dan River of 1949" was Mrs. Jewel Hall Owen. In March 30 trade and fashion magazine editors arrived in Danville to view "Four Seasons of Fashion." A New Yorker, Bill Blass, the winner of the Dan River fashion design contest, was awarded a trip to Paris, while four runners-up received $250 each.

Advertising was combined with economy in the use of clothing in the wartime booklet, *How to Take Care of Your Clothes*. One hundred thousand copies, distributed gratis, took $3,500 out of the advertising budget for 1943. *How to Get a Good Night's Sleep*, a pamphlet issued in 1944, contained scientifically sound recommendations on bedtime relaxation but strongly urged the superior qualities of slumber on Dan River sheets.[82] The first edition of *Dan River Dictionary of Textile Terms* (125,000 copies in 1944) was "a real hit," and new editions followed in rapid order: second edition (1945), 75,000 copies; third (1946), 50,000 copies; fourth (1947), 100,000 copies; anniversary edition (1947), 250,000 copies; fifth (1948), 250,000 copies; and sixth (1951), 250,000 copies—a grand total of 1,100,000 copies.[83]

Dan River "ventured into the new and exciting field of television" as co-sponsor of "The Fashion Story," beginning in November 1948 on WJZ-TV. Before this, a small amount of radio advertising, such as the

[80] Lady Astor, Danville's contribution to the British nobility, was visiting her home town about this time. President Harris made her a gift of sheets, which may or may not have been charged to advertising.

[81] To show the contrast between 1882 and 1947, some of the models displayed "Victorian garments" of "authentic 1882 styling," made of early Riverside fabrics duplicated in the pilot mill of the Designing Department. L. H. Browder argued that the 1948 show could be "made to pay off in newspaper and magazine publicity the same as the 1947 show is now beginning to do" (L. H. Browder to G. S. Harris, Dec. 3, 1947). See also: *Riverdan Benevolent Fund, Inc. Presents Dan River's Annual Fashion Show, "65 Years Young"* (booklet).

[82] The booklet was prepared by Cairns, with the help of Dr. Josephine Rathbone. Another advertising agency protested that it was similar to *This Will Put You to Sleep*, a publication prepared for North Star Woolen Mill Company in 1943.

[83] Editorial revision of the sixth edition, a pocket-size booklet of 120 pages, was in charge of Isabel B. Wingate of the New York University School of Retailing. It was widely distributed to schools for use in domestic science classes, and at least one copy made its way to Russia (through Armstrong Trading Corporation, 1948).

"Martha Deane" show on WOR, had been used. Several audience-participation shows, such as "Queen for a Day," used Dan River products as prizes; and a raincoat manufacturer identified the "Dantwill" fabric on two programs through New York stations. Direct sponsorship of a network program seems to have been regarded as less productive in sales than an equal expenditure on other media.

An advertising folder distributed to stockholders in 1943 pointed out that "without cost to Dan River . . . retailers have run several hundred thousand lines of newspaper advertising featuring Dan River products by name." In the spring of 1943 the company had contracts with sixteen manufacturers for magazine and direct-mail advertising of dress goods, and the promotion of "Prince Oxford" in 1945 called for consumer advertising in co-operation with shirt, short, and pajama manufacturers.[84] In the "best editorial . . . on any of our fabrics" *Good Housekeeping* used space to talk about Dan River spun-rayon "Pavillion" which, at advertising rates, would have cost $17,600. The editors of *Today's Woman* selected Dan River fabrics for all the children's cotton garments featured in the issue of May 1948, and the same month *Modern Screen* showed Dan River goods exclusively in its fashion section. An annual cocktail party and gifts of fabric yardage for out-of-town fashion editors helped the sales organization "keep in close contact with these young ladies" and "paid off in mentions of Dan River fabrics in their editorial columns." Working with schools which had classes in garment designing, the mill offered to "students who show particular promise" eight-yard cuts of a Dan River dress fabric.[85] In 1948 the company gave at least eight college home economics teachers trips to New York and Danville to "educate" them in the uses of Dan River fabrics for home-made garments.

Public relations

It is debatable whether an expenditure on free trips for school teachers and free cloth for students should be charged to advertising or to "public relations." Long before it had any advertising program (or an agency to lead, or push, it) Dan River spent money to defend its reputation beyond the purely commercial range of its contacts. In the

---

[84] L. R. Walls to R. B. Newton, May 9, 1945. In 1942 all but $360 of the $26,073 spent in advertising "Rivercool" suiting and "Victory" trouserings was recovered from customers, who paid an extra 5 cents per yard for the cloth.
[85] L. H. Browder to Margaret Harris Blair, Oct. 1", 1947.

decade with which we are now concerned, public relations became a
part of corporate policy: it was not enough to keep the company from
sustaining a "black eye" in the press or on the street, but planned action seemed to be called for to give the corporation a "soul." Perhaps
more important, as the mills increased in size, was the need to prevent
duplication of effort and contradictory statements in making routine
announcements of changes in personnel, operations, and policy.[86]

"Bad" publicity had a habit of popping up unexpectedly. Thus,
the Danville *Commercial Appeal* (June 9, 1947) found fault with the
"importation of boss men from other regions." President West, the
paper alleged, filled the mills with supervisors from his native New
England (he was born in Washington, D. C.), and when Harris succeeded him, a pilgrimage of supervisors from Georgia and South Carolina ensued. Why, the *Commercial Appeal* asked, if the Dan River
training program was effective, were vacancies not filled by promotions
within the ranks? A prize-winning essay by a George Washington
High School student (1947) took up and refurbished a rumor that Dan
River had successfully opposed, "several times during the war," plans
of the DuPont Company to build a plant in Danville. Although
DuPont quickly denied that it had *ever* considered locating in Danville, the Danville *Register* thought this was a good time "to either
confirm . . . or dispel . . . and, we hope, for all time . . . the old bug-a-
boo that the mills run the City Council, the Chamber of Commerce,
and fight tooth and toe nail to keep other industry out."[87] The idea
would not down. In April 1949 the educational director of the textile
union declared in a radio talk that the Chamber of Commerce backed
the mill's scheme to maintain a good labor market in Danville: "a good
labor market is one in which there are people around out of work who
will stand in line to take another man's job." The Chamber replied
with a full-page advertisement in the *Manufacturers' Record*, proclaim-
ing: "When you look for an industrial location, Look first to Danville,
Virginia, Capital City of Southern Virginia." How limited was the influence of the company in municipal affairs became clear in 1950 when

---

[86] Two cases in the fall of 1946 pointed up the need for skilled assistance in public
relations. While the company had under study several plans for employee medical care,
unfriendly and "uncontrolled" publicity got into the local papers. It was not clear whose
responsibility it was to release official statements on the matter. A considerable amount
of unfavorable publicity in regard to a veterans' housing project circulated without
effective counterpublicity (E. H. Davis to L. H. Browder, Nov., 1946).

[87] Danville *Register*, Jan. 26, 1947.

the mill and Pittsylvania County unsuccessfully opposed extension of the city limits to encircle Schoolfield.

The author of "Recommendations for a Program Designed to Benefit Local Public Relations" (typescript dated July 26, 1944) concluded, somewhat cryptically, that the "direct approach is frequently advisable, but in the case of Dan River, where the subject is full of all sorts of controversial angles, the direct approach is definitely *not* advisable." The management took no immediate steps to implement either these recommendations or the "Proposed Public and Employee Relations Program" submitted by Eunice H. Davis;[88] but in 1947 Vice-President Browder, who had been largely responsible for labor-management relations, spoke in favor of a "vigorous program" of public relations to "get our message across" to employees and the public.[89] On the recomendation of the New York office the firm of Murphy and Gapp was employed to prepare public relations advertising. In a few months this arangement became "progressively more unsatisfactory," as officers in Danville had to spend more and more time editing the proposed advertisements. Finally, the firm of Fred G. Rudge was called in to set up and direct a public relations office. In April 1949, after eight months on the job, Rudge had written the first drafts of an incentive plan booklet and a production employees' manual, prepared copy for a supervisors' bulletin, held discussions regarding a white-collar workers' organization, completed the initial training of a community relations staff, and made plans for other features of a long-range program. He submitted a budget of $168,782 for the year 1949. As sales slumped in the spring of 1949, the management found Rudge's work prohibitive in cost and decided to "discontinue for the time being our formal program of community and public relations," commending Rudge for "a very fine job."

The community relations department under John D. MacLauchlan, Jr., brought out the first issue of the *Supervisory News Letter* in September 1949. A month earlier Malcolm A. Cross came to Dan River

[88] L. H. Browder to F. E. Anderson, Sept. 12, 1946; L. H. Browder to E. H. Davis, Sept. 9, 1946. Mrs. Davis' column on "Dan River Doings" in the *Daily News Record* was found to be interesting, though it often "boomerangs" against the department furnishing the news. Harris, however, thought a Dan River newspaper might fit into the program of "improved public relations" (G. S. Harris to J. A. Cairns, Dec. 5, 1947).

[89] B. D. Browder to F. Talbott, July 1, 1947. Browder related that among 22 girls, all office employees of the company, one third could not name the president, 75 per cent failed to recognize more than one Dan River trade mark, 40 per cent did not know that the company had more than 5,000 employees, and only one person knew that the sales office was in New York.

as manager of the industrial relations division, supervising both public and industrial relations. A public relations office, directed by Louis H. Fracher, served as a clearing-house for news releases, prepared photographic material for mill publicity, wrote scripts for local radio programs, conducted tours of the mill, guided visiting textile experts,[90] and assumed responsibility for other chores, including, incidentally, scouring attics and vaults for the stuff this book is made of.

Daily mill tours had been put on a permanent basis by D. A. Overbey, Jr., in 1947, and while visitors of all types were welcomed on the two-hour trip through the mills, particular attention was given to groups of high school and college students. The annual High School Day appealed to Danville youngsters, who were given the chance to confer with the staff concerning opportunities for training and employment with the company. From August 1949 to July 1950 WDVA carried a fifteen-minute news program sponsored by Dan River at a cost of $10.50 a day.

It was never possible to measure closely the effectiveness of the over-all program of public relations. In a serious labor dispute (to be discussed below) company officials credited their streamlined publicity for successful bargaining with the union. Townspeople found most effective the weekly letter by George S. Harris, published as an advertisement, in which the president discussed Dan River's sales and earnings, talked about jobs and customers, described a loom replacement program costing the equivalent of $1,500 for every family in Danville, and, in general, expounded the theme of "Continued Security through Constant Progress."

Until 1949 visitors to Danville were welcomed in the two Dan River cloth stores, where seconds of sheets, pillow cases, yard goods, and remnants were sold at retail. As early as 1943 the New York office expressed concern over complaints from jobbers that merchants in and around Danville used the company stores to acquire "bulk lots of confined patterns." At the same time "merchants as far away as 150 miles from Danville" protested that women shoppers were patronizing the cloth stores to the detriment of their home-town stores.[91] In May 1949

---

[90] In March 1946 ten French textile manufacturers spent four days in Danville, and in June 1949 a delegation of British rayon weavers, sponsored by the Economic Cooperation Administration, visited the mills.

[91] J. M. Hughlett "Report on Cloth Store Operation," May 1, 1943. Hughlett thought that bulk sales—e.g., a lot of damaged handkerchief cloth—"have, under normal conditions, been very advantageous, and while the position of the merchandise managers [i.e., of Dan River] is fully appreciated, on the other hand, it would be undesirable to restrict

the stores were closed to the public, but they continued to supply Dan River products to employees, stockholders, and guests of the corporation.

Prices

Cotton textile prices in the 1940's developed five distinct patterns. The steady rise which followed the 1937-1938 recession raised the average wholesale price of a pound of unfinished cloth (17 constructions) from a low of 18.88 cents (April 1939) to 40.90 cents in May 1942. Price control "rolled back" the average to 40.62 cents, where it remained for two full years. Ceilings began to lift in July 1944 and, as rising wages stimulated postwar demand, the price of cloth climbed to a peak of 100.29 cents a pound in December 1947. Commencing in January 1948, prices declined steadily for nineteen months, reaching an average of 59.99 cents in July 1949. Recovery was almost continuous from August through March 1951, when the average reached 95.02 cents. (It was down again to 64.83 cents in May 1952.)[92] The volatile movements of textile prices reflect the highly competitive nature of the industry and the unstable characteristics of demand for many of the finished products. Of course, price fluctuations in the cloth market also follow, or anticipate, the erratic changes in the price of raw cotton. The two price series, however, are never perfectly correlated. In the ten-year period, 1940-1949, the ratio of wholesale cloth prices to the spot price of cotton ranged from 170.5 per cent (August 1946) to 295.4 per cent (February 1948).[93]

In the sheeting market the upward trend of prices was halted briefly in the first quarter of 1941. Higher prices were announced on April 2, when the discount off list for the "Dan River" grade moved from 35 per cent to 30 per cent (i.e., from 26 cents to 28 cents per yard for 90-inch sheeting). The discount went to 25 per cent in June, when defense orders forced Dan River to withdraw from the market.[94] On

---

the operation of the Cloth Store too drastically. It is a profitable operation and most mills in this part of the country have similar methods of disposing of odds and ends." In 1947 Hughlett suggested to D. A. Overbey, Jr., that he "refrain from writing anyone out of town about our stores when they write in to buy goods direct."

[92] U. S. Department of Agriculture, Production and Marketing Administration, Cotton Branch, *Prices of Cotton Cloth and Raw Cotton and Mill Margins for Certain Constructions of Unfinished Cloth, 1925-52* (Washington, 1953), p. 10.

[93] *Prices of Cotton Cloth and Raw Cotton and Mill Margins,* p. 9.

[94] D. L. Reardon to O.P.A.S.C., Aug. 22, 1941. "With all the firmness that exists in the Sheeting market," D. L. Reardon thought it "regrettable" that Dan River's competi-

government orders placed in April the company calculated that the price was equivalent to a markup of 11 per cent above cost. "It remains to be determined whether or not this mark up would be considered high or low by New Deal politicians."

One of the earliest contacts with the Office of Price Administration and Civilian Supply concerned the ceiling price of sheetings. President Harris and D. L. Reardon joined representatives of other firms who conferred in Washington (November 14, 1941) with a "bunch of nuts" trying to fix ceilings below cost. Tentatively, O.P.A.C.S. had decided upon prices of 20 per cent off list for Type 128, and 25 per cent off list for Type 140. "Such prices," Harris insisted, "would mean no profit for us and definite losses for the New England producers."

In May 1941 prices on Dan River staple colored goods, "in line with the market," were about 25 per cent above the lowest levels of 1940. In September, after the mills had accepted large government orders, procurement officers agreed to the following formula for pricing chambrays: 12.5 cents a yard for 3.90 chambrays when cotton averaged 15.99 cents in ten spot markets. For each change of one cent in the price of cotton, the price of cloth per yard changed one third of a cent. "This concession of 16 points," Harris said, "while painful, still leaves us a comfortable margin after allowance for another wage increase."

In June 1941 O.P.A.C.S. ordered a "roll-back" in the price of combed yarns from 60 cents to 48 cents a pound, leaving Dan River "with equipment for which we have no use and a contract in which we would never have entered if we had known the price would be 48¢."[95] Committees from the two branches of the yarn industry convinced O.P.A.C.S. that three cents a pound was the appropriate differential between combed and carded yarns, and in October yarn ceiling prices were tied to the price of cotton.

Prices for cotton goods in 1942 were generally controlled by Maximum Price Regulation No. 118, effective May 4, 1942. The maximum price on each fabric—there were exceptions—was the weighted average

---

tors continued to offer such high discounts in March. (D. L. Reardon to G. S. Harris, March 7, 1941.) For his part, Harris bemoaned the fact that "Apparently, no one tries to make what we might term a reasonable profit in sheets. Our impression is that the retailers use sheets more for ballyhoo purposes than for profitable merchandising. This makes a low ceiling that backs up all the way along to the manufacturer" (G. S. Harris to Armand May, March 17, 1941).

[95] G. S. Harris to J. P. Davis, June 25, 1941. Combed yarns, Harris pointed out, "are never in our line but when the price reached 60 cents we bought and installed, at considerable expense, necessary winding machinery to divert combed yarn from our usual production and sold it in the yarn market."

price in the base period, July 21–August 15, 1941, plus an "adjustment" of five cents a pound. Government procurement agencies could pay higher prices if the computed maximum price would not yield a reasonable return to the manufacturer. Adjustment of the maximum price was also possible in the case of seasonal goods which had an unfavorable price relationship (to the prices of other goods) in the base period.

The Dan River management had numerous occasions to protest the established ceilings.[96] In September 1941 Harris reported to Chairman Miller a "very trying ordeal" in conferring with officials in Washington. "I made the strongest presentation I could develop in an effort to prove the futility in attempting to establish ceiling prices on special weaves in style goods." But Administrator Henderson's lawyers and economists had "no conception of the problems of Industry and yet take a firm position in matters vital to us . . . Strange as it may seem, we are finding it very difficult to get these men to see the necessity of reflecting the advanced cost of cotton in these prices. When we presented the matter of future wage advances, we were told that we must use the ceilings as an argument with labor to avoid these wage advances."

Because of the "unsatisfactory ceiling," Dan River had no sheeting to offer its customers in July 1943, while the demand of the armed services for sheets and pillow cases required civilian customers "to divide the available production as equitably as possible." Type 128 sheets now sold for list less 8 per cent, an increase of 41 per cent over February 1941 prices.[97] In December the mills were "awaiting favorable action on the part of the O.P.A. to the Industry's appeal for higher ceilings," and salesmen were instructed to sell only the month's output.

Weekly operating reports show substantial back logs of orders throughout 1941 and 1942. During the last half of 1942 the average excess of unfilled orders over goods on hand was equivalent to something less than ten weeks' production.

[96] A ceiling of 12.895 cents on broadcloth (January 1942) left a margin of only .31 cents above cost. In putting a ceiling on Girl Scout uniform cloth, O.P.A. seemed "to be under the impression that only a single standard fabric has been used for this purpose." The ceiling of 36.679 cents was based on a Cannon Mills cloth, despite the fact that Girl Scout officials were "perfectly willing" to pay a higher price for the Dan River fabric (R. H. Lennox to G. J. Keisker, Aug. 24, 1942).

[97] In May Dan River refunded $1,260 to a customer who had been overcharged for sheets. The company thought a superior quality ("reinforced") justified a price differential but did not seriously contest the O.P.A. order (D. L. Reardon to D. A. Overbey, Jr., May 4, 1943.)

In August 1943 the three major producers of chambrays (Avondale, Pepperell, and Dan River) appealed to O.P.A. for a revision of the price roll-back of August 1942. "A modest advance in cloth prices" the mills said, "will have the effect of insuring a proper supply of relatively cheap work shirts. If the mills' request is not granted, the production must fall off and will surely force the worker into the higher-priced and poorer-wearing substitutes."[98] In December Pepperell's spokesman in Washington thought the three companies had "killed a bear on chambrays" and was "tickled pink over the prospect of getting 1-3/4 cents advance." Dan River failed to share his enthusiasm, and on December 20 Harris advised the directors that the company had "officially" declined to deliver chambray on its Navy contract at 16 cents.[99] The price dispute dragged on into 1944, though production continued by virtue of a W.P.B. directive. In March O.P.A. granted an increase of .875 cent per yard; but Harris, insisting that it was "not sufficient to show us a fair profit," asked O.P.A. for "prompt consideration of an additional adequate increase." Finally in July, the price administrator authorized an increase of 1.25 cents, fixing a ceiling of 18.25 cents on 3.90 Sanforized chambray. The new prices had been computed by averaging the costs and the base-period profit ratios of the two major producers, Pepperell and Dan River.[100]

Congress, in extending price control legislation, stipulated that processors of cotton should have ceiling prices high enough to pay "parity" prices for raw cotton and yet earn on their manufacturing operations a "generally accepted profit." Under this mystic formula sheet producers wangled two ceiling increases in 1944, and after June 30 Dan River's Type 128 sold for list *plus* 3.4 per cent.

At the beginning of 1944 unfilled orders amounted to 39 million yards, against a cloth inventory of only 18.4 million yards; but the gap gradually narrowed, and on August 20 unfilled orders and inventory were about equal. New orders outstripped production through the

[98] Riverside and Dan River Mills, Avondale Mills and Pepperell Manufacturing Company to J. F. Van Ness, Aug. 4, 1943.
[99] Directors' Minutes, Dec. 20, 1943. "We could get some relief by lowering our quality," Harris noted, "but the relief would not be enough to offset the danger in our future merchandising" (G. S. Harris to J. M. Miller, Dec. 2, 1943).
[100] J. M. Hughlett to G. S. Harris, July 21, 1944. O.P.A. officials, Harris commented, "fought us inch by inch and I suppose under the circumstances we should accept this new price gracefully. It is true that we were treated much better than the Denim manufacturers" (G. S. Harris to J. M. Miller, July 21, 1944). In October Harris expressed satisfaction that "for the first time, we have an Industry man [Luther Hodges, a North Carolina mill executive] in a top position in O.P.A."

rest of the year, and on December 31 unfilled orders stood at 26.4 million yards and cloth on hand, 14.7 million yards. Again, in the summer of 1945 inventory fell less than a million yards behind un-filled orders; and at year-end inventory of 22.6 million yards was close to the unfilled orders of 24.7 million yards.

Pressure for higher ceilings continued after V-E Day, and on June 26, 1945, O.P.A. allowed cotton mills to sell sheets and pillow cases with the understanding that the buyer might be billed at higher prices (but not more than four per cent higher) than those in effect on June 1. In August the Dan River sales office saw "every indication that price ceilings will be maintained"; in fact, "we do not think anyone wants to see the complete removal of price controls at this time, but we are hope-ful that O.P.A will become less and less technical and that we soon re-sume production of some fabrics which are still out of the picture be-cause of present unfavorable ceilings."[101]   Toward the end of the year cotton prices were allowed to edge upward, and in January 1946 the Cotton Mill Advisory Committee helped O.P.A. work out the corre-sponding increases in textile ceilings.   In the case of sheeting and sheets the ceiling announced in March put Type 128 at list plus 22.98 per cent (30.8 cents).   In August sheet ceilings got another boost, raising the price of Type 128 to list plus 42.35 per cent—not quite double the price in the summer of 1941.   Other fabrics were advanced correspondingly, and additional increases in ceiling prices were under consideration when, in November 1946, O.P.A. expired.[102]

On March 17, 1946, the weekly operating report showed an excess of cloth on hand over unfilled orders for the first time since 1940. Statistically, "goods at market risk" amounted to 2.1 million yards; actually, the risk was greater, since the 20 million yards of cloth in in-ventory were not entirely matched by unfilled orders.   The inventory-order position deteriorated during the summer, and on August 18 the mills had 22.5 milion yards of cloth on hand and orders for only 6.9

[101] *Dan River News Letter*, Aug. 27, 1945. Dr. Claudius Murchison of the Cotton Textile Institute observed that "the industry is totally unaccustomed to making its own prices. The government has made prices for us so long that the technique of individual pricing may have been forgotten . . . . Just as a reminder for those who are still com-paratively young in the industry, a sound price consists of only two things; the cost of production and a reasonable profit" (Cotton Textile Institute, *Confidential Bulletin,* July 1, 1946).

[102] In August the ceiling on "Ideal" chambray went from 21.709 to 24.856 cents a yard. One of the curious results of O.P.A. pricing, after it adopted dollars-and-cents ceilings, was to fix prices in cumbersome decimal fractions. Prices on sheets for instance, were carried out to thousandths of a cent.

million yards. The tide turned in the fall, and the year ended with unfilled orders of 46.9 million yards and an inventory of 21.1 million yards.

Prices in 1947-1949 moved upward once more in response to changes in costs and consumer demand. In January 1947 the Domestic Department reported that Springs Mills had advanced the price of pillow cases 15 per cent over the last O.P.A. ceiling; "but this action was not approved by the other manufacturers in the industry who are desirous of avoiding having to advance prices." Dan River preferred "to watch the situation closely," but in February announced prices substantially the same as the last O.P.A. ceilings (October 1, 1946).[103] Commenting on increases which some firms posted in March, D. L. Reardon said, "undoubtedly these goods with advanced prices will be sold, but frankly there is a lot of criticism against further advances above the average market prices at a time like this." In November, when at least one producer had gone 15 per cent over the final O.P.A. ceiling, Dan River decided to increase sheet prices "about 6 per cent."

President Harris discussed pricing policy in a prepared statement for a subcommittee of the Joint Committee on the Economic Report, convened in Richmond, on October 9, 1947. "There is no set formula," the president said,

by which prices of fabrics in our field are determined. Except in the period of government price control, prices of textile products have as a rule been governed by the action of supply and demand. Our company and our industry have passed through many periods when market prices reflected no profit and in some years a loss. When the supply has exceeded the demand, our company has had only the alternatives of accepting the prices its customers were willing to pay, accumulating inventory, or curtailing production. In such periods the opportunity for exercising any sound pricing policy was practically nil. When the present 'sellers' market began to develop, government control of prices was exercised. Since the end of price controls in November, 1946, there has been free opportunity to effectuate a price policy and from then to now our company has proceeded along these lines:

With few and minor deviations, we have adhered to the last existing OPA ceilings. The quality and styling of our products have placed them in exceptionally strong demand, and since decontrol of prices we have constantly had opportunities to sell our products at higher than our established prices. We have consistently rejected this pressure, and have also

---

[103] On the 81″ × 99″ basis, "Shenandoah" (Type 128) sold for $20.65 net per dozen sheets, and "Virginia Manor" (Type 140), $24.73 per dozen.

refused to accept premiums for spot deliveries. We have reason to believe that our trade generally considers our prices to be moderate and sound.

In the first half of 1947 production ran ahead of new orders, and on May 25 unfilled orders exceeded inventory by only 645,000 yards. A fresh spurt in sales in the summer and fall widened the gap, and on December 28 the company had an inventory of 24.3 million yards of cloth and unfilled orders for 49.3 million yards. In January 1948 production averaged slightly over four million yards weekly. The buying rush subsided by mid-1948, and inventories became uncomfortably high. At the end of the year unfilled orders of 20.8 million yards were offset by an inventory of over 30 million yards.

Although 1948 proved to be the company's most profitable year, as early as June President Harris expressed "grave concern over a definite turn in the textile market." He noted, in particular, a weakened demand for shirtings; and in October growing price resistance "confronts us everywhere," the president told the directors. Dan River might "reduce the margin of profit, if by so doing increased sales volume would result; but there is no assurance that this would happen." In January 1949 Cannon Mills "threw a bombshell into our sheet market" by offering combed percales at the same price as carded goods. Sales of shirtings as well as sheets were "very slow in the face of heavy breaks in prices," but for several weeks suiting sales continued to be "gratifying." Price guarantees on dress goods and stormwear were announced in March: "in the light of present uncertainties," Sales Manager Hughlett declared, "we felt it fair to guarantee our customers that they could enter into present commitments with the full assurances that they would be protected in the event that any price reductions should materialize prior to delivery date." It was the company's hope "to exert a stabilizing influence on the market."

In April reductions of five to twelve cents a yard in dress goods prices gave a boost to sales, while price cuts on sheets (bringing prices down to the December 1947 level) helped to reduce inventory. All in all, the "readjustments in the return to more regular conditions," which Harris had described at the annual meeting, took less time than most businessmen and economists had anticipated. No such deflation of values as followed in the wake of World War I came to pass in the uneasy years between V-J Day and the outbreak of hostilities in Korea in 1950. In his first report to the stockholders (February 17, 1950),

President Newton spoke of "a good demand for all our products, which are sold well into the second quarter of the year. We are expecting a continuation of good business for several months, and there are no signs that would suggest a repetition of the drastic readjustment of last summer."

The Dan River "price philosophy" was once expressed by the management as follows: "We must sell our goods at top prices, getting the last eighth of a cent per yard."[104] A corollary of this policy was to deplore "chiseling" and denounce competitors who took the lead in cutting prices.[105] The "Rivercool" experience showed the pitfalls of trying to maintain prices through agreements with customers; and, except for one abortive case, Dan River had no occasion to fight off a charge of collusion. In 1949 Dan River was one of forty-four firms and individuals named in a complaint of the Federal Trade Commission, charging conspiracy in fixing the price of twine products. Attorney Talbott told the directors that the company had never manufactured the products specified in the complaint; and in January 1951 the Commission dismissed the case on the grounds that the complaint had inaccurately described the commodities manufactured by the respondent firms.[106]

Cotton

In 1941 the management recommended, and the directors approved, the last-in first-out (LIFO) method of valuing cotton inventories.[107] Under LIFO cotton on hand at the end of 1940 was considered still on hand at the end of 1941 and priced at its 1940 inventory value. The excess of the cotton on hand at the end of 1941 over the 1940 inventory was valued at the cost of cotton first purchased in 1941. In successive years, unless the quantity on hand dropped below the inventory

---

[104] R. B. Newton and B. D. Browder to New York Executive Committee, June 26, 1941. Harris, however, thought that, while "we want to show as much profit for our Corporation as good business practice warrants," pricing practices should not leave "an impression in the minds of our customers that we are taking advantage" of unusual market conditions" (G. S. Harris to L. H. Browder, Aug. 23, 1941).

[105] In December 1940 the Cone Mills offered flannels for 1941 delivery at the same prices as in 1940. "This appears," Harris said, "to be contrary to good merchandising and should be unnecessary." (G. S. Harris to D. L. Reardon, Dec. 26, 1940.)

[106] *Federal Trade Commission Decisions*, vol. 47 (1953), pp. 1588-1595. Two new complaints were brought against several corporations, excluding Dan River, and cease and desist orders issued on March 26-27, 1951 (*ibid.*, pp. 1115-1136).

[107] "I adopted LIFO in '41," Harris related, "as soon as I learned that it would be acceptable to the Treasury Department. My object then was to accumulate a reserve as the market went up that would automatically shift over into our profit column as and when we owned cotton above the current market at the end of the season" (G. S. Harris to H. Lane Young, Apr. 16, 1949).

at the end of 1940, the 1940 inventory value remained frozen. Thus, the manufacturing cost of cotton consumed in 1941 was the value of the inventory at the end of 1940, plus the cost of cotton acquired in 1941, less inventory at the end of 1941, the inventory being valued at two prices as explained above. The results, since prices continued to rise in 1941, were twofold: (1) manufacturing costs were greater than they would have been under the "lower of cost or market" method of inventory valuation, and (2) earnings were "stated more conservatively."[108]

From 28.9 million pounds at the end of 1940 the cotton inventory built up, irregularly, to 72.8 million pounds at the end of 1947. At this time the value for inventory purposes averaged only 19.30 cents a pound, although the cotton on hand actually cost 34.44 cents. To compensate for an unpredictable downward swing in prices, the company accumulated a LIFO reserve, which in July 1948 amounted to $11.4 million.[109] The reserve protected the firm "down to approximately nineteen cents a pound"; that is, if cotton should drop as low as 19 cents, the "loss" from the corresponding decline in the market price of goods would be charged against the LIFO reserve. President Harris called the reserve "a cushion to catch us one of these years when our judgment in cotton fails us" and criticized manufacturers who, in the belief that cotton prices had reached permanent high levels, transferred their LIFO reserves to profit. But the reduction in the cotton inventory from 65,000 bales (December 1948) to 51,500 bales (December 1949) permitted Dan River to take $719,092 out of the LIFO reserve and add it to "Other Income" for 1949.

LIFO was no substitute for continuous study of crops and markets in an effort to determine the best time to buy the desired types of cotton for manufacturing purposes. Within a month after taking office, President Harris closed out the company's short sales of July cotton at a loss of $117,760. Although the market was bullish and Harris had sold 3,500 bales in December contracts, he submitted that the "policy of attempting to hedge cotton and finished goods with the sale of future cotton contracts should have a careful examination." In a later letter he explained his position more fully: "I am convinced that to sell future

[108] Apparently, earnings for 1941 were "reduced" by $1,441,000. When Harris told Elliott Springs that LIFO would reduce earnings by $1,800,000 but cut taxes from $1,290,000 to less than $500,000, Springs warned: "it may backfire."
[109] Although a reserve of $188,109 in 1943 and $432,000 in 1944 had been charged to "Cost of Sales," the LIFO reserve was hidden in the Reserve for Taxes, which grew steadily to a peak of $13.5 million at the end of 1948.

contracts in an effort to protect a merchandising loss in our stock of finished goods is as unsound as if one of our suiting customers were to sell cotton futures at the time he buys cloth in an effort to protect himself against a decline in the value of that cloth until such time as he produces and sells his finished clothing." Harris criticized the previous administration for including cotton in the form of stock in process and finished goods in the calculation of the net long, or short, position. "Stock in process is never sold any more than we sell the machinery that contains it, and we are not directly concerned with its value. Furthermore, finished goods . . . is an entirely different commodity from cotton, the price of which varies with the supply and demand of cloth with little or no relationship to the supply and demand which controls the price of cotton. Therefore, I would divorce entirely the finished goods and stock in process from raw cotton in determining the cotton buying policy." Finally, an effective cotton policy required "a constant study of the trends affecting cotton" in order "to average the cost of this cotton as low as possible . . . . When we find ourselves in a depressed market purchases should be made without regard to inventories of stock in process or finished goods. In other words, cotton purchases should be made against consumption and not against sales."[110]

President Harris agreed with Dan River's cotton buyer, Henry Roediger, that the best grades of cotton could generally be secured at the lowest prices at the beginning of the crop year. On occasions, as in the fall of 1941, the desired cotton could not be purchased even during the months that cotton was moving to the gins.[111] The following explanation was offered by Roediger at the company's sales convention in October:[112]

> Early in September I went to Galveston, Texas. While there I took up 5,000 bales of cotton and bought around 6,000 more at the same price . . . .

[110] G. S. Harris to J. I. Pritchett, July 2, 1940. Some of these observations echo a memorandum prepared by Henry Roediger, the cotton buyer, on July 1. Roediger believed that government cotton loans made hedging impractical, since the large quantities of cotton held by the government induced erratic shifts in the basis, i.e., the spread between spot and futures prices. "While I do not advocate speculation," Roediger said, "I do not think you are speculating when you can buy your cotton around the cost of production and when this is true, I think we should buy a large part of our requirements at a fixed price."

[111] In eleven crop years (1940-1950) the minimum monthly averages of ten spot markets came in August five times, in September three times, in October twice, and in November three times. Despite the sharply rising trend, eight of these lows were below the preceding July prices.

[112] "Notes on Meeting of the Sales Convention at the Welfare Building on October 24, 1941" (mimeographed).

The market was around 18½ cents. I left very bearish. I thought the market would go down to around 14 cents or 15 cents. But I was not bullish when it got to 18 cents. Everywhere I went I saw that the Army worms had been to work. They have ruined the crop. I bought all the old crop cotton I could find from all over Texas. When I learned that we had accepted an order from the Government for which the cotton had to be Strict Middling 1 1/32 I bought all the Strict Middling everywhere. We paid the price and got it. From Texas I went to Memphis. The army worm had still been working. I wrote Mr. Harris, also Mr. Newton, and gave them the conditions. I told them if they were not out there to see they would not believe that we would have a low grade cotton crop. I bought 20,000 bales of cotton and was fixing to come home. But Mr. Harris told me to stay. So I stayed to buy more cotton. We have stored in the interior of the Memphis territory a lot of 16,000 bales of cotton. We will have over 17,000 bales. The market is down today from what I paid for it, but you cannot duplicate it anywhere. There is no Strict Middling cotton for sale. Firms won't quote you a price for it. The Government has a big stock of cotton but it has been milked and all that is left is practically low grade cotton. I do not know whether or not we are going to get any Government cotton. I think they are going to give it all away. They are giving Canada a subsidy now and Canadians are getting cotton for around 10 cents per pound. On the same cotton we are paying 18 cents to 19 cents per pound. Also the Government is trying to fight Brazilian cotton. We are fortunate to have the supply of cotton we have. We have our warehouses full but it might be too much upper and too much lower and not enough middle. That is what is hard to get. Strict Low Middling and Strict good ordinary which is very low is on the market now. It is almost impossible to use this on most of our work. What we will do next May, June, July, and August for cotton I do not know. I have asked New York not to sell any goods made out of Strict Middling unless they know we will get the cotton.

In April 1942 Dan River sold (at a profit of six cents a pound) about 900 bales of long-staple cotton, originally purchased for making combed handkerchief cloth. But Harris found it "difficult to decide to rebuild our long interest . . . . We have been very successful in our cotton operations this season, which have contributed materially to our profitable operations. I would feel very badly if we make a move now that might nullify these results." Prices were weak during the summer, reaching a low in August; and as the market became firm, the president moved to increase the long position.[113]

From the end of 1942 to the spring of 1945 price controls held

[113] G. S. Harris to J. M. Miller, Oct. 14, 1942. "Realizing that any cotton operation involves dangers," Harris asked for the approval of the board chairman and the executive committee.

market fluctuations within a comparatively narrow range, but there were opportunities to take advantage of temporary shifts in the spread between spot and future prices.[114] In January 1945, when the long position had grown to 45,500 bales, Harris told the directors that "we have reversed our ideas and are now attempting to hedge a considerable part of our long interest in July, October and December." No genuine bear market developed; instead spot prices pushed steadily upward, rising more than 50 per cent between August 1945 and September 1946. Caught short—26,500 bales in February—the mills charged a cotton loss of $276,275 to "Cost of Sales" in 1945.

In February 1946 Harris reported, with satisfaction, a net long position of 65,000 bales. The "one-way cotton market" had enabled him to take advantage of "an opportunity presented to a mill operator once in a lifetime. Our extra earnings due to a favorable cotton policy just about represents the amount we expected to cover with long-term debt financing." But the market broke sharply in October and "a lot of people got badly burned." When prices dropped "below the reasonable floor," inventory accumulation was resumed; and in the summer of 1947, when many grades of cotton were unusually scarce, Dan River sold 14,859 bales "at a very handsome profit."[115]

Inflation, foreign aid, and the sustained demand for textiles convinced the management that the upward trend of cotton prices would not be reversed in 1947-1948. After buying 111,004 bales (at an average of 34.85 cents a pound) the mills had enough cotton on hand at the end of 1947 to operate until the end of October 1948; and the directors accepted the president's recommendation to hedge none of it.[116] A similar policy was adopted in the fall of 1948, and by November the mills had acquired 107,325 bales of the estimated requirements (to October 1949) of 146,739 bales.[117] A. B. Emmert, the company's new

[114] Thus, in March 1944, "new crop futures" were "at such discounts, it teases one to go deeper into cotton than we would ordinarily consider" (G. S. Harris to J. I. Pritchett, March 7, 1944). A. B. Emmert, who succeeded Roediger as the company's cotton buyer in July 1942, was "firmly of the opinion" that heavy purchases of fall-month futures should be made. He pointed out that over 36,000 bales of May cotton had been purchased when May was 17-25 points under March. By the first of March this month's cotton was at a premium of 45 points over May (A. B. Emmert to G. S. Harris, March 6, 1944). In October the directors approved an increase in the long position to 40,000 bales.

[115] G. S. Harris to A. W. Zelomek, Nov. 1, 1946; "Cotton Report," Oct. 22, 1947. The profit was $149,454, just about offset by a loss of $141,425 from trading in futures.

[116] "Cotton Report," Dec. 10, 1947. A gain of $16,234 on futures was reported for 1948.

[117] Consumption fell below the estimate, and during 1949 a gain of $84,834 was reported on sales of raw cotton.

cotton buyer, foresaw "an era of changing conditions and of resultant lower prices," but the threat of a break in the market was less serious than the problem of acquiring seasonally "approximately 88,000 bales of high grade cotton that major firms with comprehensive buying organizations are unwilling to sell." Although Dan River had no "large interior buying organization, and it would be impractical for us to attempt to carry one," the company "had no alternative but to buy this cotton ourselves." As Emmert explained it, the company bought the season's requirements during the early part of harvest period, when the qualities of cotton needed were usually available. Purchases were made principally from producers, with the aid of factors, which held the cost of cotton low, without the necessity of maintaining a large buying organization. Hedging large inventories of cotton would at times afford some protection; but an "inverted market," with "premiums on the near months and discounts on the distants," often destroyed the protective feature of hedges. In the fall of 1948 "further complications" were introduced by the "uncertainty of what the Federal loan program will be next season, the amount of cotton that will be consumed domestically, the size of next year's crop, whether or not our European Relief Program is continued and its scope, all of which affect both the market and the basis."

As has been pointed out often, the market price of cotton textiles is not very sensitive to changes in the price of cotton.[118] The statistics for mill margins on unfinished sheeting, for instance, show an increase of 40.36 cents a pound in eight years, 1940-1948; but the upward trend was frequently reversed, as in 1948-1949 when the margin dropped from 47.86 cents (February 1948) to 22.04 cents (June 1949). Much of the increase in the spread between cotton prices and fabric prices covered the upward march of wage rates; but "squeezing" of the margin took place in the face of stable and sometimes rising wages. Other costs, too, were subject to inflationary pressure in the 1940's. Control of manufacturing costs, therefore, involved not only sound policies with respect to purchases of raw materials, primarily cotton, but also the efficient utilization of materials, machines, and men.

[118] In a Ph.D. dissertation, "Short Run Instability in the Cotton Broad Woven Goods Industry, 1946-1951" (Duke University, 1954), Thomas M. Stanback presents elaborate data on four periods of expansion and four recessions. Generally, the prices of gray goods, which are relatively flexible, and the prices of finished fabrics, which are relatively inflexible, tend to be governed by forces unrelated to the price of cotton.

Costs

Available statistics, though incomplete, appear to support the conclusion that labor productivity gained steadily in 1940-1949 and perhaps at a greater rate than in any other decade of Dan River history.[119] A "Report of Manufacturing Division" estimated over-all output at 3.17 pounds of cloth per man-hour in 1942, 3.20 pounds in 1943, and 3.53 pounds in 1944, "in spite of constant Union resistance to progress, more inefficient workers employed and a high turnover." A more comprehensive study made by R. C. Gourley of the Standards Department showed an increase of 11 per cent in output of gray goods per man-hour between the last quarter of 1942 and the first nine weeks of 1948. In the same period the average weight of cloth per yard dropped 14 per cent while the average yarn number rose from 20.26 to 25.2[120]

In the case of ten substantially identical fabrics labor cost per yard decreased, as follows:

fabric	cost at 1948 wage rates (cents)		decrease
	1942	1948	(per cent)
"Riverside" sheeting	17.061	12.995	23.8
"Dan River" sheeting	15.276	12.177	20.3
"Starspun"	13.738	10.570	13.1
"Cordspun"	12.618	9.812	12.2
broadcloth	11.585	8.946	12.8
"Oxford"	11.377	8.116	28.7
"Ideal" chambray	7.583	6.736	11.2
drill	9.714	9.407	3.2
suiting 500	17.620	12.578	28.6
suiting 7100	22.865	16.922	26.0

The (unweighted) average decrease in unit labor cost, at fixed wage

[119] *Supra*, chap. 6.

[120] The shift to finer fabrics is also shown by loom schedules in the two periods:

	number of looms	
	1942	1948
white or piece-dyed fabrics	5,209	3,193
raw-stock dyed fabrics	1,141	316
yarn-dyed fabrics	3,834	6,598

W. H. Cousins' comparison of production in 1943 and 1944 showed the following results:

	1943	1944
gray yards produced	174.9 million	162.4 million
average loom hours per week	92.8	80.0
average employees per day	12,385	10,215
yards per man hour	6.438	7.274
average hourly earnings	$ .591	$ .626

These data indicate a reduction in unit labor cost of 6.2 per cent.

rates, was 17 per cent, indicating a gain in labor productivity of 20.5 per cent. Average hourly earnings practically doubled, but the 1948 output of cloth cost $7 million less to produce than it would have cost if labor efficiency had remained constant from 1942 on.

One of the purposes of cost accounting is to show the relative profitability of different products. A costing department study of 81-inch bleached sheeting in December 1945 revealed a wide discrepancy in the profit margins on the three qualities. At current ceiling prices, Type 128 (priced at 39.442 cents a yard) yielded only $1.35 per 96-hour loom week; Type 140 (48.613 cents a yard) returned $12.28 per loom week; and Type 180 (49.207 cents a yard) showed a profit of $7.81 per loom week.[121] In the third quarter of 1947, with price controls removed, "Ideal" chambray was sold at a loss of $1.63 per 96-hour loom week. A slightly lower unit cost and a much better market price put this fabric in the profit column in September 1948, when the return per loom week was $23.91. The following table summarizes the comparative return on 497 fabric styles at costs and prices of September 30, 1948:[122]

class of goods	number of styles or sizes	return per 96-hour loom week highest	lowest
stormwear	56	$124.55	$43.16
shirting and sportswear	155	68.39	24.80
dress	114	104.88	—.35
gray	65	71.15	55.28
staple colored	31	42.72	15.76
domestics:			
Type 128	28	38.75	15.35
Type 140	28	42.31	15.58
Type 180	11	23.57	9.82
clothing	9	130.11	54.16

Dan River's management never had any doubt about the necessity of producing at capacity in order to achieve the lowest unit cost. In a letter to the sales force (1944) President Harris stressed the need to

[121] W. H. Cousins to D. L. Reardon, Dec. 8, 1945. At this time 1,422 looms were occupied on Type 128 and 968 looms on Type 140. Cousins pointed out that "if we confined our production to Type 140, at present prices and cost, we would make one million dollars more per year than if we confined our production to Type 128" (W. H. Cousins to G. S. Harris, Dec. 21, 1945, and Jan. 2, 1946).

[122] Cost Estimates Department, "Comparative Return of Current Fabrics," dated Sept. 30, 1948, and signed by E. C. Moon.

maintain sales volume in order to spread depreciation and other fixed charges over the largest possible output. He estimated that fixed charges on 200 million yards a year amounted to 2.98 cents per yard but rose to 5.616 cents on an output of 100 million yards.[123] During the war the overtime pay and the relative inefficiency of learners and substandard workers increased the unit cost of the "marginal production." But cost studies in 1949 showed a decrease of 2.7 per cent in the manufacturing cost of combed poplin if produced in an 80-hour week instead of a 64-hour week.[124]

Depreciation showed no unusual variation until 1949, when extraordinary expenditures were made on new facilities. In 1941, the Bureau of Internal Revenue, finding that depreciation had been overstated, sent the company a bill for $37,306 covering additional taxes on income for 1939-1940. In the belief that three-shift operations required more than the normal rate of replacement of fixed assets, in December 1942 the directors authorized the management to adopt higher rates of depreciation. For three years, 1943-1945, the depreciation allowances were increased about 25 per cent, although the amounts written off in 1946-1947 were less than in 1940-1941. Despite the persistence of inflation, which encouraged many corporations to adjust depreciation charges to replacement values, Dan River took a dim view of accelerated depreciation. Varying depreciation rates, Comptroller T. A. Bassin said, gave the taxpayer "a chance of gambling on whether tax rates will go up or down." Since no asset can be depreciated more than 100 per cent, acceleration presupposes that tax rates will be lower (and earnings after taxes, higher) during the later years of an asset's life. Finally, Bassin referred to the professional advice of the American Institute of Accountants that corporation accountants should not depart from the traditional methods of depreciation based on original cost.[125]

The fact that experts disagree on the proper amount to charge for depreciation helps to explain why cost accounting must be, at best, an inexact science. It does not justify adherence to questionable practices, when improved methods become generally accepted; and in De-

---

[123] Since production in 1934-1943 averaged only 154 million yards annually, the company had "lost" $11.6 million in fixed charges alone.

[124] E. C. Moon to W. J. Fullerton, July 5, 1949. Similar figures were prepared for other fabrics. The purpose of the study was to show how profit ratios could be maintained if price reductions stimulated sales enough to permit a higher rate of production.

[125] T. A. Bassin to G. S. Harris, Oct. 25, 1948; American Institute of Accountants, *Accounting Research Bulletins*, No. 33 (Dec. 1947), pp. 268-269.

cember 1941 the president was forced to the conclusion that Dan River's accounting department was "much more antiquated than I anticipated." "A general shake-up," he decided, "will be necessary."[126] Several months earlier New York bankers had advised the company to hire a comptroller, but the president procrastinated because of the "same old problem of pulling a man from the outside and placing him in a senior position over men raised in the Corporation." Finally, in March 1942 T. A. Bassin, a Scotch chartered accountant, long associated with Price, Waterhouse and Company, became Dan River's first comptroller.

During 1942-1945 the accounting, standards, and cost estimates departments underwent major reorganizations. In February 1941 the president foresaw the need "at some time soon to re-set our standard cost, which is several years old and pre-dates some general advances in labor rates." He called in experts "to survey our cost procedure to determine its soundness," and in September 1942 a new standard cost system was installed. The company's auditors came in to assist Bassin in revamping the accounting department, but in the fall of 1943 the management found it necessary to employ the Trundle Engineering Company to work on this and other phases of the problem of record keeping and control. The Trundle investigations, continued into 1945 and recorded in several bulky volumes, resulted in improvements or changes in the methods of inventory, production and waste control, the reorganization of the standards department into four sections, and the departmentalization of the accounting system (payroll, banking, payables, traffic, etc.). Manuals were prepared to show the functional division of the various departments, and bookkeeping machines and other types of mechanized equipment were installed to speed up the processing of data and manufacture of records. The firm of A. M. Pullen and Company completed "a very big job in a very satisfactory manner" in the costing department, and one of the firm, B. D. Radford, was retained as a cost consultant.

State and local taxes reached their peak (for the period covered by this chapter) in 1949, when Dan River paid tax bills, as follows:

state intangibles (capital tax)	$208,028
real and personal property, City of Danville	117,646

[126] G. S. Harris to J. M. Miller, Dec. 2 and 15, 1941. "You can readily understand," he added, "the difficulty of modernizing this branch of our work with Mr. Ayres in charge. It probably means his retirement at an early date."

real and personal property, Pittsylvania County	101,384
manufacturers' license, City of Danville	47,389
local taxes, New York and other sales offices	58,651
sundry licenses	14,516

The state tax on intangibles was rebated in equal shares to the city and county. So far as property taxes were concerned, the company tried to hold assessed valuations at "reasonable" figures. In the case of the county, Harris believed that the mills were

doing more than our share toward the maintenance of the County government. Certainly this Company has always tried to adopt a fair attitude . . . . We have not shirked our burdens nor complained, nor asked for relief . . . during the many years of depression and losses . . . . Viewed from any fair and logical angle, I sincerely feel that our Company should not be charged with any additional increase in its tax burden when we are presently fighting such a hard battle to produce a return even for our preferred stockholders.[127]

The prospective loss of revenue from taxes on mill property led the county to support Dan River in opposing the annexation of Schoolfield by the City of Danville.[128]

All types of human effort, as well as cotton and machinery, enter into the cost of producing and marketing cotton textiles. In a sense all payments for services are wages, but it is generally useful to classify such payments by type of remuneration or function. The data in Table 9, derived from the audit reports, show under "Manufacturing" all wages, bonuses and vacation pay to operatives, supervisory personnel, and administrative workers furnishing services related to production. Commencing in 1943, payments for professional services associated with manufacturing, such as the fees of consultants on power problems, are shown separately. At the same time, the auditors divided non-manufacturing payments between "Selling" and "General Administrative" accounts and showed salaries and professional fees separately. It will be observed that salary and other service payments moved steadily upward with the growth of sales. Professional services also tended to become more costly as business expanded: more money was spent to reorganize production and administrative procedures, and

---

[127] G. S. Harris to L. Womack, Dec. 1, 1941. In 1942 the county increased the assessed valuation of land, buildings, and machinery by about $100,000, but this merely restored the assessment to the 1925 figure of $4,465,500 (F. Talbott to T. A. Bassin, July 14, 1942).

[128] "State of Virginia in the Circuit Court of Pittsylvania County: Annexation Proceedings: City of Danville, Plaintiff, v. County of Pittsylvania, Defendant" (mimeographed, 1950). Dan River Mills, Inc., was intervenor for the defendant.

more legal and financial services were required to keep up with the demands of government price-control agencies, procurement offices, labor boards, and tax collectors.

Table 9. Wages, Salaries, and Professional services, 1941-1949
(thousands of dollars)

	1941	1942	1943	1944	1945	1946	1947	1948	1949
manufacturing									
payroll	11,742	16,270	16,838	15,435	15,368	20,309	26,693	29,638	22,318
professional			234	341	284	226	240	239	161
selling									
salaries			372	430	519	668	1,106	1,457	1,311
professional			6	8		31	20	11	31
general									
administrative									
salaries	617*	863*	336	378	413	469	612	704	586
professional			32	41	111	100	104	124	132
total	$12,359	17,133	17,818	16,633	16,695	21,803	28,775	32,173	24,539

* selling and general administrative.

In 1949 more than $250,000 was lopped off the salaries, which was relatively less than the drop in the wages bill. On the average, 30.8 per cent of the amount received from sales went into wages, salaries, and professional fees. Until 1949, when the ratio jumped to 37.7 per cent, the proportion of the sales dollar distributed to wage earners and salaried workers stayed within a fairly narrow range: 27.1 per cent (1944) to 32.9 per cent (1941). The ratios are not necessarily significant; though, if studied in connection with mill margins, they may reveal how the price of cloth limits the prices paid for all the human services embodied in finished goods. Further elaboration of this point requires information on the behavior of wage rates and salary scales during the nine-year period. Inasmuch as wages were subject to collective bargaining in 1943-1949, we may now review the steps by which Dan River Mills became unionized.

The Worker

The union enters

Dan River signed its first union contract on June 25, 1943, a year after Local 452 of the Textile Workers Union of America, C.I.O., had been certified as the employees' collective bargaining agency.

T.W.U.A. came into existence, in May 1939, as a result of the merger of the Textile Workers Organizing Committee and United Textile Workers of America. At this time the two groups controlled 428 locals, of which three (452, 510, and 511) had been organized in Danville.[129] Despite the management's efforts to persuade the workers that the union could do them no good, in the fall of 1941 the president admitted that "some of our workers" were "coming out in the open on the side of the organization drive."[130] A whirlwind membership drive brought more than half the company's employees into the union, and on May 30, 1942, the union requested an election. Waiving the right of a hearing, Dan River signed the "stipulation for certification on consent election," and on June 26 the National Labor Relations Board conducted the election.[131] The results follow:[132]

employees eligible to vote	13,470
ballots cast	12,039
challenged, blank or void	120
valid ballots	11,920
for Local 452	7,204
against Local 452	4,716

Bowing before this "revolutionary change in the relations heretofore existing between the Company and its employees," the management negotiated with the union throughout the summer of 1942. As the company and the union, after weeks of bargaining, remained "far apart on several important matters," the Federal Conciliation Service was invited to Danville. Conciliation failed, and on September 26 the

[129] *Proceedings: First Constitutional Convention, Textile Workers Union of America* (New York, 1939); *Proceedings: Second Biennial Convention, Textile Workers Union of America, C.I.O.* (New York, 1941). The Danville locals sent delegates to the 1939 convention but not to the 1941 meeting.

[130] G. S. Harris to J. M. Miller, Sept. 11, 1941. In October Harris found C.I.O. organizers doing "everything in their power to create unrest among our workers . . . . We are still fighting in the hopes that we may find ways of at least delaying this organization. I am of the opinion that we are suffering more distress through this organizing period than we would after organization, but the cost to the company is not nearly so great." In other words, the Union might do the workers some good!

[131] *Decisions and Orders of the National Labor Relations Board*, vol. 42 (Washington, 1942), pp. 843-845. T.W.U.A. organizers in Danville in 1941-1942 included George Baldanzi, R. R. Lawrence, and C. W. Ervin. Douglas Eanes, a loom fixer, was president of Local 452; F. J. Wilson, a weaver, was financial secretary. On the last lap of the membership campaign, conducted by radio (from Greensboro, N.C.) and a newspaper, *Danville Textile Labor*, prizes in bonds and savings stamps were awarded to campaigners bringing in the most members. The opposition rallied under the banner of the Workers Anti-C.I.O. Association and in June inserted advertisements in the Danville *Register*, advising: "Remember 1930! Vote NO."

[132] The error in ballots cast (or in the number challenged, blank, or void) is N.L.R.B.'s.

dispute was referred to the War Labor Board.[133] Hearings were held
before a W.L.B. panel in October; the panel reported in January 1943;
and in May the Board handed down a decision, upholding the panel
report.[134] The company requested further hearings on wages and work
loads, and these two issues were left pending when the union contract
was signed in June 1943.

Section 1 of the agreement between Dan River mills and the Pittsylvania County Joint Board (the collective bargaining agency for the
three locals) provided collective bargaining for all production and
maintenance employees but specifically excluded "all executive, supervisory and clerical employees." The union recognized (Section 2) as
"management prerogatives" the right to increase or decrease operations;
remove or instal machinery and increase or change production equipment; introduce new and improved productive methods; employ, lay
off, and transfer employees; and demote or discharge employees for
proper cause. Exhibit B set forth eleven "Plant Rules" (fighting,
drinking, smoking within the mill gates, wilful damage to property,
sleeping on duty, etc.), the violation of which would be "cause for discharge or other disciplinary action in the discretion of the management." The union agreed (Section 3) that "no union activities shall be
carried on within the mills or on Company time in such manner as to
interfere with the efficient operations of the mills." The company
agreed that all employees who were members of the union must maintain union membership as a condition of employment and authorize
the company to deduct dues (25 cents weekly) from wages. Women
were promised "equal pay for equal work with men on comparable
operations where they produce a product in comparable quantity and
quality" (Section 4). The military clause (Section 5) provided for the
re-employment of veterans and protection of their seniority during the
term of military duty. Section 6 provided for the payment of time and
one-half for holiday work and work in excess of eight hours per day
(or forty hours per week) and payment of double time for any
seventh consecutive day of work. Employees required to work less
than two hours per shift received compensation for the full two hours

[133] President Harris doubted that the union wanted to settle the dispute by conciliation. "We cannot afford," he said, "to underrate the power of the C.I.O. top officials,
who consider these mills very important to them in their drive through the southern
industry. One of these officials has stated that they are purposely carrying our case to
the W.L.B. and expect to come through with a contract which they will use as a model
throughout the South" (G. S. Harris to J. M. Miller, Sept. 9, 1942).
[134] *War Labor Reports*, vol. 8 (Washington, 1943), pp. 274-295.

(Section 7). Section 8 established a procedure for the adjustment of grievances. A grievance—any complaint not settled within two days by conference with the aggrieved worker's overseer—had to be presented in writing to the overseer "for delivery by him to the department superintendent." The latter was required to confer with the union's shop committeeman; "and they shall earnestly attempt to adjust the grievance." Failure to settle the dispute at this level brought a division superintendent and a local representative of the union into conference; if they failed, the dispute was referred to a national representative of the union and the company's president or general superintendent. At this stage, either party could demand arbitration, either by an arbitrator selected by the parties or by the American Arbitration Association. The arbitrator's decision was "final and binding."

Section 11, dealing with seniority in the layoff and recall of employees, spelled out the conditions under which employees might obtain leaves of absence without loss of seniority and enumerated causes for the loss of seniority.

The union promised that there would be "no strike, slowdown, or work stoppage of any kind during the term of this agreement." The company agreed that there would be no lockout (Section 12).

Section 13 dealt with plant rules and disciplinary action. While accepting them, the union reserved "the right to utilize the grievance procedure with reference to any disciplinary action of the employer for violation of such rules."

Under Section 14 the company agreed to furnish bulletin boards for the posting of notices of union meetings, elections, and social affairs.

The company granted a week's vacation with pay to each employee with one year's service (Section 15).

The agreement was effective for one year, subject to automatic renewal from year to year, unless either party gave written notice of intention to terminate the contract.[135]

The union's negotiating committee and company officials met on June 25 to sign the contract. President Harris described the occasion as "somewhat of a love-feast."[136] The management affirmed that "from

[135] "The Riverside and Dan River Cotton Mills, Incorporated, and Textile Workers Union of America, Local Union No. 452 (C.I.O.), Now Known as Pittsylvania County Joint Board: Contract" (typescript).
[136] G. S. Harris to J. M. Miller, June 25, 1943. "Of course," the president wrote the board chairman, "we do not want to operate under a contract with a Union, but since this is forced on us, we feel that the contract as it stands is satisfactory."

this day on" it would do nothing to antagonize the union, despite its long-standing objections to such innovations as the introduction of 250 shop stewards throughout the plants. A union spokesman expressed similar confidence in harmonious industrial relations. But in August the local union, renewing its membership drive, distributed a handbill depicting a fight between the union and the "Boss Man." The caption declared: "It was a knockout." President Harris protested to T.W.U.A.'s national president.[137]

Another year was required to iron out differences over technological changes. At the hearings before a War Labor Board panel (October 1942) Dan River admitted that its system of piece-rates and incentive pay was "antiquated in spots."[138] Later, in a letter to the Board, the company explained that it had employed American Associated Consultants, Incorporated, to make "a careful, honest and painstaking study of the numerous jobs in our plants," looking forward to the adoption of a "fair and satisfactory system of work assignments." In line with the consultants' recommendation, "it was decided [September 1942] to proceed with the installation of the Unit System to all the operations of the corporation."[139] Under this plan the unit of work, arrived at by time and motion studies, was "the amount of work produced by a normal operator working at a normal day work speed with the proper fatigue allowance in one minute . . . . Once this measure has been established it serves as a basis for assigning work loads, compensation of operators and control of production." Different units carried different rates of pay, varying acording to the skill and other requirements of the job.

After the Unit Plan had been extended to twelve job classifications, a rash of work stoppages served to emphasize the union's determination to make work loads a subject of negotiation. On May 27, 1943, warp hangers refused to smash warps at the same rate of pay (60 cents an

[137] G. S. Harris to Emil Rieve, Aug. 27, 1943. "You and I," Harris said, "made a good start at the recent meetings . . . but we have not progressed far enough for either side to see the fun implied in the boxing match . . . .

"We are trying to train our management to approach all problems in labor relationships in a sportsmanlike manner. Our object is to help the stewards to function in their new position . . . but it behooves us both at this stage to avoid anything that smacks of the mud-slinging indulged in during the campaign."

[138] "For many years George Robertson handled these plants when he was unable to walk. The job-loads and rates were set up without any semblance of standardization" (G. S. Harris to B. B. Gossett, June 21, 1943).

[139] American Associated Consultants, "Engineers' Report," dated Sept. 26, 1942. A staff to supervise the Unit System was organized in the Standards Department under J. V. Verner.

hour) as for hanging warps; the next day a group of weavers stopped
their looms in protest over the grievance of the warp hangers; and on
May 31 about 100 card tenders staged a sit-down strike, protesting a
workload change which, apparently, they had willingly accepted a few
weeks earlier. The management felt that the union, hoping for concession in the pending contract, had instructed the tenders not to work
and not to leave the mill.

The union submitted a proposal for consultation on work-load
changes, which the W.L.B. rejected as too complicated; and in May
1943 the Board ruled that technological changes were the responsibility
of management, subject to grievance procedure.[140] After signing the
contract the company prepared "to fight it out with the Union until
we are entirely free to set up our job loads based on scientific time
studies"; the workers continued to make an issue of the changes introduced. In December some weavers at Riverside struck, protesting the
increase in load from 45 to 60 looms; and in February 1944 the loom
fixers at Schoolfield walked out.[141] Engineers reported that there was
"no will on the part of the operators to do a creditable job," even when
they were certain to earn more; some of the workers argued that they
had "to work too hard to make the increased money in their new assignments."[142] Despite the fear that recurrent work stoppages might lead
the government to take over the plants, the management continued
to extend the unit plan throughout the mills.[143] In May 1944 the

[140] Later the Board reversed its position, declaring that originally it had in mind only
"day-to-day changes" and that any other changes in wage rates and work loads required
union consent (G. S. Harris to B. B. Gossett, June 18 and 23, 1943).
[141] The management contended that the Riverside looms had been reconditioned and
that "careful time studies indicate these weavers can operate 60 of these looms now, with
approximately the same effort as they formerly required for 40 looms." Harris felt that
"with a few exceptions, the labor is happy after they get adjusted to the new working
conditions which enables them to draw substantially higher pay"; but he could also
show that "in every case the cost per unit has been reduced" (G. S. Harris to J. M.
Miller, Dec. 2, 1943). A change in loom assignments on "Ideal" chambray at Riverside
reduced the piece-rate from $.0019 to $.00127 per thousand picks, or about 33 per cent.
[142] Employees assigned new work loads under a different base pay were guaranteed at
least their previous rate of earnings for a period of four weeks following the change. In
the picker room the engineers had estimated that workers would increase their earnings
from 44 cents to 52 cents an hour. Actually, in one two-week period (May 1943) 62 per
cent of the 428 workers earned more than previously; 38 per cent earned less. (The
number of employees had been cut 30 per cent.) In July 1944 the C. E. Murray Company,
management engineers, reported that after reconditioning and relocating the yarding
machines in Mill No. 5, the speed had been stepped up to 110 yards per minute. There
followed the "anticipated stage of operator resistance to the change," but average hourly
earnings for the first full week were 59.8 cents—presumably an increase.
[143] The "Progress Report on Job Measurements" of American Associated Consultants
(July 1944) indicated that 8,978 workers were on jobs considered measurable, and nearly
half of these jobs had been "measured"; only 1,334 men and women were on jobs
deemed unmeasurable. In June motion pictures were made of workers on the job.

company appeared at a public hearing before the War Labor Board, presenting a prepared statement in which it charged the union with attempting "to perform a radical operation on this industrial unit by means of a demand more far reaching than any union demand hereto-fore encountered in this industry. Stripped of all euphemistic trim-ming, that demand is simply this: *That the management of the Com-pany surrender to the Union vital powers necessary to the control of its manufacturing standards and costs.*" It was "axiomatic," the com-pany contended, that management must have a free hand in four areas: (a) developing new management and manufacturing techniques; (b) utilizing its available (and presently restricted) manpower with the greatest possible efficiency; (c) maintaining job standards so that work assignment shall be properly related to the skill and ability of employ-ees; and (d) adapting itself to seasonal and style demands by changing the character of its production and the work assignments related there-to. The union, in the view of the management, had resorted to the "time-honored artifice of damnation by epithet— 'the stretchout.' " The company agreed that technological changes, defined as "changes in the equipment or machines used on a job," should be subject to collective bargaining; but it held that routine and non-technological changes should be made without prior consultation with the union, leaving the grievance machinery to resolve conflicts.[144]

The Board handed down an opinion on June 29, 1944.[145] "In the operation of a textile plant," the Board concluded, "management has the responsibility to decide upon and to institute day-to-day changes in the job assignments of employees which management deems neces-sary to meet the day-to-day requirements of its manufacturing opera-tions. . . . The union unequivocally recognizes the necessity for pre-serving this management responsibility." In the case of "technological changes" the Board observed: "Management very properly insists that it should not be hindered in its efforts to devise improved technical methods in order to maintain and improve the company's competitive position as well as to secure more economical operation of the plant." The evidence indicated the "acquiescence of the union in this posi-tion"; but it was also clear that technological changes gave rise to prob-lems of concern to the employees. "This has been recognized by the

[144] National War Labor Board, "The Riverside and Dan River Cotton Mills, Incor-porated and Pittsylvania County Joint Board (C.I.O.): Case No. 2664-CS-D" (mimeo-graphed statement at public hearing, May 18, 1944).
[145] *War Labor Reports,* vol. 16 (Washington, 1944), pp. 663-666.

company." The Board now approved a procedure, which union and company agreed to accept, for the introduction of technological changes. It involved eight steps, as follows:

1. Management will first inform the union of the change it has decided to make, giving the approximate date of institution, and the general nature thereof.

2. Management will also inform the union of the reason for the change, giving a detailed description of the proposed duties of the operators, changes in work load or machine assignments, proposed rates of pay and expected earnings.

3. Two weeks before the date fixed for the institution of the change, the parties will meet and discuss the information previously furnished.

4. After the discussion, the company has the right to install the change, for a trial period, under such conditions as it determines to be proper.

5. The affected employees have the duty and responsibility to accept the new job assignments and to cooperate fully with management in giving the work load a fair test during the trial period.

6. During the trial period, employees are to be paid not less than their previous average hourly earnings . . . or their actual earnings during the trial period, if such earnings are higher.

7. Within fifteen days from the expiration of the trial period, the union may present a written statement of any grievance as to operation under the new conditions which, if not satisfactorily adjusted by negotiations, may be submitted to arbitration.

8. If arbitration is requested, the parties are first to procure the services of a technician from the U.S. Conciliation Service of the Department of Labor . . . . In the event that the Conciliation Service is unable to furnish in ten days a technician, or the parties fail to adjust the grievance by utilization of the service of the technician, then the grievance is to be submitted to an arbitrator selected by the parties in five days, or by the Conciliation Service if the parties are unable to agree upon the arbitrator.

The Board's opinion included a recommendation "that the parties give serious consideration to the designation of a continuing Impartial Umpire to rule upon all differences over the problems considered in this case." Not without misgivings, the company agreed to the designation of an economics professor, Harry D. Wolf of the University of North Carolina, as a permanent arbitrator.[146]

[146] Harris explained to Miller that he had told the W.L.B. that the company "would welcome such an arrangement if we could find the right man." Although Professor Wolf "met with the approval of the two Industry Members of the Board who have been very helpful to us," Harris found it alarming that the arbitrator would "be in a position where he will hold in his hands our destiny, so far as manufacturing cost is concerned . . . . In our checkup of Mr. Wolf we have some favorable reports, but frankly it makes me nervous when I am about to turn over to a member of the University of North Carolina faculty problems of such vital importance, with the full power to direct" (G. S. Harris to J. M. Miller, July 21, 1944).

The decision of the War Labor Board became the basis for a company-union agreement (August 25, 1944), which supplemented the second collective bargaining contract signed on July 3. An important clause in the July agreement allowed the company to change jobs from hourly rates to piece rates without consulting the union, provided the worker received not less than his previous hourly earnings on the job. Piece rates had to be "set at such a level as to yield a proper incentive to production, in accordance with sound rate setting practices and engineering principles." If the change were made in connection with a new work assignment, the piece rate had to be "so fixed as to reflect added productivity." Data are available on the distribution of piece-rate and hourly-rated employees for the first week in July 1947, as follows:

	male	*female*	*total*
on piece rates	1,692	3,080	4,772
on hourly rates	4,239	2,473	6,712

An analysis of the wages of 428 workers whose earnings were guaranteed under the unit system showed (May 31, 1943):

217 earning more than the guarantee
211 earning less than the guarantee

average guaranteed earnings	54.6	cents per hour
average earnings	53.6	,, ,, ,,
average earnings with supplement	57.8	,, ,, ,,
average possible earnings	63.8	,, ,, ,,

Grievance reports listed 820 cases in 1943 and 611 in 1944, of which all but 72 had been closed early in 1945. Grievances totaled 339 cases in 1946, 497 in 1947, and 366 in 1948. In the latter year 88 cases were settled by departmental superintendents, 46 by divisional superintendents, 198 by the labor relations staff, and 34 by vice-president Browder or by arbitration. The following cases decided by Dr. Wolf, the impartial umpire, are representative of the disputes which went beyond the union-management grievance machinery:

1. A doffer, whose work load was excessive in the opinion of the union, was charged with slowing down production. The umpire found that the worker merited disciplining, though not for deliberate interference with production. He was awarded his wages for one of the two weeks for which he claimed back pay. (Nov. 20, 1944).

2. A fixer was discharged for refusing to lay up roving at the request of the overseer. That the employee was "in the wrong," Dr. Wolf found, "is beyond doubt." The worker was restored to his job as a fixer but deprived of seniority. (Aug. 29, 1944).

3. A battery hand who complained of illness when given a new job assignment was discharged. The "preponderance of evidence" persuaded the umpire that the employee had refused to try the new job, and the union's demand that she be reinstated was denied. (Oct. 6, 1944).

4. In the case of a picker room worker who was discharged for refusing "to run his job as directed," Dr. Wolf declined to order his reinstatement, although he considered the company "not wholly blameless" and believed that to give the worker his job would promote better understanding. (Oct. 19, 1944).

Several grievances in 1943 were refered to the American Arbitration Association, and in 1944-1945 some complaints were carried to the War Labor Board. "The facts are, "President Harris maintained, "our new workloads require an effort on the part of workers that we do not generally get from the radical element who believe that with a Union they have control of the corporation." He admitted that earnings of some workers had been reduced, but this was "because their [previous] earnings were out of line."[147] A strike threat in March 1945 blew over after Harris conferred in New York with a T.W.U.A. vice-president who was "anxious to smooth up our operations in Danville." In September the union contract was renewed.[148]

"An almost mysterious work stoppage movement" in August 1946 brought to light new charges of overloading.[149] The workers resumed production when promised that grievances would be referred to the National Labor Relations Board, but in September they voted to strike if the pending contract did not meet certain demands, including a closed shop.[150] Agreement was reached without a strike, following negotiations which both sides agreed had been remarkably free from

[147] G. S. Harris to J. M. Miller, March 14, 1945. In February 1945 the W.L.B. ruled that battery hands who had been put on piece rates were entitled to a minimum of 48 cents, instead of the 47.5 cents an hour guaranteed by the company.

[148] *The Riverside & Dan River Cotton Mills, Incorporated, and Pittsylvania County Joint Board, Textile Workers Union of America, CIO: Contract* (Danville, 1945).

[149] *Danville Bee*, Aug. 21, 1946. A weaver complained that his set of looms was increased from 12 to 28 "without any additional help of any kind."

[150] Three Dan River directors, who were also directors in the Danville Traction Company, had voted for a closed shop for the transport workers, but Harris was "determined to stand against a Union shop if it means shutting down these plants for a period of months" (G. S. Harris to J. M. Miller, Aug. 29, 1946). On Sept. 12 the president thought the mill had "no more than one chance in ten of avoiding a strike, "which would be "very bad because we now have a large group of cutting plants geared to our loom production" (G. S. Harris to E. H. Lee, Sept. 12, 1946).

acrimony. The union did not get a closed shop, but the new contract contained some concessions on the part of the company. One of these was a wage differential of five cents an hour for third-shift work.[151] The company also assumed the entire cost of the Equitable Life Assurance Society's group medical, surgical, and obstetrical care plan for workers and their dependents. The 1946 contract incorporated detailed provisions on "Workloads, Work Assignments and Incentive Systems," while the sections dealing with the adjustment of grievances were revised. Maxwell G. Copelof was chosen "continuing impartial umpire."[152]

The contract was renewed for a year (August 1, 1947), and in July 1948 a new contract was negotiated.[153] In the meantime, the Virginia "Right to Work Law" (1947) had outlawed the closed shop. Although the maintenance-of-membership clause was dropped from the 1948 contract, the company agreed to retain the check-off.[154] Dan River also promised that "there would be no legal liability on the Union for unauthorized strikes or slow-downs." The Taft-Hartley Act made it possible for the employer to hold the union liable, but the management "believed that the Union had a strong and reasonable argument to support its position in this respect."[155]

The 1948 contract was renewed in 1949. Although the recession in the textile industry had put many workers on short time, in September the union was able to dedicate its new meeting hall and office building on Patton Street. Including the land, the union headquarters cost nearly $150,000. Dan River's Vice-president Browder was one of the speakers at the dedication. Earlier in the year the Pittsylvania County

[151] In 1942 the War Labor Board rejected the union's demand for a third-shift premium of ten cents an hour.

[152] *Dan River Mills, Incorporated and Pittsylvania County Joint Board, Textile Workers Union of America, CIO: Contract* (Danville, 1946).

[153] *Agreement between Dan River Mills, Incorporated, and Pittsylvania County Joint Board, Textile Workers Union of America, CIO* (Danville, 1948).

[154] While legislation was pending, Harris wrote a member of the House of Delegates that the proposed bill was "perfect and I hope will pass without a single amendment. The Closed Shop Contract is the most iniquitous feature of our labor relations. Even an Open Shop Contract, with the usual maintenance of membership clause, enables a small minority of militant bullies to dominate a situation in industry, taking away from a very large majority of the workers the freedom of action to which they are entitled. In my opinion, if the rank and file of labor were free to vote on this issue, they would vote in favor of this Bill." (G. S. Harris to L. L. Moore, Jan. 6, 1947.)

[155] F. Talbott to J. M. Miller, Aug. 4, 1948. President Harris commented: "We worked out a Non-Strike Clause which is consistent with the Taft-Hartley Law. We also believe that our Maintenance of Membership Clause is not inconsistent with our State Law." But the company "fought through a whole basket full of fringe issues without giving up one" (G. S. Harris to B. B. Gossett, July 31, 1948).

Joint Board's Director, Emanuel Boggs, noted in a broadcast that "Dan River has been driving toward better quality since the war ended. There is no doubt that their quality has improved. This Union is wholly in accord with quality production. We are willing to cooperate." Differences between the union and the company were differences over "their disciplinary methods used in the quality control program."

Wages and earnings

Table 10 records the annual wage chronology for 1939-1950. Between December 1939 and January 1950 the average pay for an hour's work rose 192 per cent. In the same period the consumer price index of the Bureau of Labor Statistics advanced 72 per cent. Thus, the purchasing power of an hour of labor increased about 70 per cent.

In October 1939, after cotton mills accepted an industry committee recommendation to fix the minimum wage at 32.5 cents an hour, Dan River granted a general wage increase averaging 3.1 cents an hour. Average hourly earnings (including overtime) for the year 1939 were 38.9 cents; employment averaged 33.7 hours weekly.

Table 10. Employment and Earnings, 1939-1950

year	average number of employees	average hours worked per week	average earnings (cents per hour) with overtime	without overtime
1939	8,971	33.7	38.9	*
1940	9,349	34.6	41.2	*
1941	11,929	40.6	45.3	44.0
1942	13,623	42.6	53.2	50.1
1943	12,444	42.0	57.8	53.9
1944	10,257	41.7	60.2	56.0
1945	9,046	41.4	66.8	62.1
1946	10,228	40.4	81.8	76.6
1947	11,082	40.3	102.8	96.9
1948	11,563	38.5	115.3	110.8
1949	9,174	34.0	120.0	117.9
1950	10,131	37.9	124.3	120.3

* Not available.

Rates of pay for most grades of labor advanced 3.5-5.0 cents an hour in April 1941;[156] in June the Wage and Hour Administrator lifted the

[156] The increases were effective on April 28. On March 31 the management posted notice of a new committee "appointed for the Textile Industry to recommend advances

minimum wage to 37.5 cents an hour; in October Dan River advanced wage rates 2.5-3.0 cents an hour; and in December the company paid a bonus of two per cent of the employee's earnings for the year.

The payroll for the last week of January 1942 showed average hourly earnings of 46.5 cents without overtime. Anticipating the order of the Wage and Hour Administration (April 20), Dan River raised its minimum wage to 40 cents an hour at the end of March. Increases granted to those earning over 40 cents raised average hourly earnings to 49.0 cents in the first week of June. In August the company advanced its minimum wage to 42.5 cents an hour, and increases in other rates lifted average hourly earnings to 53.4 cents (second week of November).[157] The Christmas bonus amounted to 1.5-2.25 per cent of annual earnings, depending upon length of service.[158]

Collective bargaining over the wage issue broke down when the company opposed the union's demand for a 50-cent minimum wage and an increase "across-the-board" of 7.5 cents an hour, retroactive to June 15, 1942. In hearings before the War Labor Board, Dan River demonstrated that the raises effective March 29 and August 3, 1942, had increased average hourly earnings exactly 7.5 cents an hour, although individual job rates had risen by amounts ranging from 1.5 to 25 cents. If the minimum were raised to 47.5 cents an hour, there would be only 245 hourly-rated employees and 21 piece-rate workers who would not have received an increase of at least 7.5 cents since March 1942.[159] In October 1943 the Board directed the company to increase the minimum wage to 47.5 cents, retroactive to September 26, 1942;[160] and in February 1944 the new minimum wage, a number of increases in

---

in the textile wage structure throughout the nation. We are very much in favor of this move . . ." (Circular Poster no. 296). But some Carolina mills, Dan River officials complained, jumped the gun in announcing wage increases.

[157] Wage increases were general throughout the South, the management informed the directors, and it was impossible to ignore the situation and run the risk of having the employees dissatisfied.

[158] Although the president had "little disposition to pay a Christmas bonus," he hoped paying it would weaken the union's case before the War Labor Board for a contractual paid vacation. As the union pointed out, the 1941 bonus was equivalent to a week's pay; but the company wanted to avoid making it a "fixture" of the collective bargaining agreement (G. S. Harris to J. M. Miller, November 17, 1942).

[159] Harris pointed out that to add 7.5 cents uniformly to every worker's pay would "throw our wage scale full of inequalities, as it was when we started" (G. S. Harris to J. M. Miller, Sept. 1, 1942).

[160] *War Labor Reports*, vol. 8, pp. 274-285. Some 1,500 workers, earning 42.5 cents, or 44 cents, were awarded back pay under the Board's directive. In the case of Fifty-nine Cotton Textile Companies, decided in August 1942, the Board awarded an increase of 7.5 cents retroactive to June 15, 1942 (*War Labor Reports*, vol. 2, pp. 345-399) .

hourly job rates, and provision for the payment of "dead" time were incorporated in a supplementary union agreement.[161]

Vacation pay equal to wages for 40 hours was provided for in the 1943 contract; and the mills closed September 4-6, as $165,000 in vacation pay was distributed. Average hourly earnings in the last quarter of 1943 went slightly above 55 cents; with overtime, earnings averaged 58 cents an hour.[162]

In the second union contract (July 1944), the company agreed to an upward revision of wages, subject to the approval of the War Labor Board. With the consent of the Board, the following changes became effective in November; the minimum wage advanced to 50 cents an hour; other rates went up 2.5 cents an hour "across the board"; and the paid vacation was increased to two weeks for employees with five years' service.[163]

Pursuant to an order of the Fourth Regional War Labor Board, in May 1945 Dan River raised the minimum wage to 55 cents an hour, retroactive to October 1, 1944, and added five cents an hour to other rates. No wage settlement was included in the third union contract (September 1945), but in March 1946 the National Labor Relations Board authorized a general increase equivalent to 20.347 per cent, partially retroactive to April 25, 1945, and boosted the minimum to 65 cents an hour. A new union contract (September 1946) provided for a general increase of eight cents an hour and a minimum wage of 73 cents an hour.[164]

Toward the end of 1946 T.W.U.A. announced that it would press for a 15-cent-an-hour wage increase. Dan River's president guessed

[161] Learners on hourly rated jobs began at 40 cents and advanced to 47.5 cents an hour in six weeks. "Dead-time" pay commenced when a power failure or breakdown of machinery lasted as much as fifteen minutes.

[162] Weekly payroll summaries show an average of 46.5 cents for the last week of January 1942 and 55.2 cents for the week ending December 12, 1943, a difference of 8.7 cents. This was exactly the company's estimate (in a memorandum submitted to the W.L.B.) of the effect of increasing the minimum wage to 47.5 cents an hour.

[163] Vacation pay was distributed in August, but no vacations were granted because of the urgency of sustained production. The union used a paid advertisement to announce a "2 ½ Cents per Hour Raise for All Union Members," while the company issued Circular Poster No. 237 to advise that the raise went to non-union workers as well. In July President Harris admitted that Dan River scales were "less than those paid by the South Carolina Mills. I will venture the statement that this was never true before in the history of this corporation, or certainly back 20 or more years" (G. S. Harris to J. M. Miller, July 29, 1944).

[164] Newly-hired workers began at 65 cents and advanced by increments of two cents to reach 73 cents an hour after 320 hours of employment. Piece-rate workers were protected by a guarantee of 90 per cent of straight-time expected hourly earnings "but not less than the plant minimum."

that "the industry will resist more vigorously than in the case of previous demands any advancement in wages from the present levels . . . . it is clearly evident that early in '47 consumers will resist current prices. It would seem that experience must by this time have shown the heads of the Unions that continued wage demands mean higher cost of living and that the ultimate results must be a decrease in employment possibilities."[165] This bit of prophecy fell wide of the mark, and in 1947 wages advanced twice. In February the minimum wage rose to 80 cents an hour, while an agreement with the union called for a general 10-per cent increase. In another wage agreement (November) the company lifted the minimum to 87 cents an hour and raised other rates about 9 per cent.

Prior to the negotiation of a new contract in the summer of 1948, Dan River's straight-time wage averaged $1.07 an hour.[166] The union accepted the company's offer of an 8-per cent raise—"the best offer we had in the bag"—and the minimum wage advanced to 94 cents.[167] Average hourly earnings rose to $1.19 in the first quarter of 1950, only a cent less than the national average in broadwoven fabric mills;[168] and in October 1950 Dan River "voluntarily" increased wages 8 per cent.

Management believed that Dan River's hourly wage of $1.07 in the spring of 1948 was "equal to the top of the southern textile industry"; it was clearly above the southern average of $1.02, according to the calculations of T.W.U.A.[169] But statistical comparisons of the Dan

[165] G. S. Harris to H. E. Hansen, Nov. 8, 1946. Harris was also "convinced that tying wages to the cost of living means a continuing upward spiral and would be inflationary . . . . we would vigorously resist inclusion of cost of living clauses in Union contracts."

[166] *Questions and Answers for Dan River Management* (Danville, 1948), pp. 9-10.

[167] Learners were to start at 86 cents an hour and receive two cents additional after each 80-hour period of employment, until they reached the minimum. The third-shift premium was put at 5 cents an hour.

"We decided," the company's attorney observed, "that with every other important industry having granted wage increases, with the cost of living having increased considerably since last November, and with the Company making more money than it has ever made, we could not take a stubborn position denying any wage increase and still defend our decision with reason to the public and to the employees." But the company successfully opposed "*all* Union demands directly affecting our cost, such as paid holidays, increased over-time rates, enlarged social insurance, liberalized vacation pay, and paid lunch and rest periods." Success at the bargaining table was attributed in part to "the barrage of publicity that we laid down . . . . this helped convince them [union leaders] that we meant business and were preparing ourselves for a strike, if necessary" (F. Talbott to J. M. Miller, Aug. 4, 1948). President Harris also thought that "the Union's decision to accept our 8% wage advance and give up everything else was due to public sentiment locally . . . as a result of our public relations campaign" (G. S. Harris to H. L. Bailey, August 4, 1948).

[168] Bureau of Labor Statistics, *Employment, Hours and Earnings: Manufacturing Division, Textile-Mill Products Group* (mimeographed, 1951), pp. 7-8.

[169] *Questions and Answers for Dan River Management*, p. 23.

River wage with the rest of the industry are inconclusive: mills differ greatly in the composition of the labor force, as different grades of labor are required in varying proportions for a multiproduct output, rarely the same for any two mills.

A Bureau of Labor Statistics study of hourly earnings in January 1939 put the northern straight-time hourly wage at 43.7 cents, or 20.7 per cent above the southern average of 36.2 cents; in April 1944 the North's average of 68.2 cents an hour was 17.4 per cent above the South's 58.1 cents.[170] In August 1942, according to data compiled for the War Labor Board, Dan River's average rate of 53.3 cents an hour was midway between the southern average of 49.6 cents and the northern average of 57.5 cents an hour.[171] The Board took the position that it lacked authority to narrow the North-South differential; while the unions complained, especially after the war, that the gap tended to widen.

While minimum wages were rising, other rates of pay often failed to increase proportionately. In Dan River's case, the raises granted in April 1941 were graduated, as follows: 5 cents an hour on rates up to 34 cents an hour; 4 cents on rates from 34 to 38 cents; and 3.5 cents on rates over 38 cents an hour. In October this narrowing of the spread was partially offset by a wage increase of 3 cents an hour on rates over 54 cents and 2.5 cents on rates up to 54 cents. President Harris surmised correctly that the War Labor Board was "intent on making further advances to widen the differential between common labor and skilled labor, increasing this differential as we go up the scale." In February 1945 the Board raised the minimum wage to 55 cents, in a "move toward correction of substandards of living," but expressed the opinion that "the differentials now provided for between unskilled, semi-skilled and skilled occupations are too narrow for the maintenance of efficient production."[172] So-called "guidepost" rates, which in August received the sanction of the newly created Southern Textile Commission, fixed a spread of 45 cents between the minimum wage and the pay ($1.00 per hour) of skilled maintenance employees.[173] A study of south-

[170] *Monthly Labor Review*, vol. 59 (Oct. 1944), pp. 823-835.

[171] *War Labor Reports*, vol. 2, pp. 345-399. In April–May 1946 the average straight-time pay for 424,810 textile workers was 75 cents an hour, an average heavily weighted by the 74 cents an hour pay of 339,788 workers in the southeastern mills (*Monthly Labor Review*, vol. 64 March 1947, pp. 454-459). At this time hourly earnings at Dan River averaged over 77 cents.

[172] *War Labor Reports*, vol. 21 (1945), pp. 793-820, 876-887.

[173] The job differential had been greater, at least in the Reidsville-Danville area, in

eastern mills in May 1946 disclosed a narrower spread than in the guidepost rates: charwomen averaged 62 cents an hour, but the loom fixer's pay of 97 cents was barely 50 per cent above the lowest rate.[174] At Dan River the minimum wage crept up on the average, reaching 87.2 per cent of average hourly earnings toward the end of 1943. The ratio in 1948 (80.8 per cent) was practically the same as in 1939.

Very little of the narrowing occupational wage spread may be explained by the down-grading of tasks. Company files show that 25 per cent of its employees in 1940 were considered skilled; in 1942 22 per cent were so classified. In the same period the proportion of unskilled rose from 33 to 35 per cent. Total employment increased from 8,691 to 13,181; and without reclassification of jobs the proportion of unskilled workers would normally be larger in a larger labor force.

In March 1942 the mills employed 1,236 operatives at less than 40 cents an hour. After the minimum wage rose to 40 cents (except for learners) the dispersion of average hourly earnings (for the week ending September 26, 1942) was as follows:

average earnings (cents per hour)	men	women
40.0-42.5	139	53
42.5-45.0	574	339
45.0-47.5	347	398
47.5-50.0	971	839
50.0-55.0	1558	1579
55.0-60.0	641	712
60.0-65.0	564	550
65.0-70.0	529	450
70.0-75.0	473	252
75.0-80.0	158	101
80.0 and over	446	45

In any case, cotton manufacturing continued to be regarded as a low-wage industry, and the supply of textile workers fell off sharply as the demand for labor in other industries increased. In July 1943 the Dan River management observed that "in the face of many employee losses, principally due to the draft, to defense work, farming, transportation, and housing, we have had to resort to many new meth-

---

July 1943, when Class A machinists averaged 83 cents an hour, almost twice the average pay of 42 cents an hour for female doffers and charwomen.

[174] Bureau of Labor Statistics, *Wage Structure: Cotton Textile, 1946* (Washington, 1947), pp. 6-10.

ods of attracting learners and training operatives." The War Manpower Commission sent a recruiting staff to Danville in the summer of
1944, using sound trucks to tour the city and appeal to men and women
to apply for jobs at the mills.[175] The situation worsened in 1945. In
May President Harris complained that, despite promises that textiles
would "be rated as high as any other industry," the Commission had
"done nothing to follow through the statements made by Chairman
McNutt." In June Harris became "very much concerned because of
the manner in which other industries are driving for labor in our
territory";[176] and employment in the third and fourth quarters sagged
to prewar levels. As Table 11 indicates, the return of veterans and the
easing of labor shortages in war industries enabled the company to
build up its labor force in 1946-1948. The severe drop in employment in 1949 was caused by the lull in trade, not by the shortage of
help.

Table 11. Mill Employment by Quarters, 1941-1949

year	Jan.-March	April-June	July-Sept.	Oct.-Dec.
1941	9,684	10,567	10,420	11,145
1942	13,271	13,600	13,526	14,024
1943	13,788	13,185	11,480	11,056
1944	11,028	10,525	9,906	9,666
1945	9,730	9,105	8,611	8,531
1946	9,528	10,144	10,253	11,042
1947	11,201	11,121	10,485	11,531
1948	11,832	11,740	11,248	11,418
1949	10,857	8,914	7,520	9,406
1950	9,852	9,833	9,693	11,146

A concomitant of the labor shortage was an abnormal turnover rate.
Monthly separation ratios (the ratio of dismissals for all causes to number on the payroll) averaged only 3.3 per cent monthly in 1939 and 4.0
per cent monthly in 1940 but climbed steadily to 32.5 per cent for the
third quarter of 1942. At this rate, the average worker quit or was
dismissed at the end of nine months. Dan River's record in this re-

[175] *Daily News Record*, July 10, 1944. The company invested $50,000 in busses to
carry workers isolated from public transportation.
[176] G. S. Harris to K. W. Marriner, War Production Board, May 31 and June 14, 1945.
Asserting that "we need today at least 2,500 additional workers," President Harris protested the advertisements for help of DuPont and the American Viscose Company, which
put pressure on the labor market from which Dan River drew (G. S. Harris to F. Coker,
June 20, 1945).

spect was somewhat worse than that of the industry.[177] The decade ended without any striking improvement in reducing the high costs associated with the frequent replacement of trained workers. The 1948 employment and severance report showed a total of 13,366 quits, discharges, lay-offs, and other severances. In 1950 7,095 employees quit their jobs and another 2,419 were released for other reasons. Early in 1943 Dan River reported to the War Labor Board that 3,156 (out of 13,494) employees had worked for the company more than ten years; but 3,374 had been with the mills less than a year.

Employment of sixteen- and seventeen-year old girls, permitted under a revision of the Walsh-Healey Act (1943), furnished a partial remedy for the shortage of help.[178] Women and girls filled over half of all jobs for three years, 1943-1945; but the ratio dropped, as veterans returned to the mills and women went back to housekeeping (Table 12).

A less important solution to the labor-supply problem came from increasing the proportion of Negro workers. By 1946 colored employees comprised almost 15 per cent of the labor force, probably the maximum employable under the existing social limitations on jobs for Negroes in textile plants.[179]

The employment of Negro spinners and doffers occasioned a walkout in May 1944. Although the colored workers were segregated (in one room at Riverside), the union demanded that Negro production laborers be employed in a separate building. This proposal was impractical; and, after the strike had reduced production about 30 per cent, the management withdrew the Negroes from the spinning rooms.[180] National officers of T.W.U.A. planned to merge Local 452

[177] Monthly separation rates for the industry averaged 4.23 per cent in 1940-1941, 6.00 per cent in 1941-1942, 8.37 per cent in 1942-1943, and 7.75 per cent in 1943-1944 (National Industrial Conference Board, *Conference Board Industry Record*, Aug. 9, 1944).

[178] In 1942 the company began to take applications from sixteen- and seventeen-year old girls. It also had a file of 300 girls who said they were eighteen but had no proof (G. S. Harris to C. T. Murchison, May 30, 1942). The eighteen-year minimum age was restored in 1946, but the president warned the sales manager that "until labor is in easier supply" the company should not accept contracts requiring adherence to the Walsh-Healy standards. In January 1949 the sales office was advised that "we are not in compliance with the Walsh-Healy Act at our Riverside Division and have not up to this point felt it was necessary" (B. D. Browder to J. M. Hughlett).

[179] Donald Dewey, "Negro Employment in Southern Industry," *The Journal of Political Economy*, vol. 60 (1952), pp. 279-293.

[180] *Daily News Record*, June 6, 1944. Harris thought the Union had "a 'hot brick' and does not yet know what to do with it" (G. S. Harris to B. B. Gossett, May 29, 1944). "An interesting development," the president reported, was the observation of an Army procurement officer at the mills that the "solution" violated Dan River's government contract and if the Negroes complained, the Army would have to "move in" (G. S. Harris to J. M. Miller, June 5, 1944).

Table 12. Women and Negro Employees

year	all employees	women	Negroes
1940	9,566	3,244	751
1941	12,214	3,669	816
1942	13,988	5,125	881
1943	13,036	6,568	1,445
1944	11,033	5,767	1,270
1945	9,830	5,105	1,276
1946	10,239	4,990	1,505
1947	11,082	5,430	1,185
1948	11,563	5,660	1,237
1949	9,174	4,490	1,009

and the Negro Local 511, but rank-and-file opposition to the threat of nonsegregated employment killed the proposal.[181]

Despite the labor shortage, every effort was made to obtain the economies of scale through three-shift operations. Demand for sheeting made it feasible to start a third shift on Schoolfield's 72-inch looms late in 1939, and by December 1940 nearly 1,000 workers were employed on the third shift. In 1942-1943 the weekly payroll frequently reported over 2,500 workers on the third shift. All shifts commenced to work a "normal" 48-hour week in March 1941; and a seven-day work week was inaugurated in April 1943.[182] But absenteeism kept the average hours worked per week far below the available hours of work (Table 10).

One of the unfortunate by-products of increased production and high labor turnover was a rising accident rate. In June 1943 a representative of the U.S. Department of Labor surveyed the company's accident-prevention work in 1938-1942. In 1940, the best year in five, the mills had 113 lost-time accidents, including one fatality, and the accident-frequency rate was 3.9 per million man-hours worked. Much higher rates, as the following statistics show, were reached in the war years:

[181] The Dan River management observed that this movement "could cause sufficient resentment among the white workers to completely crack the Union here." If the union should attempt to force white and colored people to work side by side, "both the Company and the Union are going to have plenty of headaches" (G. S. Harris to J. M. Miller, Sept. 30, 1944).

[182] *Daily News Record,* April 12, 1943. The mills shut down at 11:00 P.M. Saturday and the third shift worked from midnight Sunday to 7:00 A.M. The following unsigned letter to the president seems to be a sample of the sporadic opposition to longer hours: "Dear Sir. If it's in your power and if possible will you please cut out the Sat. work. It will be a great help to the working people as so many are getting so they are not able to work, but it sure is helping the Drs. practice. Yours truly."

year	lost-time accidents	accidents per million man-hours
1941	178	7.0
1942	470	15.8
1943	675	23.8
1944	416	17.5
1945	343	16.5
1946	302	13.1
1947	258	11.3
1948	142	6.2
1949	123	7.5

In 1943 F. E. Murrie, the safety director, began to "think of abandoning the plan of Self Insurer and getting under the protection of a good carrier."[183] While the claims paid under the workmen's compensation law declined from $103,120 in 1944 to $43,056 in 1948, the expense of operating the company's clinic rose from $61,470 in 1944 to $97,730 in 1948. The mill's expanded safety program, including the quarterly safety meetings for the instruction of supervisors, was definitely effective in the closing years of the decade. Curiously the accident-frequency rate rose to 12.9 in 1950, the year after the company employed a safety engineer designated by the National Safety Council; but this may only represent an improvement in statistical methods.

Training

A growing labor shortage and the comparative inefficiency of workers drawn into the mills under emergency conditions necessitated a greatly expanded program of in-service training, the foundations for which had been prepared through organization of the Textile School in the 1930's. By mid-1941 supervisory personnel was "stretched to the limit due to increased hours of operations and a larger number on our payrolls . . . . This condition is much worse than it would normally be, due to the fact that in the past no plans had been made for the development and training of these men in our organization." Training classes for foremen were started, "with the idea of fitting our supervisory staff to more completely handle not only the direction of departments and production, but also that important phase of our operation

[183] Dan River became a self-insurer under the workmen's compensation law in 1931, when two insuring firms failed. According to Murrie, for a period of twelve years Dan River's accident experience was so satisfactory that a "surplus" of $175,000 accumulated from the difference between compensation payments and the insurance manual rates of premium (F. E. Murrie to G. S. Harris, Aug. 21, 1943).

which is generally known as labor relations."[184]   Plans for the fall of
1941 called for about fifty classes to train fixers and other skilled
workers.   This part of the training program met the requirements of
the Smith-Hughes act, so that federal funds covered half of the cost.[185]

A job-instructor conference preceded the inauguration of the 1943
training program, mapped out by Personnel Director W. D. Vincent,
J. A. Becher, and L. K. Fitzgerald.[186]   In the February-May (1943)
semester there were six series of classes for training in "job funda-
mentals," viz., carding, spinning, spooling-warping, slashing, weaving,
and finishing.   Classes for workers on the first and third shifts met from
4:30 to 6:30 P.M.; for the second shift, classes met from 10:00 A.M. to
noon.   Graduates of the 1943 loom-fixers' course included women
fixers.[187]

In planning the training program for 1944, company officials had
the co-operation of the Apprentice-Training Service of the War Manpower Commission.   An urgent matter, from the mill's point of view,
was the training of learners and substandard workers, numbering 859
on the payroll for the week ending May 28, 1944, since the company
normally had to supplement their actual earnings to comply with
minimum-wage laws.   (The supplement amounted to $4,036 for the
week ending May 28.)   International Correspondence Schools and La
Salle University correspondence courses were available on terms established by the company in the 1930's; Dan River paid half the tuition if
the student finished his course.   In 1945, 347 employees were enrolled
in La Salle, and 120 completed the La Salle "Foremanship for Victory"
program.

In March 1944 Dr. C. J. Schollenberger, formerly of Des Moines,
Iowa, came to Dan River as superintendent of the Training Department.   Under Dr. Schollenberger's direction the training programs
expanded, especially after the wartime emergency had passed; and by
1950 the Training Department was a euphemism for trade school, night

[184] In the fall of 1941 the company advertised in the *Textile Bulletin* for textile
graduates to take jobs as second hands and overseers—"the jobs that need strengthening."
[185] The state put up one-fourth, and the balance was met by student fees of 10 cents for
each two-hour class.   The mills, of course, furnished classroom space and equipment.
[186] *Training Tips*, vol. 1, no. 1 (Nov. 30, 1942), a mimeographed newsletter, "published"
in the Personnel Department "in the interest of training and instruction."
[187] *American Wool and Cotton Reporter*, April 29, 1943.   Riverside Division still employed a female loom fixer in 1954.   Before the war the scarcity of this type of labor
was often attributed to the fact that the weave rooms, the logical place to recruit fixer-
learners, employed too many women in proportion to men.

school, high school, and university by extension.   The organization embraced seven separate programs, as follows:

(1) Part-time trade extension.   The classes were for operatives who needed additional technical information about their jobs or wanted to prepare for better jobs within their trades.   Completion of a course entitled the student to a State Unit Card, while a certain number of Unit Cards could be exchanged for a State Diploma in Carding, Spinning, Weaving, Textile Chemistry, or some other specialty.   Tuition, a state grant, and a federal grant each paid a third of the instructional costs of these courses.

(2) Trade preparatory: classes for employees not working in a classified trade but preparing for such employment.

(3) Adult education: from the first grade through the first two years of college.   Evening classes, leading to grade-school certificate and standard Virginia high school diploma, were arranged in co-operation with the Danville Public Schools.   Tuition covered one-half the instructors' salaries, the other half coming from state funds.   College work was brought to the mills through the Extension Division of the University of Virginia.   Since tuition had to cover the entire salary of the instructor, practically any course could be offered for which there was sufficient demand.[188]

(4) Commercial training.   This program offered courses in typing, shorthand, and operation of office machines for the company's women employees.   The teachers' salaries were met by tuition and state grants-in-aid.

(5) Avocational classes.   "In many cases where a husband is going to school in the evening, his wife desires to have something to occupy her time during this period.   For this purpose we have established classes in cooking, sewing, and clay modeling, all of which tend to improve the home life of our employees."   Student fees and a state grant covered the cost.

(6) Supervisory training.   Designed to strengthen and increase job abilities, this program made available classes in labor relations, human relations, cost control, fabric analysis, conference leading, and public speaking. State and federal funds paid two-third of the instructors' salaries; tuition covered the rest.

(7) Apprentice training.   This was the training program for veterans preparing for skilled trades in the textile industry, such as machinist, electrician, carpenter, and engineer.   Applicants had to meet the approval of the State Apprenticeship Committee and fulfil the requirements of the "G. I. Bill" (Public Law 346).

A postwar program for the in-service training of college graduates enrolled 126 men, including 16 picked from jobs in the plant, between February 1946 and November 1947.   In *Dan River and the College Man* (1948), the company stated that it began "some years ago . . . em-

[188] In January 1948 University of Virginia extension courses were given in German, Spanish, and history.

ploying college-trained men on a large scale." The booklet referred to
the mills as "a young men's organization" and emphasized that over
90 per cent of those completing the training period remained with the
company. "One of the superintendents was a college senior *less than
two years ago.*"

No precise appraisal can be made of the training programs, either
in terms of increased efficiency or in such imponderable values as
morale and job satisfaction. The company gradually improved the
physical accommodations of the Training Department. The Riverside
unit of the Textile School occupied a floor in the remodeled Research
Building, and in 1948 the department acquired office space and classrooms in the subbasement of Hylton Hall. Enrollment generally maintained the upward trend begun in the war years, but the attrition rate
was high. Thus, in the spring of 1947 only 438 of the 795 completed
their courses; and in the fall of 1948, 688 enrolled and 525 completed
their courses.[189]

The Training Department inaugurated "George Washington High
School Day" in April 1947. The following editorial from the school
paper, *The Chatterbox,* explains the purpose of this step and the student response to the experience:

An organization that can make an entire day as interesting, enjoyable, and
educational as the Dan River Mills did, deserves a vote of thanks from the
Seniors. The only question in the boys' minds last Wednesday after "High
School Day" at the Mills had literally flown by was "Why hasn't this been
done before?"
Although the Mills have played an important part in our economic life
for many years, the process through which they operate has remained a
secret to the youth of Danville, so much so, in fact, that few graduates of
the High School have ever considered taking a job there or majoring in
textiles at college. Now, in one day, the secret has been revealed as not
even a secret at all, but a continual chain of cooperation, ability, and efficiency. Modern equipment, endless lines of cotton cloth, numberless
workers, and the importance of quick-witted managers and supervisors all
played their part in impressing on the boys the fact that the Mills were a
huge industrial machine and dispelled any false notions that they previously
had.
The amazing thing was that the Mills had nothing that they were unwilling
to show the youthful "managers." Correspondence, processes and all problems which came in the course of the day were readily explained to them.

[189] The Danville *Bee* (June 6, 1947) reported an attendance of 1,400 students at the
third annual picnic-outing sponsored by the Training Department. Vice-president
Browder addressed the gathering on "Dreams."

In instituting "High School Day" the Mills have made a step which will aid both them and the High School. They have brought about a greater understanding and interest among the students and influenced some of them toward seriously considering taking jobs there upon graduation. The Seniors have finally discovered that the Dan River Mills is truly "a good place to work."

Salaries

Salaries followed wages upward, and salaried employees enjoyed year-end bonuses from 1941 on. Bonus rates went as high as 50 per cent in 1948, the maximum rate applying to top salaries. The directors, who approved all salaries of $5,000 a year and over, granted increases for 1944 (subject to the consent of the Salary Stabilization Office), which put the 31 highest-paid executives in the following brackets:

$ 5,000 – $ 7,499	17
7,500 – 9,999	7
10,000 – 15,000	5
20,000	1
36,000	1

In a registration statement filed with the Securities and Exchange Commission the company made public the earnings (salary and bonus) in 1945 of those who received over $20,000. They were six, as follows:

G. S. Harris, president and treasurer	$53,000
R. B. Newton, vice-president	35,000
B. D. Browder, vice-president	29,000
A. B. Emmert, vice-president	29,000
J. M. Hughlett, vice-president and sales manager	27,600
F. Talbott, Jr., attorney	21,133

In April 1946 the president expressed concern over attempts of Dan River's competitors to hire away top personnel in New York and Danville "with salary offers considerably in excess of the salaries currently paid by us."[190] The directors responded with raises for five men in

---

[190] "It is a matter of fact," J. M. Hughlett wrote Harris, "that our salary scale for sales executives and senior salesmen is on the low side of the market," Items in the *Daily News Record* intimated that other firms were paying two or three times the Dan River scale. In April 1947 the chairman of the board was "somewhat worried" over the possible loss of "our good men. It would be difficult to replace them at anything like the same figure and probably with men not so valuable to us" (J. M. Miller to G. S. Harris, Apr. 10, 1947).

New York and five in Danville, not counting Harris, who received but did not ask for an increase to $60,000.[191] After 1944 the board passed on salaries of $10,000 a year and over, leaving the management a free hand in the lower brackets. The salaries approved for 1950 put 20 executives in the range of $12,000–$75,000.

Wartime limitations on salary increases and "the alleged low morale existing among our office employees" occasioned the formation of a permanent salary committee to review office salaries and pass on recommendations. In 1943 the War Labor Board permitted only two "merit" increases a year and held each raise to one-third of the difference between the lowest and the highest rate of pay for the job classification. As "a step toward stabilizing of office salaries," the committee collected data on seven groups of employees— administrative and executive assistants, stenographers and secretary stenographers, male and female clerical assistants, and office machine operators. Department heads were required to rate each worker from A ("worth already demonstrated with promise of further development") to D ("mediocre") and submit recommendations on changes in rates of pay. Fresh reports were to be made quarterly, but I have the impression that the work of the committee petered out. In 1944 the Trundle Engineering Company was called in to make a "job evaluation study" covering all salaried employees, excepting those in the sales division and those earning $7,500 a year or more. A point system, with a maximum score of 1,000 points was devised to rate each employee on the basis of education, experience, skill, effort, responsibility, and working conditions; and the scores were compared with the individual's salary. The anomalies revealed by the Trundle report, covering 677 salaried employees, were the product of a haphazard development in salary determination. Thus, a loom inspector credited with 437 points earned $62 a week, but a 437-point assistant section head earned only $30. A section head with 615 points was paid $25 a week, while a superintendent rated at 617 points earned $87. Of course, the whole list, comprising 188 job classifications, was not topsy-turvy: a clerk-trainee awarded 191 points earned $18 a week, while a manager of the Standards Department, scoring 793, received $115 weekly.

Bonuses, the management believed, were not the ideal form of in-

[191] When additional increases were voted in 1947, Miller remarked: "To a country man like myself these increases, of course, seem very considerable but after all I must compare them with salaries of our competitors" (J. M. Miller to G. S. Harris, May 3, 1947).

centive compensation, especially at the executive level. Although Harris once expressed a "desire to see an increasing amount of our stock held in Danville and especially by the Company's employees,"[192] both the president and the board chairman opposed using stock owner-ship in an incentive-pay plan.[193] Attorney Talbott, on the other hand, questioned the wisdom of paying year-end bonuses at rates fixed arbi-trarily by the directors. "It looks as if the Company will ultimately have to seek stockholder approval of a by-law which would formalize a profit-sharing scheme." In 1946 Harris was

wondering if the adoption of some sound plan of profit participation to include the men responsible for the profits would not be more in the in-terest of our stockholders than the retirement of our Preferred Stock . . . . We have to recognize the fact that this Corporation probably more than the average depends upon the skill and application of its executives for profits. Such skill and application is not usually bought, but needs to be stimulated. We have a group of men who up to now have been keenly interested in building our position and have given to their responsibilities everything they had. Time frequently dulls this enthusiasm. It is at this point that we should, if possible, give to these men a sizable participation in the profits.

No concrete proposal for profit-sharing was found to satisfy the manage-ment, but an alternative suggestion—to provide pensions for executives —evolved into the mill-wide retirement plan adopted in 1948. Pre-viously, some pensions had been granted, by action of the directors, in accordance with the needs or merits of the retiring employee. Thus, in 1943 the Reverend O. A. Guinn, a cotton house worker who, during 36 years of employment, had interested himself in the "social and spiritual welfare" of his fellow employees, was voted a pension of $30 a week. Three employees retiring after 50 to 58 years' service received grants of $25 a month "during the pleasure of the Board."[194]

Several pension plans were considered in 1946, but the president found none of them satisfactory and in 1947 called in Industrial Rela-tions Counselors, Incorporated. Advice was also obtained from an offi-cial of the Guaranty Trust Company. As the idea evolved, the manage-ment took a broader view of the problem and proposed a company-

[192] In July 1945 Harris wrote a sharp letter to two Danville banks, charging them with discrimination and collusion, in charging a 6 per cent discount on loans "collateralized" with Dan River stock, while loans on listed securities could be had for 4 per cent.
[193] Chairman Miller did not "think much of influencing in any way our key men to buy common stock. I doubt if any of them would be able to buy enough to any con-siderable extent influence their working" (J. M. Miller to G. S. Harris, Dec. 22, 1943).
[194] Secretary Ayres retired in 1947 at half salary despite the fact that "one-fourth his salary is in line with previous retirements" (G. S. Harris to J. M. Miller, Jan. 22, 1947).

wide plan instead of one limited to officers and key executives. Following the advice of Industrial Relations Counselors, the directors finally approved an annuity program administered by an insurance company. On January 19, 1948, the board accepted the proposal of the Equitable Life Assurance Society; and the plan was submitted to the stockholders with the reminder that "Dan River will operate at a disadvantage in competition with progressive organizations in our field if we fail to establish such a plan."[195]

The retirement plan went into effect on May 1, 1948. Eligibility was extended to all employees who had reached the age of thirty and worked five years continuously. In partial payment for his retirement benefit the employee contributed 2.25 per cent of the first $1,800 of annual earnings, 3 per cent on the next $1,200, and 4.5 per cent on earnings in excess of $3,000. Additional premiums paid by Dan River guaranteed the worker an annuity, commencing at age 65, approximately four times the amount purchased by his own contribution alone. Not counting past service benefits but including Social Security at the rates prevailing in 1952, scheduled payments run from $64.50 per month for the worker who joins the plan at age 60 and pays premiums on wages of $30 a week to $255.75 per month for the 30-year old worker with average earnings of $100 a week. Separate arrangements were made for the pensioning of the 113 employees who had already reached sixty-five when the plan went into effect.[197] The first group of 205 employees retiring under the annuity plan (1949) included eight men and two women who had worked for the company fifty years or more.

In 1948-1949 the out-of pocket cost of retirement pay and premiums on the annuity contract amounted to almost $1.5 million, distributed as follows:

	1948	*1949*
current service premium	$262,500	$390,000
past service premium	271,250	403,000
retirement allowances		84,341

[195] The directors voted in favor of Equitable six to three, the minority favoring the proposal of Life Insurance Company of Virginia. Stockholders ratified the recommendation on March 11, 1948.

[196] *Retirement Plan for Employees of Dan River Mills Incorporated* (booklet); *How the Dan River Retirement Plan Works for You* (booklet).

[197] As of August 1948 the "old timers" included William Morgan and Alice Thompson, who began to work for Riverside Mills in 1888, Mattie Golden and Eugene Bivins, who started in 1895, and E. A. Buckner, who came to the mills in 1898. The pensions of 113 workers averaged $21.40 a month.

Welfare and Housing

Numerous changes in accounting procedures make it difficult to present a consistent record of changes in village and welfare costs. On January 2, 1944, the newly created Public and Industrial Relations Division controlled the following assets:

	net book value
Schoolfield division	
houses	$279,778
coal and wood yard	9,001
Hylton Hall	114,563
Welfare Building	44,956
Y.M.C.A. Building	0
canteen	34
Riverside division	
houses	53,846
cloth store equipment	72
total	$502,250

The mill village in 1945, including company-owned houses in Danville, consisted of 958 dwellings with the rooms and sanitary facilities indicated by Table 13. Although the president told the directors that the company urgently needed housing for key men, a veteran's housing project (1946) in Schoolfield represented the only home building on company land during the Harris administration. And this represented a new departure in Dan River policy, since the forty-four houses constructed on Harris Place were immediately sold (at actual construction cost) to veterans employed by the company. Built by Allen J. Saville of Richmond, the four- and six-room houses were sold for $5,375 to $6,575.[198]

Lockwood,Greene Engineers prepared a "Village Sewage Report" in 1942, recommending the completion of the sanitary sewer system in the residential section of Schoolfield. Nothing was done about the problem, although in July and again in September 1945 the directors were reminded that "better sanitary conditions" (sewers and bathrooms) should be provided "at the earliest possible date." Inside the city the issue was forced by the necessity of compliance with municipal

[198] For the purpose of supplying the building materials, Dan River acquired a subsidiary, the Sunderland-Edmunds Lumber Company in Yanceyville, North Carolina. It was liquidated in 1946 at a loss of $45,551.

Table 13. Company Houses: June 1945

number of rooms	number of houses		
	with bath	without bath	total
Riverside Division:			
2	1	0	1
3	12	35	47
4	22	0	22
5	16	0	16
6	19	3	22
7	1	0	1
8	6	0	6
9	2	0	2
12	2	0	2
Schoolfield Division:			
2	16	53	69
3	11	308	319
4	108	192	300
5	18	1	19
6	34	62	96
7	19	0	19
8	16	0	16
10	0	1	1
totals	303	655	958

ordinances. After reviewing the cost of modernizing the dwellings occupied by employees at Riverside Division, the directors decided to sell "on easy payments" most of the company-owned houses in Danville. Appraised by an independent realty company, 94 houses were sold in October and November, 1949, to employee-occupants for $308,800. Inasmuch as the property had been heavily depreciated on the company's book, the transactions showed a profit of $235,234.[199]

Welfare in the 1940's embraced mainly the activities centered on the Schoolfield Y.M.C.A. In October 1940 an economy drive released H. E. Spessard from his post as "Y" secretary; in 1941 Mr. and Mrs. O. Andrezen were employed to carry on the programs sponsored by the "Y" and supervise social gatherings at the Country Club. The "Y" report for 1943, issued by Norman Waugh, president of the board of directors, listed the clubs, classes, scouting groups, and athletic teams

[199] The union protested the sale, without prior consultation with the union, as an "unfair labor practice." The company insisted that it was not a bargaining issue, a field examiner of the National Labor Relations Board intervened, and the union withdrew its charge.

active during the year. Membership was not reported. An innovation this year was the opening of the women's division of the Schoolfield "Y" Clubs, directed by Miss Estelle Moorefield, including the Brownies, Girl Scouts, Girl Reserves, and Young Women's Club. The Girl Reserves conducted the tuberculosis seal campaign; the Hi-Light Club, made up of employed girls, gave a Christmas party for underprivileged children; and the Health for Victory Club held monthly conferences with an expert on nutrition.

Contact was at first a newspaper, then a mimeographed bulletin, sponsored by the H. G. McGinn Post 97 of the American Legion but prepared at the mill by Dan River personnel. The paper carried news of the mill community to servicemen and featured pictures of former employees in uniform and letters from the front. The American Legion conducted a memorial service on April 12, 1945, honoring 101 former employees of Dan River who died in service.

The Employees' Benefit Association grew from its charter membership of 2,387 (1937) to 11,010 in February 1949. Dues were increased from 25 cents to 40 cents weekly (December 1948) to provide larger benefits, in view of the rising cost of hospital care. As noted above, the E.B.A. benefits were supplemented by the company-financed medical care program adopted in 1946. E.B.A. also administered a group insurance plan, underwritten by the Provident Life and Accident Insurance Company, providing death, sickness, maternity, and non-occupational accident benefits. For the year ending February 28, 1949, the Association's executive secretary, B. B. Burnett, reported collections of $144,001 in membership dues and $121,745 in insurance premiums.

Danville had an acute shortage of hospital beds, and in November 1945 President Harris brought to the attention of the directors a proposal to build a new hospital in Ballou Park. The idea was abandoned when "an impartial expert survey" showed "that the community needs would be best served by enlargement of Memorial Hospital in Danville, an existing unit of relatively modern construction, which has been well maintained and well managed."[200] Vice-president R. B. Newton headed the public drive for funds to enlarge Memorial Hospital from 170 to 275 beds. It was estimated that, apart from federal and state funds, $1.5 million would be required; and Dan River's directors voted to

---

[200] "A Message concerning Our Contribution to Memorial Hospital in Danville" (leaflet).

appropriate not over $500,000, contributing one dollar for every two dollars raised by public subscription.[201]

Although President Harris thought his predecessor, Robert R. West, had been too much of a "joiner" and turned down numerous requests to continue contributions and renew memberships, the 1941-1949 administration hardly set a record for parsimony. In 1940 the company reduced its subscription to the Virginia State Chamber of Commerce from $300 to $200 a year, but it gave as much as $5,000 yearly to the Danville Chamber of Commerce. Dan River withdrew (1940) from the National Association of Finishers of Textile Fabrics but contributed $1,200 (1948) to the Brookings Institution to help finance an economic survey of Virginia, gave $500 (1947) to the Jamestown Corporation for an historical project, and supported the work of the Committee for Economic Development, a national economic research organization. The company responded to the appeals of the Red Cross in New York, Atlanta, St. Louis, Los Angeles, Chicago, and Danville, and it contributed regularly to the Greater New York Fund as well as the Community Chest of Danville. Off-quality cloth was donated to the American Friends Service Committee, and in 1942 small sums were given to Russian and Chinese War Relief drives. In Danville, the Wesley House received the usual subvention of $500 a year, and in 1948 the annual grant of $2,500 to Hill Top Sanitarium was doubled. Dan River donated $10,000 (1948) to the Boy Scouts, many of whom were sons of employees, to help complete their camp in Nelson County. A contribution was made to the organ and manse repair funds of the Burton Memorial Church, and the Schoolfield Baptist Church was given a deed to the parsonage.

Donations and contributions charged to selling expense amounted to $8,575 in 1943; while an additional $31,010 was charged to general administration expense.

While the tax-exempt status of corporate contributions to organized charities, religious bodies, and non-profit welfare and educational organizations was never in doubt, experience has shown that the company's expenditures for these purposes tended to fluctuate with changes in business conditions. Furthermore, as early as 1941 the attorney wondered about the propriety of a textile firm's selling coal at a profit.

[201] The company's contribution was ratified by the stockholders, who were reminded by Harris that "in view of the generosity and spirited effort of our employees we think that the stockholders of the corporation can hardly afford to do otherwise."

These considerations led to the decisions to transfer the non-manufacturing assets, except housing, to a separate non-profit corporation.

In December 1943 Riverdan Benevolent Fund was incorporated as a non-stock

charitable corporation organized for the purpose of giving charitable relief to deserving persons among the employees or former employees of Lessor Dan River Mills, or their families, contributing funds to the aid and relief of churches or other religious, semi-religious or eleemosynary institutions serving such employees, forming and developing plans and financing programs for their health and physical improvement, and in general by the operations of a purely charitable corporation contributing in all possible ways to the physical, moral and educational welfare.

Officers of the new corporation, capitalized at $25,000, were R. B. Newton, president, B. D. Browder, vice-president, and T. A. Bassin, secretary-treasurer. Operations were in charge of a full-time general manager, who was responsible to a board of trustees.

By deed of lease, October 1, 1945, Dan River Mills transferred to Riverdan Benevolent Fund the following property: the Schoolfield Y.M.C.A. and the baseball park; Hylton Hall and Hylton Hall annex, including the cafeteria and sandwich shop; the Country Club; and the Schoolfield coal and wood yard. The coal and wood yard and the sandwich shop, which furnished food to the canteen service operated throughout the mills, were the principal revenue-producing assets. Disbursements were made primarily in support of the welfare, recreational, and community development programs of Schoolfield; but contributions were also made to meet unusual needs of churches, schools, and other groups. In 1948 Riverdan gave $2,516 to the public schools and in 1949 put $2,350 into the Schoolfield Community Chest. The Fund donated smaller amounts to three churches in 1948 and four in 1949.

Riverdan's balance sheet as of July 3, 1949, showed assets of $178,-329, including $64,698 in cash. This unusually liquid position apparently anticipated some capital improvement of the facilities it operated. In September 1949 John D. MacLauchlan, Jr., succeeded Ural Watson as Riverdan's general manager.

Stockholders and Dividends

Table 14 recapitulates the nine-year record of sales and earnings. From $2.1 million in 1941, gross profit on sales rose to a maximum of $27.1 million in 1948, dropping to $5.2 million in 1949, the lowest since 1941. Net earnings, which only once surpassed $1.5 million in the war years, jumped to $10 million in 1946, $12 million in 1947, and $15 million in 1948. In 1949, with sales cut by a third, net earnings contracted over 70 per cent. Earnings for the period averaged approximately 18 per cent of net worth.

Adjustments for "other income" included earnings of the coal and wood yards, gains on the sale of raw cotton, welfare and village expenses, and costs of the retirement plan. Discounts received on purchases of equipment and supplies was regularly treated as "other income" the amount varying from $70,674 in 1943 to $143,507 in 1948. A gain of $159,202 was realized on the sale of 100 shares of treasury stock in 1946.

The "other deductions" included a $305,947 write-down of the inventory of foreign-staple rayon (1947) and additions to the reserve for doubtful accounts, as follows: $250,038 in 1946, $109,400 in 1947, and $250,000 in 1948. As in former years, the loss on bad debts was insignificant; and the reserve was unnecessarily generous. In four years, 1942-1945, $2,750,000 was allocated to the reserve for contingencies to cover renegotiation of war contracts, taxes, and other items. This reserve, too, proved more than adequate, and in 1949 the balance of $1,056,386 was added to surplus. Another $134,848 was transferred to surplus from "sundry reserve balances."

In 1943 a revaluation of inventories restored $259,193 of taxable income. The net amount, after income and excess profits taxes of $180,000, was carried to surplus. At the end of 1941 the surplus was reduced by $37,306 for additional federal and state income taxes and $65,901 for federal unjust enrichment taxes, both on income prior to 1941. The premium on preferred stock retired in 1946 reduced the surplus by $500,000, and $64,159 was charged to surplus on account of the excess of cost over par value of stock acquired for the sinking fund.

It is hardly necessary to dwell on the circumstances under which federal tax collectors came to drain off larger and larger slices of cor-

Table 14. Sales, Costs of Sales, and Profit, 1941-1949
(thousands of dollars)

	1941	1942	1943	1944	1945	1946	1947	1948	1949
net sales	37,747	58,170	57,445	61,284	53,628	77,346	92,270	103,604	64,998
cost of sales	33,994	48,698	48,474	48,395	42,642	57,719	68,150	72,351	55,539
gross profit	3,753	9,472	8,971	12,889	10,986	19,627	24,120	31,253	9,459
selling, general administrative expenses	1,633	2,304	1,302	1,610	1,830	2,134	3,211	4,149	4,297
gross profits from sales	2,120	7,168	7,669	11,279	9,156	17,493	20,909	27,104	5,162
other income	263	350	289	408	302	663	360	288	1,499
other deductions	175	226	373	420	19	894	581	1,283	1,178
profit before taxes	2,208	7,293	7,585	11,267	9,439	17,262	20,688	26,109	5,483
provision for state and federal income taxes	750	5,250	5,620	9,000	7,350	7,300	8,500	11,000	2,150
reserve for contingencies		500	500	1,000	750				
net earnings	1,458	1,543	1,465	1,267	1,339	9,962	12,188	15,109	3,333

Error in total due to rounding.

porate income. Not only did the wartime requirements of the government lead to higher levies, but companies working on government contracts had to anticipate additional tax bills as a result of renegotiation. In February 1943 President Harris explained the situation to the stockholders: "the Government has reserved the right to reclaim such part of the profits on such contracts as is determined to be 'excessive.' It has not been indicated that the Government Agencies involved regard any portion of our 1942 profits as excessive. We do not think any part of them can equitably be so regarded." Nevertheless, it was the part of prudence to set up a $500,000 reserve for this contingency.

Actually, renegotiation of the 1942-1944 government contracts resulted in an additional tax bill of $1 million. The following statistics disclose the settlements for three years:

	1942	1943	1944
renegotiated sales, reduction	$630,000	$1,071,174	$2,060,224
income taxes paid, credit	510,300	871,469	1,483,361
reduction in profit, charged to contingency reserve	119,700	199,705	576,863

In 1947 the Collector of Internal Revenue reopened the company's tax returns for 1942 and 1943. Disallowing the accelerated depreciation charges shown in these two years, the Collector handed the company the following statement:

	1942	1943
excess profits tax deficiency	$430,225	$439,626
additional income tax		9,792
overassessment of income tax	52,829	
interest on unpaid taxes	107,930	91,978
total	$485,326	$541,396

Renegotiation of the 1945 sales was long drawn-out. Finally, in 1949, the Army Price Adjustment Board agreed to restore $1,439,523, which cost Dan River about $400,000 in additional taxes. But, as has been pointed out, the reserves were more than adequate to absorb these claims; and earnings available for dividends were, in fact, substantially understated for the period.

Out of the reported earnings of $47.7 million for 1941-1949 preferred stockholders received $4.9 million in dividends and interest on dividend arrearages. Back dividends were paid off, as follows: $6 per share in 1941, $3 in 1942, and $9 in 1943. No dividend was in arrears after January 1, 1944; and the market price of the 6 per-cent stock recovered from the 1940 low of 75 to more than par in 1943. Dividend distributions on both classes of stock are shown in Appendix 2.

In April 1944 common stockholders received their first dividend (50 cents a share) in fourteen years. It was long overdue, in the opinion of a persistent minority, who badgered the management with schemes for liquidating the preferred dividends in arrears. If the preferred shareholder could have been persuaded to accept stock for the unpaid dividends, common stockholders could have received a dividend in 1941 or 1942. It was also argued that common stockholders would be better off if the preferred issue were replaced by funded debt.[202]

In 1941 Chairman Miller insisted that the company was not in a position "to consider any reorganization of our capital structure at this time . . . . To do so would ventilate everything connected with our affairs." Specifically, what frightened the management was the

---

[202] Chairman Miller, a banker, bore the brunt of the attack. One critic called him "pig-headed" and accused him of running the mills for the benefit of the bankers instead of stockholders. Another stockholder threatened: "If some of the back dividends are not paid to us before very long, I propose to try to see if Westbrook Pegler will investigate the matter."

thought of filing a registration statement with the Securities and Exchange Commission and making public a far more intimate picture of the company's finances than had ever been furnished to stockholders. A bond issue to retire the preferred stock would also necessitate a registration statement; but the management had firmer ground for rejecting this proposal, since the bankers agreed with Chairman Miller that it would be "unsound."

Finally, as common stockholders continued "nagging the management," in November 1942 the directors voted to employ a "competent and disinterested person . . . qualified as an expert in the field of corporation finance," to study the firm's financial policy and suggest improvements. The expert selected was John W. Hanes, a North Carolina banker and one-time Undersecretary of the Treasury (1938-1939).

The Hanes report, submitted in February 1943, paid a high compliment to the company's financial administration and put the blame for its difficulties on the violent fluctuations in the industry and the punitive federal tax system. Dividend-hungry common stockholders "may have some merit in being critical of the financial management of the Company up to 1929," but Hanes doubted that "much fair criticism may be levied thereafter." Talk about "obsolescence of management" might have been justified in the past; there was "no basis for it at the present."

The stumbling block was the $450,000 in "fixed charges" on the preferred stock. This required earnings of about $1,250,000 before taxes, since the normal income tax, the surtax, and the excess profits tax absorbed up to 70 per cent of taxable income. The "real tragedy," Hanes thought, was the "reluctance of those charged with fiscal responsibility in our government to recognize these changes in the game and to recommend changes in the rules accordingly. Preferred stock interest is just as truly an expense of conducting business as is interest upon any other type of borrowed capital."

This led Hanes to recommend, with surprising naïveté it seems to me, "a change in the tax laws" as the most promising solution to Dan River's capitalization problem. "Take your preferred stock problem to your Senators and Congressmen without delay." Since "hundreds of corporations have the same problem," stockholders should go to Congress "with the request, or demand, that Congress take into consideration the difficulty now confronting all corporations which had borrowed money years ago on preferred stock when that kind of capital was favorable capital."[203]

The next best solution, Hanes believed, would be to raise $15 million on long-term bonds, or debentures, with a "rate of amortization so low that the common stockholder will risk no chance of losing his property in a period of depression." Such a security issue would provide money to retire the preferred stock, pay off bank loans, replenish working capital, and "make a beginning upon the modernization of your plant."

On May 15, 1943, the directors submitted the Hanes Report to an adjourned meeting of the stockholders.[204] In the opinion of the board, "the present wartime emphasis on taxation and the constant search for new sources" were conclusive evidence of the impracticability of seeking a change in the corporate income tax to permit the deduction of preferred dividends. Any movement along this line would require "strong and determined effort, with nation-wide backing"; but Dan River's directors were "not yet convinced that your corporation can afford to take the lead in such a movement." Concerning the proposed bond issue, the directors felt that "extreme fluctuations in our record of earnings suggest the danger of committing our Corporation to the fixed interest and amortization charges involved .... We have brought our credit standing to the high position, which Mr. Hanes favorably notices, gradually and after great effort. We are impressed with the danger of jeopardizing the standing by a debenture or bond issue." Until the uncertainties of the war and postwar readjustments had been removed, the directors assured the stockholders, the company would not assume the risk of a long-term debt.

The Hanes report contained other recommendations which the directors found distasteful. The first of these was to "employ the best financial man you can find as understudy to Mr. Miller." As the chair-

[203] A little needling by the Dan River management failed to change Hanes' position. On April 9, 1943, he wrote Harris that Congress could be persuaded "to give relief on the tax side. I do not agree that this is not the time to start such a movement. It is, on the contrary, the exact time .... Your corporation is ideally situated to inaugurate such a movement, and here is another example of your need for a young and vigorous financial man. I can think of no more engaging or interesting task." As though to clinch the argument, Hanes referred to his own success in getting Congress in 1942 to set aside President Roosevelt's executive order, limiting salaries to $25,000 a year after taxes.

[204] The management decided not to bring the report before the annual meeting on February 18. Anticipating a query from some eager stockholders, the chairman was prepared to say that he intended to mention it under the head of "miscellaneous business." The inquisitive stockholder was present, but the chairman informed him that the report was not yet available.

man, the president, and the comptroller were "all active in handling the financial side of the Company's operations," the board felt that another officer was not needed. Likewise, the proposal to "take your stockholders into your confidence by more frequent reports" seemed impertinent. Annual, rather than semi-annual or quarterly reports, conformed with the general practice of the textile industry. The "sound reasons" for this practice were not elaborated, but the directors promised to make more frequent reports "when such reports will further the best interests of your Corporation."

The final recommendation of the Hanes report—to "Keep abreast of developments in the field of synthetics through some recognized research organization"—was the only one to evoke more than a lukewarm response. The company's research and development committee, established prior to the Hanes' investigation, had already made gratifying progress and experience would eventually indicate whether outside research organizations should be called in to help. At any rate the directors were "impressed with the possibilities involved in this recommendation" and promised "to follow them up to the limit of our ability."

The stockholders accepted the directors' analysis of the Hanes report without criticism. But the management continued to search for a way to improve the capital structure. In July 1945 Chairman Miller proposed to retire the entire issue of preferred stock at 110. The money required—$8.25 million—would come from a common stock issue ($3 million), long-term notes ($3 million), and a reduction of working capital ($2.25 million). Since the company needed both working capital and funds for improvement, Attorney Talbott felt that it would be better to refund the preferred stock with a new issue of preferred carrying a dividend rate of 4 per cent, "if possible," and sell $9-10 million in common shares.[205] The ideas of the chairman, the president, and the attorney were not irreconcilable; eventually they agreed upon a plan of recapitalization which, after approval by the directors in April, the stockholders ratified on August 16, 1946. Changes in the capital structure, completed in September, may be summarized as follows:

[205] Another possibility, Talbott thought, would be to retire the 6 per-cent preferred with a $5 million issue of 5 per-cent preferred and the sale of $2-3 million in long-term notes (F. Talbott to S. C. Walsh, Oct. 29, 1945). The New York Trust Company offered to make a 10-year loan of $3,000,000 at 2½ per cent interest (H. F. Callaway to J. M. Miller, Nov. 30, 1945), while Chase National Bank offered $3 million for a shorter term at 2 per cent (H. E. Scheuermann to J. M. Miller, Nov. 21, 1945).

	before recapitalization	after recapitalization
preferred stock:		
shares authorized	75,000	50,000
shares issued	75,000	50,000
par	$100	$100
dividend	6 per cent	4.5 per cent
amount	$7,500,000	$5,000,000
common stock:		
shares authorized	600,000	3,000,000
shares issued	300,000	1,500,000
par	$ 25	$ 5
amount	$7,500,000	$7,500,000

The registration statement covering the new issue of 4½ per-cent preferred stock was filed with the Securities and Exchange Commission on June 2, 1946.[206] Holders of the 6 per-cent preferred were offered one share of new 4½ per-cent preferred, $5 in cash, and the accrued dividend on the old preferred. Preferred shares not offered for exchange were to be redeemed at the call price of 110. Actually, 69,615 shares of old preferred were offered for exchange, so that the 50,000 shares of new stock had to be prorated. The final adjustment of surplus in connection with the exchange of stock showed:

premium on 25,770 old shares redeemed	$257,700
premium on 49,230 old shares exchanged	246,150
premium on 770 new shares sold	—3,850
net debit to surplus	$500,000

Funds to retire the 25,000 shares of 6 per-cent preferred not exchanged for new stock were provided by earnings in 1946, without any serious impairment of working capital.

The 4½ per-cent preferred stock is subject to redemption and retirement by the operation of a sinking fund. Commencing in 1948, the company has applied 7.5 per cent of net earnings to the sinking fund and drawn by lot the appropriate number of shares for redemption at premiums of $8 (prior to October 1948) to $5 per share (after October 1950). As of December 31, 1949, the sinking fund acquired and retired 10,520 shares at a total cost of $1,216,259. The so-called

[206] *The Riverside and Dan River Cotton Mills, Incorporated: Composite Registration Statement.* P. 1-30 (the prospectus); II-1 to 9 (Part II) : and S-1 to S7 (Schedules). Also: *First Amendment to Registration Statement: Form S-1.* These were published by the Securities and Exchange Commission, Philadelphia, 1946.

"fixed charges" on the preferred stock had thus been reduced from $450,000 to $177,655.

The Richmond firm of Scott and Stringfellow, which had advised the management on recapitalization, entered into a "solicitation agreement" with Riverside and Dan River Mills. The contract made Scott and Stringfellow the manager of a group of brokers engaged in soliciting proxies in support of the recapitalization scheme and in underwriting the public offering of any shares of 4½ per-cent stock not taken in exchange for the old preferred. It cost the company about $125,000 in fees for legal and financial services to carry out the recapitalization plan.

In the charter revision, which legalized the change in the capital structure, the name of the corporation was shortened to Dan River Mills, Incorporated. The disadvantages of the "Riverside" part of the name had been recognized for some time. As early as 1942 the advertising department found "Dan River" the better of the two names to gain consumer attention. "Riverside," L. H. Browder said, was associated with too many cafes, garages, and beaneries. "In New York we now answer the telephone as 'Dan River.'"

To avoid confusion, Dan River Division was rechristened Schoolfield Division.

Apart from the financial advantages of recapitalization, the company quickly achieved a wider distribution of both classes of stock. In 1943 the *American Wool and Cotton Reporter,* much to the disgust of Dan River's officials, lent credence to the rumor that Burlington Mills was in the process of acquiring a controlling interest in Dan River. Though promptly and unqualifiedly denied by both Burlington and Dan River, the rumor was symptomatic of the "danger," as seen by the management, that some group might gain control of the thinly distributed Dan River stock. President Harris felt "very strongly" that "localized ownership" among citizens of Virginia and North Carolina afforded the maximum protection against a shift in management or control. As of August 1, 1945, stockholders in these two states owned 89.6 per cent of the preferred shares and 87.4 per cent of the common.[207] In February 1949, 1,855 shareholders in Virginia held 45.2 per cent of the common stock, while 531 North Carolina stockholders accounted for 28.1 per cent. Residents of New York, Georgia, and Pennsylvania

[207] Stockholders in Danville owned 36,895 shares of preferred (49.2 per cent) and 114,086 shares of common (38.0 per cent).

owned 7 per cent of the common shares, and there were stockholders
in forty other states, the District of Columbia, Canada, and South
America. Doubtless, a wider distribution could have been secured
through listing on a New York stock exchange, but the directors continued to insist that the company stay "free of restrictions incident to
listed stocks."[208]

Common stockholders numbered 1,050 in December 1941; 1,150 in
December 1943; 1,348 in March 1946; and 5,217 in February 1949
(when the number of shares outstanding had been increased five-fold).
On March 14, 1946, when there were 1,733 preferred stockholders, the
20 largest holders of preferred (as disclosed in the registration statement) owned 16.2 per cent of the outstanding shares, while the 20
largest common stockholders held 24.9 per cent of the shares. Officers
and directors owned 2,743 shares of preferred and 13,294 shares of
common.

On July 15, 1948, the stockholders' lists were filched from the main
office and soon after this brokers were trading the lists on the open
market.[209] This turn of events alarmed the management, now concerned about the voting strength of a "restricted group of people"
residing in a narrow geographical area, which facilitated the solicitation of proxies by non-management interests. As happened so often
in the history of Dan River, the antimanagement forces were mainly
those who thought dividends were not large enough in periods of high
earnings. Two common dividends totaling $1.25 were paid in 1944;
$1.50 was distributed in 1945; and dividends in 1946 were equivalent
to $7.25 per share on the old common. The new stock received $2.50
per share in 1947, $3.00 in 1948, and $1.12½ in 1949. Counting only
the years dividends were paid (1944-1949), the stockholders got an
average return of 7.2 per cent a year on the par value of his common
shares. Book value per share rose from twice par in 1944 to almost
six times par at the end of 1949.

Quoted over-the-counter, the common stock recovered from a low
of 6 (bid) in 1940 to 10 in 1942 and 15 in 1943. The prospect of a
dividend started a rise which produced high bids of 23¼ in 1944, 60

[208] G. S. Harris to M. E. Maybrock, April 8, 1947. The stocks were quoted, but not
officially listed, on the Richmond Stock Exchange.
[209] The lists disappeared during the lunch hour. The suspected thief was a man
registered at the Hotel Danville as Peter W. Burns, but efforts to apprehend him were
unsuccessful. In fact, the management was advised that it might not pay to find the
culprit. A legal action would call attention to the fact that the company never allowed
the lists to be examined and a curious minority might take steps to reverse this policy.

in 1945, and 110 in 1946. The new shares, after the five-for-one split, were quoted (bid prices) at 12½-17 in 1946, 14-21 in 1947, 15⅜-20⅜ in 1948, and 11¾-17½ in 1949. But the 1949 low bid price was equivalent to 58½ per share for stock which sold for 6 in 1940.

In December 1948 the auditors suggested that the surplus might be "too large for political and stockholder reasons" and recommended a stock dividend or a reverse split. Neither maneuver appealed to the management, which was confident of its ability to justify to the stockholders its policy of retaining and reinvesting a large share of earnings. Although the current ratio (1.75) at the end of 1946 was the lowest in nine years, working capital increased $1.2 million and recapitalization was achieved without recourse to long-term debt. Undistributed earnings added another $7 million to working capital in 1947; and in 1949 the liquidation of excess inventories provided funds for paying off $8 million in current liabilities, raising the current ratio to 3.51. In short, the financial policy of the Harris administration increased stockholder investment in fixed plant almost 50 per cent and at the same time forced stockholders to make a larger contribution to the working capital. At the end of 1940 the net worth was $500,000 short of covering fixed assets and inventories; at the end of 1949 the stockholders' equity was represented by the fixed assets, inventories, and practically all of the receivables.

Stockholders, Directors, and Officers

Some of the contacts between the management and the stockholders have been described in the preceding discussions of advertising, recapitalization, and dividend policy. Little remains to be said. In August 1941 the president explained to the stockholders the omission of a semi-annual report: "For the past two years, contrary to our previous policy, your Directors sent to the stockholders a semi-annual report, but at this time the Board feels it would be unwise to make a detailed statement. We find sufficient uncertainties in the immediate future to make any statement misleading." The annual reports and financial statements were issued in the traditional form—two separate four-page leaflets. In 1945 the eight pages of report and statements were combined into one booklet, and in 1949 the report and statements, including a "Ten-Year Review," were expanded into twelve pages of text and figures. For reasons which seem not altogether defensible the Dan River stockholder learned comparatively little about his corporation and would have known even less but for the publication of the registration statement in 1946.[210]

Changes in the directorate were routine, at least until after the resignation of President Harris in 1949. Harris took West's place on the board, and F. K. Nixon became a director after his election as general sales manager. The board lost two members in 1941 with the death of F. K. Nixon in April and the death of G. P. Ray in May. These two vacancies were filled by the election of L. R. Wyatt, a Danville businessman, and Frank Talbott, Jr., the company's attorney.

The next change occurred in 1947 when J. C. Jordan, a member of the board for thirty-five years, resigned for personal reasons. To succeed him, the directors selected H. L. Bailey, onetime board chairman of the textile firm of Wellington Sears Company.[211] The death of J. Pemberton Penn in October 1947 created another vacancy, which was filled by the election of Benjamin B. Gossett, an experienced textile executive of Charlotte, North Carolina.[212] In March 1950 the stockholders elected a board of fifteen members.

Largely because Chairman Miller felt "so strongly" that directors' fees should be increased, in April 1947 the board voted to raise the fee from $25 to $100 per meeting and to pay $100 per diem for each day, preceding and following the meeting day, spent in travel (plus actual traveling expenses). Every director had to own at least $5,000 par value of Dan River stock.

Top management in the 1940's comprised some men who were already on their way up the executive ladder when Harris took over and others who came into the organization upon Harris' recommendation. Of the former, none enjoyed the president's confidence to a greater degree than Basil D. Browder.[213] As assistant to the president and as

[210] The standard defense of management was that information furnished stockholders was information made available to competing firms, which might redound to the disadvantage of the stockholders themselves.

[211] Bailey severed his connections with Wellington Sears as well as with West Point Manufacturing Company, but retained a directorship in Dwight Manufacturing Company, which was not a competitor of Dan River. This seemed to satisfy the Department of Justice, which raised a question about interlocking directorates (F. Talbott to J. F. Sonnett, Oct. 27, 1947).

[212] At least as early as February 1946, Harris decided to recognize the demand of a group of North Carolina stockholders for representation on the board, but he turned down their suggestions to nominate a North Carolina banker or stock broker.

[213] Browder began to work at Dan River as a messenger and typist in 1916. His continuous employment record was interrupted by 18 months' service in the Navy during World War I. In 1943 he received the First Citizenship award of the Danville Kiwanis

vice-president (1942), Browder was responsible for general supervision of the finishing plant, industrial and public relations, and the order, billing, and payroll departments. Attorney Talbott commented on "the extremely competent and fine job which Bal Browder did" in the 1948 wage negotiations. "It fell to his lot to do most of the talking and it was he who put the proposition on the wage issue. I think that he did so in a way which convinced them that we meant business."

Russell B. Newton left a superintendency at the Bibb Manufacturing Company in Georgia to join the Dan River staff in January 1941. Appointed as an assistant to the president, in charge of Riverside Division, he became general superintendent when G. W. Robertson retired in February 1941. As vice-president (1942) in charge of manufacturing, Newton's general supervision (as of 1948) extended to the plants at both divisions (except finishing) as well as the engineering, standards, purchasing, quality control, research, and production control departments. Harris recommended his appointment as executive vice-president in July 1949, when the president, under his doctor's orders, had to relinquish most of his responsibilities.

A. B. Emmert succeeded H. Roediger in 1942 as head of the cotton department.[214] Emmert had been manager of the Texas Cotton Growers' Cooperative Association for seven years. He was elected vice-president in 1944. The three vice-presidents comprised the "team" on which Harris depended for the management of operations in Danville, and it was something of a shock to the president when the board "unanimously rejected" (1947) his proposal to make them directors.

The chain of command downward from the vice-presidents, comptroller and secretary is depicted in the Chart of Organization, dated May 1, 1948, which distributed corporate functions and responsibilities as follows:

President and Treasurer, G. S. Harris
  Controller, T. A. Bassin
    General and Manufacturing accounting, J. D. Johnson
    Accounts receivable and payable; Property accounts

Club, and in 1946 he was elected vice-president of the Virginia State Chamber of Commerce (*The Commonwealth,* July 1946, p. 30).

[214] Roediger resigned, on the "advice of physician to slow up," in order to operate his own cotton brokerage business. A trade paper noted his departure from Dan River: "Uncle Henry was easily the most colorful and best known personality of all mill buyers, though others exceeded him many fold in annual volume. Danville and Front Sheet won't be the same without him. Oh Boy! How Rody plagued Front Sheet! When he showed up on Cotton Row everybody got the jitters—just like the opposing team when Ty Cobb got on first base" (undated clipping from *Cotton Trade Journal*).

    Federal, state and local taxes
    Insurance, E. P. Bush, assistant secretary
    General auditor, P. P. Patteson
Secretary, N. J. Waugh
    Corporate records
    Banking
Miscellaneous services, D. A. Overbey, assistant secretary
Assistant to president, B. D. Browder, vice-president
    Industrial relations, F. E. Anderson
    Public relations
    Cloth store, W. W. Olsen
    Order and billing, W. J. Adams and A. L. Fox
    Payroll, W. H. Fox
    Tabulating, W. H. Fox and H. W. Bacon
    Schoolfield Division
        Finishing plant, L. K. Fitzgerald, manager
Manufacturing, R. B. Newton, vice-president
    Production control, L. M. Thompson
    Purchasing, J. L. McDonald
    Standards, R. C. Gourley
    Plant engineering, J. V. Verner
    Quality control, W. L. Clement
    Research and dyeing, H. M. Chase and H. Y. Jennings
    Mechanical engineering, F. E. Rowe
    Designing, B. B. Howard
    Canteens, W. W. Olsen
    Schoolfield Division
        Grey mills, R. E. Henderson, manager
        Training, C. J. Schollenberger
        Village
    Riverside Division
        Grey mills and finishing, L. K. Fitzgerald, manager
        Houses
Cotton, A. B. Emmert, vice-president
Sales, J. M. Hughlett, vice-president
    Cost estimates, E. C. Moon
    Clothing fabrics
    Fabric development, W. J. Fullerton
    Advertising and credits, L. H. Browder, assistant treasurer

The chart represents not necessarily an ideal plan for management but rather the culmination of President Harris' labor, over a period of eight years, to distribute talent and responsibility most effectively. What no chart can reveal are the human factors which had to be taken into consideration: the petty jealousies, clashes of personality, and inertia which sometimes kept round pegs in square holes.[215]

Chairman J. M. Miller, who prided himself on the fact that he "found George [Harris] and with the full cooperation of the Board of Directors, signed him up promptly," relieved the president of most of the details of financing. As a banker, Miller kept in touch with the money market and placed Dan River's short-term notes at Boston, New York, Philadelphia, Richmond, and Atlanta banks. But Miller also interested himself in other phases of the business and kept up a substantial correspondence with President Harris. In 1947 Miller wrote an official of the Guaranty Trust Company that he was "proud of the accomplishments of George Harris and his associates" but feared he would overwork. "Confidentially," the Chairman wrote, "I want to find a young, promising man for President, have George assume the Chairmanship of the Board and direct the mills' affairs during his lifetime." The idea had been discussed with Harris but it appeared "difficult to agree on his successor."

Time disposed of the matter but not exactly as the chairman proposed. Miller became ill early in 1948 and died on October 9. The following year Harris was stricken, and on November 23 resigned the presidency and accepted the board chairmanship. Though active as long as his strength permitted, he lost the struggle to regain his health and died on February 16, 1950, at the age of sixty-nine.

Though no one could accuse George Harris of shirking his obligations to Dan River Mills, he gave his time generously to outside activities, the last of which was the chairmanship of the Cotton Textile Institute. One of the founders of the Institute, he reluctantly accepted his election to the position in hopes of averting the collapse of this industry-wide association.[216] Specifically, his task was to resist a "determined effort on the part of the group now controlling the American Cotton Manufacturers' Association to take over the Institute, in order

[215] In May 1949 Harris acknowledged that managerial friction which combined with poor markets made "my spot much more difficult." Though ill, Harris declared that he had worked his way "out of a lot of holes and expect to get out of this one" (G. S. Harris to B. B. Gossett, May 30, 1949).

[216] "My election as Chairman of the Board," he wrote, "poses a very difficult question in my mind. While it is an honor, I cannot now be influenced by personal honors in the allocation of my time and attention. Up to now, I have give my undivided attention to Dan River Mills, and would like very much to continue. On the other hand, we have an important stake in the Textile Institute and cannot afford to treat that organization indifferently. Just what I can do, I do not know yet." (G. S. Harris to D. F. Edwards, Oct. 30, 1947).

that its policies may be dictated by the southern mills, 'because the major textile interests are in the South and we should have complete control of the policy which affects this section of the country.' " Harris favored reorganization of the Institute and the Association but believed that a solution could be found which would make membership in the new organization—"a truly national organization"—attractive to northern mills. The outcome, one may surmise—since Harris was unable to take part in the proceedings—was not altogether to his liking. On August 23, 1949, the board of government of the ACMA voted to dissolve both the Association and the Institute and create a new body, the American Cotton Manufacturers' Institute, with headquarters in Charlotte, North Carolina. After a quarter of a century in New York, the Institute at 271 Church Street folded its tent and silently crept South.

8. *Three Score Years and Ten*

I

Seven decades of growth brought Dan River Mills to a position of unquestionable leadership in the cotton textile industry. It became one of several large firms, although in cotton manufacturing bigness had never meant control of an economically significant part of the market. In 1942 Dan River had less than 2 per cent of the 27.6 million spindles in place and less than 2 per cent of the 522,127 looms producing cotton goods. But it was one of twenty-four spinning mills with over 100,000 spindles and one of eleven weaving mills with over 3,000 looms. At the same time there were 881 mills with less than 100,000 spindles each and 961 mills with less than 3,000 looms.[1]

From 1883 to the end of 1950 Riverside and Dan River Mills produced 63 billion yards of cloth. It sold $1,240 million worth of yarn and cloth and distributed $335 million in wages and salaries. From the puny investment of $75,000 the stockholders' equity rose to $58

[1] Cotton Textile Institute, *Cotton Textile Hi-lights*, Oct. 1946.

million at the end of 1950, an increase of 11 per cent compounded annually. Meanwhile, stockholders withdrew from the business $50 million in preferred and common dividends.

Financially, growth was achieved by the continuous investment of the original promoters and their associates and successors. A small amount of capital was obtained from bond issues in the 1890's, but the company never had a mortgage debt. By all odds the most important sources of long-term capital were privileged stock subscriptions and the reinvestment of undistributed earnings. In this respect Dan River emulated the generally successful pattern of financing adopted by the earlier textile mills in New England.[2] Bondholders or secured creditors might have forced a reorganization in the deep depression of the 1930's, but it seems improbable that this would have improved the company's earning power.

History is not a science, and attempts to isolate the factors of industrial growth often bog down in specious arguments or inconclusive reasoning from circumstantial and partial evidence. Probably, the only certain causal relationship inherent in the Dan River story is the fact of America's growth: Dan River Mills grew because more people needed and were able to buy more cotton goods, year after year. Even this observation is open to the obvious objection that they did not necessarily need more "Dan River" fabrics.

Plausible explanations of the company's success (which, of course, was not uniformly sustained throughout seven decades) must be sought in the quality of the product or in the efforts devoted to selling it. Until relatively late in its development the Dan River sales effort consisted largely in personal contacts, wherein friendly and fair dealings created a clientele of large purchasers of cloth who renewed their orders year after year. Since the 1890's, when Riverside Cotton Mills opened its New York office, such contacts have been maintained on a continuous day-to-day basis. While some firms have prospered, relying upon selling houses and other independent sales channels, the early decision to sell directly seems to be one of the most important factors in Dan River's rise to prominence in the industry. The specialization which a company-directed sales organization presupposes spurred the management to find markets to dispose of the quantities of goods which make a national sales organization economical. It may be equally true

---

[2] L. E. Davis, "Sources of Industrial Finance: The American Textile Industry, A Case Study," *Explorations in Entrepreneurial History*, vol. 9 (1957), pp. 189-203.

that the large-scale production of a few staples stimulated the search for the most efficient method of marketing the mills' output. The familiar question, Does distribution cost too much? was answered in the negative over a long stretch of years, when often less than two cents of the buyer's dollar went into the company's sales activities.

The advertising era in the company's history did not begin in earnest until the 1940's. In this respect Dan River was no innovator. Pepperell began in the 1920's to make market analyses and adopt product identification, "thus gaining a head start in the mad rush to become well known to consumers in the United States."[3] When the Dan River management decided (belatedly, perhaps), to enter the "mad rush" toward product differentiation and consumer identification, it became necessary to publicize the basis of the "Dan River" difference. Dan River had to do what every other producer did with his differentiated product: emphasize the difference. Although it is difficult to isolate advertising from the other components of the sales effort, advertising expenditures at some point must reach diminishing returns. Whether in practice a firm reaches that point depends upon the significance and consumer acceptability of the advertised differences.

All this points up the importance of research as the basis for innovation and product differentiation. The germ of the idea to make Dan River "foremost in research" goes back to the days of President Fitzgerald; the plan hardly got off the ground during President West's administration; it became a flourishing reality under President Harris's guidance. Advertising (and related selling efforts) to announce and explain innovations is not only potentially profitable but clearly defensible from a social standpoint. Few, however, were the occasions on which Dan River developed a product or a process so unique as to reap the gains of monopoly. Close substitutes deny textile manufacturers unusual profits from exclusive "know-how," although, in the flush of a promising discovery, mill officials may be carried away by the imagination of their own advertising agents. On one occasion a Dan River executive predicted that the development of a new finishing process would make the company an important *chemical* firm as well as a producer of textiles. If, as seems to be the case, the profit-making possibilities of one invention are of short duration, a succession of improvements, bringing to fruition a new idea before the effects of the preceding innovation have worn off, may generate a long-run phe-

[3] E. H. Knowlton, *Pepperell's Progress*, p. 372.

nomenon. This is the promise of Dan River's commitment to continuous research and development.

Research is only one of the areas of management in which knowledge, ingenuity, and leadership have much to do with the level of earnings. Another area is the one hard to describe except by the hackneyed expression "teamwork." Through conversation with the men and women who work for Dan River, and in working with the firm's records and correspondence, I have become familiar with the many sources of jealousy and rivalry with which all management has to contend. Frequently, even the casual observer may wonder whether two individuals, who make no secret of their mutual distrust, realize that they are working for the same corporation. Such instances of personal incompatibility are not peculiar to large corporations; they bedevil government and educational institutions, too. On balance, I believe that lapses from unity of purpose and conscientious co-operation were relatively few and not long lasting. Loyalty, devotion, and the challenge of leadership are not empty boxes, even in a corporation. A vigorous leadership, such as that provided conspicuously by H. R. Fitzgerald and G. S. Harris, was capable of eliciting from executives and supervisory employees the maximum of resourcefulness, application and responsibility. But the efficacy of the slogan "The Corporation above Self," which was posted throughout the mills during Harris' administration, can hardly be measured.

The quality of leadership also affects the contribution made by the worker in the mill. *Pepperell's Progress,* the pioneer history of an American cotton mill, stresses the importance to the northern firm of having "throughout its history . . . a group of industrious employees." In Pepperell's case, these were first the "Yankee girls" from near-by farms, to be replaced in time by French Canadians and Portuguese immigrants. Dan River drew heavily from Protestant Anglo-Saxon rural communities. Although this class of labor faced serious problems of social adjustment, generally they formed a community homogeneous in interests, attitudes, and social standards. People uprooted in this fashion often longed for the "freedom" of life in the hills or on the farm; but it cannot be seriously argued that they were not ultimately better off economically. The hills and fields of Piedmont Virginia and the Carolinas offered increasingly unfavorable opportunities to those who chose to remain tillers of the soil.

The men who planned and built Dan River Mills were responsible for a small-scale industrial revolution. Danville was one of many southern communities which, like New England towns half a century earlier, welcomed the "revolution"; and, as President West surmised in 1934, the Dan River story "could be made to clearly represent the change from agrarian to industrial life, which has occurred in so many southern industrial communities." In a world in which nothing is normal except change, the peaceful transformation of the means of earning a livelihood represents the positive contribution of free private enterprise.

While, as the foregoing pages have frequently pointed out, the mills and the city and county in which they operate do not make up a unified body of interests, the communities remain highly dependent upon the success of a single business enterprise. This significant, if not disturbing, situation was highlighted in a survey of Danville and Pittsylvania county prepared by the University of Virginia in 1947.[4] As of 1940, the city had 32,749 of the county's total population of 94,446. Total employment in the city and county was put at 33,772, of whom 10,351 were employed in agriculture. Manufacturing absorbed 11,509 of the non-agricultural workers; and 9,566 of these were employed by Dan River. Total income payments (city and county) were estimated at $30.9 million, of which $11.3 million were paid out by manufacturing concerns. Dan River's total wage and salary disbursements in 1940 amounted to $7.6 million. Directly, through local purchases of goods and services, the company supported an indeterminate share of other enterprises in Danville and Pittsylvania county. Indirectly, through the spending of its workers, officers, and stockholders, the mills created a large share of the employment in retail trade, transportation, and government and professional services. Different value judgments will yield different interpretations of the desirability of such concentration of economic interests. I have already indicated the reasons for believing that Dan River mills did not oppose the greater diversification of industry in and around Danville.

The mobility of workers, as revealed in high turnover rates throughout most of the company's history, undermines the argument that there was a sheltered labor market to protect, if indeed one employer had de-

---

[4] Bureau of Population and Economic Research, *Economic Summary of Danville, Virginia* (Charlottesville, 1947). The mimeographed report was prepared by Lorin A. Thompson.

termined to avoid the competition of other employers. Literacy and the automobile made even distant employers virtually as strong competitors for labor services as if they had been located in Pittsylvania county. Probably, the disadvantages of the preponderance of a single industrial enterprise in a community are more subtle than those derived from economic analysis. Men whose success depends upon experimentation in the laboratory and innovation in the market place tend to have stereotyped views on questions of politics, religion, and social relations; and these views may weave a pattern of social conformity more rigid than would be found in a community of more diversified economic interests. Whether Danville, on this account, was less "progressive" than other southern communities, I must leave to social historians. I would suggest, though, that the sociologist will not get far without a more intimate knowledge than is presently available of the development of business enterprise in southern towns and cities.

II

As we have seen, for over seven decades Dan River found in Danville and Schoolfield all the opportunities for expansion which the management deemed commensurate with the firm's position in the textile industry. The company grew by building new mills near the old ones, by introducing new methods and products, and by bringing to Danville new machinery, technicians, and laborers. No one can prove that greater geographic dispersion would have enhanced the chances for profit-making. Nor can it be successfully demonstrated that the company neglected opportunities for making its business an even greater part of the economy of Pittsylvania county.

In the 1950's the tradition of the "largest single unit mill" was set aside. The background of this new departure I wish to discuss briefly, leaving to another historian the full story of Dan River since mid-century.

Dan River was nearing seventy years of corporate life when death ended the career of its seventh president, George S. Harris. His successor, Russell B. Newton, resigned in September 1952, leaving the chief managerial responsibility in the hands of the executive vice-president, Basil D. Browder. In July 1953 William J. Erwin, vice-president and general manager of the Reigel Textile Corporation, was elected president and treasurer of Dan River Mills.

The company's net sales in 1951 set a new record: $112 million, as compared with $104 million in 1948. In the following four-year period, 1952-1955, sales ranged from a low of $81 million to a high of only $92 million, despite the continued upward movement of prices.

In the postwar decade the textile industry experienced much the same cyclical instability as had characterized the years after World War I. The following pattern of expansion and contraction has been identified:

period of expansion	*period of contraction*
August 1945–November 1946	November 1946–September 1947
September 1947–May 1948	May 1948–July 1949
July 1949–March 1951	March 1951–April 1952
April 1952–June 1953	June 1953–May 1954
May 1954–April 1956	

From the lowest point in a period of contraction to the peak in the following period of expansion output of cotton goods increased as much as 47 per cent; from the peak to the subsequent trough production fell off as much as 35 per cent. While the cyclical movements in recent years were still short in duration, they appeared somewhat less violent than in 1919-1940, when production rose as much as 77 per cent in the upswing and fell 63 per cent in the downswing.[5] As in the 1920's, many mill owners sought a remedy for instability in mergers.

In August 1956 Dan River joined the parade of corporate consolidations, which had gotten under way before the end of World War II. All of the outstanding capital stock of Iselin-Jefferson Company, Inc., was acquired by Dan River in exchange for 202,020 shares of 5 per-cent preferred stock and 1,164,020 shares of common stock. At the same time 428,121 shares of Dan River common stock were exchanged for the net assets of Alabama Mills, Inc.

The new acquisitions resulted in the establishment of the Alabama Division of Dan River Mills, with plants in Aliceville, Clanton, Dadeville, Fayette, Greenville, Wetumpka, and Winfield, Alabama, and Rome, Georgia. The Woodside Mills, the manufacturing subsidiary of Iselin-Jefferson, brought under Dan River management mills in Anderson, Easley, Fountain Inn, Greenville, Liberty, and Simpsonville, South Carolina. Iselin-Jefferson Financial Company, a factoring

[5] T. M. Stanback, Jr., "The Textile Cycle: Characteristics and Contributing Factors," *Southern Economic Journal*, vol. 25 (1958), 174-188.

subsidiary of Iselin-Jefferson Company, was also brought under Dan River management.

The purposes of these acquisitions, as explained to Dan River stockholders in the 1956 *Annual Report,* were "to secure greater diversification of product lines, more diversified manufacturing facilities, and broadened distribution." It was also contemplated that integrating the Alabama mills operations with the Danville plant would yield "substantial operating economies and more efficient manufacturing in the Alabama plants." Iselin-Jefferson Company continues as a separate organization, selling the products of the Alabama Division and Woodside Mills. In addition, Iselin-Jefferson sells the products of other textile mills on a commission basis, while Iselin-Jefferson Financial Company engages in factoring for both Iselin-Jefferson mills and for other manufacturers and distributors.

The consolidated balance sheet for 1956 shows an increase in total assets from $71.1 million (1955) to $139.7 million, while net sales rose from $91.7 million to $122.4 million. In 1957, the first full year of operations for the consolidated firm, sales rose to $164 million. Eighteen thousand employees were running 800,000 spindles and 18,000 looms.

In 1955 the House of Representatives Committee on the Judiciary took cognizance of the merger movement in the textile industry. "The basic question" considered by the committee was "whether the mergers which have been taking place tend substantially to lessen competition or to create a monopolistic condition in the textile field." The committee's "Staff Report"[6] concluded that

the textile industry is in a state of transition. Several years ago the industry could be described as unconcentrated and highly competitive. By a process of painful liquidations and mergers the industry is becoming increasingly concentrated. This is apparent from the emergence of a small group of large firms employing an increasing percentage of the workers in the industry. These large firms are sharply differentiated from the smaller firms which make up the balance of the industry. The diversification, size, advertising and selling potential in addition to financial resources give a distinct advantage to these larger firms. These advantages present the threat of further concentration in the future. If continued unabated, increasing concentration will likely result in substantial future antitrust problems in the textile industry.

[6] *The Merger Movement in the Textile Industry: A Staff Report to Subcommittee No. 5 of the Committee on the Judiciary, House of Representatives* (84th. Cong., 1st Sess., Washington, 1955).

A decade earlier the *Textile World* reported a "prevalent" belief "that the industry is entering an era of larger mill groups and that consequently fewer men will control the majority of its equipment and its products. Some extremists even forecast that the time is coming when a mere five or six companies will dominate the textile field just as has come to pass in the automobile industry."[7] What the "extremists" forecast scarcely seems realistic. For one thing, the economies of scale in the two industries are realized at radically different levels of output; technical efficiency is still possible in relatively small and specialized plants. Diversification of products, "forward" integration, and a "full line" of fabrics are sought for the sake of achieving stability in sales, earnings, and employment; a higher rate of return on invested capital is a secondary, though not unimportant, consideration. Thus, it is the considered judgment of one writer that there is "little prospect that [mergers] will result in . . . the disappearance of the prevailing competitive structure of the industry" and, consequently, "there is little warrant for the application of special measures of control to, or intervention in, the cotton textile industry."[8]

On the seventy-fifth anniversary of the founding of Riverside Mills the management declared that "The drive and vitality that characterized the earlier days have not faded with time; there is still the pressing urge to move forward, to grow bigger as well as better."[9] The expressed determination of business organization to become better is a tacit recognition that it has faults. No prophet can be trusted who pretends to know whether in striving to become a better corporation Dan River must be bigger; or whether, growing bigger, it will necessarily be better.

[7] *Textile World,* vol. 96 (July 1946), p. 101.
[8] A. M. McIsaac, "The Cotton Textile Industry," in *The Structure of American Industry* (New York, 1954), pp. 72-73.
[9] *Annual Report,* 1956.

548

Appendix 1. Balance Sheet Summaries
(thousands of dollars)
Assets

Riverside Cotton Mills, 1882-1908

end of year	plant	inventories	receivables	cash	other assets	total
1882–1887	*	*	*	*	*	*
1888	726	*	*	*	*	*
1889	*	*	*	*	*	*
1890	1,193	175	111	38	10	1,528
1891	1,218	212	68	29	5	1,532
1892	1,223	153	100	31	16	1,522
1893	1,471	271	127	102	40	2,011
1894	1,704	319	108	34	50	2,215
1895	1,894	278	209	34	60	2,475
1896	2,024	269	181	20	108	2,603
1897	2,056	237	194	23	115	2,624
1898	2,085	230	211	27	105	2,658
1899	2,000	387	345	23	157	2,912
1900	2,000	415	249	34	153	2,851
1901	2,000	276	208	43	159	2,686
1902	2,000	317	330	29	203	2,879
1903	2,000	348	377	33	206	2,964
1904	2,000	319	407	73	558	3,358
1905	2,000	252	314	60	598	3,224
1906†	2,000	279	377	65	600	3,321
1907†	2,000	239	552	139	590	3,520
1908†	2,000	451	568	282	590	3,891

Discrepancies in totals due to rounding
* Data unavailable
† December 1

Dan River Power & Manufacturing Company, 1903-1908

end of year	plant	inventories	receivables	cash	other assets	total
1903	584	0	402	35	0	1,021
1904‡	870	0	416	109	0	1,395
1905	1,853	146	199	47	14	2,259
1906†	2,317	171	271	78	8	2,845
1907†	2,964	190	479	151	8	3,791
1908†	3,224	541	429	220	8	4,423

Discrepancies in totals due to rounding
† December 1
‡ July 1

Riverside and Dan River Cotton Mills, 1909-1945

end of year	plant	inventories	receivables	cash	other assets	total
1909	5,701	1,759	978	440	600	9,478
1910	6,914	1,450	1,186	462	600	10,611
1911	7,114	989	956	312	270	9,641
1912	7,517	1,622	1,185	671	90	11,085
1913	8,468	1,726	1,130	310	90	11,724
1914	9,648	1,645	1,946	335	90	13,664
1915	9,782	2,620	1,264	335	90	14,091
1916	9,930	3,450	1,647	309	90	15,426
1917	9,864	4,369	2,757	811	252	18,054
1918	10,076	5,504	2,442	669	1,681	20,371
1919	9,940	7,087	3,650	490	2,594	23,761
1920	13,905	5,415	3,645	903	3,074	26,943
1921	17,604	4,535	3,884	828	98	26,949
1922	17,626	6,398	4,106	616	107	28,853
1923	18,751	6,668	4,469	1,118	144	31,150
1924	18,703	6,076	3,000	345	146	28,270
1925	18,570	5,832	3,219	379	149	28,149
1926	18,222	4,607	2,276	421	548	26,074
1927	18,023	5,902	2,747	504	122	27,298
1928	17,878	6,376	2,652	494	109	27,509
1929	17,800	5,123	2,430	475	101	25,929
1930	18,198	2,944	1,098	673	101	23,014
1931	17,973	2,320	1,885	645	187	23,010
1932	17,706	3,093	1,305	433	167	22,705
1933	16,812	4,362	2,573	449	147	24,342
1934	16,112	5,858	2,530	403	168	25,071
1935	15,770	5,644	2,955	201	171	24,741
1936	15,514	7,231	3,776	229	206	26,956
1937	15,833	9,737	2,737	205	218	28,730
1938	15,405	8,586	2,855	201	229	27,276
1939	15,186	6,960	3,805	214	372	26,537
1940	14,691	7,808	3,935	819	220	27,474
1941	14,665	10,460	4,965	462	159	30,712
1942	14,484	11,611	6,732	972	519	34,318
1943	13,903	11,415	4,804	1,060	3,475	34,656
1944	13,335	13,445	4,203	1,475	6,547	39,005
1945	13,446	18,617	1,588	1,079	7,405	42,134

Discrepancies in totals due to rounding

Dan River Mills, Incorporated

end of year	plant	inventories	receivables	cash	other assets	total
1946	15,555	19,538	7,055	1,990	5,335	49,472
1947	17,277	26,323	7,215	3,527	3,240	57,582
1948	19,825	28,467	8,946	3,797	4,883	65,919
1949	21,000	22,795	5,850	4,413	4,247	58,306
1950	21,579	32,323	12,500	3,716	3,903	74,020

Discrepancies in totals due to rounding

Capital and Liabilities

Riverside Cotton Mills, 1882-1908

year	common stock	preferred stock	surplus	bills payable	other liabilities	total
1882	78	None	*	*	*	*
1883	150	"	*	*	*	*
1884	186	"	*	*	*	*
1885	225	"	*	*	*	*
1886	233	"	*	*	*	*
1887	500	"	83	*	*	*
1888	612	"	125	*	*	*
1889	650	"	134	*	*	*
1890	1,000	"	127	211	190	1,528
1891	1,000	"	172	170	190	1,532
1892	1,000	"	190	142	190	1,522
1893	500	1,000	93	228	190	2,011
1894	500	1,000	89	436	190	2,215
1895	800	1,000	64	421	190	2,475
1896	1,000	1,000	45	368	190	2,603
1897	1,000	1,000	91	343	190	2,624
1898	1,000	1,000	267	200	190	2,658
1899	1,000	1,000	372	241	300	2,912
1900	1,000	1,000	442	109	300	2,851
1901	1,000	1,000	346	41	300	2,686
1902	1,000	1,000	485	94	300	2,879
1903	1,000	1,000	584	80	300	2,964
1904	1,000	1,000	601	457	300	3,358
1905	1,000	1,000	639	285	300	3,224
1906‡	1,000	1,000	597	424	300	3,321
1907‡	1,000	1,000	650	571	300	3,520
1908‡	1,000	1,000	820	771	300	3,891

Discrepancies in totals due to rounding
* Data unavailable
‡ July 1

Dan River Power & Manufacturing Company, 1903-1908

year	common stock	preferred stock	surplus	current liabilities	total
1903	1,000	0	21	0	1,021
1904‡	1,352	0	43	0	1,395
1905	1,500	500	128	131	2,259
1906†	1,500	1,000	313	32	2,845
1907†	1,500	1,000	634	657	3,791
1908†	2,000	1,000	650	773	4,423

Discrepancies in totals due to rounding
† December 1
‡ July 1

Riverside and Dan River Cotton Mills, 1909-1945

year	common stock	preferred stock	surplus	current liabilities	total
1909	2,500	4,500	414	2,064	9,478
1910	2,500	4,500	572	3,039	10,611
1911	2,500	4,500	839	1,803	9,641
1912	2,500	4,500	1,163	2,922	11,085
1913	3,000	4,500	1,588	2,636	11,724
1914	3,000	5,500	1,266	3,898	13,664
1915	3,000	5,500	2,016	3,575	14,091
1916	3,000	6,000	3,433	2,993	15,426
1917	4,000	6,000	4,886	3,168	18,054
1918	4,000	6,000	7,286	3,086	20,371
1919	6,000	6,000	7,995	3,767	23,761
1920	6,000	7,500	9,901	3,542	26,943
1921	6,000	7,500	8,715	4,735	26,949
1922	6,000	7,500	10,121	5,232	28,853
1923	6,000	7,500	11,222	6,428	31,150
1924	7,500	7,500	8,367	4,903	28,270
1925	7,500	7,500	8,446	4,703	28,149
1926	7,500	7,500	8,355	2,718	26,074
1927	7,500	7,500	9,095	3,203	27,298
1928	7,500	7,500	8,309	4,200	27,509
1929	7,500	7,500	7,129	3,800	25,929
1930	7,500	7,500	6,014	2,000	23,014
1931	7,500	7,500	6,110	1,900	23,010
1932	7,500	7,500	6,080	1,625	22,705
1933	7,500	7,500	6,870	2,472	24,342
1934	7,500	7,500	7,195	2,876	25,071
1935	7,500	7,500	7,159	2,583	24,741
1936	7,500	7,500	7,346	4,610	26,956
1937	7,500	7,500	7,333	6,397	28,730

552

Riverside and Dan River Cotton Mills, 1909-1945 (Cont.)

year	common stock	preferred stock	surplus	current liabilities	total
1938	7,500	7,500	6,316	5,960	27,276
1939	7,500	7,500	6,538	4,998	26,537
1940	7,500	7,500	7,031	5,443	27,474
1941	7,500	7,500	7,465	8,246	30,712
1942	7,500	7,500	8,267	11,051	34,318
1943	7,500	7,500	8,501	11,155	34,656
1944	7,500	7,500	8,943	15,062	39,005
1945	7,500	7,500	9,382	17,753	42,134

Discrepancies in totals due to rounding

Dan River Mills, Incorporated, 1946-1950

year	common stock	preferred stock	surplus	current liabilities	total
1946	7,500	5,000	16,281	20,691	49,472
1947	7,500	5,000	24,494	20,587	57,582
1948	7,500	5,000	34,878	18,540	65,919
1949	7,500	3,948	37,450	9,408	58,306
1950	7,500	3,727	43,450	19,343	74,020

Discrepancies in totals due to rounding
* Data unavailable
† December 1
‡ July 1

Appendix 2. Sales, Earnings, and Dividends
(thousands of dollars)
Riverside Cotton Mills

year	sales	net earnings	dividends	
			preferred	common
1883		$6		
1884	$130*	15		
1885	170*	33		
1886	200*	n.a.		
1887	225*	n.a.		
1888	390*	63		
1889	410*	49		$49
1890	620*	100		49
1891	785*	126		80
1892	985*	208		80
1893	1,100*	193	$50	100
1894	1,200*	189	100	50
1895	1,300*	206	100	50
1896	1,327	120	100	80
1897	1,591	187	100	0
1898	1,695	356	100	80
1899	1,785*	369	100	80
1900	1,975*	351	100	80
1901	1,673	148	100	180
1902	1,905	319	100	80
1903	1,956	339	100	140
1904	2,010	217	100	100
1905	1,841	238	100	100
1906	1,829	108	50	100
1907	2,070	253	100	100
1908	2,265	371	100	100
1909	2,550	342	100	75

* Estimated

Dan River Power & Manufacturing Company

year	sales	net earnings	dividends	
			preferred	common
1905	475	128	16	0
1906	1,230	231	46	0
1907	1,838	381	60	0
1908	2,316	530	60	80
1909	3,351	450	195	180

Riverside and Dan River Cotton Mills

year	sales	net earnings	dividends	
			preferred	common
1910	6,147	622	270	159
1911	6,759	557	270	231
1912	6,348	718	270	241
1913	6,420	646	270	275
1914	6,643	308	330	300
1915	7,985	1,380	330	300
1916	11,335	2,077	360	300
1917	13,845	2,783	360	1,470
1918	18,695	3,559	360	800
1919	22,523	2,269	360	1,200
1920	29,962	4,156	450	1,800
1921	18,790	164	450	900
1922	22,660	3,056	450	1,200
1923	24,501	2,751	450	1,200
1924	16,486	—905	450	0
1925	20,354	1,279	450	750
1926	17,789	1,109	450	750
1927	18,861	1,939	450	750
1928	13,690	117	450	750
1929	16,166	20	450	750
1930	11,713	—665	450	0
1931	10,882	94	0	0
1932	9,818	29	0	0
1933	14,554	737	0	0
1934	19,032	780	454	0
1935	21,364	189	449	0
1936	23,745	1,279	1,314	0
1937	23,346	1,270	1,049	0
1938	16,390	—1,017	0	0
1939	22,762	447	225	0
1940	21,815	391	0	0
1941	37,222	1,458	920	0
1942	57,555	1,543	742	0
1943	57,445	1,465	1,310	0
1944	61,534	1,267	450	375
1945	53,930	1,339	450	450

Dan River Mills, Incorporated

year	sales	net earnings	dividends	
			preferred	common
1946	78,009	9,962	388	2,175
1947	92,531	12,188	225	3,750
1948	103,892	15,109	225	4,500
1949	64,998	3,333	201	1,688
1950	88,155	7,144	173	2,250

Appendix 3. Production of Cloth
(thousands of linear yards)

Riverside Cotton Mills

1884	2,013	1895	29,872
1885	2,816	1896	32,824
1886	3,797	1897	37,163
1887	4,024	1898	42,754
1888	7,132	1899	44,385
1889	7,994	1900	42,959
1890	11,205	1901	27,819
1891	14,529	1902	34,023
1892	16,585	1903	34,216
1893	17,573	1904	33,781
1894	21,266		

	Riverside Cotton Mills	*Dan River Power & Manufacturing Co.*
1905	32,666	9,793
1906	31,908	19,248
1907	31,716	26,809
1908	36,956	33,025
1909	37,844	40,414

Riverside and Dan River Cotton Mills

Riverside division		Schoolfield division
1910	39,464	41,337
1911	39,869	49,783
1912	42,176	49,208
1913	48,295	47,727
1914	46,028	53,454
1915	49,503	66,827
1916	54,877	82,150
1917	52,928	78,792
1918	45,808	68,555
1919	48,500	69,220
1920	50,977	78,069
1921	52,167	78,025
1922	75,276	75,051
1923	76,665	85,084
1924	44,502	62,378
1925	57,265	84,149
1926	53,612	76,498
1927	65,799	92,767
1928	49,826	65,634
1929	53,927	79,074
1930	34,387	55,401
1931	40,871	58,542

Total: both divisions

1932	112,260
1933	127,803
1934	140,218
1935	142,915
1936	165,512
1937	167,260
1938	116,536
1939	121,285
1940	128,491
1941	184,188
1942	199,248
1943	174,917
1944	162,400
1945	136,242
1946	151,148
1947	176,416
1948	188,863
1949	125,429
1950	177,700

Index

Abbott (machinery); *see* Machinery acquisitions

Abington Textile Machinery Works, 427-428

Absenteeism; *see* Labor turnover

Accidents, 172, 408, 510-511; *see also* Safety

Accounting; *see* Cost accounting systems

Adams, W. D., 213 n., 279 n.

Adams, W. J., 536

Advertising, 142, 211-212, 229, 348, 370-371, 460-466, 541

Agricultural Adjustment Act, 346, 366, 385-386

Alabama Mills, Inc., 545

Aldox Laboratories, 344

Alfriend, K. T., 455

Allis-Chalmers, 74, 76, 125, 331

American Arbitration Association, 500

American Associated Consultants, 495

American Association of Textile Chemists, 452

American Cotton and Wool Reporter, vi, 370, 531

American Cotton Manufacturer's Association, 97, 143 n., 213, 325-326, 346, 365, 416, 537

American Cotton Manufacturers' Institute, 538

American Federation of Labor, 51-52, 263 n., 294, 296, 299, 302-305, 314, 320, 323, 393

American Institute of Accountants, 371, 488

American Legion, 521

American Moistening Co., 337

American Red Cross, 148, 247, 320, 522

Amoskeag Manufacturing Co., 206-207, 218-221, 339

Anderson, B. P., 455 n.

Anderson, E. A., 457

Anderson, F. E., 536

Anderson, R. I., 25-26, 28, 54, 98 n.

Anderson, W. D., 9 n., 220 n., 241-242, 278 n., 361 n.

Andrezen, O., 520

Annexation; *see* Danville, city limits

Anti-Tuberculosis League, 247

Appalachian Electric Co., 331-333, 429, 432

Archives; *see* sources

Army Price Adjustment Board, 526

Associated Factory Mutual Insurance Companies, 119

Association of Cotton Textile Merchants, 206, 215, 218

Atlantic & Danville Railroad, 8

Audiffren Refrigeration Machine Co., 270

Audits, 83, 118-119, 129, 157, 173, 489

Avondale Mills, 436, 476

Ayers, F. C., vi

Ayers, W. W., vi, 176, 211, 267, 489 n.

Babson, R., 313

Bacon, H. W., 536

Bad debts, 40, 157-158, 210, 229, 348, 389-390, 524

Bailey, H. L., 534

Bailey, J. L., Co., 215 n.

Bailey Meter Co., 333

Balance sheet summaries, 548-552

Ballou, C. A., 10, 23

Ballou Park, 252

Baltimore and Ohio Railway, 148

Baltimore *Evening Sun*, 318

Bankers Trust Co., 414

Barber, W. H., 53

Barber cloth, 355, 382-383, 443

Barber-Colman; *see* Spoolers and warpers

Barnes Textile Associates, 329, 336, 380

Barrow, Wade, Guthrie, 83, 118-119, 152, 173, 193 n.

Bartell, F. E., 451

Bassin, T. A., viii, 488-489, 523, 535

Beavers, John and Elizabeth, 14 n.

Bebeau, M. E., 344

Becher, J. A., 198, 200, 512

Bedspreads, 200-201